D0932912

Lamy of Santa Fe

BY PAUL HORGAN

NOVELS

The Fault of Angels • The Habit of Empire • No Quarter Given
The Common Heart • Main Line West • Give Me Possession
A Lamp on the Plains • Memories of the Future • A Distant Trumpet
Everything to Live For • Far From Cibola • Whitewater

Mountain Standard Time
(*containing* MAIN LINE WEST, FAR FROM CIBOLA, *and* THE COMMON HEART)

OTHER FICTION

The Return of the Weed • The Saintmaker's Christmas Eve
Figures in a Landscape • Humble Powers • The Devil in the Desert
Toby and the Nighttime (*juvenile*)
One Red Rose for Christmas • Things As They Are

The Peach Stone: *Stories from Four Decades*

HISTORY AND OTHER NON-FICTION

Men of Arms (*juvenile*) • From the Royal City
New Mexico's Own Chronicle (*with Maurice Garland Fulton*)
Great River: The Rio Grande in North American History
The Centuries of Santa Fe • Rome Eternal • Citizen of New Salem
Conquistadors in North American History
Peter Hurd: *A Portrait Sketch from Life* • Songs After Lincoln
The Heroic Triad: *Essays in the Social Energies of
Three Southwestern Cultures*
Maurice Baring Restored • Encounters with Stravinsky: *A Personal Record*
Approaches to Writing
Lamy of Santa Fe: *His Life and Times*

LAMY
OF
SANTA FE

HIS LIFE AND TIMES

Paul Horgan

THE NOONDAY PRESS   NEW YORK
Farrar, Straus and Giroux

Copyright © 1975 by Paul Horgan
All rights reserved
Fifth printing, 1988
Printed in the United States ot America
Published simultaneously in Canada by
McGraw-Hill Ryerson Ltd., Toronto

Library of Congress Cataloging in Publication Data
Horgan, Paul, 1903-
    Lamy of Santa Fe, his life and times.
    1. Lamy, John Baptist, Abp., 1814-1888.   I. Title.
BX4705.L265H67 1975   282'.092'4 [B]   75-5870

In Homage and Affection
to
Henry Allen Moe
and
to
the memory of
Harriet Christy,
a promise fulfilled

Contents

Illustrations

Note: *Many of these photographs came from Miss Isabel Echols, who received custody of them from the estate of E. Dana Johnson, the distinguished editor of* The Santa Fe New Mexican.

Benedictus qui venit in nomine Domini

I

FRANCE

1814 – 1839

NOTE

Letters by Lamy have been transcribed here without alteration in any way. He always expressed himself plainly, and often eloquently; but his English, except when polished for public use, did not always conform to common usages of capitalization, punctuation, and spelling. However, his mild aberrations in a language not native to him seem to bring his presence more immediately before us; and out of respect for this advantage, I have felt justified in letting them stand.

P. H.

i.

The Fugitives

DURING THE HOURS BEFORE SUNRISE on 21 May 1839, Jean Baptiste Lamy, accompanied by his closest friend and former school-mate Joseph Priest Machebeuf, made his way on foot through the silent streets of the old Roman town of Riom, in the Massif Central of France. With his companion he was walking toward the Paris highway, crossing the northern arc of the great drive which circled the city after the manner of roads laid upon buried Roman fortifications. Within the town were small dark enclaves of medieval stone—gray, damp, impregnated with rank airs from the barnyards on the green hillsides all about. Beyond in the dimness sat the low, small-timbered mountains of Auvergne.

Lamy was not well. He had recently risen from a sickbed to join his friend in Riom, but his determination was calm. The better not to be noticed, he was dressed as a layman, and so was Machebeuf. In their usual dress, since they were both priests, they would be marked that night if anyone should see them. Lamy, the younger, was twenty-five years old and had been ordained only six months before. Machebeuf, twenty-seven, had received final holy orders two years and five months earlier. Their states of mind and emotion were high. With baggage for a journey of thousands of miles, they were going to the open highway in the pre-dawn twilight to await the fast coach from Lyon to Paris, and the first stage of an expedition.

In spite of their care, they were even at so early an hour seen and recognized by a former fellow student. He queried them. They now risked telling him of their plans, shaking hands in farewell. Their interceptor later reported their emotion as they parted—the unexpected friend perhaps on his way to early Mass, the other two walking to the outskirts, where there were houses to pass even after the new travellers should be safely aboard the coach.

They were fugitives from home who understood that if their plans were known, one of them might have to face obstacles which would be difficult, perhaps impossible, to overcome. As in every joint exploit, one was the mover, the other the recruit. In this case it was Machebeuf, small and impulsive, who had laid the long train of arrangements which brought them both to the coach stop, and whose consequences were to last their lifetimes. But it was the other, Lamy, taller, deliberate and mild, who was destined to become the leader in lifetime terms. What these were to be, they could not foresee except in the most general way, yet were compelling enough to make the young men take flight. For occasions of defeat or hazard, the patois of their homeland had a proverb which made people laugh in self-recognition when they heard it spoken—*"Latsin pas!"*—and behind it lived the spirit which moved the fugitives to set aside, for their own purposes, home and those they loved, for it meant, "Never give up."

The coach came and bustled to a halt, they entered, and rolled on. There was one more peril—the road led directly past the house of Machebeuf's father, who was Riom's leading baker. Day was now breaking. Machebeuf had the impulse to halt for a moment to take leave; but higher obedience prevailed, and passing his father's door he threw himself to the floor of the coach in the rue de la Charité to avoid even the chance of recognition. Lamy knew how he felt, for, though his parents were aware of his plans to go, he himself had come away without saying an outright farewell to them when he had seen them the day before in their village of Lempdes, to the south, below Clermont. Now he tapped Machebeuf on the shoulder to sustain his resolve. Soon it was safe to come up off the floor of the diligence and face toward Paris—a drive of over two hundred miles—and the future.

Within them rested a rich cumulation of history, tradition, belief, inherited ways, which had made them what they were; and despite the shocks of change they would meet in a new world, they took with them out of the past all to empower them for the life ahead.

ii.

Caesar and Vercingetorix

AUVERGNE—the people today bound it as *"tout le Massif Central"*—
is a great plain raised above surrounding France. It reaches south toward the borderland of the ancient Languedoc region, and in its place
names, pronunciations, and patronymics, continues to echo the hard,
clicking style of Languedoc speech, as against the more elegant and
fluid idiom of the old *Langue d'Oïl* of Paris and the northern provinces. Great hill systems, with woods, ravines, glens, wide meadows,
keep a bucolic aspect, all set off by ranges of distant wooded mountains whose dominant peak is the noble cone of the extinct volcano
Puy-de-Dôme, after which the political district is called.

Under so much open sky, settlements remain sparse and far apart.
Their distance one from another seems matched in the people by a
reserve perhaps imposed by a history of separation. To reach each
other, as Caesar wrote, the early Gauls, when they had matters of note
to communicate in that landscape, shouted over meadows and through
districts, asking neighbors to continue the relay afar, across high green
acres where voices could carry on long cries. Early Gallic settlements
were rough stockades, in high ground for protection against raid and
for periodic market gathering. Life came from the earth and even in
spirit returned to it. Caesar saw the Gauls as the most "religious" of
men. Rivers, woods, springs, and mountains, in their various mysteries
of source and atmosphere, all had their gods. It would not be strange
to see the isolated rise of the Puy-de-Dôme itself as a great altar,
whether almost lost in summer haze or lighted by clear winter. To live,
propitiate, propagate, and die, remote from the sophisticated Roman
energies which stirred to the south toward the Mediterranean; to take
the earth's yield and defend the land when necessary—such tasks
and impulses governed life in the ancient Averni of pre-Roman Gaul,
and seemed eternal.

But in a half century before Christ the Roman drive across Europe
under Caesar intruded its superb array into Auvergne. Independence
was threatened. The Averni resisted, and found their leader in the
son of their king. He was Vercingetorix, who, making a coherent force

out of what Caesar dismissed as "rabble," stalled the conqueror. The tribal prince reached to the spirit of his people, led them to heroic measures, such as burning their own rude stockade towns to deny the invader protection and stores, and defeated Caesar's attempt to take Gergovia (Clermont) in 52 B.C. The defenders put the torch to more than twenty of their own towns in a single day in one district. Other states did much the same. "In every direction," wrote Caesar, "fires were to be seen."

In the end, Rome's wits and resources were too great to withstand. Overwhelmed by a huge Roman reserve force of men and supplies, Vercingetorix acknowledged defeat. He sent for his chiefs to let them decide whether they should put him to death for his failure, or deliver him alive to Caesar. Since this was a matter for the conqueror to resolve, messengers were sent to him to ask him his will. Caesar received them enthroned before his camp, demanded their weapons and the delivery of Vercingetorix, whose style was equal to the event. Wearing gold-studded armor and riding his finest mount, he presently pulled up before Caesar and in silence threw down his arms and regalia and became a living trophy in captivity. Caesar took him everywhere for five years to display him in defeat, and then had him executed. Rome's Gallic wars succeeded. To native pastoral paganism was added imperial pagan politics in that remote frontier, and it was not until after the Christian baptism of Rome by Constantine in 312 A.D. that the Gauls began to come under Rome's new faith.

...
iii.

Romanesque Heritage

IN THE ENSUING CENTURIES the Christian energies radiating from Rome achieved a far wider and more enduring conquest than any imposed by an armed Caesar. The social and spiritual precepts of Christ struck deep into the individual person, touched veins of spirit through which he found a new sort of identity with fellow beings in the worship of God. The Church evolved, and with it, all its expressions in religious orders, liturgy, theology, and the arts. Christian Rome was the fount, her stream of faith flowed everywhere, and heroes of holiness became even greater objects of veneration than kings and warriors. Long worshipful before the visible, man began to find paths of aspiration linked to what lay before his immediate comprehension. One sure way to satisfy such desire was to make a pilgrimage to a holy place associated with a saint, and obtain the blessing of a human spirit in place of that of a stream, a tree, a mountain. Both pagan and Christian impulses were fervent; the latter one exalted humanity itself in the image of God.

Along with Rome, the great shrine of St James of Compostela in Spain drew pilgrims from all Europe. Their myriad steps confirmed the main roads from France to the Peninsula. Other paths also grew within the confines of France. At intervals along such ways, rest-houses evolved into monasteries, each with its church. A principal road for pilgrims led through Clermont, the old city of Vercingetorix. In many reminders, classic Rome survived there, nowhere more so than in the form of the churches; for, bringing home the ordinary news of travel, pilgrims renewed their recognition of the Roman style long ago established in aqueducts, theaters, walls, council halls *(basilicae)*, during the centuries of the unconverted empire. But the monuments to their faith built at home by the medieval believers referred not only to old massivities of Roman power, but also to the familiar and simple elements of the life all about them. Out of their experience at Compostela and other Spanish shrines, the travellers brought, too, echoes of Iberia, with its own remnants which were Moorish, and memories of these gave various details to the Romanesque style as it was evolved above the Pyrenees and the Alps.

By the twelfth century the Romanesque was widespread in Europe and its character became ever more local, until not only the ancient empire but the identity of cities and fiefdoms in their own regions found expression through representations of living creatures as parts of otherwise inscrutable architecture. Humanism entered visibly into engineering by way of prayer and its fortress. All expression sprang from faith. All safety lay in charity. All strength rose through the combination of these, in the mainstream of the inherited culture. Available through the Church, this was the culture of peasant and lord alike. Anyone growing up in it—while he might not even be aware of secular learning—was yet the possessor of a central body of the historical tradition of post-Roman Europe; and the single most powerful recorded analogy of life was the Holy Scripture.

As it was common to all, so must be its monuments. The churches were self-images of their makers, combining aspiration with recognizable images in stone taken from daily experience—the humble realities of what was loved and what feared, ranging from the human person to grotesques out of the world of demons. The Romanesque style made its daily and lifelong impact less through the refined aesthetic than through expressions of power—durability, seemly strength, and impregnable shelter; and what was sheltered was man's spirit against all threats the world could offer in every life until that life should end. The patience needed to do the work of the early medieval style seemed to prefigure a promised eternity, even if what made it believable in its mystery were the very motes of daily life represented in carved ornament.

Rome gave its arches to the fabric, and where in classical times they had seemed to hang great weights of masonry high in the air, now in the Middle Ages they brought to mind the earth-bound body of man, braced in stone to endure with blunt shoulders man's earthly passage. If God made Christ in man, other personifications of Christian attributes and saintly individuals came as a logical step from life to art, and back to life again, by way of the vision of those who gazed at either the smallest or the largest of sacred artifacts—a chief function of iconography. Romanesque sculptured ornament—celebration of man and the common sweetness of his visible world—joined with the craft of the mason to hold constant in the great dark churches the power also of that which was invisible, yet describable. Faith itself seemed anything but abstraction.

In fixed quiet, Romanesque ornament celebrated all living things— animals, fish, men and women of the day at their work; plants of the earth in branch, leaf, fruit, as well as figures of the Passion and the personification of the demonic unseen which thus became as real as the rest. Anywhere, from the capital of a double column, or the base of a font, or the frontal of an altar, or the almost hidden groin of a twining stairway, suddenly one could recognize a common face in stone gazing forth as an angel, a fiend, a saint, one of the Holy Family, in constant reminder of how the world went, and how in his own essence one carried these, containing all: the capacity for the divine; for evil; for safety, either through imitation in prayer and act, or perdition through mortal caprice. The powers of piety were inescapable, whose ideal persisted in familiar expression from the times of the earliest religious pilgrimage until, eight centuries later, interpretations of the essential forces of life would take a new turn through the physical sciences.

In Auvergne, as in other regions with strong local flavor, the Romanesque style evolved its own variations. The churches were often made of the dark volcanic stone of the Puy-de-Dôme. Rounded external chapels leaned in support of central chambers like foothills against mountains. Articulated bare columns and arches were lofted to sustain interior galleries of lesser arches. At Clermont, Notre Dame de Port, one of the oldest "Roman" churches in France, created out of its rude ingenuities an abiding grace of deep shadow, shafted height, and a simplicity as powerful as it was unambitious. Its circular ambulatory and side aisles, where the vision was symmetrically interrupted by pillars, offered visible analogy of processions, like those of life itself, which in the liturgy reenacted the ceremonies of worship in all their references to the mortal and the immortal.

The carved saints and the living world merged for the worshippers. At Mozal, the Holy Women at the Sepulchre are peasants in stone, with their strong, almost manly, faces, their voluminous folds of hardy cloth, their hands like those of farmers, all brought to pray in a stubby working grace. Elsewhere, a medieval bishop, already a figure of high consequence by his station, was the apostolic succession made visible; from the earliest time a figure of celebration and authority, in sculpture or fresco often represented as benign in expression, despite awesome mitre and crozier. In medieval glass the light of day was held like "the light of Christ, as in the Gospel." Color was always an element, no matter how greatly time might turn all gray with age, so that to later eyes the medieval epoch, except for its glass, seemed all monotone. Posterity judged and admired age, failing to see the original youth. Was the glass of the Romanesque an echo of the first Gospel of John— the *"lumière de lumière"*? It was perhaps the prime glimpse of what was to come in the lofting Gothic style. But in its abiding character, the Romanesque seemed rooted to the earth, while the Gothic sought to leave it.

So the earlier forms were bound to the common land rather than to the aspiring pinnacle—cavern, glen, hill; tilling or feeding creatures, bent in their own small bodily arches to their tasks. Mortality is present; but in terms of supplication, even in the romance of the time—the *Chanson de Roland* itself:

> *Save my soul against all threat*
> *The which my life's sins may beget.*

> *Upon his arm he sinks his head,*
> *He joins his hands and he is dead.*

Fatality inescapable; but in the very admission of this, in spirit, form, observance, lay appeal to what rested in the common eternity—the promise of life from life, light from light. It was the same spirit which raised the round Roman arch to the Gothic spire, and gave central conviction and unity to a whole vast and various society.

iv.

Auvergnats

ANTIQUITY MARCHES FORWARD in a procession of persons, creating a
tradition whose depth of culture formed belief, character, and vocation
for centuries. Gergovia, once the capital of Celtic Averni, became the
city and see of Clermont, whose founding bishop was St Austromonius,
believed in his land to have been one of the "seventy-two disciples of
our Lord, who came to Rome with St Peter." Before the tenth century,
twenty-three of Clermont's bishops were canonized. One, Innocent VI,
became pope (1332–62), five of its monks were saints, five popes passed
through the city of whom one was Urban II mounting a crusade in
1095, and in his exile Thomas à Becket visited Clermont. Now the provincial metropolis of central France, the city is called Clermont-Ferrand. By 1262 its Gothic cathedral rose above the old medieval quarter,
where to this day a weekly street market is set up with bright booths
and counters to which country people come to mingle and trade with
the townsmen.

A feeling of remoteness attaches to the city—removal from the
energetically forwarding affairs of Lyon to the east, Paris to the north.
In architecture there are echoes here and there of the grand palace
manner of Philibert de Lorme and the seventeenth century, and in
intellectual history abides the luster of Pascal, who came from Clermont, and Massillon, who is commemorated by an important school
there. The Loire château style, bastioned and towered, carved and
vaulted, with doorways under ogee arches, is visible in the foliaged
ruins of the great castle of Tournoël on a long ledge far overlooking
the valley where a tributary of the Loire flows on pale sand through a
green spread all the way to the horizon. The greens are dense yet
various—silver of willows set against yellower grasses under the black
shade of groves. Dürer-like scapes of river and hill, villages, spire, roof,
all glow in that palette in which gold seems to underlie all other
colors. In the fields and meadows creatures are bent to earth, men and
women, two or three in a group, cultivating, horses grazing, and black
and white cows, uniting in a Virgilian cycle the recurrent antique with
the pathos of what is fugitive:

The people—broad of face, reserved in manner—suggest a temperament born of the silence and the space of their great elevated plain. When they used their experience in their music, it was to imitate shepherds' dialogues across the same fields where Caesar heard their ancestors calling. Songs of sowing and harvesting set little piped scales under monotonous melody in simple repetitions made to carry over bucolic distance. Mountain flageolets imitated the spinning wheel, and bagpipes groaned the toil of market carts along the road. If they merged into dance figures, the Auvergne folk tunes sometimes clattered with Iberian effect, recalling the long-ago link with the Spanish pilgrimages. Cradle song and lover's lament both seemed to bear an underlying stoicism touched with a poor sweetness, as by those who worked hard to meet simple needs in a land beautiful, yielding, but demanding, where in winter the plain lies open to harsh weather, in summer to hazes of heat which all but erase the horizon mountains.

Much in the present, then, seems constant from the past. In June the cherry orchards show their enamelled fruit hanging along branches with long leaves. A dead crow dangles from a planted stick as a warning to other crows in a ripening field. From the corner of the eye a shuttered flash—the white stripes on the wings of great blackbirds against the bright haze. In the open country, pale villages look like houses of cards, with their red tile roofs. Red poppies echo the color, amidst the green checkerboards of the fields. Within the city of Clermont, the same tile-red housetops, accented by shutters to close against heat or cold, seem to make a common roof if seen from any small height. The streets rise and fall on many contours, and turn with inner hills, and like those of any ancient city seem to lose their narrow way in hidden districts and secret enclaves. Where these open out, as at the Place de Jaude, a prospect of state makes a sweep of elegance for great shops and municipal palaces, for a park, for sculpture, and there, at the head of the vista, rises a heroic statue of Vercingetorix on his "finest mount."

A street bearing to the south presently leaves city houses behind, and turns dusty, entering the country to lead to small villages, one of which, forty-eight kilometres away, is called Lempdes.

V.

The Home Village

THERE—TO RETURN TO THE NARRATIVE from the base upon which it rests—Jean Baptiste Lamy was born on 11 October 1814, in a clay-plastered house on an earthen street.

His parents, described as *"paysans aisés"*—well-to-do peasants—were Jean Lamy and Marie Dié. They represented old and respected families of the countryside—the father at one time was mayor of Lempdes. Of their eleven children, only four survived as adults. Two sons—Louis and Jean Baptiste—-became priests, a daughter Marguerite entered the sisterhood, and a third son, Etienne, fathered Antoine and Marie, who in turn became priest and nun.

The family house sat flat-faced and flush with the other houses on its street. It presented a scatter of windows at random heights, some square, some small, others large and shuttered (oddly suggesting the fenestration in the church of Ronchamps by Le Corbusier of the twentieth century). A single-span door opened into the house at one end, and a wide double door at the other was the entrance to the concealed animal and wagon yard and barns behind. There were three low storeys, rising to the dusty vermilion roof like that over all the other houses.

Lempdes sat on a gently domed hill above the right bank of the Alagnon River. Its narrow streets, all uncobbled, wound about on low slopes as if established by the meander of domestic animals. Proper narrow stone sidewalks were edged by running gutters. Heavy old masonry was revealed here and there through broken plaster. An occasional flourish of style was added by a wooden balcony at a second storey, and, open, an old sagging wooden doorway gave on to a fortress-like courtyard entered through broad arches high enough to admit farm wagons and horses. Two-wheeled carts, tired with iron, used wheels as high as the cart cages. Far in the narrow aisles curving between houses, glimpses showed of a forge, or a crib full of hay, or, in a miniature enclosed farmyard behind a house, a byre, straw, droppings.

Near the entrance of the village, and at its highest point, the public square presented a row of flat-fronted buildings painted in a succession of pale fresco colors—blue, beige, rose, white. Flower pots stood in summer along the pavements. If there was an air of poverty, it had the dignity of self-sufficiency, and if there was pride, it was centered in the modest Romanesque church which dominated one end of the small square. This was the home of the village patroness, Our Lady of Good Tidings—Notre-Dame de Bonne Nouvelle. On her altar in her side-chapel she stood in diadem and free-flowing carved robes, holding her naked child, who wore a little crown as He gazed upward into her broad-cheeked face in which lingered a composed merriment. She looked like a farm woman of Auvergne. Her healthy face glowed with simplicity above the gold leaf of her amply folded and tucked garments. Her eyes were dark, her high cheekbones were marked by smile shadows, and her closed lips seemed to indicate that she knew what she knew, and that what she knew was good. She was about ten inches tall. Jean Baptiste became her familiar at the age of five, when he began to pay her long and frequent visits in a *"grande dévotion"* which was later recalled when his childhood was mentioned. Their silent dialogue established a meaning—a view of life—never to change for him.

A certain pathos dwells in the localism of childhood—who could know what horizons awaited far away, not for all, surely, but perhaps for one or two? But the children of Lempdes, innocent of futures, must always have seemed much the same at any period, and thus Lamy, where they played—limpid small boys with shining caps of hair and dark clove-like eyes and ruddy cheeks, in the dusty walled streets, where tiny kittens blinked and dozed, and hens wandered loose with gravel in their voices, and dogs lay in the center of the lanes in perfect confidence of rest undisturbed. No life was precisely like every other; but in the village, as in that part of the great world to which it was attached, all human matters drew order from a common source so strong that its flow of influence could not be separated from any act.

For the people prayed not only to God, in that equation which had no true form but inner conviction, but also to history. From the dawn of the Middle Ages until the century of Lamy's birth, the Church had grown to be the teacher of all things—the proprieties of custom, the styles of philosophy, the seemliness to be searched for in the relation between body and soul, earth and the unseen. Man's single life, and the life of the state, the life even of the Church's own servants, could show every range of human capability, from good to evil, throughout the centuries; yet the mystery of the need for truth and communion beyond the self persisted in an unbroken line of faith whose very monuments seemed as eternal as what they repre-

sented, in all their variety, from the Islamic striped arches in Notre-
Dame de Port, dating from 1099, to the groined elements meeting like
hands in prayer high above the floor of the cathedral of Clermont.
The church building made of this world's materials by men's hands
was the gateway of prayer which led beyond death. To enter those
dark caverns of worked stone and lofting shadow, those aisles where
light shifted high in the air under the passage of the day, those obscure
corners by pillar or arch, and to face the altar where the body of God
could be addressed privately in the tabernacle where it lived, was to
draw a secret line from the cares and hopes of a short life to eternal
mercy.

Every age marked by a distinct historical style is an age of faith.
The object of faith may change, but the impulse to define and live life
in terms of a system of belief is constant. Great acts have been done in
the name of many different beliefs. To understand any such act and
the individual who gave it interest for us, it is necessary to take as a
given element, regardless of our own relation to what we see as reality,
the absolute and sometimes glorious significance of the faith which
moved him.

The Catholic form of this view in Lamy's time lay at the foundation
of the state, the town, the family, and the person. It was as naturally
expressed by believers as life through the act of breathing. Believed in,
its formalisms were not burdens but aids to a divine end, through a
culture both intensely local and fervently strong because it was by
definition universal. Familiarly but awesomely, a life given to the
Church brought anyone, whatever his original lot, to take his vocation
with a sense of immense privilege and with it a calm assumptiveness of
power whose duties embraced all terms of life, death, and eternity.
Nothing long-lasting was done without religious conviction. Piety was
an energizing force, and a clear gaze into the mystery showed forth in
early Auvergne fresco paintings of the saints drawn in formalized
conventions which called on the manners of the old Roman, the
Byzantine, the Iberian, the Arabic, the Mozarabic, in resemblances not
entirely accounted for by historical linkages. Who in the presence of
such silent witnesses staring from a painted apse, seeing them from his
earliest life, would not retain in imagination something of their
suggestive power?

With the turn of the eighteenth century, the age of piety seemed for
many to be ended, in the name of reason. But still, for vastly many
more, the motive of Christian belief survived, and for them the offering
of self in its behalf remained an act of unquestioned reasonableness.
Without that, much in any chronicle of a religious life might seem
implausible and unmeaningful. With it, achievements in its name

could be recognized, taking for granted that spiritual conviction lay behind them.

It need not be further explained to the broadly skeptical taste of a later time why men and women in religious commitment thought it worthwhile to bring the works of faith, hope, and charity to strange lands and changing societies. Once they have recognized their gods, men have always served them.

From childhood, Jean Baptiste Lamy, gazing from the tilled fields well to the north of Lempdes, across bluing hills, to the farthest line of the land where the solitary profile of the Puy-de-Dôme rose in the distance, could see between near and far the hazy cluster of the city of Clermont-Ferrand. The only constant and distinguishable features which he could pick out were the two spires of the cathedral side by side, there, at the end of the country road leading from Lempdes to the city and the world. At that angle, in certain airs and lights, they might fancifully suggest the twin spires of a mitre, such as worn by a bishop, a lord and teacher.

vi.

The Two Friends

LAMY'S VOCATION came alive in his childhood. Equipped with the simple learning of his family, he was enrolled before the age of nine in the Jesuit *collège* at Billom, a short distance from Clermont-Ferrand. Billom, like all the regional towns, was ancient, and its school, older than any in Clermont, was the first which the Jesuits administered in Auvergne. After their order was suppressed in 1773, the school was conducted by secular teachers. In 1814 Jesuits again took charge.

Nine years later, now with study for the priesthood his clear purpose, Lamy was entered at the preparatory seminary of Clermont, where he took the usual classical curriculum and presently, for the long course of theology, he was admitted to the diocesan seminary of Mont-Ferrand, which, administered by the Sulpicians, occupied a mass of seventeenth-century buildings on the outskirts of the city. Later used in turn by the *gendarmerie* as a barracks, and finally by Clermont's Ecole Supérieure de Commerce, the seminary in 1832 was still a closed world of studies and devotions, under strict discipline. In its long echoing corridors, under its mansard roof, and within its high interiors and general institutional darkness, the seminarian on entering could look forward to six years of separation from the open life to which he would one day be returned as a leader, fixed in purpose and sure of his means. In such an institution, the opportunity for personal affinity remained formal; but in a class two years ahead of Lamy was the seminarian who became his closest friend, then, and for life.

Outwardly, the two could not have been less alike. Lamy was taller than average, with a long-boned frame and a large head with dark hair, a tall wide brow, and a strongly modelled square-jawed face. Photographs later showed him as a gravely handsome man. His temperament reflected the country life he came from—orderly if not rapid in thought, mild in expression, strong and patient in a mind made up. He was so gentle with his early school companions that they nicknamed him "the Lamb." If he generally looked serious, he could be robustly humorous. Behind his eyes lay emotions which could be powerfully stirred and at times become exhausting. He knew what hard physical work was, and when necessary he expended reserves in effort which sometimes left him ill. Strong as he looked, he was peculiarly subject to periodic bad health, which was not always entirely physical in origin, but arose from a nervous fragility which he came to ignore through hard work. He seemed all simplicity, but he was woven of many strands—warm intelligence, charm, modesty, with a certain hardnesss veiled by habitual patience. Slow-moving, he went about his days with long strides at the pace of a countryman who thought in seasons rather than in days or hours.

By contrast, his fellow seminarian, Machebeuf, born in Riom south of Vichy on 11 August 1812, the elder by two years, was conspicuous for his small size, his pale hair and eyelashes (his nickname was "Whitey"), and his liveliness. His mind darted from notion to notion. Mischief played about in his gaiety; his small, plain, clever face was animated by a venturesome spirit; his little body hated to be still. He had come to his priestly studies despite early distractions—at one time, seeing a grand military review, he was all for a soldier's life; but ever after his mother's death during his ninth year, the priesthood held a powerful call, and despite the trials of his youth, *"pleins de chasmes et illusions,"* as someone wrote of him, it took him all the way to Mont-Ferrand. But even there, the confining regimen soon threatened his health and he was forced to spend a brief time away from the seminary to restore himself in free action. His resolve held, he returned, and like Lamy after him, completed his course.

It was a time of the religious revival under Louis Philippe, after the iconoclasms of the first Revolution, followed by Napoleon's self-serving rapprochement with the Roman Church. Religious orders and education had been secularized, the Papacy had been bent to the parvenu emperor's will, and the energy of the new politics was still animated by doctrinaire idealism. Alexis de Tocqueville was examining for the Old World how democracy was working in the New. America was becoming a world factor, calling to the religious mind as well as to the political hopes of the increasing tide of colonists who went to be free and rich—partners to the open promise of the new republic overseas.

Taking his "course of philosophy and theology" at Mont-Ferrand, where he distinguished himself "by his talents and above all by his exemplary life," Lamy spent much time reading of the missioners abroad in the *"Lettres Edifiantes"* of the Society for the Propagation of the Faith, and the heroic endurances which at times were required of them.

He was not alone in his thoughts of far places. Machebeuf had also thought of missionary life, always with America as its imaginary scene. France had already partaken of America in determining ways—early exploration, support for the ideal and act of the American Revolution, and more lately the religious colonization of the new states by clergy who had fled revolutionary France.

French missioners returning from across the Atlantic reported news and marvels of the sort to challenge youth. The seminarians at Mont-Ferrand heard a certain Lazarist, John Mary Odin, who first became bishop of Galveston and later archbishop of New Orleans, tell of hardships and needs on the barbaric coast of the Gulf of Mexico. Begging for money and men, he was rewarded also with stirred imaginations. In 1833 an old bishop—Benedict Joseph Flaget, who long ago was a seminarian at Mont-Ferrand—came back to his native Auvergne from Kentucky and spoke to his young successors of how he had spent his forty years in America. In his time, the Appalachians had been breached, the westward map was slowly unfolding. He was consecrated bishop of Bardstown, Kentucky, by Archbishop Carroll in Baltimore in 1810, and his first cathedral—in a Roman and Gothic town they heard him tell of this—was an open log cabin, and his diocesan parishioners consisted of four families in an area half a dozen times as large as Italy. He was at times companioned by Algonquins, and slept in the open air or in the conical hide tents of the Indians. His work in Auvergne while Lamy and Machebeuf were still seminarians was to give zest to others who would follow such a path as he had walked in all weathers—the exhausting prairie summer heat, the blizzard of prairie winter, the slow progress through vast pathless woods. The old bishop looked frail but was hardy as dried rawhide, and his seamed old face suggested gem-hard wits mixed with Latin gaiety, rather like traits seen in such faces as those of Voltaire and Leo XIII. During the early 1830s, at the express wish of Pope Gregory XVI, he worked for two years in France and Sardinia, stirring alive America and her needs in the aspirations of the new generation of clergy and religious. His authority was that of the survivor of far and dangerous enterprise; his vision was of that sort which kindled youth. Lamy and Machebeuf often talked together of the appeal of that distant life, and not only they—other seminarians were drawn toward it, until their priesthood converged with the needs of history. Their ordeal of preparation must be so solemn, under ancient ways, as to be an irrevocable source of strength.

vii.

To Go

IN THE MONT-FERRAND SEMINARY chapel Machebeuf was ordained by Bishop Féron of Clermont on the Ember Saturday of Christmas week in 1836, Lamy two years later on the same feast. They were assigned to small parishes in the diocese of Clermont, Lamy at Chapdes, Machebeuf at Le Cendre.

Presently, in 1838, a letter reached the Sulpician rector of Mont-Ferrand, Father Comfé, from a former student who had worked under him in Paris years ago. It came from the bishop of Cincinnati, Ohio, John Baptist Purcell, who wrote from Rome. Returning now to Ohio, he would come to France on the way, where he hoped the Father Rector, his old spiritual counsellor, could help him to recruit a party of young priests to go with him to work in America. He stood in great need of more missioners.

The Father Rector lost no time. He spoke to Lamy, Machebeuf, and other young priests of their classes, whose interest in America was known to him. Their response was eager. Machebeuf evidently led the enthusiasm. Along with three others, Lamy and he resolved to go, and readily obtained approval of Bishop Féron of Clermont-Ferrand. Even before the arrival of Bishop Purcell in Paris, their plans and conjectures for departure were taking form. They were soon, as Machebeuf said, "notified to be ready to go in the spring with Bishop Purcell to Cincinnati." Gathering their few belongings, they thought of the furious winters of America, and took the precaution of buying lengths of heavy cloth of the sort from which the Auvergnat mountaineers made their cloaks.

Their arrangements went forward with a certain secrecy. The seminary rector feared that Machebeuf's father might under parental authority forbid his son to go so far from home, and when it was time to go, he put Machebeuf under obedience to depart without taking leave of his family in Riom. Matters stood differently in Lempdes— there Lamy was able to disclose his intentions without meeting obstacles. Even so, saying a final goodbye was hard in his weakened state after the recent illness which had followed upon his great decision. But affairs had been set in train, there was no time either to grieve, or to ease what must be done, for the date had been set when the young Auvergnats were to meet their new bishop at the Sulpician Seminary in Paris.

So it was that they were northbound in the Paris diligence before word of their flight became general. Friends were astounded, and Machebeuf's father, the leading baker of Riom, was enraged as well as hurt when the young priest who had seen the fugitives waiting for the coach before dawn hurried about town with his news. But by then nothing could be done to reverse matters. Lamy and Machebeuf reached Paris safely, reported to the seminary at number 120 rue du Bac, where they were received with "paternal and affectionate cordiality," and settled down to await the bishop of Cincinnati.

They found a remarkable population of missioners on the alert— eight priests preparing to depart for China, Cochinchina, and Tong-King in Siam. Other parties had already gone to the Orient, and still others would follow. According to seminary gossip, the endurances awaiting in China made those expected by the Auvergnats destined for America seem less formidable. It appeared that priests going to the Asian kingdoms would be obliged, in order not to be noticed, to wear Chinese garb, and smoke a pipe four feet long all day, and never be seen to read the breviary, and use a small stick of ivory for a fork, and sleep on the floor with a simple mat for a bed—all this in addition to the chance of persecutions rumored to be far worse than any elsewhere. It was comforting news, of a sort, to send to the home villages left behind near Clermont. Meantime, Lamy and Machebeuf took from their bundles their supply of heavy Auvergnat mountain cloth. They first had it dyed black, and then ordered cloaks made from it, with extra linings of black cashmere for warmth in unknown America.

In a day or two Machebeuf heard from his sister at home that their father was inconsolably chagrined that his son should have left home without taking leave.

"Very dear Papa," he wrote at once, "let me assure you that it was not through indifference or lack of consideration for you, but in reality through obedience to the Superior of the Seminary, who enjoined upon me the most inviolable secrecy. In the face of all the longing which I had to tell you goodbye, he insisted that the interview would be too painful for both of us.... The sacrifice was great for me, but my course was marked out and I had to hold to it...."

When Bishop Purcell arrived in Paris from Bordeaux, he learned that one of his recruits was in disgrace at home, and wrote on his behalf.

"Dear Sir," he addressed the elder Machebeuf, "my heart feels fully the sorrow that the departure of your dear son for the missions of America has caused you," and went on to speak of a father's love which on occasion must include sacrifice. Begging him to forgive his son, the bishop offered an august consolation.

"It was in this manner," he wrote, "that the great Apostle of the Indias, St Francis Xavier, passed the house of his parents without saluting them, to go to a barbarous land much farther away than ours," and he closed by assuring the baker of Riom that he would love his son for him, who would pray for him and render him blessed on earth and in heaven by the souls who would be saved by his ministry. Then, "pray for him, and for me," concluded Purcell. Full forgiveness came from Riom in early July, along with a gift of five hundred francs to the young Father Machebeuf, who reported that the bishop was delighted. It would be possible to go to America with a lighter heart.

Purcell was a large-natured man with whom Lamy and his new followers were able to establish lifelong confidence and affection. Born in Ireland in 1800, he emigrated to the United States in 1818, where he began his theological studies, completing them and receiving ordination in Paris in 1826. At thirty-three he was made bishop of Cincinnati, and when he joined Lamy and the others in the rue du Bac, he was thirty-nine years old, a well-fleshed man with dark expressive eyes under black brows, an amiable mouth, and a strong chin.

There was much to organize for the voyage westward. The party was to consist of fifteen people, including old Bishop Flaget, who was returning to America for the last time. In addition to five priests (four of whom were to become bishops), three nuns were emigrating. Purcell made a hurried trip to London, and from there would proceed to Dieppe, where Machebeuf was instructed to join him for various duties. On a Thursday morning Machebeuf left the rue du Bac to reserve his seat in the Dieppe coach and attend to his passport.

Lamy did not accompany him on the errand. Suddenly, during the little while that Machebeuf was absent arranging for his ticket, Lamy collapsed, "deprived of all his strength," evidently on the verge of falling seriously ill. On his return from his brief errand, Machebeuf was astonished at the change in Lamy, put him to bed at once, and sent for the seminary doctor, who questioned the patient extensively and concluded that there was nothing critical to be concerned about—it was only a curious weak spell. But Lamy's fever kept rising, and Machebeuf remembered a letter he had had a few days before from a fellow priest in Clermont who told how Lamy was "always ill," had been bled twice, and treated fifteen times with leeches on the abdomen. Behind that serene control, that lamb-like gentleness, and within his square peasant frame, Lamy's tendency to nervous response sometimes appeared in moments of irrevocable commitment.

Privately, Machebeuf feared Lamy might not be well enough to sail with the mission party on 8 July, and only hoped that if this were so he might follow with another party sailing ten or eleven days later. Hard as it was to leave his friend ill in bed, Machebeuf must go to meet Purcell. After all, he said in practicality, as he put Lamy in the care of others, he had already reserved his coach seat. When he met Purcell at Dieppe, he could describe how affected the bishop was by the news of Lamy's collapse.

But there was much to do—the bishop had tasks in the neighborhood, and Dieppe was a port where Machebeuf had his first glimpse of the sea, and ships, and above all a steamship—a sort of amazing vessel which, in addition to sails, had a tall chimney to carry away smoke. It was a beautiful ship, he said, handsomely decorated with a green interior, and a chocolate-colored exterior with gilt-work. But Lamy was in his thought, and a week or so later hurrying back to Paris without the bishop, who was to proceed to Le Havre where they would all embark, he was relieved and amazed to find Lamy happily "promenading after supper," talking about him, as it happened, with the remaining colleagues who had arrived from Auvergne to join the expedition—Fathers Rappe and De Goesbriand. With them, Lamy had spent recent days in seeing the sights of Paris. He was well enough now to make the Atlantic crossing.

viii.

America

By 7 July 1839 they were at Le Havre, waiting to sail on the following day. Purcell was there already. Sailing day, Monday the eighth, was stormy, and the boarding was postponed until eight o'clock the next morning. In the deeply land-locked harbor, masts and spars made a web of fine lines like bare trees against the sky. The sail packet *Sylvie de Grasse* was at her dock. Her captain, an affable master from Bordeaux, knew Purcell, who as a seminarian fifteen years earlier had crossed to France with him in the same ship.

The captain now oversaw the boarding of his complement of passengers—the ship would be full—and at nine o'clock, as the deck-hands sang their capstan song under a fine sky, while a crowd watched from the quayside, and a blessing was given from the pier, the voyage began. The *Sylvie de Grasse* made her way down bay, past the great stone fortress, moving so slowly (the wind was set against her) that a steam tug was summoned to help her out of the narrow harbor entrance. Presently the wind changed, the tug cast off, and the wooden ship leaned and made for the open sea under her own sail, though still so slowly that not until night was falling did the voyagers lose sight of land "and then," said one, as distance and darkness engulfed France, "we began to get acquainted with the other passengers."

There were about sixty, mostly Protestants, in that part of the ship where the bishop's party were cabined. They included young men and women returning to the United States after studying in Paris, and solid businessmen emigrating to establish themselves in America. In the steerage were emigrant Germans—Catholic, Protestant, Jewish. They were all crowded into one open space separated from the crew's quarters by a partition. There they slept, cooked, passed the time. Their fare—150 francs—did not include food. They brought their own. The ship provided only wood and water. The air was so foul in the steerage that a visitor was forced away in a hurry—though he noted that all the Germans seemed healthy enough.

Comforts were greater for Purcell and his people. The captain seated them at his own table, to honor their calling and to spare them the

company of ordinary passengers, most of whom appeared to be wanting in manners. The captain's guests had "everything of the best which
one might find at a Parisian hotel"—fresh mutton, fowl, imported
wines, oranges in abundance, bread baked fresh daily, milk, butter;
and potatoes with every meal, a serving which the missioners enjoyed
most of all. The chef was a Negro, "very clever at his profession." His
supplies included enough fresh fruit and vegetables for the first eight
days of the voyage, which was expected to take four or five weeks.
Below decks, in addition to storerooms for provisions, were pens for
sheep and cows.

The *Sylvie de Grasse* presented unexpected style. Mahogany panel-
ling, with pilasters whose bases and capitals were finished in gold leaf,
lined the dining saloon, the ladies' saloon, and the sleeping cabins.
The staterooms were only six feet square, and though ordinarily they
accommodated two passengers, the missioners were assigned six to a
room, in three levels of two bunks each. With Lamy, Machebeuf, and
their Auvergnat companions, a Bavarian Franciscan was quartered.
The stateroom looked like a "fruitstand with its many shelves." If she
was typical of the ships of her time, she was under two hundred feet in
length, and of about a thousand tons gross weight—a three-masted,
full-rigged veteran of the North Atlantic run.

Several of the party felt the sea at first and spent their days in their
bunks. Lamy was among them—his seasickness lasted three weeks.
Another missioner was resigned to die until Machebeuf took him up
on deck, where he rapidly recovered. The marvel of the voyage was
old Bishop Flaget, who kept everyone in spirits with his nimble gaiety
and his edifying example of long daily devotions. He was always the
first one every morning to say his orisons in the little deckhouse. Even
when a heavy timber rolled loose across the deck and struck the old
man in the leg he dismissed the pain with a word. Machebeuf, too,
was in danger one day while studying English on deck—Lamy and the
rest also worked on the new language they would need—when a piece
of rigging broke aloft, a heavy iron-bound block fell nearby and a
thick rope, falling forty feet, struck Machebeuf's leg, which swelled and
gave pain for two days. A passenger who saw the accident said, "a few
feet closer, and Machebeuf's mission would have ended."

On the Feast of the Assumption, 15 August, Low Masses were quietly
said by the two bishops and the Bavarian friar—these in place of the
traditional ten o'clock High Mass which Purcell decided not to sing
out of recognition of the views of the surrounding Protestants, who
did not hold with the cult of the Virgin Mary, and who would have
thought the Catholics absurdly deranged in their practices. But that
evening the travelling clergy privately sang the litany of the Virgin

Mary and other holy canticles as the ship leaned her way on westward.

Sunrise and sunset at sea were the great events of the day. Imaginations worked to find celestial mountains and castles in the clouds, and flocks of sheep, bands of great horses, parades of soldiers; and then the light would change and there would remain only sea and sky, day on day, for forty-three days.

But on the forty-third day, they heard the captain cry out, "Land, land!" and all strained to see. Those without spy-glasses saw nothing at first, not having the eyes of mariners; but when at last they saw Long Island, in the evening of 20 August, they rejoiced in the sight of houses, farms, forts, woods, lighthouses, telegraph pylons, and knew that by the next morning they would disembark at the port of New York after a voyage of forty-four days.

As they came up the bay, which was "magnificent," they began to see the spires of the city. At the quarantine station in the Narrows, the *Sylvie de Grasse* anchored offshore. A steam lighter came to take passengers off—all but the steerage Germans, who must remain on board for two days to fulfill quarantine requirements—and brought them to the docks of South street, where the bowsprits of moored ships extended like a lattice roof above the clamorous traffic on the cobblestones below.

Purcell and his party, all in good health, were conducted across town by two friends from Cincinnati to pay a call upon Bishop Dubois of New York. After more than six weeks of inaction at sea, the travellers felt animation and purpose. They would leave the very next day on their journey inland. Purcell was not one to waste time, and there were still three hundred leagues to go until they should come to Cincinnati, nineteen days later. Their first duty on the inland journey was to pay respects to Archbishop Eccleston at Baltimore.

Going by canal, they found themselves in a cabined flatboat which resembled Noah's ark in a child's drawing. The barge was drawn by horse teams on the tow paths, the movement was at the pace of a horse's walk, and the passengers from France had their first view of farther America as it went slowly past the narrow windows of the cabin. The barges of the day combined flourishes with discomforts. Some of them contained small musical organs on which itinerant "professors" played concerts. In 1842 Charles Dickens travelled in a barge in whose common cabin men and women were separated only by a drawn curtain. The sleeping bunks were let down from the wall, were sixteen inches wide "exactly," and had to be vacated soon after daybreak to serve as seating benches. Dickens was obliged to wash in dirty canal water poured into a tin basin which was chained to the wall for the use of all passengers, and to dry himself must use the single roller towel provided for all. If the weather was mild, passengers rode on top of the cabin, and on moonlit nights, passing through hills or gorges—for the canal boats went along by day and night—saw how the wilderness scenery held every gleam and shadow of dreamlike strangeness, in the manner of romantic painting.

At Baltimore, the party transferred to stage coaches pulled by four horses at a fast sustained trot. There were three ranks of seats within, the sides of the coach were open except in rain when leather curtains were buttoned to wooden window frames, and the coach rocked on unimpeded. The coach was slung on leather straps instead of springs, and many occupants found the motion distressing.

Heading for Wheeling [West Virginia] the missioners crossed the Alleghenies and at a cost of one dollar for every sixteen miles followed the rude roads through continuous forests and woods, with only an occasional village to reassure them with the sight of boulder and log houses by day, and a lighted window or two by night. At Wheeling they took passage on the steam packet down-bound from Pittsburgh, which would carry them with many twists and turns of the Ohio River in a generally southwestward course to Cincinnati.

As they voyaged downriver, Purcell prepared the newcomers for what they would see at the journey's end. Cincinnati was a cathedral city—but like none they had ever seen at home. It was embraced by a great curve of the Ohio River, whose banks rose away to the north with only a few streets, and on those, only scattered buildings. The waterfront where the steamers tied up presented a row of shops, chandleries, and warehouses. Here and there the hillsides on which the city spread showed a few sizable houses, some of brick or masonry, but most of wood. There was much open land, with trees, within the town. The first church—a barn-like affair—had been built of logs outside the town limits because of a local ordinance prohibiting the erection of a Catholic church within the town proper. Bishop Flaget had built it, for Cincinnati had then belonged to his see of Bardstown, Kentucky. He had later managed to have the ordinance repealed and the log church brought into the town on rollers and resituated there.

Cincinnati had grown in response to river traffic—people still believed in 1839 that it was destined to become the greatest inland city of America—though a skeptical early settler, according to a family legend, when offered the entire site of Cincinnati "in exchange for his whiskey and molasses, . . . turned it down on the grounds that it was a hog wallow, and went up the Licking River and raised strawberries." In 1821 the outlandish riverside town was declared a bishopric. Its first bishop was the Dominican Edward Fenwick, whom Flaget consecrated in 1822. He was succeeded by Purcell eleven years later. Whatever was there now, all stemmed from Flaget, who said, "When I arrived I had absolutely nothing, except the benedictions with which the venerable Archbishop Carroll of Baltimore"—the first American bishop—"clothed me." Even now, Purcell seemed to be saying to his recruits on their Ohio River steamboat as they wound their way toward the next stage of an undertaking begun in the heart of France with so much filial regret and inner uncertainty, there was not much to find.

It was the rivers, in their great size and grand currents, which conveyed a sense of the vastness of the continent, in a scale of nature new to the Europeans, as they entered the last lap of the journey, beneath towering smokestacks, and to the rhythmic splash of steam-powered paddles which recalled the sound of village mill-wheels. Slowly, the strangeness, amplitude, and beauty of sparsely settled America began to make claims upon the newcomers.

Lamy, like the others, could retain a sense of what lay behind him in his venture so far from his ancient home—the form of the organized, world-wide structure of the Church, in its administration, its resources, its experience in how the world ran, which would give him support when he should need it. Its purpose was not to be questioned, for it was at the center of his life, nor were its methods, for he was their minister. At home, in Roman France, or here, established however meagrely beyond the wilderness riverbanks going by, lay the same source of conviction and energy.

II

THE MIDDLE WEST

1839–1850

i.

Cincinnati

THE PADDLE-WHEEL RIVER PACKET warped its way to the waterfront of Cincinnati on 10 September 1839, to its berth amidst other moored riverboats, with their tall twin smoke pipes and wide decks, bearing such names as *Car of Commerce, Ohio Belle, Belle Creole, Cincinnatus, Brooklyn,* and *New Orleans.* The missioners saw the straggle of stores, shacks, and mansions rising away on the slope in the midst of open fields. Not yet a half century old, it was, with almost fifty thousand people, the greatest city of Ohio. It all looked raw. They left the ship and proceeded to the "little seminary" where Bishop Purcell was already training local youths for the priesthood. There the newcomers were to lodge, and, they hoped, there they would have a chance to advance their study of the language of America. How could they be at home until they could communicate, or preach, or feel like Americans?

But the few faculty members of the seminary were so busy with their duties of teaching resident seminarians and also carrying on parish work that they had no time to give English lessons, and little for conversation. To their dismay, the young Frenchmen met with the community only for a short while after supper every evening.

There were strangenesses to become used to. In America, it appeared, priests were addressed as Mister. When priests went into the city, they changed from cassock to the dress of laymen—a long frock coat, a high-buttoned waistcoat, and (the Frenchmen laid aside the black tricorne as worn at home by Monsieur l'Abbé) a tall hat of brushed silk nap or a shapeless felt headgear with a wide drooping brim. If they looked to Purcell for continued companionship like that of shipboard they found him endistanced by work—people even invaded his mealtimes to talk business, and only now and then was he able to join in the after-supper gatherings. Lamy and his friends were left "without anything special to do." The inaction of their days was far different from the visions they had made of America and the sanctifying sacrifices that would be demanded of them. Now it was Machebeuf's turn to fall ill—he was ill for fifteen days and he wondered if he would ever become accustomed to America.

But at last, after three weeks, the bishop had orders for them hardly less amazing than the disappointments of Cincinnati. He saw how weary they were of inaction, and how their first eagerness might be wasted. Despite their inexperience, their lack of the language, and the state of the country, he suddenly assigned all the new Frenchmen to certain mission parishes in Ohio which had no regular pastors. It would be their duty to bring scattered settlers together to form parish groups, and to build churches. Others at the seminary wondered at the assignments—young men in their twenties given pastoral charges?

But Lamy and his fellow countrymen assumed the inland wilderness of the Middle West with restored spirits. Each was given a central location to develop—a little cluster which might one day be a town—from which other settlements could be served. Lamy was given Danville, in the wooded middle of the state; Machebeuf, Tiffin, which lay to the north, on the flat lands not far from Lake Erie. One thing which "astonished" them was that they had been sent so quickly to separate assignments. Each was to be on his own.

ii.

To the Forests

OHIO LAND was generally flat, the horizons were almost level; the rivers unbridged, the woods and forest uncleared but for widely separated farms and small communities; the roads cloudy with dust, or flowing with mud. When streams rose their woodland banks became marshes. The whole state—it was admitted to the Union in 1803 as the seventeenth state—was almost entirely covered with forest. Summer's heat was sultry, the air glistening and humming with insects, the temperature often passing a hundred. In winter the cold was so great that trees cracked under ice, and lakes were crossed by sledge, and snow lay on the ground in layers of ice for weeks, making travel by wheeled vehicle or horse chancy and by river impossible. It was odd, to the stranger, to find a land subject to such extremes of weather, yet settlers sought it out in great numbers, cities were promised, the imagination looked westward, and by the 1830s, Ohio's population numbered almost a million.

But such a figure did not suggest the isolated farm or the forest-lost settlement, often named after a single family, which in time might become a village, then a town. One such was Sapp's Settlement, later to be called Danville, to which Lamy went in the autumn of 1839. Purcell already knew it well.

Before 1810 George Sapp and his wife, Catherine, emigrants from the Catholic Maryland of Lord Baltimore's descendants, came to the Middle West, and "on a beautiful spot," declared their grandson in a narrative which came down through the family in manuscript, "by one of the most beautiful springs God has caused its waters to flow," they built a small log house. Catherine said, "George, right here we will build our cabin and live and die."

So they did, "but not until God had blessed them with a large family. I have said a noble family. I will say one of the most remarkable Familys that has ever been raised in this vicinity. They were kind and agreeable together, truly brothers and sisters."

Not far away a few other Marylanders came to stay. The presence of the settlement could be detected, from a little distance, only by the blue smoke of its cabin fires rising above the woods. In all things life must be sustained from what the wilderness alone could provide. There was a sense of contentment in the slowly gained knowledge of this. Bare necessities were mingled with sport—there was no other entertainment. A few books and spoken prayer met non-material needs.

George Sapp told his grandson, then a boy, about hunting at night. His very language conveys the time.

He has, while hunting, come across an old bear and her young cubs and he would run towards them and hallow and all the noise possible and by so doing the cubs would run up a tree and the mother bear would then run away for some distance and then Grand Father would shoot the cubs and they would have some good meat. At one particular time Grand Father and a friendly Indian went out to watch a deerlick on a bright moonlight night and on the way to the lick they made an agreement not to talk any after They arrived at the Lick. And also each one would climb separate trees on the west side of the lick so that They would have the lick between Them and the moon, when it came up, in order that They would have full view of the Lick and surroundings. They were up in the trees waiting patiently when to their surprise They heard something climbing a tree over the Lick and could not Tell what it was until the moon gave sufficient light for Them to Discover what it might be and it proved to be a panther perched upon a limb waiting for Mr. Deer. They all three kept quiet and it was not long until They Heard and seen the Deer, but as soon as the Deer came to the Lick the Panther leaped upon Him and killed him quickly and then the Indian shot the Panther and made the remark to Grand Father that was the way to watch a Deerlick.

In the log house of George and Catherine there were not "any cradles for rocking Babys." Consequently, their first son "had a bresh heap for his resting place." The scattered settlers longed for community. It would come, and one of its chief tracks was the "Great National Road," the highway which was conceived by General Washington. It was also known in various of its sections as "The National Pike," the "Cumberland Road," and finally, and prophetically for Lamy, as the "Santa Fe Trail." Its Ohio portion was financed by Congress when the state was admitted to the union. Even as early as 1825 its extension to Santa Fe was authorized by Congress. Eventually the several states it crossed assumed responsibility for its local maintenance. It had a roadbed thirty feet in width and its earliest portions were surfaced with crushed stone and gravel. The rest of it was plain dirt. "Tree stumps eighteen inches high were left in the road but trimmed and rounded with an axe so that carriages could safely pass over them." Along its tracks went "a steady stream of two-wheeled carts, Conestoga wagons, farm wagons, men on horseback, men on foot, men driving cattle, hogs, horses and mules." Parts of the road were traversed by Purcell in his earliest visits, and when Lamy went north from Cincinnati, he too travelled upon it for a while. But on the straggling earthen tracks which were tributaries of the Great National Road, travel for anyone was precarious, with many creeks to cross which were often swollen in warm weather and treacherously frozen in cold. Some of these passed by curious low hills of symmetrical shape, which later proved to be Indian burial mounds holding the secrets of life in the wilderness as it was lived long before the Easterners came.

George Sapp gave part of his homestead land for a church and burial ground in 1822. Though he himself was not baptized, others of his community were, and in any case, settlers gathered together on whatever possible occasion, and so it came to be that when first, Father Fenwick of Cincinnati, and later, Father O'Leary and Father Alleman of distant parishes, rode from their stations to hold services, they found a loosely organized parish at Sapp's Settlement with a log church called St Luke's. A town was growing a dozen miles to the west—this was Mt Vernon, and there, too, settlers had made their congregations, in the beginning largely Methodist.

When Purcell became bishop of Cincinnati he went through the country where later he would send resident pastors. In some places, he encountered impassive hostility from those who were not Catholics, in others, all people of whatever confession gathered to see him, to hear him preach, and to take the sacraments from him if they were eligible —baptism, communion, confirmation. In the nation at the time there was lively animosity against Catholics, who kept arriving by immigration from abroad in swelling numbers—people mostly of the laboring class come to make their fortune and find new identity in republican America. Purcell, in his forest clearings, preached on the "vulgar prejudice against the Catholic Church," refuting its "pretended [i.e., supposed] opposition to Scripture and civil and religious liberty" and defending "the much abused and calumniated convents." Lurid rumors about the latter were feverishly enjoyed by Protestant extremists. Purcell was warmly greeted. On one journey to Sapp's, he "preached twice from a rudely fashioned pulpit in Mr Sapp's orchard," and when he went to Mt Vernon, said Mass in private houses for the first time— in 1834. When the Methodist church there was refused him on one occasion, he used a private chapel built by a well-disposed Protestant. Crowds met him also in Newark, and Zanesville, sometimes so eager that he had to preach twice a day—once in the morning, and again in the evening "at early candle-light," for two hours at a time. For many of his listeners he was the world coming to see them—they who lacked news, and theatres, and any music but their own half-remembered, half-invented songs and airs.

. . .

iii.

The Pattern

At Danville, as the Sapp settlement was now called, Lamy found a fine country of great shady groves, set in a sequence of wooded valleys where morning mists lingered paler and paler at each farther ridge. To reach his village, he had to cross the Walhondling Creek, which took its slow course to the south. In autumn, when he arrived, the creek was mild; in winter it could be an icy obstacle, in spring a treacherous flood. He found St Luke's log church, and not far away Grandfather Sapp's cemetery, which sat on a fine hill looking to all directions. The village was laid out on streets which rose and fell on the folding hills.

By what followed rapidly, it was clear that the people took him to themselves from the first. Since there was no place of his own in which to live, he stayed now with one, now another, of his new families. He was charged with mission settlements at varying distances from Danville, and he rode or walked to make himself known—he thought nothing, said someone, of walking from Danville to Mt Vernon and back in a single afternoon, a journey of twelve miles each way. In his halting English, of which he must have seen the humor even as he regretted its limitations, he held his meetings, and performed his routine duties, and brought his followers to join him in the matter of the church building.

Walls and a roof had been put up by the settlers, but the church was far from finished. He led them in continuing the work, and considering his difficulties, it progressed rapidly. About a year after his arrival, he wrote from Danville to Bishop Purcell, by the uncertain mails:

I am in the hope that you received the letter I wrote to you two months ago. I told you that I was most [?] uncertain whether we should go on or not, for our new church at Danville, because it's so hard times this year; but we are going to finish it. we have many hands, and I hope it will be quite done perhaps before the last week of next month. You recollect that you promised me hundred dollars to help this congregation; and as I cannot have the least doubt about your word I have already engaged myself to pay the plaster. this will cost from 60 to 70 dollars; I am going also to get the altar made. be so good as to make me an answere, and let me know how you will do about that help for our church. when I came here for the first time, the building was under the roof, and since, we have expended more than three hundred dollars. you know, it is a frame building fifty feet by thirty-eight.

Furthermore, it had a choir gallery, and the altar was to be "handsome," and there was to be an altar railing. The plastering was "remarkably well done by two good Irish Catholics." The front centered on a sturdy, square tower, with a latticed belfry, topped by a cross, all in vastly simplified Gothic. Not much wider than the tower, with windows in pointed arches, the rest of the church reached back under a peaked roof. There was nothing like it thereabouts, and by 15 November—two weeks before Lamy had planned—it was, though not fully completed within, ready to be dedicated.

The bishop came from Cincinnati to perform the ceremony. He saw that the church stood on "a beautiful eminence visible for a great distance," and that it was established on a two-acre plot. It was touching that many Protestant neighbors had helped in one way or another toward the building of the church. Almost more than a monument to religion, St Luke's was a mark of organized society such as had never before existed in Sapp's Settlement. Bishop Purcell gave first communions, confirmations, baptisms, and preached on the Holy Eucharist, and celebrated a solemn Mass, and in the congregation pride was mingled with righteous fatigue after great effort. Lamy was at the center of it all. By now he was revered and loved by those whom he had led in the building of the temple and all it stood for in the way of civilization.

Two days after the dedication, Purcell moved on to Mt Vernon, where, at the request of Protestants and Catholics alike, he preached and held services. There was not yet a church there—to build this would be Lamy's next task. Meantime, he set about making a rectory for himself on donated land opposite the Danville church.

The whole pattern of his work there established the terms of his labors over the next years. He had looked no farther than Ohio—except for one occasion which seemed to threaten the continuation of work so faithfully begun.

It had to do with an impulsive notion which Machebeuf, in his parish of Tiffin in northern Ohio, seemed ready to carry out. He had been visited by the celebrated Jesuit missioner P. J. De Smet, who was already celebrated as "the Apostle to the Indians" (their name for a Jesuit was "Blackrobe") and who brought, from his expeditions into the Far West, much of the earliest knowledge of the upper plains and Rocky Mountain regions to the established public east of the Mississippi. Machebeuf, he urged in Tiffin, should join him in his vast western missionary travels, with all its dazzling hardships and holy dangers. But what would become of Tiffin, where a little parish church of native stone was being erected? Bishop Purcell heard of the plan to go West, and knowing of the close friendship of Lamy and Machebeuf, sent Lamy to Tiffin to dissuade Machebeuf "from a project which afflicted the heart of the bishop and father."

After hearing Lamy set forth the views of his bishop against abandoning Tiffin and going West, Machebeuf "contented himself with asking his friend,

" '*Eh bien! mon cher,* what would you do in my place?' "

Lamy—whether placing an even graver responsibility on Machebeuf or simply expressing his innermost feeling—replied,

"What would I do? All right. If you go, I will follow you."

It was a deterrent which Machebeuf was unable to ignore. Yet the episode held a prophetic note for them both, even as they remained with their own present duties—building churches, visiting their dependent missions. Purcell knew upon whom he could depend, and how to use friendship as an instrument.

iv.

Those Waiting

IN 1840 LAMY SET ABOUT the building of a small brick church in Mt Vernon. Its substance began with his creation of a sense of community among the people there. Someone gave land, another was to take the lead in bringing timber, others worked to use the roads and canals of Ohio to gather other materials. As resident pastor of Danville, Lamy could not give all his time to Mt Vernon—or even to Danville itself— for he was charged with mission duties also in Mansfield, Ashland, Loudonville, Wooster, Canal Dover, Newark, and Massillon, in addition to even less coherent communities by the waysides.

In the hot, white, diffused mists of summer, and the cracking and often howling winters alike, he and Machebeuf both had to forward their home parishes and attend to their missions. As Lamy wrote to Purcell, "I have bought a horse, and I am now a great 'traveller'; for I have many places to attend, and I don't stay more than two Sundays a month in Danville."

Machebeuf, too, had acquired a horse—*"beau et excellent"*—from a German priest at the exorbitant rate of one hundred dollars. His letters home were full of lively details about the life of the missioner— typical of what Lamy, too, was experiencing, and all the other young Auvergnats who had come away with them.

In their own parishes they wore their cassocks, but travelling they put on their oldest clothes, and when they came to towns they dressed more neatly in order not to invite scornful comments from entrenched Protestants. They used a long leather bag in which to carry vestments, Mass vessels, and other supplies, and the bag was thrown over the saddle. Where roads permitted, a four-wheeled wagon served the missioners and then they could carry a travelling trunk. In the very beginning, they had to "preach by their silence" but it was not long before they were able to get along in English, to the delight of their listeners. Sometimes it was so cold that the ink froze in its bottle as they wrote at night by firelight. The visitor often had to sleep next to his horse to keep warm. Coming to a house where he would spend the night, the missioner was given a bed, "sometimes very good, sometimes only passable." In the morning, children would be sent in every direction to tell other remote homesteaders that the priest had come, and, so soon that it was amazing, the people came gathering, settlers from Germany, Ireland, France, and the eastern states, and it was time for the sacraments and the Mass and the sermon. The listeners were "not savages, but Europeans who are coming in crowds to clear off the forests of America." And then on again to the next cluster of those waiting for what the visitor alone could bring them. It was a matter of literally keeping the faith, at whatever cost to the traveller—on one occasion Machebeuf used the frozen Toussaint River as his highway, until the ice broke and he went through into water five feet deep.

Danville and Tiffin were eighty to ninety miles apart and there were few occasions when Lamy and Machebeuf could see each other. Sometimes they would converge at Cincinnati on visits to the bishop. Now and then they were prevented by illness from visiting each other— Lamy was ill several times, once "dangerously for several days," but when he was well enough he joined Machebeuf for a visit to the Irish canal workers on the Maumee River, and exclaimed over American enterprise which was constructing a canal forty feet wide. One day Lamy heard that Machebeuf was dead of cholera, and "heartbroken" went to bury his oldest friend. When he arrived, he found instead that Machebeuf was simply recovering from a fever. There was joy all around, and another of the French missioners referred to the invalid who had deceived death as "Monsieur Trompe-la-Mort."

Loving all which they were overcoming in the name of what they believed, they were content. Machebeuf wrote to Riom, "I declare to you that for all the gold in the world I would not return to live in Europe," and Lamy in one of his letters written from abroad some years later, said he was preparing himself "to return to my Beloved Ohio." Still, the call of their early home was strong in their early days in the Middle West. They had fine plans for a visit to Auvergne. They knew how they would go—the Lake Erie steamboat from Sandusky to Buffalo, the great canal to the Hudson River and down to New York, and from there, no such antiquated an affair as a ship under canvas but a steamer, which would reach Liverpool in fourteen days. "From Liverpool to Paris by railroad and the Straits of Dover, two days would be enough," wrote Machebeuf to his father. "Then from Paris to Riom is but a hop-step-and-a-jump for an American. This is the way Father Lamy and I have fixed up our plan." Yet there was a condition which had to be met first. "But it cannot be carried out until we have each built two churches, [Lamy] at Mt Vernon and Newark, I, at my two Sanduskys [then known as Upper and Lower Sandusky]. So, if you can find some generous Catholic who can send us at least eighty thousand francs for each church, we can leave within a year. *Merci. . . .*"

V.

Self-Searchings

AND THERE IT WAS—the material struggle from which neither would ever be free. Lamy knew moments of self-doubt—there was "grade deal to be done"; he wrote the bishop in 1841; "if I had only that sacerdotal zeal." He need not have worried—the bishop referred to him as a "fervent pastor."

Yet the obstacles were not merely local. The nation was undergoing a great financial depression, and despite all the good will, strong arms, and community work in the remote countrysides, materials still cost money, labor must be paid; the pressing needs of a growing population always increased the goal to be achieved. Machebeuf wrote to his brother, his sister, and his father in turn, describing the national condition. "Since the declaration of independence," he declared, "no one ever saw here such stagnation in business affairs. Not only is this true of Ohio, but in all the States of the Union." There was not a tenth of the money in circulation in 1842 which had been known in earlier years. Most of the banks failed; those which survived would not lend money; paper money, much mistrusted as issued by banks which later failed, destroyed confidence; employers defaulted on wages to workmen. Through the months, work was discontinued on all large enterprises. It hardly paid to raise grain crops. Food prices were depressed, but those who raised their own could not starve. Immigrants kept pouring in, not to take jobs, but to claim land and cultivate their own produce. It was obvious that support of existing churches and the construction of new ones was almost impossible. Machebeuf—and the same must have been true for Lamy—had the greatest trouble keeping up his own dwelling, and said, "I have had to sell my dear little buggy which was so useful."

Yet, all sharing, the pastor's work went on, however humbly. Lamy's rectory at Danville was "pretty well finished" in April 1841. He later said to someone else that he found it harder to furnish a house than to put it up out of rude materials.

Even before St Luke's at Danville was completed, Lamy was continuing work on his new church at Mt Vernon. He called it St Vincent de Paul's, after his "favorite saint." While it was going up, he said Mass in various private houses. Overseeing the erection of the church, Lamy had a helper in "old Squire Colopy," who was "in such good earnest, that he has scarcely any rest, till he sees it enclosed. It will be a very handsome building. at the moment I write to you," Lamy told Purcell, "they have employed 60000 bricks. We think that it will be an ornament to the town."

But people were not always as strong as bricks. Squire Colopy fell ill, and a Mr Brophy had to take time from his own work to oversee the construction. Lamy to Purcell in December 1841:

> this church in Mt Vernon would have been enclosed two months ago if it was not for the accident that happened to Mr Brophy (the little Irish tailor) he had one day a fall, and has been lame since, though he is getting better. he was the man to attend to the building, but after he had that fall, the church was little neglected; Mr Colopy has not been very well, there was only Mr Morton who has done all he could; the mecanics that had to put on the roof have also been sick. but now all that is wanting, is to have the shingles on. all the timbers for the roof are fixed on the wals that church looks very handsome.

The church was finally roofed and plastered when fire, "by some unknown means," on the evening of 2 March 1844, burned away all but the brick shell of St Vincent de Paul's, and that was weakened.

Purcell came to see the wreckage, preached in the court house to a large crowd, and the citizens subscribed six hundred dollars to rebuild the church. The rebuilding would be slow—"not so much for want of means as of materials, in the getting out whereof some unavoidable delays have occurred."

But Lamy was already at work on plans for his new church at Newark, twenty-four miles from Mt Vernon, thirty-six miles from Danville. He was in constant touch with Purcell, projecting hopes, reporting progress, asking permission for various moves. In December 1841, there was as yet no deed to the Newark property where he meant to build. He wanted this settled before spring, so that he could count on beginning the work when the weather broke fine. He would be able to buy windows and altar from the church at Zanesville, and he intended to get them "very cheap." If he had to go into debt to build, might he have permission to sell a portion of the deeded land?—for the deed, in February 1842, was now secure—though it would be the last measure to take, if necessary. The church went up, and the next question was where the priest might stay—Lamy came every fourth Sunday to Newark, had been staying with a certain family. But there was now illness in their small house and he felt it imposing on them to return each time. How would it be if he carefully chose another good family, asked them to build a house on church property, keep a room for him, and after the equivalent of his room and board had paid for their share of the house, let it all revert to the parish of St Francis de Sales, as he had named it? There was "good spirit" in his people. His plans went forward, even to the great matter of fine music. Newark was largely a German parish. The congregation had music in them, and he was able to report: "We have then a very good choir of German Catholics with some fair instruments. [There was no organ.] They sing very well, but almost all in German, except the Kyrie, Gloria and Credo in Latin, till they get some books of church music." Like the early Franciscans in a place he had not yet heard of, he seemed able to do everything, even to rehearsing the choir, for it had "greatly improved" under his instruction. Would the bishop please send books of liturgical music? A cheque for two hundred dollars would also be welcome at Mt Vernon, whose people were rebuilding St Vincent de Paul's after the fire. He was happy to report that at Newark, "we have got a little help from the Widow McCarthy."

So it went, in all his missions, in much the same set of problems, ingenuities, endurances. There were always the Widow McCarthys, the Squire Colopys, the Mr Brophys, to give support and help lead others in the itinerant pastor's plans. Machebeuf, in the north, was moved from Tiffin to Lower Sandusky, and later given Upper Sandusky, and eventually the two parishes met and merged simply as Sandusky. In his turn, he kept Purcell informed and asked him for money. His first church was a vacant storeroom. The one he built as soon as possible was called after the Holy Angels. Its timber and stone were brought from across Sandusky Bay where a curving peninsula reached out into Lake Erie. Even before it was finished, it was too small for the congregation—a mixed success. He had benches sitting back to back to accommodate whom he could. It was a rudely Gothic church, forty by seventy feet in dimensions, with a steeple 117 feet high. The cross at the top, said Machebeuf, was "made by an English Anabaptist, gilded by an American infidel, and placed upon a Catholic church to be seen shining by mariners far out upon the lake."

Throughout their labors in separated places, Lamy and Machebeuf kept up their comradeship as well as they could. Despite their infrequent visits to each other, they never lost the strong root of their friendship. Each knew what the other was accomplishing at every step, and both kept in touch with their fellow Auvergnats. Each reported news of all the others in writing to France. Lamy went to see Machebeuf begin his stone church, Machebeuf reported Lamy's growing number of conversions, including a highly placed English family now reduced to poverty, and referred to him as "my dear colleague," and "neighbor," despite the ninety miles which divided them. The grave charm of the younger man and the spritely wits of the older still complemented each other like nourishment. Machebeuf regarded himself at moments with some accuracy, noting the "liveliness and inconstancy of my character." He told his brother that "even if the Devil is often in my purse, I am happy." As for his formidable tasks, "when will we finish them? This question I ignore."

Lamy's self-searchings were of a somewhat different character. Purcell had become not only his lord, but his confidant. ". . . If I was a priest or minister according to the heart of God," he wrote the bishop in 1841, from Danville, "the Divine seed would bring forth fruit, though sown by a pour [sic] sower. I beseech you that you pray God that he may enable me to be a good priest, and to persevere in that state, that I may procure the glory of God, and the salvation of those souls which he has redeemed at so great a price." Was momentary discouragement to be read in this? Or such temptations as might threaten his vows? Or perhaps a simple humility which—as he was a meditative man—let him see human weakness as an inescapable state? It took a certain stalwartness to know oneself in honesty and still go forward with affairs in the world for the sake of others.

Most distasteful, as always, was the unending quest for money with which to do a job. To the utmost extent possible, the parishes had to support themselves, appealing to Cincinnati only as a last resort. Machebeuf went to French Canada in search of funds in 1843 to pay for building debts of his new church. Surely there would be some inevitable appeal in a common ancestry? He travelled by what he called "clerical post," putting up at rectories wherever possible. Lamy went to see him on his return in April, and the news was both good and bad. Machebeuf had managed to raise money for most of his debts. But he had had a disagreeable adventure on the way, which was reported in the press:

We regret to hear that the Rev. Machebeuf, the pastor of Lower Sandusky, was shipwrecked on Lake Ontario, whilst on the way to Quebec. The crew and passengers saved their lives with difficulty and landed on an Island. They applied for shelter where all were kindly received until the owner discovered that a "Popish Priest" was among his guests. Our Rev. friend after much solicitation was graciously permitted to sleep *on the floor!* Such *christian charity* deserves to be remembered. Even the Heathens of old were more merciful.

The newspaper went on to cite the Acts of the Apostles, Chapter 28: "And when we had escaped, then we knew that the Island was called

Melita. But the Barbarians showed us no small courtesy. For having kindled a fire, they refreshed us all, because of the rain falling, and of the cold. . . ." If there was any satisfaction for the two friends in the episode, it was that of entering into such an experience as had come to St Paul himself.

Lamy now had four churches and was making arrangements for two more, and though the parishioners were generous, times were still hard and means limited. He must turn to Purcell. "If you give me permission I will go on a begging expedition, though I am not very bold. . . . I am willing to go and beg, but before could you not send me a little help to settle some of the more urging affairs." He went to St Louis, and thought of going to New Orleans from there, and a letter from the bishop would be helpful. "I hope that difficulties will only enlarge my courage. . . ."

He had heard of a woman of means at St Louis, a Mrs Biddle, called upon her, and was at once involved in an absurd financial tangle. "I proposed to borrow 300 dollars from her if she would let me have that sum without interest for some years. She consented but would not give me the money until a certain priest from Illinois would return to her a sum which he had borrowed from her for some years. She was to send it to me after my departure from St Louis, but I never received the money, I didn't think she sent it at all." But evidently she considered that she had Lamy's note for the amount, and later queried the bishop about it. Explaining further, Lamy said, "I left the management of it to Father Glaizal but this father will not write me a word about it. She could not then by no means have my note it must be a misunderstanding." As the sole result of his interview with the prudent matron of St Louis, he came away with ten dollars she had given him. The bishop was not to pay off any such note, though Lamy was grateful to him for cancelling another held by a "young man Mr Creighton for the 5 dollars he gives me." Five dollars—it was hard to ask even for that.

He tried to see both sides of the financial difficulty of the parishes—what was needed, and what could be given. But there were moments when he was tempted to use his priestly powers, even if unworthily, to force money troubles toward some resolution. He once put it to the bishop this way:

. . . There are times which goes very hard with some people of those settlements to help toward the church when some thing is to be done, and also to contribute a little according to their abilities for the support of the clergyman. in regard to this last point I do not know what to do with a number of them. I wish you would advise me some means to make them do. Could I not tell them, that if they do not help [a] little, even if they are not able to do much, they have no right to the services of the priest? could I not try to scare some of them refuse to hear their confessions once or twice? you will oblige me very much if you suggest what I could do in such a case. . . .

It was a harsher thought than he usually expressed. Whatever Purcell told him in reply—there is no record—Lamy was more like himself a few years later, when, still struggling with issues of discipline, he appealed to the bishop for a decision about how to respond to renewed sick calls from lapsed Catholics who when they recovered decided to return to their sinful comforts. Should he go? Or should an example be made of such persons? His own character was clear when he wrote, "I know the way of mildness is the best. . . ." The Church had her conditions to be met, people were weak, authority was often puzzled, the material and the spiritual met at odd boundaries on occasion. Perhaps his qualms did him as much credit as his strictness.

He was still more like himself when he reported to Purcell on certain other sick calls. "These last two months I had some sick calls, for some people who were not Catholic, two men married, and a boy of twenty years. They were very low, they have got well; and the poor innocent creatures think that my visit did them more good than all the medicines; they now come to church regularly, and I hope, they will be good Catholics. . . ." There he spoke as the shrewd peasant, the faithful mystic, and the pragmatic Frenchman, together.

But if problems never ended, neither did they end in frustration. He was still young, comradely, energetic, and comely. On one of his infrequent visits to Machebeuf in the north, they always traded troubles and surmounted them with high spirits, saying to each other in their old Auvergnesc saw, *"Latsin pas!"* and in 1843, Machebeuf wrote to his sister the nun in Riom that his friend was *"toujours gaie [sic], grand, gros, et gras"*—"always happy, hearty, huge, and hefty."

vi.

The Materials

INCREASINGLY, LAMY TURNED TO PURCELL in friendship. At the outset struggling to learn English he asked the bishop's pardon if he ventured to write him in the new language—*"Monseigneur, je prie votre*

*grandeur** de vouloir bien me pardonnant la liberté que j'ai prise
de vous écrire quelques lignes en mauvais Anglais—"* and went on to
another language difficulty, for there were so many Germans swarming
into his territory that he said, "one thing is wanted for me, it is the
german language, and though I speak but very little English, could I
speak the dutch so well, it would be very good." He was then boarding
at the house of George Sapp's son, where they gave him a room. He
longed to see the bishop, "could I be so happy as to see you, I would
have it for the greatest blessing; I have so many things to tell you. . . ."

Through the years there were "so many things," and also so many
requests and needs. He needed altar stones—one for his home church,
others for the missions. They could be broken. He had broken one.
He needed vestments, a ciborium, a cheque, for the hard times continued, though to be sure the churches were flourishing, and even in
its first year St Luke's at Danville saw a thousand persons present at
the Feast of the Resurrection, most of whom were not even Catholics,
and the sermon, in imperfect English, was a challenge. "However," he
said, "I did not get scared; and as I had before prepared mon petit mot,
I did my best to deliver it." At about the same time, he could report,
"Great many in Danville have joined the temperance Society, and some
in Newark"—a national movement whose earnest power had reached
the forest frontier.

In 1842 he had "yet another thing" to ask the bishop. What was to
be done if a Catholic girl would insist on marrying a man who was
not baptized? In the small community of Danville such a case of
relentless love, before which man or woman was often helpless, was
now Lamy's concern. He told the girl she ought not to think of marrying her lover, and seemed at first able to turn her mind in the righteous
direction. But he was "afraid that she will have the man," who, he
declared, had "lost his moral character." But "suppose the marriage
must take place?"—in other words, what if she should be with child?
What then should he do? Would it be better to let them go to the
Squire—the Justice of the Peace—or to marry them himself after all?
The matter might, for reasons hinted at, be urgent. "Answer as soon
as possible, what I can do . . ." So an ancient blind power spoke
through his own concern, in the little grassy town with its new spire
and its cemetery hill. It was not always simple to be the mediator
between what these monuments represented.

In 1844 Newark, his second mission, demanded increasingly of Lamy
more than he reasonably could give to it from Danville. The town

* *Votre grandeur*—the English usage is "Your Excellency."

was growing faster than Danville, yet the church at Newark had not even yet been plastered. Had he been overambitious in building? "Perhaps I ought to be blamed to do so much in these hard times. in this case I beg your pardon but I do hope good intention will be some excuse"—for he had gone ahead too with a modest rectory and by summer the first payment on it would be due—a hundred dollars. Perhaps he should move to Newark from Danville, though he still had "great many places to attend," and was almost "constantly on horseback." He was not complaining of the labor and the fatigue, for he was "as hearty and strong as ever."

Action was urged upon him from many directions—the newest one was the "already contracted" plan to build a railroad from Mansfield, Ohio, to Lake Erie. Mansfield would grow much faster than either Danville or Newark, and yet—he thought it important—"there is no regular clergyman who attends Mansfield regularly." He had been there four times, it was only twenty-nine miles from Danville, yet he had hardly any time to go there. The matter was urgent—"Many protestants, I have no doubt would help to put up a church for this very circumstance of the railroad coming there."

If he was "very thankful for . . . the particular kindness you have showed to me," the bishop, in his turn, must have been grateful to have a man in the field so alert to all the implications of a fast-growing society. Lamy was not only a good priest, he was also a reliable manager and observer of the hard facts all about. It was a quality to be kept in mind by Cincinnati for what the future might bring.

It was satisfying to report in the midsummer of 1845 that the burned-out church at Mt Vernon was under roof again. To rebuild it, everyone had "struggled very hard, but especially our warm friend little Mr Brophy. his zeal which he proves 'by the act' cannot be praised enough." But the problems at Newark were still nagging, and a priest with whom he alternated one Sunday a month proved to be disinterested in "the temporal concerns of the church," such as building, care for the property, the finances. Possibly the Dominicans, who had many priests, might take over the place, if he might make a suggestion? After all, they had once controlled Newark, and would probably be glad to assume even Louisville. But of course, "Bishop, you know yourself what is best to be done." He still blamed himself for perhaps assuming more at Newark than could be redeemed, and he felt so unhappy about it, and so responsible, that he would gladly pledge a substantial portion of his inheritance in France, whenever it should come to him, to help with the problem. It was a comfort, however, to be able to be frank with Purcell. "It is to you, Revd Bishop that I must open my heart. You have always been a father to me, and I bless the divine providence that I am in this diocese" and "I have the honour to be your devoted child, J. Lamy."

But the materials of his work were first of all the men, women, children who looked to him through the years for what they could not achieve by themselves. In his four principal stations, he had three hundred families for which he was directly responsible, and there were many more in the missions to which he rode, often swimming his horse across unbridged or swollen rivers. Once crossing in an inadequate boat, he almost drowned with fourteen other persons. People knew the bothers he undertook for their sake; and when they came together with him on some great day, such as Christmas in Danville, all sighed with satisfaction. He wrote the bishop the day after Epiphany 1844 that though their hard times were not so great compared to those in "some other country, I have great deal of consolation for a missionary. our little church of Danville was ornamented at Christmas with garlands of evergreen all around with a kind of lustre où [*sic*] bien chandelier fixed also with evergreen hanging from the ceiling with the lights on it. we had a great illumination for Christmas. quoique ce ne fut pas merveille our good catholics in their simplicity thought there could be nothing better, nor more handsome. I have heard some say that at the first mass which was at 5 o'clock, they were almost transported to heaven. These three holy-days and these three Sundays our church has been very much crowded." For graces in the wilderness, all gave thanks, including the pastor, who could measure their simple ardors against splendors he had seen long ago, far away, in the same purpose.

vii.

Private Concerns

FROM THE FIRST it was comforting to Lamy to receive much help in the building of his churches and the making of his communities from numbers of non-Catholic settlers. Yet there were always others who glowered hot-eyed from the periphery, hissing of "priest-craft," and rejoicing in the national "Know-Nothing" movement which sought to discredit Catholicism in the growing society. Convents were burned in various sections of the country, and lurid books, such as that by "Maria Monk" which professed to describe horrors of every sort in the conventual life, were popular among those who feared "popery." Lamy and his colleagues were aware from the first of such a hostile climate in certain quarters, and had to meet it face to face now and then. The only answer was to go on modestly and calmly in the work of the Church, without mounting counter-attacks of any sort. In the end, such a posture won tolerance, which was all the Catholics asked, sure as they were of what they preached and sought to live by.

Lamy, receiving converts, reported that "the Methodists were furious about here"—Danville—and went on to say, "they are holding quantity of meetings to stop as they call it the progress of popery." Machebeuf, in upper Ohio, in his early days there, said Mass in Toledo in a private house, and declared that at the same time and in the same house, the Methodists held their services, and "following their honorable custom, the minister made such a din and such howlings that we were singularly inconvenienced." The Catholics were upstairs, the Methodists on the first floor. Machebeuf disliked knowing what thoughts were going on under his feet, he said. But at Lower Sandusky, where every Sunday he could hear the singing of nearby Presbyterians in their services, it often happened that many of them would attend also the Catholic Mass, and some even vouched for Catholic credit at the banks, and he saw with gratification that as prejudices lessened, priests were no longer regarded as "monsters," and Catholics as "ignorant and superstitious idolaters." He had an ingenious theory why Catholicism became gradually acceptable—it was that the great number of conversions effected in England at the time of the Oxford Movement gave Americans reason to examine a religion which hitherto they had known only through "the most atrocious calumnies."

But as always, while public matters went along, private concerns bore heavily at times; and when in October 1843 Machebeuf received word that his father was critically ill at home in Riom, he resolved to go to France to see him before the end. He would need Bishop Purcell's permission, but since the bishop was himself abroad at the time, the vicar general of the diocese must act for him. Machebeuf submitted his request. It was denied—justly enough, as Machebeuf had to admit, for at the moment there was no replacement for him in Sandusky, and he had committed the parish to so many works that must be continued. Moreover, he had no money for the journey. Writing home for "two hundred piastres," he was forced to say that he had only five in his pocket. The baker's family sent him the necessary funds—but still he could not leave. He wrote to his father, enclosing the letter in one to his sister if the old man should be too ill to read it for himself, hoping that a beneficent Providence would grant a few more weeks of life to the invalid so that he might see him once more before he died. Meantime, he was saying Masses for him, and could only add, "Farewell, dear papa, we shall meet, I hope, either in this world or in heaven." His heart was heavy, his friend knew it, and when work allowed, Lamy journeyed to Sandusky to console him, offering to come there whenever he could, during Machebeuf's absence, if arrangements for the journey should ever be managed.

So they were, when Purcell returned from abroad. He at once gave permission for Machebeuf to go—but in addition to his merciful purpose, the bishop added an important mission to be carried out in France. Purcell charged him with the complicated task of recruiting clergy and religious for the Cincinnati diocese—priests for the missions, Ursuline nuns to found a convent in Brown County, Ohio. Finally, in June 1844, nine months after the first word of his father's grave condition, Machebeuf was able to set out. It was to be a year before he returned. In due course, Lamy learned, as he did in all matters concerning his closest ally, the adventures of Machebeuf on the first journey home made by either of them since they had left France in 1839.

viii.
Machebeuf's Intrigue

MACHEBEUF SAILED FROM NEW YORK in the second week of June 1844, and arrived at Le Havre on 6 July, not knowing whether his father still lived. But there were Ursulines at Boulogne-sur-Mer only fifty-six miles up the coast, and he had been directed by Purcell to commence his mission there. It must come first. He left Le Havre the next day to begin the affair, hoping to reach Riom during the following week without even pausing in Paris.

He carried with him a letter of introduction from Father Louis Amadeus Rappe, of Toledo, Ohio, who had come to America with him and Lamy and the others in the first place; and this he presented to the Mother Superior of the Boulogne Ursulines in their "large and magnificent convent and academy." What could one expect offhand? There were no commitments, only a possibility of further discussions.

Machebeuf hurried south to his family home in Riom—but arrived too late. His father was dead. It was a cruel loss, after all the delays of the past year. Machebeuf, his brother Marius, their sister the nun Sister Philomène at the Convent of the Visitation, consoled each other, the necessary family decisions were taken, and then duties continued.

There were other Ursulines at Beaulieu, near Tulle. What to do but write their spiritual director, M. L'Abbé Graviche, and open the subject of enlistments with him? An animated correspondence ensued over the weeks. Father Graviche seemed to favor Machebeuf's appeal. But it was clear that locally there was great opposition to any "disestablishment" of the Ursuline convent of Beaulieu; and Boulogne, allied in a common order of religious, also remained reluctant. In the meantime, there was the other purpose of finding priests or seminarians and Machebeuf fixed upon the Grand Séminaire of Avignon as a promising source. He proceeded to Lyon, where he spent a day with his brother Marius, who lived there, and went on to Le Puy, where he arrived with a cold which he caught passing through the mountains of the lower Loire—the Monts du Morvan. A good sweat set him right and he was soon as good as ever, and he now returned to Lyon, as there turned out to be no direct route south from Le Puy. At Lyon he embarked on a Rhône steamer. The river was high, the steamer was a mean affair compared to "our American boats." To pass the time he fell into conversation with a pair of Englishmen who spoke bad French, and who appeared to seek him out merely for the sake of a French lesson. They picked his brains about the country they passed through, about which he knew no more than they. The "Irish Question" came up with one of the English travellers, and Machebeuf confounded him so triumphantly with remarks of the injustices visited upon Irish Catholics that he retired to his English carriage, which was lashed to the deck. Docking presently at Valence-sur-Rhône, the steamer picked up more passengers, including an English family one of whom was a young man of twenty-five. When he heard Machebeuf talking in English he was delighted, they talked incessantly, Machebeuf dined with them all when they reached Avignon, and the young man, who hoped in the next year to go to America, vowed to seek out Machebeuf and renew the acquaintance. It was all most agreeable.

Interviewing faculty and seminarians must have revived memories of Clermont and Purcell and Flaget and the student days at Mont-Ferrand. Again there was a hiatus in arrangements, and Machebeuf went to Marseilles, with the great purpose of proceeding to Rome, where he arrived in November. Immediately he had marvels to report.

He said it would take volumes to describe what he saw. The churches of Rome were the greatest of things to be seen there. His very first visit was to St Mary on Minerva—a richly marbled and gilded church built on the ancient site of a temple to Minerva. He had to go five times to St Peter's to feel at last its tremendous primacy over all other churches in the Holy City. There he descended to the tomb of the first pope, amidst the remains of the original basilica, and there, on the anniversary of the dedication of St Peter's, he said Mass on the altar over the grave of the first of the apostles. He did the same at the altar tombs of St Paul, St Stanislas, and St Francis Xavier. At St John Lateran's—so he said—he saw the original table of the Last Supper, and the great baldachin containing the martyred heads of Sts Peter and Paul, and went twice to the cell where St Peter had been imprisoned, and he offered Mass in the very room where St Ignatius died. At St Peter's he ascended into the cupola and even into the sphere, large enough to contain two persons, which supported the topmost cross in Rome. By his descriptions, in their vivacity and emotion, it was plain that he knew spiritual exaltation.

But the greatest experience was yet to come—he was granted an audience with the Pope. Was it on 17 November? In any case, he was encouraged to present a detailed recital of all the missionary work in Ohio. He evidently spared his listener nothing of the hardships, the gallantries, the discouragements, the absurdities, the near-despairs and the poverty and the persecutions to which the young Frenchmen, laboring away in a new land, knew as their daily lot; for when he was done with what surely was a vivid performance, Gregory XVI said to him, "Courage, American!" and gave the Apostolic Blessing, for him, and for all his Ohioans. The exhortation was the greatest of powers which Machebeuf took away with him, one which in all after years he would remember and invoke when courage should be needed.

Going on to Venice, then, he had as travelling companion a French Franciscan who "burned with desire" to join the American missions, but Machebeuf was not sure he would do, for one could not be too careful in electing recruits, and this one seemed "too eager" and "not sufficiently prudent." In Venice, he would consult various priests about the suppliant. In the end, the French Franciscan was not added to the party Machebeuf was laboriously assembling.

Once again in France, Machebeuf came together with Graviche to develop plans. Finally, on 20 January 1845, they went together to see Bishop Bertaud, of Tulle, to ask him to issue letters of obedience to the nearby convent which would direct that eight nuns be enlisted for America. The bishop was hesitant, his callers persuasive, and agreement eventually prevailed. But there were still difficulties. What of the Ursulines of Boulogne, who, belonging to the same order as those at Beaulieu, came under a central authority? Letters flew from Beaulieu to Boulogne but without firm issue. March first had been decided upon as the date of departure, and Machebeuf optimistically hastened to Bordeaux to arrange for the westward crossing for himself and his party. It was all to no purpose, for Boulogne did not capitulate until 10 March, when suddenly the Mother Superior consented to release three sisters—two English (both converts) and one Irish. A new departure date must be set, and in the end, could not be arranged before May, in a ship from Le Havre. Machebeuf must make another journey to Tulle in late March to resolve final qualms, difficulties, conditions. There was strong local resentment, now, in the town of Beaulieu, against the departure of any of the Ursulines. All was not yet smoothly arranged.

But Machebeuf had still another errand, and went about it in Paris during the first days of April. He had written to the French royal family begging financial aid to speed him and his party across the Atlantic. He was presented to Queen Marie Amélie, and, giving an account of himself and his needs, he mentioned Bishop Purcell. The Queen exclaimed, "Oh! that fine man! I remember him well." She promised Machebeuf a contribution, the King would also contribute, and Princess Adelaide, King Louis Philippe's sister, promised by letter to make a donation. Machebeuf had written to her, and also to the King's son, the Duc d'Aumale, "who is so rich," and the Princess de Joinville, a royal daughter-in-law, an American. Hearing nothing, Machebeuf, dining with the pastor of St Roch, which was the regal parish, asked him to remind the royal personages of both requests and promises. Nothing came from the King and Queen, or the so rich royal duke, or the American princess; but Madame Adelaide sent—guess what? Two thousand francs? "Just cut off one zero," remarked Machebeuf, noting bitterly that with all her riches two thousand would have been little enough. There was nothing to do but shrug and proceed with further begging, and, for his part, to use some of his father's bequest to pay expenses of the voyage.

But it was still almost unimaginable what had to be contrived to get the Ursulines away from Beaulieu. They had to leave in two groups —one the newly designated superior of the mission accompanied by a sister, the other the remaining six. At night, in the disguise of peasant countrywomen, carrying bundles containing their concealed habits, they stole away, trudged back roads, knew panic when tollgate keepers seemed suspicious, had monstrous difficulties finding lodgings, but at last some reached Paris, and the others were met by Machebeuf at Brive la Gaillarde and conducted to Paris to join their sisters. When their flight was discovered, there was anger at Beaulieu, but too late. All were safely in Paris in religious houses, except for the three from

Boulogne who would join the company at Le Havre for the sailing, which was now firmly set for the Feast of St Monica, 4 May. At five in the morning, Machebeuf said Mass and gave communion to all. Father Pendeprat, a priest accepted for the Sandusky parish, said Mass in his turn, the nuns had breakfast, and at seven o'clock they all went to the pier, boarded the packet boat *Zurich,* and knelt on deck to receive the blessings of the two Mothers Superior of Beaulieu and Boulogne, who had come to send their charges off with all good feeling. As the *Zurich* made way down the narrow channel of Le Havre, the sisters on board watched as long as they could the carriage of their superiors "until it was lost in the crowd," and France was absorbed by the "blue distance."

It was a fine day, with, "I understand," said Machebeuf, "no danger of stormy weather." He had collected sixteen people—eight nuns from Boulogne, four from Beaulieu (evidently one more than spoken for earlier), and four priests or seminarians, three of these having sailed earlier. For the remaining members and all their luggage, he struck a bargain with the ship's captain for reduced rates. The total was 5750 francs. The ship was full, and the other passengers paid full fare. They included (among the few lay Catholics aboard) a merchant from Lyon on a business trip to New York, an American lady with her small daughter who had been sojourning in Paris, the mother of an Italian singer who was a member of a New York opera company, and a French modiste on her way to open a shop in New York. All went out of their way to show respect to the venturesome nuns, for whom the "ladies' salon" was reserved exclusively. Their staterooms were small but comfortable. Machebeuf felt they were happy in their choice of their vessel—it was "one of the largest, most beautiful, and best sailors," as Marius Machebeuf could attest (he had come to see them off), and her "rooms were of an extraordinary sumptuousness . . . all gilt and rosewood." What was more, the food was as good as the ship's fittings. Machebeuf conducted the usual daily services, and one unusual one: on the Feast of Corpus Christi, when custom ashore required a formal procession bearing the Host through the public streets and into the church, he led his little congregation in a solemn march in and out of their staterooms, and declared that it must surely have been the only Corpus Christi procession ever held "upon the immense ocean."

Despite his confidence on sailing, there was heavy weather ahead. The *Zurich* encountered two furious storms in her crossing of twenty-nine days, and both times had to heave to and ride out the weather, while all prayed, and Mother Julia—her seasickness lasted for the entire voyage—felt worse than ever. She recovered immediately when on 2 June the captain said they would soon sight land, and an hour later the cry of "Land ho!" sang out from the lookout on the forward mast. As the vessel came up the Narrows, a steam lighter came to take the Machebeuf party off as soon as their customs and quarantine examinations were complete. At the South street docks there were carriages waiting, and all were promptly lodged in the boarding house of Madame Pilet, a Frenchwoman, whose accommodations had been recommended by a fellow passenger. A week later they were on their way by stage, canal, small inland steamer, until they reached the Ohio and boarded one of her great stern-wheelers, the *Independence*. The weather was stifling in the June days. Everyone slept on deck for three nights, until finally on the nineteenth, they docked at Cincinnati to be received by Bishop Purcell at his house, who led them to the new classical revival cathedral of St Peter's and preached over them a brief homily of welcome and exhortation to their new duties. Their journey had been a lucky one, for if Machebeuf's first arrangements had been carried out, they would have sailed not on the *Zurich* but on the packet *Emerald,* which departed from Le Havre eight hours earlier, and reached New York five days after the *Zurich* with her masts shattered, and all her sails torn by storm. Machebeuf wrote Sister Philomène that her prayers must have saved him and his party.

If there was any disappointment connected with the whole venture, it was that Father Pendeprat, who had been expressly brought along to assist Machebeuf at the Sandusky missions where many parishioners were French, was soon dispatched to Toledo to assist Father Rappe. For the rest, the journey was a model for many later ones to be undertaken by Lamy and Machebeuf, and for the same purpose—to find adventurous and dedicated leaders who would meet the needs of an ever-growing society in whatever quarter of the land.

ix.

The War

INTENSELY AS THEY WERE OCCUPIED with their local responsibilities, the missionaries, along with their parishioners, were increasingly concerned with a grave and complicated matter which grew upon the whole nation throughout 1845 and which, in 1846, came to a state of crisis.

Ex-President Andrew Jackson stated the issue when he said, "You might as well, it appears to me, attempt to turn the current of the Mississippi, as to turn the democracy from the annexation of Texas." For Texas had applied several times for statehood under the American republic, had been refused, had declared herself an independent republic by an act of secession from Mexico; and now, in 1844, Texas was willing to give up her own sovereignty if allowed to become a state of the United States. The Democratic nominee for president in 1844 was James K. Polk, who ran principally on the plank of admitting Texas to the Union. Only days before his inauguration Congress admitted Texas as a state. The act made inevitable a declaration of war against the United States by Mexico, which had never conceded that the vast Texas lands were independent, and now considered them wrongfully acquired by the North Americans. Polk ordered troops south to the Rio Grande border of Texas-Mexico, and Mexico City in turn ordered forces north to the opposite side of the river. Inevitably they clashed, and a war fever swept the States. Congress authorized the raising of a volunteer force of fifty thousand men, and President Polk declared, "A portion of this force was assigned to each State and Territory in the Union so as to make each feel an interest in the war." For the hundreds asked for from each state, ten times in the thousands flocked to volunteer.

Ohio and all of Purcell's diocese felt the call. Troops moved down the Ohio River and others boarded river steamers at Cincinnati for the voyage to New Orleans, the Gulf, and the coast of Texas. Barges of coal needed by the armies so far from home also took the route of the rivers, and all who remained at home felt the national quickening and saw the troop movements and the great flow of supply, and had a new place name by which to reckon the loneliness of separation, worries, news of victories, and messages of death—the Rio Grande. Just where was it? Evidently it divided Texas from Mexico, and ran down from the high Rockies all the length of New Mexico, as the northernmost inland state of the Mexican nation was called. So far away—nobody knew what the land out there was like except the traders who since 1824 had been voyaging across the prairies to Santa Fe, and down to Chihuahua. It all seemed to move closer when news came that on 18 August 1846 the American General Stephen Watts Kearny had captured Santa Fe—peaceably, as it turned out—and with it, for all practical purposes, the whole of New Mexico. The act was the first in a sequence which, though without meaning for Lamy until three more years had passed, was to determine his work for the rest of his life.

Meanwhile, what was nearest seemed larger. Father Pendeprat, who was intended for Sandusky to help Machebeuf, would soon be reassigned to Louisville by Purcell—hardly a matter for rejoicing in the north. In April Lamy suggested to Purcell that he station a permanent pastor at Newark, and announced that his presbytery at Danville was completed and that Mrs Brent and one of her daughters were established as his housekeepers. "The old lady does great deal for me and yet she will be no burden to me she finds her own provisions and says she is quite happy to do it for she is now near the church and can go to mass often. I am really edified by this regularity and piety. I have also an orphan Irish boy about 14 years old. I can buy in general but the Catholics of this congregation have furnished me with provisions such as they have." Lamy later converted Mrs Brent's young son, took him to Rome to be educated for holy orders, and years afterward Father Brent, in turn, became pastor of St Luke's.

Northern Ohio was growing faster than the central counties of the state. Machebeuf—with an air of complaint—reported to Sister Philomène at Riom that Purcell had, since his return from France, assigned to him all the duties of Norwalk in addition to those he already struggled to meet. He would have to take charge of everything— assembling materials of all kinds, keeping all accounts, spending almost a month at Norwalk making a general canvass for funds to protect the church from being sold on demand by "a protestant fanatic who had furnished various materials" and who obviously had not yet been paid.

A momentous response to the leaping growth of the lake cities and inland towns of northern Ohio came in the summer of 1846. The American bishops petitioned Rome to separate the area into a new diocese, to be taken from Purcell's great domain of Cincinnati, and proposed Father Rappe of Toledo as the new bishop-designate—the first of the original party from Auvergne to be raised to the mitre. The decision would throw both Danville and Sandusky, among other settlements, under a new bishop so soon as he should be consecrated—presumably in the autumn. In his own group of parishes, Machebeuf was desperate for more help. Lamy was named by Purcell to go to him if only for a month, and wrote Purcell in late August that he was daily awaiting his own replacement at Danville. "Everybody," he said, "except in my own congregation knows that I am going to Sandusky City . . . one thing only I regret it is to be cut off from the diocese of Cincinnati. but whether I stay at Danville or be removed to Sandusky City I will belong to the new diocese of Cleveland, but if I must be out of your jurisdiction . . . I shall never forget the kind attention, the paternal affection which you have always showed to me."

Sandusky was in need of every sort of governance. "Dreadful scenes" went on in public, drunkenness, street fights, sometimes reaching even to the church door. One of the rowdies was so out of control that he bit off the nose of his father-in-law, an old man almost seventy. Machebeuf, small as he was, often had to separate such fighters. Lamy would be a great reinforcement, with his powerful, quiet presence. Not only would the public peace be resumed, and the missions attended, but the two great friends would be united, as they had always hoped to be on leaving home together.

But this was not to be. In September Lamy wrote to Machebeuf to report that Purcell had felt obliged to rescind his decision. Lamy was not to go to Sandusky. Machebeuf was downcast, wrote Purcell that he accepted the will of Providence, and did not know how he could now carry on against civil disgraces and religious neglects all of which brought ill repute upon the Catholic name. Purcell wrote to Machebeuf twice—once evidently to explain the change of plan, to which there was no answer from Sandusky; and again to hope that Machebeuf was not angry at him for what had been done. The answer to both letters was late in going off to Purcell, but its manner was somewhat stiff—sorry if Purcell had been made to "think that I was displeased with you." Protesting his devotion, Machebeuf went on to add, "To say that I did not feal [sic] disappointed in hearing that I was to [be] deprived of my very dear friend Rev. Mr. Lamy would not exactly be true, but I did my best to resign myself." He could not forbear mentioning one other matter of grievance—it seemed to him that he might have had the "consolation of assisting at the forthcoming consecration" of his "worthy and beloved neighbour"—Bishop-designate Rappe— but he had not been invited. Ah, well. Machebeuf's spirited nature could be testy as well as merry. Also, on occasion, discreet. He was baptized Joseph Projectus Machebeuf. The Latin middle name was translated into French as "Priest" (with no connotation of *prêtre*). In all his early life he used the French middle name, but during his Ohio years he dropped it, since in an anti-Catholic atmosphere it seemed open to invidious use, and for it he substituted his baptismal middle name of Projectus. (To avoid confusion, his original style of Joseph Priest Machebeuf is here used throughout.)

For Lamy, it was a sorrowful year. He received word from Lempdes in the course of the autumn that his father had died there on 7 September 1846. Writing this news to Purcell, he said that his father's family "urge me very much to go to France, but I have no desire of going," and ended by asking his friend the bishop to "be so good as to pray for the repose of his soul."

x.

To Covington

"THE WEATHER," wrote Lamy to his bishop on New Year's Day of 1847, "was very bad this last Christmas and the mud very deep." Even so, the little Danville church was as crowded as ever—people came from many miles through the abominable roads, many of them in the dark, for again he said his first Mass at five o'clock. The church was "as well decorated as we were able. For the illumination we had 150 candles burning almost all sperm [whale oil] or wax candles." (From Sandusky City, a more exuberant account of the Christmas feast there went to France—Machebeuf told Sister Philomène in all the detail dear to a nun that never had Christmas been celebrated at Sandusky with such "pomp and solemnity." The church was solidly lined with greens, there were *three hundred* lights, and the sanctuary vault— all Gothic—was sparkling with innumerable stars cut out of gold paper. And the music! The choir had been practicing for two months under an excellent director, accompanied with an old piano as there was no organ.)

It was the wettest winter and spring in years—travel was worse than ever, when all the rivers and creeks flooded the countryside. Bridges went out, canals were ruined, animals were borne away and those that lived ended by pasturing far from their home farms, and the wheat crop was given up. Barter took the place of currency paid, and parishioners brought produce and goods to their churches instead of money. Machebeuf remarked with irony that it was obvious that it was a land of milk and honey—and added, apropos honey, that Lamy paid him a visit in January and brought him a gift of "an enormous pot" of it. Lamy was adding a small belfry to his Danville church, where it was now clear he would remain, and himself pledged a bell of 400 pounds to hang in it. He was well, so was Father Pendeprat, and Machebeuf himself said his only illness was an "excess of health."

What never ended was the growth of the state. Lamy gave Purcell a three-year summary of his records of baptisms, Easter communions, marriages, and deaths, and in each category, the figures of the first year were about doubled for the third year. Machebeuf's parish grew even faster, for northern Ohio had the lake, and shipping, the immigrant workmen kept arriving, and more than ever, more than even Lamy himself, he needed a new assistant. None was at hand. When in February Lamy and some other priests went to Niagara Falls to see the great cataract, their route by-passed Sandusky, which came as a "shock of electric current" to Machebeuf, who would have gone along but for two reasons—he could not afford it, and he had too much to do at home.

But a larger concern brought a shock which needed no exaggeration when the Ohio priests heard that despite the petition of the American bishops and Purcell's own urgent description of the need, Cleveland was not in all probability to be separated after all from Cincinnati by Vatican decree. It was an embarrassment for Father Rappe, who had been nominated for the mitre, and it showed a typical bureaucratic lack of imagination (such as often operated in central governments and military headquarters far from the field) of the realities behind the requests of those who struggled daily with distant problems. In six years Sandusky's original twenty-five or thirty families had grown to about two hundred. The need of a bishop at the opposite end of the state from Cincinnati was obvious. Rome deliberated. In time, the issue would be properly resolved with the creation of the new diocese after all. Meanwhile, one had to do with what one had.

The national news was stirring—Taylor's army of Northern Mexico had won a great victory at Buena Vista in late February 1847, a week later on 1 March General Wool took the city of Chihuahua, and before the month was out, Winfield Scott and his amphibious force received the surrender of Veracruz and started inland for the heart of Mexico and her capital, as the summer wore on.

In July there was distressing news for Lamy. Evidently the fact that central Ohio was not growing so fast as the northern counties moved Purcell to decide that after all Lamy should go to Sandusky permanently for city parish work. In reply to the proposal, Lamy wrote a long and eloquent plea to be allowed to remain at Danville. He reminded Purcell that a year earlier when he, Lamy himself, had proposed moving north, the bishop had said he wished the idea had never been thought of, and it was dropped. But now, Lamy begged to have his weighty reasons for *not* moving listened to—he was deep in arrangements to build a new brick church at Danville; he had contracted for the land; procured six thousand feet of lumber; "made a bargain with a man to burn a large kiln of bricks"; the congregation had already given him money, even the children; the shingles were ready; everyone felt "in good spirit about the new church." He had been with them all for eight years, they were all as dear to him as children were to their own father. Now, unless the bishop had decided that his services had become useless among those people, he must earnestly and most humbly "entreat" Purcell to grant him the favor of not removing him. Yes, and moreover, he had almost completed the restoration of the burned Mt Vernon church, and though he would be "in some debt," he had "better prospect" before him. He piled reason upon reason in a flow of emotion such as he rarely revealed. City parish instead of the mission rides despite their hardships?

"I could not bear the idea, unless compelled by obedience, to be confined. I know it would be very injurious to my health. providence seems to have fitted me for a barbarious [*sic*] and extensive mission," he added in innocent prophecy. "I do not complain of hardship, and if my congregation are poor I should thank God to have given me an opportunity of practicing a virtue so dear to my divine master." More, "If I was to consult my taste I should be obliged to say that I have a great dislike to be charged with the cure of a community on account of my inexperience and of my age for I am only thirty-two."

"Dear Bishop," he pleaded with passion so unlike his customary calm, "please bear with me a little longer. You have too great idea of my capacity as far as I know myself I would be afraid to exercise the ministry in a town or city. You might be too much disappointed in your expectation, if there is a certain good done where I am, though only a little, suffer me to remain here. would it not do more harm than good to remove a general from the army when there is accord and union between him and his subjects, and a great desire on both sides to perform some achievements according to their number, strength and means? Now Dear Bishop I must acknowledge that never before in my life was I compelled to write a letter with so much repugnance as I have this for I never wished to go against the will of my Superiors, neither do I wish it now. But I hope that whatever I have observed you will believe that I had not the least intention to be disrespectful. I have only candidly expressed my own feelings, knowing well that you would take it in good part. please, excuse me if I have said anything that would give you the least suspicion of my disposition towards you. you have often said that you would not oppose a reasonable desire of any of your priests . . ."

Could it have crossed the bishop's mind that his suppliant protested too much? Gave too many reasons where one good one would do? In any case, what appeared to be Lamy's overriding purpose was to avoid —but let his own words resume:

"Your brother (Father Edward Purcell) has likely told you that Mr [Father] Senez desires very much to return to this diocese provided he would be welcome and have great deal to do. he has written to me on the same subject, but before I consent to the condition which he seems to require, for me to live with him, I want some time to reflect upon it. I know, Mr Senez is a good, pious, talented priest, I have been long enough in his company to be convinced of it, but I would be afraid to say without serious consideration that it would be for the greater benefit of both of us to be together. but I would not wish him to know it. . . ."

His final point, unelaborated though it was, seemed to have carried more weight than all the earnest arguments which came before it; and a few weeks later Lamy wrote with relief to Purcell, "Your answer to my last letter delivered me of a great anxiety of mind. I was very much afraid to have displeased you." On the same day he took out his United States citizenship, and when within a week or so he received another plan for his transfer elsewhere, with Father Senez uninvolved, Lamy agreed with abounding alacrity and willingness. He told Purcell on 20 August 1847, now with no talk of bricks, timber and shingles,

"As you desire me to go to Covington [Kentucky] I am ready to leave Danville at your first orders. You may dispose of me as you please, my duty is to obey cheerfully. if you think I will do better I am perfectly willing to try. one thing which consoles me is to know that I will be so near you . . ." His work had prevented him from writing to Father Senez. He had heard that some feared Senez would not come at all if he had to stay alone. Would Purcell please write him? As for himself, he would like two or three weeks to settle some affairs at Danville, chiefly concerning the new church. A week later he wrote to the chancellor at Cincinnati giving his final report on Danville, Mt Vernon, Mohican, Pine Run, Mansfield, where he had congregations totalling two hundred fifteen families. Was he to wait for a replacement or come immediately? In any case, he was ready. His new assignment at Covington, which was directly across the river from Cincinnati, would put him distant the whole length of Ohio from Machebeuf at Sandusky. He left his forest parishes with feeling which was returned to him by them all. Something of him remained alive for generations in Danville. In a lovely phrase, Francis Sapp, grandson of the founder George, wrote in reminiscences set down in his last years, that Lamy's "name is held in benediction by all the old residents of the county, irrespective of creed." Francis Sapp, a waning old man, speaking with a childhood's returned simplicity, said that "Father Lama" was a man "so good that everybody loved him. I was a very young boy when he was pastor here, but had such a high esteem for him I thought that God would not let him die but take him to heaven a live body and soul. . . . He baptized me and called me Francis Sapp. . . . I think him the most lovely priest I ever knew. . . . I have sat upon his knee many times. . . ." It is the earliest picture of Lamy at work in the New World.

xi.

Lamy to France

BY AUTUMN 1847, many concerns were resolved. For the nation, the Mexican War drew to a close when Scott took Mexico City on 14 September. In December, at the call of the United States military governor, the conquered and ceded province of New Mexico held an election to vote on joining the Union as a territory. The vote carried— mostly by the ballots of United States troops stationed there, and the mercantile resident-traders of the Santa Fe Trail. Peace was signed on 2 February 1848, with the Treaty of Guadalupe Hidalgo roughly indicating a new boundary between Mexico and the United States. Other sovereignties would be affected by this vast geographical change and soon enough would be dealt with, along with individual destinies linked to it. In Covington, Kentucky, Lamy, the new pastor of St Mary's, was at work on the tasks he had rehearsed so often before— acquiring land, moulding together a community, planning a church (to stand where the Covington cathedral would eventually be built). He placed the temporal responsibilities of Covington in the hands of a committee, headed by Mr Doyle, father-in-law of Mr McClosky, and including Mr John White and Mr John O'Donnell, among others.

As always, it was slow work, but it went along in Lamy's familiar pace of deliberate, daily steps which reflected his patience with the day and his long view of the future. He could be in closer touch with Purcell now, for it was only a ferry crossing to Cincinnati, in the passage of the river just above the great bend which turned east and then west again between rolling hills which came down to the banks. The affairs of his new charge seemed to proceed rapidly. The fast-growing city across the river from Covington was a source of supplies far different from those of the wooded upper counties, where canals and muddy roads had to haul materials from far away. In the spring of 1848, Machebeuf, in one of his most euphoric moments, wrote to his sister of the "little earthly paradise" where he was working, where a new church was paid for within a matter of two or three years, where begging often produced results beyond expectation, where a presbytery of eight rooms aside from kitchens and pantries and basements was put up, with garden and cistern, as if by magic, and where the cathedral of Cleveland—for Rome had approved the new diocese and Rappe had been consecrated after all—was already two years old: how different it all was from the decaying Catholicism of Europe, France itself, where the "new republic" was established—a word to make any authoritarian shudder. In Covington, Lamy found it possible to make plans for a journey to Europe on family matters calling for settlement since the death of his father.

In May 1848, on his way abroad, he paid a surprise visit to Machebeuf, who decided to see him off on a lake steamer from Cleveland. He gave to *"mon cher compagnon et mon cher ami"* a list of errands to do for him, and later wrote after him to buy church supplies for him in France. In Cleveland Bishop Rappe also asked Lamy to act for him abroad in finding three or four young priests in Clermont to bring back to Cleveland. Lamy would try. In New York on 29 May he made "a little excursion" to St John's College, and there found old friends—one in particular—who had taught him in the Jesuit *collège* at Billom. He wrote Purcell that the Catholic churches of New York that he had seen were "not so handsome in my opinion as those of Cincinnati," though the interior of "the French church" was "very pretty," and he said Mass there on Sunday. He sailed 1 June on the "fine packet" *Duchesse d'Orléans* after nine years in America. While he was gone, the question rose again of whether he should be assigned to another parish, possibly in the Cleveland diocese, but the possibility came to nothing when Bishop Rappe wrote to Purcell, "I feel more inclined to let everything in status quo."

Lamy reached home in Lempdes in early July. Everyone was eager to see the man who had left as a youth, and he had so many visits to make that he had little time so far to stay with his brother Etienne and the family. He thought Etienne had treated him fairly in the matter of their father's estate, though to be sure the new American offered his brother more than generous terms. "My brother has not been so hard to deal with as I had suspected." The American Lamy offered all his rights in his share of the father's estate for at least a third less than they were worth, and moreover asked just now for only half the payment due to him. His sister Margaret—a nun of the order of the Miséricorde at Riom—did likewise. Etienne thus became the sole proprietor of the family land. "In this manner the union and good understanding between relations will be maintained between us and my brother's family," wrote Father Lamy. He was happy to add that now he could repay Bishop Purcell a sum on account for what he owed to him for various advances, and asked for instructions—should he deposit one thousand francs to Purcell's credit in the hands of M. Carrière, treasurer of the Society for the Propagation of the Faith in Paris, from which mission funds were dispensed about the world?

But alas for the dear homeland: France was in a "very uncertain state" under the current republic. Lamy feared insurrections could be expected at any moment, thanks to higher taxes, anti-clericalism, and absolute rule by Louis Eugène Cavaignac, the dictator who was vested with "supreme power." "It is nowadays a saying," wrote Lamy, "that in Europe two men are Supreme Masters Nicolas in Russia and Cavagnac [*sic*] in France." He had heard on good authority and he hoped it was true that Cavaignac "approaches the Sacraments." Even so, "we are far from being in security, everybody is looking from some dreadful explosions . . ." For himself, Lamy was preparing to return to what he called "my Beloved Ohio."

Unluckily the seminarians of Mont-Ferrand were on vacation, and he could find no one to pledge to America. But there were others. There was a Father Caron at Boulogne-sur-Mer, a friend of Bishop Rappe, who would come to Cleveland, and a priest in Clermont agreed to come to Cincinnati (though Lamy felt obliged to note with regret that he was already thirty-six years old), an excellent priest who was a *"maître de conférence"* at Mont-Ferrand in Lamy's own time. He still hoped to bring two or three younger ones "who could learn English with more facility."

In early August he wrote Purcell that he was thinking of bringing his sister to America with him—she was hoping to be dispensed by her superior so that she could join the Brown County Ursulines of Ohio. His niece Marie might come too—to be brought up by her aunt in that Ohio convent. The little girl was strongly drawn to America and the religious life. On the twenty-seventh he wrote the bishop, "I will not tarry much longer." He was happy to report that everyone in Clermont remembered Purcell very well and many had congratulated Lamy for belonging to Purcell's diocese. He would see to the few articles Purcell asked him to buy in France.

Machebeuf, too, had his list of requirements, one of which was word from home. Lamy had written him three times with all the family news. He, whom Machebeuf regarded as his *"plus intime et sincère ami,"* was to beg some financial help from Riom, which was duly sent in the amount of "two or three thousand francs." This, it appeared, was not enough, but for which, in any case, Machebeuf sent his family his best thanks. Sister Philomène was to send to him by way of Lamy "a pair of dalmatiques, white overall, with sides of different colors and

trimmed with galoon, either of real gold or imitation. Also another alb
of netting"—all to make it possible at last to celebrate the ceremonies
of the Church with "pomp and solemnity." Lamy had another list.

After these errands, he pursued the more important ones, and ended
by finding three Ursulines at Boulogne who would sail home with him,
as well as his sister—the bishop of Clermont had approved her going
—and his niece, Marie. Julius Brent, from Danville, studying for the
priesthood in Europe, had arrived in Clermont, and would lead him
to England, where Brent family members wanted to receive them. It
was, for Lamy, "a great opportunity to speak English again." The nuns
sailed from Boulogne under the protection of Father Caron, Lamy and
Brent went to London, and when the time came, Lamy, with his sister
and his little niece, sailed for New York from Liverpool. Years later
they still told at Santa Fe how Marie, when the ocean was stormy,
would climb up to her uncle's embrace and hug him for safety against
her fear of the sea. He too, now, had made the first of many voyages
between America and Europe.

He was home in Covington by early autumn 1848. The work which
followed growing immigration was heavier than ever—in Ireland the
famine was on, and the diocese was increasing by astonishing numbers.
Not only did these desperately poor searchers for comfort and freedom
need the attention of their Church, thus heavying the burden upon
it, but their coming had an odd secondary effect on the furious attempts of the Church to keep up with its task which required additional revenues: for, finding work, however humble in America, the
new Irish Americans made a practice of sending part of their wages to
those, hungry and destitute, whom they had left at home.

As soon as he could, Lamy went to see Machebeuf in Sandusky. The
two old friends would have much to talk about, eager questions, keenly
deliberate replies. Family news. The state of France. And the fulfillment of errands. What had Lamy brought home? One item which
required particular care—cuttings of the best grape vines from Auvergne, muscats, Damas, Gamay. Wine was wanted for Mass, and also
for the table. Lamy was a lifelong gardener. But more: he brought
some fine vestments and six beautiful gilded candlesticks and a chalice
of gold-plated bronze, with the cup lined in vermeil. Fine as they were,
Machebeuf, poor as he was, later had to go to Detroit to sell them.
But "the pity was," wrote Machebeuf, that Lamy had "forgotten to
bring the two white dalmatics" which he had particularly asked for.
A disappointment, but there were larger matters to talk about. The
railroad had reached Cincinnati, and the flood of middle western
settlers from the East and abroad increased even more as a result.
It was agreeable to report that a priest could have a pass which would

allow him to travel *gratis* at any time. Only nine years ago, travel had been a matter of jolting along ruts, wet or dry, or breaking through woods, or halting at some forest cabin during blizzard or downpour. Material development was so rapid and widespread and called for such strong measures to meet it that Machebeuf, writing in May 1849, to Sister Philomène, declared that "at the moment when I write these lines, Bishop Rappe and all the other bishops of the United States are gathered at Baltimore" a crucial provincial council. They were to debate the resolution to ask Rome to create new archbishoprics—there were only two—one at St Louis, the other at Baltimore, which was the ranking U.S. see. In their session, these prelates, by their very convening, were creating a national character for the Church in the United States; and among the results of their debates was a decision which neither Lamy nor Machebeuf could have imagined, if they contemplated their futures.

xii.

After the 1846 War

THE SIGNED TERMS of peace laid out new boundaries which yielded a vast domain from Mexico consisting of Texas and California, and all lands between, which embraced the province of New Mexico as it then included present-day Arizona. The southern border of this huge territory was defined in a provisional way by the Rio Grande from the Gulf to "the whole southern border which runs north of the village called Paso," as the Vatican copy of the Treaty of Guadalupe Hidalgo stated. From there the boundary would go west until cut by the first arm of the Gila River, and proceed to its confluence with the Colorado River. From the point where the rivers met, the boundary would be drawn to the Pacific Ocean along the existing line which divided the provinces of Upper and Lower California. The agreement was shown in the adjustment of a map published by one J. Disturnell in New York in 1847. By treaty terms, both nations in due time were to set up a joint boundary commission which would conduct a proper survey and permanently fix legitimate possessions of both nations.

Something of the difficulties of defining a conclusive boundary was reflected in a letter written by an Army officer and quoted in a speech on the floor of the House in Washington by Congressman Truman Smith of Connecticut. "The boundaries of the territory have never been very exactly defined, as a great share of the line lies over desert countries, where very little importance can attach to an exact location. Whilst in Santa Fe I endeavored to ascertain the exact southern boundary of the territory, but I found that various lines had been claimed both by New Mexico and Chihuahua. All agreed, however, in considering the settlements to the north of the 'Jornada del Muerto' ('Dead Man's Journey') as belonging to New Mexico, whilst those to the south of it were considered as belonging to Chihuahua." The congressman for his part spoke sentiments which to one degree or other were shared by a vocal minority of his fellow citizens. He announced that the common people were very ignorant, the women less educated than the men, and both sexes were, as he understood, "under the control of the clergy to an extraordinary degree. The standard of morals is exceedingly low . . . the country is little better than a Sodom." He thought the whole acquisition of the territory a disaster. "The moral desolation which exists in Northern Mexico must long continue; . . . I am free to say that if all the vices which can corrupt the human heart, and all the qualities which reduce man to the level of a brute, are to be 'annexed' to the virtue and intelligence of the American people, I DO NOT DESIRE TO BELONG TO ANY SUCH UNION." The congressman ended his grand periods by saying, "It is apparent that we have extorted a bargain from Mexico at the point of a bayonet, and cheated ourselves."

In any case, such a political separation, imprecise as it had to be in its first phase, and relying on self-interest as well as lines drawn on a map, brought another serious matter for debate; and that was the question of religious jurisdiction in the new United States territories. All lands that had been ceded had been administered by bishops of Mexico. What should now be decided? Should this, could this, old ecclesiastical authority continue, even across national boundaries?

The American bishops nearest the problem were those who presided at New Orleans and Galveston. Bishop Blanc of New Orleans had given much thought to the question, and had gathered what information he could. In January 1849, he wrote to his colleague and far neighbor, Bishop Odin of Galveston. "New Mexico," he stated, "is under the Bishop of Durango [in Mexico], who is there at the moment (in New Mexico) and plans to spend six months there—it seems that matters there are not good—and in general are even worse than those in California." Durango was fifteen hundred miles from Santa Fe, the civil and ecclesiastical capital of the province of New Mexico. But there, too, was California, dependent on the bishop of Sonora. Texas—

at least the eastern Gulf portion—was independent of Mexican jurisdiction, having been established under the Texan Republic. But the
Mexican bishops were as concerned as the American, and, wrote Blanc
to Odin, "having jurisdiction over the ceded parts of their territory,
have consulted Rome to know if they should continue their control
of those lands which are now American."

Rome's reply was astonishing, and bore the seed of years of legalistic
wrangling. Rome "answered the Mexican bishops in the affirmative"—
they were to continue to exercise their episcopal authority north of
the border. "No doubt," said Blanc, "it is for this reason that the
Bishop of Durango went off to New Mexico, on ecclesiastical affairs."
Bishop Blanc had been told that the Mexican bishops were extremely
responsive to everything which must interest them concerning the
spiritual good of those provinces. Blanc thought two very capable men
were needed in those territories—men who spoke both languages,
English and Spanish. He did not specify their nationalities—but that
was nothing new, since a bishop from far away often was sent to preside over a new diocese. He ended with a local bulletin: the cholera
epidemic at New Orleans was drawing to its close, after having carried
off at least between twelve and fifteen hundred people.

But the territorial problems were not to be readily resolved. How
could Rome, in her great distance from the scene, grasp the realities of
the scale of the land, the needs of the people, indeed, the fallen
state of the Church herself in the ex-Mexican states? At Baltimore three
archbishops and twenty-three bishops assembled in synod to enter
into more than the recommendation of additional American archbishoprics and dioceses.

They gathered in early May 1849 in the archbishop's residence at the
rear of Latrobe's superb classical cathedral, which though not completed (the pedimented portico was not yet built) was the finest Christian monument in the country, symbolic of the earliest Catholic colonization, seat of the premier bishop, who at the time of this convening
was Archbishop Eccleston. Led by a crucifer, and wearing mitres and
copes, carrying their croziers, and following a long column of lesser
clergy, attended by acolytes, and watched by a crowd of citizens, the
women in crinolines and the men uncovered, the prelates processed to
the opening session from the archbishop's house, along the south side
of the cathedral, around the corner, passing a locally admired iron
fencing which enclosed the premises, and entered by the main doors
on the west front. The cathedral's serenely unadorned lines were enriched within by nine large religious paintings sent from Rome in
1824 as a gift from Cardinal Fesch, Napoleon's uncle, and by two even
larger donated by the last Bourbons of France. Under the noble cof-

fered dome of the cathedral and before the high altar with its classical pillared apse, the bishops, conducting their business in Latin, entered upon their agenda.

The matter of the new archbishoprics would not have taken long to deal with—the developing provinces were immense, several bishops were needed in each, and a presiding head, or metropolitan, must assist with the making of policy for each suffragan bishop. But more difficult, perhaps even more urgent, was the question of the Mexican territories now within the United States, their proper administration, and the state of the Church within them for the past many years. There was much to be brought forward about the latter point, before the territorial issue was to be taken up.

Shocked observations of Mexican life had been made by soldiers who had gone to the border war. Many such men were officers who recorded their impressions. Some drew faithful if not wholly skilled pictures of aspects of the Mexican life now so abruptly incorporated into the American territories, and some accounts had been published. The Mexican society and—so far as the Council was concerned—the Church could only be described as outlandish in their condition. Thousands of Catholics—Mexican and Indian—who had inherited the faith so laboriously and successfully implanted by the Franciscans between the Spanish conquest and the early nineteenth century—when they had been withdrawn from the vast area now annexed to the United States —thousands lived in scattered sites, far removed from each other, and almost totally without spiritual succor. Even where this was present, as in the older settlements of New Mexico, in particular Santa Fe, the lives of the priests appalled visitors from the States and from abroad. It was the bishop of Durango in Mexico, fifteen hundred miles from Santa Fe, who was responsible for the whole of New Mexico as part of his immense diocese, and he had paid only three visits there in the twenty years before the war. An English traveller reported that to come there, the "good old man was glad to return [to Durango] with any hem to his garment, so great was the respect paid to him . . ." It was thought a miracle that he escaped death at the hands of Apache or Comanche warriors in the course of his three-thousand-mile round trip over an empty landscape which was a seemingly endless repetition in sequence of desert, parched river, and mountain barrier.

New Mexico's condition was incredible, as the bishops at Baltimore considered what was needed. Her churches were for the most part in ruins, and all of them had been built of earthen walls and roofs. There were no schools. Most of the parishes made no proper observances. There were only nine active priests in over two hundred thousand square miles. The deportment of most of these was reprehensible.

United States Army officers had often been startled by what they had seen—reverend fathers drinking, gambling, dancing with their most carefree parishioners, and even betraying their vows by living in concubinage, or even open adultery. A soldier wrote in his diary, "I have no respect for the priesthood in this country, and I think it a desecration of God's temple, that a priest of New Mexico should be permitted to officiate in one." A United States lieutenant paying a call upon the pastor of Albuquerque saw that "a lady graced the apartment" quite openly. The missions of the Pueblos were abandoned, and the town parishes, poor as they were, felt the burden of extortion when certain pastors levied outrageous charges for pastoral services at birth, marriage, baptism, and burial. There was still a pathetic spark of faithful need for the Church among the Latin population, and many families did what they could to pass along to their children the outlines of Christian doctrine and history; but memory played tricks, and truth was lost in local fancy, and where form survived it was often corrupt and without substance. Thousands of men and women lived unbaptized, unmarried though in cohabitation, unconfessed, unconfirmed, and at the end, unshriven for the human errors of a lifetime. The state of affairs, the Council concluded, could hardly be worse.

In Texas, similar conditions prevailed along the Rio Grande frontier, with only the diocese of Galveston to serve the huge territory. After the peace settlement with Mexico in 1848, Bishop Odin of Galveston had written to the Vatican to ask how far his responsibility must reach now that the national status of Texas had been settled as part of the United States. His reply came in the following year, just as he was setting out for the Baltimore Council of 1849. It told him that his diocese must include all of Texas and extend as far in New Mexico as to include all territories east of the Rio Grande—the old political boundary claimed by Texas from the beginning of her moves toward independence and subsequent statehood.

At the synod, Odin reported this ruling to his colleagues. They debated the Roman wisdom in creating a diocese so immense; and in the end, the bishops appealed to the Holy See to revise its vision of the great Southwest, and provide for more manageable units to be administered by added bishops or vicars apostolic.

In the more settled portions of the United States, the annual growth was so astonishing that some estimate could be made of what would be needed there—the synod reported to the Society for the Propagation of the Faith at Lyon that two hundred fifty thousand Catholic immigrants arrived every year, and that to meet this pace, three hundred priests a year must be sent, in order to build annually three hundred churches and three hundred schools. The Charity of Christ, the wants of society, required no less. It could be assumed that in time the desert West would require its share of support from the world church.

Completing its work through many days, the synod on 13 May 1849 sent its conclusive appeal to Rome. *"Beatissime Pater,"* wrote the bishops to Pius IX, "Most Holy Father," asking that for the states and territories of the United States, there be erected new archbishoprics in New York, Cincinnati and New Orleans, and new episcopal sees in Savannah, Georgia; Wheeling [West Virginia]; St. Paul, Minnesota; Monterey, California; and that a vicariate apostolic be erected to encompass "the territory called ROCKY MOUNTAINS which is included neither within the limits of the states of Arkansas, nor Missouri, nor Iowa" (loosely indicating an immense central area of the nation which in time would be occupied and defined as perhaps half a dozen states); and further that "there be elected a Vicar Apostolic, dignified with an episcopal consecration, for the Territory of New Mexico, and its see established in the city of Santa Fe." Thus the oldest Spanish Catholic lands now within the nation would receive extraordinary attention. Presently, with their deliberations concluded, the prelates returned to their cities and began exchanging lists of candidates for the new bishops whom Rome must appoint to administer whatever new dioceses might be created.

xiii.

A Bishop for New Mexico

THE QUESTION OF ESTABLISHING a bishopric for New Mexico was not a new one—though now as a consequence of the Mexican War it had again come forward, at last to be answered. The matter had been agitated periodically under Spanish rule ever since the 1630s, through two and a quarter centuries. Fray Alonso de Benavides, the early father custodian of the Franciscans in New Mexico, pursued it tirelessly at Madrid and at Rome from 1630 to 1636. In a number of petitions he besought Philip IV to erect the Santa Fe diocese under the power held by the Spanish crown to appoint bishops. He argued skillfully, trying to make the far country he knew so well come alive in the impenetrable royal imagination. How far away from the nearest bishop was the capital of the Rio Grande kingdom—five hundred leagues, for Durango already had its cathedral. It then took almost a year to make the round-trip journey between Durango and Santa Fe, it was not possible to procure the holy oil every year, and sometimes five or six years passed before it was brought to the New Mexican missions, whose people lacked the sacrament of confirmation, which was "so necessary to strengthen the souls of the faithful." The journey was not only long, it was perilous. But if a bishop were established at Santa Fe —it was "desirable that he remain always at Santa Fe, where the governor and the Spaniards reside permanently"—then what benefits must follow! Beyond the spiritual, what wise economies! For "if there were a bishop to consecrate churches and to ordain priests from among the native Spaniards of that land," who knew its languages, wrote Fray Alonso, then His Majesty "would be spared the heavy costs in sending friars." As for supporting a bishop, the discovery of silver mines and the increase of population, with additional farms and cattle to feed the people, would yield enough money in tithes to maintain his lordship without a call upon the royal treasury.

Everything was available locally, even the person of the bishop himself, insisted the father custodian in the seventeenth century: the bishop should be appointed from among the Franciscan friars already at work in the river kingdom. After all, there was precedent for such an appointment among Franciscans. "Your royal predecessors," wrote Fray Alonso to the King, "gave them the first bishoprics of the Indies, and, assuming that the same reasoning applies . . . may your Majesty be pleased that the one appointed as bishop in these kingdoms and provinces be of the same order. . . ." He could readily name four New Mexican friars any one of whom, "though devoid of human ambitions," would be suitable candidates, and there was a fifth whom in all modesty he would not name, but whose brilliant statement of the case surely would bring him to mind.

In 1631 the father custodian had reason to think the matter was about to be settled, for the King seemed "determined on the erection of a bishopric in these parts and decreed that a brother of St Francis should be nominated to be prelate," and even seemed ready to ask Pope Urban VIII to confirm the establishment. But a matter of such weight could not travel swiftly through the labyrinths of policy at the Escorial and the Vatican, and nine years later, with the question still unresolved, a bishop of New Spain presented to the King damaging evidence that the New Mexican friars were exceeding their authority as simple priests. The bishop had been told that "the Franciscan friars in New Mexico are using the mitre and crozier," behaving for all the world like bishops, even "administering the sacrament of confirmation, and also conferring ordinations in minor orders." Nobody had yet given them authority to do any of these things. Perhaps they were beyond patience at not having been given a proper bishop. When chided, they lamely explained that they had an official paper of some sort granting them authority to "give orders." This they took to mean *holy orders,* when all it could have meant even to a child's intelligence —the complaining bishop was disgusted—was routine authority to exercise priestly discipline over parishioners. Examiners of the case in Madrid found that there was no town in New Mexico great enough to contain a cathedral, and further, that the province was so poor that its tithes would never support a prelate. In any case, the friars made too much of their need, and their father custodian presently received no more than an apostolic grant empowering him to administer confirmation.

The matter was allowed to gather dust in official files for twenty-eight more years, when once again it was looked into, and now again with favor, for the kingdom of New Mexico had prospered until in 1666 it seemed likely that a bishop could be properly supported at Santa Fe. Royal and papal approval gathered strength for the next fourteen years; but then, in 1680, the calamity of the Pueblo revolt swept away the New Mexican colony, its Spaniards, and their parishes, and accordingly all chances for the bishopric. The river kingdom was left under the jurisdiction of the bishop of Durango, in his famous and lamented distance of fifteen hundred miles from Santa Fe. Generations would go by without an episcopal visitation to the exiled north after the Spanish restoration in New Mexico in 1692, while the mission friars struggled to hold their authority against that of the civil governors, and even broke into quarrels with their distant and invisible bishop. When in the last hours of the Spanish dominion in the New World, New Mexico was allowed to send an elected delegate to sit in the *Cortes* in Spain, he proposed once again, in 1810, but in vain, a bishopric for New Mexico. After the revolutionary secession of Mexico from Spain in 1821, the long process of secularization began, and without a bishop to guide it on the scene, the Church fell upon unhappy days. The absence of a spiritual leader seemed like a symbol of the abandonment of the province. Who cared?—so far, so outlandish, with only a handful of Spaniards (now Mexicans) amidst a diffused population of inscrutable Indians—New Mexico was lost in its golden distance, and the world did not appear to miss it. Without leadership in the affairs of the spirit, the society lost any motive larger than that of simple survival. Without food or purpose for the aggregate mind of the colony, ignorance was the birthright of each new generation. Without education to foster the works of betterment in people's lives, and to create a sense of a future for the young, the very heart of the society was oppressed. When the last Franciscans were withdrawn in the 1830s, and a mere handful of the secular clergy was left, not only the people, but even many priests forgot the laws of the Church.

Now, in 1849, letters circulated between American chanceries and converged upon the prelate at Baltimore, who would forward to Rome the recommendations from among which the names of the new American bishops would be chosen. It was not a matter for parish priests to enter into; their presiding prelates kept the affair in their own hands. Lamy in Covington went about his modest but demanding labors, as yet knowing nothing of what was coming to a focus.

For each new bishopric, three nominations were drawn up by the conciliar bishops, were discussed by letter, and the names forwarded to Baltimore. Lamy, in his undemanding obscurity, was brought to light on several lists, which presented candidates in preferential order for first, second, and third rank in every case. For the new diocese of St Paul, he was ranked as second choice, with the notation, "Joannes Lamy, a Frenchman, 35 years of age; well versed in the doctrine; especially praiseworthy for his mild character, zeal for the salvation of souls." For Monterey, California, he was again ranked in second place; but for Santa Fe, he was, by preponderance of recommendations, placed first, with the supporting statement, "Joannes Lamy, Native of France, 35 years old, for many years already working in the Diocese of Cincinnati, well known for his piety, honesty, prudence, and other virtues." On 16 April 1850, Archbishop Eccleston of Baltimore wrote to Purcell that Lamy was "first on the list for the Vicariate of Santa Fe." His nomination was submitted to Pius IX, while as summer deepened, Lamy, all unaware, wrote to Purcell on 25 July 1850 on routine matters in Covington, and added that "the cholera is not so bad in my little congregation"—St Mary's—"I have had only two deaths in this month . . . but the weather continues excessively hot."

No one in America yet knew it, but six days earlier, on 19 July, Pius IX, recently returned to Rome from his sanctuary at Gaeta, where he had fled from Garibaldi, had established by decree the vicariate apostolic of New Mexico, and further, on 23 July had issued a papal bull naming as its vicar apostolic Father John Baptist Lamy, of Covington, Kentucky, with the title of bishop of Agathonica, *in partibus infidelium.*

xiv.

These Two Vicars

LAMY WAS AMAZED when first the suggestion came his way, probably from his friend and superior Purcell, that he had been nominated for the mitre; but it was best to put thoughts of all that aside and get on with parish duties until the official bulls should arrive from Rome during the summer. His elevation then became a certainty which the self-doubts he felt could not affect. Of one thing he was immediately sure—to a place so far away, so outlandish, of which so little was known and that little discouraging enough—he could not go alone. He had communicated to Machebeuf what might be coming to pass, and they were keeping it between themselves. But when the "great news" finally arrived, he wrote to his old friend at Sandusky asking him to go West with him "not only as a missionary, but as an intimate friend on whom he could count and upon whom he could lay a part of his burden—in short, as his Vicar General"—a post which would place Machebeuf next in authority to the bishop. In his usual "simplicity and humility," Lamy wrote to him, "They want me to be a Vicar Apostolic, very well, I will make you my Vicar General, and from these two Vicars we'll try to make one good pastor."

For Machebeuf it was a harder decision than for Lamy, who had no choice. Privately, Machebeuf was disposed to follow his friend, but for himself, he felt "neither the necessary talent nor the courage, nor even the *patience*" for the move. He struggled throughout ten days before he could reply to Lamy's appeal. During that time he went to Cleveland to ask Bishop Rappe and the other cathedral clergy what to do; but they felt that they must leave the decision to him—he must interpret God's will in the matter. It pained him to think of leaving Sandusky where his ten years had been so binding. Just now he was about to build his first school, everyone was relying on him, the news that he might go dismayed them. Lamy wrote a second time, and finally Machebeuf was brought to decide. He went to Cincinnati at last to see the bishop-elect himself and to make all arrangements with him.

The moment he arrived at St Mary's in Covington, Lamy seized him by the hand and reminded him of the pledge they had made to each other years before—*never to be separated.* A certain memory had some effect—when Machebeuf for a moment had considered going to the Rocky Mountains with the illustrious Jesuit missionary De Smet, and Lamy had been sent by Purcell to deter him, what had happened? Machebeuf had asked Lamy what he would do if he were unable to change Machebeuf's mind about going to Oregon, and Lamy had said, "I will go with you." The positions were now reversed, but the pact was as strong as ever. Together they would proceed to Santa Fe.

But much came first—Machebeuf's parishioners sent delegations to plead with Purcell not to let their pastor go. They could not see the bishop, who was making a retreat at the Ursuline convent in Brown County, in Ohio. The decision was not reversed. Plans for Lamy's consecration went forward at Cincinnati. He himself went to the Ursulines to make his own spiritual preparations for the consecration which would take place on 24 November 1850. His sister Margaret, the nun who was at New Orleans Ursuline Convent, and his little niece Marie, were coming for the ceremony, after which they would return to New Orleans with him. Margaret Lamy must go home to France, for her health was alarmingly poor. Marie would remain in the New Orleans convent to continue her education.

The question of how to travel to Santa Fe had its complications. There were two possible routes. One led to St Louis and across the prairies with a merchant train along the Santa Fe Trail, which could take up to ninety days. The road led through Indian country, and by now there were hazards from Indian attack, as a result of brutal encroachments by some of the later trading caravans, where the earliest waggon parties of the 1820s had given and received little or no hostility in the plains empire of the Indians. The other way to Santa Fe was more complicated and lengthy. It would require a voyage to New Orleans, another on the Gulf of Mexico, and another from there to Indianola, Texas, followed by passage overland to Port Lavaca and San Antonio. Once there, an accommodation must be made to travel with a United States Army supply train as far as Fort Bliss opposite El Paso del Norte on the Rio Grande; and then must come a northward turn to follow the Rio Grande for many days, until a final, and brief, deviation led northeastward to the unimaginable capital, all of which would take six months.

By 21 September Lamy's plan to follow the second of these routes was known. Not everyone thought this a wise decision. Archbishop Blanc of New Orleans wrote to Archbishop Purcell—both had been promoted—assuring him that Lamy would be well received in New Orleans, but he could not imagine why Lamy had chosen the longer and more complicated road over the shorter and swifter. In any case, he must be given all possible assistance, and Blanc wrote also to Bishop Odin at Galveston to send helpful details of how Lamy should plan his journey to San Antonio, and how to meet supply requirements for the further approach to Santa Fe. It seemed that a certain officer had arrived from Cincinnati with a hundred soldiers, some of whom were destined for Santa Fe; and he advised that Lamy would do well to buy at New Orleans the mules he would need for the overland passage, as they cost much more at San Antonio. Did Odin agree that this was so?

Meanwhile the solemnities planned for 24 November 1850 were taking form. It was always moving to see within daily circumstances the extraordinary acts of elevation by which, in any society at any epoch, the high priests were brought to be dedicated to their office. Ancient ways, preserved through empowering ritual, were let into the common day, not only as an act of the affirmation of a person—but also as a celebration of a collective need above personality.

Cincinnati in 1850, as seen from Lamy's Covington, where St Mary's steeple rose a few blocks from the river front, was a far greater city than that which the new arrivals from France had seen in 1839. Tall industrial chimneys by the dozen gave out announcements of progress into the otherwise clear air. The river was densely busy with every sort of craft—the ferries from Cincinnati to Covington, sailing sloops, steam tugs, barges in tow, the great house-like paddle-wheelers with their towering stacks. On the Cincinnati shore, the city had spread widely across the hills which met the river, and two great buildings stood out in the panorama. One of these, on the highest hill, was an astronomical observatory dedicated in 1843 by President John Quincy Adams, and the other was the new St Peter's Cathedral which had been dedicated in 1845.

The cathedral was a monument to that American mood which from the beginning had seen the nation as an offspring of the classical learning of Greece. Purcell had built it. "The Cathedral I would propose," Purcell had written to the Ohio architect Thomas Spare of Somerset, "to have about 70 by 100 feet, grecian style of architecture, with portico and colonnade in front, with vestibule, all about 30 or 40 feet deep, and with a steeple carried up from the foundation. . . . These specifications, I presume, will be sufficient." They were enough for Mr Spare, and by 1850 all was complete in hard Dayton limestone except for the portico, which still had to be built. But the centered steeple rose in six diminishing octagonal blocks to support the high thin needle. Corinthian columns supported the clerestory and the coffered ceiling within; a pair of marble kneeling angels flanked the altar. They had been commissioned by Purcell from the American sculptor Hiram Powers, who at eighteen had been manager of Dor-feuille's "museum" at Cincinnati but was now living abroad in Flor-ence. Above the tabernacle was a large painting of St Peter in Chains, which was another gift to the Church in America by Napoleon's uncle. Modern times brought additions and other changes to St Peter's in Cincinnati, but it remained a moving testament to the energy, taste, and style of frontier America. It was, in effect, the ecclesiastical capitol of interior America between Baltimore and St Louis. So many bishops were consecrated there—to the number of twenty-one, most destined for new dioceses to the Far West, a few assigned to the even farther Orient—that St Peter's was known among the clergy as "the bishop factory."

Here, on 24 November 1850, Lamy entered, following a long proces-sion of religious, priests, bishops, and his consecrators, to endure the second ceremony of commitment to his life's design. It would take three hours, and he would be at its center as the victim and protagonist of an office which reached him through the centuries by the touch of St Peter. He was, so, the heir of Christ's own words to the first of the apostles, and himself became on that November day a successor as bishop to symbolic custody of the Rock upon which the Church was built.

Before the public, and in the presence of many of his peers, he was subjected to an examination of his faith, and then to the act of con-secration, and finally to the investiture with the regalia of his office— pectoral cross, mitre, crozier, gloves, and ring. Bishop John Martin Spalding of Louisville was his consecrator, assisted by Bishop James Maurice de Long d'Aussac de Saint-Palais, of Vincennes, Indiana, and Bishop Louis Amadeus Rappe, as co-consecrators.

Bishop Spalding and his mitred assistants officiated at the central altar. For the bishop-elect a smaller altar was prepared to one side, where as the ritual proceeded he celebrated those portions of the Mass to which, after long and exhaustive passages of the sacral process, the ceremony returned. The event proceeded with a dream-like slowness, woven of countless lights against white stone, and vestments in color brocaded in silver and gold, and figures moving in traditional order from one prescribed position to another in the sanctuary which was clouded with the smoke of censers amidst which the distant voices of the celebrants seemed like disembodied sounds.

When the members of the procession were all stationed according to their function and rank, seated or standing, Bishop de Saint-Palais rose and approached Bishop Spalding where he was seated on a fald-stool in front of the high altar facing the church. *"Reverendissime Pater,"* he said, presenting the candidate for promotion to the burden of the episcopate, *"postulat sancta Mater Ecclesia Catholica ut hunc praesentem Presbyterum ad onus Episcopatus sublevetis."* Speaking, as did all throughout, in Latin, Bishop Spalding asked,

"Have you the Apostolic Mandate?"

"We have," replied Bishop de Saint-Palais.

"Let it be read."

A notary took the papal bull from the co-consecrator and read aloud the text by which Pius IX promoted Lamy to his bishopric. When he was finished, all said, "Thanks be to God."

Now Lamy came to kneel before Bishop Spalding to read his oath as a new bishop. He vowed to sustain with all his power the Pope, the Papacy, the Church and its decrees; to attend synods when called and to make his visit *ad limina* to Rome and the reigning pope every ten years at which time he would account fully for his stewardship, or if prevented from coming by legitimate reason, he would send a qualified representative from among his clergy; and to guard strictly all the Church properties in his care; and "if through me any . . . alienation shall occur, I wish, by the very fact, to incur the punishments contained in the constitution published concerning this matter."

Bishop Spalding sat facing him, holding open the books of the Gospels so that Lamy could see them. Lamy concluded,

"So help me God and these Holy Gospels." Saying this, he touched the pages of the Gospels with both hands, completing his oath, and Bishop Spalding said, "Thanks be to God."

All now being seated, Bishop Spalding conducted Lamy's examination. In a preamble, he restated the ancient rule that anyone who was chosen for the order of bishop should be diligently examined, and with all charity, concerning his faith and his fealty to his duties, for the Apostle had said, "Impose hands hastily upon no man."

"Therefore," declared Bishop Spalding, taking cognizance of human frailty, "with sincere charity, we ask you, most dear brother, if you desire to make your conduct harmonize, as far as your nature allows, with the meaning of the divine Scripture."

"With my whole heart I wish in all things to consent and obey," replied the bishop-elect.

There followed seventeen questions, some humbly concerned with mundanities, others tremendous in their citations of the Deity, all of them requiring an affirmative reply. The examination done, and witnessed, Lamy was conducted to his separate altar where in his first assumption of the bishop's insignia, he received his pectoral cross, and unlaced his stole so that its bands hung straight down instead of being crossed, as simple priests wore it. After being fully vested, he then began the Mass. At the *Alleluia* he was again taken before Bishop

Spalding, who, wearing his mitre—an act which always signalized that the wearer was performing in his authority as a bishop rather than as a simple priest—said to him,

"A bishop judges, interprets, consecrates, ordains, offers, baptizes, and confirms," and then prayed that all present would intercede for Lamy that he receive the abundance of God's grace in his duties.

The consecrating bishops and Lamy then prostrated themselves upon the steps of the altar in an act acknowledging their submission to higher powers than they could, as men, aspire to; and the litany of the saints was recited.

After this invocation of the great forebears, all rose, and Lamy came to kneel before Spalding. The consecrating bishops then took the books of the Gospels and laid them upon the bent neck and shoulders of Lamy so that the printed words touched him. So receiving the Gospels as their custodian, he was ready for that other touch which transmitted, to one who believed as he did, more than symbolic tradition. Spalding, and his assistants, all wearing the mitre, laid their hands in turn upon Lamy's head, and Spalding said,

"Receive the Holy Ghost."

It was the essential act by which the creation of a bishop, as of a priest, was done.

Now the Mass was resumed with the intoning of the Preface, in the course of which the acts of Moses and Aaron were recalled, and the power of their symbolic vesture in their sacred functions, and the text went on to declare, ". . . the adornment of our minds fulfills what was expressed by the outward vesture of that ancient priesthood, and now brightness of souls rather than splendor of raiment commends the pontifical glory unto us. Because even those things which were sightly unto the eyes of the flesh, demanded rather that the eyes of the spirit should understand the things they signified. And therefore we beseech Thee, O Lord, give bountifully this grace to this Thy servant, whom Thou had chosen to the ministry of the supreme priesthood, so that by what things soever those vestments signify by the refulgence of gold, the splendor of jewels, and the variety of diversified handiwork, these may shine forth in his character and his actions."

Visible splendor was neither to be scorned nor valued for its own sake, but for what it represented in the gift of reverence.

"Fill up in Thy Priest," intoned Spalding, finishing the Preface, "the perfection of Thy ministry and sanctify with the dew of Thy heavenly ointment this Thy servant decked out with the ornaments of all beauty."

Lamy's head was now bound with a white cloth; Spalding knelt facing the altar and began to intone the hymn *Veni Creator Spiritus,* calling upon the Holy Spirit to be upon them all, as He had come to the apostles at the first Pentecost. As the hymn proceeded, Spalding anointed Lamy upon the head with the chrism, and upon the hands, at great length reciting manifold duties and invoking graces. He then blessed a crozier and presented it to Lamy, and then blessed his episcopal ring—it was a large amethyst surrounded by small pearls—and placed it upon the ring finger of his right hand, and once again gave him the book of the Gospels; and finally raised him up and gave him the kiss of peace, saying, *"Pax tibi."*

Lamy returned to his altar, cleansed his head and hands of the holy oil with bread crumbs presented to him in a dish, and resumed the Mass, and when the time for the sermon arrived, Purcell preached on the appropriate theme of the apostolic succession. At the end of the Mass proper, Lamy was again presented to Spalding, who, having blessed a mitre, placed it upon Lamy's head, with the weighty words of commitment,

"We, O Lord, place on the head of this Thy bishop and champion, the helmet of protection and salvation, so that his face being adorned and his head armed with the horns of both testaments"—the front and rear spires of the mitre—"he may seem terrible to the opponents of truth, and through the indulgence of Thy grace may be their sturdy adversary, Thou who didst mark with the brightest rays of Thy splendor and truth the countenance of Moses thy servant, ornamented from his fellowship with Thy word: and didst order the tiara to be placed on the head of Aaron Thy high priest. Through Christ our Lord," and all replied "Amen" to this second invocation of the powers in the Hebraic Old Testament. Spalding then blessed the new bishop's ceremonial gauntlets and placed them upon his hands, and Lamy, now fully vested as a bishop, turned to the people and gave them his first episcopal blessing, making the sign of the cross over them three times, "May the Almighty God bless you, the ✠ Father, the ✠ Son, and the Holy ✠ Ghost." After this, he faced Spalding and intoned three times, at a rising pitch with each utterance, and genuflecting three times, "For many years . . ."

And now he was released from the passive role of victim of the ancient powers enacted upon him throughout the three-hour ceremony; and wearing his mitre and walking with his crozier, he went to his separate altar and recited the Last Gospel, *"In principio erat verbum,"* at the end of which he was divested of his ceremonial garments. He turned and bowed to his consecrators with thanks, and all departed "in peace."

In St Peter's, the people moved, the church was emptied, the episcopal colleagues and their friends—along with Lamy's sister and his niece (surely Machebeuf was present)—gathered to sit down together at table, and the concerns of the common day were eagerly resumed after the timeless impersonality of the just completed ritual.

Bishop Rappe undertook to do "all possible to persuade the new bishop to go to Europe" (instead of setting out for New Mexico) "to seek after new priests who knew Spanish." The attempt was useless. Lamy was firm in his plans. He would leave tomorrow for New Orleans, and then he would begin his arrangements for his long journey westward. At New Orleans he would wait for his new vicar general to join him whenever Machebeuf should have resolved his affairs at Sandusky, and they would then set out together for Santa Fe.

III

TO SANTA FE

1850–1851

i.

New Orleans

ON 25 NOVEMBER 1850, Lamy sailed from Cincinnati by river on the first of the several long stages of his way to the Far West. His ultimate destination was that whole immense area of the Rocky Mountains and the high plains which was lettered in a sweeping arc on early- and mid-nineteenth-century maps as "The Great American Desert." Since the end of the war in 1847, and the discovery of gold in California in 1848, travel to the West had increased vastly, by many alternate routes, including trails straight westward overland; Atlantic travel by ship to Mexico or the Isthmus of Panama, followed by an overland passage to the Pacific, and again by ship north to the California gold fields; or, by ship, all the way around Cape Horn. News came eastward, not too much of it accurate, but people responded. Inevitably settlements took root along the westward trails, and new details soon came to light on later maps. But beyond the Mississippi much was still alive only in the imagination, and impressions owed as much to legend as to fact. Lamy had little detailed knowledge of the continent, other than that known at second hand to the fellow bishops who had elected him.

How full, as preparation, had been his work in the intimate forest villages and their confined landscape during the past ten years? He had no way yet to measure this, and it was not in his nature to indulge in imaginative speculation, and in any case he had little enough to go on to form any true idea of what lay ahead. Habitually he met the occasion of the day, under the calm sense of confidence and guidance which animated him.

His river steamer wound slowly away from Cincinnati, taking the great double bend of the Ohio to the south and west of the city. The populated slopes were soon lost to sight. Wilderness America followed, with its rolling hills and winding valleys, broken only now and then by wide flat fields on each side of the river, and an occasional farm house in Indiana and Kentucky. On the Ohio and the Mississippi, the river voyage to New Orleans would take nine days. The paddle steamer would pass many others of her general sort. They all made a brave sight, with their fancifully crowned stacks, showing dense smoke by day, and sparks and even flames by night. They were capacious ships— some had room for over fifteen hundred passengers—with luxurious fittings and flattering service which were meant to rival those of the wooden scroll-saw hotels in the inland cities.

Lamy's sister Margaret, and Marie, the daughter of his brother Etienne, saw with him much to wonder at during the voyage, now with amusement, at other times with sorrow and distaste—and so did Machebeuf, who followed on a river steamer some weeks later in January 1851. Machebeuf was a lively and constant letter writer, and his own observations of river travel captured the typical.

There was always a mixed passenger list—American, Dutch, English, French, Pole, Italian, Irish, Catholics and Protestants, priests, laymen, and Negro servants who were slaves. The crews were both white and black. To the animation of the persons aboard was added the dense animal presence of more than 160 mules or horses, 100 beef cattle, 400 sheep, 60 or 80 fighting cocks which had been bought for twenty-five francs each at Louisville and were destined to amuse the spectators of New Orleans. There was other cargo: 400 bales of cotton, 200 or 300 tons of wheat—and Negro slaves for sale.

Lamy used river-time to study a new language. English or French would not, it was supposed, be generally useful to him where he was going. Spanish was the language of the people, and had to be learned, as English had had to be mastered for Ohio. As the wide, fancy-decked, scroll-sawed steamer wound slowly southward Lamy would work at his Spanish, and later he and Machebeuf were amused to compare notes on the resemblances they found between that language and much of the common speech of Auvergne, despite differences in pronunciation. *"La vida"* seemed to them close to *"la vie,"* *"aqua"* to *"l'eau,"* *"la mitad"* to *"la moitié."* Putting the language together in discourse would, however, be another matter, as they would learn.

The steamers hove in for passengers and cargo all down the river. While the ship was docked for several hours at Memphis, there was an event not to be forgotten by strangers, though it was familiar enough to others. In the evening her cargo of slaves was taken to the slave market by the trader in charge, who, in a "revolting scene," sold two young black women to a local customer. This buyer examined his prospective goods thoroughly. He directed them to walk, to speak, asked them what they could do, why their previous owner had sold them, and, finally assured that he would get his money's worth, paid

650 piastres each for them and led them away in their rags. It moved the observer to compassion to see them walking slowly off behind their new master. (Machebeuf naively felt obliged to add—having no doubt heard as much from cordial southern passengers—that many slave-owners took great care of their human property, and that even if offered their freedom many slaves would never leave them.)

Here and there when the steamer tied up at the bank to take on wood for her furnaces, the travellers could see some of the great Mississippi plantations, which often looked like small villages, centered about the great two-storey brick mansion of the master, with the slave quarters set to one side, where they stood thirty or forty feet from each other. Each Negro family had its own cabin and little garden, and the inhabitants were obliged to work for nothing in exchange except their food and coarse clothing.

As the voyage proceeded, the climate gradually changed—overcoats even in mid-winter were no longer needed, the trees bore leaves, and the land was green, and as they drew close to New Orleans, the travellers would see orange groves before nightfall. The river widened. The city would be both a destination and a point of departure. Lamy's sister was ailing so rapidly that on arrival he must enter her into the hospital of the Sisters of Charity, where she could await the sailing of the ship which would take her home to France, back to her motherhouse, for she was no longer able to be active in America. Little Marie Lamy would go to school to the New Orleans Ursulines with the blessing of her uncle the bishop. He cared greatly for her, and during all his life she would be devoted to him.

They docked at New Orleans in early December and carried out their arrangements. Lamy was lodged with Archbishop Blanc, who had a lively interest in his affairs. From Blanc's experience and the letters of Bishop Odin of Galveston, Lamy could draw on a great fund of advice. Blanc had already written to Purcell at Cincinnati that he expected Lamy, and would receive him as a "friend and brother," but could not understand why he had to go to Santa Fe by way of New Orleans, as the St Louis route was so much quicker. It may have been that those who always raised the question did not know of Lamy's sense of responsibility for taking proper measures himself for his sister and his niece at New Orleans, or if they knew, did not feel so strongly as Lamy in this duty. Another possible reason for the New Orleans route was that soon after arriving there, he was to go to Mobile, Alabama, to assist at a consecration; and New Orleans was the most suitable place from which to go to Mobile.

Once in New Orleans to plan his next steps westward, Lamy had plenty to do. The city was busy—an ocean and river port both. The waterfront was clustered with steamers for the river trade, and also with others which voyaged into the Gulf of Mexico and into the oceans. The Mississippi was as wide as a sizable lake. Signs of industry lined her shores. Canal street was like one half of a great Parisian boulevard with two traffic lanes separated by a park with walks, lawns, lamps, and trees. Horse-drawn passenger cars moved along parallel to the river; and in the inner streets, winding between gas lamps and houses with lacy iron balconies, the glass hearses and black broughams of funeral processions bearing away cholera victims could frequently be seen by people on the sidewalks—men in frock coats who bared their heads at the sight, bonneted women who said a prayer, a black woman carrying on her head a round basket of flowers for sale. Facing the river across a formally planted park, in the midst of which General Jackson in bronze doffed his cocked hat while his charger reared beneath him, was the Cathedral of New Orleans. Its tall central spire and two lesser ones were almost black in color, above an ornate façade of pale plaster. Behind the cathedral was an enclosed garden with great trees and flowering bushes. There Lamy, like his host, could read his daily office, or enter the rear door of the church to say his Mass.

Waiting for Machebeuf, he went ahead with his preparations.

ii.

S.S. Palmetto

FROM A LOOK AT A MAP, he could see where his course would take him next, and from a search of the New Orleans newspapers—the *Picayune* and the *Commercial Bulletin*—he could work out a schedule of the Gulf steamship sailings. "For Galveston and Matagorda Bay—Regular N. Orleans and Texas U.S. Mail Line of Low Pressure Steamships," read the announcement of the shipping line of Harris and Morgan, 79 Tchoupitoulas street. "The public are respectfully informed that hereafter a steamship of this line will leave New Orleans for Galveston and Matagorda Bay on the 5th, 10th, 15th, 20th, 25th, and 30th of every month." Additional announcements advertised the "Superior coppered and copper-fastened Steamship PALMETTO, J. Smith, Master," to leave "as above" for "Galveston, Indianola, and Port Lavaca." An added note stated that passengers for all points in Matagorda Bay—

which was where Lamy was going—would be landed at Indianola. Ships would dock several hours at Galveston for unloading and loading of passengers and freight, during which time through-passengers would be required to stop on shore. Lamy could plan to spend his day in Galveston with Bishop Odin. At the end of his sea voyage, he could look forward to the transshipment of his luggage and other cargo from the port at Indian Point, also called Indianola, and to his passage overland to Port Lavaca, Texas, where Gulf steamers could not dock.

Bishop Odin knew from Archbishop Blanc that Lamy was coming, and wrote practical suggestions for the entire trip, dispatching these to Blanc by an eastward run of the *Palmetto*.

Odin would be "charmed" to see Lamy at Galveston, only regretting that the hospitality he could offer would not match that of Blanc at New Orleans. He wished it were possible to accompany Lamy as far as the western boundary of the Galveston diocese—at that time the region of El Paso—or at least to San Antonio, but duties and lack of funds had to prevent this. He confirmed that the quickest way for Lamy to go must be by one of the Gulf steamers from New Orleans to Galveston, and from there to Port Lavaca. The ships docked at Galveston in the morning, and resumed their voyage in the evening, arriving at Port Lavaca at mid-morning the next day. He wished Lamy would spend a week with him, leaving his first ship and taking the next one westbound—same expense. If he were to do that, he should send all his luggage straight through to Port Lavaca, addressed to Major Kerr, though the ship's captain would no doubt plan instead to unload all at Indianola, twelve miles over a wretched road from Port Lavaca. From Lavaca, he should transport all his belongings to San Antonio by "Mexican or German carts," which would cost up to a piastre and a half per hundredweight. Lamy and his companions—at first, he expected to have three priests with him—should then go direct by the stage coach to San Antonio. Odin advised that he not buy mules at New Orleans, as the Gulf voyage would be hard on them; better to buy them at San Antonio, where, if they were not so powerful as United States mules, they were anyhow less expensive. As for the overland trip from San Antonio to El Paso, Odin had little to suggest, except that Lamy should conclude arrangements with the United States quartermaster to travel with an Army train, and buy whatever he needed at San Antonio, where merchandise was plentiful. He ought to engage a Mexican waggon to carry his books, vestments, and altar vessels. If Lamy was not used to riding a horse, he should buy at New Orleans a travelling carriage, and then, perhaps after all, two mules used to the traces. Odin had made a journey of two thousand miles during the previous summer using only one horse all the way, but the season was good, the grass abundant; but now in winter, and crossing the plains westward, there was little grass, water, or wood. Only mules could subsist on the land. In any case, said Odin, "I am an old enough Texan to predict" for Lamy "great fatigue and many obstacles on his hard journey, and I whole-heartedly wish him a good and heavy purse. . . ."

It was excellent advice, and Lamy followed most of it. All it lacked was a useful plan for a calamity no one could foresee. At New Orleans, Lamy discussed accommodations on an Army ship with the commander of troops who would sail for Indianola, and later form part of the overland train with which Lamy would travel. The officer said the Gulf voyage was offered to him *gratis,* a great saving. Lamy accepted, even though it must mean leaving New Orleans ahead of Machebeuf.

He made his farewells in early January. His sister, at the hospital, was by now extremely ill. Their leave-taking was particularly sad. Marie, at the Ursulines, would see her uncle again when his travels permitted him to return to New Orleans. He bought a beautiful small carriage for his later land journey, but no mules. When he went to embark on the Army transport, he found that he had missed her sailing by two hours. The consequences would be unhappy.

In haste, he made new arrangements for his passage and the shipment of his carriage for the following day, 6 January 1851. The Harris and Morgan liner *Palmetto* was sailing and he would be on board. She carried "829 bbls. flour, 147 do whiskey, 4 do brandy, 110 sacks corn, 100 do coffee, 70 boxes cheese, 110 kegs lard, and sundries." Lamy's trunks and boxes held his sizable collection of books, his ecclesiastical objects, and clothing.

If it was not openly talked about, there were those who knew that the *Palmetto,* for all her "superior" low-pressure head of steam and her copper-fastening, had been condemned as unseaworthy; yet the Harris and Morgan line continued her scheduled operations.

Having left a letter for Machebeuf with orders to follow as soon as possible to meet him in San Antonio, Lamy saw New Orleans recede under the nacreous skies of the delta as the *Palmetto* on schedule was piloted away from the sloping levees and the tangles of moored shipping there. The three black towers of the cathedral rose highest on the city's skyline. Low brick warehouses lined the waterfront. The river was heavy with earth roiled by the current. He was leaving much behind to which he was devoted—but he was carrying with him much experience to give him confidence in the unknown lands of his mission. One always saw the strange through the vision of the familiar. Any departure was likely to make the heart go somewhat heavy. The city grew smaller and smaller—the three black spires stood clear, but steadily diminished. On the low right bank: little habitation, wide grassy flats, groves of trees. The *Palmetto* steamed along cautiously, for the river was always full of heavy debris—logs, foundered small boats—which were carried along just under the opaque surface by the current. Presently, on the left bank: Jackson Barracks, with its reminders of the battle of New Orleans a generation ago.

At the rate of her movement, the *Palmetto* must take a long while to reach the open Gulf. Looking back to New Orleans—and even beyond—time, distance, had strange new aspects, as if related to another life. The clouds of the littoral were low and changed slowly, light seemed different in a long progression of changes; at Nine Mile Bend, the city was lost to view. Only the future was in sight, and that only in the faulty imagination. The New Orleans *Commercial Bulletin* for 6 January 1851 listed that the "steamship *Palmetto,* Smith (master), for Galveston, Harris & Morgan," had cleared the harbor, and before nightfall, the ship paused at Pilot-Town downriver, at the mouth, a community of plank shacks, marsh grass, long wooden jetties, where the pilot was discharged in a row-boat for shore. Captain Smith took over, the *Palmetto* turned westward in the Gulf in the long twilight.

. . .
iii.

Interlude at Galveston

ON 8 JANUARY in the morning, she tied up at Galveston for a day's dockside work. Lamy went ashore to find Bishop Odin.

When they met that morning, Odin saw his visitor as *"ce cher Seigneur,"* and was at once animated with extensions of his original advices and also with new persuasions. He listened to Lamy's immediate plans. Lamy intended to hurry to Santa Fe, make a brief appearance there, ostensibly to secure his throne, and then leave very soon for Europe to recruit a band of clergy upon whom he could lean from the very beginning of his mission.

Odin disagreed with this program, and could not help saying what he would do in Lamy's place. He made a well-argued case for his differing view, and he urged it upon Lamy with all the force of experience and shrewdness. It would, he said, be a mistake to go to Santa Fe initially without the support of from six to a dozen zealous and entirely devoted newly imported priests. He explained his reasons. In New Mexico, Lamy would find scandalous native clergy, and a public, especially among the Anglo-Americans, who were waiting for reforms with the arrival of the new bishop. What could Lamy do alone and without support? If he should have occasion to banish a recalcitrant priest, without having someone to replace him, might not the people protest, and perhaps insist on keeping the excommunicated priest in defiance of their bishop? If he should succeed with God's grace in peacefully taking possession of his see, would it not be more suitable to remain at his post, at least for a few years? A brief appearance, followed by a long absence, might do immense harm to his mission.

Therefore, continued Odin in the warmth of his conviction and the pleasure of his foresight, he must counsel Lamy to go—immediately —not to Santa Fe, but to France (as Bishop Rappe had also advised), and to bring back with him a number of priests who would absolutely be needed. Moreover, during such a journey to France, he could perfect himself in the study of Spanish, so that he could speak the language adequately upon at last entering his mission. Yet more—he could procure new vestments and the rest to replace the old rubbish which he would find in all the New Mexican churches, and he would thus instantly correct a great scandal in that country. Odin himself had been shocked, on his own journeys up the Rio Grande, on seeing the filth of the churches in which he had officiated. Time and again he had had to use his own portable vestments rather than the dirty and torn ones offered him locally. To go on, then—on arriving at Santa Fe (under the ideal plan so far proposed), Lamy would not need to take any precipitate action, but could await the moment when conscience and prudence should move him to act. If there were incorrigible priests, he would have replacements for them. In a parish—there were many such—where the congregations were too large, he could add one of his new young priests. Even if all the clergy of New Mexico were worthy of his trust, the new priests could be sent about to hold missions, which were greatly needed in that land where the word of God was never preached.

Lamy was hearing a rich account, through what was urged, of what was needed. Polite and respectful, in his usual habit, he heard Odin to the end.

Preaching, even in imperfect Spanish, on his Rio Grande travels, Odin had found that it was impossible to imagine the joy with which his little exhortations had been received. If Lamy's new men did no more than simply teach, this would be a work which would bear fruit. He might deceive himself, but Odin would hate to see Monseigneur Lamy go west without stout reinforcements, and above all Odin could not bring himself to believe that it would not be actually imprudent to absent himself too soon from his apostolic vicariate after having merely shown himself there. No doubt the mission would briefly suffer by a delayed arrival after a trip to France, but Odin thought it better to keep the *status quo* for five or six months rather than to go there at once without the means to introduce necessary reforms.

The bishop of Galveston at last rested his case. In the end, the eloquent arguments made no difference—Lamy must follow his own intention, and, indeed, would not even stay out the week and take the next boat west, as Odin urged, but would reboard the *Palmetto* that evening and sail on for Port Lavaca and the overland trail to San Antonio and Santa Fe.

Lamy was Odin's peer as a bishop—there was no question of orders to be given by the older man. Resignedly, Odin turned to other matters, described conditions to the west, and assigned three Mexican villages near El Paso del Norte which lay in his jurisdiction, under Lamy's episcopal care. It was obvious that places so remote could hardly be well administered from Galveston. Lamy would see them on his westward journey. They were Socorro del Sur, Isleta del Sur, and San Elizario, on the north bank of the Rio Grande. Lamy accepted the charge. The two prelates parted as sailing time drew near.

But Odin did not give up easily. Three days after Lamy left him, he wrote to Blanc at New Orleans, having told Lamy he would do so, outlining the advices he had urged upon Lamy, and suggested that if the archbishop agreed with them, he might make this known to Lamy, who would in any case have to delay two months at San Antonio waiting for the departure of an Army supply train, and such time could be used to go to France. Ships regularly sailed for French ports from New Orleans. Moreover—Odin thought of everything—if the vicar general whom Lamy would await in Texas should call on Blanc, why not send him straight off to San Antonio, where he could remain until Lamy's return from France, using the time himself to learn Spanish and come to know the kind of people whom he would evangelize in New Mexico?

On the evening of 8 January 1851, the *Palmetto* made her way out of Galveston, scheduled to arrive off the mouth of Matagorda Bay on the ninth, and once again Lamy was on board.

iv.

The Wreck at Indianola

THE GULF OF MEXICO COAST of Texas described a long southwestward curve from Sabine, past Galveston, to Brownsville at the mouth of the Rio Grande. At about midpoint of the curve lay Matagorda Bay. Like most of the coastal region, it was separated from the great Gulf by long, extremely narrow islands of sand and sea grass broken by occasional small inlets giving access from the open sea to the mainland harbors. The land—old sea beds almost at the level of the Gulf—was flat, and shaped into dunes by the wind. Greasewood grew there sparsely, and occasional rows of tall palm trees—the palmetto—stood with their tousled heads trained inland by the sea winds. On cold mornings a silvery fog diffused the sun into a pale disc. Winter there was the season of the lesser Canada goose, the egret, and the avocet. Looking to land from the sea was like looking toward another sea, so level was all, and so lost in vapory distance. The coastwise vessels paralleled in their passage the long curve of the occasionally broken rope of sand islands. The temper of the sea close to shore, where the water grew shallower in a long gradual rise of the Gulf bottom, was affected by weather both from out at sea and from far inland. In January 1851, pilots at the Gulf ports reported tides to be much lower than usual, because of strong northerly winds, which made entrance through the inlets to the bays more difficult than ever.

But given ordinary conditions, the ships managed successfully, until late during the night of 9 January 1851 one of those sudden and violent storms known as Texas northers struck out across the land toward the Gulf, bringing with dawn inky blue skies, wildly high winds, howling rain frozen on contact with anything, and driving the tide outward at Caballo Pass, the inlet for the Matagorda Bay ports of Indianola and Port Lavaca.

The Pass was a sea arm bridged underwater by a high sand reef which at the best of times gave trouble to the port pilots. During the storm of 9 January, the current in the gut, always dangerously swift, was running especially fast, and the tide, blown out to sea by the blue norther, lowered the clearance level perilously. Added to this hazard were others—shifts in the underwater bar caused by the work of the northerly winds, and the recent relief of pilots familiar with the passage by new pilots assigned to the station at Caballo Pass who had had little experience in the local waters.

Out of the storm, during the forenoon of 9 January, the *Palmetto* came toiling into sight and hove to off the bar of Matagorda Bay. Captain Jeremiah Smith signalled for a pilot. Despite the furiously high waves, pilot Thomas Harrison reached the ship and took charge. In the uproar of wind and sea, he had to measure his chances and maneuver the ship for several hours, but finally at twenty minutes past three he was at the inlet, and he pressed toward the bar. In the attempt to cross over, the *Palmetto* struck bottom, and struck again, repeatedly.

Harrison tried to back the ship into the Gulf, but failed at his first efforts. Just then the winds increased and the waves grew wilder. The *Palmetto* thumped bottom again and again, until, according to the *Picayune,* "her thumping became alarming and it was deemed essential to force her over." Harrison at last was able to take her off the bar, running back some three hundred yards into open water, and then again approached the inlet. There again she struck bottom and a leak was opened into her weakened hull. The waves rose still higher and carried her at last over the bar and through the inlet, but it was clear that the ship was beginning to sink. She had been fighting to gain the passage for almost three hours. At seven in the evening, she ran for the empty beach, grounded a little distance offshore, and was "almost instantly filled, the sea breaking furiously over her decks."

A ship's boat was lowered, a line was taken ashore and secured, and the passengers—there were over a hundred—gathered to take to the remaining boats. The women went first, then the men passengers, and finally the officers and crew. The sea was combing wildly across the tilted decks. The wind, said Lamy, was blowing gales and the sandy surf was running high, but no life was lost. The whole company were soaked through. Men went to work trying to make a beach fire of washed-up timbers—some from the *Palmetto*—and by the time they succeeded, Lamy remembered, everybody was "white with frost and ice." Night was coming down. Some of the ship's freight pounded toward shore. Most of the passengers' baggage was sighted and some saved. Frozen and shaken between dismay and relief, men on the beach hauled out of the water some baskets of champagne and kegs of brandy which they broke open. Before long a great number of the survivors were roaring drunk, a sight which Lamy deplored. In the presence of their revelry and profanity he found himself unable to say his daily office.

Among the debris borne toward shore he thought he saw his trunk containing his books and vestments. When sure of it, he asked a strong young Negro in the crowd if he would venture into the shallows, where the sand-colored surf pounded away, and try to bring back the trunk. The matter was accomplished. Lamy paid his helper out of his pocket with what little money he carried—otherwise the rest of it, and all his other possessions, including his "beautiful little carriage," were destroyed in the wreck.

Going about among the freezing beach party, Captain James Cummings, the principal pilot of Caballo Pass, whose house was three miles inland, gave what comfort he could. He had seen the *Palmetto* go to her end, and during the rescue work had built beacon fires to guide the boats; and now he offered his house—the only one for miles around—to the number it could accommodate. Among them was Lamy, who, with others, went to take food and drink with the pilot. They would stay with him until he could arrange for boats to come and carry the survivors to Indianola, in the next day or two.

On the morning after the wreck, all that could be seen of the *Palmetto* was "one wheelhouse remaining above water." The ship, a total wreck, was not insured, being a condemned vessel. One thing all agreed upon—Captain Jeremiah Smith had performed his hard duties during the disaster with "intrepid, cool, and humane conduct." When three days later the shipwrecked company reached Indianola, several members came together to memorialize their thanks to Captain Smith and Captain Cummings. On 12 January, they drafted and sent to the *Daily Picayune* at New Orleans "A CARD—TO THE PUBLIC," which the paper printed in its issue of 21 January 1851:

We, the undersigned, passengers by the steamboat *Palmetto* feel it incumbent upon us to publicly express our warmest gratitude and thanks to Capt. Jeremiah Smith, all the officers and crew, for their gallant conduct during the whole of the dreadful catastrophe that occurred to that boat on the 9th inst. No set of men ever made greater exertion for the safety and well-being of those under their care and could not have had less regard for self than did these heroic men. Capt. Smith during the whole time displayed the greatest coolness and courage, and but for his excellent judgment and self-possession, we fear that we would not now have this opportunity of thanking him, deeming it more than probable that we would have been lost. Nor can we permit this opportunity to pass without returning our sincere thanks to Capt. Jas Cummings, who, after rendering as much assistance at the scene of the disaster, kindly afforded all possible relief to the sufferers at his house near the beach, and did much for making them comfortable under all the circumstances.

Eleven men signed the "card," of whom the last was "Rev. J. Laury" —a misprint for Lamy, who in his calligraphy of that time wrote the "m" of his name in three small peaks which together looked like "u" and "r."

Galveston citizens presently followed with another printed testimonial in praise of Captain Smith—he was their fellow townsman— and in the courtly rhetoric of that formal time, he sent his reply to the *Galveston News*, 14 February 1851:

Gentlemen: I have this moment received your note of today [10 February], in which you manifest the feelings of the citizens of Galveston towards me, as commander of the late Steamer Palmetto. If anything, Gentlemen, could have added to the kind feelings which I have always enjoyed towards my fellow citizens, it certainly would have been the tenor of your note of invitation to a public dinner, as expression of the estimation in which I am held there; and while I feel a pride in your manifestation, I regret that I have not words to express, in accordance with my feelings, the satisfaction I have in the knowledge of your confidence. This confidence shall to the best of my experience, be preserved unblemish'd under which circumstances I cannot refuse the compliment; therefore I will name Friday next, 14th inst., as the day on which I shall have the honor to greet you, with a seaman's heart, overfull from your kindness, and remain respectfully, your obliged fellow citizen and sincere friend, J.S.

The amenities concluded, those at Indianola gradually managed their next steps. The little town was a rival of Port Lavaca as the seawater harbor for San Antonio, which lay inland a hundred and forty miles westward in a direct line. Indianola was soon to be thought of as "a great railroad terminal between the Atlantic and the Pacific." Centuries earlier, Matagorda Bay had been the scene of an ambitious colonization by the French, when on 31 August 1685 La Salle had established Fort St Louis on its protected shore. But none of such great enterprises came to fruition, and Indianola itself vanished, to become only a name on antique maps.

The Gulf flats, in all their sea hues of oyster-colored sand, olive and russet bush, and gray grass, where a single tree even as far as eight miles inland was an event, gave way now and then to dunes in regular intervals of rise and fall—waves of dune made by wind just as waves of water. In the cold of January, over a sandy trail which dragged at wheels and feet, the stranded travellers made their way finally to Port Lavaca. Lamy reflected upon his losses in money and objects, and knew that he must appeal for their replacement to an arm of the Church with which, now, as a bishop, he would correspond directly.

This was the Society for the Propagation of the Faith, with offices at Paris and Lyon. He would lean on it heavily for help in all the years ahead.

v.

San Antonio

MERCHANT TRAINS OF WAGGONS went from Indianola to San Antonio. Two-wheeled, covered carts were available for hire, pulled by three-mule teams. Lamy arranged for a "German or Mexican" cart to carry him inland. The old "Cart Road" was well established via Victoria, Goliad, and Floresville. All the way to San Antonio, crossing gentle land swells and little rivers, it rose in shallow ascent on the ancient sea bed whose character changed from the Gulf-side barrenness. Bladed marsh grass gave way to live oaks and scattered prickly-pear cactus. Mistletoe and Spanish moss clung to the gray trees, and cardinal birds whistled and streaked among them. The gray-green hills, where the earth was exposed, showed pale coral pink and beige color. The air grew warmer. After many days on the commercial road, Lamy and his fellow travellers forded the Salado River and came into a broad shallow valley and saw San Antonio with its low church domes and blunt towers, and the flat roofs of the one-storey town, among green groves which cooled the earthen streets.

San Antonio was the largest United States military outpost in Texas, with a population, mostly Mexican, of thirty-five hundred in 1851. The parish church of San Fernando (later a cathedral) faced the military plaza. Mingled with the flat-roofed adobe and masonry houses of the Mexican period were new, pitched-roof two-storey houses and stores built by the eastern Americans. Scars of the Texan war of independence were still visible—the empty mission of the Alamo faced its plaza in a ruined state. The town was ringed by four other great stone missions, also unused and broken since the change of sovereignty in 1836. In Commerce street, business was lively—merchants sold French candies, German toys, Boston biscuits, silks, champagnes and liquors, all brought by the Gulf steamers to Matagorda Bay and carted overland. There was an active market in hides and wool, reflecting the ranching of the region. It was an inviting town with its mild climate, the grace of its Latin people, and the style of the United States garrison.

There Lamy reckoned up what was lost, and wrote to the Society at Paris, asking for a loan of five thousand francs. This letter never reached Paris, and he had to write again later, citing the total sum of ten thousand francs, most of it borrowed, some of which had gone to pay for all he had bought for his journey, the rest to be held for its continuing expenses, which "will be three times greater than I expected." Until help should come from Paris, he must again take out loans to send him forward. "Poor Bishop Lamy has made a disastrous beginning to his labours," wrote a priest of Cincinnati to Archbishop Purcell, who was in Europe that spring, ". . . but he is an apostolic man and God will certainly guide and protect him in his most arduous labors . . ."

Once again Lamy set about organizing his approach to New Mexico. He made the acquaintance of Major General William S. Harney, commander of the department of Texas, whose headquarters were at San Antonio. It was to be a useful connection. At regular intervals the Army sent supply trains across the southern plains to the garrison near El Paso and others up the Rio Grande in New Mexico. With one such supply train Lamy and his small party were welcome to travel when he should be prepared to go. One thing he must replace was his New Orleans carriage. While waiting for Machebeuf, he bought a stout Mexican waggon and a span of "bronco mules," and gave further thought to his long day with Odin at Galveston; for on 8 February Odin was writing to Archbishop Blanc, "I received a letter from Monseigneur Lamy. I think you will see him at New Orleans soon again. He will decide, as soon as he receives your letter, to go to Europe. He awaits only a word from you to take his departure . . ."

Meanwhile, Machebeuf had arrived at New Orleans on 21 January, only to read in that day's issue of the *Daily Picayune* of Lamy's shipwreck. He found Lamy's letter urging him to follow to San Antonio, and he at once made arrangements for passage to Matagorda Bay for the next Saturday, 25 January, the day, he noted in a letter to his sister, consecrated to the Blessed Virgin, who, he hoped, would protect him, in his turn, against all danger. He went with sad news for his old friend, for he would have to tell Lamy that on the day after he had sailed on the *Palmetto,* his sister Margaret (Soeur Marie) had died in the hospital of the Sisters of Charity at New Orleans.

Whenever "these two vicars" came together after being separated, they usually had much news for each other, and it was so in early February as Machebeuf arrived at San Antonio. He found Lamy an invalid, laid up with his leg so badly sprained that he would be unable to move without great pain for six or eight weeks. What had happened was this: since Odin had given him authority to make religious visitations in the Galveston diocese, Lamy had gone about, with the added encouragement of General Harney, to various Army posts in Texas, driving his new "bronco mules." He found eager response among the officers and men and their families. He often travelled with detachments of troops moving between the outlying posts and the San Antonio headquarters. Recently returning, he had set out after the soldiers, and approaching San Antonio, wanting to overtake them, he whipped up his team. Unluckily he came to a rough place in the road. The mules now running wild—they were broncos, after all—dragged the waggon on a reckless career. Lamy thought he was sure to be overturned. Seeing a sandy patch by the road, he jumped for it, and on hitting the ground, wrenched his leg so seriously that he couldn't move. Someone came along and found him, and he was carried to his quarters in the city.

The accident, aside from being a general nuisance, had direct results. One was that a quartermaster caravan for El Paso, with which Lamy had expected to set out in February with Machebeuf, left without them, for Lamy could not yet travel. They must wait for the next train. The other was that, as he could not go to Santa Fe, so he could not go to Europe. Odin received word of this setback and wrote to Blanc from Galveston on 17 February, "Monseigneur Lamy will start for Santa Fe at the beginning or the middle of March . . . I write in haste."

But a departure in March was also impossible, for reports from the plains told of how meagre the grass was. The Army must wait for more fodder before setting out across a country where even in the best of seasons grazing was sparse.

During the delay Lamy wrote an important letter—one difficult to write since he knew so little of the state of affairs in Santa Fe and in Durango. Yet courtesy required him to inform Bishop Zubiría of Durango that he had been appointed by Rome to preside as vicar apostolic over New Mexico; and that he would in due course assume his duties in what had been, until now, Zubiría's northern province. He also stated that he would soon go to Rome "to practice *consualia*" —the traditional visit to the Holy See in the course of which his new estate and assignment would naturally be recognized. As he wrote on 10 April 1851, and since he would be departing from San Antonio for Santa Fe in May, an answer, considering the state of the mails in northern Mexico, might not come before he should leave Texas.

There was a sense of well-being during the delay at San Antonio.

Lamy and Machebeuf studied their Spanish together, and rehearsed it among the Mexican population. The parish priest—there was only one, himself a Mexican—was "very kind" to them, and gave his "hospitality with the greatest cheerfulness." The congregation of San Antonio was the largest in Texas. It had a new convent. Bishop Odin owned a large building which he rented to the government for use as a barracks, at $1800 a year. Lamy heard that Odin was later to make a college of it. Though there was an occasional day of cold wind, Lamy found the weather generally delightful, and said that "the boundless prairies of Texas are a beautiful sight, and the rivers and springs are also admirable. We have two rivers which run through San Antonio, one of which gives its name to the place, the other called San Pedro." He thought that below the point of their confluence, the river which they made together—the San Antonio—would be navigable.

Texas was recovering from the 1846 war which had destroyed the local commerce until the population had begun to increase through the arrival of colonists from the East. Odin had built eighteen little churches or chapels since his arrival at Galveston in 1840, but for the forty thousand scattered faithful of the following decade they hardly sufficed. When overland gold-seekers began to hurry westward across Texas after 1849, the state's population grew again, until in 1851 a hundred and twenty thousand new settlers arrived each year. The new communities and Army posts lacked spiritual administration, and Machebeuf, like Lamy before him, took up some of the waiting time at San Antonio by going out in April and early May to remote little stations along the Rio Grande.

By May, Lamy was recovered well enough to complete his plans to join the Army caravan which was to leave for El Paso and the upper Rio Grande at the middle of the month. General Harney figured large in his arrangements, for the department commander granted the bishop and all his party the assimilated rank of officers, which carried with it the issue of rations. Since his shipwreck Lamy was travelling light, but Machebeuf had come with all his possessions intact. These included three great chests in addition to smaller pieces of luggage. He had arranged for the transport of all of them, but at the last minute, the quartermaster captain refused to take along the three large chests in government waggons. (Lamy's own waggon was full as it was, and he and Machebeuf went by horse when the time came.) Machebeuf could only hope that his important pieces would follow him by the next waggon train.

On 13 May, Odin wrote to Blanc, "I don't know whether Monseigneur Lamy has left San Antonio. He was still there some days ago.

I believe that the caravan is almost ready, and that he won't hesitate to take to the road . . ." It was a report which the bishop of Galveston made "despite great reluctance."

In fact, it was only a matter of a few days until the long train of two hundred waggons, each pulled by six mules, accompanied by twenty-five other non-military waggons, including Lamy's, equipped with provisions of all sorts to last six or eight weeks, and escorted by a company of dragoons, set out from the dusty streets of San Antonio for the plains west. The soldiers wore newly prescribed uniforms: single-breasted frock coats; tall hats with chin-strap, orange pompoms, and level black leather visors; trousers of sky-blue kersey, "made loose and to spread well over the boots." The troopers were forbidden "under any pretense whatever" to wear mustaches. The pace of the train was set by that of the slowest animals in the traces. They had six hundred miles to go through Comanche territory before reaching El Paso. The journey was the first lesson for Lamy and Machebeuf in the character of the country of the rest of their lives.

vi.

To the Rio Grande

THEY LEFT THE VERDANT, stream-sweetened country of San Antonio to go along the arid military trail which led due westward for the first two hundred miles. The black earth supported mesquite and low trees with mistletoe. On a middle-distance ridge, small clumps in silhouette might either be trees or something else; and if they moved suddenly, and vanished in the low rolls coming toward the train, it was a signal to go on guard, for they might be Indians, however unlikely an attack against such a great caravan. The waggons crossed many dry creeks with white pebble bottoms, and the black earth gave way to plains the color of dried animal dung. The scrub trees showed black winter twigs. Only distance forgave the harshness of the land. Strong winds arose at times, carrying the plains dust, and dried the skin, the inside of the mouth, pressed against the vision, made time seem endless.

The trail presently turned northwest to a great speckled land of rolling flat plains. Every waggon carried a water barrel; a stream bed with flowing water was a rarity. But there were some, and at such places, they caught fish, often with their bare hands, a sporting delight, to be followed by a feast. Where there was great scarcity of water, wrote Lamy, "we generally travelled at night." The weather for the most part was fine, with "some days rather too warm, but the nights were delightful." And then they would sleep in the open air, using their saddles for pillows, under the stars—*"sous la belle étoile,"* in the phrase which Lamy and Machebeuf used often, then and for years after. At first Lamy felt stiff from sleeping on a blanket over the rough ground, but when he got used to it, he said, "I never enjoyed my rest better." He was briefly ill with a mild cholera, like many others of the party who had drunk impure water along the way; but Machebeuf "never had the least indisposition." In any case, one or the other said Mass every day in the tent which General Harney had provided for them, and which they rarely used for any other purpose. They were under "many obligations to the officers," who were "invariably kind." They enjoyed the officers' mess, where they had fresh beef three times a week, and milk every day, and their own waggoner was at times able to offer them venison, rabbit, duck, and partridge. The country, as a scientific observer saw in 1849, was "exceedingly rich in reptiles." The most famous of these was the great diamond-back rattlesnake (genus *Crotalus terrificus terrificus*). Another creature less dangerous, but one which the Mexican muleteers seemed to dread particularly was the *vinagrón* (*Telephonis giganteus*), a large black scorpion which when squashed gave off the penetrating odor of acetic acid.

After more than a month's slow travel to the northwest, the caravaners saw far off a great range of mountains. Clearly at last they saw fifty miles to the north the Guadalupe Range with its highest point, Signal Peak, at its eastern end. It was on the crest of this peak that the Comanches built their signal fires on their autumnal strikes across the Rio Grande to steal Mexican horses, and it was that range which Indians used as sanctuary from which to raid passing caravans. The Guadalupes made a long rocky barrier lying north and south. They were the first considerable mountains which Lamy saw on the boundary of his own domain.

The military road—now abandoned—turned westward at the base of the Guadalupe foothills a hundred miles from El Paso del Norte in Mexico, which was sometimes referred to under its parish name of Santa María de Guadalupe. Presently the train went along near the Rio Grande toward the North Pass, with its cluster of villages downstream, and its road north which led upstream to the heart of New Mexico—and Santa Fe.

As they drew on toward El Paso, Lamy and Machebeuf could reflect that in their six hundred miles of overland travel they had seen hardly a single sign of habitation. Soon they began to see the mountains of northern Mexico which continued across the Rio Grande in the distance.

During the last week of June 1851, Lamy's company arrived at the river towns of San Elizario, Socorro, and Isleta. The latter two had been founded in 1680 by refugees from towns of the same name in New Mexico during the great Pueblo revolt, and it was these three villages which had been confided to Lamy's charge by Odin of Galveston in whose diocese they belonged by treaty.

Word of Lamy's approach had reached the settlements. People came out on the road for several miles to meet him. He passed through San Elizario, the first village, and on reaching Socorro, "a fine town," he wrote later to Purcell, "they gave me a grand reception." As he came to the first houses, he saw a newly erected "triumphal arch under which I had to pass." The village mayor, the local pastor (a Mexican), a band of music, and the national guard came to meet him. The land was restful after the desert passage. "This little spot," wrote Lamy, "and the vicinity for a few miles on the Rio Grande, is truly beautiful; particularly so to me, arriving from a journey of six weeks over barren plains, and mountains without a tree to conceal their rocky precipices." He was "delighted to find a country covered with verdure, the fields waving with grain, and the trees loaded with fruit."

But these three towns in Texas, under the instructions from the Vatican which Bishop Zubiría of Durango had received in 1849, had been given by him into the charge of the local Mexican pastor, all unaware of Odin's disposition of them. "The *padre,*" noted Lamy, was not "overwell liked by the people"—though he treated Lamy and his party with great kindness. And there, in those border settlements, Lamy saw the actual places which for years, in jurisdictional confusions established in good faith among Rome, Galveston, and Durango, would constitute an exasperating problem among the many others which awaited him.

In Socorro on 24 June—the Feast of St John the Baptist, his own name day—the bishop said Mass for a great crowd in the village church. At the proper moment, he asked the Mexican pastor to speak for him in thanking the people for the great respect which they had shown for the episcopal office, refusing to take to himself the honors they had shown him. The *padre* complied—but went so far with personal compliments that Lamy felt obliged to interrupt him. "I then," said Lamy, "made my first public essay in the 'Lengua de Dios,'" preaching in Spanish.

He moved on to El Paso, on the Mexican bank of the river, and was at once established under the famous hospitality of Father Ramón

Ortiz, who was well known to a generation of traders and soldiers who had passed either way across the Rio Grande between Mexico and what had so lately become United States territory. Here Lamy and his people had several days' respite. It was a particularly rewarding place to pause, after coming out of the wilderness. Lamy thought Father Ramón "very intelligent" as well as most cordial. The El Paso pastor—a handsome and charming man—was full of advice and information about the journey to Santa Fe which still lay ahead, and generously reprovisioned the bishop's party for the long way still to go. After years of never seeing a bishop, Father Ramón now entertained his second within nine months, for in the preceding autumn Monsignor Zubiría had paused at El Paso on his way home to Durango from his last tour of New Mexico. By the time of Lamy's arrival, the Mexican bishop's vast northern lands had already been transferred by the Holy See to an ecclesiastical jurisdiction within the United States —but he did not know it then, and the pastor of El Paso, discussing Lamy's credentials with his new visitor, could not say if Zubiría knew it even now.

On the recommendation of Don Ramón Ortiz, Lamy wrote of his coming and his new post to the pastor at the other Socorro, on the Rio Grande up north in New Mexico, and the letter was relayed to all parishes farther along on the road to Santa Fe. He wrote his official news also to the Very Reverend Monsignor Juan Felipe Ortiz, who was Bishop Zubiría's *vicario foráneo*—rural dean—at Santa Fe, representing the Mexican episcopal authority there.

Lamy saw El Paso in Mexico as "a scattered village, of at least eight thousand souls. Though it seldom rains (for they have had scarcely a drop of rain for three years), yet, by a system of irrigation, they have managed to make their country like a garden. Their wine is excellent, also their peaches, apples, apricots, and pears. . . . The houses are low and remarkably clean, and well arranged for commerce, and to suit the climate." He noted that they were built of "mud." The churches, he saw, were large—the largest was that in the plaza at El Paso (now Juárez). It was a great block-like construction of adobes, with a flat roof over the nave and a higher rise above the sanctuary. A free-standing bell tower—later demolished—with slender arches, cornice, pilasters, and a tile dome and lantern, rose at the left front corner of the church. The sacristy and priest's house were attached to the rear of the building, and the whole was surrounded by a low adobe wall. The plaza was enclosed by other low, flat buildings with porticoes roofed with cut branches. Mexicans in wide hats, wearing serapes across one shoulder, and with their loose white cotton trousers bound with leggings, rode small ponies on the dusty square, and women in long

voluminous dresses sat by their wares in the shade of the porticoes. The
sky was open and hot, and Lamy observed that "it is so warm that
many go half-naked." Flocks of blackbirds turned in their sudden
accord about the bell tower. Lamy thought the churches might have
been better kept. So far as he could see, the people were well disposed,
and showed a strong attachment to their religion, "especially to its
exterior observances." It would take him more time to know more of
"their customs and practices," of course.

In the evening, when the air chilled, and the sun fell behind the
great sierra west of the town, dust in the air made wonders of the
sunset. The mountains became a mysterious violet, the skies were
streaked with dusty gold under the high lingering daylight blue, and
all was shadow on the streets, roads, and houses. It was then that the
other character of El Paso and the lower villages came free; for the
transcontinental migrations continued westward since 1849, and to the
volatile temperament of the natives was added the lawlessness of the
transients. Violence and vice of every description were met at any
moment. Gamblers, thieves, even murderers were abroad; and the
fandangos—dances held in private houses or public halls, to the rude
music of scraped violins and violated guitars—were scenes of every
ardor of romance among the swaying couples. Fury often broke out
at the gaming tables, with sudden death as ready as a hand on a pistol
or a knife. With little organized preservation of the law, posses of
citizens were convened, trials were swift, and murderers were often
hanged within an hour of their conviction. Was Santa Fe to be like
this? "From what I have heard," wrote Lamy to Blanc, "and the little
I have seen here, no doubt I may expect to meet with serious difficulties
and obstacles . . ."

He had over three hundred miles yet to go, and he understood that
after advancing one third of the way, he would reach the pueblo lands,
and would see at least half of his district before reaching Santa Fe.
It was soon time to march again. The military escort from San Antonio
—presumably including the troops earlier assigned from Cincinnati—
was now divided into two detachments. One was to remain at the
military post near El Paso (later Fort Bliss) for eventual return to San
Antonio. The other was destined for upstream New Mexico. Accompanied by the new increment for Santa Fe, Lamy and his personal party
set forth in early July 1851 on the Rio Grande road—that stretch of
the *Camino Real* reaching from Mexico up to Santa Fe over which
the waggon trade had been moving since the seventeenth century.

The north road took them at every five or ten leagues through New
Mexican parishes for the first time. In all the towns, the reception was
the same, as the bishop's waggon and his horsemen appeared with

him from the dusty road—a road as pleasant, said Machebeuf, as the other passage across Texas was tedious, except for the eighty-mile stretch which they would encounter called the Dead Man's March. This was a desert crossing divided from the river by a range of mountains which began shortly north of Las Cruces and ended a little way below Socorro, at a point where the mountains sloped down to the plain, and the road joined the riverside again.

While Lamy was on the way, the Santa Fe rural dean Juan Felipe Ortiz, having received his letter, wrote to various pastors along the way the amazing news of the American bishop's progress northward. The word spread rapidly among the people; and at town after town they marshalled their poor best to receive him in honor. "Everywhere I had to go," he said, "they erected triumphal arches across the road, in village after village," and, as he had put it concerning the same honors at San Elizario, he "had" to pass beneath them. Entire villages came out to meet him and escort him in procession to their local churches. In certain towns the women laid their shawls or wraps on the ground before the church doors to make a carpet for him, and men, women, and children came to receive his blessing and kiss his ring. It was clear, said Machebeuf, that they had not come to a non-Catholic land. They thought the people's devotion survived from the time when the first Franciscan missionaries from Spain had "watered the Mexican earth with their blood and sweat."

But the further they advanced, Lamy and Machebeuf saw that their first impression was not wrong—the zeal and piety they saw was only on the surface. The people went to Mass, observed the feast days, kept their religious sodalities active enough, but for the most part failed to adhere to the sacraments, upon which all else depended. The reason was not far to seek: the general disarray was the fault of the clergy. For the Catholic population of seventy thousand, Lamy in the end would encounter only fifteen priests, six of whom, enfeebled by age, were inactive. As for the other nine—he soon saw that they were either lacking in zeal or were actually so scandalous in their lives that the state of affairs could not be worse. He would need prudence, zeal, and devotion if he was to administer such a vicariate. The people were sweet as children in their response to the priest, and if the Mexican clergy who were still active could be moved by good intentions, it would be the easiest thing in the world to lead their people back to the full practice of their religion. "But alas," exclaimed Machebeuf, "the great obstacle to the good which Monseigneur wants to do comes not from the people but from the Mexican clergy who dread any reform in their ways. . . . One of the worst of their neglects of their duty to their parishioners was that they almost never preached the

Gospel . . . and," he demanded, "how could such priests dare to preach?"

As they progressed northward, the bishop and his vicar general did what they could to begin meeting needs long neglected. Lamy whenever he could offered the Mexicans "edifying words in poor Spanish," and Machebeuf, when they came to any of the United States Army forts along the river, brought his spiritual offices to the soldiers who asked for them. On they went ("Goodbye to railroads, steamships, passenger coaches, and so on," exclaimed Machebeuf, "in New Mexico there's no way to travel but in your own wagon, if you were lucky enough to have one, or on muleback") through the villages of Socorro, Lemitar, Belen, Tomé (where they saw the parish records which Bishop Zubiría had signed on his last visit on 30 May 1849), and the pueblo of Isleta, and the Rio Grande town of Albuquerque under its great dome of cottonwoods, and again on to Bernalillo (Coronado had wintered across the Rio Grande there in 1540–41), and to the pueblos of San Felipe and Santo Domingo, where they left the river and began to climb toward the escarpment of La Bajada. There the narrow road led in precarious double curves up to a great plain, and they came in sight of the Sangre de Cristo Mountains twenty miles away, in whose foothills lay the ancient and famous city of Santa Fe and the end of the journey.

vii.

Triumphal Entry

EARLY ON SUNDAY, 9 AUGUST 1851, they were drawing near enough to be able to see the city. Lamy had thought it probable that "some of the faithful" would come out to meet his party, but he was astounded to see many thousands advancing at a point five or six miles from the first houses, and his first assumption was that the local garrison was leading a welcome to the troop detachment which accompanied him. In another moment he must accept the welcome on his own account. Most conspicuous in a magnificent carriage was the United States Territorial Governor James Calhoun. He greeted the bishop warmly. The resident Mexican rural dean came forward—Very Reverend Monsignor Juan Felipe Ortiz—"a large, fat-looking man" with reddish hair

—to pay his respects to Lamy, and the governor took the two into his own carriage. All the civil and military authorities were on hand, and leading citizens, riding in the finest carriages gathered from the city and the country for miles around. Among the festive thousands were ranks of Indian dancers, each group in its own characteristic costume, who "performed their evolutions" along the way.

As the elated procession came to the city, the American artillery at Fort Marcy on its height commanding the plaza fired cannonades in salute. The road of the bishop's entry—evidently San Francisco street leading directly to the parish church of St Francis, which would become the cathedral—was superbly transformed into a lane of "beautiful cedar trees, which the day before had been brought in and planted for the occasion." All the houses were decorated with their best fabrics— silks and carpets hung from the windows, doors, and balconies—while the animated populace attended the progress up the earthen street.

Going direct to the church of St Francis, the bishop entered the sacristy to change from his dusty travel clothes. The church was filled, the women kneeling on the floor, with black shawls over their heads, while the men stood at the rear. The principal church, it was in poor repair. There was no floor but the packed earth. Particles of the adobe ceiling and walls flaked down. Whenever at rare intervals there should be rain, mud puddles gathered on the floor. The nave was long and narrow, with dim transepts establishing the shape of the cross. On each side of the main chamber were life-sized wax figures left behind from the time when Franciscans administered the province. These were effigies of painted friars with tonsured heads, one group wearing white habits, the other blue, all cinctured with the knotted Franciscan girdles. The altar was a garish bower of ornate mirrors, paintings or colored prints, and brightly colored hangings. Colored glass high up in the walls cast a reddish glow over the interior. A Mexican string orchestra waited for the bishop's entrance, with all the available clergy, for the singing of the Te Deum. He was now robed in his purple cassock, surplice, mozzetta, and a heavy white stole embroidered in gold bullion. Machebeuf, as his vicar general, accompanied him.

Looking upon him clearly now, the people saw Lamy in his early middle age, with the signs of ten years of hard, maturing work on him. Gaunt and sparely built, he was weathered from his travels. His manner was mild but when he met their gaze, his dark eyes sparkled. His head was broadly modelled, with deeply porched eyes and strongly shadowed cheeks, outlined by his long, dark, curly hair. In repose his wide mouth wore a melancholy expression, but when he smiled people felt the illumination of his nature. Patience, civility, and intelligence marked his face. His jaw was bony and square, and his chin was resolute. He seemed young—and in fact was, at thirty-seven—to be a bishop. His vicar general looked older than he. They saw that Machebeuf was shorter, and how his thin little frame seemed to quiver with controlled animation. His hair, long and brushed straight back from his spacious brow, was light. His face was as plain as the bishop's was handsome. Over his deep-set little eyes he wore small spectacles rimmed in metal. His face was lean, with marked cheekbones, and his mouth was a trifle protuberant, with a thick lower lip. A large mole made a lump on his right jaw. His collar was too large for his thin neck. Through all this, his witty and compassionate nature charmed people's spirits when they looked at him. However curious a pair they were to come before strangers whose ways and wants were so different, the Santa Feans paid respect to their offices now.

The Te Deum was sung, and in the liturgical intervals, the music of the fandangos—for it was the only music available—twanged forth from the string players. Lamy at the end gave his triple blessing, and was then conducted to the adjacent rector's house of Monsignor Ortiz. What Lamy found there amazed him. The house, as both he and Machebeuf remarked, was transformed into a veritable "Episcopal palace"—presumably with rich furniture, hangings, and rugs. Ortiz had moved out in order to accommodate the bishop, and had taken up residence under his mother's roof. The rectory looked like a suitable lodgement and Lamy resolved to live there.

Now followed a "magnificent dinner" to which came all the leading authorities and citizens of the town, including Mexicans and immigrant Americans, Protestants and Catholics alike, military and civil. It was such a feast, declared Machebeuf, as to cause Lamy and himself to forget entirely their long journey across the Texas deserts.

The day needed only one more blessing to make it memorable. As at El Paso, and all the length of New Mexico, the drought over Santa Fe had been ruinous. Fields and ranges were scorched, cattle and sheep were dying of starvation, the hardest of times faced the people. Like everyone in New Mexico, the guests at the ceremonial dinner were all concerned at the disaster which threatened. And then, on the very day of the bishop's arrival, clouds appeared from across the mountains, and rain fell in torrents until the earthen streets ran like brown rivers. The downpour was general. Crops would revive, the grass ranges be saved. The year would be one of plenty after all. In the common thought, could it be anything but an omen?

The day's welcome could hardly have been more joyful, and, in terms of what was to be had in Santa Fe, extravagant. But if Lamy thought it an auspicious beginning for his new labors, he was wrong.

IV

THE DESERT DIOCESE

1851–1852

i.

Defiance

A LEADER IN THE JUBILANT WELCOME given to Lamy, Juan Felipe Ortiz, the rural dean (or vicar forane) at Santa Fe, reserved until later the most unexpected news he had for the new bishop. Having paid all proper respect to mitre and crozier—Lamy was undoubtedly a bishop —Ortiz, and the local clergy over whom he presided, suddenly maintained that Lamy was not the bishop for Santa Fe, and refused to recognize him as such.

It was astonishing to be told this after all the triumphal arches, the episcopal palace of mud placed at his disposal, the public excitement. How could this be?

Ortiz stood his ground, believing he had good reason to do so. Only a few months ago, his own bishop, Zubiría of Durango, had been in Santa Fe, when the two discussed the ruling given to Durango by Rome—that Mexican bishops should "continue to exercise their episcopal authority north of the border." What else (as Bishop Blanc had noted earlier) could have taken Zubiría to New Mexico after the 1846 war?

But the papal bulls, the faculties vested in Lamy, all set forth in the documents which he carried with him?

Well and good, conceded Ortiz; but he had had no word from Durango that the episcopal power was to be transferred, and lacking such direct authority, the dean would continue to disavow Lamy as his ordinary. His local clergy would do the same, for it was to him that they looked as the representative of Bishop Zubiría. As rural dean since 1832, Ortiz had been responsible for the entire administration of the Church in New Mexico—the duties of the clergy, the upkeep of the churches, the keeping of parish records, the strict observance of the liturgy, the care of sick priests, continuous visits to his parishes, and the making of annual reports to his bishop. Ortiz had shown no zeal for his duties, and under his régime his clergy had lost theirs. But in the matter of a change of bishops, he was suddenly zealous, legalistic, and rudely stubborn.

Lamy, in his amazement, yet considered the matter from the dean's point of view and patiently concluded that the dean was technically justified in his position. Conferring with Machebeuf, he wrote to Zubiría in Durango asking for a swift confirmation by letter of Rome's new appointment.

The news of Lamy's presence and pretensions went to Zubiría from another source—the pastor of Taos, Father Antonio José Martínez. "Your illustrious lordship," he wrote, "perhaps knows that New Mexico has been erected as a bishopric [actually vicariate apostolic], and Fr. Juan Lamy was appointed to be its bishop. . . . I have regretted a great deal the separation of New Mexico from the diocese of your Illustrious Lordship," and he hinted that a "superior authority"—evidently referring to the territorial United States governor—was behind the move.

Durango lay five hundred leagues to the south in Mexico. A letter from there must take time to arrive. Meantime, Lamy could not remain idle. His documents made one matter binding—he had in them a legal claim to the Church properties of New Mexico; and even the dean must bow before this. The new bishop moved swiftly to take custody of Church buildings, chapels, and other properties, and succeeded in all but one case. This instance, before it was resolved, was a scandal, a farce, an occasion for the public passion for which the citizens of Santa Fe have always been famous. The case had to do with the Chapel of Our Lady of Light on the south side of the earthen plaza of the old city. This was popularly called the *"Castrense"*—a word signifying that which belonged to the military.

It had been the old military chapel of the Spanish/Mexican garrison of Santa Fe, and, in much disrepair, it had been appropriated by the United States territorial government after the 1846 war, evidently without protest by the rural dean. A United States lieutenant in 1846 noted it as "the richest church in Santa Fe," though it was then in ruins, the roof fallen in, and bones of parishioners once interred below the earth floor lying about in random exposure. He saw the carved stone reredos, dated 1761, with its panels of saints and a central bas-relief of Our Lady of Light "rescuing a human being from the jaws of Satan whilst angels are crowning her." He fancifully detected Egyptian influence in the ornamental carved columns which enclosed the central panels. By 1849, the roof had been repaired, and the building was in use as a storehouse by the United States authorities.

Within a few days of his arrival, Lamy had already taken steps to bring the chapel into his possession. Writing to Purcell, he said, "It is not very large but admirably proportioned, and the sanctuary is enriched with a great deal of fine work in stone. The military authority seems to allege a claim to this property, though the territorial legislature has relinquished all right to interfere. I hope I shall not have much trouble in its recovery. . . ."

But on a Sunday night soon afterward, while Lamy was still awaiting a reply from Zubiría, the presiding judge of the Supreme Court of New Mexico, Chief Justice Grafton Baker, ruminating drunkenly over Lamy's campaign to take the *Castrense* from United States jurisdiction, declared that he would never yield the chapel to Lamy and Machebeuf; on the contrary, he would have them both hanged from the same gallows.

It was the wrong thing to say in the presence of a few Mexican Americans who with others were drinking with him that evening; for like their fellow Latins of the time, they held the Church and its priests in reverence. They repeated abroad what the chief justice had threatened to do. On Monday morning a petition was swiftly circulated which demanded the return of the chapel to the Church. Over a thousand citizens signed it—Catholic, Protestant, civilian, military; and a great crowd came together out of nowhere and marched on the profaned chapel where the chief justice had taken refuge. "Fearing for his life," wrote Machebeuf to his sister much later (she had heard of the episode even in France, which astonished him), the judge demanded military protection from the American commandant at Fort Marcy, the United States fortification. His plea was disdainfully refused, and an officer came to the bishop to assure him that if he should need protection (presumably from the court) the entire garrison would be at his disposal. Feeling ran so high during the day that Machebeuf and a Catholic officer of Fort Marcy took up a position at the door of the church to protect Chief Justice Baker until he asked for safety and vowed to yield to the bishop. That Monday evening, "the poor judge, wholly humiliated and abashed, went to make reparation to the bishop, and proposed to return the church to him with all possible solemnity."

So it was that on Tuesday morning, in the presence of the governor and all the military and civil authorities, "they surrendered the building," declared Lamy, "according to all the formalities of the law; the court itself sitting in the church, myself being present, they gave me the keys. I said few words in Spanish and English, and right on the spot I got up a subscription to repair the church in a decent manner. the governor and the chief justice liberally subscribed the first ones and in a short time, we had upwards of thousand dollars our list is increasing every day . . . I hope to say mass in it in three month, when I come back from Durango . . ."

For there had been no word from Zubiría and Lamy began to see that he must go himself to show his documents of appointment to the old bishop and try to bring him to cede what had so far been denied in Santa Fe.

ii.

The Society

AT STAKE WAS HIS AUTHORITY over a diocese larger than France. New Mexico still loosely included all of present-day Arizona, and other areas imprecisely defined, which were part of the Mexican cession after the war. Lamy had already seen much of his new diocese, whose overall size was about two hundred and thirty-six thousand square miles, and if the desert seemed to predominate in its character, the country around Santa Fe had great variety. It lay at an altitude of seven thousand feet in the foothills of the Sangre de Cristo range, which rose nearby in the east—wooded mountains which took the sunset light in such color that the early Spaniards named them for the Blood of Christ. To the south were rolling hills dotted with piñon and juniper trees. Sixty miles away across a vast plain rose the superb arc of the Sandía Mountains at Albuquerque, and on the northern horizon was the grand line of the Jemez Mountains, beyond great barrancas of sandstone and earth, the color of rosy flesh, through which ran the Rio Grande on its two-thousand-mile course from the Colorado Rockies to the Gulf of Mexico. Overall was a light so clear by day that prehistoric Indians named the place of Santa Fe "the dancing ground of the sun." The air was pungent with the exhalations of mountain forest and desert bush; and every play of mountain sky, with light and cloud, and every gradation of blue in the mountains from near to far, and the rustling cool under cottonwood groves in summer, and the warm sunlight of even the coldest winter day, when the smoke from hearth fires of piñon wood gave a resinous perfume over the town, brought a sense of thoughtless well-being to most people, and an awareness of unique beauty. The bishop found some four thousand residents in Santa Fe, out of a total of 65,984 as reckoned in a census taken for New Mexico five months before his arrival.

The city seemed humbly like a very element of its natural surroundings. From a little distance, its houses merged into a likeness of some eroded earth outcropping, for they were all made of earth itself, in the form of adobes, or large shallow bricks moulded from a mixture of mud and straw which when dried were strong and durable. To soldiers and traders from the East, the buildings seemed like wretched hovels, and Lamy himself said that his Mexicans had no other architecture but that of their mud houses, which used no boarding, and had almost no windows, and as for the churches, of which Santa Fe had five, they reminded him of nothing so much as "the stable of Bethlehem." (There was only one house in town with a peaked roof and shingles; it was put up during the war and was known as *"la casa Americana."*) Streets and houses both were of earth material, and met the weather in the same way, wet or dry, muddy or dusty.

Yet there were graces and strengths in the local building style, for once off the street and through a blind door, which might be richly panelled and weathered to a silvery gray, the visitor saw a patio within, with trees rising above the flat-topped one-storey rooms, and covered walks leading outdoors from one room to the others, for the rooms rarely opened into each other; and in the plaza of the town, the whole square was lined with such covered walks, or *portales,* for protection from sun, rain, or snow.

The plaza, a rectangular park in the center of the city, was once the parade ground, or *plaza de armas,* of the Spanish garrison. In 1610 the government palace was built along its north side, and remained the official residence of governors for over three centuries, under three régimes. As Lamy arrived, it housed also the chambers of legislation, the post office, the territorial library, and the ruins of a jail. The palace was a greatly enlarged version of the typical Santa Fe house. Its outer *portal* measured over three hundred feet in length, along one whole side of the plaza. It was the most impressive structure in the capital, and history had made it oddly beautiful. Always called the Governor's Palace, or the Old Palace, it would become in later times the historical branch of the Museum of New Mexico. High cottonwood trees towered within the patio gardens to shade the flat, low rooms. The whole town looked like those through which the bishop had come after reaching the Rio Grande at El Paso del Norte. If there was a prevailing character to those places, it was the appearance of untended poverty—the color of dust over all, the crumble of dried mud between the annual seasons of replastering with new, wet earth, the straggle of animals loose in the earthen alleys, the meagre and flyblown markets.

Though Lamy's birthplace of Lempdes also had the look of the earth on which it stood, it was thriftily neat, and its ways were adapted from those of the cathedral city of Clermont only a few miles distant over long-cultivated fields. He carried within him the medieval styles of central France, and of the fresh, young towns of the forest clearings in Ohio, so lately affected by the comforts increasingly brought by developing canals and railroads. Santa Fe, as he found it, showed no such effects of technical civilization. All was as alien to him as though he had been sent to a missionary station in remotest Africa. It must seem that he had only the primal materials of human society with which to work. In his vocation they were what counted most; but surely he must, when he could, work to bring them the bounties of such worlds as he had left. . . .

If the people he saw had variety in their looks—Mexican residents, United States traders and trappers and prospectors, Indians who wandered in and out of town on obscure errands—there was still a prevailing look to the majority. This was the Latin-American look. Santa Fe, all New Mexico, were still vastly more Mexican than anything else in appearance, ways, beliefs, degrees of knowledge, and language. On the average, the people were smaller than those persons who came for varied reasons to live among them. Their complexions were swarthy, their hair dark, their eyes black and vivacious in captured light, their gestures by turn restrained—a lift of the chin to indicate a direction was enough to answer an inquiry—or extravagant, and generally polite. A soldier thought them "the most abject contemptible objects" he ever saw, but allowing for various levels of prosperity, their dress reflected lively vanity. The men wore a brightly striped shoulder blanket or serape over a short jacket and ruffled or pleated shirt. Their trousers, thigh-tight, were held about the waist by a wrapped silk band. Among the relatively prosperous, the trousers were studded all down the outside seams with silver buttons. Horsemen by need and tradition, they strode and rode in boots high-heeled to hold securely in broad wooden stirrups, and their spurs were often of silver, with spiked ornamental rowels twice as big as poker chips. Topping all were "those everlasting big hats," as a trooper said—tall-crowned affairs, with very wide brims turned up at the edge, and traced with embroidery of gold or silver lace and little spots of mirror or bright metal. Their women went, by day, in blouses and skirts of varied color, and black shawls or *rebozos* which covered their hair and often their faces as a fold was flung about across a shoulder. Many of the poorer went barefoot. In the evening, at a fandango, where everyone danced and all smoked, men and women alike, the men wore long-tailed coats, pale full trousers, and small, pointed shoes, and the women then appeared in bright fabrics, and widely spread skirts, with heavy face powder which over their dark skins took on a pale violet hue; while half a dozen tunes by violins and guitars, repeated all night, set the steps, most often those of the *vals despacio,* or slow waltz.

Cut off from most of the world, and from prepared education, these people were ignorant though quick-minded and passionate. What education they had came only up to a certain point, and this was received at home; though a very few of the more prosperous families sent sons to colleges in Mexico and the nearest United States metropolis, St Louis. When Lamy arrived there were already four Protestant ministers working to establish education where seven eighths of the population were illiterate, and to wean the Mexican Catholics away from their religion of ritual and ardent practice.

And yet there had already been a long heritage of teaching the Indian people, from the time of the sixteenth-century Franciscans to the 1840s. Adolph Bandelier—a sort of southwestern Humboldt—wrote in his journal that a Cochiti Indian, Juan José, "told me about olden times. He says that, previous to the years 1845 and 1846, there were schools at the pueblos, under the direction of the Church." A handful of Indians could read and write, though "paper, books, and ink were extremely scarce, so scarce that the writing material was mostly sheepskin or tablets of wood." To write upon these, the pupils flattened a stylus out of a leaden bullet, and drew lines with it, and then using a quill wrote their exercises, with ink made from powdered charcoal, mixed with saliva, or water, held in deer-horn inkwells. But "after the American invasion, the schools were gradually cut off . . ."

The society's greatest concern was the constant yet unpredictable threat of raids by Indians of the roving tribes—Apaches, Navajos, Comanches, who were called by one observer in 1846 "the real masters of the country." A year before Lamy's arrival, a United States officer tallied losses to Indians of almost fifty thousand animals, valued at $114,050, and added that this, a conservative estimate, could be increased by fifty per cent. All too often inseparable from the incursions of raiding Indians after horses, mules, cattle, and sheep, were murders of their owners and destruction of property. A year later the territorial governor called by proclamation to able-bodied men for the establishment of a Volunteer Corps "to protect their families, property and homes."

The Territory was working to form itself politicall —committees and conventions met, a New Mexico Legislature was formed, lobbyists were sent to Washington by groups of private citizens, the territorial spokesman R. H. Weightman, elected by the Legislature, struggled to bring before the Congress the outlandish realities of New Mexico, and in 1850 a citizens' memorial was presented to the Congress declaring:

We were promised at the time New Mexico was taken possession of by the American forces, in 1846, the extension of civil government over us, and protection against the savage foes, which on all sides surround us; and under the treaty with Mexico we were *assured* of our being speedily placed under the full protection of the constitution, with all the rights and privileges of citizens of the United States. We relied confidently on the promises held out to us; we relied still more on the treaty stipulations; but in all we have been disappointed. Twice have we appealed to Congress, and as often we failed to obtain its favorable consideration of our situation.

We are without protection from our savage foes. Barbarous invaders drive off our flocks and herds by thousands; our citizens, men, women, and children, are murdered or carried into captivity, and hundreds are now suffering a bondage worse than death; our communications from town to town and village have become dangerous; everywhere is met the lurking foe; all enterprise and industry is paralyzed, and many of our citizens are abandoning a country thus insecure and unprotected, feeling, notwithstanding all the promises held out to them, that, in regard to protection against our Indian enemies, New Mexico is now in a worse condition than it has been for the last fifty years.

Our population is diminishing, our wealth is decreasing, and unless we are soon relieved by the favorable consideration of our condition by the government of the United States, ruin to New Mexico must inevitably follow.

Feeling conscious that in this representation of our condition we do not exaggerate, we, as citizens of a common country, entitled to the same rights with all, claim your protection.

Together with our appeal to you for the adoption of our [Territorial] constitution, and our admission into the Union, we earnestly claim from the government an adequate military force, to be properly stationed for the protection of our frontier, and to aid in the extension of settlements on the many fertile valleys of our valuable public domain, now utterly impassible on account of our barbarous enemies.

Never having received donation or aid from the general government, we confidently rely upon the justice and liberality of Congress, upon our admission into the Union. . . .

But sixty-four years were to pass before the Territory would become a state, and now in mid-nineteenth century, emotional turmoil still lingered following upon great and dislocating events—Mexico's final separation from Spain in 1821, New Mexico's separation by war from the mother country of Mexico in 1848, the fast-growing commerce from the states across the prairies: in short, the intrusion of the world upon a land which for so long had lived on hearsay, with all its irrealisms.

Much of the Mexican population was hostile to the power of the United States and its representatives. When Lamy arrived, representing still another non-Mexican power, they must however unwillingly accommodate to it, and to the disciplines which soon enough began to come clear.

Still, in the meantime, there were immediate events exciting enough to make a day or a week festive and memorable. When a trading caravan neared the city after its long trudging journey over the plains, the waggoners whipped up their oxen to make a grand entrance into the plaza, circling the park, while a crowd of citizens, among whom local merchants were the most concerned, cheered and thronged. The arrival of a stage coach was even more spectacular, for its horses could gallop where oxen lumbered, and the stage drivers yelled, the escorting horsemen fired pistols, and the plaza became a circus ring. Goods and mail came with drivers and passengers—and with them, the world. Think of steamboats on water, declared a leading Santa Fe citizen (a Señor Baca) who had been as far away as Matamoros and New Orleans in the 1840s, and of "little steamboats on land!" The American officer he was talking to recorded that he turned around and said, "What is there in the whole world that shows more beautifully the wonderful genius of man than steamboats and steam cars?" Visionaries of progress were already (1846) placing "a high value" on New Mexico as "affording a highway from the United States . . . to California," but a skeptical observer, not even dreaming of the steam cars, believed that a roadway was "the last purpose to which this country will ever be applied."

What struck such a person as primitive seemed so also to Lamy, even as he felt the warm temperament of the people, and the improvised graces and precautions of their way of life. They feared robbers, quizzed those who knocked at the street door, but those who were admitted knew entire hospitality, however small the means at hand. The Mexican rooms were plastered with the native earth, which was whitewashed. The whitewash would rub off on anybody leaning against it on the beds which during the day were rolled up to provide banks to sit upon, in the manner of Moorish ancestors of centuries ago. To keep the whitewash off, the walls were covered with calico reaching well above the height of backs and shoulders. Above hung mirrors and pictures. Bleached muslin was tacked to the overhead beams to keep the earthen roof from powdering down. A small, hive-shaped fireplace was located in a corner of the room, and, burning the pungent and light, lovely piñon wood, threw an intense heat.

In a large house or a public hall, a room so furnished would be the scene of the society's favorite diversion—the fandango, or dancing party. Here officers and men of the American garrison joined with the citizenry to dance the slow waltz, the "Italiano," the *jarabe,* the *cuna* (or imitative "cradle" dance), while the women in their brilliant shawls turned the air blue with the smoke of their corn-husk cigarettes and "gazed around the room with great complaisance." In 1850 a letter to the St Louis *Republican* described the fandangos as "low," and linked them to "troops drunken and reeling in the streets," for El Paso wines and brandy were served at the parties, and leaving them, the soldiers went "winding their tortuous way from one den of iniquity to another," and murders were "common," and gambling establishments flourished, and the dispatch added that the native Santa Feans were "all heartily tired of the presence of troops" among them. Others saw how the native dancers often went direct from the fandango to early Mass, followed by the same musicians who had played for the party, and who accompanied the Mass with the same tunes, which served also as funeral music when a burial procession went marching briskly through the streets. There were other amenities at the United States garrison, when at evening parties in the Governor's Palace, "all the luxuries of an eastern table were spread before us. At the sutler's one can get oysters, fresh shad, preserves and fine champagne."

It was, then, a society of contrasts, with its graces, luxuries, scarcities, and disgraces. The stores on the plaza and the open markets in the square sold melons, peaches, grapes, onions, piñons, red peppers, cheese, light bread, dark bread from Taos, wood, and fodder. Dry goods brought by the prairie waggons filled the shelves of shops established by enterprising German Jews who came with the early traders and who brought cultural styles and educated ways from Europe. In the clear late afternoons the daily promenade was staged, when young men walked together in a circle one way while young women walked in the other way, that they might face each other as they passed, and take to each other in word or glance. Mounted on tiny burros, which in the daytime carried every sort of burden from bundles of firewood from the mountains to goods to be delivered for the shops, men and women trotted about during the social evenings.

The American conquerors had need of a hotel, and one—the Exchange—was built and later called La Fonda. "If you wanted an American visitor, you went there." It was, like the other local buildings, a one-storey adobe affair, with long windows and wooden posts under its *portal.* Loungers sat there in their black American broadcloth, rakish hats, and full whiskers, tilting their chairs back with their feet up on the *portal* posts in native American manner, picking their teeth after a family-style meal. The local newspaper, the Santa Fe *Republican,* edited by a soldier who had come with General Kearny in 1846, advertised other accommodations including the "best of liquors, oysters, and sardines," and carried a notice to say that "Mrs. G. de Habile, recently arrived from New Orleans, La., will be pleased to receive a few more gentlemen as boarders and flatters herself that her efforts to please will, as heretofore, succeed." Lamy could see about twenty-five stores, a printing shop, many saloons, two tailor shops, two shoemaker's stalls, one apothecary, a bakery, and two blacksmithies. On a hill to the northeast, only a few hundred yards from the plaza, and so commanding the heart of the city, stood the artillery emplacements and riflemen's traverses of Fort Marcy, built in 1846. The United States garrison did not live there—their quarters were below, in the town, behind the Governor's Palace, where troops had always been housed since the early Spanish settlement.

The Third United States Infantry now occupied the garrison, and the local department commander, Colonel E. V. Sumner, who had arrived about a month before Lamy, was in open conflict with the civil territorial governor, J. S. Calhoun. The governor asked for arms from the military to distribute to the volunteer company of United States citizens he had raised by proclamation for their own protection against the Indians, particularly the Apaches and Navajos. Sumner refused; but the governor was persistent, and the problem of Indian terrors was too real to be ignored on behalf of bureaucratic wrangling.

"The Navajos are a terror to all the people around," wrote an American soldier, "they descend from the mountains and sweep away the *caballadas* [horse herds] of the Pueblos and Mexicans, who look on unresistingly." Another saw in 1850 that "the hillsides and the plains that were in days past covered with sheep and cattle are now bare in many parts of the state, yet the work of plunder still goes on! The predatory operations of [the Navajos and Apaches] are even now carried on in the close vicinity of our military posts; the shepherds are pounced upon and shot with arrows to prevent their carrying information, and with their spoil the Indians dash with speed to the mountains and are beyond reach before the loss is known. In this way (I mean now the Apaches only) they run the flocks from seventy to one hundred miles in twenty-four hours. And, consequently, out of ten thousand sheep that may be started, probably not more than one thousand will reach their destination. As the overdriven animals falter from exhaustion those that do not fall dead by the wayside are lanced as the Indians pass to prevent their falling again into the hands of the Mexicans. . . . The more provident Navajoe [*sic*] is more careful, because his principal object is to increase his stock at home. . . . They were on several occasions pursued by the troops, but without success." For several decades, there had even been traffic in the sale of Mexican children abducted by Indians.

Governor Calhoun wrote to President Fillmore, "Until the Apaches and Navajos are completely subdued, we can neither have quiet or prosperity in this territory. You are aware that our treasury is empty, and that we are without munitions of war." Calhoun believed that if given munitions and other means he could, "in a few months, secure a lasting peace with the Indians in this territory, and locate them within fixed limits." He had been an Indian agent before being designated territorial governor, and he believed he understood the problem —from which he exempted the Pueblo Indians. These people were peaceable in their "archaic city-republics which line the Rio Grande," and were "intelligent, moral, sober, and industrious"—this by a soldier in 1850—"and, generally speaking, better off than the lower class of Mexicans."

Pressing for his volunteer company, and a supply of armaments from the military, the governor was able to persuade Sumner to agree in the end—but with conditions: the colonel stipulated that whatever arms he supplied must be given only as a loan, that they be returned to the military authority on demand, and that no expeditions of protection or reprisal be made against Indian raiders unless volunteers should be "acting in conjunction with the regular troops." The conditions attached by the colonel were unacceptable to the governor; not only for practical reasons, but because in 1849 responsibility for disciplining Indians had been transferred by law from the military establishment to the Department of the Interior, to which territorial governors reported. It was a live issue at the time of Lamy's arrival at Santa Fe.

But it could not be one whose solution must engage him to any extent personally—though he would often enough be exposed to its perils. He established courteous relations with Calhoun—and with all succeeding civil authorities—but his concern lay with the physical condition of his churches, the spiritual state of his parishes, the social and moral ignorance which flourished in Santa Fe's isolation from the world, and finally in every aspect of the waywardness all too evident among the local clergy.

Lamy chose the parish church of St Francis as his cathedral. This was adjacent to the dean's house, where he took up residence at the beginning, and was a walk of two or three minutes from the plaza, at the head of San Francisco street. Rising above all the flat roofs with its twin towers crenellated in mud bricks, it was the largest building in the city. It had transepts lower than the nave—all the churches in Santa Fe, reported Lamy, were in the shape of a cross; and all were built of the same humble material as the houses. It was amazing how old some of these were, and how long the dusty or muddy walls could stand against the weather, even without the annual replastering of earth which it was the local habit to apply. But all were in poor repair, like those he had seen on his journey northward from the Mexican boundary. Dried earth sifting downward by the day between the wooden beams which supported the packed earthen roofs—it was a metaphor for the constant decay and necessary renewal of the Church itself in that land.

And yet among the native families there were seeds of faith and learning which took root where they could grow, however obscurely, in the minds and habits of children. A later churchman saw how the culture of Christianity was transmitted from adult to child, at home. The invisible company of Christ, the Holy Family, the saints, became a reality to those who could not read or write, but who could listen, who could look at the carved and painted wooden household figures of the sacred company of history, and form a second world where the heart and soul could dwell intimately with greater affairs and higher manners than the rude conditions of daily life. "Prayers and catechism," wrote the churchman, "were taught orally to the young children by some member of the family or by some trusty person of the neighborhood, and repeated word for word, question after question, until some part of the lesson would remain in the memory of the hearers. This was a hard work, but a meritorious one, and one of great value to the missionary, who had only to explain the mysteries and the chief points of our religion to the children thus instructed at home. . . . Every evening it was customary to make the children say some prayers which always terminated with the words: '*Bendito y alabado sea el Santísimo Sacramento del Altar* (Blessed and hallowed be the most holy Sacrament of the Altar).' After this, the innocent creatures, still kneeling, had to kiss the hand of their parents and receive their blessing before going to bed."

Adults used holy ceremony even in casual moments. Visiting, when a door was opened to them, they said *"Deo gratias"* or *"Ave Maria Purissima,"* and whoever admitted them replied, *"Para siempre bendito sea Dios y la siempre Virgen María—pase adelante* (Blessed be God and the ever Virgin Mary—come right in)." Simple greetings were invocations—*"Buenos días* (or *Buenas tardes*) *le dé Dios* (God give you good day [or evening])." and the reply came, *"Que Dios se los dé buenos a Ud.* (May they be good to you from God)." In a casual meeting, the first one to say *"Ave Maria"* could properly expect the other to recite the whole "Hail Mary" for his intention. The most immediate terms of history were those of the passion of Christ, with all its characters. Holy Week was a drama lasting seven days, with the crucifixion and the resurrection as their climaxes.

But the amenities were light-hearted, too, in suitable seasons—at

Christmas fandangos, when the roof-lines of houses were traced by rows of *farolitos,* or candle lights protected from the wind, and bundles of piñon faggots *(luminarios)* were lighted to outline the plaza, the dancers within, wearing masks, played a famous joke. Young women holding eggshells filled with scented liquids pursued men on whose heads they smashed the eggs, in mixed compliment and mockery. "Another evidence of the Catholic Church in New Mexico," wryly noted an Easterner who spoke as a United States puritan, "was the attendance at Mass of devout women, of whom not one was supposed to be virtuous"; and other traders and soldiers concluded that the native women were for the most part prostitutes—an unfair assumption based on the newcomers' lack of acquaintance with the seemly private life of most colonial Spanish and Mexican families. But if a certain class of females was available to invading frontier males, it was not to be wondered at, with the introduction of thousands of newcomers who had money to spend in a society so poor and by temperament so ardent in character and so indolent concerning work. A complacent observer who came with the American occupation thought that he could presently discern, "here in Santa Fe, the diminution of filth in the streets, and the improved dress and personal cleanliness of the people, together with the cloaking of immorality," which "showed that precept and example [were] not altogether thrown away upon them."

And yet others felt the "kindness of the people—they loaded us with presents," tobacco, food, and always showed politeness. There was true poverty in a land of potential riches. As Lamy wrote to Paris, twenty days after his entry, "it is a mistake to think the country is rich . . ." Perhaps it was so in agriculture, "but gold mines and copper mines are in the hands of Indian tribes, who are ferocious and spread throughout the country," and he concluded that the country had "suffered greatly since the declaration of [Mexican] Independence. Franciscans [had been] obliged to abandon their posts. To replace them, secular priests were sent from Mexico, but in insufficient number—there were 15, 6 of whom are now old—But these priests, under any respect, could not replace their predecessors; even now they are either incapable or unworthy . . ." There was scarcely anything which Lamy met which might encourage him. "Almost everything needed to be created," except the touching and curious grace kept by the annexed Mexicans despite their poverty and the new ways to which they were subject after the war which their country had lost, and which had brought their new bishop among them.

iii.

The First Needs

So in his first weeks at Santa Fe, Lamy learned of conditions and needs which would compel his acts in the years ahead. In a sense, his work in the Middle West had been a rehearsal for what now faced him —but on what a different scale, and under what different responsibilities. Where he used to appeal to his Ohio neighbor, Bishop Purcell, he must now work directly with Rome, Paris, and Lyon, and now not as a missioner priest, concerned with a county or two, but as a missioner bishop charged with duties in an area six times as large as Ohio. In the summer of 1851 all he knew of it as yet was Santa Fe—but this was the place to begin; and he wrote to the Society for the Propagation of the Faith at Lyon to say what he had found, and to Paris, what he needed, and—the habit was strong and the response certain to be sympathetic—to Purcell at Cincinnati.

His first concern was education, not only in book knowledge, but in Christian amenity. "The state of immorality in matters of sex is so deplorable that the most urgent need is to open schools for girls under the direction of Sisters of Charity." He had already begun to look for a site on which to establish a convent, and he declared the need for a school for boys in every parish, "since the Mexican national vice" was ignorance. He must have money—fifteen thousand francs—for he could not repeat too often that riches were not to be had locally. He made his own census of his people—sixty-eight thousand Catholics, two thousand "heretics," thirty to forty thousand "infidels," eighteen missions (in the pueblos), twelve native priests, twenty-six churches, forty chapels. There were eight or nine thousand Catholic Indians, and perhaps thirty thousand in want of conversion. If only he had some zealous French missioners, he said to Lyon, to meet their needs —and indeed, those of another six thousand Indians wholly abandoned only a hundred leagues from the capital (possibly referring to the Navajos in the west). Schools and religious workers—these were his first responsibilities there, as he said long later. The next concern was the state of the local clergy, which would bring him exasperation and regret for years.

The first Franciscans in the old kingdom to preach the Gospel had been men of God, he said, but they were gone long before his arrival, and the bishop of Durango had come to Santa Fe only three times in twenty years, which no doubt explained what Lamy found. "On my arrival in N. Mexico I found frightful abuses among the clergy." Of these there were many kinds. "What," he asked Purcell, "would you think of a priest who does not preach to his congregation but only once a year, and then at the condition that he will receive $18? Such is the case here, and it grieves me to tell that this is not the worse yet. . . ." Another contemporary witness—a layman—observed that "the priests of New Mexico were noted for their corruption and profligacy, and instead of being teachers in morals they were leaders in vice. Their lascivious pleasures were quite as public and notorious as their priestly duties, and there was hardly a priest in the country who did not rear a family of illegitimate children, in direct violation of his holy vows and the laws of religion and morality."

As to cases, they could be cited. Machebeuf wrote Rome about the "guilty indulgence" of Ortiz, the rural dean, and went on to report about a certain Father Lujan, who had had a succession of mistresses. Upon the death of the last one, he scandalized all by giving her a "funeral ceremony as solemn as possible," to which he invited all the dignitaries of government and Army, "while he followed without his surplice and crying. . . . It is quite certain there was no piety in all this."

In Albuquerque the pastor, José Manuel Gallegos (a New Mexican born), was famous for his convivial ways and was regarded as highly intelligent and able, though also as vain and pretentious. He dispensed grape brandy and cakes and changed gold pieces for the rare currency of the province for friends, was a convivial crony of the leading traders and politicians, and had for his housemate a married Mexican woman who had been the mistress of two Mexican officers in turn, by whom she had three children. To her alliance with him she brought four thousand piastres and together they ran a general store, which they kept open all day Sunday.

"It was," said Machebeuf, "a great scandal for the people to see a woman such as that in the rectory, travelling alone with the priest in his coach, and active in his business. . . . The parish administered by a priest so scandalous and so given to business and politics finds itself plunged in the most profound ignominy and corruption." Even many local residents were appalled by his conduct. As for his intellectual brilliance, aside from what Machebeuf called *"son amour pour les plaisirs du monde,"* Gallegos illustrated this moderately enough in the presence of an American officer. "The priest asked us if we knew anything of astronomy and mathematics. I answered, 'A little.' He drew forth paper and pencil, and I expected some astounding problem, when he drew some of the simplest figures and asked their names. His questions answered, we were at once looked upon as astronomers and mathematicians."

But even such poor learning as Gallegos could show was unusual in New Mexico, and was perhaps exceeded only by that of the pastor of Taos—Father Antonio José Martínez—a much older man under whom he had studied before being further educated in Durango and ordained by Bishop Zubiría. Martínez was in fact one of the most gifted and interesting men in the territory. He was fifty-eight years old when Lamy came to Santa Fe, and he had long occupied a position of eminence in churchly and political affairs in New Mexico. This he deserved through the incessant activity of his career and the general enlightenment of his mind. Born in the village of Abiquiu on the Chama River of a respectable provincial family (a grandfather was a Mexican general), he was taken to settle at Taos at the age of twelve by his parents. From the first he was interested in learning, and was largely self-taught, reading whatever he could find. In 1812, when he was nineteen, he married; was widowed the next year, and left with a daughter, who lived only a few years. In 1817, he went to study for the priesthood at Durango and was ordained there in 1822—his twenty-ninth year. In the following year he returned to New Mexico, first to Tomé. Later he moved to Abiquiu, then Taos, then Abiquiu again, and finally to Taos, where he spent the rest of his life.

In that village surrounded by ranches on the great Taos plain, he managed to find useful outlets for his energetic intelligence. He opened a school for boys and girls, with emphasis on preparing the boys for the priesthood. Twenty of his students became potential seminarians. Books were needed. He bought a printing press—the first in New Mexico—from its owner at Santa Fe, moved it to Taos, and produced his own textbooks, catechisms, and missals. For fifty subscribers, he established the first newspaper west of the Mississippi—*El Crepúsculo de la Libertad (The Dawn of Liberty)*, a name which directly expressed his own strongly libertarian and independent nature. The newspaper, for lack of wider support, died out after a few issues.

But in any case, Father Martínez's most powerful organ was his personality, and it took him into public affairs as strongly as it moved him in affairs of the Church. He urged separation of Church and State for Mexico, which almost brought him censure from his Mexican bishop. He was said to have been active in the minor rebellions of 1837 and 1847 in New Mexico—the first a bloody riot over a court case in the remote town of Santa Cruz which resulted in the execution of the

New Mexican governor by a mob which marched on Santa Fe; the second a conspiracy at Taos a year after the American occupation which led to the massacre of the United States governor, Charles Bent, and eleven others, in an effort to upset American rule. Martínez was known to be hostile, like a great number of New Mexican natives, to the United States régime, and yet during the Taos Massacre he gave refuge in his house to many fleeing its violence. He eventually entered the American territorial legislature—earlier he had served as an alternate legislator of the national Mexican congress.

In his isolated world, he was famous. His birthday was celebrated by the people, the bishop of Durango had empowered him with the faculty of giving confirmation, and as a man of learning he was revered by the less enlightened. His library, for its time, was distinguished if unavoidably meagre—it included a Latin copy of Thomas Aquinas printed in 1750 and bound in vellum. Martínez had even served as Chaplain of Dragoons in the 1837 uprising, and before the brutal execution of the governor had heard his confession. He was a strong friend to Bishop Zubiría and in regretting Lamy's appointment and arrival in his letter to Durango on 28 August 1851, Martínez gave direct notice of his feeling against the new authority in New Mexico— a portent of exhausting struggles which would last through years to come.

In the *Paroissien romain,* published in Paris in the mid-nineteenth century, Lamy could find in the epistle for the first Sunday of Advent (Romans 13) august support in all the troubles which lay ahead: *La nuit est déjà fort avancée, et le jour approche. Renonçons donc aux oeuvres de ténèbres, et revêtons-nous des armes de lumière. (Already the night is almost done, the day is near. Then let us renounce the works of darkness, and vest ourselves in the armor of light.)* If the spirit against which Lamy must cast his powers was all too worldly, the means he must use were all too pathetically material. A historian of the conquest of New Mexico who had come with the colonists in 1598, and was soon afterward dean of a Spanish church in Rome, published a history of New Mexico in 1602. Referring to the ancient cosmographers and their proved errors, he said of the early Franciscans, "we are not to ridicule those learned men as ignorant, since it was their chief purpose to reveal to men not the secrets of the earth, but the path to heaven." It could have been a motto for Lamy as he went about his immediate tasks.

One of these was to make a brief tour, with Machebeuf, of the villages and settlements scattered in the open country about Santa Fe —some of them at considerable distance. Coming up the river the first time, he had seen typical pueblos. Now he used back roads and trails, across plains, into arroyos, and the foothills, which lay below mountains visible in mystery wherever he looked. The people living in such places had need of almost everything which was generally thought of as civilized. There were chapels, yes; but who served them? There was no school anywhere. If the people turned toward Santa Fe the capital, there was scarcely anything there, either, to make a fabric of society for them. Remote for centuries, ignored for decades since the loss of the Franciscans, the people of the removed ranches and haciendas and the citizens of Santa Fe alike made demands, merely by existing, which Lamy in conscience must meet.

In early September 1851, he wrote to Purcell, begging him to help in a search for commitment by teaching nuns who would be willing to come to Santa Fe—Sisters of Notre Dame, Sisters of Charity—with all their expenses paid and a good house with pleasant grounds provided near the principal church, as he called what would become his earthen cathedral. He must also have new priests. If only such persons could come to help, he was sure there would soon be a change for the better, "as the people seem so mild and docile," and he had already seen "good dispositions." He was confident that citizens of every kind in Santa Fe would give their support to the establishment of new schools. He had already written to Lyon for aid, but his report was evidently not sufficient—they asked for "a true statement of these missions." He promptly sent more information in the hope of receiving help "next year." Purcell had spoken up in his interest, he was as ever grateful. Surely Lyon would listen.

Nothing could come too soon for his purposes from either Europe or the eastern states; but the most pressing of matters could not wait. As no religious teachers were available, he engaged one E. Noel as a schoolmaster, set up a boys' school in his own residence, gave it in charge of Machebeuf, to whom he also assigned the repair of the *Castrense* until it should be ready for use again as a church; and, with his own vicar general left behind to continue to do what could be done in the face of the disobliging attitudes of the rural dean and the other native clergy, in the third week of September 1851, Lamy set out on horseback, with one lay attendant, down the Rio Grande to El Paso and across unknown mountains and deserts in Mexico, for Durango, fifteen hundred miles away, to confront Bishop Zubiría, from whom he had heard nothing.

iv.

The Durango Journey

WHAT HAD HE WRITTEN in Ohio four years before to Purcell? "Providence seems to have fitted me for a barbarious [*sic*] and extensive mission." Perhaps these words crossed his mind now, as he rode forth across Santa Fe plain with his attendant, who must surely have been a man who could serve as guide with knowledge of the long road to Durango. By necessity they travelled light. The bishop's travelling bag was probably much like that which he used on later overland journeys. It was fashioned of black leather, about fourteen inches long, with a fastener and lock at the top, and a shoulder strap. It was wide enough to contain the simplest of Mass vessels and a set of thin vestments, among other objects.

Leaving the Sangre de Cristo Mountains and Santa Fe behind, the riders passed by La Cienega, with its farms and low red bluffs and scrub piñon, and passed down the escarpment of La Bajada on the Albuquerque road. Sixty miles to the south rose the Sandía range. Lamy was never to be out of the sight of mountains on the entire passage. He was fortunate in the season of his journey. New Mexico in autumn was a time of special comfort for the senses. Lamy, if he had any capacity to express exalted feeling, left no record of it; but even the most stolid of travellers there had been known to respond to the particular beauties of that landscape; and it would be strange if a man such as he who so much loved the open country—one who "could not bear the idea . . . to be confined"—did not respond to the wonderful vistas, by day and night, of his new land. His present journey would reveal to him every aspect but that of extreme summer, which he already knew, with its great dome of white light and parching heat; and now of the autumnal desert, river course, and mountain wilderness, where scattered so widely lived the human creatures he had been sent to serve.

Riding down to Albuquerque, he passed black-crested mesas rising above pink earth, and came into river groves along the Rio Grande at Algodones and later at Bernalillo and Albuquerque itself where the cottonwoods and willows made islands of cool shadow, and the fields

by the shallow river gave off a damp rich air; and always at the end
of vision were the blue mountains, and the rolling silver clouds which
they brought into being through the interaction of earth and sky.
Storm often rode over valley and plain from such heights, and then
every fantasy of light and distance, obscurity and brilliance, changed
the vast vision of what was to be seen, and, in private thought, what
was to be felt. Riding his horse at a sustained walk, alone but for his
guide, it might be that Lamy, halting to say Mass in the desert, felt how
the exaltation of the *Gloria* would be made manifest by the splendor
of the earth and sky in their immense changing aspects. The liturgy
would speak to him in French as well as Latin:

> *Les cieux et la terre sont remplis de Votre gloire:*
> *Hosanna au plus haut des cieux,*

and before the blessing at the end of Mass,

> *. . . Si Vous êtes un abîme de majesté,*
> *soyez aussi un abîme de miséricorde. . . .*

Always plain spoken, and in writing simple and direct, Lamy might
not express himself so grandly; his eloquence was that of act, not word.

His first one hundred thirty miles took him down the old Royal
Highway along the east side of the Rio Grande—the same which had
brought him north six weeks before. In central New Mexico there
were villages—Placeres, Peralta, Valencia, Tomé, and a few more,
some scarcely more than ranches of one or two families—where he
might find hospitality for the night and a tortilla and a mug of hot
chocolate the next morning. But such places were not spaced out for
the convenience of travellers, and more often than not, all the way to
Durango, he would spend the night in a blanket, on the ground, under
"*la belle étoile,*" like any plainsman. There might be occasional trains
of traders, or a mail rider—though the latter was a rarity, for there was
no regular system of mails, and the carrier was willing, for "a slight
douceur," to open his bag to let his tipper examine the letters within,
and do with them as he liked. The road in New Mexico was merely
a trail, so limited was the travel on it. Yet it had its attraction for raiding Indians, who watched for the waggons of traders or the drives of
cattlemen. More than one person at Santa Fe thought the bishop
"heroic" for setting out with only a single companion through country
which had been terrorized for generations—even before the arrival of
the American invaders—by Apaches who preyed not only on travellers
but on Indians of the pueblos.

But by his acts, he seemed to say that every journey could only add to his immediate knowledge of his desert diocese, as he went on his way. His road on the east bank crossed to Socorro on the west, and then back again, on high ground above the Rio Grande. He passed Fort Conrad, which was a United States Army post established only a fortnight before on the opposite bank of the river, and soon came parallel to the mountain called Fray Cristóbal, which was named after an early Franciscan who had died near the place; for the mountain's outline curiously seemed to show in rock the profile of a man's face, which his companions thought looked like Fray Cristóbal himself. This was the northernmost end of the mountain system which, rising close upon the east bank of the Rio Grande, made travel by road impossible along the river; so that travellers had to turn eastward at that point, and for the next seventy miles, follow a course separated from the river by the mountain range. Lamy had come north by that path—it was the *Jornada del Muerto,* or Dead Man's March, and it was the dread of all who passed that way from the time of Juan de Oñate, the colonizer of New Mexico in 1598, to the bishop's time. The character of such country was expressed in the names put upon it in various places— Dead Man's Lake, Dead Man's Spring. Water was so scarce that parties often had to leave their direct route north or south and go west to the mountains which separated them from the river to find a spring or a little natural reservoir. Finally, the mountain chain dwindled southward, and at the southern tip, allowed Lamy to come to the river again at a place variously called San Diego or Robledo, approximately sixty miles north of El Paso in Mexico.

Here near Robledo ran, east and west, the old boundary between New Mexico and the Mexican state of Chihuahua. Within a few miles of each other, the villages of Doñana and the *ranchos* of Mesilla and Las Cruces bordered on the river. Sparsely occupied, these adobe settlements would finally assume, for Lamy, a grave importance for many years to come, when additional problems of his jurisdiction in territory led to wrangles and intrigues reaching from Santa Fe to Rome, Rome to Durango, Durango to Sonora, and Sonora to Santa Fe.

But as he rode past these settlements Lamy had as yet no reason to consider their site as significant. He saw that it was a barren land with two small villages removed from the world. Durango, which had long held them ecclesiastically, was still more than a thousand miles away to the south; Santa Fe, to which they belonged by political treaty, was over three hundred miles away to the north. Both villages lay in a vast district also referred to as Doñana, like the hamlet of the same name, and out of this confusion of names, a persistent problem would result—especially after the third village, La Mesilla, would be established two years later, whose name would also be popularly and even officially used to designate the district, or *Condado,* or county, of Doñana. But for the moment, Lamy could only wonder how such little clusters in such remote territory could ever be given the comforts of church and pastor.

The United States Army, though, viewed the area as strategically important: Lamy could see across the Rio Grande, as he went by, the construction of Fort Fillmore in its early stages. The ford at Mesilla was logically the place to extend the road from California and the West across the Rio Grande at that point. One day, California—a third of a continent away—would be joined by commerce to Arizona and New Mexico. The whole immense Southwest must come into Lamy's vision.

Entering the state of Chihuahua as he went south from Robledo, the bishop saw abandoned and ruined villages in the desert between the Rio Grande and the Organ Mountains to the east. They had been destroyed by Apache raiders who had swept down from their heights and canyons in the Sierra Blanca and who still must be watched for by anyone travelling that way—especially anyone almost alone. He crossed the river, taking the ford six miles above El Paso, and came again into that pastoral valley where he had been so well received before. Now he came without a powerful escort and he knew nothing of the country from there to the south. Here, for the moment, was refreshment in shade, with his journey to Durango almost one third done. El Paso del Norte was the source of the famous "Pass wine" and "Pass brandy," which went up the trail to Santa Fe and Taos in the trading waggons. Lamy, always an agriculturist, may well have thought of cuttings from the vines for his use when there was time for such pleasant refinements.

At the nodding pace of his horse's walk, he took the Chihuahua road and after a day or two came to the formidable passage of sand hills called Los Medános which reached as far as the eye could see. The sand so fine, the dunes so endlessly wave-like, were entirely without vegetation. A trail wound through the shifting valleys of the dunes. It was the sort of country which led a traveller to wonder if it would ever end; but when it did, he found a road which a trader described as "firm and beautiful." Yet it was the sort of land which was either parched or flooded by the desert sky. Sudden cloudbursts would send the arroyos running, and would mire the road for miles. It was said of the state of Chihuahua that in its hundred thousand square miles there were no more than two inhabitants for each square mile, and fewer than twenty square miles were under cultivation.

Comanches knew the road well and, working out of their retreat in the Bolsón de Mapimí to the east (a great purse-shaped desert valley roughly 150 miles long and 100 wide), had their way with passengers who had no refuge. Where there was an occasional ranch, it was centered on a hacienda built like a square fort, with sentries on the flat roof, and marksmen's portholes, and a great timbered double door-way bolted and barred every night. Once accepted within, travellers were treated to good food, ingenious song and dance accompanied by guitars, and even folk plays in pantomime. By day men worked in the close-lying fields, while women cooked or sewed; but an Englishman passing by such a wilderness lodgement remarked that "severe labor is unknown to either men or women." The United States citizens who had taken Mexican territory north of Chihuahua were known locally as "the barbarians of the North."

Lamy met a continuing sequence of land forms as he went. In effect, all of that Mexico which he travelled was a vast repetition of land which in many ways resembled New Mexico—there was a great terrestrial rhythm which repeated mountain, desert, and river course (whether wet or dry), which he crossed innumerable times as he rode. Such a sequence of land supported a great variety of animals—the grizzly and brown bears, big-horn sheep, elk, many kinds of deer and antelope, the peccary, rabbits, and the wolf, and the coyote who sang dolefully at night. He could see fantastic birds—the *paysano* or chapar-ral cock, the great cranes of the sand hills, quail—a wonderful variety of insects, including the centipede, and the tarantula; and the rattle-snake, the copperhead, the horned toad, and the scorpion "whose sting, was sometimes fatal to children or," noted the Englishman with origi-nality, "persons of inflammable temperament." Where anything grew from the ground, it was likely to be the mesquite or greasewood, unless near a ranch or in a wet arroyo a few willows or *alamito*—little cotton-wood—were to be seen.

With human habitations so far apart, it was occasionally reassuring to see in the distance—which diminished so slowly—an occasional wayside chapel, with a tiled dome, pink or blue, and a corner tower, and a frame of trees; and yet seen more closely, it would show a black cavern of an open door in its ornamented plaster front, the doors awry on their hinges, or thrown down, and within, drifts of desert sand and cracked walls—the work of such Indian people as never stayed, but who must destroy the works of strangers on the land.

It was a welcome, if implausible sight, in that vast vacancy, to dis-cern at last, two hundred thirty miles south of El Paso del Norte, the city of Chihuahua, which lay against dust-colored hills. It was built on rolling land, and its Spanish aqueduct, with its "stupendous arches," whitewashed houses, and the towers of its churches and its reaches of trees rising from patio gardens under the pitiless sun, made it seem larger than it was. Not as old as Santa Fe, it had a population of perhaps ten thousand. It was the most considerable town of northern Mexico, where trade routes converged from New Mexico, Sonora, and California, and where silver from thriving mines in the sierra to the west was hauled into town. What was known as the Santa Fe Trail, which began at Independence, Missouri, actually ended in Chihuahua, with Santa Fe as a midway point. A merchant city, Chihuahua was twelve hundred and fifty miles as the crow flies from the capital city of Mexico, but even in its isolation it had been reasonably well sustained by the viceregal government of Spain. Since the independence of Mexico, the city had been left more or less as a wilderness outpost, to live on its own resources.

Lamy rode into town through streets laid out in squares, unlike those of Santa Fe, which had seemed to follow the trails of animals seeking the meagre watercourse of the Santa Fe Creek. The houses of the Chihuahueños were of adobe, but many were cornered and corniced with cut stone from the dusty hills about. At the center rose the cathedral, with its towers over a hundred feet tall, whose bells marked the many services of the day. The great bell, said a Santa Fe trader, could be heard at a distance of twenty-five miles. Lamy could see that the façade of the cathedral, which the English traveller said was built "in no style of architecture," displayed niches which contained life-sized figures of Christ and the twelve apostles. Behind the grand façade was an interior which bore "striking marks of poverty and neglect." Across from the cathedral was a *portal* or portico running the whole length of one side of the plaza. It was the habit of the residents to string along the *portal* roof the scalps of raiding Indians which had been taken by hunters paid by the local government. Not long before Lamy's passage through town, one hundred and seventy fresh Apache scalps had been paraded through the streets by a procession of men, women, and children. The display was a daily reminder of what a journey away from the protection of the city might mean. Americans and "Northerners" were not warmly welcomed in Chihuahua either—the Chihuahueños, from the governor on down, still remembered "every class of excesses" committed against them by the invading army from the States in the recent war.

Lamy now had five hundred miles left to go across the open country. In long stretches the road became a trail which was at times hard to follow. Having crossed mountain, desert, valley, in the familiar sequence, by now he had become a plainsman who knew how to watch for features of the land which would serve Indians as hiding places. Space and silence and pouring light by day; and sometimes in optical illusions the strange, imagined presence of savages—a species of cactus which had a thick body and stood at about the height of a man, crowned with spikes which at certain distances and lights looked startlingly like an Indian with a great crest of feathers. By night, under the stars, a sense greater than ever of the vastness of the land and its emptiness, and its silence, until the long cry of the coyote came over the distance; or, nearby, the obscure crackings and rattlings of shelled insects alerting the ground sleeper.

He passed the small town of Camargo, where the church was distempered in pale yellow, while its tower was rose-pink and the dome over the sanctuary a faded blue, all against bare rock mountains in the distance. There were hardships and glories in the weather—sometimes came storms which seemed as wide as a continent, the airy equivalent of the desert reaches in size; and then the riders took shelter beside their horses. Again, there were storms of light itself, breaking through clouds above mountains, and standing rays of gold air against distant blue, and trailing far veils of rain which often never reached the ground but seemed to become part of the very light itself; and infinity, perhaps even eternity, had an image.

Coming to a settlement days apart from any other, the traveller might find himself in the midst of an alarum—Indians had been sighted and lost and seen again, and the hacienda within its fortress limits was a turmoil of action, as the master and all his household prepared to resist attack. Animals to secure within the walls; children to put safely away; food to be cooked and stored by the terrified women; water drawn; weapons cleaned and loaded; prayers recited; farmers called in from the fields; and then the long wait. And if it was a needless scare, then what followed would be relief expressed in festivity, with music and abundant food dipped with tortillas out of common bowls and all hospitality for the harmless stranger. He found the ways of the house much like those of Santa Fe—some furniture left over from the Spanish centuries, and some from memories of the Moors.

If Indians did not come, traders sometimes did, and then the household spent hours going over goods, bartering for stuffs, pulling silver pieces out of buckskin *bolsónes* to buy utensils or pretty trifles. Everyone had stories to exchange—odd weather, escapes from Indians, good advice as to landmarks and passages for anyone travelling alone, locations, and of these, like the Arroyo de los Indios, where the rider might find enough water, caught in deep places, and cool, and perhaps shaded by a high bank from the hot sky, where he could pause for a bath, even then keeping watch for those after whom the arroyo was named, for they had made a trail which crossed it.

It was a land rich in mines—the road passed through Hidalgo del Parral, where pale tailing lay against the slate-gray mountains from which the ore was taken. The village had a three-tiered bell tower rising above its small, square adobe houses which were washed in many different colors. Durango state was a center for iron mining. If Parral seemed like an outpost of Durango city, it was not quite half-way there from Chihuahua.

But still the days passed in long thought and patience, and finally Lamy came to the hacienda of El Chorro, where there were salt licks for the horses, and lodging. There the news, along with that of vigilance *"por las novedades que hay* (for the troubles about)," was that Durango lay only twenty-eight miles further, beyond the corn fields where the great sand-hill cranes flew making their strange hoots by day or night.

v.

Confrontation in Durango

LAMY CAME ACROSS the arid plain which surrounded Durango, and, through the formal grid of the streets which were arranged according to the uniform plan for colonial cities issued through the centuries by Madrid, found his way to the bishop's palace. This was a long, low building with plaster walls washed in pink. The façade had strength and elegance—a cornice, window frames, footing, and a main door-way carved from an ochreous gray stone. The windows and the main entrance were barred with iron grilles. A stone cross surmounted the entrance, whose double doors were made of heavy wood, richly carved, in which a lesser, single door could be opened for inspection and in-quiry, and closed for dismissal. Through the little single door a great patio was visible—the palace was built about a grand inner square where trees grew and a running portico hung out from the walls as protection from weather. From without, the building was inscrutable. In its general design it was not unlike the 1610 palace at Santa Fe; but it had an air of greater majesty—spoke of a finished style nearer the center of affairs; and in fact Durango was the northernmost ex-tension of Spanish Mexico proper. All that lay above it on the map might as well have been a colony lost in distance and trifling in value. Lamy, his five-week journey ended, asked to be admitted to the pres-ence of Bishop Zubiría.

José Antonio Laureano López de Zubiría y Escalante had been bishop of Durango for twenty years. He promptly received his visitor, and confronted a lean young man about half as old as himself—Zubiría was seventy years of age, having been born in Sonora in July 1781. All he knew of Lamy were a certain letter he had received from him months before, and various rumors abroad during the pastoral visit to the northern provinces in the previous year—Zubiría's third such tour, following the first in 1833, and the second in 1845. He knew well the country across which Lamy had just travelled, though Zubiría himself had not done it alone; had gone, in fact, with a heavy escort, which was wise under the prevailing conditions.

The old bishop received the younger with every kindness. Zubiría impressed others with his benevolent and intelligent expression. His face was fleshy, his hair dark, his eyebrows strongly marked above black eyes which had a narrow Mongolian slit to them which suggested the typical Mexican admixture of Indian blood, and also a reserved shrewdness. His nose was long and slender, above a wide mouth which in repose was turned down at the corners. In his age, his body was heavy, with a full throat which rolled over the edge of his frilled jabot. He loved to talk, his affability and grace of manner were remembered, and he had the reputation of a conscientious prelate much concerned for his people and his duties. He recalled with gratitude the official courtesies given him in his recent New Mexican visit—the military escorts, the great public reception, crowds unable to obtain entry in the churches where he preached.

Despite the United States victory in the 1846 war he had never expected what was made known to him first by rumor, then by Lamy's letter of 10 April 1851 from San Antonio. On the contrary, he, with other bishops of the Mexican North, had been expressly ordered by Rome to continue their jurisdiction over the full extent of their original diocesan limits despite a new political boundary.

Charm and courtesy were his natural responses, and so, as the years would make plain, was a legalistic stubbornness concerning his responsibilities. He and Lamy had matters of common experience and light courtesies to exchange, but Lamy had really only one mission of immediate importance which had brought him to Durango. If Lamy had come prepared, Zubiría was no less sure of his own ground, and he had one further issue to raise with his visitor—and with Rome. First, however, he saw to the comfort of his guest, establishing him in the bishop's palace.

The crucial exchange of information followed. When Lamy's Spanish was inadequate, they conversed in Latin. Zubiría had written to Lamy on 12 June, in reply to Lamy's letter of 10 April from San Antonio.

ABOVE: San Francisco street, Santa Fe, much as Lamy first saw it in 1851. At the
end of the street is the old adobe parish church of St Francis, which became Lamy's
first cathedral. BELOW: A sketch of Santa Fe by an anonymous soldier in a company
morning report, c. 1846–1850. The crenellated towers of the old parish church are
indicated to the right of center

The south side of the Santa Fe plaza, looking east on San Francisco street, with parked caravan waggons attended by traders and citizens

Characteristic nineteenth-century adobe houses in Santa Fe, with haystack, bare ground, cottonwoods and poplars, and a faint line of mountains beyond—the pastoral look within the city

The plaza at La Mesilla, with its church and famous twin bells, trader waggons on the Santa Fe–Chihuahua Trail, and a woodsman with his burro-load of wood. From an anonymous painting of the period, c. 1860s

The plaza at Santa Fe, showing its soldiers' monument, a concert in progress by the 9th U.S. Cavalry band, cavaliers, the fountain playing. From an anonymous painting of the period

LEFT: The stone reredos carved in Santa Fe originally for the Spanish garrison chapel (*castrense*) in the plaza, seen here as later installed in the old cathedral in 1859. It is now the altarpiece in the noble modern church of Cristo Rey, designed by John Gaw Meem. RIGHT: The chapel of Our Lady of Light in the convent of the Sisters of Loretto, completed in 1881. Its French architect had in mind the Sainte-Chapelle of Paris. To the left is a glimpse of the sisters' academy, to the right a corner of their convent

LEFT: The exterior of Villa Pintoresca, Lamy's retreat in the hills of the Tesuque Canyon, about three miles north of Santa Fe. It was one of two places he loved best (the other was his famous garden in town) and there he lived when he retired. RIGHT: Villa Pintoresca consisted of only two rooms—a bedroom-study, and this very small chapel where Lamy said his daily Mass, often served by students from St Michael's College whom he would invite for a day in the country

ABOVE: Panorama showing the stone cathedral of St Francis under construction. Lamy laid the cornerstone (which was stolen a week later) in 1869. The north tower is shown rising. The old adobe transept of the previous cathedral can be seen, and to its left the early St Vincent's hospital, and a portion of the convent and orphanage of the Sisters of Charity, c. 1880s. BELOW: Lamy did not live to see the new cathedral completed; but he brought to it his inherited style of the Romanesque, with its Moorish echoes, and he had the satisfaction of seeing installed in the finished north tower the bells of the old cathedral

Lamy had never received the answer—the mails were notoriously inefficient.

Lamy's letter was the first notice he, Zubiría, had had concerning Lamy's new mission.

Rome had never notified him?

Never. The only word Durango had received of his supersession was Lamy's letter from San Antonio, and, in fact, as a Vatican memorandum noted, Zubiría had written in protest to the Pope, declaring that such notification from another bishop instead of from the Holy See, and, in fact, from a council of the North American bishops acting as though they had the authority to do what was Rome's to do, was hardly to be regarded as official. If the Holy Father had answered this protest, Zubiría had never received the answer. There was, to be sure, always the possibility that one had been sent, and that it had been lost in transit. Moreover, Zubiría had, however mistakenly, assumed that Lamy would have gone to Rome to make his duty to the Pope before proceeding to New Mexico. Out of such a visit, official notification might have come, in case none had already been sent. Again, if bulls had been sent to Durango, they, too, might have been lost in the mails.

Lamy, of course, had gone direct to Santa Fe, where his reception by Zubiría's vicar, with the refusal to recognize him as the new ecclesiastical authority of New Mexico, had made the present visit to Durango necessary.

Quite necessary; but Zubiría insisted that without specific orders from himself to his clergy in New Mexico to transfer their allegiance, they were entirely within their rights to withhold such allegiance.

Lamy agreed that this was so, even though he had shown them his papal document to attest to his appointment. He now laid it before Zubiría.

"I knew nothing about it officially," said Zubiría, "but this document is sufficient authority for me and I submit to it."

It was what Lamy had come fifteen hundred miles to hear.

Now, if the affair of the episcopal title to Santa Fe was settled, neither of the bishops knew what had caused the confusion in the first place. But in the Vatican archives lay evidence of a bureaucratic misconception central to more than one aspect of the transfer of churchly authority across the emerging national boundary after the 1846 war. When Pius IX granted the request of the Baltimore Council of 1849 to create the vicariate apostolic for Santa Fe out of certain Mexican territories, and gave it to a new bishop, the Vatican duly sent notice of the change to Mexico—but to the wrong Mexican bishop. Not Durango, but Sonora, was notified. Rome was far away, maps were imprecise, lordships grandly but loosely defined. The fact was that a great portion of the western half of New Mexico then embracing modern Arizona) did belong to Sonora, but without precise demarcation. If New Mexico was to be the new vicariate, then Santa Fe as its ancient capital must surely be the seat of the bishop (thus the Vatican) since northern Sonora had no town above the border, but only a few missions long abandoned. If Santa Fe implied New Mexico, and if New Mexico had reached deep into Sonora, then to a Vatican official who did not know that for centuries Durango had controlled the great eastern half of New Mexico while only the western half had come under Sonora, it might seem a satisfactory disposal of the whole adjustment to notify the Sonoran bishop, Pedro Loza, at Hermosillo or Culiacán. If Loza received the decree, he did not, beset as he was by Yaqui Indian troubles, make any reply to Rome; nor did he communicate to Zubiría at Durango any word of the error of the Roman bureaucracy. But at last, "in reality," said the Vatican's internal review of the confusion, His Holiness, "through the sacred Congregation of Extraordinary Affairs, ordered that the Bishop of Durango be clearly informed . . ." And so he was, in a decree dated 12 November 1851. But by then Lamy was already returning northward to Santa Fe, having himself settled matters with Durango.

With Lamy's position at Santa Fe now firmly recognized, he and Zubiría had two other affairs to discuss. One touched on that southern area of New Mexico and its poor settlements—Doñana, Las Cruces, and the Mesilla valley—which Lamy had seen on his way to Mexico. The other concerned the little river villages in far western Texas which Bishop Odin of Galveston had given into Lamy's charge.

The state of Chihuahua (which under the Spaniards had been known as New Biscay) had by tradition extended to the Mesilla-Doñana area forty-odd miles north of El Paso del Norte; and accordingly this area had always belonged to the see of Durango. Yet everything Lamy had understood from the deliberations of the Baltimore Council and his papal bulls of appointment concerning the extent of his vicariate stated his responsibility as fixed by the Treaty of Guadalupe Hidalgo, which indicated all of New Mexico to the Rio Grande near El Paso.

But Zubiría did not hold the same view—and with some reason. For a later map correction and a revised international boundary had actually assigned the lower east-west New Mexico area to Chihuahua in exchange for an agreement by which the United States could retain within a new north-south line the region of Santa Rita, formerly in Mexico, and its rich silver and copper mines a hundred miles west of the Rio Grande. Durango therefore had real claim territorially to "Mesilla-Doñana," and Zubiría considered himself still its bishop. He and Lamy each assumed that his own interpretation of territorial limits was correct.

But what would be served just now by making a change in their jurisdiction? Were not the populations too meagre and too impoverished to form a new parish? If formed, how could it support a pastor? Zubiría knew the places also—had passed through them on his visits to New Mexico.

Lamy could rely on only two priests in his entire diocese. He must admit that he had no one to send to Doñana for priestly work. What was more, Socorro, the nearest New Mexican town to those villages, was a hundred miles away across the desert—the *Jornada del Muerto*—and no travelling vicar could visit them without a long passage through that extremely dangerous Indian country. El Paso, across the Rio Grande to the south, was less than fifty miles away from the settlement. If any priest could serve those remote settlements now and then, it was surely more feasible to send him from El Paso rather than from the north.

In the face of such facts, common sense urged that Lamy and Zubiría should decide to leave the southern villages of New Mexico under Durango rather than transfer them to the authority of Santa Fe. The two bishops so agreed. But in agreeing to this point, Lamy unwittingly established the basis for a legalistic wrangle which would exasperate him for decades, as populations would shift, local resources would be differently evaluated, and finally, new treaty boundaries would soon alter local sovereignties.

As for the other question—the Texas river villages—these were only a few miles from the Mexican El Paso, where the rural dean of Chihuahua lived. Granted that Odin, almost nine hundred miles away in Galveston, could hardly service them; but could Santa Fe, almost four hundred miles to the north, do much better? The villages had been Mexican until the Rio Grande's change of course had left them within the United States boundary. But in a practical sense, they were still Mexican and pendant to Durango. Let the matter rest there—so Zubiría would argue; and again, limited by his resources, Lamy must agree for the time being.

If, for a few days, Lamy presumably enjoyed an interlude of rest and content after his journey southward and his long debates with his host, and went to see something of the city of Durango, Bishop Zubiría was not idle. He was a responsible man, and if his benevolence was admired, the experience of his long episcopate had prepared him for the exercise of all his imaginative shrewdness. He put it to work now.

While Lamy was still his visitor, and after the joint resolutions of their common problems, Zubiría threw himself into the composition of a most carefully worded letter to Rome which must have cost him and his reverend secretary Doctor Luís Rúbio hours of cautionary debate to insure that all concessions of the present would not cloud certain vital reservations for the future. Beginning with ceremonial rhetoric, Zubiría soon enough put more plainly what concerned him.

I, the present Bishop of Durango, José Antonio de Zubiría-Escalante, as hereafter subscribed [he began profusely], owing to the honor of my having as the guest of my house the Illustrious Lordship Don Juan Lamy, Bishop of Agathonica *in partibus infidelium* and Vicar Apostolic appointed for the Territory of New Mexico, by our reigning Pontiff, the Supreme Bishop Pius IX, may whose reign be long and filled with God's blessings, for, since God possesses all power and facility to do so, may he so deign; and, since, assuredly, God will so do: and whereas such concepts being clothed as they are with mere words, and these are so susceptible to change and variance within the human intelligence of mankind: obviously, then, despite this frailty of human communication, I have no choice accordingly but to accept this medium through which to express my message, and it is thus written, as follows . . .

Then, in points here much simplified, he set forth in six sections his positions on several matters.

To begin with, he stated that Lamy's letter from San Antonio had first told him informally what he now knew officially—though he admitted that the San Antonio letter had left no doubt that he was being "legitimately relieved" of his responsibilities in New Mexico.

Second, though he had never received the "special mandate" for which he had asked Rome, Zubiría now felt that Lamy's documents were enough to permit him "licitly" to await it, but he would cease to depend upon the "long-awaited letter," and would "recognize, as of now, as Vicar Apostolic of New Mexico, the said Illustrious Lordship, Señor Don Juan Lamy." But Zubiría cautiously added that he was "only reserving for myself actually seeing the answer which should arrive soon from Rome," for this, he thought, might possibly contain details or modifications yet unknown.

Third, he would personally instruct his former dean, Señor Don Juan Felipe Ortiz, the established pastor of Santa Fe, that Zubiría by his will now required him to submit to Lamy and to lead all others to submit with him.

Fourth—and here arose the matter which it would take years to resolve—he asked that the precise limits of his diocese be defined. They should, he urged, reach as far north as the present—the treaty—boundary between Chihuahua and New Mexico; and no civil decision like that of the treaty, made before the Baltimore Council's creation of the new vicariate apostolic of New Mexico, should be altered to extend the limits of New Mexico, "even for a Vicariate."

Fifth—he had learned in conversation with Lamy that Odin, the bishop of Texas, had allotted to Lamy's care those three small towns along the Rio Grande southeast of the "Villa de El Paso." Political acts had given these towns to the state of Texas; but *in ecclesiam* they belonged to the diocese of Durango; Zubiría had never had from Rome any letter or notice taking them from him; the Texas bishop had been appointed to his see long before those towns had come under the civil authority of Texas and hence Odin had no claim to them; and moreover, the diocese of Texas could not now be enlarged.

And sixth and last—he avowed that points four and five (those concerning churchly dominion over certain territories) were really the important points in his letter, yet (by his vehemence he made this clear) he would nevertheless, in the sight of God, submit to and obey any contrary decisions issued by the Holy See; and, he wrote, "should there come to me, by some legal way, other information referring to the said cession of the above-mentioned places, be it for the authority of the Bishop of Texas, or be it to the Illustrious Lordship, the Lord Vicar of New Mexico, it shall be so done."

Dating his letter "Durango, November 1st, 1851," he stated also that he was informing Lamy of all which it contained, "so as to save me in this way from any further responsibility of conscience."

So, from the beginning, the question not only of Lamy's recognition, but the matter of definition of territorial limits arose out of Lamy's journey of 1851 to the former ecclesiastical capital of all New Mexico.

Durango itself, he saw, like others before him, had its curious aspects. Out of a population of nearly twenty thousand, all but a thousand or so were "rogues and rascals." The city was further celebrated as "the headquarters, as it were, of the whole scorpion family," and it was odd that when these poisonous arachnids were removed a few miles from the city, their venom seemed to lose strength. A local society paid youths of the town three cents for every one of the creatures they killed. The churches were handsome outside, filthy within, though the case was just the opposite with the houses, which if they were dirty outside were cleanly kept inside—though from a distance their white or ochre plaster showed handsomely under the hot sun. Lamy could see the great profile of the Sierra Madre to the west of town, across barren hills from which rose a curtain of dust. The iron mines of the district were in those mountains. From them came much of the city's commerce, and perhaps many of its rogues and rascals. The great native drink, derived from the maguey cactus, was pulque, which, taken temperately, raised the spirits and induced nausea, and, more freely, changed the temperament suddenly and for the worse.

At the center of one side of the main plaza stood the cathedral, several squares away from the bishop's palace. It was a towering block plastered in pale yellow, with twin towers rising to a great height through three diminishing arched, square elements to identical domes and lanterns. In the façade between the towers was a three-storey entablature of pale stone carved in the Churrigueresque style. Above its center rose a wrought-iron cross. The great center double doorway was of timber with rows of iron studdings. The nave, lighted by the sky through plain glass, rose to a noble height, and rose again in the dome over the sanctuary. Square pillars supported arches which upheld the dome and its pendentives frescoed with sacred images. Over the main altar was a baldachin on tall slender white columns, decorated with sunbursts of gold leaf. There was nothing remotely so splendid in Santa Fe. Europe, through Spain, and modified by Mexico, spoke to Lamy again.

If he wondered what was happening so far away in Santa Fe, there may have been grudging items of news when the rural dean and established pastor Ortiz arrived in Durango on his own, to argue his position with Zubiría, to whom he still held allegiance. The bishop of Durango decisively instructed him—possibly in Lamy's presence—to make his religious duty henceforth to Lamy, and to require all others in New Mexico, clergy and laity alike, to do the same in good faith.

Armed with the knowledge of this, and with a written decree from Zubiría yielding to him what he had come to receive, Lamy in early November took to the return trail. Knowing something of the country now, he must have found that the northerly journey seemed to go more rapidly than his trip south—though of course it did not do so. When he reached El Paso, he came upon the camp of Major William H. Emory, the chief astronomer (and later the leader) of the United States section of the international boundary commission set up to survey and correct what should become the official borderline between Mexico and the States. Lamy impressed Emory as an "excellent" man. They talked shop, and Emory was left with the notion that "the Bishop's purpose on his trip was to see the Bishop of Durango and adjust the territorial limits of their respective dioceses to make them conform to the altered boundaries of New Mexico and Texas"—an incomplete conclusion. What was Durango like? "The Bishop stated that the wealthy State of Durango must soon be depopulated by the Indians. Haciendas within a few leagues of the city that once numbered one hundred thousand animals were now abandoned . . ."

Continuing northward along the Rio Grande, which was entirely dry for much of its course, Lamy was soon on his own ground. Machebeuf expected him home by Christmas.

vi.

Disciplines

IN FACT, he reached Santa Fe on 10 January 1852, as inconspicuously as he had set out almost three months before. The round-trip journey of three thousand miles, alone but for his guide, was a hardening experience for the years ahead, when his desert diocese would require much travel of the same kind, often quite alone, across the empty splendors of his dominion. Though ostensibly robust, he would for all his life be subject occasionally to the sudden and unexpected strikes of physical collapse which he had known in youth; but by will alone he overcame these and pursued his far-flung duty.

Machebeuf, eagerly awaiting his news, had some of his own. The contrasting styles of their exchanges can be deduced from their various letters to others. Machebeuf infused his information with a dancing vitality, in which he always saw himself. Lamy never seemed to see himself—only the task before him—an extension of character from the daily to the long view. To Machebeuf every event, most satisfyingly, was a *scandale,* while to his bishop, it seemed more like a tile in a pattern. Machebeuf saw with his imagination; Lamy with a sense of recognition. Their friendship, their working partnership, were the stronger for these complementary traits.

Lamy's first act on his return was to circularize to his sullen subordinates the ruling of their former bishop in Mexico. In a body, and officially, they showed a degree of submission; though individually, soon and late, they would act otherwise, in some cases with extreme consequences. Meantime, Machebeuf had both farcical and serious matters to report to Lamy, which would lose nothing in the telling.

Imagine him all alone in Santa Fe, he reported, speaking wretched Spanish to the natives, and conducting, rather better than otherwise, a steady correspondence in Spanish dealing with dispensations, and other parish affairs. The pastor of one of the four chapels in Santa Fe, a Father Lujan, introduced him to the congregation. When it was time to preach, Machebeuf did his best in Spanish; but nobody understood him. It had to be assumed that he was saying the proper things, while representing the absent Lamy. But after Mass, what a comedy: some of the people, lingering outside, said that since he did not speak as Christians do, he "must be a Jew or a Protestant." Someone else shrugged—"Who knows?" But there was no doubt that he sang the Mass in Latin, and it was added that he sang better than the local priests. The affair was resolved by a sensible, if simple, woman, who joined the discussion. Why, she asked, was there any doubt about "the religion of this man? Did he not give proof that he is a Catholic by the way he made the sign of the cross before giving his sermon?" The others were silenced. But what an index of the primitive mind and local experience all this revealed!

With both Lamy and Ortiz away, those few native priests still present had been no more amenable than before. There were affairs to report about the pastors of Taos, Albuquerque, Pecos. As Lamy had seen before his departure, the clergy were for the most part "incapable or unworthy." He had then given such pastors admonitory advice, hoping that they would begin to mend their ways which had so shocked him, and many a newcomer before him. Now it was disturbing to hear that while he was away in Mexico, the "greatest number" of the New Mexican clergy "did all they could to make the people believe" not only that he held no real authority, but that he would never even return from Durango.

Now, however, on seeing Bishop Zubiría's letters which declared that Durango no longer held jurisdiction over Santa Fe, and that Lamy was the true ecclesiastical superior of the New Mexican clergy, and that they must submit to his authority, they had, said Lamy, shown him "good face." But it began to be clear almost at once that he must bring them to submit by force rather than by good will. Rather than comply, some preferred to leave New Mexico—Machebeuf knew this for sure. Lamy hoped God would speed them, for, he said, "they are more in the way than help." "But, what shall we do for priests here?"

Then there was the affair of the pastor of Pecos which had reached its finally intolerable state in November, during Lamy's absence. The pastor, an old man of sixty-five, was an addicted gambler and an adulterer, and last November, after mounting his horse while drunk, he was thrown when the horse shied. The old man's leg was broken in three places. Providence, decided Lamy, had punished him in the very act of drunkenness.

Machebeuf could report that he was already at work restoring the *Castrense* with the fund raised by Lamy after the rout of the chief justice in August, and stood ready to serve as its pastor, at least for the present, unless the bishop decided to use it as his own church, in which case Machebeuf could administer the old parish church of St Francis, which had become the cathedral. It was still true that religion, whatever its local peculiarities, played a great part in the whole life of the people. What Lamy and Machebeuf both could see now was what had persisted for generations. When the Americans came six years before, the natives were promised by President Polk and General Kearny, the conqueror, that their practices of faith would rest undisturbed.

But certain practices were alarming—those which survived in the village chapels of the Rio Arriba, the upper Rio Grande district. In one form or another these had persisted since the days of the Spanish colonists of 1598 in the cult of the Third Order of Penitence, patterned after the laymen's Third Order of St Francis, but not identical with it. Even now, the Brothers of Penance, or "Penitentes," as they were conveniently called, observed Holy Week each year in the snowy, juniper-speckled foothills of northern New Mexico, by flagellation, even to the bloodied use of scourges, upon each other and themselves, and rituals of terror, and initiations by mutilation, and, it was believed, on Good Friday the actual crucifixion of a chosen victim as the Christ —a great honor bestowed upon a man adjudged worthy of the role. It was said that he was tied rather than nailed to the cross; but even so, if a village Christ died under the ordeal (as tradition insisted was the case now and then) his family, mourning him, were yet consoled by the thought that through his mimic sacrifice, he and they both would go to heaven, when their time came, without passing through purgatory. How to end these cruel observances, even though they were inspired by piety?

In his first pastoral visit in 1833, Bishop Zubiría had been horrified by the penitence of blood and its sanction by the New Mexican churches; and he had forbidden it in a sermon before the people and a letter to his priests: "We command, and lay it strictly upon the conscience of our parish priest in this Villa, the present one and those to come, that in future such assemblies of Penitentes shall not be allowed under any pretext whatsoever. . . . I forbid for all time to come those brotherhoods of penance—or, better still, of Butchery— which have been growing under the shelter of an inexcusable toleration . . ." But his orders never took full effect. The penitential abuses which had been lodged within the church buildings were simply transferred to non-sanctified chapels called *moradas* where the rituals of the cult were carried out. Zubiría protested again in his second visitation some years later, again in vain; for after the Franciscans had been withdrawn in the early nineteenth century, the Penitentes, in the absence of enough parish or mission priests, often administered services of blessing and prayer, though no sacraments; and so deeply rooted were the penitential savageries that these, too, persisted. The discovery of all this by Machebeuf and Lamy presented a problem never resolved, for the Penitentes began to take refuge in self-protection as an almost secret society.

Beyond all this, Machebeuf was able to report that he had been working hard—had given a retreat in a chapel "30 leagues from Santa Fe" which seemed to produce "an immense good." Finally, as Lamy himself would learn, "the most savage Indians, the Navajos," were at peace, and it seemed "a fine time to establish missions among them."

This conclusion was more ideal than real—who would serve the missions? And how long could those Indians be expected to keep the peace? Lamy, if he looked for satisfactions, could find at least one small one, for his school for boys was doing "pretty well," and he wrote Purcell—he continued to write Purcell for years, to share experience with him, and often to ask for help—"We have ten little boys who sing Mass with the organ most every Sunday."

For the rest, he must go to work. One of his first pastoral visits took him to Pecos, where the large mission church of the seventeenth century served eighteen villages in the upper Pecos Valley. On this visit, Lamy suspended the broken-legged old pastor from all his functions; but as he was the *parochus proprius*—the permanent pastor of Pecos, to whom local revenues were due for life—Lamy permitted him to keep one third of these.

This first act of discipline had its risks—the old pastor was a powerful member of the territorial legislature; but Lamy hoped that it would be seen as a warning to the other unworthy priests. There were several other cases he knew of which also deserved "the same severity"; but, so he wrote Purcell, "as they have not been caught in the very act, I must wait with patience, and try at least to keep them under fear, perhaps that some of them will change." He felt "obliged to go very slow, and to be very prudent," for the local clergy had "not only a great influence," they had actually been "the rulers of the people."

He must come to know the people himself, and let them see him as their father and servant. On 5 February he left Santa Fe for a journey through some pueblos and towns of the north which he had not yet seen. Again he came upon isolated villages with their crumbling earthen chapels, in some of which he found statues, paintings, and wall decorations done by native artists. To his eye these were touching evidence of the need of the faithful for saints—but what he preferred were the

Gothic and Romanesque treasures of his youth. Here were pieces of cottonwood carved and painted, with staring eyes and raw colors, and flat entablatures of holy figures whose features looked like those of the people themselves in the dark mountain villages of the north. Such religious art had been fabricated by saint-makers, the first of whom had been taught by Franciscans how to carve and to use color, and what they created was needed to replace the European works which had been destroyed by the Indians of the Pueblo rebellion of 1680, when the Spanish colonists had been driven all the way south to El Paso, their churches profaned, their signs of faith obliterated, their civil order and its symbols either abandoned or used in mockery.

To Lamy and Machebeuf the native Mexican attempts to bring back the saints after the Spaniards recovered the kingdom in 1692 must have seemed as pathetically primitive as the very houses of the local style. Later times have seen them differently. As works of art the native paintings and carvings of sacred presences—the *santos*—were a victory over technical limitations; for the passion that begot them had more power to express than the technical ignorance of their creators had to constrain. Yet, however different in style, the *santos* were closer in spirit to the earliest medieval Romanesque than the Frenchmen could have recognized. As for chapels and houses of mud, as Lamy and Machebeuf so often called them in letters to Europe, they were less failures than triumphs, given the only materials at hand, and the prime necessities they met. But all newcomers brought their definitions of propriety with them; and the bishop was no exception. It was no wonder that his ideal was to create, if he could, a little of France in this wilderness of neglect. In any case, it was his task to visualize and make manifest for people what they addressed inwardly. Such a purpose lay at the heart of his problems, with their material urgencies all too plain.

In the parishes where he came on this journey, he would see the adobe chapels, some of which tapered like coffins in form, prefiguring that death whose promise was so large in the Mexican awareness, and he would discover that all too often the poverty of the priests was less than that of the parishioners. The people were called on by the local pastor to bring him a great part of their produce—seeds, animals, whatever commodities they had, but of course no money, as hardly any was circulated in the territory outside the major towns. Much of such tribute stayed in the hands of the local pastors. The rest, converted into money through bills of exchange, went, up through the year 1851, to the bishop of Durango. None of such tribute was used for the good of the whole province of New Mexico. One parish simply might be less poor than another, which in turn might be almost destitute. Recent times had been hard—harder than usual. The year 1850 was plagued by locusts which destroyed field crops almost entirely, and the general drought (temporarily broken on Lamy's day of arrival at Santa Fe) reduced the crops to a tenth of the expected yield. Collections were next to impossible—though, as Father Martínez wrote Zubiría from Taos, in the previous August he had "on two holidays" obeyed Durango's command to read to the people "the official order" on the collection of tithes, and the dreadful penalties, spiritual and temporal, which would fall upon those who failed to pay. It was a system long-established and expected by the congregations—but the degree of its demands amounted to extortion and every parish suffered under it.

Lamy, coming upon such conditions again and again, concluded that he must devise a system of maintaining the Church by which each parish would help to support all, at much lower levies, with the common resources deposited at the bishop's office. Moreover, he found that the local pastors charged fees for sacred ministrations far greater than people could afford for marriages, baptisms, burials. The more he thought about what such fees were ultimately used for in gaming, drinking, and worse, the firmer he became in his intention to establish an orderly and more equitable means of support for the clergy, and services to the people, across the whole vast vicariate.

The matter was directly related, too, to the behavior of the most prominent native priests. Since his return from Durango, where he had lost his case, the Very Reverend Dean Ortiz was visibly resentful, but so far no firm evidence against him had come to light of personal misbehavior. But Father Gallegos at Albuquerque, Father Lujan at Santa Fe, Father Salazar at Santa Clara, all deserved, and received, firm and direct but on the whole gentle admonitions from Lamy to mend their ways. They all knew what open scandal must lead to— the alcoholic old pastor of Pecos was a ready example. The bishop was reluctant to discipline any more priests—he had too few to spare, and moreover, it was not in his nature to impose punishment lightly. Clearly, his hope was that they would follow as strictly as he would lead, so that the notoriously loose customs of the society would gradually improve under seemly example.

But meanwhile, the February weather was "like spring"—it had been a mild winter. His new country was beginning to cast its spell on him. His vision of what he must do first was clear. Ignorance was the first enemy, even more than impiety, for the latter must recede before knowledge, he was certain. He must have teachers. He could think of none finer than Jesuits and nuns. On 1 February he wrote to Father Roothaan, General of the Jesuits at Rome, asking that certain Spanish-speaking priests—two of them—be sent to him, but neither was available. One was pursuing his studies at Georgetown, the other was fully occupied as president of St Louis University. But the bishop already knew the Loretto nuns in Kentucky.

The opportunity was soon coming for him to go in search of teachers, for the bishops of the nation were to convene again at Baltimore, and he planned to be with them. He would leave Santa Fe on 1 April. He hoped he would arrive in time for the sessions, but ahead of him lay his first journey over the plains, and he had no experience by which to judge the conditions and times of such travel. Matters at Santa Fe would temporarily have to be left to the native clergy, though he gave Machebeuf a certain task to perform.

This was to find and prepare a house in which to install whatever teaching nuns he could recruit, where they might live and hold school. Casting about, Lamy fixed upon a large house belonging to "a rich Frenchman" of St Louis which would be a suitable residence and convent school. It would be costly—sixty-five hundred piastres—and Lamy wanted to enter at once into negotiations for it, but before his departure for the East there would be no time for this or for his actual acquisition of the property. He gave the negotiations over to Machebeuf to accomplish during his absence. It was a notable house in the road immediately adjacent to and at right angles to the cathedral of St Francis (Cathedral Place). It measured two hundred feet along the front, with a patio within under a portico on all four sides, like a cloister, and it had twenty-six rooms of which five or six were *"très vastes."* Most advantageous of all, the house was surrounded on three sides by streets, so that there was little chance of being hemmed in by neighbors. The Frenchman was so well off that he could allow time for extended payments on the purchase. Machebeuf had no notion of where the money would come from to buy the place, but he hoped Providence would see to it. The house was to be ready for Lamy on his return with his teachers. As Machebeuf put it, "since the source of evil is the profound ignorance of the people, undoubtedly the first remedy will be to teach and to establish Christian schools for both sexes . . . and religious houses staffed with devoted people filled with the spirit of sacrifice. . . ."

He looked forward to a flourishing religious community in Santa Fe, for there were already more than thirty young people of leading territorial families impatiently awaiting the opening of Catholic schools on the bishop's return. Meanwhile, Machebeuf, with no fixed duties, took to the road down the Rio Grande where the landscape enchanted him with its valley greenery, and its mountains crowned with sempiternal snows lying far back on either side—so he wrote home from

Peña Blanca. Everywhere he saw a romantic and picturesque vista which surely promised rich fields of wheat and corn and vineyards. He was already used to crossing mountains and fording rivers. The Rio Grande was "limpid," but could not support the great steamships of the Ohio which he knew so well—no, now he went along on his beautiful little Mexican pony; all of which called for descriptions and demanded poetry. But his muse was a rebel, he said, which refused to ascend Parnassus. Raptures aside, he was content to go among the abandoned (he intended the pun) villages to preach and give the sacraments. For years, when new friends whom he travelled to serve asked where he lived, Machebeuf would reply, "in the saddle . . . they call me *El Vicario Andando,* The Travelling Vicar, and I live on the public highway." Lamy could always say the same.

vii.

The Plains Eastward

ON 1 APRIL 1852, Lamy set out eastward from Santa Fe across the plains which he would see for the first time. He had written to the Jesuit provincial at St Louis, Father Murphy, his old teacher from Clermont-Ferrand, that he hoped to see him on 1 May at St Louis. The dates imply a journey of four weeks, and seem to indicate that he would be travelling by stage coach, as a waggon train on the traders' trail would take longer. It is possible that he may have gone, mounted, with a small escort—there was no record of his mode of travel on that east-ward journey. The weather was usually opening up by that time of year, after the heavy snows and high winds which forced the waggons of the Independence–Santa Fe–Chihuahua trade to suspend most of its operations during the winter months.

The plains crossing was the national adventure of the time. A "pleasure trip on the plains," for a view of the great prairies attracted many in addition to those who toiled across the vast level inlands in search of new life, new settlement, independence, and wealth. The stage service, which had been started in 1849, took two weeks to go from Santa Fe to the Missouri River at Independence, Missouri, and cost two hundred dollars per passenger, meals included. Armed out-riders kept watch for Indians. It was a needed precaution. Without it,

and general safeguards on a wide scale, New Mexico, wrote its governor that winter, "instead of becoming settled with an industrious
and thriving population, will be left in a howling wilderness, with
no other inhabitants than the wolf, and the birds of prey, hovering
over the mangled remains of our murdered countrymen. . . ."

The old Santa Fe Trail led eastward by a circuitous route as it left
town, and then made its way through the far-scattered Sangre de
Cristo foothills dotted with piñon and juniper. Lamy saw some of his
ranchos and villages lost among the mesas, until he came to Las Vegas,
where high meadows gave the first sign of the great open lands ahead.
Reckoned as space, the plains seemed flat, and in general they were;
but western Kansas was not flat as a table—there were low rolls, dips
and gullies, any one of which could afford concealment to Indian
watchers or attackers. The travellers, though they could see, it seemed,
to infinity, were often limited in their foreground vision to the low
ridge just ahead. It was country about six hundred miles in extent,
reaching to Council Grove, and in its spaces lived the immense herds
of bison which if they were still or grazed slowly, often, from a great
distance, resembled groves of trees; and there too lived in their roving
way tribes of the Comanches, Apaches, Cheyennes, Arapahoes, Pawnees,
and Kiowas, from whom the traveller had most to fear. The distance
from Council Grove to the end of the trail at Independence was a
hundred and fifty miles. In that span, the Indians—Shawnees, Kaws—
were more friendly, and Lamy could see an occasional cabin where a
settler had planted himself far beyond the connected frontier. Such
a house was likely to be a dugout, rising with sod walls a little above
the ground.

From Independence, stage travel would continue to St Louis, or, if
he had time, the traveller could board a Missouri River steamboat for
the continued journey of several days to the Mississippi.

Lamy had already established relations with an imaginative and
adventurous member of the university. The Jesuit father P. J. De Smet
(known all over the West, among whose Indians he had travelled as
far as the Pacific) had written to Lamy from the university in November 1851 of plans to come to New Mexico, and to visit the Comanches
on the way, and finally to obtain the bishop's blessing at Santa Fe.
The visit never took place, but contact by letter would soon be followed by valuable meetings as Lamy passed through St Louis on his
later east-west travels.

There was no continuous rail travel eastward from the Mississippi
to the Atlantic coast until 1857. Lamy therefore proceeded by stage
to Louisville, then by river to Cincinnati, from there to Pittsburgh by
river, and finally by rail to Baltimore. There the bishops of the United

States were to hold their first plenary council, and Lamy for the first time would sit with them as their peer.

With Francis Patrick Kenrick, archbishop of Baltimore presiding, the council convened on 9 May 1852, in the beautiful cathedral of Latrobe. Those of its deliberations which concerned Lamy began with an all too familiar issue. The young bishop set forth a review of the conditions of his immense vicariate, and went on to describe the difficulties which he had discussed with Zubiría in Durango seven months before. These included the matter of the confusion surrounding his final achievement of his proper authority, and also the curious matter of the uncertain ecclesiastical boundary between Durango and New Mexico. The treaty was recalled, and Lamy's bulls of appointment, which gave him all of New Mexico, including the southern villages. Yet Zubiría had held out for his own continued control of those remote places, and Lamy, wearied by his journey to Mexico, and perhaps relieved to have the episcopate, at least, resolved, had informally agreed to a *status quo*.

But now—now the problem of a defined area for New Mexico arose under a new motive; for the assembled bishops "decided humbly to ask" Pius IX "to elevate the above mentioned Vicariate to [an] Episcopal See of the City of Santa Fe, which would be subject to the Metropolitan church of St. Louis, and that as the Bishop of this new diocese the present Vicar Apostolic of this territory, the Most Reverend Johannes Lamy, be appointed." But more: the bishops asked that "all the territory of New Mexico, which by established boundaries belongs to the Federal Government of the Federated States of America, be subject to" such a new diocese, "including in it also that part of the Territory which, although it belongs to the Federated States of America, remains subject to the diocese of Durango." The geographical matter had now passed beyond an informal agreement between two bishops, and was thrown into the great machinery of policy at Rome. The consequences would be achingly protracted.

But behind the council's move was surely a sense that religious authority, save that of the Papacy, could not expediently cross national political boundaries; and the assembled bishops had another similar case in the disputed authority over those villages southeast of El Paso with which Odin had charged Lamy on his way west. This, too, was referred to Rome, with Odin's eloquent statement of the case, in which the ancient habits of the desert Rio Grande played the decisive part. The "three small parishes, San Elizario, Socorro, and Isleta (del Sur)," had formerly been in Mexico. But "the Rio Grande, having changed its bed, these three parishes, instead of lying to the west, are now found to be east of the river and consequently"—again the treaty provision which defined the middle of the Rio Grande's river bed as the boundary line—"belong to Texas [and are] civilly governed by the laws of that state. [But] the Bishop of Durango seems to want to conserve jurisdiction on them because they were formerly part of his diocese." But as Lamy had been given all of New Mexico, so had Odin been given all of Texas. Only Rome, so far away, with no information but that offered by contending prelates, could pronounce a decision. The lost hamlets, their bishops, former and later, must await it, in both cases.

The plenary council, having had other work to do, concluded all its affairs on 20 May 1852. The final resolutions of those attending were signed by thirty-two bishops, of whom the twenty-ninth was "John, Vicar Apostolic of New Mexico, tit[ular] bishop of Agathonica," who, when his work was done at Baltimore, hurried to New York on business, before he must depart for the South in his search for teaching nuns.

From New York he wrote to the Society for the Propagation of the Faith, with its dual offices in Paris and Lyon, saying that he would recruit Loretto nuns in Kentucky; and to bring home the lesson of his general needs in the desert, he went on to cite the state of his properties. "My poor churches or chapels to the number of 65 are neither plastered nor floored, and are almost all without windows." With great trouble he had found a few vestments and chalices with which to celebrate Mass, but there was not a candlestick deserving of the name— in fact, destitution was everywhere. The Society's Paris office would have some idea of the condition he faced when he told them that in New York he had had to obtain, "on credit," imperatively needed supplies to the amount of "at least ten thousand francs." These included chasubles, dalmatics, candelabra, altar vessels, and the like. His lifeline from the desert diocese reached all the way to Paris and Lyon. "I hope that you will not forget me," he pleaded, and gave his next address as the University of St Louis, in care of the president; for his homeward journey would once again take him by that way.

But first to Kentucky: he went by coach to the Allegheny station in Pennsylvania, then by the Baltimore and Ohio Railroad to Cincinnati, and on by steamer to Louisville, and again by road to Bardstown, Bishop Flaget's old city. Flaget was long since dead, but with his second successor, Bishop Martin John Spalding, Lamy opened the matter of sending teaching nuns from the Loretto motherhouse at Nerinckx, Kentucky. He would ask Spalding to arrange for the sisters to leave their community, which had been founded in 1812 by Charles Nerinckx, a Belgian priest who had left home because of religious intolerance to serve under Flaget. Like Flaget's first cathedral, the first convent of the Lorettines in America had been built of logs. Lamy was promised his teachers.

He did not linger long in Bardstown, where Flaget's later cathedral, with its classic portico and arched apse, and the town's eighteenth-century stone tavern, and the hilltop mansions, were so unlike anything at Santa Fe. Returning to Louisville, he took steamer for New Orleans, where he came to see again his niece Marie at her convent school. She was now two years older than when he had left her—a sweet-faced and lively girl. He must have given her many tales of his life in the old earthen town where much—"everything"—needed to be done. Marie thought her uncle worth the service of anyone's lifetime. There was more than a family's bond between them—Marie already had a sense of vocation. He left her, when he must, to proceed to St Louis, where he expected his party of Lorettines to meet him for the westward crossing of the plains.

For their part, the Loretto sisters set out on 26 June 1852, on their way west. They went to Bardstown along roads winding through dark pine and oak woods, and in their turn took the steamer *Lady Franklin* down the Ohio, and up the Mississippi to St Louis. They were received by the archbishop, Peter Richard Kenrick (brother of the prelate at Baltimore), and lodged at the Loretto convent of Florissant, at the edge of the city.

St Louis was the center of the inner continental river network. As Anthony Trollope observed a few years later, it boasted of commanding "46,000 miles of navigable river water, counting the great rivers up and down from that place . . . chiefly the Mississippi, the Missouri, and Ohio . . . the Platte and Kansas rivers." It was, in the report of an earlier Englishman, the novelist Captain Frederick Marryat, "a well-built town," and its levees were "crowded with steamboats, lying two or three tiered." By moonlight, said the captain, the Mississippi had "a candle-like beauty." A remarkable city, St Louis was a place where an alligator committed suicide by throwing itself out of a third-storey window of a "museum," leaving four other alligators who "fought each other to death eventually." One was preserved, and, "to make him look more poetical," he had "a stuffed Negro in his mouth." The city was a frontier crossroads for the outlandish, the optimistic, the vicious, and the visionary nature of the American character on the frontier. William Makepeace Thackeray, on his profitable lecture tour, arrived in 1856 in a steamboat which had caught fire twice and also offered as entertainment the presence of Mrs Julia Hayne, who was billed as "the American giantess." Thackeray (who was reading Marryat's books—"a vulgar dog but he makes me laugh") declared that the giantess was eight feet high and that to make her a dress required "one hundred and fifty-four yards and three *quarters* of ordinary dry goods." He underlined the *quarters* as the ultimate monstrosity. Marryat's candlelight river he saw as that "great dreary melancholy stream," and somehow found in her a matronly character, for he spelled her as the "Mrs. Sippi."

But St Louis was also a commercial and ecclesiastical crossroads, and Lamy had much business there when he arrived from New Orleans. His first concern was to let Paris know that six sisters of Loretto were indeed with him now at St Louis, and he was sure they would be of inestimable value to New Mexico—they represented the first establishment of their calling there. He had high admiration for them, for by their commitment, they undertook to meet with courage the rough and dangerous plains journey ahead of them. He thought two months would do for the crossing of what was called in the States *"les plaines et les prairies."* They would go by river for six hundred miles on the Missouri, and then would come the open land. They would go slowly, because of the great heat of summer on the plains—he was writing in July. As he must, he cited the great expenses he would have to meet, and as always he put his trust, "after God," in the Society at Paris, for aside from other expenses, to cover the cost of transporting only the nuns, with their luggage, provisions, and the two "strong waggons" for them and the people who must take care of them, he had to say that he would need thirteen thousand francs.

He made a good stroke of business in St Louis by arranging for Father De Smet to act as his agent for all purchases and payments. He still hoped De Smet would presently come to New Mexico, but meantime, since Santa Fe was so far removed from financial or marketing centers, it was an advantage to have someone so able as De Smet to receive drafts from France, make payments, and place orders for supplies.

Before going westward, Lamy wrote out a legal instrument: "By these I authorize P. J. De Smet to sign for me, and negotiate any draft that comes from France. The house or bank which sends them is aware that I have appointed the same father as my agent, and that he can act in this respect as myself. John Lamy, Vic. Ap. of N. Mexico, St. Louis this 10th day of July 1852."

He had already run up an account in orders and purchases, part of them incurred on his way eastward to the council in April. De Smet kept a careful reckoning for such items as a pair of slippers ($1.25), a box of water paint ($3.00), a gold watch ($5.00), clothes ($3.00), board and room at a St Louis hotel ($19.00), telegrams (75¢ to $1.10), a draft payable to Mgr Purcell $500 [evidently a repayment], a horse at livery stable (85¢), books ($21.75), freight for a trunk of Mgr

Machebeuf ($50.25), and more, the whole coming to $2103.00, which when paid left in his account "a balance in favor of Monseigneur Lamy, $849.84."

He and Father De Smet hit it off agreeably, and it was an added advantage to have as his agent one who knew the frontier as well as anyone in America, and yet who could manage financial affairs, including international drafts, which could not be handled in Santa Fe. If Paris drafts should arrive in the absence of De Smet, they were to be processed by Lamy's old teacher Father Murphy, who described his former pupil now as "an amiable and holy prelate." The bishop now drew two hundred dollars to cover contingencies of his westward party, which consisted of twenty-one persons, and in addition, bought two carriages from Edgar's of St Louis for five hundred and ten dollars.

His plans were careful in the face of the unknown, for he was the commander of the expedition, and though he had come East over the plains, he had travelled by stage, had had no experience of the long slow travel which a waggon train would take, and fast-rolling stages had given little of the real nature of prairie life. He would go West now with a heavy heart on one particular account—one who was to have gone with him, an old friend from the days in the Middle West, Father Pendeprat, died of cholera at the Jesuit College in St Louis. Sad, the event was also ominous, for the disease was everywhere and fear of it was as prevalent.

viii.

Westward Prairies

ON 10 JULY 1852 Lamy took his party on board the steamer *Kansas* at St Louis for the long, meandering voyage on the Missouri River to Independence, where the overland trail began. The river passage would take eight or ten days, through generally flat country. Lamy lost no time in beginning to teach Spanish to his nuns as the steamer went upstream on the winding river. There were hazards which had to be planned for, on a scheduled basis. The river steamers travelled only by daylight. Lacking navigational aids of a mechanical nature, they must keep watch for sand bars, "boils," timber snags, or changes in the channel, which could not be seen by night. Further, anchoring for the night, the steamers hove to in midstream for safety, not so much from Indians as from bandits who roved the shallow banks expecting to rob passengers and cargo.

But a greater danger was at once upon the *Kansas* and her company. Cholera was aboard in epidemic proportions. Lamy's little party of teachers fell victim to it. Two days short of arriving at Independence, after six days on the river, Sister Matilda, the superior of Lamy's "little colony," died and three other sisters "were attacked by the same epidemic." Fear of contagion took hold. Lamy and all his party were ordered to leave the ship at Todd's Landing, six miles east of Independence. There, he declared, they were obliged to "lodge in an old store"—a warehouse—"stripped of its merchandise." It was the only shelter in the neighborhood, and there, "during a dark night," he told Paris, "with the mortal remains of the sister superior, and another dying, a magistrate of the nearby town [of Independence] was sent to me to forbid us from passing through town, even to bury the dead." Expenses, he said, were enormous—it was next to impossible to find draymen and others for service jobs because of their fear of the sick.

The caravan soon moved out of the warehouse and camped with tents in the woods near Independence, and there they were beaten by torrents of rain which destroyed many of their supplies and damaged some of their cargo. Lamy "lost nine of his best animals"—his two waggons were pulled by mules. The other nuns attacked by the cholera slowly recovered, but one was too weak to go on later to Santa Fe and had to be returned to St Louis, to Lamy's "great regret." He must look forward to nine hundred miles of prairie travel with his reduced party, and with two of his six teachers lost to him and the future. He was himself "very much fatigued," but his "strong constitution" had withstood the "labor and care" of his concerns. He could not help remembering that two years ago, when he had asked Bishop Odin in Galveston to visit him one day in New Mexico, Odin had replied that this would be impossible "unless he had 30,000 francs to cover travelling expenses," and now Lamy—for the benefit of the Paris Society—had to declare that from his own experience he could agree with Odin's estimate.

Toward the end of July the saddened little caravan began to organize again for the westward advance. From the camp near Todd's Landing, Lamy once again appealed for Jesuits to join him in New Mexico—again directly to the General of the order, at Rome. He spoke of De Smet, and the "generous hospitality" of the St Louis Jesuits, and he made a strong if veiled suggestion when he said that De Smet "has a particular grace for the conversion of the Indians. . . . And so I entreat you for God's glory and the salvation of souls, do all in your power to send some of your Fathers to a field where the harvest is already so ripe, but is being lost for lack of workers. . . ." In the event, Jesuits were not able to come to New Mexico for many years.

Before moving on with the westward journey, Lamy called one of the nuns, Sister Mary Magdalen, to join him for a little talk. They sat together on the bank of the Missouri River, and there he asked her to succeed Mother Matilda in the post of mother superior of the establishment he planned for Santa Fe. She agreed, subject to the approval of her motherhouse in Kentucky, and he forthwith invested her with the pectoral cross of her office, and in due course she was confirmed by Nerinckx.

Once more organized, the bishop's party moved westward again on 1 August 1852. One of the party—a Mexican priest—was still so weak that he must be carried in one of the ten waggons. They bypassed Independence, but within a few miles, an axle broke on one of the waggons, and a day was lost in making repairs. That night the open country was swept by such a storm of thunder, lightning, and wind that the party was unable to pitch tents. The women stayed all night in the waggons, which were buffeted like boats at sea by the gale, and the limitless prairie darkness was repeatedly shattered by the lightning. By dawn all was quiet if drenched, the axle was repaired, and the little train moved on. When Sunday came—8 August—they halted during the morning while the bishop said Mass and preached on charity, and the nuns renewed their vows before receiving communion. It was an act which gave them strength for the unknown which lay ahead, after all they had heard of the hazards of the prairie voyage.

Yet they were all now part of that great adventure of the time, which had its beauties and exhilarations, its curiosities and its rewards, as well as its dangers. Many a person found health itself in the open life of the trails West. The new lay everywhere about them. Where before, except upon the ocean, was such a vista to be seen? The endless grass rolled like waves under the wide movements of the air. Many chroniclers of the prairie experience used metaphors of the sea to describe their travel. Landmarks were few, and after the third day out from Independence, when they passed the one called the Lone Elm—a great solitary tree visible for miles—first voyagers had nothing ahead to measure distance by except their daily reckoning. It was those whose work took them back and forth on the trails, soldiers and traders, who came to know the lay of the land—its creeks and rivers hidden until the traveller was almost upon them, the deceptive gradual rises low enough to be lost against the level horizon yet deep enough to conceal an Indian band, the illusory watering places caused by mirages, the actual water catches so few and far between. It was an ocean of extremes, between the blasts of winter and the beating heat of summer; the splendors of the sun at rise and set, and the vacant sky by day; the simple breezes of clear weather and the searing dust storms and the electric tempests wildly playing between all horizons.

The vast land had its intimacies, too, in plant and creature life. There were creeks where thick grass grew whose edges were lined with sharp teeth which could cut when grasped. Insects abounded. Worst were the mosquitoes which came to sing and sting all night. Mosquito nets were needed, and often in the morning were heavy with dew. Horseflies tormented the hauling animals, and myriads of grasshoppers cracked underfoot and flicked through the air. Crickets came to the camp. They were uncommonly large—a soldier once measured one an inch and a half long. The travellers saw a wonderful quantity and variety of birds. There was an abundance of quail—the little birds whirred up through the steps of the mules and horses, which shied. By day meadowlarks sang, and owls hooted by night, and the bishop's party could see and hear in the wide country a marvellous variety of other birds—crows, doves, bluebirds, flickers, buntings, cowbirds which rode on the backs of the waggon mules, screaming catbirds, robins, bluebirds, high-diving hawks, plovers, thrushes, the kingbird, grouse, and even parrakeets. Of animals, the most curious were the little prairie dogs who watched passers-by from the tiny hillocks of their sandy towns. The coyote, the rabbit, the famous rattlesnake, the antelope, the deer, were all to be seen, and wild horses; though if anyone in the party sighted the solitary white stallion which roamed the plains, appearing and disappearing like someone's thought—which is all it may have been, yet one so powerful as to become a well-loved legend—no one recorded the vision. Of all animal creation, it was "those numberless ferocious animals," wrote the new Mother Superior to her sisters back home in Kentucky, "called cibolos or buffaloes" which "told us of the power and greatness of the Creator." Hunting parties returned to camp with buffalo meat. She wrote also of how for the most of one day the bishop's caravan was watched by over three hundred Indians who rode along a little distance away; never came nearer; and finally, after giving the travellers a day of uncertainty and some fear, vanished. Thereafter, the bishop ordered that they would rest in the daytime and travel by night, "as the Indians did not usually attack after dark."

On the road one day Lamy's train saw far ahead another which seemed to have halted. Overtaking it, he saw that someone from the train—it had twenty-five waggons—was being carried by Mexican teamsters into an abandoned sod hut. Lamy asked questions of others in the earlier party. This, they explained, was a merchant trader from

Santa Fe. His name was Levi Spiegelberg. Lamy knew who this was—he had already met Levi and his four brothers, whose general emporium did a thriving business in the Santa Fe Plaza. What was being done to Levi now? The Mexicans explained—they were sure he had cholera, and out of fear, they refused to travel any further with him. Lamy went to those who were carrying Levi away to leave him in the ruined hut and spoke to him.

"Good friend," he said, "we willingly make room for you in our covered waggon, and we will nurse you until you regain your strength, for we could not think of leaving you here in this lonely prairie cabin. We do not believe you have cholera, and [even] if you [have] we are not afraid of contagion."

The orders were given. Spiegelberg was taken into the bishop's train, which then moved on. In a week he was cured, and had a story to share later with his brothers—handsome and cultivated men—which bound the Spiegelbergs to Lamy in lifelong friendship.

In their slow time, they reached the Arkansas River, and crossed it safely, though the Arkansas fords were often the sites of sudden attacks by Indians, and moved on to the Cimarron River, where they paused for two days of rest. A few days later, on 14 September, about six weeks after starting out, they came to the Red River, saw horsemen, looked cautiously, and then recognized Machebeuf with an escort and fresh horses. It was a gallant welcome, still so far from Santa Fe. In three or four more days they came to an Army outpost, a fort where they slept "under a roof for the first time in two months." On the following day they came into the meadow town of Las Vegas, and the nuns had their first sight of Mexican adobe houses, clustered around a clay chapel. All went to Mass there, and at the elevation of the Host, the nuns heard what they thought was faraway thunder; but it was only the sound made by the devout Mexicans as they thumped their breasts at the sight of God's body. How foreign it all was, with men in their striped serapes, the women wrapped in their long black shawls, head and body.

The same day Machebeuf led the main party ahead to the small way station which Lamy kept at the place which long later became the railroad junction bearing his name. The bishop had matters to attend to in Las Vegas, but soon joined them for the entry into Santa Fe on 26 September. Once again this was treated as an occasion, for the arrival of Santa Fe's first nuns was something to celebrate. Writing to De Smet four days later, Lamy said "the people made them a grand reception. A great number of persons, more than a thousand, went out to meet them," and conducted them into town and through "triumphal arches" to the old cathedral of St Francis, while the bells in its twin adobe towers rang out over town. It was "a reception such as we had never seen before," reported Mother Mary Magdalen.

At the cathedral door the rural dean awaited them. Vested in surplice and stole, Vicar Ortiz offered them the asperges, and then all proceeded to the altar to sing the Te Deum to the *baile* music of violins, guitars, and drums, which was now given sacred intention by being played in a slow wailing tempo. At the end, Lamy gave his newcomers the episcopal blessing, and with that, the first move toward building his new era was made and sanctified.

The second, which followed almost at once, broke over the diocese and himself with the echoing fury of a high mountain storm.

V

THE ANTAGONISTS

1852—1856

i.

The Pastoral Letter

THE FEES WERE "ENORMOUS," Lamy exclaimed. He was referring to the
levies laid upon the New Mexicans by the priests for the occasions
which both marked the stages of life and supported the clergy. His
intention to reform abuses included this one, and he seemed to have
given it much thought during his long travels East and West during
the summer of 1852. If a couple asked to be married they were charged
from twenty to twenty-five piastres (a coin, or its equivalent in goods,
equal to the Mexican peso, then worth more than ten of today's United
States dollars). If they wanted a child baptized, the fee was one and
a half piastres. If they must bury the dead, each interment cost sixteen
piastres. In the pathetic values of most families such fees in the aggregate of a lifetime's pious needs amounted to a fortune. What was
more, the native clergy kept for themselves most of such revenue, and
made extraordinary charges for other occasions—there was that pastor
who said Mass only once a year for his people and then charged eighteen dollars for it. Again, the collection of "tithes" yielded money
equivalents for the diocese of Durango, yet with a great share retained
by the local clergy. The worst of penalties were imposed upon people
who refused to pay, or simply could not: they were deprived of the
spiritual formalities without which they believed their lives were not
blessed.

The problem for Lamy was, accordingly, in part ethical, in part
practical. In the first place, the Church was the most wanted of institutions among the New Mexicans; it was one designed to serve human
good, and Lamy was committed to this purpose; but if it was to function, it must be supported materially. In the second place, how could
material support best be obtained? He would always receive some aid
from Paris—but by no means all that was needed. The rest of it must
come from the direct beneficiaries of the Church—the people. He

must bring them whatever relief he thought just, he must ask for some share of their goods for the continued support of the whole of his diocese (Durango's share no longer existed) and even like his predecessor, he must impose firm means of insuring such support. As he worked toward his solution for the problem in the autumn of 1852, it became clear that the people must gain by it, and the clergy lose their direct control of their benefices which they had abused and enjoyed through custom so long established as to seem a vested personal right.

Once he knew in detail what he would command, he gave it substance in his first pastoral letter, to be read in all the churches as soon as possible. Printed as a pamphlet for distribution, and appearing in the columns of the *Gaceta de Santa Fe* for 1 January 1853, it confirmed what he had verbally announced in part on other occasions. It revealed his own character even as he devised that of the reforms he proposed.

Addressing his "much beloved brothers," he began his letter by reminding all of his establishment of the school for boys, and the convent school for girls. Both schools, especially the new one for girls, had not yet called for great expense, compared to those which had been needed for repair of the old garrison chapel of the *Castrense*. Whatever had been undertaken so far was for the spiritual and temporal good of the faithful of the territory, and for the seemliness of divine worship. Let all put their trust in God, who knew the purity of "our intention," without which nothing could prosper; and at the same time let it be hoped that the faithful would take advantage of opportunity now given them to give their children a decent and religious education; for "the greatest heritage which parents could leave their children is a good education which is worth far more than the most brilliant success, since riches without education do more harm than good."

Now, therefore, continued the pastoral letter, the bishop judged it suitable at this time to publish the ensuing regulations which would take effect on New Year's Day 1853—the following week. In effect, the costs for church services would be reduced approximately by two thirds: eight piastres for a wedding, one for a baptism, six for a burial. Moreover, for those who could not pay in full, they could pay half at one time, the rest later.

So far, so good, for the laity.

The next regulations were aimed at the clergy. What was now required made plain what had been amiss before.

When requested to conduct particular services or ceremonies, each pastor would respond according to his discretion; sung Masses would be conducted as usual, except that the pastor was not to receive any recompense *before* the day of the service, and the same provision would apply to all other services. The pastor henceforth would say Mass once a month on any convenient day of the week in every chapel which was more than three miles from the parish church and which had a neighborhood of thirty families. (This had never been observed before.) The pastor's share of the parish revenues was now *lowered to one fourth,* which would provide an appropriate and decent subsistence for the holy ministry. Knowing the poor state of the church buildings, the new regulations reserved another quarter of the total revenue for their restoration and for those furnishings so necessary to the proper offering of divine worship; but such funds would be expended *under the bishop's supervision.* Knowing also the costliness and scarcity of candles in the territory, the poorest persons and areas were dispensed from the use of candles in the holy services.

After the compassion and realism implied in such new rules, the bishop hoped, in his letter, that the faithful would approve of his use of the church revenues for the decent maintenance of the bishop and the clergy, the proper observance of divine service, and the establishment of schools—all to be supported by the system of tithes long established in Catholic countries by Vatican decree. True enough, there was no civil law to compel anyone to pay his share of these; but Catholics properly instructed in the obligations of their religion knew that they were required in conscience to give in proportion to the gifts they had received from Almighty God, and all were under the obligation to obey the Church in this matter as in others. Satisfaction was to be taken from the knowledge that in the past year the greater part of the faithful had met their obligation, and it was hoped that the few who had failed to do so would not oblige the imposition of severe penalties for their disobedience. But if anyone persisted in ignoring this law of the Church, and the ecclesiastical authority, he would, as heretofore, and with great pain and regret, be denied the sacraments, and be regarded as outside the fold.

Those difficult specifics firmly established, the bishop must proceed to matters more general in the society, for he was responsible before God for the souls of "his much beloved brothers," and he would fail in his duty if he did not in all loving-kindness bring up certain scandals which were most common in the territory.

"I wish to speak," he wrote, "of divorce, dances, and gambling."

He hoped that no one would take in bad part his admonitions, for which he would draw freely from the Gospels. Therefore:

No matter what was permitted by man's own laws, divine law taught, concerning matrimony, that "whom God hath joined let no man put asunder" (Matthew 19:6). Further, said the bishop, those who did not keep the conjugal fidelity promised in the sight of heaven and earth could not hope for a happy life, or anything but divine punishment. As for dances, he proceeded (now touching on a local indulgence whose disorder was a scandal to all foreign observers), they were conducive to evil, occasions of sin, and provided opportunities for illicit affinities, and love that was reprehensible and sinful, and—citing the exhortations of St Francis de Sales—were a recreation closer to paganism than to Christianity; in fact, a school of immorality and vice. How many persons who habitually frequented this profane diversion had lost their fear of God, their innocence, their honor?

Concerning the way gambling was practiced here, unworthy of any Christian, it was "absolutely and essentially evil and reprehensible," and for such reason prohibited by both civil and Church laws. Let it be remembered that Sarah, that holy woman, when proclaiming her innocence before God, declared, "You know, Lord, that I have never trafficked with gamblers."

Then, "much beloved brothers, let us conclude with the Apostle," he wrote finally, arranging excerpts from Ephesians 4: 27–31. "Neither give place to the Devil. Let him that stole steal no more . . . let him work with his hands that which is good. . . . Let no corrupt communication proceed out of your mouth, but that which is good to the use of edifying, that it may minister grace unto the hearers. . . . Let all bitterness, and wrath, and anger, and clamour, and evil speaking, be put away from you, with all malice." And I Corinthians 6: 9—"Be not deceived, neither fornicators," he quoted, and then adjusted the text to his hearers, "nor adulterers, nor highwaymen, nor those given to drinking, nor blasphemers, nor thieves, shall inherit the kingdom of God . . . therefore glorify God in your body."

"We direct that this pastoral letter shall be published in all the parishes on the Sunday after it has been received," stated the printed circular, and it ended, "Given at Santa Fe, Feast of the Nativity, 1852," and was signed, "✠ *Juan, Vicario Apostolico de Nuevo Mejico.*"

ii.

Rebellion

THE DUTIFUL, clear, firm pastoral message was like a hot coal touched to a fuse, and the explosion was immediate. On reading Lamy's words, Dean Ortiz forthwith ordered him out of his house—the "bishop's palace" into which the rectory had been turned so grandly in August. Where must he go? Lamy had no other house but the "Frenchman's house." A small corner of it would do for him. But there was a more serious issue—Lamy believed that the principal church should be his cathedral, and this was where Ortiz had presided since the 1830s. Surely the rectory would belong to the cathedral, and the bishop must have a right to residence there?

But no. Ortiz furiously declared that the house was his personal property.

But how could this be? On parish land?

It was his, Ortiz insisted, because he had bought it years ago from Bishop Zubiría, and he had a deed to prove it.

If so, this was inconvenient; for at the same time as he published the explosive pastoral letter, Lamy made known his official decision to divide the parish of Santa Fe, keeping one half to administer himself, and designating the old parish church of St Francis as the cathedral. As a gesture of fairness, he offered Ortiz the other half of the divided parish.

Nursing his rage, Ortiz refused, stating that he was the *parochus proprius,* the established life pastor of the whole parish, and that no one had the right to deprive him of this status. On the same day as Lamy's proposal, he gathered all his close friends in a crowd—"most of them corrupt in every aspect," as Machebeuf said, for they included the native priests under discipline by the bishop. In a troupe they came to Lamy's house, crying, shouting, threatening to chase him out of town; and only fear of the civil authorities, who were Anglo-American, kept them from outright violence. When Lamy tried to explain to the mob his policy concerning the parish division, Ortiz cried that he would not accept it—he would rather give up everything than accept such an insult. At last the mob dispersed, and Ortiz and

Gallegos spent the next week in composing elaborate complaints against Lamy to be signed by selected citizens and in due time to be forwarded to Pius IX. A general, now open, controversy was ablaze with all the enraged vitality of which the old dean was capable, and countered with all the formidable calm in Lamy's nature.

As for the deed to the rectory, Lamy asked to see it, and when Ortiz complied, it was to show only a very small scrap of paper on which a few lines, supposedly written by "a priest who claimed to be authorized by Mgr of Durango, in 1831 or 1832 . . . gave everything to Ortiz." The land—"much land"—attached to the parish church was sold to Ortiz "for 300 sheep" which "he was supposed to give [i.e., return to the church] after his death or his resignation." By this act there was scarcely enough land left on which to build a new rectory. Consulting local residents, Lamy was told that the people of Santa Fe were witnesses that the property had belonged to the church of St Francis since the foundation of the missions; the dean's present claim "astonished" them all. In the same manner as the affair of the parish church, Ortiz had acquired personal possession of the ancient chapel of San Miguel. Everyone in Santa Fe, said Lamy, considered the whole thing a mystery. He himself assumed that Zubiría at Durango had been misinformed in whatever transaction took place, and that the church properties were lost through misunderstanding.

He did his best to propitiate and recompense Ortiz, now offering him more than half of the parish area for his lifetime, a pension, and one of the houses which he had built on other church land; but instead of accepting any arrangement from Lamy, the dean demanded thirteen thousand dollars of him, which of course was out of the question. Lamy was offered—by whom is not clear, but probably by a Santa Fean who remained loyal to Ortiz—the three hundred sheep which was the [originally] arranged price, but the bishop said, "I have refused to accept them as I do not think the sale was legitimate." He believed he must finally resort to a lawsuit to regain the disputed properties.

For the moment, however, Lamy thought that patience and belief in the right would serve him better in the end than legal measures, and himself took the lower portion of the parish which he had offered to Ortiz. The *Castrense* was well enough restored for him to use it as his diocesan church. He left St Francis and its properties to Ortiz, and the parish division became, if not satisfying to either, firmly in effect.

After the pastoral letter, in which the native clergy had seen their habits, customs, and privileges attacked outright by its every implication of strict reform, they were more than ready to oppose Lamy, and Ortiz in his fury was girded to lead them. Some of them were already disposed to challenge the bishop—those whom he had suspended from their duties after earnest warnings about their ways of life. One of these was the pastor of Albuquerque, who had continued his inadmissible indulgences while Lamy was in the East. Another was D. B. Salazar, pastor of Santa Clara, who, said Machebeuf, was "so guilty that he did not reply with even one word to charges of almost daily drunkenness and adultery." The bishop had charitably reinstated him to give him another chance, but Salazar fell at once into "his old vices," and Machebeuf fully expected him to be struck dead at the foot of the altar "on pronouncing the opening words of the Mass" (*O God, sustain my cause; give me redress against a race that knows no piety; save me from a treacherous foe and cruel*).

Another, the Santa Fe priest José de Jesús Lujan, had long previously received censure from Zubiría. Lamy, in his early months in Santa Fe, learned that Lujan was "living in a most scandalous manner, keeping a very young and beautiful married woman in his house." Her husband would come and plead with her to come home, and even went to the bishop for help, but Lujan refused to send her back where she belonged, even when Lamy ordered him to do so. Lujan, instead, sneered at Lamy as a hypocrite and worse, and the bishop suspended him for two years. But the great need for curates soon obliged Lamy to send him off to another parish whose pastor had died; yet no sooner there than Lujan sent for his mistress again—though he took the precaution of lodging her next door to his own house. When the pastoral letter reached him, Father Lujan refused to read it to his people. Lamy ordered him directly to do so, sending Machebeuf to hand it to him already "all unfolded" at Mass; but Machebeuf was met with insults. The bishop promptly suspended Lujan. Along with Ortiz, Gallegos, and the famous pastor of Taos, Antonio José Martínez, Lujan signed a letter of protest to Lamy about his division of the cathedral parish. Two other curates—Jesús Baca and Antonio Otero—resigned immediately on receiving the pastoral letter, and went about declaring that they had been deprived of their parishes. Lamy gave them a month to reconsider. Neither did so. With that, Lamy formally suspended them also.

By then, Ortiz had refused his services to the vicar apostolic, and, equipped with the written accusations to send to the Pope, had "departed resentfully" for Durango. He would be absent from Santa Fe for two years.

Since 1839, when Lamy came to Ohio, and 1851, when he went to New Mexico and began to comprehend the daunting dimensions of the land and its astonishing social problems, he had had plenty of experience of obstacles and difficulties; but these were of an impersonal kind and in facing them he neither gave nor felt enmity. But now he encountered hatred which was pointed straight at him. As it was induced by his view of his duty under divine and Canon Law, it obliged him to spare none who would oppose that. But the energies released by the enmities which now divided New Mexico represented two ideas of justice, both sincere.

The New Mexicans saw themselves as victims of a complicated set of oppressions—those left in the wake of the 1846 war; the increasing dominance of their lives and ways by the fast-growing commercial power of the plains traders and settlers from the East; the separation of their religious character from its original center in Durango; and now the invasion by still another set of foreigners who respected almost nothing of the local nature and who indeed could scarcely speak its language. What right had anyone—so the passionate New Mexicans felt—to despise their mode of life and impose rigors upon it quite foreign to its habit?

On the other hand, Lamy, in his rectitude deeply rooted in the ancient faith and discipline of provincial Europe, could not condone what made mockery of the very sacraments of matrimony, ordination, and penance. If at first his touch was light, it grew firm as he worked to turn his new people and their priests away from their accustomed path; but it was the new direction he demanded, not its mode, which gave rise to the two images of justice to the territory at the outset of 1853. Both sides inevitably insisted that justice could have only one. The initial clashes led to stubbornly held positions.

With Ortiz gone, the leadership against the bishop fell to others, whether among clergy or laymen. The initiative came from an unexpected quarter, on a surprising pretext.

During Lamy's absence of the previous year, Machebeuf, leaving the capital to the unresponsive local clergy, had spent his time and services among the people of the outlying districts. First of all, he kept an eye on Albuquerque, where Father Gallegos was going his own way; but in general visiting the pueblos of the middle Rio Grande Valley and the *ranchos* and other village settlements of the river country he found so beautiful. He said Mass, preached, administered the sacraments, entered into the territorial life with his simple gaiety and came to know local affairs intimately—so intimately that when these scandalized the Church, he worked to set them straight.

Now, suddenly, in January 1853, these works of his became the means through which certain powerful laymen decided to assail the bishop. The first onslaught, significantly enough, was led by a brother-in-law of the vanished rural dean. This was Francisco Tomás Baca, of Peña Blanca, who became the spokesman of the ranchers downriver from Santa Fe in a savage attack upon Machebeuf.

Citizens of the parish of Cochiti/Santo Domingo—an area which included the Indian villages so named, and principally the settlement of Peña Blanca, which contained important families—sent Lamy a bill of complaints against Machebeuf accusing him of neglect. How they suffered for want of a regular pastor since the death of the previous one! Machebeuf came, stayed only briefly, and went; and "since he is such a wide traveller," the spiritual needs of the people were neglected. "He is no sooner here, than he is already at Taos, Mora, San Miguel, Albuquerque, or elsewhere." Worse, even when he tarried in Peña Blanca, he seemed to think his only duty was to harangue his hearers on the Fifth Commandment, that was, to dwell on money matters, "as if this was the only obligation for the faithful." Then came the most shocking accusation—that if Machebeuf touched on "other matters it was to reveal the secrets of the confessional."

No graver charge could be brought, and the petitioners made more of it than of their other complaints, such as that he compared them to "all kinds of savage animals, who work only for their temporal life and not for spiritual ends." They had been forced to tolerate his actions only by their respect for the priesthood, and certainly not for any personal respect "for the man," who used his "hurried visits" chiefly to "amass" levies, "harvests, really," of tithes, within the space of twenty-four hours before dashing on elsewhere. Unless they were granted a resident pastor, they predicted a great falling away of the faithful, and they asked Lamy for one, saying "we do expect Your Lordship seriously to consider this, our just application, even though the information might possibly be disagreeable" to him.

Lamy instantly responded. His letter in reply was both frigidly correct and wrathful. Before speaking to the presentation and accusation "against the Vicar Don José P. Machebeuf," he wrote on 14 January, "it is necessary to see what kind of defense he can make in his own behalf, since such matters are of themselves so very grave that they would seem to require juridical proof; and until such time as I am given proofs of what lies behind your demands, I shall consider the presentation as a calumny of the most malicious kind that could ever be made against the character of any priest; and accordingly, it shall be my duty to punish such persons who have made such accusations," and he signed himself, omitting the usual blessing, with "Adiós! Your friend and Vicar Apostolic, Juan Lamy."

His anger brought a change in tone in the correspondence, for two days later, Baca, now revealed as the principal spokesman, hurried to say that Lamy had "not quite understood the petition," which was not meant as a "direct accusation" against Machebeuf but only as "a request for a resident pastor." Calling on all the Hispanic talent for legalistic niceties and obfuscations, Baca hastened to add that as soon as the bishop gave him opportunity prescribed by Canon Law, "and counting on the obvious intelligence" of His Lordship, if he required proofs, he was prepared to proceed, if only to prevent "the slandering of any priest," and further "to prevent the threatened punishment upon those who subscribed to the letter." He therefore would ask only that the bishop address himself solely to "the said two points in question"—presumably the request for a pastor, and opportunity under Canon Law to testify further.

To this Lamy replied promptly, demanding answers "to the following questions: first, when and where was the violation of the seal of the confessional made?; second: to whom was it made?; third: what things were revealed?; fourth: the name of the person whose sins were thus revealed? Send me the answers, with proofs, as soon as possible. Adiós."

A few days later, Lamy wrote again to Baca, stating that his vicar general could justify himself in the face of the accusations made against him, once proofs were submitted. "Then we will have finished with this business!" Lamy then attempted to close the correspondence: "Now permit me to inform you that when it will be necessary to write me, I will so advise you. I will have great pleasure in receiving any of your letters," but, he could not forbear to add in the face of Baca's wrangling rhetoric, "please write in easier style." Yet more, and now sternly, "And please do not interfere with or meddle with the operation of my administration but say and write only what pertains to the case in point."

For Baca had also castigated the bishop for his suspensions of certain curates, and Lamy reproved him forcefully: "The priests who have been suspended by me, as you yourself should well know, were dismissed because they well deserved ecclesiastical censures, by reason of grave faults well known throughout the Territory. How then can you accuse me of having punished some priests without proof, and without having received any information except that given in simple conversation?" Lamy expressed regret that "a gentleman of good education and honor as I think you are" did not quickly dismiss such ideas against the bishop's administration. "I don't remember ever having given you offense on any occasion; and I hope that from now on you will not oblige me to instruct you as I have. . . . I can assure you that I don't have any resentment against you, but I believe you have written as you have under some sort of presuppositions."

If this last statement was a quiet suggestion that Baca was further-

ing the enmity of his brother-in-law Ortiz against Lamy, Baca was
quick to answer (even though not invited to do so) that his acts had
"not originated from an ecclesiastic," and went on for many pages in
his old style to elaborate, and veil, yet restate the charges, and the
requests, now with a tone of "the highest respect," while pointing out
the difficulty of offering the sort of "proof which is given before a
certain class of authority, be it civil or ecclesiastical," and not exclud-
ing the possibility that the charges could be seen in certain contexts
"as malicious"—and such, and more, even to the point of stating that
since the original petition, other papers had come into his hands which
(so Baca now advised Lamy with the air of an ally) should lead the
bishop to "demand proofs" for the good of the particular person
against whom new charges had been made.

But nobody was deceived, for Baca soon enough returned to press
the original charges against Machebeuf, and even, when the vicar
general came to Peña Blanca on his rounds, refused the sacraments,
"and seemed . . . to be quite opinionated." As for an "easier style,"
Baca in a later letter said that his temperament being as it was, "I
will never be able to use any other kind of language," and again
denied being influenced by anything but his own feelings, "written
without any kind of persuasions."

He was almost finished with his stream of letters; but before he was
done he felt obliged to report that Machebeuf, while staying at Peña
Blanca as his house guest, sounded a defiance in which he had offended
the people of Peña Blanca, against whom he directed all of his sermon,
and had used these words:

"Since you want to threaten me with presentations to the bishop,
let me tell you this; that he and I grew up together; that we were
ordained together; that we have missioned together in the United
States; and that he knows me well, and this for many years; and as
a consequence, the Bishop never does anything without first consulting me . . ." Baca drew the fine point that this was unseemly because
among the listeners were some who did *not* agree with those who
signed the original petition against Machebeuf, who was therefore
attacking such citizens unjustly. He then renewed accusations of the
betrayal of confession, citing cases—Machebeuf publicly, from the
altar, referred to information about a ten-year-old boy, and matters
concerning a man who had lived in incestuous adultery with a sister-
in-law, and another irregular marriage case, and a case of a man who
hadn't been to confession for eight years; all of whom, being absolved
in confession, were then publicly commented on by Machebeuf, who
rejoiced for their restorations to grace in such a way that all knew to
whom he referred.

How, then, could that of which he spoke been known to him except under the seal of confession? Moreover, Baca went on, if Machebeuf was so sure that the charges against him were slanders, why did he take steps to incite others to write to the bishop in his defense? If Machebeuf was as close to Lamy as he claimed, and if they acted as one, and if His Lordship did not intend to "administer carefully" the scandals under discussion, then he would have to be considered guilty of "wilfulness and arbitrariness" for which he would be held responsible; and if misfortunes should occur, as seemed likely, in consequence, then—Baca now made a significant threat—"we shall have to appeal to higher powers, in behalf of the faithful whom I might have to represent." Upon which, in closing, Baca offered all his consideration and respect, as the bishop's servant and most attentive friend, who kissed His Lordship's hands.

Lamy was, then, served notice that serious representations would probably be made against him to Rome.

In the following month, another powerful antagonist was in the forefront of spreading struggle. Martínez, the pastor of Taos, wrote to Lamy making "the gravest accusations" against Machebeuf, again having to do with betraying the confessional. On his return from a mission journey, Lamy showed the letter to Machebeuf, who at once replied to Martínez, cited cases, and declared that all which might have been learned in the confessional had already been given to him in ordinary discussion—even, in some cases, in the presence of others; and furthermore, that all the matters discussed were common knowledge. If the people had put two and two together, and concluded that what they knew anyway had also been confided in confession, it was the common knowledge which had made revelations, not himself, even when he publicly rejoiced that certain sinners had come to grace.

It was a measure of Martínez's general intelligence that he promptly wrote Lamy saying, "I remain satisfied with what Señor Machebeuf answered," though this was not by any means the end of the opposition which existed in Taos, for it was not long before Martínez was again assaulting Machebeuf and the bishop with charges that various suspensions of the clergy had been made by Machebeuf, in Lamy's absence, for the purpose of obtaining for himself the benefices belonging to the suspended curates. What was more, Machebeuf, though he obviously regarded himself as "very persuasive" in his sermons, actually only seemed "to annoy and bother his hearers," which did not produce "the necessary good fruits or results," and in fact, he might well have tried to be "more moderate in his approach, according to the ordinary rules of oratory." If such rules existed, they were essentially foreign to Machebeuf's spontaneous temperament. While notarized depositions against Machebeuf poured forth from Taos, Martínez went on to execrate him in the affair of the parish of Albuquerque and its popular pastor, Don José Manuel Gallegos, which would soon come to full boil as the most notorious event of the next two years.

Meanwhile, no matter how violent and demanding the agitations of the outlying parishes, Lamy had other matters which also required his attention, and Santa Fe itself was lively in its own traditional ways.

iii.

Diocesan See

THE UNITED STATES SECRETARY of the Territory believed that half the population could not read their catechisms or write their names. How could they make their own laws with any intelligence? "It was," he observed, "always the policy of Spain and Mexico to keep her people in ignorance, and so far as New Mexico was concerned, they seem to have carried out the system with singular faithfulness . . . the education of females has, if anything, been more neglected than that of the males . . ." However, "a slight change for the better has taken place, in an educational point of view, since the country fell into the hands of the United States. The boarding and day schools at Santa Fe, under the care of Bishop Lamy, will, in time, produce a good effect in the Territory. . . ."

Lamy himself reported to Purcell that "the school of the sisters and that for the boys are doing pretty well," and showed signs of increasing. The convent school of Our Lady of Light opened in January 1853 with ten boarders and twenty-two day students. In both boys' and girls' schools, the pupils were "instructed in ancient and modern languages, music, drawing, and other branches of a useful and polite education." Instruction in religion and decorum was allied to all the other subjects. The sisters were planning to establish an asylum for orphans. The majority of pupils in the boys' school came from among the poor. Looking to the future, Lamy watched for "children showing signs of ecclesiastical vocation."

For he saw that the present critical need for priests would extend far into the years ahead, and he never ceased working to find them, near or far. He believed the prospects for missions among the Indians were good, but the expenses were "enormous," because of the great distance of the territory from any other, and from one Indian locality to the next. In that spring, the vicariate had resources of sixty-five thousand francs, and expenses of eighty-eight thousand. It was clear that he must live in debt for years. De Smet replied to an appeal for Jesuits that none was available, and was obliged to dun the bishop for bills due in St Louis for everything from waggons, carpets, medicines, and a watch to chalices, ciboriums, and a piano. But Lamy thought that if the Paris Society would repeat last year's subsidy of twenty thousand francs, he could hope to be out of debt in two or three years. It was a hope never to be fulfilled. He wondered, too, if he might "borrow" two priests from Purcell; the present need was made the more acute by the suspension or defection of so many of the small band of native clergy, a number of whom had, like Ortiz, departed for Durango. Purcell was unable to comply.

The need, the whole climate amongst the clergy, were more agitating than ever. In Easter week, six or seven of the remaining clergy held a meeting against the bishop, and sent him a letter which four of them signed. They proclaimed their open insubordination, and announced that henceforth they would consider "null" any act of his administration. Further, they intended to appeal to "superior authority"—by which they meant the Vatican. Lamy was sorry they chose to desert him, for, as he wrote Zubiría, into whose jurisdiction so many had fled, "up to the present time I have treated them not as inferiors but as equals," but added, "I can not tolerate their foolishness any more." He informed His Lordship of Durango that if their claims ever reached Rome, the Holy See would already know the true circumstances of the whole affair, for he had himself already sent full reports concerning it, and his information would be seconded by "several bishops, three archbishops, and a Jesuit"; the last-named was De Smet, who would be in Rome that spring.

Lamy wrote also in detail to Purcell, describing the whole sequence of events since the rebellion of the clergy had broken out early in the year. Fully informed, Purcell (one of his supporting archbishops) would, he hoped, use his "great influence" on his behalf by writing to counter whatever might reach Rome from the insurgent priests. If only he had even "three or four Spanish priests"—and he still had hopes of some Jesuits. Could not Purcell lend him "for two years" two priests, or even two advanced seminarians? To find more of such help, he planned to go to Europe as soon as he felt it prudent to leave Santa Fe.

He wrote in similar vein to Cardinal Barnabo, now the Prefect of the Sacred Congregation of the Propaganda Fide in Rome, warning him that the Mexican dissidents would try to make their case against him there in a "highly florid style *(un style bien fleuri),*" adding, "I thought it prudent to inform Your Eminence on this matter, so that if their complaints ever reached the Holy See, you would be informed already, and from a good source, as to how these things happened, and that the critical circumstances I was in and the abuses I witnessed obliged me to be severe and to interpret the ecclesiastical law in favor of order and religion. As God has witness, I have experienced a great sorrow, but my duty and my conscience have forced me to take these measures. Now I hope that Your Eminence will do me the honor of examining my motives, and if I must depend on your protection, I ask that it be available to me."

He wrote also to another of his archbishops—Archbishop Francis Patrick Kenrick, at Baltimore, who not only wrote to Rome in his support, but used Lamy's facts as "another reason why there should be created an Episcopal See in the city of Santa Fe, and that the illustrious Prelate be invested with full powers and authority, as was also the opinion of the Plenary Council" held in Baltimore a year before. It was not yet known in America, but Santa Fe, with Lamy confirmed as its bishop, had already been raised to the full status of a diocese by Pius IX on 29 July 1853.

Before that news reached Santa Fe and Durango, Ortiz, at Durango, had sent a "folio" of documents to Rome containing letters of accusation against Lamy. Not trusting matters so vital to the regular mails in which they could so easily be lost, he dispatched them by way of Archbishop Clementi, the apostolic delegate at Mexico City. But the self-exiled rural dean of Santa Fe and his fellow dissidents could not have been as happy in their reception by Zubiría as they surely expected to be, for Lamy reported to Baltimore that they had been "coldly received" at Durango.

At home, the awkward issue of tithes was still making trouble. Though the system had been in effect long before Lamy's time, and Lamy's only offense to the clergy was to halt their abuses of it, and reduce the parish tariffs and terms of payment, his enemies behaved as if he himself had invented the very idea of tithing.

The scandal over the issue became general, and non-Catholic settlers from the East had their views about it. They regarded the institution of tithing as an offense. A heavy burden fell on the poor people, and some had refused payment. It was commonly believed that the diocesan collection amounted to eighteen thousand dollars a year, some of it received in kind; that an agent who made the collections was paid fifteen per cent for his work; that the bishop retained half, and that the other half was divided between payment to the priests and expenses of repairing and maintaining the churches. A newcomer admitted that the bishop did not spend his portion in "sumptuous and extravagant living" but used a great amount of it for the upkeep of the religious properties of Santa Fe.

A native who defied the tithing rule outright was one of Lamy's tormentors—once again, Baca of Peña Blanca. In May the bishop wrote to him:

Dear Sir: having been informed by one of my collectors that you have as yet not completely paid up the different parts which correspond to tithing, it is now my duty and obligation to inform you that as long as you obstinately refuse to pay your just debts, I cannot then allow any priest whatsoever to celebrate Mass in your private chapel at Peña Blanca.

Baca's reply was extraordinarily insolent in tone, but it stated a view held by many:

Monsignor: I have before me your note of the 17th of the present month of May, and so in adequate response, let me say to Your Lordship: that it is now and will be my firm resolve not to pay any kind of tithing fee, as long as it is demanded of me as some sort of contract payable by me for spiritual administration, the present powers of which may well be within the powers of a Catholic bishop; and this being so I see no reason to worry about the same; since, for over a year now, we have been given bad administration; and so I now beseech and even advise you, first to consult what you owe to your own conscience, for I suspect there is some prejudice in Your Lordship against my own family. Therefore, let Your Most Illustrious Lordship quit your vengeful censures. Though you use such reprehensible means to force me to make your plans effective, first with your now usual threats, and then later with your denial of spiritual ministrations, such procedures, let me inform Your Illustrious Lordship, don't impress me in the very least; not only because of the notorious injustice which the Monsignor [Lamy] habitually uses in these serious matters, but also because the sheer mercy [to] and piety of all Christians do not depend on the blatant use of absolute power that your Lordship commands, as I've learned from others of the Faithful in New Mexico.

He signed himself in the full panache of his heritage, "Francisco Tomás Cabeza de Baca."

But as summer deepened, Lamy thought he detected a lessening of hostility. Even if "serious difficulties" remained between him and the clergy, he thought the laymen's movement against him was losing vigor, and he told Purcell that "the vast majority in the territory is in our favor." In early autumn he received the official word that Santa Fe had been raised to the rank of a bishop's seat, and he hoped this would "give the last blow to any opposition" when he should publish the news. An incoming territorial governor, Meriwether of Kentucky, who was received at Santa Fe with a Te Deum sung by the bishop in thanksgiving for his safe arrival—an "imposing ceremony" which he had never seen before—said that Lamy was "most deservedly popular in this town," though the new governor saw also a great deal of hostility between certain factions of the American and Mexican populations.

Meriwether soon saw how things stood concerning Indians. There had been a United States Army battle against Apaches north of Santa Fe a few months before his arrival in which the soldiers had been defeated with heavy losses. Mexican shepherds were in constant danger from Indian raiders. Meriwether officially recommended to the Indian Office at Washington that the Indians should either be impartially fed and clothed to a certain extent or chastised decisively. Neither course was followed. The suspenseful combination of general Indian unrest broken by periodic outbreaks prevailed.

But the Indians soon had their own view of Lamy. He wrote to Paris about a recent event which touched him. "Our good Indians are of a primitive simplicity. Lately a few chiefs [presumably from various pueblos] came to visit me." He showed them the chapel of the Loretto sisters—"a simple room with a few decorations"—liturgical objects—which he had brought from the recent Baltimore trip, and they were astonished. They knelt and asked if they might touch the sacred articles with their lips. The bishop gave each of them a medal and a rosary, "but then I saw on their faces that they were still expecting something, so I asked them to tell me what they wished for." One of them said to him in Spanish,

"Grandfather, Father of prayer, we came from far to see you, we are hungry, and therefore you must give us bread to go back to our family."

The bishop replied,

"I am poor, but I will try to give you some provisions."

"You poor!" said the chief. "See the beautiful red robe you wear"—pointing to the bishop's cassock—"while we are scarcely covered with scraps of fur. . . ."

Long later, Lamy's nephew Hippolyte, reminiscing about his uncle, said that Indians regarded him highly—"for them, he was the Great Captain."

As always, Santa Fe remained a city with its own special character; and when strangers were not noticing the Indians who came and went, they were making observations on the local morality, which offered enlivening differences—in public, certainly—from the customs of the Atlantic coast. Immigrants from that quarter were fluent in their descriptions and judgements of the Santa Fe society.

At mid-nineteenth century, "the people of New Mexico," noted the United States territorial secretary, "have never received moral training, in the American sense of the word." They had been allowed to grow up from infancy to manhood without being taught that it was wrong to indulge in vicious habits, and he particularized: the standard of female chastity was "deplorably low"; prostitution was carried to a fearful extent; it was quite common for parents to "sell their daughters for money to gratify the lust of the purchaser." The catalogue, as evidence, supported Lamy's findings, and his ameliorative efforts. Gambling flourished, and its presiding professional in Santa Fe was Señora Gertrudes Barcelo, a native of Taos. She made such a success of her work that she became a member of the city's best society. When she died during Lamy's early days in New Mexico, mortuary honors were heaped upon her and the high style of her funeral scandalized an Anglican bishop who later happened to be in Santa Fe and heard about it. He told his diary that the funeral of this "notorious prostitute and gambler [was] utterly disgraceful to Bishop Lamy," for "she was buried with great pomp. Streets swept clean, grand procession. Bishop's bill on record in court . . . amounting to $1597." Though done in Lamy's name, the obsequies, according to later evidence, seemed to have been the work of Ortiz, the rural dean.

Other spectacles also interested newcomers. The daily market in the plaza was lively. Country ranchers and Indians from the pueblos brought their produce to sell in town, displayed it under the porticoes of the plaza, and sat all day by their wares. They strung their meat on lines attached to the pillars of the *portales,* put their vegetables in rows on the ground, in season offered daily bundles of fresh-cut hay weighing twelve pounds at twelve and a half cents per sheaf. The shoppers could find mutton, a pig, "red peppers, beans, onions . . . enormous . . . milk, bread, cheese, and in the proper season, grapes, wild plums, and wild berries." Winter brought fresh game shot in the mountains above town—venison, turkeys, even bear. At the Exchange Hotel the family-style table was spread with such provisions, and even, at times, "luxuries." On Sundays crowds gathered to watch cock fights, with the glaring birds cheered on by everyone from beggar to priest.

Amidst all this local style, New Mexicans, like Americans everywhere in their time, hoped for the coming of the great quickener of the national life—the railroad. Even in the early 1850s the New Mexico territorial assembly asked that a memorial be laid before the House of Representatives in Congress "in favor of the establishing of a national railroad from the Mississippi River to the Pacific Ocean." The memorial "very briefly gave the reasons why the road in question should be located so as to pass through New Mexico." First, New Mexico was centrally positioned and would be a connecting point with several western lines; second, construction would be cheap as the track need not cross "a single elevation"; third, the New Mexico route would never be "impeded by snow"; and finally, the region had an abundance of "stone coal" for locomotives. The memorial hoped also that the electric telegraph could be constructed across New Mexico. The petition was referred to the Committee on Printing. Lamy himself said in June 1853, "There is great talk of the Pacific railroad, and some hopes that it will run through New Mexico. Then"—he was writing to Purcell—"you might come and see our beautiful mountains, and breathe purest kind of air. . . ." (Almost three decades were to pass before the tracks would come that way.)

Meanwhile, Santa Fe was animated by other than mechanical means. All people took pleasure to one or another degree from ceremony; but the Mexicans of Santa Fe, in their world-remoteness, poverty, and innate public style, responded perhaps more than others to the delights of spectacle. The ancient rituals of the Church had been locally enfeebled for generations. Lamy now gave demonstrations in the streets of the city of the veneration owed by Catholics to the very heart of their faith. Spectacle alone may have moved some of the populace, but for the great majority, what was within outward form began to be reawakened in meaning. Writing to Purcell, Lamy gave a simple account of how all responded.

Sunday within the octave of Corpus Christi [1853] we had a solemn procession of the Blessed Sacrament. the weather was beautiful, the streets had been well cleaned, and before every house and store where the Blessed Sacrament was to pass, they had put ornaments of every kind. the Americans who have fine stores most all round *la plaza* were not behind the Mexicans, they showed a fine spirit. Seven beautiful repositorys had been made in different places, and at each one I had to stop with the Blessed Sacrament. I had deacon and subdeacon with a master of ceremony for the procession. the choir composed of ten small Mexican boys and their two teachers performed well, accompanied by the harmonium. we had eighteen enfants de choeur, four censor-bearers, and some to throw flowers. a great number of banners were carried in the procession. the commanding officer was kind enough to lend us some cannons, and from the evening before until after the procession was over they fired several rounds. the people seemed to be delighted with the ceremony. a good lady from one of the best families of this place said in the evening: *ahora tengo gusto para rezar,* now I feel a pleasure to say my prayers. All passed off with good order. at high mass which is said every day during the octave, after which benediction is given, we have a great number of people and of communicants.

So in the midst of his stern attention to disciplinary needs, he had the reassurance of "a good lady" that his deepest purpose was taking effect. With the bishop in mitre and cope bringing up the rear, the procession would sway down the well-swept earth of San Francisco street. Fringed and tasselled banners took the breeze, spectators crowded the rooftops and streetsides, and at the head of the street, the old *parroquia* loomed with its fortress-like towers; and far beyond, the green-blue air of the mountains glistened in the sun. As Lamy was then using the old *Castrense* as his church, the procession would return to it in the plaza after winding past the improvised shrines in the principal streets.

But if this was a first fruitful demonstration, life could not be sustained by processions; and Lamy was making plans to go to Europe in January 1854 "to obtain missionaries and also some help"—the latter in finances. Other help he was powerless to administer—that which was needed to meet the perils of the open country. On 1 August he wrote: "the Indian neighbors . . . only few days ago they killed four or five Mexican shepherds who were herding their animals at some distance from the settlements, and took away, according to the report, about ten thousand sheep. I don't know if some measures will be taken to chastise them; I hope, the people will raise en masse to recover their property, if the government suffers passively these murders and depredations, as it has done for some years past."

For his own work, he summoned Machebeuf to join him at his small ranch in the country a few miles out in Tesuque Canyon. There he gave his orders to Machebeuf for the administration of the church during his absence. The place enraptured Machebeuf—not the house, it was no palace, he wrote to his sister at Riom. What almost defied description was the romantic and picturesque beauty of the site—"the accidents of the terrain," as he put it. There Lamy would often go for private study, meditation, rest after long journeys, and renewal of his countryman's spirit.

The elevation of Santa Fe to diocesan status was a matter of open news when the Cincinnati *Catholic Telegraph* published it, but with a curious error. It announced the new bishop of Santa Fe to be Don Juan Felipe Ortiz, who had for so long been vicar there. A highly necessary correction was published, in Spanish, for all to read, in the Santa Fe *New Mexican* for 3 December 1853, making it clear that the matter was a simple confusion of the titles *vicar forane* (Ortiz) and *vicar apostolic* (Lamy), and that the most reverend bishop of Santa Fe was of course Lamy. On the Feast of the Epiphany, 6 January 1854, the bishop published a pastoral letter which announced the new status of the diocese and himself. The change from that of vicariate apostolic was taken to be a great honor to come to Santa Fe and its spiritual leader; and "the dullness of Santa Fe was somewhat broken in upon by an entertainment given in the vestry-rooms of the parish church to Bishop Lamy, on the eve of his departure for Rome."

It was a formal party, with cards of invitation for five in the afternoon. The governor attended, along with the top military command, leading citizens and merchants, and members of the two houses of the legislative assembly. At the proper moment, a committee went to fetch the bishop and escorted him to the vestry, where all rose at his appearance "with the respect due to his personal and official character." An hour of genteel conversation and seasonal compliments followed until supper was announced at seven o'clock, to be served across the patio in another building. The guests were met with "an abundance of the necessaries and the luxuries of life," including various kinds of wines. The bishop said grace, the guests fell to, a group of students made music, and at the end of the banquet, while the wine still went round, a deputation of schoolboys read a farewell address to the bishop in English, French, and Spanish. Words, they said, were but the faint echo of their heartfelt feelings; but in looking upon the present concourse, His Excellency could perceive what their lips were unable to express. A grand motive carried him to Europe. The speakers were convinced that he would defend their interests with dignity, and they were certain that the smallest shade of an eclipse would never darken the brightness of his character. Their fervent prayers would ascend for his happiness and success in his journey, surrounded as he would be by numerous cares and troubles at every step in the discharge of his high duties. They begged him to remember that he would be leaving there, in his true country, souls innumerable who sought his personal happiness, and who prayed God that the same hand of Omnipotence which would conduct the bark which would carry him over the boundless ocean seas would, in his return to these shores, cause to shine on his noble brow the rays of a new star on its appearance in the heavens.

Excessive adulation was to be listened to impassively. If such rhetoric of the period gave more pleasure to those who made use of it (the nuns who, carried away, probably wrote it, and the scholars who spoke it) than to the listener, it was his nature to accept reverence more for the pleasure of those who gave than received it. His plans for the journey were completed. He was taking with him two promising Mexican youths to further their studies in the classics and theology at Rome. They would come back as priests to Santa Fe "to help prune away that portion of the Lord's vineyard so covered with brambles and thorns," as Machebeuf put it. With him also he took as his trusted chaplain and secretary Father Eulógio Ortiz, the old vicar's brother.

Two days after the farewell party he published another pastoral letter —14 January 1854—admonishing pastors and people about proper preparation for the sacraments, matrimonial conduct, observance of tithing support, and a firm command that "not a single peso of the holy parish fund was to be spent for theatrical comedies, dances, and other profane diversions."

Soon afterward, Lamy left for the plains, the Atlantic, England, Rome, and France, while Machebeuf remained in charge as vicar general, with the particular charge of consolidating Albuquerque in its recovery from the style, clerical and secular, of Father Gallegos. This, for the past two years, had been largely Machebeuf's to cope with, while under assault from clergy and citizens almost everywhere.

iv.

Trouble at Albuquerque

EVEN BEFORE HIS JOURNEY to Durango and back in 1851, Lamy had received petitions against Gallegos from some of the more concerned citizens. These were grave enough to induce Lamy to confront Gallegos with them, who rather wittily replied that any improprieties on his part were "exaggerated"—this despite the public knowledge of his irregular domestic life, his love of gambling, his involvement in private business affairs to the detriment of his duties as pastor of San Felipe de Neri at Albuquerque. Lamy sent him warnings for a year which he more or less appeared to heed; but no sooner had the bishop gone to the Baltimore Council than Gallegos, openly indifferent to the authority of Machebeuf acting for Lamy, resumed his old habits, including his lively involvement in private mercantile ventures. In the late summer of 1852, as Lamy was returning from Baltimore, Gallegos was completing arrangements for a journey to Mexico. A prosperous trader, he would take seven waggon loads of merchandise. Letting it be known that the vicar general had, in the name of the bishop, given him permission to make the trip, he delegated his parish duties to Father José de Jesús Lujan, and was just about to start when he heard that Lamy had returned to Santa Fe. It was too late for Gallegos to abandon his intention. He departed as planned.

But it seemed after all that he had gone without permission, and

Lamy swiftly sent Machebeuf to take charge of the Albuquerque parish, and to publish a decree of suspension against the absent Gallegos. Machebeuf ordered Father Lujan to remove himself from parish affairs, declaring that he himself would henceforth administer them exclusively, even if this must mean intermittently, as he would also have to be absent on service to the lesser towns of the Rio Grande.

The resulting outcry was immediate. Martínez wrote Lamy from Taos making charges of violation of Canon Law and once again animating the old accusations against Machebeuf. Through a spokesman, Ambrosio Armijo, probate judge, nine hundred fifty citizens of Albuquerque sent a petition to Lamy in defense of Gallegos, making their case out of what he had told them, and of what they now suffered. Gallegos, they claimed, had gone to Mexico on "important business" with Bishop Zubiría. He had gone with the permission, he insisted, of the vicar general, leaving Father Lujan to act for him. Imagine their sorrow and misfortune when a few days later Lujan had been removed, leaving them to spiritual abandonment in the "infrequent visitations of Señor Machebeuf," who "under the fictitious guise of an apostle" neglected everyone, even those needing the last rites for the dying. Think of the many who had died without this consolation. More, in his "boring and annoying preachings," Machebeuf threatened denial of the sacraments to all who did not pay tithes. If he began his sermons with the Gospel, he ended up with "the private lives of the Faithful." He was driving Catholics into the arms of the Protestant churches. Disgracefully he appropriated benefices for his own appetites. But two weeks ago—on 1 March 1853—Gallegos had returned from Mexico. They hailed him with joy and love, and they now begged the bishop to restore their pastor to them and to withdraw Machebeuf, and they kissed the hands of His Illustrious Lordship.

Two days later Lamy, addressing Judge Armijo, replied curtly. "The rehabilitation of Father Gallegos will be very difficult indeed, at least for now, because he did not obey my orders during my absence, and furthermore, he left his parish without the permission of his superiors. As for the removal . . . of the Vicar Machebeuf; let me tell you this: that this is my business alone, and I myself will decide what is to be done about the errors of which you accuse him. At the same time, let me give you some advice in all charity: that you ought to adhere closely to Ecclesiastical Authority; otherwise, you place yourselves in the gravest of difficulties."

After a hiatus of six weeks, the correspondence was resumed with Armijo protesting that his petitioners recognized the bishop's authority "as such," but they were surprised that the Ecclesiastical Authority now worked so hard "thus to intimidate them with threats of future difficulties, in order that they should now begin to keep the necessary silence." To this Lamy replied, "I don't want to threaten anybody, even though I have been threatened myself"; and he dismissed complaints against Machebeuf by declaring that the vast majority of the people gave him their support—they went to confession in such numbers that they kept him in the confessional "until very late at night," which they surely would not do if they feared for any betrayal of the secrecy of the confessional.

But Gallegos and those who believed in him were not done with measures of resistance. One day Machebeuf, on a visit to Indian parishes seventy-five miles from Albuquerque, had it on good authority that on the following Sunday—it was sometime in early spring 1853— Gallegos, under a claim that he was not legally subject to removal as pastor, intended to dispute Lamy from the altar for possession of the parish of Albuquerque. What was more, Gallegos had returned to take up his residence again in the rectory to which he no longer had any right. It was the most direct of challenges, and it fired Machebeuf to the most energetic of responses.

He instantly sent by swift courier—so he said with delighted animation in reporting to his sister all that followed—to Lamy at Santa Fe, asking for a paper to confirm the suspension of Gallegos, and once again, and most clearly, to state his own authority to govern the parish. Machebeuf arrived at Albuquerque from the country on Saturday night. On Sunday morning, an hour before the usual time, he went to the church on the Albuquerque plaza to be ready for whatever might come, and found to his astonishment that Gallegos was already there in the pulpit.

Gallegos in his middle years was a spare man with a bald head, tall brow, dark side-hair and sparse side-whiskers and eyebrows. His eyes were pale, pouched with suggestions of fleshly comforts. Below a rather flattened nose, his mouth was wide, with downturned full lips, framed with creases in his narrow cheeks. In repose his face had a sad, rather used look, mixed with an expression of shrewdness, and a hint of a suppressed skeptical smile. Taken altogether, it was a rather amusing face and it was not hard to understand his reputation as a good companion and a man of superior wits.

The church was almost full with the adherents whom Gallegos had secretly notified, and whom he was stirring up to rebellion, or at least to resistance. They barred Machebeuf from entering the sacristy by which the rectory and the church were joined, so that he was obliged to go around to the front of the church to enter by the main door. "Armed by courage," he ordered all, like the rightful master, to stand aside and make way for him. He went forward through the crowd with a commanding air, and passed beneath the pulpit just as Gallegos was uttering his name and Lamy's with the "most atrocious of accusations and the most insulting of insinuations." Coming to the altar level of the sanctuary, Machebeuf stood there giving conspicuous attention to these.

When Gallegos fell silent, the people turned to Machebeuf for his reply.

With the utmost exactness, he refuted "all of the alleged accusations and with supporting facts proved that Gallegos was guilty of the scandals which had caused him to be punished"; and to settle all with a single stroke, Machebeuf drew from his pocket the letter from Lamy which his courier had delivered to him at midnight. Now he read it in a loud voice. When he was done, he called upon Gallegos to defend himself, or at least to reply, if he had anything to say.

Silence. Without a word, Gallegos, ignominiously, could do nothing but "slink away like a fox," leaving Machebeuf in undisturbed possession of all. Like a proper pastor, then, Machebeuf celebrated the Mass and preached upon the Gospel of the day, making no reference to what had happened.

But Gallegos was not quite ready to accept defeat. A few days later, to salvage what he could out of his humiliation, he went about the countryside beating the drum to stir up the people and managed to collect twenty or thirty of the most influential of the well-to-do ranchers and his intimates who were "followers of the Devil." Taking advantage of the absence of the local prefect of the peace, who was on Machebeuf's side, Gallegos sent his crowd to Machebeuf's residence and there, insolently and brutally, ordered him to get out of the parish, and if he refused, declared that they would "have recourse to other measures."

Wonderful, exclaimed Machebeuf: at one and the same moment, God gave him both power and patience quite foreign to his nature. He replied resolutely that he was there by order of the supreme authority to take possession of the parish, and that in the absence of other orders from the same supreme authority, they were at liberty to take whatever "measures" they deemed suitable, but being, as it were, on sentry duty, he would never quit his post, and as shepherd of souls, he was ready to give his life for his flock before he would abandon them. "This brief but energetic response," he reported unselfconsciously, disconcerted the little mob. They had not a word to say, but left in a body to serve notice upon Gallegos of the failure of his "embassy." "The poor creatures!" exclaimed Machebeuf. "They didn't know I was an *Auvergnat . . . Latsin pas!*"

They had hardly dispersed when the municipal prefect, who had

been sent for, arrived in a furious state. He had already ordered the
arrest of the demonstrators, but Machebeuf persuaded him to drop
the whole matter, assuring him that further action would do more
harm than otherwise for him; and actually, this magnanimous gesture
worked so well in his favor that soon from all the outlying villages
came deputations offering to defend Machebeuf in case of need. All of
that happened on a Saturday, and on the following day, Machebeuf,
with only his sexton, went to the church, and everywhere the people
greeted him with much more respect than before. It turned out that
of those who chose to take part in the "mutiny" only three men
belonged to Albuquerque proper; the rest were from the largest and
richest outlying district which was known as Ranchos de Albuquerque.

Observing the customs of the Mexicans, Machebeuf deplored nothing so much as the style of their Christmastime celebrations. It was a
local habit to hold a novena in honor of the Blessed Virgin Mary in
the days just before Christmas; but instead of an occasion for piety,
this period had been one of carnival—"dances, orgies," every sort of
license. He felt strongly the basically good dispositions of the people,
even in their ignorance, corruption, and superstition; he knew they
hungered for the word of God. Like Lamy, he exclaimed over what
could be accomplished if only there were enough missionary priests
available. Still, alone, one did what one could. Now, after his survival
at Albuquerque, he proclaimed the usual novena before the next
Christmastide, and was overjoyed to see, instead of hordes of merry-
makers, throngs of the faithful coming to confession, who kept him
in his latticed stall till long after midnight every night. Even the rebels
of Ranchos de Albuquerque came, and many another who had been
among the most fierce opponents of Lamy and himself. He could only
invoke the father and the prodigal son as he thought of them. So
complete was the union of the people with him that when, in due
time, he would have to leave them for Santa Fe because his duties
must keep him nearer to the bishop, the Albuquerque parishioners
would come in crowds, weeping and begging him not to desert them.
He would vow to come to them for one Sunday a month all year and
how he would rejoice to be with his *rancheros* again!—the very men
who had come insulting and menacing him in his own room. Until he
must leave, he delighted in his pastorate at San Felipe de Neri.

Gallegos, however, had no part in the grand reconciliation. Instead,
he moved suddenly into another venture. He threw himself into politics, and, as he "did not lack ability," observed Machebeuf, he managed through "every kind of fraud and intrigue" to get himself elected
as delegate from New Mexico to the Congress of the United States.
As a territory, New Mexico, until proclaimed a state (an event which

would not occur until long after Lamy's time), had a single non-voting delegate in the House of Representatives. In the summer of 1853, soon after his expulsion from the Albuquerque parish, Gallegos declared himself a candidate, running against Dr William Carr Lane, the former territorial governor. Lane's successor, Governor Meriwether, noted that "the Nominee of the Democratic Party is a Mexican. Some object to him because he does not speak the English language, and charge that he has been suspended by the Catholic bishop . . . on account of licentious conduct. Ex-Governor Lane is the opposing Whig candidate, and he is generally popular with the American residents."

Meriwether found Gallegos "to be a shrewd, intelligent man," whom he agreed to instruct in the political principles of the Democrats, and in a spirit of fairness—Meriwether was a Whig—provided him with an interpreter to translate his campaign speech at Santa Fe, in which the candidate made "a very favorable impression upon the audience." In fact, Gallegos had so impressed his followers that they hanged straw-stuffed effigies of Meriwether and another Whig—Judge Davenport—from the flag staff in the Santa Fe Plaza. The election was close—the count showed Gallegos ahead by 445 votes out of 9497 cast. On 19 December 1853, Gallegos's credentials were presented to the House of Representatives, and he was duly seated. But Dr Lane contested the election, and the House referred the issue to its Committee on Elections. Extensive debate followed in the House. On further study, it appeared that if "Indian ballots were counted, Lane was the winner." But Congress disallowed Indian votes, thereby throwing the victory to Gallegos. On 27 February 1854, Gallegos asked that he be allowed to bring an interpreter with him into the House chamber, but the request was denied.

It was another aspect of Gallegos's situation which concerned Lamy, who touched upon it in a letter to Archbishop Francis Patrick Kenrick at Baltimore, identifying Gallegos as "one of those unfortunate priests that I was obliged to suspend." Lamy believed that the archbishop should be aware of this in case Gallegos should appeal to him in a certain matter. "It may be that he will ask permission to say Mass, and some gentlemen of his party may plead for him, saying that he has been punished unjustly, but he deserves well his suspension, and he cannot show any authentic recommendations."

But if Gallegos maintained relations with any bishop but Zubiría of Durango, there is no record to say so. Evidently he still considered Zubiría his prelate. From Washington, on 2 June 1854, Gallegos wrote a long and devoted letter to him, which began, "To satisfy the wishes of my countrymen I decided to come to this capital to occupy the place of Delegate," and he went on to say that he had been well received by his colleagues, who listened "attentively" to his requests. He had obtained an appropriation of $127,000 for New Mexico. He had made a swift tour of the northeastern states—*terra incognita* to Zubiría—and reported on the benefits of industry and nature to be seen there. Catholics were present, but were greatly outnumbered by Protestants. He was not impressed by the general calibre of the priests —though he excepted the Jesuits, in their "intelligence and zeal." Indeed, he often visited their college at Georgetown, near Washington. More interestingly: toward the end of March, "His Illustrious Lordship Lamy passed through here on his way to Rome. I assume he is going to justify his behavior before the Holy Father. I am afraid he will discharge upon us the weight of his imputations, so leading the Holy Father to a belief in contradiction of the true facts." Gallegos held one hope, however. "May it be that the petition of the New Mexico clergy had been expedited before his arrival"—the packet sent by Dean J. F. Ortiz from Durango by way of the apostolic delegate in Mexico. But patience. "I will soon be informed about everything," wrote Gallegos in an astounding revelation, "by Father Eulógio Ortiz" —a brother of the furious self-exiled dean—"who is accompanying Bishop Lamy; and then I will give Your Illustrious Lordship all the news." It was plain evidence of a continuing intrigue against Lamy, and it seemed to implicate his priest-secretary, as well as his fellow bishop in Mexico. If so, perhaps patriotism as well as sacerdotal concern held the intriguers together. Gallegos proceeded to declare that his informants in New Mexico told him that "the position of my Catholic countrymen is getting worse every day." In their resentment against Lamy and his vicar, many had "defected to the Protestants." He hoped Mexico, whether in part or in entirety, would never be annexed to the United States. "The position of Mexicans would be lamentable if they were in the Union; their character, language, religion and other personal circumstances are diametrically opposite to what the North Americans feel about them." He perceived fairly a social situation long to endure in the conquered Southwest. He added that he thought the United States would go to war against Spain to annex Cuba—it was true that there was sentiment, even in Congress, and, he said, in the White House, for such an imperialistic move. Public opinion was divided. "God willing," wrote the delegate, "within two years [i.e., at the end of his term in the House] I'll have the pleasure of visiting Your Illustrious Lordship and receiving your orders."

But Zubiría heard also from another quarter concerning the affairs of Gallegos. Connected to the rear of the Albuquerque church stood the long, one-storey adobe building with its many rooms and its spacious patio which served as the rectory, and was loosely called the *"convento,"* as it contained also the sacristy. It had a certain spacious elegance, despite its primitive materials. The main door and the street-side windows were topped by Palladian pediments of wood. Panelled shutters adorned the windows. The slightly peaked roof was topped by a little open cupola ending in a pyramid. The great room, or *sala,* within had square-cut wooden beams. The walls were washed with a neutral distemper, and the dado, running around the room above the adobe banquette, was of pink muslin printed in a pattern of bluish squares. The banquette and floor were covered with another material in varied stripes. A panelled double door, decorated with a valance and heavy curtains, opened into a room beyond. Paintings hung on the walls of both rooms.

This was the residence of Gallegos, and despite what had happened to him at home, and what required his presence in Washington, he refused to abandon it. Upon his suspension he was asked several times to vacate the church property by Lamy, who even offered to pay him a certain sum to do so. Gallegos insisted that the property had been deeded to him personally by Zubiría.

Machebeuf now wrote to ask Zubiría in May 1854 if this were so. He had already filed suit against Gallegos to recover it. Gallegos had asked for a postponement of the legal action to enable him to "look for his documents," which the court granted. He produced his papers in April, at the same time asking for a change of venue, which seemed odd to Machebeuf. Moreover, Gallegos had originally applied to the municipal town authorities of Albuquerque for a permit to build his house on the church lot, and had been given it. How, if he had had Zubiría's deed, would he need also a municipal title to the place? What Machebeuf asked was Durango's answer to all this, after, in his turn, "by various pretexts," having secured another postponement of the trial, now to give him time to write to Mexico and obtain a reply. He wrote a second letter in June, in case the first had been lost.

In due course the reply came. In the "most clear and satisfactory manner possible," Bishop Zubiría officially declared that he had never sold the house to Gallegos. "Behold the impostor unveiled!" exulted Machebeuf, and promptly moved into the rectory. The claim to the place was eventually settled out of court, with Lamy making a certain payment to Gallegos to reimburse his personal investment in the property.

Now Machebeuf was free to rehabilitate his parish, repairing and redecorating the church. Now the people were proudly helping him in his work of renewing their temple. What was yet to be improved was the execrable native music at the services. One of the parishioners heard from Machebeuf what proper liturgical music must be like; and because he was so moved by Machebeuf's labors to bring seemliness into all possible aspects of the church's conduct, this citizen now offered to present a pipe organ to the parish. Machebeuf gratefully accepted—but who would play the sacred instrument? No one in Albuquerque could do so. At just the right moment, a letter came from the old organist who had played in church for two years in Machebeuf's Sandusky parish, saying he wished he might come to New Mexico to be with his former pastor. Might he come? Machebeuf said that he must. Organ and organist arrived simultaneously in Albuquerque and soon in church "the music fairly enraptured the Mexicans."

v.

Disputed Boundaries

AT LAS VEGAS, NEW MEXICO, going eastward in January 1854, Lamy and his party joined up with a waggon train setting out for the plains. By March he was in St Louis, visiting Archbishop Peter Richard Kenrick, who wrote to Purcell as Lamy left for Cincinnati, "He is a truly Apostolic Prelate, nor could a happier selection have been made for Santa Fe," and he added that Dr Lane, the former New Mexican territorial governor now living in St Louis, "has the highest esteem for the Bishop to whom he refers as belonging to the class of heroes."

The journey continued to Ohio and Kentucky. Once again he was at Bardstown, and this time he went on to the Loretto motherhouse at Nerinckx, where he reported to the members on what their sisters were accomplishing at Santa Fe, and where he asked for others of the community, now, to be ready to go back with him to Santa Fe on his return from Europe in the late summer. With the promises of several, he made his way to Boston, and sailed on 29 March. "We had a short and good passage," he wrote to Purcell. "We were on the sea only nine days and one night."

He disembarked first in England. In Birmingham, where he hoped to see Father John Henry Newman, he was disappointed, as Newman, briefly home from his troubles in attempting to found a university in Dublin against the opposition of the Irish bishops and clergy, was spending the whole day in Bishop Ullathorne's retreat house. But

Ullathorne, regretting that he could not release any priests for Santa Fe, was hospitable, and showed Lamy "through the city of Birmingham to see some of their Catholic institutions." Lamy noted that the diocese of Birmingham was making "immense progress."

Coming next to France, he landed at Boulogne and at once paid a call upon the Ursulines there, whose community had invested so richly in Ohio a few years ago: how long ago all that seemed now, and how much had happened since to the two young French missionaries who had persuaded them earlier. Now Lamy found that the Ursulines "were pressing upon me so much to stay with them, that I was near missing the cars that day for Paris." Finally away, he sent messages to the Ursulines of Brown County, in Ohio, of his visit, and arriving in Paris, went to stay once again with the Sulpicians in the rue du Bac. In the Paris headquarters of foreign missions, he thought it advisable to leave his two young New Mexican seminarians for their schooling, and he hoped Purcell might be able to pay their tuition. Perhaps later Lamy could reimburse him for the account of one of them, if the seminary at Clermont should also be able to contribute. He was sorry to presume on his old friendship. Where else to turn? As for other news, it seemed that the new Emperor was very popular, often went through the streets alone, and it was professionally reassuring that Napoleon III kept at court a bishop and chaplains, and that recently they gave a retreat there.

By early June, Lamy was in Rome for his first visit *ad limina* to the Pontiff, and for his own recognition in person by the Vatican offices with which for so long he would have so much business from so far away.

The Eternal City was a meld of three elements—the ancient pagan imperial Rome, much of whose remains had been half-buried by the risen earth of centuries; the domed and palatial Christian city of the popes; and the very countryside itself. Groves of trees and open fields and much bare land were mingled with the works of man. Hillocks of earth rose gently upon the exposed upper portions, in marble or tawny brick, of ancient ruins; and everywhere he looked Lamy could see rising above the dirt streets the great baroque domes and tiled roofs, palace façades, and square stuccoed towers of the later city, while the open Campagna lay in view from any hilltop or at the end of any straight way. The via del Babuino leading from the Porta del Popolo to the Piazza di Spagna had country airs proper to a village street.

Lamy's affairs were focussed in the great bureaux of the Sacred Congregation of the Propagation of the Faith whose immense offices were housed in a brown sandstone palace restored by Bernini at the end of the Piazza di Spagna where the street divided to flow past its walls. Its shallow stairways were wide and sweeping, taking the visitor from one pale vista of grand vaulted corridors to another, until he came to the reception rooms and finally the great inner office of the Vatican official who directed world-wide the Catholic mission activities. These continued in countries (of which until 1908 the United States was one) where the local Church was unable to sustain itself materially or to find itself so securely a part of national life as to justify separation from Rome in routine administration. Rome remained the fount of spiritual powers and hierarchical dispositions; and in her Christian history and the visible splendor by which she celebrated it, lay weighty confirmation of her authority for all her servants to see. Lamy, coming from his all but hidden diocese of towns and chapels built of the humblest dust, could be seen as a minister of the faith which bound the simplest of human situations to the might and glory of Christian Rome evolved through its own centuries from its underground beginnings to the universal Papacy of his own day.

His duties now began in the office of Alessandro Cardinal Barnabo, Prefect of the Propaganda Fide, with whom he would exchange a voluminous correspondence of increasing warmth and good feeling for many years. The Vatican palace and St Peter's lay far across Rome from the offices of the Propaganda Fide, where in rank upon rank of shelves, through vast, lofty open chambers, the archives of all the foreign missions, including his own, were kept in folios of heavy sheepskin tied with rawhide thongs and lettered and dated on their thick spines by quills holding brown ink. Until his period of brief exile, ending in 1850, Pius IX had lived in the Lateran Palace. Since his return from Gaeta he had occupied the Vatican, and at the proper moment, Lamy would be conducted there for his first audience with the pontiff who had decreed him bishop. The Cardinal Prefect of the Propaganda was received twice a month by the Holy Father. Perhaps Bishop Lamy would be presented on one such occasion.

But before that there was much to lay before Barnabo—one affair in particular, and Lamy came prepared with documents. This was the still-disputed ecclesiastical jurisdiction over the villages and county, known variously as Mesilla or Doñana or "*Condado,*" whose names were taken by different parties, according to whose interest was involved, to designate either a cluster of villages, or one village, or a great tract of almost thirty thousand square miles across the southern area of New Mexico–Arizona. The civil jurisdiction of the tract had first been agreed upon in the Treaty of Guadalupe Hidalgo in 1848, which on faulty map lines gave it to Mexico. But later boundary surveys raised serious doubts, and the New Mexico territorial government claimed the land all the way to the northern line of the state of Chihuahua, running due west to the Pacific from the Rio Grande's southeastward bend at El Paso. The Mexican government refused to recognize this claim, and in March 1853 Governor Lane of New Mexico, on his own authority, had sent volunteer territorial troops to occupy the area. President Santa Anna of Mexico responded by ordering Mexican troops north to keep it by force of arms. Just as a new war with Mexico seemed imminent, the matter was resolved when Senator James Gadsden, of South Carolina, who had been sent to Mexico by President Pierce to negotiate the purchase of the disputed land, concluded his mission. The Gadsden Purchase, made final on 30 December 1853, for a payment by the United States of ten million dollars, provided a new southwestern boundary and made possible a railroad line to the Pacific within United States limits. The troops were withdrawn, the civil crisis was over, and the final official act relating to the 1846 war with Mexico was done. New Mexico was firmly defined in her permanent boundaries, within which lay Doñana, Mesilla, and the *Condado*. Under the terms, and within the logic of the Baltimore Council's original request urging the establishment of the vicariate apostolic and now recently the diocese of New Mexico, by which the national political jurisdiction would be matched by the ecclesiastical, it was clear to Lamy that no obstacle could possibly remain to his administration of the disputed areas.

But Zubiría of Durango had claimed these same areas in his conversation with Lamy and his letter to the Vatican in November 1851, and he had no intention now of changing his views on the issue, no matter what boundary commissions, treaty officers, or international purchase agreements might decide. Lamy had "tried many times to reach the Most Reverend Bishop of Durango and discuss this matter," but got nothing in return but "elusive answers" from the see of Durango "which they thought would satisfy . . ." Now, after the conclusion of the Gadsden Purchase, Lamy's only hope of affirming the integrity of his proper diocese lay with the Vatican, and he set out the case in the grand chambers in the Piazza di Spagna. In doing so, he reiterated details which he had already written from Santa Fe before coming to Rome.

He recalled to Barnabo that the papal bulls named him as bishop of New Mexico with "no exceptions" of territory within that diocese. It was therefore natural that he should reclaim as belonging to his diocese that important part of the New Mexico territory which was always included within it. The part in question was the *Condado de Doñana,* which enclosed the southern limits of the territory of New Mexico and the northern limits of the state of Chihuahua. The *Condado* was always included in New Mexico before the latter was set up as a bishopric. Now that it belonged by purchase to the United States, it inevitably became a part of the diocese of Santa Fe. Practically speaking, the county was very far from Durango, and much nearer to the city of Santa Fe. Moreover, it was not hard to imagine the difficulties which could be expected for the United States government if a Mexican bishop would attempt to exercise a jurisdiction in United States territory. What was yet more, the Mexican government "never pretended to make laws for Doñana," and (since the end of the recent war) "the inhabitants always voted in the New Mexico civil elections." The people of Doñana could not "understand why the exception has been brought up, especially since they are in New Mexico, nearer to Santa Fe, whence they can receive spiritual aid, whereas they are hundreds of leagues from Durango and the roads leading there are exceedingly dangerous. . . ." The disputed county was increasingly populated by Anglo-Americans who resisted Mexican jurisdiction. Lamy feared that such people would "manifest their displeasure by refusing to accept the sacraments from the hands of priests from Durango," and he feared also that if Mexican priests should come, they might even be mistreated by the Americans.

Careful minutes were made in the Propaganda of all such points, and in due course were relayed to Bishop Zubiría for his comments. The matter would take time, thanks to the slow ocean crossings and the deliberate pace of bureaucratic affairs. When Lamy's statements reached Zubiría from Rome instead of from Santa Fe, his first reply would be simply to send to the Vatican, in all respect, a notarized copy of his original letter of November 1851, quite as though no significant events concerning the matter had since taken place. How much time the dispute would subsequently take, in groaningly slow exchanges between Santa Fe, Rome, and Durango, nobody foresaw in 1854. For the long moment, there was a lucid Vatican memorandum: "It must be decided if to Santa Fe there belongs what in New Mexico belongs to the United States. . . ."

Lamy had other affairs to discuss which referred to Zubiría, revealing serious doubts concerning funds and properties belonging to the parish church of St Francis and the chapel of St Michael, "both in the city of Santa Fe," which had recently been taken from them. In the first instance these had been possessed personally by a priest "by the name of Felipe Ortiz" and, in the second, by his mother.

In the light of Lamy's description of the relation of the former rural dean to the diocese of Durango, Cardinal Barnabo wrote flatly to Zubiría on 17 June 1854, while Lamy was still in Rome, "I trust that Your Excellency will understand that in view of the office and the authority given to the Bishop of Santa Fe, it is right and just that all the goods pertaining to his churches be administered by him. I trust that you will help to clear this situation and make sure that all which is due to the above-mentioned Bishop will be arranged to his satisfaction." With this instrument, ex-Dean Juan Felipe Ortiz entered into the long memory of the Vatican, and Zubiría was given notice of the official position toward Lamy. If Ortiz, or any other disaffected New Mexican, had made representations to Rome against Lamy before now, there was no record to indicate that any discussion of any such act took place. Soon enough, such concerns were to come under examination in the Propaganda, and not Lamy, but his vicar general, would speak to them.

But meanwhile, Lamy was in good health and occupied with other matters. The bishop shopped for furnishings for his churches, acquired some paintings which he planned to take home with him, and found a Spaniard, Father Damaso Taladrid, who would go to New Mexico with him to stay. Finally came the moment for Lamy's audience with Pius IX.

The papacy—and its occupant—gave Rome its greatest spectacle, as Henry James saw soon after Lamy's first Roman visit. "Open-mouthed only for visions," James left the breakfast table to observe, in the Via Condotti, "the brightest and strangest of all." The perspective was suddenly emptied of traffic by "mounted, galloping, hand-waving guards," and while all doffed hats and knelt, he saw (less reverently than a Roman) "the great rumbling, black-horsed coach of the Pope, so capacious that the august personage within—a hand of automatic benediction, a pair of celebrated eyes which one took, on trust, for sinister—could show from it as enshrined in the dim depths of a chapel."

Lamy found Pio Nono genial, keen, and generous. The Pope was a man of fine looks and great charm. An Oxford college master thought him "a capital fellow." He was also a hero of auguries—on his way from his old episcopal see of Imola to Rome for the conclave in which he was elected to the chair of Peter, a dove had repeatedly fluttered down to the roof of his coach arousing the acclaim of the faithful. He was also a suddenly conservative survivor of the republican furies which had ended the temporal rule of the Papacy over most of Italy. An aristocrat, he always presented an impeccable appearance. His voice was famous for its fine sound. An affable smile lighted his full and handsome face and his large dark eyes. He was sixty-one years old at the time he received Lamy. Of more than officially devout habit, he held great veneration for the Virgin Mary, and was already formulating his plans to promulgate as dogma the doctrine of the Immaculate Conception. People referred to him as "the Pope of prayer." It is likely that he felt Lamy's quiet devoutness, in all its peasant simplicity and episcopal dignity. Lamy made only one reference later to their exchange in the audience: among the matters he discussed with Pius was the flagellant brotherhood of the Penitentes in his diocese. What to do about them? The Pope made it clear that the bishop should try to disband the order—a view with which Lamy was in sympathy.

For the rest, the Pope signalized Lamy's audience in a superb and concrete fashion. He presented his forty-year-old bishop with a chalice out of the papal treasury. It was attributed to a goldsmith of the sixteenth century and spoke richly of the Renaissance style in its design. Its height was over eleven inches, the mouth of the cup measured four and a half inches in diameter, and the base six inches. The cup of the chalice consisted of two parts—the vessel proper, which was of gold as plain and pure as water in its brilliant reflections, and an embracing support of worked gold which, like the major knurl and the base, depicted sacred subjects in carved medallions—variously, St Peter with his keys, St John with an eagle, St Paul and his sword, the crown of thorns, the monogram for Ave Maria, Christ and two apostles at the Last Supper, Gethsemane with an angel holding the cup of agony and Christ gazing at it, and the crucifixion with St John and the Holy Mother at the foot of the cross. It seemed clear that by a gift of such magnificence the Pope intended to show particular favor to his visitor, whose report of the desert diocese could refer to few enough of even the simplest sacred accessories. The chalice, for all its rich repoussé, was extremely light in weight. It was fitted upside down into a carrying case of black leather lined in red baize. The lid was locked with brass hasps, and to the top was affixed a brass handle, by which the case could be strapped to a ring on a saddle when in future years the chalice might accompany its new owner on pastoral journeys across the reaches of his desert. For the moment, Lamy consigned it to the care of Barnabo at the Propaganda.

On 30 June, his Roman duties done, Lamy wrote to Barnabo from Civitavécchia, where he was about to embark for France with business in Clermont, Lyon, and Paris. Father Taladrid was there to see him off, and to carry the letter to Barnabo in person. "I am again writing you to entrust the chalice to the Spanish priest Don Domaso Taladrid who is going with me to New Mexico and who must leave in about eight days to meet me in Paris. . . ."

In Clermont, Lamy knew all the emotions of homecoming, and of visiting as a bishop the seminary of his youth. With the support of the bishop of Clermont, he carried the same appeal now to the seminarians and young priests which he had heard from Purcell in the same place so long ago. His description of his needs brought a good response. In addition to Taladrid the Spaniard, he could now add to his homeward party three priests, Pierre Eguillon, N. Juilliard, and Antoine Avel; Jean Guérin, a deacon; Eugène Pollet and Sébastien Vaur, subdeacons (all of the diocese of Clermont); and also two laymen—another Vaur, who was a brother of the subdeacon, and Rimbert, their cousin. The latter two would go to Santa Fe, and there begin their studies in a *"petit séminaire"* to be founded by Lamy.

Etienne Lamy, the head of the family, and the father of the young Marie, was in Lempdes, and the bishop went there to see him. Their parents were both dead. In this visit, Etienne agreed to lend his brother twenty-five thousand francs, to be repaid in four years. With this fund to give him a degree of certainty, Lamy moved on to Lyon, presented his case for more help, and received assurance there from the council of the Society for the Propagation of the Faith that he could "rely on extraordinary help" from that quarter. From there he proceeded to Paris, where he stayed once again with the Sulpicians. There he found Father Taladrid waiting for him, with his papal chalice, and there he spent most of his time with the Paris office of the Society, trying to give them in detail a description of a state of affairs they could not readily imagine.

How to make the priestly administrators at Paris see his land? The distances, the remoteness of the people in the great landscape, the heat of summer, the year-round droughts, the poor clay villages lost in the hill-folds under the mountains, the spiritual life once manifest under the Franciscans now all but asleep under the Mexican clergy, and the consequent uninstructed gaieties and vices of the population, the hovels which served as chapels and churches? What must be thought of altar candles made from sheep fat and set into discarded bottles for candlesticks? The diet of cornmeal and jerked meat on which the parish pastors had to subsist? Church revenue consisting of donations of animals and grain which the diocese must then sell in turn to the United States Army quartermasters in order to obtain money which was to be divided among the parishes in order to provision the priests and pay expenses for repair and maintenance of the chapels? In the pueblos, the Indians farmed little gardens to sustain the missioners who rode by the Rio Grande or over the deserts to visit them. There were ten thousand Catholic Indians to serve in their pueblo churches which had been empty of resident pastors since the withdrawal of the Franciscans in the 1820s.

Even the positive aspects of his report led to the same purpose—the need for funds, priests, and religious. The small community of nuns at Santa Fe were "doing well," but he was already in debt for four years on their account alone. He expected three more Loretto nuns to join him to go West. When the Paris Society allocated twenty thousand francs in reply to his appeals, he thanked them earnestly, for he needed it immediately to buy "many things at as low prices" as he could—catechisms, prayer books, school books, whatever else might be needed for the new preparatory seminary he would establish for the "many vocations for the priesthood" which he hoped to find locally, for he thought he would never again return to Europe.

For her brother's sake, he had planned to visit Sister Philomène at Riom, but was prevented by demanding business, and also by a spell of poor health. But in making his regrets, he told her of his chalice, and of how, without knowing of the gift, the Abbé Mousset, vicar of Clermont, had presented him there with "a very beautiful pair of cruets," to complete the furnishings of his own chapel. Gold-plated, like their little tray, they were identical, except that the one for the wine had on its lid a distinguishing tiny bunch of grapes in red enamel. His work done in Paris and his party assembled, he could inform her that they would sail for New York on an American steamer from Le Havre on August first—a twelve-day crossing.

From New York his party set out at once by rail, stage coach, and river, going direct to Independence, Kansas, and in its prairie neighborhood to the west, established a camp at Willow Springs. There Lamy was to await the arrival of the sisters from Kentucky who had agreed earlier to join his convent in Santa Fe. He was delighted to find that Machebeuf had sent four Mexican carters and "thirty good animals" to meet him at Willow Springs. It was good to hear that the rainy weather he had found in the East had reached across the plains, for travellers coming by from Santa Fe told him that there was no trouble in finding water and grass for the crossing.

The month of waiting wore on—the sisters were expected daily but did not appear. The party in camp sent out hunters for buffalo meat. Returning from one of these expeditions, Father Pierre Eguillon, "while putting his gun into the wagon, it slipped through an opening in the [waggon] bed, exploded, and the unfortunate priest received the whole discharge in his right hand." Taken to Independence for help, he was told by doctors that the hand should be amputated. He refused, clinging to the priesthood which must have him whole. In camp, he was nursed but remained seriously ill.

One day "a bearded stranger" in a long linen coat and carrying a rifle arrived in camp, having heard some of the party speaking French. He asked who they were. They told him, and, assuming he was a hunter, asked his name in turn.

"I am Bishop Miège," he said, "vicar apostolic of this area."

Lamy appeared and made him welcome. They had met at the previous Baltimore Council. Miège's vicariate—known as the "Indian Territory"—was huge, like Lamy's. It embraced a great portion of the plains and all of Colorado, and it bordered on Lamy's diocese on the east and north. He had no town, no cathedral, but lived in a hut at the Jesuit mission near the site of the later Topeka, from which he made his journeys across his empty lands. He was even poorer than Lamy—his sacerdotal equipment consisted of one yellow silk chasuble, which he would lend to other missioners.

The plains hunter went on his way, and Lamy expected to move within a week—his company had been under tents almost a month waiting for the nuns from Kentucky, but he could not risk the coming of hard weather on the plains in autumn, and it was time to go. But another circumstance would have kept him at Willow Springs for a while longer in any case, for he had a spell of illness in late September. Soon recovered, he decided he must not wait any longer for the Lorettines. But what to do with Father Eguillon? He was hardly strong enough to travel, but begging not to be left behind, said he would rather die on the way to the new mission than among strangers. On 5 October, Lamy gave the order to break camp, had Eguillon lifted on a mattress into one of the waggons, the caravan moved out, and before the journey was ended, Eguillon was well again.

Lamy had ten canvas-topped waggons with mule teams, twenty-eight people in his immediate party, and he was the only European in the group who had previously crossed the prairies. But his companions showed fortitude in all conditions of the journey, which would take five weeks. Because water was, after all, hard to find, the stages of the passage were long ones, often lasting until after dark; and in the dark, they often saw Indian campfires only a mile or so away, and in the daytimes, they would often see fresh trails made by Indian parties, and they were always on the alert for attack, but luckily none came. The plains—"those solitudes"—presented, he said, a monotonous aspect, but even so, they were magnificent, "vast and undulant as the sea." During a certain week the caravan saw not thousands, but hundreds of thousands, of bison in herds so immense that they solidly blackened the prairie in all directions. It took fast horses and crack shots to kill when bison were needed for fresh meat. On every Sunday and feast day the bishop said Mass in his tent and all came together to worship God and ask His protection in their travels. At last, seeing the mountains of New Mexico, they saw also a little crowd of New Mexicans who had ridden to meet them. They gave the bishop's party a good welcome; but it was left to Santa Fe to mount the most brilliant reception. It was so notable that when news of it reached St Louis, De Smet wrote to Santa Fe of his "pleasure in reading about it in the papers."

With all the civil and military authorities in attendance, several thousand citizens turned out as the party approached Santa Fe, and a company of United States dragoons in full dress with guidons and bugles rode out to form an escort. Dragoon William Drown caught much of the scene in his diary, along with the superior, even contemptuous, tone which the conquering Easterners took toward the older population.

Under the entry for 18 November 1854, he wrote: "We have had a splendid turn-out today. We received orders from the Adjutant-General's office yesterday to be in readiness to start today at twelve M. on the road to Fort Union to meet the Bishop (Lama), who has just arrived from Rome. . . . We all drew new horse equipments yesterday, and were thereby able to make quite an imposing appearance. We started at twelve M. accompanied by all the bigbugs of the city and about 3,000 of the poorer class of Mexicans, who met the Bishop about five miles out of the city, where we were all wheeled into line—the dragoons on one side of the road and the citizens another, and the mob most anywhere where they could get a good sight at their 'dear Bishop.' " The Loretto nuns with their pupils also rode out in coaches. As soon as Lamy came in sight of the city, the bells of Santa Fe began to peal. "The dragoons were the first to salute, with presented sabres and flourishing of trumpets. The Bishop halted opposite our center, and very gracefully returned the salute by taking off his sombrero—which" when he bowed "exhibited the dollar-spot on the summit of his cranium—and thanked us for our kindness to him. He then proceeded on a few yards further, and proceeded to pay his respects to the citizens of the city—about 100 of which were Americans and Europeans—for their uniform kindness and attention. Our company was then desired by him to move in front, and he would be very happy to follow us into the city . . ." He asked the dragoons to take him into town by the road which led past St Michael's chapel, the oldest church. "We accordingly started off at a full gallop, and the Mexicans crowded in upon the Bishop so close to get a good sight of him that we could not see him at all. He at last sent an express to us, desiring us, if we pleased, not to ride so fast, as he was at least a mile behind us. . . . We then pulled down to a walk and allowed about fifty ugly faces to pass us. As we neared the city, the whole population was standing in crowds on both sides of the road—men, women, children, dogs, burros, and in fact every living thing that composes a Mexican family, but they, being on foot, were no annoyance to us. We proceeded on into the city by the very road we had gone out about an hour before," but now what a transformation. An hour ago, the road, all the streets, had been just as usual, plain adobe walls along dusty lanes. But now, "in an hour all was most beautifully ornamented. Arches of beautifully colored silks, gold crosses, artificial flowers, mirrors, etc. were thrown over the streets in all directions. I noticed that none of the Mexicans dared or did not pass under the arches until the Bishop had passed; but not so with us: we had the honor of being No. 1 and the Bishop No. 2." They drew up in front of St Michael's, saluting as the bishop dismounted and entered the chapel. There was a brief struggle over who should hold his horse—at least fifty people tried to do so. Drown was given charge of the prelatic horse by his lieutenant and said, "I began to feel rather monkish myself." Presently Lamy reappeared, now in vestments, which were "truly rich and beautiful." He remounted and all moved on to the *Castrense* in the Plaza where the bishop sang the Te Deum. When he emerged the procession conducted him to "his residence which . . . stands in a very narrow street—so much so that we were obliged to charge upon the Mexicans in order to enable him to get to his own house. But he soon saved us the trouble; for as soon as he spoke to the Mexicans himself, they broke like quarter-horses, nearly breaking one another's necks to see who should have the honor of getting out of his way first. When we arrived in front of his gate, we were again wheeled into line to give him a farewell salute, which he returned with many bows and thanks, and we were dismissed. The Bishop is about forty-five years of age [actually forty]; of very prepossessing appearance; speaks English well, and is by birth a Frenchman."

Before the afternoon was over, Lamy and all the new foreigners paid a call of respect at the now overcrowded little convent, and pupils gave florid addresses of welcome. This was followed by "a sumptuous supper," as Mother Magdalen reported, which was held at the home of Father Carlos. It was a joyful homecoming.

But on the very next day, another procession was held, this one a march for the dead, for on the night of their arrival, Lamy's new subdeacon, Sébastien Vaur, died of the cholera which had made him ill during three weeks of the plains crossing. The Mother Superior said he was buried "with all the solemnity possible." Machebeuf preached. His companions had all grown fond of the young man "of many talents and eminent virtue." They buried him in St Michael's chapel, and Lamy reported his loss to Paris.

But work was waiting, and within a few days the new assignments had been made for parishes by Machebeuf—Juilliard at Belen, Martin at the pueblo of Isleta south of Albuquerque, while Avel was stationed in Santa Fe. By the end of November, Machebeuf returned to *"mon cher Albuquerque"*—dear to him as the scene of trials which he had overcome to gain the devotion of the people. The bishop was worried about the great cost of caravan travel—other dioceses in America had means of transportation and communication which he could not call upon. He hoped for additional material help from Rome and Paris. De Smet reported from St Louis that "a great number of boxes have arrived for your lordship and are in care of Mr Walsh." There were also two small cameos addressed to Purcell, which De Smet, who was going to Cincinnati, would deliver for Lamy.

vi.

The Old Dean

IN MARCH OF THE FOLLOWING YEAR, 1855, Machebeuf left for the East to collect the three Loretto nuns who had failed to meet the bishop at Willow Springs. One additional sister from St Louis was now to join the others. All was arranged for their emigration. The vicar general, homeward bound, took the occasion to visit the Ursulines whom he had so dramatically removed from France to Brown County, and their pupils now entertained him with a performance of "the beautiful play of 'Uncle Tom's Cabin,' " while he sat in their midst "as pleased and happy in listening to their simple play as if he knew nothing of the danger and sins of border life and Indian camps, or the hardships of travel over desert plains." Soon he was again at St Louis, where the Lorettines were to meet him. On 7 June they took ship aboard the *Genoa* on the Missouri River, for Independence, Missouri. Once arrived at the edge of the plains, they made all the familiar preparations for the plains crossing in company of a trading caravan.

They were well on their way when on 16 July during a halt for breakfast a cry was raised—"Indians! Indians!"—and the travellers looking to the east saw a rise of the land covered with horsemen painted for war. "They swooped down upon us like so many eagles," declared Sister Ann Joseph. The nuns were hurried into their ambulances which were in the center of the circle of parked waggons. The heavy canvas tops were lashed down. The caravan animals were herded to the center also. It was hot—ninety degrees; and a great stillness was over all. The waggon drivers sat on their high benches. Soon the Indians penetrated to the inner circle and tried to look under waggon covers. Whenever they did so, the drivers cracked their long rawhide whips with the sound of pistol shots. To mollify the Indians, the caravan traders made them gifts out of their masses of merchandise —blankets, calicoes, manta, sugar, tobacco, molasses—and Machebeuf freely distributed holy medals. He saw a young Mexican boy with the Indians, assumed this was a captive, and tried to have him released, but without success. Inscrutable, willful, and curious as cats, the Indians wrought fear in those whom they came among at such times. If their souls were the immortal charges of the missioners, what they posed as threats to the living were to be met if necessary with outward as well as inward acts. Machebeuf knew Lamy's pastoral circular of the previous February which, citing government orders sending the Army at last into the field to subdue Indian depredations, had decreed that for the duration of hostilities, the prescribed prayers "in time of war" be read at all Masses "for the success and triumph of our troops." The Collect: "O God, who bringest wars to nought, and by thy mighty protection rousest the assailants of those who trust in thee, help us thy servants who entreat thy mercy, so that our barbarous enemies may be brought low and we may never cease to praise and thank thee: through our Lord."

By four in the afternoon, half of the Indians were gone, but the remainder "hung around" the camp until an hour later. At last free to move, the caravan went on to find an encampment for the night. When they pulled up, the nuns were freed from their day-long imprisonment, and found that for some time they could not stand, after being so cramped in their breathless and prayerful confinement. Machebeuf had ways of restoring their spirits and showing them regard. Often he would send a small detachment ahead of the main body when trees were sighted so that they could take up and plant farther ahead a few trees where the party would make camp. There he would himself be found waiting to welcome the nuns in their "little garden or grove." He liked to find wildflowers to bring them, and little collections of shells which linked the dry prairies to their ancient sea beds. High water at the ford of Las Vegas briefly endangered them, but they arrived safely at Santa Fe on 24 July 1855.

During Machebeuf's absence, Lamy had been canonically installed as bishop of the new diocese of Santa Fe. For those who understood it in general, this signified a rise in dignity for their old city and kingdom. For those with a special relation to their hierarchy—the native clergy specifically—it seemed to make less difference than Lamy had hoped.

For "the old ex-vicario Ortiz has returned from Durango, and we receive new vexations from him every day," wrote Lamy to Purcell. Ortiz had spent two years in Zubiría's diocese, but finally must return to Santa Fe. He had a hard journey—fever and dysentery troubled him all the way to New Mexico. As he came up the Rio Grande he heard that Lamy was making pastoral visits as far south as Tomé for confirmations. When the bishop returned to Santa Fe, Ortiz paid him an official call. But already there was a complication to be dealt with. His cousin, Father José Ortiz, called away by affairs, had asked him to officiate in his place on the important feast day of St John's eve in June, when the acequias—irrigation ditches—were blessed for the coming growing season, processions held, vigils observed. After singing the vespers on the saint's day, Ortiz received a brief suspension from the bishop for having assumed faculties not properly granted him.

The dean wrote to Lamy in self-justification. One of Lamy's measures in dealing with those whom he had disciplined was silence thereafter. He sent no immediate answer to the letter from Ortiz. But a fortnight later Lamy sent word to him that it distressed him to deny the old dean his priestly functions, and invited him to call for the purpose of reaching a reconciliation.

"I went, and he received me kindly," said Ortiz, who then brought up the reason for his return to Santa Fe: he asked Lamy for his old Santa Fe parish.

To this Lamy replied that he would "speak in all frankness." To prove that he would "forget the past," Lamy offered Ortiz, for his parish, instead of Santa Fe, the rich river lands reaching from Peña Blanca to Algodones, which contained haciendas and villages as well as Indian pueblos.

To this, Ortiz said he, too, would speak "in all frankness," declared that he would accept no charge which was not in Santa Fe, and took his leave.

Lamy's answer once again was complete silence. They were still in conflict, and Ortiz, once more acting out of the same spite he had shown in leaving Santa Fe before, now seized "several holy vessels and some church ornaments which belonged to the parish," and again left Santa Fe. He took also "a bell which is not his property," reported Lamy to the Vatican "(for we have the testimony of the person who gave this bell to the church)." But Ortiz had a brother-in-law, the municipal prefect of Santa Fe, who promptly gave him a writ of possession of the bell, and "the bell was taken down by violence." Lamy felt powerless, "as the authorities are on his side, and I must say are rather scandalous Catholics, we have to suffer these abuses. I am telling you these facts so that if you receive in Rome some documents on the subject, you will have already been informed . . ."

For his part, Ortiz wrote copiously to Zubiría, making a furious case.

Ortiz declared that he would "almost certainly" leave New Mexico again. If Zubiría would once again receive him in his diocese, please let him be assigned to El Carrisal. Beyond such personal affairs, let him report that he had rescued from the Santa Fe cathedral those properties which—as he saw it—belonged to him in a sense, since they had been given to the church in the first place by his relatives. He had done this because many fine objects which he had known well for years were now missing from the church, chalices (one of which he said he himself had given), a censer, a pyx, and some of these things, he had heard, vanished with a silver box and were taken to Europe. Why, he did not say. Furthermore—the list of outrages continued—many of the cathedral vestments had been burned, along with forty different costumes once used to dress the statue of Our Lady of the Rosary. But more—the cruel old matter of the division of the Santa Fe parish was now seen to be a fraud, since the *Castrense* church which was supposed to be the seat of a new parish was now empty, its bells silent, the place in disuse. The bishop was now using the original church of St Francis as his cathedral, after all, and it remained the chief parish church. Ortiz was sorry to send Zubiría such an "annoying and tiresome" report, but he thought it might be useful to him, and besides, he added to "his" bishop, "you sent word for me to write to you."

By his behavior in Santa Fe, Ortiz was evidently giving new energy to those local priests who opposed Lamy, and Lamy resolved that he would be obliged to withdraw the license he had given Ortiz to say Mass. As he wrote to Purcell, "Some of our Mexican *padres* are more troublesome to us than the 'know-nothings' with you"—for Purcell was having his own difficulties with organized anti-Catholic sentiment in the East. But, added Lamy, "we have not all roses in New Mexico . . ."

Still, he went steadily ahead with his measures of rectitude. Late in the year he issued a new pastoral circular touching on several matters. The first of these was to order that the Feast of the Immaculate Conception be observed in December with the greatest solemnity, for the entire Catholic world had received with "unanimity and thanksgiving the Dogma of the Immaculate Conception" which Pius IX had declared in the previous year. All, therefore, should prepare to receive the sacraments in honor of Our Lady, "thus truly trying hard to imitate the purity of Mary." But he sternly took this occasion to remind everyone of the discipline he had announced several times before— "any family which does not fulfill the fifth precept of the Church"— to support the Church materially—"will not have the right to receive the Holy Sacraments. Let us again inform you that we consider those as not belonging to the Church who do not observe this precept; and we likewise would take away all faculties to say Mass and administer the sacraments from all Pastors who failed to sustain and provide for the maintenance of religion and its ministers, in proportion to the goods which God has given them." He was obliged to note further that such support was now "such a small part" that it seemed "more an insult than the fulfillment of an obligation."

It was still another direct challenge to the native clergy, and by its forthrightness, it indicated that harsh measures were still needed to produce the support without which the diocese could not function. Curiously enough, the circular brought a gratifying response from the pastor of Taos—Father Antonio José Martínez—who had earlier joined with Ortiz, Chavez, and Gallegos in opposition to Lamy. Martínez read the circular to his two churches in Taos immediately, the people received with much joy the "plausible news" of the newly defined dogma of Mary, and they also gave vigilant notice to the demand for tithings, and would "literally" observe it. Martínez could report that he had already given the collector, Don Antonio José Valdes, "twenty-two dry measures" in grains of corn, and also four pigs, and four more measures of corn, together with payments totalling twelve pesos. He signed himself saying, "May the life of Your Excellency be in the hands of God for many years, Your servant and Obedient follower who loves you and kisses your hands." Was Taos— was Father Martínez—now in filial obedience and peace? What hope.

But four pigs? Twelve pesos? Twenty-two dry measures [about forty-one bushels] of corn? To redistribute to the institutions of the diocese and support a share of the growing measures of learning and charity? Paris sent what money it could, Rome provided procedural and doctrinal guidance; the rest was Lamy's to provide. Somehow he must sustain the primary school for young boys; the pre-seminary school for twelve older boys destined for the priesthood, where already a handful of students were ready to begin their Latin studies; the convent of Our Lady of Light of the Lorettines, which was now augmented with both teachers and students so that Lamy moved out of his own *Casa Americana,* which Machebeuf had bought for him during his absence. The bishop now gave it to the sisters for their living quarters, classrooms, student dormitories, and chapel. With it went extensive grounds on all sides of the cathedral, except the front, which faced San Francisco street.

These were measures undertaken in only a single town—the largest, to be sure. But in addition, there were the now annual journeys over the plains for supplies and recruitment, each of which cost in the thousands. The long-neglected outlying churches and chapels needed renewal—needed everything. The immense lands to the west and north which were also his responsibility remained *terra incognita;* when time —and peace at home—would allow, he must go to see them, learn their wants, and provide for them. For help, he clung to that older and more experienced friend who never failed him—Purcell, under whom he had learned his way. "Your charity and your great kindness to me of which I have had so many proofs will excuse me [i.e., rescue him] on account of my embarrassed condition being under very heavy expenses, and with everything to establish. . . ."

In the same letter, he told Purcell, "Most likely Rev. Mr Machebeuf is to go to Europe next spring." In search of new clergy and seminarians, yes—but more: to present, in Rome, Lamy's replies to charges and intrigues against him on the part of his antagonists at home. For Santa Fe was home, now, and forever, with all which that could mean.

VI

SCANDAL AT TAOS

1852–1861

i.

Martínez Rampant

IF THERE WAS EVERY REASON FOR LAMY TO BELIEVE that his enemies
were intensifying their representations against him at Rome, he had
more comforting reason, in January 1856, to hope that peace might at
last settle upon his relations with one who was potentially his most
formidable, because most intelligent and even least corrupt, adversary.
This was the pastor of Ranchos de Taos, Father Antonio José Martínez. Father Martínez had worked for a quarter of a century for his
people in Taos—Indians of the pueblo as well as the Mexican families
of the *ranchos* and the central village. He had tried, long before Lamy,
to find native youths who could be trained for the priesthood, and
had found some—the notorious Gallegos of Albuquerque had been
one of them. Martínez, too, had had his fling in local politics, and,
remote in his high mountain village on Taos Plain, he had kept up
a lively life of the mind, with strong opinions dating from his years
as a seminarian at Durango. Now, after his skirmishes with Lamy,
over the issue of the division of the Santa Fe parish, and with Machebeuf, over the accusations of betrayals of the confessional oath, he
seemed to have subsided, despite his deeply entrenched local patriot-
ism and pride of race. Further, he was beginning to feel the infirmities
of age coming upon him, and he fell to considering proper arrangements for a diminishing future. He wrote to Lamy about all this in a
temperate spirit.

Sending his letter by way of his cousin Joaquín Sandoval, who
brought with it for the bishop a chalice of silver "worth thirty pesos,"
he went on to say that he was troubled with rheumatism which, especially when riding, gave him great suffering in his legs. He had to keep
himself warmly dressed even in the house. More—his nights were
greatly distressed by urinary difficulties—"I am unable to void all that
I need to," and falling asleep became impossible. Lying in bed until

three in the morning was all he could do. He was troubling Lamy with these disagreeable personal matters because "if such ills continue," he must sooner or later vacate his benefice—when, who could say? But it might be in the near future, though until such time he would of course give due attention to his duties. In short, "I might find myself obliged to resign because of poor health," and he remained at His Excellency's disposal, and was his most true subject and faithful servant.

To this recital which seemed to cry out for sympathy there was no reply from Santa Fe. Lamy was alert to other concerns, and he wrote of these to Barnabo at Rome; for he had evidence that the legislators of New Mexico, and other laymen, under the sponsorship of Gallegos and J. F. Ortiz, were readying a huge bill of complaints against him to be addressed to Pio Nono. In the light of recent history, he may still have had doubts about Martínez. In any case, instead of answering Martínez, he wrote to Barnabo, "Perhaps the legislators of New Mexico who, though Catholics in name, are far from honoring religion by their moral conduct, will send you a representation against me and some of the rules which I established. I think it my duty to warn you of this, for all this opposition is plotted slyly by two or three Mexican priests"—could Martínez be one?—"who do not easily pardon me for the fault of having come to trouble them. . . ."

In a month or so Machebeuf was to leave for Rome. He and Lamy were taken up with the preparation of documents which would present the bishop's case at the Holy See. Father Martínez, with his tall, oval face, framed in black receding hair, his black eyes with the lids drawn down at the outer corners, his lean dour mouth, his jutting cheek bones, the uncertain look oddly lodged in his strong features, above his black neck cloth and his velvet-faced black cloak, was not the foremost of the concerns which now held Lamy's attention. Once again preparing to manage without the presence of his vicar general, Lamy, as he had written to the Society at Paris, would have to do everything himself—"*Je suis alors curé, vicaire, secrétaire et enfin factotum, mais grâce à Dieu j'ai une santé robuste. . . .*"

He armed Machebeuf with "a long letter" in his own defense which the vicar general was to present at Rome. He gave him a letter to Pius IX asking permission for his travelling priests to say two Masses in one day—keeping the fast—at far separated missions, during the pre-Christmas novenas of the Virgin Mary, for he feared that without this privilege, certain places would be deprived of the devotions which alone could save the feast day from lapsing into merely secular celebration. Once more, he wrote an outline of the entire dispute with Zubiría over "Doñana" or "*Condado*," patiently supporting the logical, indeed legal, claim which Santa Fe held to the still unassigned area. In February he had already written again to Barnabo, hoping to hasten the decision, and pointing out that "the inhabitants of the Condado are astonished that I do not exercise my jurisdiction in this part of the Territory as in the other parts . . ." Now Machebeuf would press the claim again. So far, if Lamy had not taken possession of the disputed lands, it was only to "avoid any controversy with Mgr. Zubiría," and also to permit the decision to come from Rome. But it was to be noted that "several bishops and archbishops of the United States" were joining him "to demonstrate to the Holy See the justice" of his appeal. For the rest, "M. Machebeuf will expose to you the various reasons why the Holy See should deign to grant my request, for the order and general well-being of our holy religion." In another matter, finding himself "financially embarrassed," he asked permission to sell a small piece of Church property—evidently the *Castrense* chapel, now unused since the departure of Ortiz and the reconsolidation of the parish of Santa Fe. In addition, and of vital importance, he gave Machebeuf a general document authorizing him to recruit, wherever he might go, "priests, seminarians, brothers, nuns, or monks," to meet the "immense need" of the diocese. (Machebeuf kept the paper all his life.) Counting on success in such enrollments, Lamy asked the Society at Paris to stand ready to pay the travel expenses of those who would return home with Machebeuf. Not for the last time Lamy had to turn to the Old World to succor the New; for all America was still a missionary district and his diocese was remote from everything but the concern of Paris, Lyon, and Rome.

In bitter weather and heavy snows, Machebeuf travelled eastward over the plains in March. Everyone had adventures, but his always carried, in his accounts, a particular kind of pleasurable amazement. His carriage was upset in the snow four days out of Fort Union. He must abandon the carriage and in order not to overload his other cart, which already carried luggage and rations, he and a companion had to walk for two days through the snow, at last joining up with a waggon train of merchants, American and Mexican, who were bound for the St Louis markets. They "took pity on him" and gave him and his equipment travelling room in an enormous waggon containing six other passengers and fodder for twenty animals, pulled by ten mules. It could be imagined how all this was less than agreeable or thrilling, but preserving a dignity becoming to a Frenchman and a missioner, he showed himself satisfied none the less, and did not allow his "good humour to suffer."

There were compensations, for, in return for inconvenience, he was witness to the marvels of the snowy plains: buffalo, deer, antelope in the thousands; and he revelled in the adventures of dining now and then with the plates laid on the snow, but for the most part, they all ate "like the Israelites"—standing, with their weapons in hand. They slept at night under two buffalo robes with an added cover of five or six inches of snow, while great packs of wolves circled the camp, eating what was left, even to bits of harness. One of his fellow travellers told him he had seen wolves prowling several times about his bed, but he neither saw them himself, nor paid attention, for soundly asleep he was "not of this world." (Between St Louis and Cincinnati in April, he wrote this account to his sister from the steamboat *Sultana*, a ship which blew up nine years later when her entire battery of boilers "went," killing 1647 persons in the worst steamship disaster of the inland rivers.) He would proceed first to Paris, then Clermont, then Rome.

At Santa Fe, by the beginning of April, after the long and hard winter, which had brought much extra work in keeping the adobe houses and churches with their mud roofs in repair, fine weather came to the mountains and brought the first easing of spring, when everything stood clear and sharp to the eye, and the air wafting down from the high pine forests lifted the spirits. Lamy—had he been struggling already for five years there?—seemed to see a few signs of progress.

The cathedral parish church was now "pretty well repaired." He had a good lot and house for the sisters, and as much for the school for boys, and he began to think that his heavy expenses might be over, so that he could begin to "square" some of his debts. "If on one part we have troubles," he told Purcell, "on the other we meet with some consolation. where I have good priests, the improvement is sensible." People were able to resume the sacraments; children were being taught and catechized; new churches were being built, others restored; schools were improving, "particularly that of the sisters," whose pupils were steadily increasing in numbers. "The priests I brought two years ago, and to whom you yourself gave hospitality in Cincinnati are doing great good. they are animated of the right kind of spirit. I hope Mr Machebeuf will bring me a few more of that kind. . . ."

True, expenses continued to be dreadful, chiefly because of the high cost of transporting everything over the plains. There seemed no possibility of letting up on his means of raising money through church fees. These seemed harsh not only to the old residents, and their priests whose benefices had been reduced and divided, but also to other observers. The secretary of the Territory wrote,

In the spring of 1856 a young Mexican gentleman was buried in Santa Fe according to the rites of the Catholic Church, and a friend afterward handed me a copy of the bill the officiating priest presented for the services, which, though considerable in amount, is quite reasonable compared to that previously mentioned. As a matter of curiosity, I append an exact copy of the bill of fees, viz.:

Dobles (tolling the bells)	$10.00
El sepulcro (the grave)	30.00
La cruz alta (the grand cross)	1.00
La capa (high mass vestments [cope])	3.00
La aqua bendita (holy water)	1.00
Los ciriales (candlesticks)	1.00
El incensario (vessel for incense)	1.00
Las mesas (resting places [bier])	3.00
El intierro (the interment)	30.00
La Misa (Mass)	20.00
El organo (use of the organ)	15.00
Los cantores (the chanters [choir])	6.00
El responso del oratorio (response of the oratory)	10.00
Más al diacono (the deacon's fee, additional)	10.00
	$141.00

It must be borne in mind that these charges are solely the dues of the Church for the religious services of the burial, and the bills are made out in mercantile form and duly presented for payment. From this showing, it is an expensive matter to die and be buried in New Mexico, and appears to cost quite as much as it does to live. There is no doubt about the right of the Church to charge for the burial service all the people are willing to pay, but we may fairly question the propriety of making such simple and necessary rites so expensive. . . . Facts of this kind are a strong argument in favor of the abolition of the system of tithing in New Mexico, and instead giving the priests a fixed salary, as is the case in other parts of the United States.

Where the income for such salaries was to come from, the secretary did not say.

"Though the time rolls on," wrote Lamy, "the strong opposition raised altogether by few of the old *padres* does not seem to stop." For one thing, Gallegos was campaigning furiously for reelection to the post of delegate to the Congress, spending money, making splendid promises. His opponent was a young man of a great old family, the Otéros. He was well educated, he spoke sensibly, and he saw the society as Lamy did; but Gallegos by an early reckoning was in the lead and his party, said Lamy, were "trying all they can to embarrass us."

But even more extraordinary—Juan Felipe Ortiz was again agitating the scene. In his condition of suspended priest, he was the principal one who had induced the members of the legislative assembly of New Mexico to "make a petition to the court of Rome" against Lamy. But—Lamy could not forbear to report the most astounding absurdity—Ortiz "had the humility to propose himself to Rome as Bishop of the Diocese and to have us suspended or at least removed. This very week"—the last week of April 1856—"he wrote me an insolent letter, asking me to show him a Document of the Sovereign Pontife [sic] by which I could prove that I was authorized to take this parish." The hysterical unrealism of such a performance, which alone must guarantee that Rome would never view Ortiz as a potential bishop, moved Lamy to add, "From these facts you may have an idea of their ability. I have to pray for them that the Almighty will change them."

In the same month, Martínez wrote again to Lamy from Taos. His maladies persisted. He hoped a priest might be sent to relieve him— not for the sake alone of his health, but for the fact that he felt unable to fulfill his duties properly. In fact, he had a candidate, and he proposed him to the bishop: Father Don Ramón Medina. He said he was asking for Medina "because the people are terribly worried about the priesthood that is not native to the country"—an admission which said much, if tactlessly, about the local opinion of the French clergy. He hastened to add that the parishioners regarded the new clergy as Americans, and did "not believe in them." Recognizing their fears, Martínez did what he could to allay their suspicions, "but," he said, in the end, "it is a sort of general preoccupation which they do have." He thought, therefore, that if Medina, a native priest, could be sent, he could learn his duties and the local obligations under Martínez's supervision, and, surely, would in a short time be able to continue alone as pastor. "At this time," said Martínez, "I would formally resign."

It was an adroit proposal (he accompanied it with sixteen pesos due to the bishop) by which in effect Martínez would retain control, the cabal against Lamy could be maintained, and the ways of reform could be resisted; but it failed of its purpose.

Lamy, moving swiftly, gently, and with finality, within a fortnight notified Martínez that his resignation was accepted, saying that he wished to accommodate him, and "contribute with all in my power toward the recovery of your health, since you say . . . you feel quite unwell and unable to carry out the duties of the administration." He was therefore sending a priest to Taos to assume the pastorate—not Don Ramón, for this young priest was not yet experienced enough for such a post. But instead, the bishop was assigning Taos to the mature

Spanish priest, Don Damaso Taladrid, who had come with him from Rome two years ago, and already had had much experience "in the priestly ministry" of parish duties. To make his point quite clear, Lamy added that under this new arrangement, Martínez would be "without responsibility, and, relieved of cares," could, out of consideration for his advanced age, accept the ease and rest he deserved.

A stunning rebuff, the reply was anything but what Martínez expected. Consequences painful and protracted for both him and the bishop would not be long in coming.

ii.

The Advocate at Rome

MACHEBEUF, MOVING ABOUT HIS AFFAIRS with his usual *brio,* was at Mont-Ferrand in Clermont by the end of May, where he enlisted six seminarians for the New Mexico transport. While there he undoubtedly paid a visit to his old home, and to Sister Philomène, his sibling and constant correspondent, in her Convent of the Visitation, at Riom. By 7 June he was in Lyon, a week later he was in Paris, and in both cities he made requests for financial help for the return journey to the West. He had thought to be in Rome earlier, but being delayed, he did not expect to arrive there before the end of June, and accordingly, he sent Lamy's documents ahead to the papal court, and would soon follow to support their contentions with his own testimony.

He had four main lines of argument to pursue—one, concerning the attacks upon Lamy; two, attacks upon himself; three, reports on leaders among the rebel clergy; and four, the stubborn affair of Doñ-ana and the *Condado,* and the proper assignment of their ecclesiastical control.

By the time Machebeuf reached Rome, Pius IX had already asked for a report from the office of the Propaganda Fide about the formidable documents addressed to him, with elaborate enclosures, by Gallegos, whose covering letter summarized the accusations against Lamy, mourned the lost epoch under Zubiría, and strove to anticipate and nullify any efforts Machebeuf might make to justify the state of affairs at Santa Fe. Writing in Spanish from Washington on 24 April 1856, Gallegos said:

Most Holy Father:

I have the honor of presenting to the special consideration of Your Holiness the attached pages which were consigned to me by my constituents of the Territory of New Mexico.

The complaint which they contain against His Illustrious Lordship Lamy is true, just, and honest; for which reason I believe they will merit the worthy attention of Your Holiness; so that by estimating the deeds in their just merits, Your Holiness may then resolve them in the most rational and suitable manner.

With all my soul I regret to find myself the one to reveal such sad truths, which should always be hidden in the pages of history. But their revelation has become necessary, since the spiritual and temporal welfare of the Catholic Faithful of New Mexico depends upon it.

The conduct, Most Holy Father, the hostile conduct of his Illustrious Lordship Señor Lamy without just cause, and without observance of the necessary rituals as demanded by Canon Law, has violently deprived the permanent pastors of the Church of New Mexico of their proper benefices, while substituting in their places other ministers newly emigrated to this country, whom he has favored, conferring on them many benefices, thus leaving our poor previous ministers without their posts of spiritual administrations, and forcing them into the hard position of having to work in menial and crude tasks, in order to make a living.

Our Christian Towns of Indians (converts of Catholicism, as they are), and numbering some 18 towns, are thus also left without spiritual administration, harshly abandoned to their own ignorance; and I have no doubt that within a short time they will revert to their primitive and savage state of idolatry.

With respect to the spiritual administration by Señor Lamy and the greater number of his protected ministers, let me inform Your Holiness that I do not err in stating that even in the barest simplification [my present statement] contains the aspect of truth.

I have been informed that no sooner was Señor Lamy apprised of the accusations thus made than he immediately ordered the Vicar P. Machebeuf to hurry to Rome, for a reason which we suppose was the principal object: to try to mislead with false information, which we hope Your Holiness will not credit, and will consequently take needed action on such an important matter.

Most Holy Father, permit me also to declare that our shortcomings in the past were always excused when we were dependent on the pastorship of the Illustrious Lordship, Señor Zubiría, the Bishop of Durango; for this virtuous Prelate, with his true Apostolic zeal, was able to hold our loyalty and satisfy our spiritual needs; and he carried forward unalterably a good program of peace which certainly prevailed in that most memorable time, throughout all our Towns.

I hope Your Holiness will have the goodness of communicating to me your decision in this important matter, sending it to Santa Fe, New Mexico, so as to satisfy with your decision the desires of my constituents.

May God Our Lord preserve in His grace the inestimably important Life of Your Holiness: such is the petition of this,

Your most loving son, who humbly implores Your Blessing, and who attentively,

Kisses Your Hands,
J. M. Gallegos,
Delegate of New Mexico
in the Congress of the Union.

Supporting his letter, Gallegos enclosed that lengthy catalogue of charges against Lamy and Machebeuf which he had drawn up with Ortiz, and which was signed by twenty representatives and ten members of the legislative council of the legislative assembly of New Mexico, and by three country prefects. The fact that the signers all bore Spanish names dramatized the social animosities of the diocese. In their ten accusations they greatly elaborated their charges: Lamy had annulled certain marriages despite earlier dispensations; had "without fair cause" first divided the parish of Santa Fe and then entirely taken it away from its pastor of twenty years, Juan Felipe Ortiz; had deprived at various times, against the wishes of their parishioners and without canonical warnings, certain named priests of their curacies; had ignored many petitions sent to him (with, in some cases, duplicates to the Holy See) by eminent pastors. The accusations insisted that Machebeuf had been guilty of faults of "much gravity"; that Lamy's imposition of tithes and heavy penalties for non-payment were harmful to the very Church; that four native priests had been retained by Lamy because they had bribed him to do so; that he had condoned Machebeuf's offensive characterizations of certain native marriages; that he had "contrary to our public statutes" taken part in and interfered in political affairs; that Lamy was guilty of other infractions not particularized in order not to "presume upon the High attention of Your Holiness." The petitioners were sure that what they had already cited must be enough to prove that if Lamy went unchecked, then schism must follow and Protestantism would flourish.

"Wherefore," they concluded, "Most Holy Father, with all such remarkable facts, and they are so of a certainty, for causes so serious and grave and just, we do beg Your Holiness, and we pray in the most humble and respectful way, that You deign to decree for us, according to our petition, the removal from his place as Bishop of Santa Fe, His Illustrious Lordship Lamy; and the nomination in his place of the Vicar Don Juan Felipe Ortiz, in which individual, we have no doubt in telling Your Holiness, that those qualities stipulated

by Saint Paul as necessary for the exact fulfillment of the heavy episcopal responsibilities, are found. . . . Such a substitution will return
the peace and tranquility to our Church, and will preserve us firm
and stable in our true Catholicism, producing at the same time great
joy and happiness for the majority of the Faithful of this Bishopric."

In Rome, all the charges were laid before Machebeuf, and, asked
to comment, he hurried to a desk in an office at the Propaganda to
work on written refutations. In the loose scramble of his handwriting,
his pages looked as though his pen could not keep pace with his
thoughts.

"Firstly," he wrote, in a general rebuttal of the legislative attack
sponsored by Gallegos and others, "it is necessary to observe that the
inhabitants of New Mexico are generally deprived of all schooling and
are little accustomed to governing themselves according to the law of
the United States to which they submit since 1846. The immense
majority do not know how to read and those who are able to sign
their name are considered educated . . ." He could therefore describe
the legislative assembly as "composed of ignorant men, most of them
corrupt, dishonest, who hold the people in fear of them, as their old
priest has told us. These people are mostly related to each other by
different degrees of affinity and the corruption of this society illustrates
their prejudice toward a foreign bishop who is obliged to reform their
morals." Out of fear, he declared, "many people sign written contracts
without understanding the contents." It followed, in respect of the
charges laid out in the assembly's letter, that it was "not wrong to say
that several signed the presentation without knowing what it meant."
The inference to be taken was that Gallegos and Ortiz had drawn up
a case to suit themselves for which they had rounded up signatures.
(It was clear that this conclusion was sustained by the rhetorical style
of the petition itself.)

Going on to specific charges, the vicar general declared that when
Lamy was accused of making his famous journey to Durango without
specific authority to do so, it was vitally important to consult with
Zubiría if he was to function at all. In the matter of the division of
the Santa Fe parish, it was necessary only to recall the reason naively
attributed to Lamy by Ortiz—that was, for personal gain. The charge
would remind anyone of what Ortiz stood to lose for himself. Concerning the claims that Lamy had deprived certain priests of their
parishes without warning, "half the territory" knew that on the contrary these pastors, in consequence of the first pastoral letter requiring
reforms (which Machebeuf quoted), *had resigned,* "declaring they
would never submit" to the bishop's rules. Even so, Lamy gave them
a month to reconsider. When they refused to do so, Lamy properly

suspended them. (In certain other more notorious cases, the bishop had suspended certain pastors, because of their scandalous lives, without strictly observing the canonical periods of warning, but at the time he had explained to Archbishop Purcell that matters were too flagrant to permit a delay of discipline.) The accusations against Machebeuf himself were "absurd," the people themselves had supported him, and even Padre Martínez of Taos, who was one of those against the bishop ("document attached," showing his signature with those of Ortiz, Lujan, and Chavez), defended Machebeuf in this instance ("document attached"). As for the theological questions raised by the legislators, these displayed the ignorance of men who didn't know what they were talking about, and who perhaps could not even read. For example, what they said about the two annulled marriages was false. "Mgr Lamy had perfectly examined the circumstances." The charge that Lamy was "playing politics and favoring Protestantism" was simply not so. "His only policies have been to preach the word of God and to work for the salvation of souls, and in this pursuit he has been unjustly attacked by ignorant, dishonest, and corrupt men." Machebeuf then, as if to illustrate the sort of persons he meant, gave brief but devastating sketches of such as Fathers J. F. Ortiz, Salazar, Lujan, Gallegos, and Martínez, scrupulously adding, about the pastor of Taos, that "we cannot prove anything about the accusation against his morals, but we are certain that public opinion is against him," and that "his character is so false and deceptive, so *hidden,* so *flattering,* that while seeking to destroy Mgr Lamy, he appears as his best friend in front of other people. Duplicity is thus his dominant trait." Still, "the truth obliges me to say that he has never failed in a show of personal respect towards" the bishop. A secretarial digest, which did not presume to reach a judgement, was promptly made of Machebeuf's memorandum and was forwarded by Barnabo to Pius IX in accordance with the Pope's command.

All of these loyal arguments were undoubtedly supported further by much spoken discussion between Machebeuf and the office of the Propaganda, and so, too, must have been another matter which in turn had its written statement made at the time in Rome by Machebeuf.

This was of course the wearisome affair of the disputed territories of the border. Zubiría had already proved himself a master of procrastination, and he was far from finished with it as an instrument of policy. At about the time Machebeuf was arriving in Rome, Archbishop Clementi in Mexico City—the apostolic delegate—was writing to the Vatican to say that Lamy was "anxious to hear the outcome about a controversy with the bishop of Durango," and requesting a Vatican decision based on Zubiría's statement of 1854, which had never been acknowledged. Clementi therefore sent another copy now. It merely repeated Zubiría's original position—that the *Condado* belonged to him.

Machebeuf in raising the issue again (which he had already reported to the Society in Lyon) cited new factors which since 1854 had radically changed the rationale for a decision—the Gadsden Purchase and the new, and final, borderline between Mexico and the United States. But more—immigration had steadily increased, he said. There was a new county named Doñana now, not only a town by that name, the population had reached close to five thousand, and the people had no spiritual ministrations except infrequent visits from priests from Mexico, below the Rio Grande. Within the year, he cited, a hundred and sixty persons had died without the sacraments, and there had been repeated requests to Lamy, "whom they recognized as their bishop," for priests from his diocese. But Zubiría had not budged in his position. All Machebeuf could do was to keep the issue alive. He received no decisions, either, to his other protestations while in Rome. But he had done his best. He knew the Court of Rome moved in a stately measure, and in order not to miss his all-important date for catching the last of the autumn crossings westward, he had to hurry off to France in early August to gather up his new party destined for America.

iii.

Martínez, Gallegos, Politics

FATHER DAMASO TALADRID had promptly followed Lamy's letter by moving to Taos to assume his duties as pastor—an act which inspired Padre Martínez to new heights of irascibility. Ill and aging, he already felt put upon, for Lamy clearly had outmaneuvered him. Perhaps there was that in his temperament, too, which reflected the historically unstable character of Taos. There were three related communities in the great Taos Plain. The pre-Hispanic pueblo rose at the base of the mountains to the north. Three miles away to the south, the principal Spanish village of Don Fernando de Taos, scattered with its whitewashed adobe houses, was the seat of the parish and the civil authority. A few miles still further south was the much smaller settlement of the

Ranchos de Taos, whose massive chapel of St Francis served the farming families in the little houses and corrals clustered about it.

In the mid-nineteenth century a United States soldier recorded his view of the area: "the inhabitants of the Valley of Taos are the most turbulent in New Mexico, and the Indians of the Pueblo of Taos still entertain a smothered feeling of animosity against the Americans, which it is well to keep under." The same could have been said of the recently annexed Mexicans, who had a tradition of revolution and massacre, the latest of which had been thrown against the United States authority only nine years earlier than this summer of 1856. In that, as well as in the revolt of 1837 under the Mexican régime, Martínez was thought to have been active on the side of the rebels. The only authority which he felt necessary was that which he honored in himself. His state of both mind and body, then, disposed him to resentment against Taladrid.

But more—Taladrid himself invited this response; for, a Spaniard born, a familiar of Rome, who had served as a missionary in Africa, he viewed New Mexicans as mere colonials, and as colonials of a low order, at that. He was not slow to show this attitude toward Martínez, who with justice regarded himself as a superior individual, a man of education; indeed, an intellectual man, if measured against his neighbors. Now, instead of the junior recruit he had asked for whom he could train in his own independent Taos attitudes, he had to contend with a mature, sophisticated, and unmannerly priest who, moreover, was the personal choice of the bishop to replace him.

His provocations were already great, but, for the moment, Martínez held his temper, and occasionally officiated solemnly at ceremonies in his former parish church. But he had an ally in the pastor of Arroyo Hondo, twelve miles north of Taos, Father Mariano de Jesús Lucero, and it was not long until they spoke out together against Taladrid, bishop or no bishop. They had strong native constituencies, and they set about to do everything possible to undermine Taladrid's authority and prestige.

Almost immediately, then, Martínez's powers as the great man of Taos and Taladrid's as the licit pastor came to clash. For one thing, long ago, Zubiría had given Martínez certain faculties as chaplain and custodian—perhaps as a restraining influence—for the Brotherhood of the Penitentes; and since this mandate was made to him, Martínez said, as a personal sub-delegation, and not as "a priest of Taos," he had not transferred this function to Taladrid, though he had duly notified him of the matter. Otherwise, Martínez felt that he had "with the best disposition" handed over all the other parish rights and duties to his successor, as Taladrid surely must have reported to Lamy.

But Taladrid was not convinced that Martínez's abdication was sincere or complete, or that the parishioners were ready to welcome him. Actually, certain persons had made trouble by reporting how freely Martínez had spoken against him. Taladrid was often suspicious as well as disdainful, even when Martínez protested that he had done his best to bring the people into a respectful attitude. To no avail. "Señor Taladrid," declared Martínez in a letter to the bishop, "does not behave well toward me, defaming me behind my back, even in some of the outlying missions of the parish." Taladrid, for his part, wrote to the bishop about Martínez: "The only human thing about him is his shape." It was the old case of the pot and the kettle.

A hard summer was in the making. Taladrid not only abused Martínez's reputation—he caused him physical discomfort and even suffering. The old pastor still liked to say morning Mass in the church but the new pastor often made this as difficult as possible for him. Taladrid, even though he knew that Martínez in his illness could not sustain a long fast before Mass, would instruct the sexton to delay the preparation of the vestments and vessels so that Martínez would be obliged to wait, "in order to mistreat me"—so the sexton himself had told him. One morning in May when Martínez went to Taladrid at home to beg him to let him say Mass early, Taladrid seized hold of him, cried, "I know how to hit hard and fight!" and added that the bishop was so fixed in his anger against Martínez that he held him forever "in reprobation." To this cruel statement Martínez answered that it was not from animosity that he had been relieved of his post— it was for consideration of his health, and he had Lamy's letter to prove it.

Now smarting with an aggravated sense of injustice, Martínez published an open letter in the Santa Fe Spanish newspaper—the *Gaceta* —to give his side of the row—at the very least an unseemly public act. It discommoded and angered Lamy, who took to the Taos road himself to try to bring about a reconciliation between the two priests.

It was a difficult road, impossible for carriages, while even freight waggons had to take a laborious detour under half-loads. The bishop rode his horse up along the Rio Grande, through Taos Canyon, coming at last onto the sweep of the Taos Plain, so flat that the cut of the river's deep gorge looked from a distance like a cloud shadow.

Unable to effect a lasting peace in Taos on this first visit, Lamy made a second trip later in the summer, once more with no success. Taladrid had further gravely offended Martínez, who had a strong patronal family feeling, by treating a Martínez cousin "as a heretic"; and even though Taladrid evidently made a sort of redress, the enmity was sealed. Because of all the provocations Martínez had been made to accept, his final act of rebellion came in a form which Lamy, even in his patience, could not long condone; for in his visits to Taos, the bishop learned that Martínez had remodeled his own residence to contain a private oratory, and that there he conducted services and officiated in other ways as an independent pastor. His native following—including his large collection of relatives—provided him with a regular congregation for whom he exercised his priestly powers without any authority from Santa Fe. In all his trials with the recusant clergy—particularly Gallegos and Ortiz—Lamy found Martínez "worse than these two together."

For throughout the summer Ortiz and Gallegos had been working with reckless zeal to secure the latter's reelection as New Mexico's delegate to Congress. The campaign aroused strong partisanships. A priest, one Cárdenas, who had been suspended even by Zubiría for moral reasons, wrote to the *Weekly Gazette* of Santa Fe from London to support Gallegos. The paper, "independent in all things, neutral in none," published an editorial against Gallegos in both English and Spanish which said,

We ask the people of New Mexico in the name of all that's just, to look at the acts of Bishop Lamy since he came into the Territory. Has he done anything that is not calculated to elevate the Church, and to advance the interests of the holy Catholic religion? Has he not relieved the people from oppressive Church exactions levied solely to maintain a corrupt and profligate Clergy, who were in many cases a moral curse to the country? Pause, Mexicans, before you cast your votes for a man who would stop the progress of this glorious reform, in which you are so much interested for yourselves and your children in all time to come.

Miguel A. Otero ran against Gallegos and lost in the final tabulation of votes; but with evidence of fraud at hand, he challenged the election, even though Gallegos had been seated in the House again. Once there, Gallegos laid a speech of great length before the House, in which he directly defamed Lamy. Denying in his speech a charge that "the influence of the Roman Catholic Church was brought into the contest at the polls to secure my election," Gallegos went on to write:

—In point of fact, this is the precise converse of the truth. A clergyman of that church, I found myself, previous to my first election to this body, deprived of my living in common with all the other native clergy of New Mexico, excepting four only, by the new French bishop, to make way for imported French priests of his own selection. The attempt to vindicate our rights only served to secure the whole weight of ecclesiastical influence against us, one and all. At the [second] election, now the subject of contest, it is notorious that the foreign bishop did, in fact, intermeddle, by himself and his priests, not to support me, but to crush me, and to secure the election of my opponent. And I have now the original memorial, signed by upwards of thirty of the thirty-nine members of the two Houses of the Territorial Legislature, addressed to the chief bishop of the Roman church [Pius IX], praying the removal of one who has shown himself capable of prostituting his office.

Mr Speaker, these topics are not willingly introduced by me, nor do I believe that they will be acceptable to this House; but they are forced upon me, and I am compelled thus to notice them. I leave them now to such reflections as what has been said may suggest to the minds of honorable members.

He then discussed the criteria for counting ballots in New Mexico, and touched upon the legitimacy of 131 ballots cast at La Mesilla village, in the Doñana *Condado,* which had been disallowed as votes cast by Mexican nationals—again the old ambiguity of the civil status of an area within the United States but still in popular ways allied to Mexico.

In his turn, Otero rose as contestant to address the House. He first made the statistical claim that Gallegos had been returned by a fraudulent majority of 578 votes, and then challenged his opponent's claim to represent faithfully all New Mexicans; for Gallegos had based much of his campaign on anti-Anglo-American sentiment, since the Mexican population was still in the majority. But, Otero declared,

For many years past there have been two parties in that Territory—one calling itself the Mexican party, and indulging in great hostility against the institutions of these States; the other denominated the American party, and looking to annexation as the only security from the perpetual discords and civil wars of Mexico. These visions commenced before the late war between the two countries, and continue to the present day as the fundamental distinction between existing parties. I confess I have always been attached to the institutions of this country, and to have been taught from childhood to look to this quarter for the political regeneration of my people. Though of unmixed Spanish descent, I received my education in this country; and I am happy to entertain the thought that I am the first native citizen of that acquired Territory who has come to the Congress of our adopted fatherland, and address it in the language of its laws and its Constitution. And I am proud to know that my own people at home do not consider me the less qualified, on that account, to represent them in this body, whatever may be the opinion of the sitting delegate. . . .

There is one topic, Mr Speaker, which ought not to have been introduced here at this time, and which I should not have noticed at all but for the attack of the sitting delegate upon the Catholic Bishop of New Mexico. I have asserted in my notice, and it is perfectly notorious in the Territory, that the corrupt priests did exert the influence of the church to secure the election of my competitor. This fact cannot be denied by any honest man who is acquainted with the facts. But I utterly deny that the bishop was guilty of any interference whatever, unless that could be called an interference which sought merely to restrain the priesthood from the scandal of an active and zealous participation in the canvass. I myself carried to the bishop a petition signed by several influential and respectable citizens of the sitting Delegate's native county, requesting that the priests who were actively interfering in the election might be forbidden to use the power of the Church for so corrupt a purpose. Not without hesitation and reluctance, the bishop wrote a mild letter to padre Ortiz [the old ex-dean] of San Juan, which letter I also carried to said prelate, advising him to abstain from taking an active part in the contest. The hypocritical padre, while professing obedience to the wish of his superior, utterly disregarded the instruction given. He was a zealous partisan of the sitting Delegate, and made use of all the influence of his position to aid him in the election.

So much for the election. But Otero felt obliged in conscience to do more. "I feel it my duty," he declared in the House, "to go further, and to defend the bishop from the charges unjustly made or insinuated against him. I believe him to be eminently worthy of respect for his piety, intelligence, and public spirit, and I should feel myself culpably negligent not to vindicate his reputation here." Otero went on to quote Gallegos's congressional attack upon Lamy's treatment of him and his fellow dissidents, and then resumed,

Now what is the truth in reference to this matter? It is no part of my purpose, as it certainly would be unbecoming of me, to make any allusion to the private character of the sitting Delegate. I do not wish to be so misunderstood. But the occasion requires me to say that, at the time of the acquisition of New Mexico by this country, when the new bishop was sent out, he found the Church sunk into the most deplorable condition of immorality. The priests themselves were notoriously addicted to the grossest vices. They were, in many instances, the disgrace of every gambling house and drinking saloon, and the open frequenters of brothels. In a word, they personified vice in all its hideous and revolting aspects. The good bishop, seeing how the holy office had been prostituted and the Church disgraced, proceeded at once to remove the delinquent priests, and substituted others in their stead. This is what the bishop has done: "this is the head and front of his offending."

But Lamy had gone still further, and done "what was never before so effectually done, since the days of the pious padres who first settled the Territory."

He has established schools upon a good foundation, and has begun the education of the young, both male and female. It is not surprising that the corrupt and degraded priests, who were formerly the worst enemies of the people, imposing upon their credulity and cultivating their prejudices, as the means of attaining their wicked ascendency, should find fault with the measures of reform adopted by the new dignitary. But in spite of their complaints, all good men will approve the change which deprives them of power and position, so much abused and perverted by their vices. This much I felt it my duty to say in vindication of a pure and good man, who has faithfully served the best interests of his Church, and has labored for the good of the people over whom he has been placed. I know the responsibility under which I speak: I vouch for the general accuracy of the facts stated.

Mr Speaker, I should never have felt authorized to allude to any of these subjects but for the singular production which the sitting Delegate has caused to be laid upon your tables.

Returning to the election issue, Otero further consolidated his arguments in contest. The question was again put before the full House, Gallegos was unseated, and Otero took the oath of office as the new delegate from New Mexico. This debate in Congress was a public vindication of Lamy's whole administration thus far; and further, it might give him one more measure of strength in the Doñana problem, since this had been shown as a matter which clouded not only ecclesiastical but even civil jurisdiction in the diocese. Lamy was yet again awaiting Rome's decision in the matter.

As for another decision, more immediate and distressing to make— Martínez was forcing Lamy to it; for in spite of demands from the bishop that he publicly retract his violent and rebellious statements in the *Gaceta de Santa Fe* (signed with his pseudonym "Santistevan"— his mother's maiden name) he had not done so, though eventually he apologized for his "excessive" language. Further, ordered to cease conducting the affairs of his private "parish," in which Father Lucero of Arroyo Hondo openly supported him, he disobeyed; and finally, on 27 October, Lamy sent to Martínez a writ of suspension of all his priestly duties. Martínez defied even this, refused to discontinue his ministrations, and so entered into a state of open schism. What could only follow would be further—and extreme—action on Lamy's part, after Machebeuf's return to Santa Fe, expected a week or so later.

iv.

Machebeuf and Company Returning

WITH A PARTY OF THIRTEEN IN ALL, Machebeuf had sailed from Le Havre in the *Alma*, Captain Bocandy, in early August, bringing from Mont-Ferrand the seminarians J. M. Coudert, Gabriel Ussel, Fialon,

Fayet, Rallière, and Truchard. The crossing was marked at first by the seasickness of the young men, but soon over that, they were all able to join in a jubilee on 15 August, when, before an improvised altar arranged at the bridge deck by Captain Bocandy, and made festive by the flying of the flags of five different nations, Machebeuf was ready to celebrate the Mass of the Feast of the Assumption, but sudden violent storm sent them all below to celebrate Mass in the main saloon. It was also the national holiday of the Emperor Napoleon I, and the Frenchmen lent their gaiety to it. In the evening, Truchard, who had a great bass voice, intoned the *Ave Maris Stella,* uniting for all the mysteries of ocean and heaven. "A splendid dinner" was given by the captain, marked by "the explosions of champagne corks and many hilarious toasts."

In New York, Machebeuf wrote to Lamy giving his schedule of travel, and arranging for the date of arrival at Kansas City, where the bishop would have waggons waiting for them all. During a delay at the customs house, the seminarians, unable to be of help to Machebeuf because they knew no English, toured New York by horse car. When it was time to start West, Machebeuf must visit his old town of Sandusky, and on the way, show Niagara Falls to his young charges.

They found the falls "really overpowering," even grander than what they knew from Chateaubriand, whose descriptions they had read in the seminary: how from the distance he heard the frightful thunder of the falls, and saw clouds of mist rising as from a great fire, shot through with every color of the rainbow; how the pines on the banks rose like phantoms in the mist, while eagles soared high and low on the violent air currents, and how Chateaubriand gazed in mixed terror and pleasure at the spectacle with its gulf in awesome shadow four hundred feet below. He rode close to the edge for a better view, and at the very brink, his horse, suddenly terrified by a rattlesnake in a bush nearby, reared, and was saved at the last second from plunging into the current only by his rider's desperate pull on the bridle, until both were safe again on land. An adventurous youth, Chateaubriand must have a closer look at the falls; saw vines growing along sloping rocks beside the cataract, and began to climb down, when suddenly the rocks cut straight below and the vines went no further. He was left holding to the last of them, unable either to climb up or down, feeling his fingers losing their grip and the weight of his body growing heavier, while he saw death awaiting him. There were few men, he later reflected, who in all their lives knew two such minutes as he had known, suspended above the gorge of Niagara. Finally his hands opened and he fell—but by preposterous luck, he found himself alive on a rocky ledge, "half an inch from the abyss," with an excruciating

pain in his left shoulder. How fortunate: his guide, above, saw his
signal, went for help, and with immense difficulty he was rescued by
Indians of the neighborhood. In the end, all he suffered was a simple
fracture of the arm, which was set right with two splints, a bandage,
and a sling. Along with other travellers on the rocky edge in frock
coats and top hats, or bonnets, shawls, and parasols, the young Frenchmen of 1856, like Chateaubriand in 1791, staring at the unimaginably
swift and deep glassy emerald brink in its eternal pour, must have felt
the dangerous spell of its hypnotic pull.

If Sandusky, next, was less exciting, it provided them with a glimpse
of how beloved Machebeuf was in his former parish, for his welcome
there gave them, said one, "a higher idea of our good Father, and a
greater love for him." In St Louis, they met De Smet, watched Machebeuf lay the cornerstone of a new church in the woods, nearly capsized
in their waggon on the way to the ceremony, and recovered at a dinner
later in a nearby farmhouse. Machebeuf was waiting to hear final plans
from Lamy for the plains crossing, and when after some delay these
arrived, he took his people (including a new recruit, Thomas Hayes,
in minor orders) by river steamboat to Kansas City.

There the waggons sent by the bishop were waiting. Late in the day
on 4 October the party set out for the plains, and had their first night
of sleeping on the ground, hearing the doleful ruffles of the roving
coyotes all night long. In the morning they grumbled to their leader
about the animal chorus. Machebeuf replied, "You dread the monotony of the plains; these are a few of their many distractions. You ought
to be glad to have a free band to serenade you. If you do not like the
music, Mr Truchard with his magnificent voice can intone the *Ave
Maris Stella,* as he used to do for us in the ship." Truchard obliged;
they all joined with him; and the song became "their regular hymn
during the trip," except when they feared to attract Indians. Still,
whenever they relapsed into moody silence, Machebeuf would say to
them,

"Well, young men, what is the matter? Have you lost your voices?
You do not seem to be enjoying your breakfast; perhaps the coffee does
not agree with you? Well, let me work a miracle."

So, reported Gabriel Ussel, Machebeuf went to his waggon for "some
good wine, and it brought our spirits back like a charm."

On 6 October—the second day out on the plains—Machebeuf said
to his young men, each of whom, along with the Mexican carters, had
an assigned task in the order of the camp,

"Why don't you speak Spanish with our men?"

They said they did not know how.

"Oh, yes, you do!" replied Machebeuf, "and I shall prove it to you.

Now, here are the conversation books; I shall read the *Credo* very slowly while you follow me in Latin." He then recited some "very simple rules for the formation of words," the strangers mastered the system in five minutes, and thereafter "had no great difficulty in conversing" with their Mexicans.

Travelling about twenty miles a day, they met only the peaceful conventions of the prairie experience—herds of bison, visits from Indians whose chief interest seemed to be greedy curiosity, nocturnal forays by wolves in packs, parties of United States cavalry on reconnaissance. On 3 November, twelve miles from the first habitations of New Mexico, Machebeuf took a moment late at night, by a good fire, in the midst of woods and surrounded by snow, while all his companions were sound asleep, to write a word to his brother which he could post next day at Fort Union.

"I have only a moment to write that we are all in good health, we have not had the slightest accident, we have twice been visited by Indians but they did not seem hostile and were satisfied with a little sugar, wheat, and some biscuits. We hope to reach Santa Fe before Sunday. . . ."

It was 10 November when they came to the city, to receive the traditional welcome out on the road, and to attend the bishop's Te Deum in the cathedral. The six young seminarians were highly important reinforcements for Lamy's company of priests and teachers; and a month after their arrival they were all ordained in final orders by the bishop in the humble chapel of the Loretto convent, and assigned their posts in the field. Young Father Gabriel Ussel was assigned to Arroyo Hondo, replacing Lucero.

Machebeuf brought, too, items of good news from Rome. Barnabo had sympathetically heard his defense of Lamy against all the charges made against him. He had brought also written permission to sell the *Castrense* for the benefit of diocesan finances. Barnabo had been elevated to the cardinalate and promoted from secretary to prefect of the Sacred Congregation of the Propaganda Fide. Lamy wrote to congratulate him on these honors, and to thank him for his confidence and favor; and at the same time, though without offering further defense of his own case since this had been well managed already by Machebeuf, he forwarded to the cardinal marked copies of the election contest speeches in Congress by Gallegos and Otéro—exhibits which spoke for themselves well enough. He thought it well to add, since the matter had come up in the civil context of the voting process, "I hope also that the disputed area between Durango and Santa Fe will soon be decided. . . ."

v.

The Excommunications

AND NOW MACHEBEUF heard of the collapse of relations between Martínez and Lamy. Letters had again begun to pour forth to Lamy from the pastor of Taos. Always observing the complimentary conventions of salutation and conclusion, Martínez, in between, went far beyond the honest indignation of a man who felt put upon. Making charges suspiciously like those already lodged at Rome, he declined on 12 November 1856 to retract the rebellious arguments he had published in the *Gaceta de Santa Fe;* accused Lamy of attempting to impose censorship; undertook to instruct Lamy on the Canon Law requiring three formal warnings before imposing penalty upon a subordinate; cited civil as well as theological rights; edified the bishop with references to scriptural sources; reminded him of the rights of a citizen of the Republic free to express his opinions; attacked him again about his tithing policy and other provisions of the pastoral letters; advised him to imitate his predecessor, Zubiría, in administering the office of bishop; and ended with the most preposterous statement of all, which was that if Lamy would change his policies, lift the "censorship," and abandon the existing system of financial support for the Church, he, Martínez, "would agree" to make public apology for the transgressions he had committed in his open letters—quite as if these were the only matters at fault, when the schismatic chapel continued to flourish at Taos.

Since there was nothing to say in reply to any of this, Lamy made none, and Martínez wrote again five days later, admitting that in his manner of expression in his public letters he had gone "over the limits of moderation" and exercised "bad behavior in his precipitous writings"—but changed none of his views, leaving support for their rightness to public opinion. If there was an attempt at a mollifying tone in this letter, it was supported further by a postscript stating that he and Taladrid had "repaired" their arguments and had "mutually forgiven" injuries.

But Martínez was unable to leave matters at that, and ten days later, he was again at his desk, laboring through his repetitious and convoluted style to probe old injuries anew. With an air of riding his chair in outrage, he now raked up the manner of his replacement at Taos. He had not, he stated, actually resigned in his first letter of the year, or in his second—he had merely *proposed* that he would resign, but only after the successor *he* had named (Medina) had been properly proved at his task. Then, and then only, would he feel he could vacate his office. Further—by implication—he felt that he had been tricked by the bishop, in sending a "foreign" priest instead of a "native" one: this had been the cause of all the trouble. Moreover, he cited Thomas Aquinas—out of his famous vellum copy of that doctor's works—to indicate that even in suspension, he still had the right to perform such priestly functions as absolution and burial, and he let it be clear that he intended to continue doing so. It now appeared that Taladrid was still "defaming" him, and Martínez said he suspected that this was with Lamy's knowledge and approval. He charged, too, that Taladrid had formed a party of defenders of himself and Lamy made up of the survivors of the Taos Massacre of 1847 in which Martínez had played a role. Martínez saw in this a cabal against himself. He also informed the bishop that church vessels of silver had been spirited away from Taladrid's church and replaced with others made of tin, to the scandal of all. Then, there was the matter of the Penitentes—the Fraternity of Penitent Brothers. Reminding Lamy that Pius IX expected him to "quench" the Penitentes—for Lamy had once told Martínez in Santa Fe that he had discussed this with the Pope in Rome in 1854—and alluding to the mood among the native people who were making trouble over the suspension of their chaplain in the Brotherhood, Martínez warned the bishop to take care, be impartial, and correct the wrongs which would attend his announced course. (In the event, folkways persisted, and the Penitente cult survived.)

Impassive silence at Santa Fe. But Lamy poured out his troubles to Purcell, writing him in March 1857 to report that "the opposition we met at our first coming here, and which manifested itself on several occasions, is far from being crushed down. Their number, we hope, are diminishing, but unfortunately, the less they seem to be, the more head strong they are getting. the few native clergy that are out of their office keep up a bad spirit against us," and he named Gallegos, Ortiz, and Martínez—all three suspended, Martínez since the preceding October. They were working to embarrass Lamy "in every way," but chiefly by unceasing efforts to incite the people to refuse to support the Church through tithings. Lamy had to admit they were succeeding all too well. They had nothing to lose—removed from their benefices, they each had "already got a handsome fortune from the church," and they knew that if Lamy were deprived of the only local temporal means of support, he could not expect to succeed in his work for very long. But "the large majority is on the side of order," he wrote, there were now good priests leading several congregations, and through the children, the future might be secure. Further, there was not much to "fear" as yet from the Protestants who were opening schools and missions in the wake of the eastern American colonization. To the Society in Paris, the bishop said more forcefully, that the suspended clergy were "making war to the death against us, but nevertheless, Mexicans are for the good order."

Certainly Machebeuf found them so on this return to his "dear Albuquerque" to resume his pastorate. Sixty horsemen and the county prefect received him three miles from town, and escorted him to a great party enlivened by many bottles of "good Mexican wine." His assistant was the young Father Coudert, who had just come with him from France, and between them, they had to visit on a weekly basis a line of missions consisting of twelve churches, chapels, or oratories, some of which were sixty miles apart. "Imagine," he exclaimed, "the need for railroads there! But we have no other steam but the sweat of our *little* Mexican horses pricked by the *big* spurs of this land . . ."

But Martínez could not long remain silent in his impotent rage. On 13 April 1857 another enormous missive descended upon Lamy, scolding him for ignoring Martínez's previous letters; declaring his own suspension "a nullity" because it had not been preceded by "canonic admonitions" and proclaiming his immunity under "canonic rights"; declaring himself "free of suspension," who was to be "recognized as the rightful priest of Taos," and demanding the removal of Father Taladrid as pastor—all of which was elaborated repeatedly, and with vehemence, while, kissing the bishop's hands, he remained "the servant and follower" of His Illustrious Reverence.

When there was, as usual, no reply to this, Martínez wrote to Machebeuf, attacking the bishop once again for his pastoral promulgations and Church rules, and flatly stating that Lamy in suspending him was guilty of "disobeying the laws of the Church." (It was no wonder that Taladrid, writing in his turn to the *Gaceta,* called him "a Voltaire, a Rousseau, . . . egotism personified," with his "depraved maxims.") Martínez went on to complain that there were tensions in Taos, with rumors that he was to be threatened by civil authority, and that "armed forces" of certain inhabitants seemed to be ready to move against his personal safety.

What he referred to in the last instance was ominously true; for, tried beyond further patience, Bishop Lamy had come to the end with Martínez, and his ally, Lucero. In June 1857, he set in motion formal proceedings of excommunication against both Father Martínez and

Father Lucero; and when Machebeuf arrived to publish on three successive Sundays, at both Taos and Arroyo Hondo, the "canonic" admonitions demanding for the last times the submission of the defiant recusants, excitement and emotion among the people threatened to explode into violence. Martínez had his partisans, Lamy his. The pastor mounted a guard over his oratory, which he heard had been threatened with arson. Serious members of a strong faction which supported Lamy had made known their intention of preventing expected danger to Machebeuf from Martínez's followers, by armed force, if necessary.

Those who stood with Lamy and Machebeuf included both American and Mexican Catholics, whose leaders—all residents of Taos—were formidably determined and known for their prowess. One was Céran St. Vrain, a famous scout and trader, another was the French Canadian Charles Beaubien, whose son Narciso had been murdered in the Taos Massacre of 1847 in which Martínez had been a prime mover, and the third was General Kit Carson. Beaubien said, "Martínez had always been treacherous, and is now afflicted with the bighead. Let him look out!" and Carson said, "We shall not let them do as they did in 1847, when they murdered and pillaged. I am a man of peace, and my motto is: Good will to all; I hate disturbances among the people, but I can fight a little yet, and I know of no better cause to fight for than my family, my Church and my friend the Señor Vicario."

Martínez knew his people—their emotional loyalty to their own race, to him as their great man, and their resentment of the "foreigners" who had come to dominate them—and he was not now slow to arouse their anger in his defense when Machebeuf began to carry out his dangerous duty. For his part, Martínez made no response to Machebeuf's public calls to retreat from his revolt, nor did Lucero. Taos, under its dark mountain, and in its habit of violence, was waiting.

On the final Sunday, with Martínez still within his own silence, Machebeuf appeared in the Taos church to celebrate High Mass and to pronounce the excommunication. Tension was almost tangible. The church was filled, and people stood outside to hear the ceremony and to watch each other, and to see who had guns. When time came for the sermon, Machebeuf explained the meaning of excommunication, of which most of the people had no understanding except that it was the Church's ultimate discipline; and then he read the instrument itself to a hushed congregation, finished the Mass, and announced that he would remain in Taos for several days to help Taladrid in hearing confessions—a calm invitation to any who had joined the schism to return to the bishop's fold. In silence, the listeners dispersed. There was no disturbance, though everyone had felt the precarious atmosphere, and later, at Beaubien's house, when he and Carson and the others commended Machebeuf for his courage, they heard him answer, with the effect of a shrug, "Why should I be afraid? I only did my duty." Taos was left with two churches—one licit under the bishop, the other illicit under Martínez, who would keep his followers and would never give up his independent parish while he lived.

Machebeuf next had to proceed to Arroyo Hondo. Carson and the others proposed to go along to protect him in the foothill village; but he declined their help, and again, in a tense but quiet scene, he imposed the excommunication on Father Lucero, who left to join Martínez in spiritual exile. Father Ussel now presided alone at Arroyo Hondo. Done with his difficult and dangerous assignment, Machebeuf said to Ussel before returning to Santa Fe and Albuquerque,

"It is always the way. Bishop Lamy is sure to send me when there is a bad case to be settled; I am always the one to whip the cats (fouetter les chats)."

Before the excommunications, Lamy had seen the necessity of replacing not only Lucero with Ussel, but Taladrid with Eulógio—the young priest (brother of the old belligerent vicar) who had, in all loyalty, travelled abroad with the bishop. Taladrid was reassigned to Isleta. As the new pastor of Taos, Juan Eulógio Ortiz, a native New Mexican, could do more to keep the peace in Taos parish than the Spaniard Taladrid. In early July, he tried to report to Lamy in Santa Fe, but the bishop was absent, visiting outlying parishes, including that of El Vado de San Miguel, on the Santa Fe Trail. Ortiz wrote him subsequently, and had a curious tale to tell.

One day Martínez sent him a message asking if he would go so far as to receive a visit from an excommunicant. Ortiz replied that since he was now the rightful pastor, with all proper faculties, he was of course able to receive "even the condemned." Martínez came and they talked for an hour, inevitably about the recent events of his disgrace. Ortiz asked him "hard questions," evidently to give him opportunity to admit the justice of his penalty, to which Martínez replied each time in affirmation of his guilt, "Amen, amen, amen." When asked why he had so furiously opposed the bishop, Martínez said he had "done it out of pure caprice," in hostility to Father Taladrid, and then handsomely added that now, since circumstances were not the same, he recognized Ortiz as the rightful pastor, and would not again interfere in any act of the ecclesiastic administration. It was a gesture of ingratiation.

But it meant nothing, reported Ortiz; for Martínez forthwith returned to his own chapel to continue his old ways. Ortiz felt, though, that these could not continue forever, for Martínez was "growing weaker." To comfort the bishop, Father Eulógio Ortiz declared that he, though naturally under suspicion by his own brothers in the Ortiz family who opposed Lamy, would always serve him loyally. "Even though I am not of much use, I will be on your side. . . . It is true, Most Illustrious Lord, that I have other faults, but of that sort which can be publicly condemned, I want none."

It was a measure of the pathetic degree of poverty, in regard to tithes over which Martínez—and others—raised such furor, that Ortiz in the same letter declared that when he came to Taos to assume his pastorate, it was an unpropitious time, since Martínez had already predisposed everyone against Taladrid, and little had been contributed; so that now there remained for the bishop only seventy-five sheep, a young bull, and a calf. Was he to send them to Santa Fe, or sell them, and remit the proceeds?

But it was still evident that Martínez and his allies among the clergy were not yet subdued, even after the excommunication; and Lamy foresaw what would ensue if he should die, leaving the bishropic vacant: the native clergy would at once surge back into power and life would revert to the state of ignorance and worse, which he had found six years ago. To counter such a possibility, he asked his metropolitan, Archbishop P. R. Kenrick of St Louis, to forward a petition to Rome proposing the creation of a chapter of cathedral canons for Santa Fe. Their appointment would rest under the discretion of the bishop. They would of course be members of the clergy loyal to him and his reforms. It was the custom in Mexican dioceses that the chapter elect its vicar, who would temporarily succeed a bishop until his successor was named by Rome. As vicar general, without the chapter, Machebeuf would succeed Lamy; but the Mexican clergy would surely refuse to respect his authority. In that case the cathedral canons would govern in any interim. Since the matter seemed so urgent, Kenrick added the suggestion that, if a chapter were not approved by Rome, at least a council of consultors might be created under his archdiocese which would hold the authority to act in place of a chapter at Santa Fe, to protect the see of Santa Fe in the event of Lamy's death. Cardinal Barnabo duly forwarded the proposal to Pius IX.

That it was not acted upon at once was an indication of how difficult —how almost impossible—it was to make real the actual state of affairs, the vast extent of the land and its scattered needs, the primitiveness of all conditions, to those across the world who could see only through clerkly reports, and who, in their great bureaux and palaces, must consider most affairs as abstractions, in a world-wide structure which had to be governed as a whole, rather than in terms of its parts.

vi.

Schism

AND STILL CONTINUING was the nagging indecision about Doñana—the *Condado*—La Mesilla (the interchangeable terms which helped to confuse the Vatican for years). Lamy wrote to Barnabo in January 1857, begging once more for the final assignment of the great strip of territory across southern New Mexico/Arizona, making the point now that an area under the civil control of one nation (the United States) could never be satisfactorily managed in ecclesiastical matters under the control of another nation (Mexico). The bishop added, "Please note that the priest who is administering these areas was the one [Ortiz?] who revolted against my authority and who has sought refuge in these parts." The implication was strong that Zubiría was content to have him there to hold the district for Durango.

Barnabo replied to Lamy in February that he had never had an answer from Zubiría to his letter of three years earlier asking for Durango's view of the dispute, and said that it was the Vatican's wish to help Lamy "in any way possible." Lamy then wrote asking for a copy of Zubiría's letter of 1854, which Barnabo sent, asking for Lamy's comments on it. Lamy's arguments were familiar, and again, in May, he asked for news of a settlement by Rome; but now he went further: he declared that in his opinion the bishop of Durango was "hardly able to write because of his age," and, added Lamy, "I have very strong reasons for suspecting that one of the vicars from the neighborhood of El Paso is allowed to interpret various orders after his own fashion, even to the decrees from the Holy See." Yet once again a silence of months descended upon the affair.

Lamy spent much of the summer in the open land, visiting distant missions. He returned to Santa Fe to carry the Blessed Sacrament in the procession of Corpus Christi, when the garrison band marched and played ahead of him, and "the discharge of cannon balls also added much to the solemnity," and to the felicity of the Mother Superior.

On the following day Machebeuf left for the Mississippi to meet two new priests from the diocese of Le Mans, in France, and others who would return with him to Santa Fe. He travelled by the mail carrier's coach. There was no armed escort. He thought Indians on the whole were well disposed, though when gathered in great numbers were emboldened to do ill, but generally they were "indolent, they stole out of need, and rarely attacked except in self-defense, or to avenge those of their people who had been killed!" So far, he had never had a misadventure with Indians, and felt entirely safe with them.

For all his courage and gaiety, Machebeuf's sense of what was fun had on at least one occasion that streak of mockery or cruelty which newcomers often showed to races whom they saw as inferior. One day a dozen or so Indians appeared in the mail carrier's camp during the halt for a meal of ham and biscuits. As one of them already knew Machebeuf, he brought friends to join him for dinner on the ground. Machebeuf offered them salty meat, which they refused. An Indian then saw "a little gray powder and he wanted some of that. I gave him a spoonful of it, and he gave us a free exhibition of facial contortion which was interesting and amusing. The powder was pepper! Another spied a bottle half full of what he thought was whiskey, and he wanted a taste. I gave him a big spoonful, which he swallowed, but he threw the spoon away and began to cough. He said that such whiskey was good only for dogs. He had tasted of my vinegar!" When his little jokes were done with, Machebeuf gave his guests some coffee, sugar, and biscuits.

He met with a disappointment at St Louis—the bishop of Le Mans had at the last minute withdrawn permission for the two expected priests to sail for America. He went on to Louisville, where Lamy's niece Marie, and another girl her age—she was then fourteen—were waiting for him. Both would return with him to Santa Fe, to enter the Loretto convent there, first as students, later as postulants. Marie by now had spent six years with the New Orleans Ursulines. She was a lovely, round-faced child, with the dark hair and brilliant dark eyes of the family. She wore discreet little gold earrings, and when dressed up for a daguerreotype to send home to France, a short-caped black bombazine dress. Gravity, charm, and intelligence shone in her expression. Joining her uncle out West was the great adventure of her life. She was, said Machebeuf, "innocent as an angel."

His westward party included also a French gardener from Versailles, who had already spent two years at Santa Fe and was now going back again, three Mexican servants to attend to the vicar general's two carriages and equipment, two Frenchmen from Besançon, an Irish seminarian, and others to the number of ten. Two caravans had started out on to the trail on 7 September, but they went slowly, and Machebeuf with his people would leave on the tenth to overtake one of them which had an Army detachment of four hundred and fifty men, whose commanding officer he knew well. It was not in his nature to fear anything for himself, but with the two girls in his care, he was glad to have the protection of the soldiers. "You will understand the reason," he wrote to his sister. A few days out from Kansas City they passed the Last Chance Store at Council Grove—a one-storey stone building by a single cottonwood tree—and slowly drew away into the empty distance of the prairie crossing.

At Santa Fe, Lamy heard strange news from Mexico—it seemed that in Chihuahua, things were in "a very bad state," and that some of the local clergy wanted to be allied with Santa Fe. He had thought earlier in the year that he might travel to Mexico to try to raise money for his diocese, but duties had kept him home, visiting his own missions in their isolation. He went by horseback, often alone. In his saddlebag he kept bread, crackers, and a few hard-boiled eggs. For the rest, as he said, he lived on the "fat of the land," by which he meant the principal fare in the Mexican diet—"*el bendito frijole y el santo atole* (the blessed bean and the holy corn mush)." On a visit to a Pueblo mission he was obliged by his good manners to eat a piece of a butchered dog which had been dragged out before him as a special delicacy.

New villages were founded every year, and when attended by a newly assigned missionary, could serve as bases for restoring the Church to the various pueblos. A dot on the map here, another there, where before nothing had been, would in time make a network of society possible, and with it, increased safety from the thousands of unsettled Indians who, as Lamy told Purcell, made it perilous to venture out even six miles from the capital. To be sure, there were United States soldiers stationed here and there, but not as many as needed, and moreover, he remarked in his dry style, it would require, to be effective, ten thousand men "a little more accustomed to fatigue and hardship" than those already on station. Meanwhile, there were conversions among the troops. Lamy noted that Machebeuf baptized them, and also a "very intelligent negro, who is free, as we have no slaves here."

Distance and poverty were not so fully disposed of in those years as the long troubles with the clergy revolt. Lamy paid what he could of his accumulated debts to Purcell, and regretted that in his old church of Covington he had been obliged to leave other parish debts behind him, but hoped these would be assumed by Bishop Carrel of that diocese. Meanwhile he must see that new seminarians were educated for New Mexico—the two young Mexicans at Clermont, whose board of a thousand francs per year must be paid by the Society at Paris, and another young man named Peter Hart, whom he was sending to Purcell for theological studies. Hart had already been ordained subdeacon by Lamy, and was an "excellent young man . . . not of bright talents but his application and his virtue will make up for that."

Not all problems were dramatic but for all that, must be heeded—to work with what was at hand; to measure time itself by patience when snows closed the direct trail eastward for months at a time and mail had to be sent by way of the New Orleans courier; to educate children free whose family had nothing; and in fact, to help establish free public schools for the territory at large (Lamy was one of the three commissioners who would guide free public education into being in New Mexico). Satisfactions had to be modestly measured: "our schools are going on pretty well, specially the sister's." He had given the Lorettines a deed, now, to the house he had vacated for them: the land, the buildings and furniture, including fifty bedsteads with bedding, chairs, carpets, and pianos, all for three thousand dollars to be repaid in three years (without interest) from the fees of pupils who could afford to pay. He hoped to procure "a good Mexican pony" for Purcell, which he would send him next year—it was too late for this year as the autumn of 1857 was drawing into winter when the trail would be precarious. Political affairs looked auspicious, now that Gallegos was out of power in Washington.

But it was too much to hope that Martínez could long remain silent. In October he wrote to Lamy, reporting—surely to make trouble—that Pastor Ortiz and he had come to an agreement about dividing the parish duties of Taos, quite as though Martínez had now assigned to Ortiz what was already and only his. As an afterthought to his old dispute with Lamy, he could not resist raising again his position on tithing, to point out that as long ago as 1829 he had made his familiar objections on the subject to the "High Mexican government," and had newspaper clippings to prove it. He wrote also to Ortiz to bestow on him a share of the Taos priestly duties, citing an agreement he said Ortiz had given him in writing, and magnanimously noted that he, Martínez, had already referred to Ortiz one case of a marriage and another of a burial, blandly in the tone of one reputable professional to another. He chided Ortiz for presuming to call at the house of a Martínez brother to collect tithes, and for stating that those who would not pay would not be granted the sacraments, and accused him of working to establish for himself an "emphyteusis" or personal domain. It would be a disastrous document to fall under the eye of a superior, and Ortiz replied indignantly the next day, refuting every statement— "I have never consented to your administering any Sacraments to any persons"—and stressing further that in respect to tithes, that "he who does not pay what he owes, because he cannot pay, will certainly not be condemned."

Driven by enmities which tormented him long after he could have any effect, Martínez again turned to the public print in the *Gaceta de Santa Fe,* and in a series of tracts in pamphlet form which he issued from Taos. Variously, in such publications, he pursued Lamy for years with shrieks all the louder for their impotence. All the old charges came forth again—Lamy was concerned only with "money, money, money," Lamy "profaned the sacred temples," Lamy had collected for his own party "one hundred thousand dollars" (1859); Lamy was not a true religionist but a "fanatic," while Martínez took to himself the new rationalism of "this century of light"; repudiated the bishop as his religious superior; called him a liar; accused him outright of simony; of "acting against the laws of the church"; and referred to him and Machebeuf as "ravening wolves"—Matthew 7: 15,16 (1860); justified his own schisms by quoting from Thomas Aquinas to prove that even a layman could absolve sinners (1861); all in frenzies of rhetoric which reflected his ceaseless miseries of mind.

For there could be no doubt that Martínez, seeing himself in the libertarian posture (similar to Diderot's definition of *liberté naturelle* in the *Encyclopédie*), was wretchedly unhappy in his schism. His whole life, with its often generous efforts to civilize in isolation the oncoming generations through his own diligent but restricted learning, had been set awry by several forces any one of which he might have been able to face peacefully, but which together brought him only torment against which he was powerless, if defiant.

To begin with, his ire was undoubtedly patriotic—that of an educated native full of resistance to foreign authority—a double authority at that. It was bad enough to come under Anglo-American control, but when to that was added another foreign domination through the presence of a strict French prelate, Martínez (like his colleagues) could not contain his sense of injury. Further, a whole tradition of patronal style was being heedlessly discredited: everything Mexican was treated as inferior by the two sets of newcomers. Mexicans, rich or poor, ignorant or informed, were as proud as the Spaniards and Indians of their heritage, and as properly resentful of slights. Martínez saw himself as a learned man, a social benefactor, and when made to feel inferior, he was bitterly offended. Again, he felt himself, though a sincere churchman, an exponent of the modern civil enlightenment; and it was galling to submit to the rectitude of a conservative bishop to whom the anti-clericalism of the French Revolution and its aftermath was disgraceful. Acting against Lamy, Martínez oddly invoked the sanctions both of scriptural precedent and libertarian tolerance. And finally, his intemperate behavior might have been a result of his increasingly bad health in the malaise of premature old age. The chronic toxicity of his affliction may well have exacerbated his mental distress, inducing him to the cholers which embittered his last years, until he was left with only the ashes of the old consuming conflict, in the pathos of learned agonies spent for a footless cause.

But if Martínez was the protagonist of one culture, the bishop was the custodian and exemplar of another, which under his responsibility for the general good had to win the day in both spiritual and temporal affairs. Though the belief and vocation of both men stemmed from the same source—Rome—the modifying forces to which each was subject in his own history accounted for most of the differences between them.

Lamy was closer to the source than Martínez, and as bishop must speak with finality in its name. Post-Revolutionary France had revived the piety, the social rectitude, which the Enlightenment had discredited for a generation or two. Lamy came into his fullness of mind after the reign of libertarian principles, and during the restoration of the Church.

Martínez, on the other hand, so far removed not only from Mexico, but from Europe, was the victim of that cultural lag always suffered by the provincial: his ideas had been formed by imported styles of mind long after they had lost novelty at the point of origin.

Martínez thought of his basic ideas as modern. Lamy believed his own to be eternal. In any case, beyond theological and cultural differences, the temperaments of the two men inevitably must have clashed; for one was a supreme egotist, a master in a little house who could never be a servant, while the other, self-disciplined in mildness, was a servant in a great domain who knew, when necessary, how to be a master. The bishop's Romanesque mysticism, embedded in the sacred traditionalism of both peasant and priest, met head on the imperfectly assimilated spirit of the Mexican effort to create its own character out of tumultuous elements—rebellion against Spain, survivals of the Indian strains in the mixed blood of post-Cortez Mexico, the struggle to retain its proud native nature by a Mexican population subject to recent waves of conquest and condescension in several forms.

In the end, Lamy, once his dismissal of Martínez was done, simply had to ignore him and his allies thereafter, and get on with work more demanding and productive, in a frame of responsibility as vast as the lands, with their far people in desert and mountain, awaiting what he had been sent to bring to them across the whole desert Southwest.

VII

THE COLONISTS

1858–1863

i.

Niceties of Geography

"LA COUR DE ROME"—IN MACHEBEUF'S WORDS—"*dont les lenteurs* sont bien connues," had yet to resolve, in its "well-known procrastination," Lamy's official claim to his Gadsden Purchase lands. In the spring of 1858, nobody yet had a clear legal right to act as spiritual proprietors of Doñana (the village or the county), Las Cruces (the town), La Mesilla (the valley or the village), or the *comitatus* or *condado* (the *whole* ill-defined "county"). None of the parties to the dispute understood in common what these terms precisely designated. Rome heard them referred to interchangeably by Durango, and such was the practice of the local people themselves. Lamy knew exactly what he himself meant—all that land granted to the United States under the final boundary survey, by which he should control the religious aspects of everything from El Paso–Fort Bliss on the Rio Grande west to "Arizona," and north in a parallel line which passed through Las Cruces at the southern end of the Dead Man's March. All the rest of New Mexico was already in his diocese, which was taken unofficially to include what later was demarked as Arizona. It was not that the Vatican was ignoring the issue, but that all its machinery moved in such agonizing indecision. The affair was under study there in March, in an exhaustive review of the whole problem, and the Propaganda Fide slowly concluded that Lamy's claims were the more legitimate, and recommended to the Pope that his petition be granted, and that the disputed lands be assigned to him. Pius was inclined to agree, and the bureau was gratified to learn at last that Zubiría seemed willing to yield out of his knowledge of his earlier visits to the area. But he and Lamy and Rome were still all talking about different niceties of geography, thanks to the old confusion of place names. Debate on these points consumed months and a firm decision was not yet promulgated.

Meanwhile, nearer to home, other old trials had their reminders.

Martínez wrote from Taos in March to say that his successor, Eulógio Ortiz, was committing sacrileges, acts of hypocrisy, and persecution against him; and he was therefore proclaiming anew his own ministry, in his own chapel, giving sacraments, and in general treating with the bishop who had unfrocked him quite as though with his proper ordinary. There being no other arm to use against him, Lamy in silence left him to the opinion of Providence. Gallegos, in his turn, had come back to Santa Fe, was living in a fine house in Washington street near the cathedral, "trying to do all the mischief he can." Lamy, hearing from the northern territory "between us and the Mormons," recorded that "the Utahs, a powerful tribe . . . are going to give us some trouble this year. . . ." It had been a "very hard Spring." Extreme drought held the country. Over a hundred thousand lambs were lost "for cold and want of grass." Lamy had spent four months travelling in the open lands and had seen the hardships of the *rancheros,* which he took to heart.

And always he had the future in mind, and always he saw that he must have more help in his task. Recruits from abroad must still come, and would come; but he thought the greatest need was for a seminary of his own, where he could educate his own priests. There were excellent candidates—he had several already who gave him "great hopes." The sisters' school was "still increasing"—there was no doubt about it: a pressing need existed, as this growth demonstrated. The old mountain capital, with its awakening amenities, took increasing pride in the refinements taught by the Lorettines. A sense of order was growing at Santa Fe, without destroying the unique character of the city in its exhilarating air and the splendor of its landscape.

But an era of sorts had suddenly come to an end when the Very Reverend Juan Felipe Ortiz, the displaced old rural dean, and brother to the pastor of Taos who had gone to Rome with Lamy in 1854, died suddenly of apoplexy late in the morning of 20 January, at the age of sixty-one, after receiving the last rites. "Some Friends of the Deceased" signed a necrology which made no mention of his intrigues and disgraces, but recounted how for three days a great crowd paid respects to his body in state at his own residence, and thronged to his requiem Mass in the cathedral, where he was buried. The governor, the United States military commander, and the entire legislative assembly (in which he had served in his time), were in attendance, and the "Friends" were at pains to note that since "the year by ecclesiastic authority he was elected Vicar of this territory," he had given "special satisfaction to the wise and virtuous Bishop the Right Revd. Dr. Zubiría"—quite as though Lamy had never been heard of.

ii.

The Poisoned Chalice

IN MID-SUMMER 1858 a provincial council under Archbishop Kenrick was to be held at St Louis. Lamy must attend. It would mean another long absence during his round trip on the plains, and also another visit to Kentucky to enlist more Loretto nuns for his ever-increasing school. Further, he was devoting more and more time to travels in the diocese; and the still untouched question of Arizona to the west and Colorado to the north would call for journeys in the field. To act for him in Santa Fe, he sent for Machebeuf to return from Albuquerque to preside as rector of the old adobe cathedral of St Francis.

While Machebeuf made ready for his transfer, he could report a series of loving protests by his parishioners—the very ones who had once reviled him. There was *"un* meeting *monstre"* at which plans were made to demand that he remain. A petition signed by two thousand persons was addressed to the bishop pleading that the pastor not be removed. Not a delegation, but a great crowd descended upon Machebeuf, rich and poor, children and elders. Hearing that he must leave within two days, they commanded him to remain long enough for a committee to carry the petition to the bishop at Santa Fe. When he laughingly replied that he knew every inch of the way to Santa Fe and could escape at will, despite their command, the women cried that they, they alone, would guard the Santa Fe road, as sentinels all the way. He was obliged to grant three more days' delay, while two successive letters were sent to Lamy pleading for a change of orders. In vain. Lamy was immovable, Machebeuf departed with a mounted escort through ardent farewells far out along the highways, while his heart swelled with feeling. Arriving in Santa Fe, he was further swept by emotion when he was received with the usual delegation of officials, religious, priests, pupils, as the four bells of St Francis, and all those of the four other churches of Santa Fe, rang out to announce his arrival as rector of the cathedral. His triumphal entry made him feel "as Napoleon III must have felt in the Boulevard Sébastopol." After the reception at the cathedral attended by an immense crowd, Lamy crowned the event with a collation of little cakes and "a good bottle of wine to settle the dust. . . . You will see," wrote Machebeuf to his brother Marius, "how we do things in style in New Mexico. . . ."

There was more ceremony to mark Lamy's departure for St Louis, to be gone all summer and well into the autumn. The convent study was "prepared and adorned" as only nuns could do it, and, seated under a canopy, Lamy listened to addresses of occasion in Spanish and English by convent girls, who demonstrated not only sentiment but scholastic progress. In return, he granted the students a holiday "on the longest day of the year" soon to fall due, and then cut two large cakes "with his own hands presenting a slice to each person in the room," along with a small portion of wine, joining all in taking the refreshments. When it was time for him to depart a day later, on 12 June, he passed the convent, where all the nuns and pupils were standing in line. He blessed them; and, said the Reverend Mother, "our eyes followed him until he was lost from our sight." The longest day of the year turned out to be the feast of St Aloysius Gonzaga and the students duly had their "recreation." The day afterward was the bishop's name day—the feast of St John the Baptist—which reminded all "forcibly" of their "dear absent Father." Set down in a private letter, such sentiments spoke for more than perfunctory respect.

Once again to cross the plains: "indeed I am used to such travelling," wrote Lamy to Purcell, adding in his understated way, "and I think I enjoy it." He was a man to whom eloquence did not come naturally; but his perception ran deep, like his convictions, and his responses in action were firm and patient with something of the rhythms of the seasons about them—the peasant's ancient knowledge of the cycle from seed to harvest. The moment meant less than the years, and the years than eternity. In the solitude and wilderness of his vast empire, perhaps he found a vision of his particular spirituality and grace; and an affinity for the dimensions of the deserts which in the end led him to his mastery, so often alone, of the great lands in his charge.

Increasingly he was off in the grand distances. In the spring of 1858 he made his first trip to Colorado, and there, in its southern plains, he found intimate little passages reminiscent of Auvergne. The little streams ran shallowly over pale gravel, bordered by willows and cottonwoods, and in and out of cooling shadow the water was slate blue or diamond white, and beyond lay the tawny sweeps of the great San Luis Valley, and still beyond, the mysterious, and beckoning, visions of the Colorado Rockies, where cloud shadows played and weather and rivers were immensely formed in the union of sky and land. On the Conejos River, Lamy erected the first Colorado parish with a chapel built as a *jacal*—open to the sky, an enclosure of walls made from slim cottonwood stakes with bindings of salt-cedar branches. It was the first move of the spiritual colonization of Colorado which would soon proceed from Santa Fe.

Now in the summer of 1858 he moved on eastward to Kentucky, reaching there toward the middle of July after a journey of about four weeks. Bishop Spalding of Louisville told Purcell, "Bp Lamy, in fact all these missionary bishops, are never at rest, only this be *in mortem.* He stayed in and about Louisville for some days, but we saw little of him. He had to make an excursion to Loretto and back in the interim" —where actually he found more Loretto nuns willing to go West with him for the rest of their lives.

In September he was again in St Louis for the second provincial council, and celebrated the Mass at the opening of one of the sessions. Of the matters discussed by his colleagues, the one which interested him most was his old boundary dispute. He set forth all the arguments which he knew so well, with the result that his colleagues voted to petition Pius IX to issue a decree settling the matter once and for all by ordering the disputed lands politically under the United States to be assigned to Santa Fe. What they did not know was that the Vatican, on 10 June, had written Zubiría, complimenting him on his "brilliance of mind and right judgement," and declaring it expedient "that the Holy Father through the Apostolic Authority officially incorporated the county of Doñana and the parish of Las Cruces into the jurisdiction of the Bishop of Santa Fe." A copy of the papal decree was sent with the letter—and another went to Lamy at Santa Fe, which he would see on his return home.

When he finally saw it in the autumn all might have seemed in order. Rome had finally acted on his many requests, and also had accepted the graceful capitulation of Zubiría in reversing his previous claims—but there was still a nice technicality to which the bishop of Durango would now cling: his earlier and handsome decision to give up Doñana and Las Cruces, and Rome's decree requiring this, had made no mention of the word, and the locality of, La Mesilla. Therefore, at that moment, and for years to come, Zubiría held that this village (or the long pastoral valley of the same name in which it was situated on the Rio Grande) still belonged to Durango; so the pretext was splendidly laid for another triangular contention between Santa Fe, Durango, and Rome, while the familiar confusions about what the very names designated remained unresolved. The village of Doñana lay ten miles north of Las Cruces, the village of La Mesilla five miles south of Las Cruces. Doñana was often taken to mean the whole vast district north of Mexico from the Rio Grande west—but so was La Mesilla. The Vatican had granted "the county of Doñana and the

parish of Las Cruces" to Lamy. He inevitably understood this to include the town of La Mesilla. Zubiría chose to except, and to retain,
the town of La Mesilla because it was not specifically mentioned. But
Lamy did not know of this view as yet.

On this return home he had to hear of another event—strange and
tragic—which had happened in his absence.

"Last August third," he told Barnabo, "while I was at the council
in St. Louis, one of my priests was poisoned at the altar."

He was the young Father Antoine Avel, who had come with Lamy
from France in 1854, had served on the cathedral staff for four years,
and then had been assigned as pastor in the village of Mora, to replace
a certain priest who gave scandal. In the village was a woman who
lived outside of marriage with a man named Noel. One day she fell ill,
was in fact dying, and sent for the priest to administer the last rites.
This was Father Munnecom, who though replaced as pastor by Avel
was still in Mora. By chance, Father Avel was absent on a mission
visit. Munnecom would go to her only on condition that she renounce
her lover. At death's door, she consented, sent Noel away, was given
absolution, and died. Noel, the lover, was distracted with grief and
rage, and threatened revenge against Munnecom.

A few Sundays later, when Munnecom was scheduled, as usual, to
say the nine o'clock Mass, he was absent, and Father Avel unexpectedly
took his place. He heard a few confessions, began the Mass, and on
swallowing some of the wine at communion, knew it had been polluted.
He sent the acolyte to the sacristy for fresh wine, and was barely able
to complete the Mass; by now he knew he was poisoned. In tremors,
he returned to the altar to pray. A few people were still present, and
he said to them, "Pray for me, I am dying poisoned."

Noel came forward to take Avel to the sacristy, where he tried to
administer an antidote, at the same time telling Avel that Father
Munnecom must have poisoned the wine, in revenge for having been
displaced. Avel knew his end was near. Someone proposed to find
Munnecom to give him the last sacraments, but Avel replied that he
could not confess to a priest who had poisoned him. A priest at Las
Vegas was sent for, but arrived too late. Avel wrote his will, leaving
his library to Bishop Lamy, and a sum of money to help found a
hospital at Santa Fe, and, forgiving his murderer, died.

Then, abandoning his sheep and pasture, Noel left in haste for Las
Vegas, where he met Machebeuf, who was hurrying to Mora to investigate the case. There Noel told the vicar general of Munnecom's jeal-
ousy, made a mystery of Munnecom's absence from his usual Sunday
Mass, and then disappeared, to be unheard of for years, until news
came that he was murdered in southern New Mexico. "We suspect,

with good reason," wrote Lamy before the case was resolved, "not a Mexican priest, but an unfortunate Dutch priest . . ." In the end, Munnecom was cleared by the chancery and by the courts, served many years as a worthy pastor elsewhere, and finally retired to his native Holland.

But it was still the larger, and crucial, matter of territory which concerned Lamy above all; for not only had the Vatican decree granting him the Gadsden Purchase areas of New Mexico (which the decree called "La Mesilla") arrived in August—another in the same month placed the immense and empty lands of Arizona under his jurisdiction. There was no established boundary between New Mexico and Arizona, and the Gadsden territory ran westward across both as far as California.

But there was a complicated parallel to that presented by the claims of Durango; for Arizona, until the war with Mexico, and even now, in 1858, was under the authority of the bishop of Sonora and Sinaloa in Mexico, whose proper see was in the ancient city of Culiacán over seven hundred miles south of the all but abandoned shack settlement of Tucson in Arizona. If Lamy was to assume the administration for Arizona, the bishop of Sonora, Don Pedro Loza, must concur in the transfer. It would be 1851 all over again—months of agonizingly slow progress across thousands of miles of desert wilderness to consolidate a new dimension of responsibility.

Lamy moved promptly. He relieved Machebeuf of the post of vicar general, for he had a new duty for him, and appointed in his place Father Eguillon, who had been pastor of Socorro on the Rio Grande. Concerning the Vatican decree awarding him his southern lands at last, he wrote—not to Zubiría as usual, whose competence he had already doubted on account of old age—but to the vicar general of Durango, to say that the "political troubles of the unfortunate Republic of Mexico" were a great obstacle of communication, for the revolution led by Benito Juárez was interrupting even the most random of Mexican affairs, and the Church was under open persecution. It was possible that papal briefs might never reach their destination there. Lamy hoped there would be "no difficulties" in the matter.

Now the decision must be ratified locally. Lamy lost no time in sending Machebeuf to annex officially the parishes in the Gadsden Purchase. In El Paso, Zubiría's rural dean was the same pastor Don Ramón Ortiz, who, with his fine looks, delightful charm, and open-hearted hospitality had shown the Mexican style at its best to the captives of the disastrous Texan–Santa Fe expedition of 1841 as they were marched from northern New Mexico through El Paso to the wretched life of Mexican jails far to the south. He had also generously entertained Doniphan's Missouri troops who had gone by on their way to Chihuahua in 1846, and he had received Lamy and Machebeuf with every kindness in 1851 on their way to Santa Fe.

As Don Ramón was the Durango official nearest to New Mexico, Lamy wrote to him to say that "I have received a decree from Rome, whereby "Doñana" (the quotation marks are significant as indicating more than the village of that name) and *Las Cruces* belong to the jurisdiction of Santa Fe. I am sending my Vicar General Sr. Don José P. Machebeuf to take possession of the said places. I hope that His Lordship of Durango will have received notice of this matter"—i.e., from Rome. "I shall be very grateful to you if you will be kind enough to inform the afore-mentioned Vicar of the present situation of these ecclesiastical affairs, and if you would help him, in case any difficulty should arise."

But the atmosphere of difficulty between Mexico and the United States was more than local. President James Buchanan, in his recent annual message to Congress, had proposed that the Mexican states of Chihuahua and Sonora be seized by the United States in lieu of ten million dollars in reparations left over from the 1846 war. Congress had tabled the proposal; but political suspicion and national pride may have emphasized attitudes along the border.

Machebeuf, with two Mexican riders, left Santa Fe on 3 November 1858 for the Rio Grande road, pausing for nostalgic visits at Albuquerque and other missions, and finally came to present himself to Don Ramón Ortiz in his oasis-like home south of El Paso. Don Ramón received him warmly "as a friend and colleague"; but when it came to surrendering "Doñana" and the rest, he made every sort of difficulty "under the pretext"—familiar enough since 1851—that he had never received from his bishop any order to yield the requested jurisdiction. He had not seen Lamy's letter to Zubiría's vicar general. Who knew if Zubiría had ever heard from Rome? Machebeuf showed Don Ramón the actual original of Cardinal Barnabo's decree which added to Santa Fe all of the Arizona parishes. Ortiz made a copy of it, promising to send it at once to Durango, and to act immediately upon receiving orders from his bishop.

For the moment, there was nothing further to be accomplished at El Paso, and Machebeuf, visiting Fort Bliss on the United States side of the Rio Grande to say Mass for the garrison, heard of an Army detachment which had left only recently for Arizona. It was providential, he thought; and after three days of hurrying after them across the flat desert he arrived at their bivouac at nine o'clock at night. Safely answering the challenge of the sentries, he went to the tent of the commanding officer, who chose not to leave his bed, but ordered for Machebeuf and his two men all they needed. His new mission was to find the bishop of Sonora, wherever he might be—whether in Culiacán itself or somewhere else in the 190,000 square miles of Sonora/Arizona—and obtain his obedience to the papal separation of his diocese according to the civil boundary between Mexico and the United States; for as New Mexico had been, in relation to Durango, so Arizona was to Sonora.

. . .

iii.

Quest in Sonora

"DO YOU REMEMBER," Lamy once asked Machebeuf in Santa Fe, "that when we were in Ohio we used to long for the chance of getting beyond the lines of our narrow parishes to do missionary work on a grand scale? Well, our wishes have been so fully granted here in the West that there is nothing left to be desired in that way. There is nothing beyond us now but to leave civilization and travel with a band of roving Indians. . . ."

The two friends were by now masters of the grand scale in wilderness. If in their travels protection might be at hand—a band of soldiers or a caravan going their way—they would take advantage of it; but if not, they went on their way, in reasonable caution, alone. Machebeuf now learned that the way to Arizona was for the moment peaceful—the Apaches were quiet. The soldiers he had overtaken would move too slowly for him. With only his two young aides, he struck out for the next Army post, which was Fort Buchanan, southeast of the old settlement of Tucson. He had travelled by horse about six hundred miles from Santa Fe. When anyone asked him where he lived, he would reply, "In the saddle. . . . They call me *El Vicario Andando* (The Travelling Vicar) and I live on the *Camino Real* (the public highway)." He usually took along a spare saddle-horse, a mule loaded with blankets and other necessities, and a large valise stuffed with trifling religious articles to give away to Indians or Mexicans, by which he invited an initial welcome among isolated people.

At Fort Buchanan, he was made welcome as a priest, remained for several days, said Mass daily, and then moved on to Tucson, coming first to the decaying but spacious mission church of San Xavier del

Bac, which had been founded in the eighteenth century by Jesuits. It was now abandoned, though a scattering of Papago Indians lived in brush huts in its shadow. He first saw it across parched yellow flats, as it stood white against bluing foothills and far purple mountains. He inspected the empty church and was astonished at its considerable size, its high brick walls, the richness of its Churrigueresque façade, its general beauty. It was the only surviving mission of the seven which had once flourished in this northern part of Sonora.

The village of Tucson lay twelve miles to the north. There Machebeuf found about four hundred inhabitants. A few years earlier the United States boundary commissioner saw that "half the buildings in Tucson are tenantless and falling to ruin," thanks to the indifference of the population, of whom he said, "A more lazy and idle set of people I never saw." Since 1827, when the last Franciscans had been withdrawn by the Mexican Republic, the people had had no continuous religious life, and it was not known when a bishop of Sonora had ever visited Tucson. Machebeuf was warmly received, administered to the people, and announced that their province now belonged to the bishop of Santa Fe.

The town's life was primitive and turbulent, yet it was being increasingly settled by men who looked for fortune in silver mines a little way to the south. Their trials were great, for to work the mines they must bring huge and heavy machinery across the deserts all the way from Port Lavaca on the Gulf of Mexico, on roads mostly created by infrequent cloudburst run-off in rocky gullies. Apache attacks were frequent, many travellers were killed, and the garrisons at the far-flung Army posts could patrol only local areas. The one at Tucson was said to be of little help. According to an early observer, it "confined itself to its legitimate business of getting drunk or doing nothing." Everyone went armed. Arizona, not yet under United States territorial law, was a haven for fugitives from justice. The immigration from Sonora consisted largely of murderers and robbers; and what the Apaches left undone in the way of pillage, the invaders finished. "Tucson," wrote the observer—a man engaged in the mining business—"became the headquarters of vice, dissipation, and crime."

Machebeuf paused only long enough to state his ecclesiastical claim over this "paradise of devils," and set out on 20 December for the south to find Bishop Loza. The bishop, he had been told, was not at his city of Culiacán, because of the state of revolutionary troubles there, but was probably somewhere nearer Arizona, for he had reestablished his cathedral temporarily at the Spanish colonial silver-mining city of Alamos, far to the south of Guaymas, and inland from the Pacific.

Until he should reach that sea, Machebeuf would proceed at the pace of his pack animal, across deserts, and companioned by mountains, near or far, which had every sort of fantasy of light, distance, sky turbulence, or bearing stillness. Sonora had a character all its own, with few of the lyric enclaves of the New Mexican Rio Grande, and in color, more of the hue and temper of a volcanic land which seemed reflected even in the temperament of the people there. In their color, the mountains suggested dead fire—ashy blue or rose, with hills as scarred and golden as the pelts of mountain lions. He rode past the dead Mexican fort of Tubac, with its empty mission church, came to the ruins of Tumacácori a few miles farther on and saw its empty belfry and the earthen burial chapel and the white dome of the mission, and the "miserable population" which clung about each place. Farther south, beyond the border, he passed Imuris with its own mountain, and the ruins of the San Ignacio mission, and the famous canyon of San Ignacio, which was a rallying point for Indian raiders or Mexican bandits—"nature never designed a fitter location for the destruction of unwary travellers." But as he went, he became part of every village and town through the exercise of his priestly powers and concerns. At Magdalena, amid tamarisks and palms, lying in a shallow cup of land, the pink bell tower and the blue tiled dome of the church rose against a high gravel hill, and there he sang midnight Mass in a private chapel on Christmas Eve, with the local pastor assisting.

A party of travellers were setting out from Magdalena, and Machebeuf with his men joined them, pausing to see Governor Gándara of Sonora at his "magnificent hacienda" and then moving on to Hermosillo, where at Epiphany the Christmas folk play of *The Shepherds* (*Los Pastores*) was being given by parishioners, and Machebeuf watched it—the history of faith preserved in the humble verse drama of the Holy Family's search for shelter, the denial of it to them, their refuge in a stable, the birth of their child, the visit of three kings, while shepherds saw and sang of portents in the stars, all as it had been acted through untold time by the forebears of that night's village actors.

It was a hundred miles from Hermosillo, with its bougainvillea, lime trees, and flowering bushes, to Guaymas. The mountain profiles far away grew ever more fantastic, showing through vast notches to others in succession which paled into the distance in every degree of blue. Harsh as it was, a prison of space and distance, the land was there to be conquered and finally loved. It was the land of the Yaqui Indians, where each village had its little church established in the previous century by Jesuits, whose order was expelled in 1767. The

Yaquis subsisted on a sporadic stream or in a little canyon by farming, keeping rituals left over together from their ancient ways and
their Catholic time; and in its recurring season, war took the men out
upon the country in ancestral ferocity. Machebeuf made his way safely
through their land, and after many days, the desert sky, its beating
light, began to change, grew hazier, and he could see among the distant peaks immense canyons like far chambers, diminishing one past
the other—a great range whose other side sloped down to the Pacific,
and at last the mountain barriers were drawn aside slowly by his
advance, and the sea scent came through the open channels of the
canyons and gaps; and then finally, from a far height, he could observe
the sea—a table of light. Coming to the edge, he rode along the empty
shore of Bacochibampo Bay and after a curve of the land entered the
seaport of Guaymas.

There, even in that "miserable Mexican sea-port town, containing
at that time about 3500 inhabitants," was a grand church whose twin
spires and dome tiled in sky blue rose between noble mountain ter-
races of red rock and the squalid waterfront. Machebeuf, in his habitual conviviality, met up with a Californian surveyor. This was a
Brigadier General Stone, who was in the employ of the Mexican government to lead a team of topographical engineers in exploring the
west coast of Mexico. It was a lucky encounter; for when a steamer
due to arrive from Mazatlán, and to return there, failed to appear,
one of Machebeuf's ultimate plans was threatened with failure. He
had intended to make the voyage to Mazatlán, and then ride across
the Sierra Madre del Occidente to Durango, where he would show
Zubiría the Vatican documents of assignment concerning "Doñana"
and Arizona.

But here General Stone—a Catholic convert—showed his power.
He lent Machebeuf one of his company's sailing vessels, commissioned
him captain of it, provided him with a crew, and sent him south by
sea. Once his own master, Machebeuf decided to halt at the River
of May, which entered the Gulf of California at Navajoa, and ride
inland to Alamos, to search for Bishop Loza, who might well be there
at his interim cathedral. Leaving the seaside palms of the Gulf, and its
sunsets of fire quenched by the sea and the immediate dense night, he
crossed forty miles of a wide brushy plain toward the vast profile of
the Sierra lying north to south. Where in such mountains could a city
be? As always, on entering mountains, he had to follow their turning
ways. At last they revealed a church tower in three tiers of masonry
and plaster, and after passing Los Tres Frailes—a small mountain with
three distinct humps named after three friars—he rode through close-
walled streets into a large plaza at one side of which was the cathedral,

built of mottled rock, with its single tower and its bell, which in ringing the angelus and the Mass sounded cracked. At the cathedral there
was no sign of Bishop Loza, and Machebeuf must decide to wait.

Alamos was a town of great beauty. In the tropical heat of midday,
all was quiet. The sun beat down, but on two sides of the plaza arched
colonnades, plastered in white, covered the deep walks with cool dark-
blue shadow. It was a rich silver-mining town, the houses were miniature villas or palaces, and rising above the elegant blind fronts with
their iron-grilled windows, were tall palms and tamarisks and other
trees which spoke of garden patios within. Stray Yaqui Indians came
and went by day. At night, an almost menacing stillness prevailed,
except for the inquiring song of some distant dog.

But Machebeuf's immense passage was not for nothing. The day
after his arrival—it was a Saturday—he heard that Bishop Loza was
at a village three miles to the north of Alamos to administer confirmation. Going at once, he found Loza at the house of a Don Mateo Ortiz,
and at last was able to lay forth his purpose, which he did with his
usual wit and persuasiveness.

Loza was cordial as he heard the case, saw the briefs, and without
argument agreed to write the necessary documents, adding that he
would present Machebeuf with all faculties permitting him to exercise his priestly functions within Sonora. Machebeuf heard him preach
on the following day and saw him confirm a large number of people
who had gathered from everywhere about. Within a few days, the
papers were ready.

The instrument of cession let further light in upon the territorial
confusion; for Bishop Loza, naming not only the missions of Tubac,
Tucson, San Xavier del Bac, and Arizona at large by name, also
specified "La Mesilla within the *condado* of Doñana," and "any other
settlements . . . pertaining to this our Diocese." At one stroke, he made
clear that he considered the entire Gadsden Purchase, under the name
of "Doñana" from California to the eastern portion of New Mexico, as
his own territory to dispose of in ecclesiastical authority. He thus included more than merely the Arizona portion.

On 16 January 1859, "in this parish of Alamos," he signed the paper:

> *Firmado*
> *Pedro*
> *Obispo de Sonora*
> (flourish)

and Machebeuf, with his aim achieved, was ready to return to his
sloop at Navajoa, sail on to Mazatlán, descend upon Zubiría at Du-

rango, and lay to rest, with the paper he now held, the exhausting issue of territorial jurisdiction.

But Loza advised against this journey. Mazatlán, and the state of Sinaloa, which fell within his diocese, were in a state of civil war, and indeed, he himself had been forced to depart for the north as a "half-fugitive" because of "differences" with the governor of the state of Sonora. Machebeuf would do far better to return to Arizona rather than risk travel to Durango across the warring southern lands, where Catholic priests were particularly in danger.

How should he go then? He was informed that the strong current in the Gulf flowed southward, and this with the prevailing winds would make a return to Guaymas as captain of his own ship arduous if not perilous. He would do well to vacate his captaincy, dismiss the sloop, and return northward by the coastal road.

This he did, proceeding overland to Hermosillo. He met ardent welcomes wherever there was a chapel with a little population, or a tribe of religious Yaquis, to whom he ministered. He arrived without memorable troubles at Tucson, sent word of his achievement to Lamy by the Butterfield stage, and set about the business of a missioner in a wild town which must have order if it were to recover from the decline which had set in after the original Mexican presidio, founded in 1781 as the nucleus of the settlement, was abandoned.

Machebeuf was given a little house of two rooms by a leading Mexican citizen, and volunteers soon added to it a sizable wooden porch which became the first church to be established there under Lamy's diocese. It was soon too small to hold all who came to Mass, and one Sunday, when only a fourth of those attending could find room within, he preached in English from the doorway on the unity of the Church, appealing to all denominations represented in the throng. He called upon the Mexicans to build a larger church, promising them a regular pastor in return. In short order, men quarried rock in a hillside a mile and a half away, women of zeal dragged the blocks to the church site, Protestants gave money and materials.

Machebeuf moved regularly between Tucson, San Xavier, and Tubac. If there were no bells to summon the worshippers for Mass, guns were fired off to signal them. San Xavier was the center of his interest. Though badly in need of repair, it was still a noble building, with its heavy towers, fine dome, walled churchyard, large sacristy and rectory, and a sanctuary dimly rich in gilt-work, statuary, and carving, reminiscent of the great churches of southern Mexico. The Papago Indians living close to the mission had kept alive by tradition the prayers and even some melodies of the liturgy; and one of the tribal elders revealed to Machebeuf a treasure of four silver chalices, a gold-plated monstrance, two gold cruets and lavabo, a pair of silver candlesticks, two silver incensers, and the old sanctuary carpet, which he had kept to protect them against theft. It was a moving sign of belief in tradition.

In one of his sermons, given with even more than his usual vividness, Machebeuf thought it well to denounce the crime of murder, which was common enough in the scarcely governed town. The homily was more appropriate than he knew, for in the church that day was a man who had committed murder the very night before. He was at once convinced that the sermon was directed against him, which he felt to be unjust, since he considered that he had killed in self-defense. Later the same day he waylaid Machebeuf in a wood, raved against his supposed accuser, and began to draw his pistol. Machebeuf leaped on his horse and galloped away, which gave him the advantage, since his enemy, following in a buggy, could not keep up with him. In his sensible flight, Machebeuf spurred his mount so hard that he knocked off the heels of his boots. Ever after, so long as he was in town, as he went about his duties, by day or night, to the church or elsewhere, he was guarded, without his knowledge, by men of his parish.

With much to describe to his superior, he left for Santa Fe in early March, though suffering from malaria which had infected him in Mexico. Again he had to cross the Apache lands where only a few days earlier several soldiers had been killed by the Indians. He and his little party came to Apache Canyon (later the site of Fort Bowie). Machebeuf left his waggon and mounted his saddle-horse to ride ahead of his companions to the top of Mount Chiricasca, where a stage station had been established. It was raining hard. As he came alone to the stage house he saw that it was surrounded by belligerent Apaches. The chief rode to meet him and asked,

"*Tu capitán?*"

"*No capitán,*" replied Machebeuf, holding out his crucifix.

"*Tu padre?*"

"*Si, yo padre.*"

"*Bueno! Como le va?*" said the chief, sealing his how-do-you-do with a handshake, and sent for his warriors, all of whom shook hands in turn with the visitor. The chief then wanted to know if Machebeuf had seen any troops along the way.

"Certainly," said Machebeuf, and reported that even now, a detachment was on its way up the mountains.

The Indians held a conference and thought it expedient to depart, calling out, "*Adiós, padre.*" From the stage house three Americans emerged whose lives they said Machebeuf surely had saved. They took him in out of the rain, fed him, put him up for the night, and saw him off next morning for New Mexico, which lay twenty-five miles eastward.

At the village of Doñana the malaria gave him a troublesome spell of fever, but he was soon ready to travel, and he arrived at Santa Fe on 24 March, where Lamy "congratulated him heartily" upon his successful undertaking. For two months the malaria and, probably, the accumulated fatigue of his hard journey, kept him resting in Santa Fe. Now both he and Lamy, on similar missions, had travelled to what must have seemed like the ends of the earth, and, having achieved their aims, had come home with enough travellers' tales to last a lifetime.

iv.

Again to Auvergne

THOUGH BY NOW, in 1859, Lamy had firmly established eighteen parishes with the young clergy he had successively brought from Europe, he knew this was only a beginning for the design he had in mind, which, however ample, would have to be thinly spread over the endless and wonderful spaces of his land. He had not only the land to conquer, but the future.

While Machebeuf was in Arizona and Sonora, Lamy had written to the Society at Paris to say that he was sending Father Peter Eguillon, his present vicar general, to France to find still more priests, and to enlist a group of members of the order of Christian Brothers for the purpose of establishing a permanent school for boys. It was true that from the beginning he had had a boys' school, "more or less flourishing," but the faculty consisted of priests who had other pressing duties than those of the teacher. He had seventeen possible candidates for seminary training, and there were a few elementary schools with sixty small scholars. But not all of this was stable, and he needed to have new teachers. He already had a house ready for them if they should come, and he hoped the Society would come to his aid to help pay for their expenses on the long voyage to Santa Fe, if they could be found. He capped his plea with an argument certainly calculated to stir response in Paris—with an educated body of youth in the province, the future would be protected against the "incredible efforts" of Protestant proselytizers who unless opposed would render the young Catholics indifferent, or even turn them into non-Catholics. Luckily, so far, "little damage" had been done; but meanwhile, the young people of the territory really were exposed to "grave dangers." Sending Eguillon was a sacrifice, as he wrote to Purcell, for he would be left with only one young priest to attend to nine thousand Catholics, half of whom were "scattered through the county," with "some villages forty miles distant . . . we will be pretty busy." It was still evident that he was "very much in need of priests."

Like Lamy and Machebeuf before him, and Flaget and Purcell before them, Peter Eguillon went direct to Clermont, where he had been educated, and began making his own vivid appeals to the new generation of seminarians at Mont-Ferrand. Irresistible attraction seemed always to lie in eloquent accounts of the worst conditions of hardship, peril, and every obstacle of poverty and isolation. Imagine—and then would come challenging accounts of experience which lost nothing in the telling: the searing travels over endless lands with Indians behind every rock, hunger in the desert, thousands of souls starved for the means of salvation, primitive peoples and their alien ways, a vicious society waiting to be cleansed, the test inherent in the vision of one hardy young man serving God alone in the wilderness. . . . Hard as they worked, said Eguillon, the few priests of New Mexico were incapable of meeting more than a fraction of the great need which existed.

His eloquence was effective. Almost at once two young priests, Jean Baptiste Salpointe and François Juvenceau, agreed to join him if their bishop would release them; and soon three seminarians also joined up. In addition, and directly in response to Lamy's most urgent appeal, Eguillon was able to enlist four members of the Clermont establishment of the Brothers of the Christian Schools—Hilarien, Gondulph, Geramius, and Galmier Joseph—who were picked by their superior as the best teachers of his local group. Brother Hilarien already knew Spanish, a great advantage. With four more pre-seminary youths, and Father John B. Raverdy from Reims, Father Eguillon had a party totalling fourteen persons—one of them was to become the first vicar apostolic of Arizona, and, later, second archbishop of Santa Fe. They all embarked with him at Le Havre on 17 August in an American steamer, the *Ariel*, so old she was considered barely sea-worthy, and was soon afterwards scrapped. But the voyage, which took fourteen days, was without notable incident.

They travelled by rail to St Louis, then to "a small village" called Kansas City, and set out from there for the plains adventure. Salpointe saw "the green prairie undulated by the accidents of the ground, and

representing well enough a sea becoming swollen by a rising wind."
As usual, Lamy had sent waggoners and equipment to meet them, and
the party now had seventeen men. The report was that Comanches
were making war, so the newcomers waited for a caravan, found one
to join, and were surprised to meet with cold wet weather, and even
more so, to discover that Lamy had sent them heavy overcoats and
thick boots in anticipation of just such a condition. After the usual
marvels, observed in peace, the party came to Santa Fe on 27 October
1858, seventy-one days out of Le Havre, and were received by Lamy.

They were all amazed at his "affable simplicity," for of a lord bishop
they expected the grand manner. He gave them their first supper at
his own table. Excited over their arrival, and eager to work, and, as
one of them said, feeling at home, they "commenced to speak like
Frenchmen, and, of course, exclusively in French." The bishop sternly
interrupted them.

"Gentlemen," he said, "you do not know, it seems, that two languages only are necessary here—the Spanish, which is spoken generally
by the people of this territory, and the English, which is the language
of the government. Make your choice between the two, for the present,
but leave your French parley for the country you have come from."

The young men were abashed and fell silent, eating "with as little
noise as possible, and with a kind of lost appetite." The bishop
watched them for a moment as chastened they bent their heads over
his table to take his fare. Remembering what it was to be young,
without experience, in a strange land, he felt a pang of compunction,
and breaking into laughter, reopened the conversation—in French.

Even so, he admonished them to study Spanish and English, and
sent them to bed in a large dormitory room where they spread mattresses on the floor, though they would have preferred despite the late
hour to visit the town. Reporting on their arrival, Lamy told the
Society at Lyon what the young men had been spared—that all un-
knowing they had passed through a summer of terror, when many a
massacre by Indians had occurred among the caravans, and that
Providence had protected them "in an altogether special manner."
His new school was assured, and work began immediately to organize it.

Since May, Machebeuf was again in Arizona, with plans to visit all
the western portions of New Mexico and even to push on to California. New silver mines were discovered over the area, and immigration began to increase. Once recovered from his malaria, he had
wanted to set out for the West again without delay, but Lamy kept
him in Santa Fe. When Machebeuf asked him why, Lamy replied,

"Oh, there was nothing in particular, and you were so long away
that I was lonesome for your return. Just stay here with me for now

a while and rest. It will be pleasant to talk over old times. We have not had too much consolation of this intimate sort and I feel that we need some now. In a short time you can go again."

There it was again—patience tempering impulse; but Lamy knew when to judge his friend ready for the road, and let him go. Machebeuf was off to the West again travelling now along the Gila Valley, in its long course from its source country in the Mogollon Mountains to central Arizona. He visited even the most isolated of settlements along the way until he came again to Tucson, having left the Gila, which ran itself to its confluence with the Colorado River. He stayed in the Tucson country for two months, and during that time began the repairs which would eventually bring much of its original state back to the mission of San Xavier, where he said Mass often, ministering to the Indians whose little *jacales* clustered about its heavy walls. He was arranging to go farther west when word came from Lamy calling him back to Santa Fe once again. Dutifully he returned—but not before he heard of remarkable discoveries of gold in Colorado, far north of Pike's Peak. It was information which would bear upon the rest of his life.

V.

Quarrel with Durango

BUT BEFORE MACHEBEUF reached Santa Fe in early summer, the continuing paper battle over the disputed southern areas of the diocese had flared alive again. Rome had sent Lamy a decree, in the hope that it was final, which recognized the cession granted by Bishop Loza, and equated it with Zubiría's action in yielding up "Doñana and Las Cruces." In other words, Rome had given Lamy the entire *comitatus* or *condado*—the vast *county* of the entire Gadsden Purchase, assuming that Zubiría and Loza were in agreement in the matter.

Yet even now Zubiría had not agreed that he yielded all; he retained "La Mesilla," simply because it was not *specifically itemized* in the Vatican decree. La Mesilla was far the most important area in the entire region—both the village of that name, and the long agricultural Mesilla Valley, which stretched southward along the Rio Grande for thirty miles and sustained the densest population of the region. As it lay within the boundaries of "Doñana" the county, i.e., the Gadsden

Purchase, how could La Mesilla be kept as an enclave of Durango? But this was precisely what Zubiría demanded in a letter to Rome on 16 May. Lamy had assured him in April 1859 that Bishop Loza of Sonora had ceded the entire area, *including* La Mesilla.

Daily the matter was becoming more urgent, since a new American town called Franklin was growing up around Fort Bliss on the American side of the Rio Grande, opposite the old El Paso—a name which finally crossed the river to designate the new Franklin as it grew, while the old El Paso was eventually renamed Ciudad Juárez. The growing population of Franklin was Anglo-American—the Mexican priests of the old El Paso, or the parish of Santa María (as Zubiría always called it, after its tutelary saint the Virgin of Guadalupe), could not successfully serve the new English-speaking population.

Lamy at last was out of patience. If Durango did not accede to the Roman decree, he told Zubiría, "I will be obliged to notify the Holy See in Rome of the poor attention given to their Apostolic authority." He hoped Zubiría would forgive him for speaking so frankly.

In an angry reply on 28 June the bishop of Durango confirmed that he had ordered his northern vicar at Santa María to retain La Mesilla, he disputed Lamy's interpretation of the meaning and extent of the *comitatus/condado,* and he bitterly took notice of Lamy's threat to report him to Rome for disobedience.

"This is not the first time," he declared darkly, while the image of the old rebellious Vicar Juan Felipe Ortiz rose in the background, "nor the only proof made to me, of the discreditable image I seem to invite from the first Titular Bishop of Santa Fe of New Mexico"; but he thanked God that "in Rome they think very differently of me than you do."

He then had an astonishing rebuttal to exhibit: only a week after receiving Lamy's offensive letter, into his hands had come a document from Barnabo which quoted the St Louis synod's petition for the aggregation of the southern territory to New Mexico. The Holy Father had seen it and approved it, *and there had been no mention in it of La Mesilla,* even though Lamy himself had been at the synod and could have made the specification. Moreover, how could Tucson, Tubac, and other localities of Arizona legitimately belong now to Santa Fe? Zubiría strongly implied that Bishop Loza had been the victim of "the lack of exact news" and what was more, had been given wrong information—*videlicet,* lied to.

Once again—the exasperating affair raged on all summer and winter in 1859—Lamy had to write Barnabo explaining the whole situation, declaring, as to Arizona, that Zubiría "goes so far as saying that the Bishop of Sonora was wrong and that we have no jurisdiction whatsoever in the places he has ceded to us"—this, even though Rome had directly charged Santa Fe with jurisdiction over Arizona. Pressing his claim later, "the Bishop of Durango still wishes to keep three-quarters of the same *'condado'* (Doñana)." There was also the issue of the three small villages on the Rio Grande southeast of El Paso on the United States bank which lay at the extreme western tip of Texas. These, too, Zubiría still claimed, never having recognized their transfer to Lamy's care in 1851 by Odin of Galveston. The fact was, they also lay within the confines of the Gadsden Purchase, and should accrue to Santa Fe. But Zubiría in refusing to yield them declared, in truth, that their population was still largely Mexican, and required Mexican clergy. He went further, claiming that they were still territorially Mexican, which was not the case any longer, since the shift of the course of the Rio Grande—a notoriously vagrant river—had moved to the south of the villages, thus depositing them within United States limits. If Zubiría may have had a cultural claim to the three villages, they now belonged not only politically but geographically to the United States. Lamy therefore once more begged for a new decree for the whole of the *Condado de Doñana,* without excepting any of the places attached to Santa Fe or the county of El Paso in Texas.

Months later, Rome was still inviting contrary interpretations from Durango and Santa Fe; and a year later still, Lamy, writing to Barnabo, said, "I am afraid I have tired you of this affair" but "Durango had kept three quarters of the inhabitants of the county despite the decrees of the Holy See"—so slowly did some matters move between the hemispheres.

But not all.

Now struggling to meet the spiritual and cultural needs of Santa Fe, and all New Mexico and Arizona, Lamy on returning from a seven-week tour in the desert, was suddenly presented with a great new responsibility.

vi.

"Pike's Peak"

WHEN IN THE 1850S GOLD WAS DISCOVERED in Colorado—or, as the whole area was popularly called, "Pike's Peak"—immigration was sudden and numerous. "Pike's Peak" was part of the huge vicariate apostolic of the Indian Territory and the plains. The Kansas bishop—it was still J. B. Miège, the hunter who had turned up alone one day five years before in Lamy's prairie camp—was unable to visit Pike's Peak regularly, or send clergy in residence; and accordingly requested Archbishop Kenrick of St Louis and the other bishops of the province to ask Rome to assign the new gold country to Santa Fe, which was much nearer to it. Kenrick notified Lamy that he had petitioned Rome to make the new assignment to him.

It was an unwelcome surprise. Lamy was hardly able to manage what he already was responsible for. On hearing about the affair, he wrote immediately to Barnabo declaring that he had no "desire to extend the jurisdiction" of his diocese—though he had to agree that he was much nearer to Pike's Peak than Miège. Rather, said Lamy wryly, it would be far more suitable to have all of his own legitimate territory firmly assigned to him *all the way to the Mexican border* than to add another vast empire to the north. He regretted bringing the old nuisance up again, but there it was, even now not resolved. The Vatican, at its blandest, replied that they had received Lamy's letter in which—they quoted—"you indicated that you are unable to take any care of the spiritual needs of the Catholics in the territory of Pike's Peak." Rome cited the reasons he gave; and then, with no further reference to his unwillingness, recalled that he had admitted that "a priest should be sent" to Pike's Peak, and firmly gave him "the information how to proceed legally" in this matter. Almost as an afterthought, the Vatican added, "As regards the county of Doñana, the question is already sufficiently settled and His Eminence, the Prefect of this Congregation, has sent his reply to the Bishop of Durango." In whose favor? They did not say.

Rome then wrote to Miège, approving his proposal of the Pike's Peak transfer. Miège in his turn had sent Lamy a description of his recent visit to Denver City, the largest mining town of the area, and had done his best to have the people begin the building of a church. But there were 100,000 people in the region, more towns were going up, the need was severe, however exaggerated it may have been in Bishop Miège's reckoning of figures. Lamy told Barnabo, "It is true that I am much closer than is Mgr. Miège, and we have good routes going there as well as large towns all along the route. It is only five days in walking from one of our missions"—for Lamy and Machebeuf had both penetrated lower Colorado much earlier. There was nothing for him to do but agree, conditionally. "I consent to it until the new order," he wrote, evidently expecting that the diocesan lines would soon be redrawn and he would be relieved of the Pike's Peak area.

Barnabo duly thanked him "sincerely." Nothing more was said about Doñana.

Lamy took the matter up in detail with Machebeuf. The problems were almost unthinkable: the extent of the new territory; the lack of civilized resources in rude frontier shack towns; the distance—almost four hundred miles—from Santa Fe, which was the responsible see; above all, the question of whom to send, and where to find him. At last, "I see but one thing to be done," said Lamy to Machebeuf, and a sigh of resignation seems to breathe between his words. "You have been complaining because I sent for you and have kept you here at Santa Fe—now, don't you see that there was something providential in all this? I do not like to part with you, but you are the only one I have to send, and you are the very man for Pike's Peak."

In his familiar impulsive way, Machebeuf replied,

"Very well. I will go! Give me another priest, some money for our expenses, and we will be ready for the road in twenty-four hours."

It was the sort of flourish to make the bishop laugh at his closest friend, for nobody could be ready that soon. A companion in the field had to be found. Lamy appointed the young John B. Raverdy, who had come from Clermont as a deacon in 1858, and had lately been ordained. The equipage was presently in order: "a waggon with the necessaries of church service in [Machebeuf's] new field where he might have several chapels, a few personal effects, blankets and buffalo robes for their bedding, and provisions for the journey. This, with a lighter conveyance called an ambulance, for their personal comfort and for later travel among the mines, was the preparation, and four mules, including the span of mules, furnished the locomotion." Once again Lamy, sacrificing his strongest friend and helper to the wants of others, would be left to govern New Mexico, Arizona, and now Colorado, from Santa Fe with only one or two priests in the capital.

On 27 September 1860, in his own hand, he wrote out two documents for the expeditioners. The first read, "To all those whom it may concern we make known by the presents that Very Rev. Joseph P. Machebeuf has received from us all the faculties necessary to administer the Sacraments of the holy Catholic Church in the various districts towns and settlements of Pike's Peak and also that he has the same extraordinary faculties which he has had as Vicar Genl in our Diocese these nine years." The second stated, "This is to certify that Father John B. Raverdy has received from us all the faculties necessary to administer the Sacraments as assistant missionary to our Vicar Genl Very Rev. Joseph P. Machebeuf, in the new towns and settlements of Pike's Peak country." Both were signed "✠John B. Lamy, Bp of Sta

Fé." In his own administration Lamy retained the Conejos River area of Colorado.

All the rest—one half great slow-rising plains, the other half the abrupt highest mountains of the Rockies, with their vast interior parks, great range systems, and uncountable secret valleys and canyons—now awaited Machebeuf and his assistant. There the rude, fast-growing settlements were small, obscure agitations of society to be sought out and civilized.

The bishop and his vicar general were colonists in the broadest sense, and the lands they must claim for the values they held had to be trodden upon by each in turn across the whole Rocky Mountain and desert Southwest. The pattern of Lamy's life was a slowly continuing opening out of widening space, from a closed village world in Auvergne, to metropolitan France, the Atlantic, the Middle West, the Texas Gulf country, New Mexico, Mexico, Arizona, and now Colorado. For him the future was explicit in every day of the present. The works of both needed his patience as well as his vision. Whatever the need, large or small, he seemed to meet it under the precept of a later teacher of his faith who said, "All our raw material of sanctity is in the now, just as it is. . . ." He saw the small, plodding, inadequate equipage of his deputies draw away up the road to Taos toward known and unknown Colorado. He would hear their news only now and then; but what they found and what they did belonged to him, the father, who must know all out of duty, and the friend, out of love.

Machebeuf and Raverdy came into the wide golden southern plains of Colorado, passed Fort Massachusetts (later Fort Garland), crossed the Huerfano River—a mild flow of reflected sky bordered with cottonwoods turning yellow and willows fox red for the coming winter—and saw mountains at great distance both east and west. Often they looked like clouds on the horizon, but what they saw was snow on the far crests. There was a year-old settlement called Eldorado City in the foothills of Pike's Peak, and there in camp they said the first Mass to be held in their new territory. As they walked their way again, pushing northward, the great splendor of the Rockies to the west—the "Front Range"—drew closer, and in the evening light of 29 October Machebeuf had his first sight of Denver City, a "village . . . composed of little [mining] works (fabriques), wooden cabins, Indian tents and wigwams on the banks of the Platte, and only two or three brick houses."

He was expected. A new friend who had a store in a small wooden building "on the corner of Fifteenth and Holladay" put him and his curate up for the night, and after a good night's sleep under a roof, they walked around to see the town. Machebeuf was astonished to find that a small congregation, impatient for his arrival, had obtained a gift of two lots on the outskirts of town from the "express company, worth about $15 each, and had given the contract for the erection" of a brick church fifty by thirty feet in size. The specification gave the legal site as in "Denver City, Arapaho County, Kansas Territory." Machebeuf said, "What folly to build a church so far from the town" —for it stood actually on the prairie. He put up a seventy-five-dollar frame house behind the church, and soon enough both would be engulfed by the spreading city.

In 1858, a party of Kansas prospectors working near Pike's Peak had heard that gold had been found to the north, on a tributary of the Platte River, had made their way up to the site, had created a township and corporation there, and had returned to Kansas to excite prospective immigrants. In their absence, another party struck gold, set up their own camp of Aurora (named for their own town in Georgia) and soon a third party from Kansas arrived with a charter to organize a settlement given them by General James W. Denver, territorial governor of Kansas. The third place was named for him, and in due course all three areas merged in population as word spread and gold-seekers arrived in a growing rush. Gold in grains was to be had simply for the washing of the sand in the clear, shallow creeks of the region. Other gold was locked away in underground veins and was more laboriously mined by tunneling and by refining the mother ore. The earliest comers had no thought of settling—only of making quick fortunes and getting out. The rush came in a flood of people in 1859. Uncle Dick Wootten, a famous scout, opened the first saloon, serving the whiskey known as Taos Lightning, and a second soon followed under the name of the Hotel de Dunk.

It was a spontaneous society. Thieves or other criminals were given summary mob justice, and—the usual frontier style—were often shot to death or hanged within minutes of their crimes. As always, there was an element which stood for law and order, but vastly the greater population consisted of lonely men, living a hard life, and taking loose pleasures in compensation, though at high cost. Gambling, whoring in dance halls, horse-racing, gun-fighting, claim-jumping and consequent killings, were common. The promise of riches and the less material but almost equally strong pull of the West as an idea brought party after party over the plains into the mountains. Many never forgot their first view of the Rockies from a hundred miles away— again the illusion was of cloud, often of a symbolic golden hue. Guide books were rushed through eastern presses to help the emigrants. Indian tempers were uncertain and many a survivor arriving at the camps could tell of massacre and pillage on the way.

But the energy of the whole nation seemed to be behind the movement westward, and already the shores of the continent were connected by a vital link which closed the gap between the steamboat terminus of St Joseph, where the Missouri River was almost four hundred yards wide, and the ports of the Pacific. This was the pony express. The riders went in relays of twenty-five miles each, taking two and a half hours, mostly at headlong gallop. Fresh horses waited at each stage, the saddle-bags were transferred, and the courier was off again, never to pause for any reason until his span was complete. A Colorado immigrant in 1860 after weeks on the plains longed for news, and seeing the Pony Express—he capitalized it—approaching in a thunder of hooves, hoped for a little exchange. But "the Pony Express returning from San Francisco . . . passed us like the wind and we could not get a single word of news." It became a familiar, possibly comic, sight, the rider leaning forward in his saddle, scowling in the importance of his mission, his hat brim pressed flat against his crown by the wind, his driven pony, like the rider, distracted by nothing, as the pony's loyal triple beat faded at the gallop into the empty distance.

Beyond the open Platte River valley of Denver City rose the wonderful mountains with their infinite complexity of form. Entry into them followed creek and river beds, which were soon accompanied by the rudest of roads, leading to side canyons or hardly accessible slopes where mining camps were put up out of raw timber. The miner's life could hardly have been harder; yet camp after camp grew into village, then town, and in some instances, cities which endured.

In the beginning, Denver City was the miner's only change from the camps, and with a nugget, or a little pouch of gold dust, he went, when he could, for the violent relief to be had in a town whose chief industry was the assuagement, in various ways, of the hungers of lonely men. One such remembered coming to town from the lost gulches.

We made a most woeful appearance. When we started out we had a gay suit of miner's dress. Only two weeks passed and we came back our clothes hanging in shreds from our backs, our hats in ribbons and scarcely affording us any protection from the sun. Our boots were left behind more than twenty miles back and our feet entirely bare and cut from the sharp jagged rocks. They had a thousand questions to ask us but before we would answer any of them we made them get us something to eat and a change of clothing. We did not have one for two weeks. It was almost as good as renewing life when we got new clothes and I felt as if it was worth going through all those hardships for the rare enjoyment of that hour.

By the time Machebeuf arrived, the city was already swelling with commerce and growth. Overland waggons brought goods to the wooden

The young Bishop Lamy of Santa Fe in the 1860s

Marie Lamy, while a pupil in the Loretto Academy, entered the novitiate, became a nun as Sister M. Francesca. She later became mother superior of the Loretto Convent at Santa Fe, and outlived her uncle by twenty-four years, dying in 1912

Marie Lamy, the bishop's niece, as a young girl. She came to America with
him in 1849, was put to school with the Ursulines in New Orleans, and in
1857 joined him at Santa Fe as a pupil in the Loretto Academy

Christopher (Kit) Carson as colonel of the First New Mexican Volunteer Infantry during the Civil War period

Joseph Priest Machebeuf, Lamy's lifelong friend and lieutenant, as Bishop of Denver in his late years

The aged and ailing Archbishop Lamy in retirement

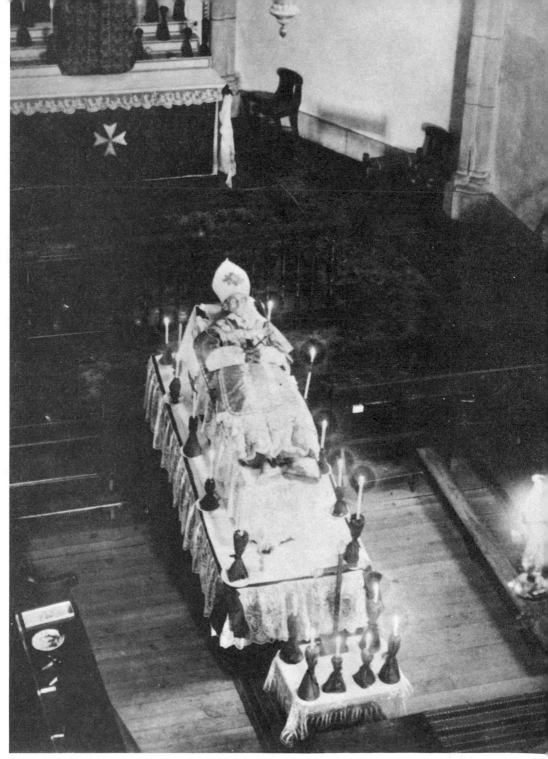

Archbishop Lamy lying in state in the Loretto Chapel of Our Lady of Light, night of 13 February 1888

Statue of Lamy in front of his cathedral in Santa Fe, which was unveiled in 1915. Willa Cather thought he looked "well-bred and distinguished...there was about him something fearless and fine...."

warehouses, including "to some extent the luxuries" of life. Hundreds
came not to find gold in mines but in the pockets of the miners—
billiard-hall proprietors, the milkman ringing his bell as he went along
the mud streets, even a theatre manager whose place was running "full
blast with the Bateman sisters as the great attraction." The United
States mail had a regular route to Denver, and men lined up a hundred
at a time to get their letters. The *Rocky Mountain News* already had a
two-storey building with a pitched roof and a great sign at one end
which read PRINTING. It was a mark of Denver's isolation when a miner,
"coming round one corner . . . found an auctioneer in full blast, selling
as cheap and cheaper he said than the things could be bought *in
America.*"

Machebeuf—like Lamy—could readily countenance the common
longing of people for material things. It was an energy which given
opportunity worked toward commercial civilization. As powerful was
that other energy which called for the unseen spirit of men and women
to be given visible form. Once again in an alien place Machebeuf went
to work in its behalf. Before a year was out, he wrote to his brother
Marius,

Since you are the head of the family, I send you this little sign of life to give
to all the others. . . . Here I am, firmly established at the foot of the Rocky
Mountains (at least for a while, as I don't know where I'll die). This evening
I leave for my eighth trip across the Middle and South Parks. N.B.: consult
a map and follow me if you can, even though I have to cross the highest
range several times to visit our poor Catholics, who are almost buried alive
in the depths of the mines. I am very well. Providence has given me strength
according to the need. To get to California Gulch, which is on the western
slope of the mountains, I often have to sleep under the stars, sometimes
surrounded by snow, as in last July, but thanks be to God, I sleep there as
soundly as in a feather bed. Besides the principal parish, established at Den
ver, we have begun another in the center of the mountains at a flourishing
place called Central City. I go there next Sunday to say Mass for the first
time in our temporary church [it was the hall of a lodge called the Sons of
Malta]. After several days there I'll go on to South Park—and from the crest
of the Snowy-Range (or chain white with snow) I'll be able to see through
the gorges far off the territory of Utah where the Mormons live. I'll be returning only at the end of September [1861] to pass a few days at Denver and
Central City, and then, in October, I'll move on again to the same South Park,
and New Mexico, Santa Fe, and Albuquerque [*sic*] & after procuring some
vestments which the nuns are busy making, and some good Mexican wine for
Mass, and for the table now and then, I'll return to Denver by Christmas
at the latest.

"Father Machebeuf," observed Lamy, "seems to be in fine spirits."

vii.

Marie, the Convent, the Country

WHEN MARIE LAMY came to her uncle at Santa Fe in 1859 she was a "parlor boarder." At sixteen, she gave herself airs, tossing her freshly laundered collars back to be washed again if they did not suit her. The convent suffered her—she was lovely, she was the bishop's niece, and there was that moving within her which led her to become a postulant on 1 October 1859, two years after her arrival. She wore silk dresses—this was remarked upon—but even so, she never shirked her duties, however unpleasant, for they included the responsibility of cleaning the outdoor toilets. When Lamy received her into the first stage of the sisterhood, he was proud. She assumed the name Sister Mary Francesca. With her addition, the membership of the Loretto convent reached twenty-six. There were those among them who eventually came to think of Sister Francesca as a saint. One who grew to a great age kept all her life a towel with Francesca's name on it. The lovely child from the Ursulines was growing into a remarkable maturity.

"Our little schools are on the increase," Lamy had said in 1859, "we have at least two hundred children, between boys and girls." What he had to offer was being eagerly taken, and the nuns were pleased to present their curriculum of "Spanish grammar, English, French Reading, Orthography, Spanish Geography, Maps, Spanish and American History, Pizarro's Dialogues, Mythology, Copybook Penmanship . . . Piano, oil painting, crocheting, and"—what appeared to be an especially nun-like craft—"embroidery on perforated paper."

If parts of the course seem mystifying, occasionally there was more in the convent by which to be both mystified and edified, as in the case of Sister Hilaria and the Devil. It seemed that Mother Magdalen, in order to improve the instruction in piano, which was in the charge of Sister Hilaria, engaged a professor of music to teach her the art, in which she "showed much promise." As a matter of course, she was always chaperoned by another nun, usually Sister Filomena Lujan, when the professor came to the convent to give the lessons. Both sisters were young, and Sister Filomena did not understand English and so missed certain meanings in the remarks made by the musician to his pupil, who, young as she was, also did not take what was meant for what it was—an infatuation on the professor's part. "One day he asked her to go to a concert being given in the town and she asked and obtained the permission. The Professor called in his carriage for Sister Hilaria and her companion." An appalling revelation then took place. "As she was about to enter the vehicle, Sister Hilaria looked down and saw cloven hoofs where the professor's feet should have been." As fast as she could she turned and followed by Sister Filomena ran back into the convent. *To think*—! It was an inexhaustible subject within the walls. Changing her name to Sister Rosanna, Hilaria never again left the convent.

It was gratifying to Loretto that "a smart and fine young lady," the heiress of one of the richest native families in New Mexico, entered the order. Lamy remarked that her father and grandfather "could beat the patriarch Job for the number of stock, out of the increase of their sheep, they have sold upwards of seventy thousand heads in few years . . ." When she died some years later, she left her property to the nuns, and her will was contested by her family, but was finally upheld by the courts. By 1861 there were over three hundred pupils in Lamy's schools, and it was plain to see that the holy training of the children had its good effect on their parents also. The convent property was being improved through the years—"Our place is beautiful," said Mother Magdalen, who had assumed her unknown responsibilities on the bank of the Missouri in 1852, "everybody says there is not another such in the Territory." A wall was built around the grounds, the trees grew so tall that they could soon be seen from a great distance, water flowed in acequias to the flower and vegetable beds and Sister Catalina was kept busy in the garden. To add to the convent fruit trees, Machebeuf brought oranges from the West in 1860.

A year before the arrival of the Christian Brothers with Vicar General Eguillon in 1859, Lamy had made ready for them, asking Rome to let him exchange certain pieces of church land so that he would have a convenient place in which to receive the Brothers and start their boys' school, which would grow in its educational reach until it became a college named after St Michael the Archangel (and which long later in an act of administrative expediency changed its name to the College of Santa Fe). When they arrived the Brothers must be content with "an adobe hut with four walls," five mattresses, five blankets, two tables, a few benches and some old carpets. They were invited to share Lamy's table until their own kitchen should be ready. The bishop presented them with a contract, assuming all their debts until they should become self-supporting, paying them eight hundred dollars a

year, and perquisites including board and laundry. The contract specified that for breakfast they should be fed bread, meat, and coffee; for
dinner, bread, meat, vegetables, dessert, and on occasion, wine. Within
a month of their arrival they were open for enrollment, took in at
once thirty boarders and more than a hundred and fifty day scholars.
It would be, thought Lamy, a "pretty good school." The Santa Fe
newspaper took pleasure, daily, in seeing what had never been seen
there before: "the cleanly, joyous little fellows, going and coming from
the place"—the school stood next to San Miguel's, the oldest church in
Santa Fe and probably in the nation—"where they receive the seeds of
instruction, from which shall grow the future rulers, teachers and
business men of New Mexico." Lamy would have the school grow, and
asked Purcell to procure him a loan of "four or five thousand for five
years. . . . I have got good property to answer for it" as security. Above
all, he kept urging, the great need for a seminary remained.

But even if matters moved forward in the long view, there were
setbacks. In 1861 a smallpox epidemic greatly reduced the school enrollments, and an outbreak of Indian troubles (so dreadful that Lamy
called it "war in the west") endangered the daily life of the territory.
The mail service, monthly until 1858 and weekly thereafter, and all
other communications, were cut off—even the Army received no official papers from the government. Twenty men were killed at one
mission, where sheep, cattle, and other supplies were stolen. Citizen
volunteers mobilized to fight the depredations. It was, said the bishop,
"a reign of terror." A speculative soldier decided the Navajos were
descended from Welsh families cast away long ago on the Texas Gulf
Coast. "Persons," he said, "who speak the Welsh language find no
difficulty in understanding them and being understood by them . . ."
Such interesting knowledge did little to help the general situation,
which was even more difficult because of the effects of a drought which
for three years had held the country. Produce was scarce, prices "were
frightful"—so high that many poor people were in great want, said
Lamy. Increased illness of all sorts kept reminding him of the need
for a hospital.

Meanwhile, the routine of his office—administrative affairs with
Rome, and now Denver—kept him at his desk for long hours when he
was not out on the dusty highways to the remote missions.

He seemed to ignore his none-too-robust health, but there were
moments when it failed him. In 1859 he had fainted at the altar while
saying Mass on the Feast of SS Peter and Paul in the convent oratory.
Mother Magdalen was present. During the Epistle she heard a great
noise and looked up. The bishop was not in sight. She ran forward.
He was lying unconscious, face upward, across the top step of the altar.

She tried to raise him but could not, and then ran to fetch camphor. By the time she returned, some men had lifted him up. He regained consciousness and sat down for a little while, bathing his hands in cold water; and then, "though with difficulty," he completed the Mass. Afterward he drank a little coffee and was helped to his house. "You can imagine," noted Mother Magdalen, "better than I can describe what I felt on seeing his Lordship prostrated in his vestments as though dead. . . ."

Within a short while he was writing as vigorously as ever to Barnabo pursuing the elusive decision on the Gadsden Purchase. His life continued in Spartan simplicity, and one time on returning from his little ranch four miles north of town where he had been ill, he found that the Mother Superior had installed a stove in the chapel where he said Mass, the better to keep him warm. It was instantly removed when he said that "if he was to say Mass there, that stove should be taken out."

But he knew, too, when to provide warmth and gaiety himself for his helpers, and after school term in 1860 invited the nuns and others to a picnic at his *ranchito,* thirty-two of them. They took their lunch with them, some sat on the floor of the little two-room stone cabin where he had already planted trees by the porch. Nobody was left to take care of the convent but "the little musician Francis." Lamy loved the country and stayed several days after the picnic.

At his desk, he conducted his entire correspondence by himself until very late in life. Always clear and deliberate, changes in his handwriting reflected the labor and the passing of the years. Routine reports (there was still opposition, though lessened, among some of the native clergy); finances (he regularly consulted Purcell about business plans and when he had to borrow from him said he would rather help Purcell than ask for help); regular, if modest, payments of Peter's Pence to Rome; whenever possible repayment by installment of his debt to the Society in Paris by requesting them to withhold what he could afford to spare from their annual allocation to him, which was for him "a great pleasure."

After ten years of struggling with the tithing regulations, he wrote to Cardinal Barnabo: "Here the principal revenue of the church comes from the tithe. A good number of worshippers give it reluctantly and almost never completely; an even greater number refuse to give it at all. All this makes the administration very difficult. Could we be authorized to change this custom and to adopt rules more suited to our present circumstances, after having consulted our clergy on the matter?"

Meanwhile, to the delight of all, Santa Fe's old customs continued, such as the manner of celebration on great occasions. On St Francis's eve—he being the patron of the old New Mexican kingdom and the cathedral—Lamy recorded: "about sundown, first vespers," then "grand illumination in the whole town, made with small piles of pine wood on the top of every house—the poorest families will have several piles. on the roof of the Cathedral we will have not less than forty fires. We are ignorant of the use of fire-engines. I never witnessed here a house on fire for our buildings are fire proof"—Lamy's first admission of any value attached to the old earthen architecture of New Mexico.

He seemed to like best to be off in the country on his pastoral visits. On those of the early 1860s he could see "some amelioration" in both substance and spirit in the missions, whether in the northern chapel towns in their dark mountains or in the leafy Rio Grande Valley, where rudely but passionately made images of Christ and the saints were both portraits of the people and likenesses of their lurid visions of blood made sacred in sacrifice. He saw eight new churches being built, and in several tours of "our poor mountain country" many were "being newly repaired," and a great number of the people lived by the sacraments. As soon as a newly arrived priest knew enough Spanish for simple exchanges with the people, he was sent out to a country parish which had usually several missions attached to it— visitas they were called. Some of these were days away, and required several nights in the open country. As in the frontier Army, the missioner's chief valued utensil was his tin cup. He cooked in it, drank from it, showered himself from it with cool water. Wild game or fowl he roasted over a burning stick or two. When he came to take charge of his new parish, his reception was festive, in whatever degree the poor means at hand allowed. Fiddlers, drummers, guitarists, and the general people met him outside his chapel, and often a local rhymer addressed him with complimentary verses "which did not always bear the stamp of novelty." When he could, the new pastor replied in kind, and then all entered the chapel to hear his first Mass. When Lamy came, often riding alone out of the tawny distance like his newest recruit, the ceremonies were much the same, but enhanced by the noble Latin liturgical observances, with mitre and crook, which accompanied a bishop at Mass, confirmations, and consecrations, and which moved even those observers who could not yet explain them.

viii.

The Civil War and Santa Fe

ARCHBISHOP KENRICK called a provincial council of his bishops to be held in St Louis in May 1861. Lamy took the opportunity to travel to St Louis by way of "Pike's Peak," where he could see for himself all that he must learn about his new territory, and hold a reunion with Machebeuf, who would be his guide in all the new activities radiating from Denver. He travelled by way of Las Vegas, Mora, the Huerfano, and saw how rapidly Colorado was being settled.

He spent two weeks with Machebeuf and Raverdy at Denver. The population was growing so fast—Lamy thought Denver City might have as many as seven thousand inhabitants—that Colorado had already been admitted to the Union as a territory in the previous February. Machebeuf showed the bishop his "nice brick church"—a simple box with a wooden vestibule in front and a wooden lean-to for sacristy in back—"in a beautiful situation." Machebeuf had secured additional property close by. The city was "nicely laid out," and already had "many fine buildings."

After Easter Machebeuf took Lamy to see the mines. "Some of them are within few miles, but the most stirring place I saw is what is called Gregory diggings forty-five miles northwest of Denver in the midst of the highest mountains." Central City was nearby. Lamy was struck how each of the mining camps had only one street of "crowded houses in the steepest gully you could imagine," reaching three or four miles in length. "Quartz mills, stores, shops, dwelling houses, all is mixed up." Mines were still being discovered daily. He visited some of the mills at work—the "most curious sight" he ever saw. Some of them made as much as five hundred dollars a day. He noted that Denver was over three hundred miles from Santa Fe, and he believed that if the mines continued to produce, the territory of Colorado could not fail of becoming important, with its many rivers, and the land generally good for cultivation. He saw "a great number of farms, already fenced in, some of them with good houses." The climate was mild and pleasant but for the spring dust storms. Fine timber covered the mountains, and the plains were "very rich with pasture." No wonder he saw on the road a "great many immigrants who were going there." Machebeuf and Raverdy, one or the other, were generally out visiting mountain chapels. Lamy, writing his impressions to Purcell, said "Father Machebeuf would be thankful if you would have the kindness of publishing in the *Telegraph* the information which I give you here about Pike's Peak."

Seeing it at first hand, Lamy now saw how Machebeuf's work would be concentrated mostly in the Denver region; and so realigned the boundaries of the Colorado division of the diocese, taking under Santa Fe a large portion of southern Colorado, including the site of the later Pueblo, and the lands of the rivers Las Animas, Huerfano, and San Carlo, and assigning all this to the New Mexico parish of Mora, north of Las Vegas. It was an exhilarating visit to wonderful country, but he had to leave in April to cross the plains for the St Louis council.

Now a veteran of the prairies, he arrived without incident, only to discover that he had made the crossing to no purpose; for while he was on the trail, southern states had seceded, Fort Sumter had been fired on at Charleston, and the United States was in the first weeks of the furious upheaval of the Civil War, with allegiances newly divided, and two governments improvising with every confusion the wildly complicated order of troops for the battle lines, and, behind them, the support in states and cities and farms which nobody had been ready to organize. From St Louis on 10 May 1861, Lamy wrote to Purcell, "When I arrived here, our Archbishop had just sent a notice to his suffragants [*sic*] that on account of the political troubles there would be no council. I intend to return in a few days."

In the following forty-eight hours St Louis was torn by massacres, for the city was divided into the two loyalties of North and South. Martial law ruled. Lamy said the tension was running high. The nation's war was repeated in desperate miniature within the very city itself. Anthony Trollope, there at the time, said, "The only trade open is the trade of war . . . Sick soldiers, who have never seen a battlefield, are dying by hundreds in the squalid dirt of their unaccustomed camps," and he was indignant at the "terrible dishonesty of those who were trusted" to take care of them. Lamy observed that "we are in a very dangerous time," and he was thinking of his journey homeward, for at Kansas City a party of six priests and three Christian Brothers from France were waiting for him to take them across the plains.

He felt it urgent to return, for he had heard of "troubles" in New Mexico, and, in fact, the Confederate Texans were moving into positions about El Paso, other Confederate forces were mobilizing in Arizona, and a march of conquest up the Rio Grande was clearly in the making.

He took time to write to the official Jesuit visitor to the United States, the Very Reverend Father Sopranis in San Francisco (which would be hand-delivered by Father De Smet), asking for a Jesuit establishment in his diocese. He could promise little in money, but there was a good house to offer in Santa Fe, there was fine church farmland, and heaven knew there was enough to be done professionally, and he cited not only the needs of New Mexico but of Colorado. He reminded the Father Provincial of the great Jesuit work done long ago, and still remembered longingly, by the people of Mexico. He himself had seen ruins of the fine Jesuit churches of northern Mexico which had been not quite destroyed in the various waves of the Mexican revolution.

In haste Lamy left St Louis for Kansas City, presently found his party there, and set out for Santa Fe on 21 May.

They made a forced march. The summer heat was particularly dreadful. They sometimes omitted meals, often marched thirty miles without pause, took turns riding in the waggons or on horseback, and had particular trouble crossing rivers—once one of the waggons broke apart in the ford and Lamy feared the loss of the supplies it carried. But these were rescued at six in the morning, and it was not long until at every camping site each newcomer knew a particular job to do, taught him by the bishop. They made the whole crossing in "18 days" —an extraordinarily rapid rate for a passage which often took six weeks or more. He arrived home to find "troubles" on two fronts—"on one side, the Indians, and on the other, the inhabitants of Texas, making war against us. Thus, we may expect great ordeals," not the least of which would be the financial upheaval and hardship sure to come with the war. He had not heard from the Society at Paris for a year, which gave him reason to worry about his treasury; and he asked them to carry over his debt of twelve thousand francs for another year without any of the usual, and gradual, deductions.

By the time Lamy returned to Santa Fe the sentiment of many citizens was against taking any part in the emerging Civil War. The *Gazette* asked editorially, "What is the position of New Mexico? The answer is a short one. She desires to be left alone." But the Texans were already mobilizing.

The Confederacy did not want New Mexico only—the goal of the forming campaign was to use New Mexico as the road to the Colorado gold fields, and from there, to turn west and capture California and its great gold deposits. It was a large strategy, for it would give the Confederate States seaports on both oceans, and at one blow, a land mass one third of the nation in size, and most desirable of all, the gold with which to pay for the war—so essential to the North itself

that Lincoln called the western gold fields "the life-blood of our financial credit." First take Santa Fe, then Fort Union to the east, then on
to Denver—this was the Confederate plan. The approach was already
open, for even before the declaration of war, people at La Mesilla had
held a convention and voted to ally southern New Mexico to the Confederacy. Santa Fe heard of the invasion of the southern part of the
diocese by a small Confederate force under Colonel William Baylor,
which captured Fort Fillmore on the Rio Grande near Mesilla. On 1
August, Baylor proclaimed Mesilla the capital of a new Confederate
state taking in southern New Mexico and Arizona—once again the
Gadsden Purchase lands.

At this point, New Mexico spoke out. The territorial governor proclaimed New Mexico's loyalty to the Union and ordered conscription
of "all males from 18 to 45 in age" for her defense. A grave war issue
had already gone through several phases. Though in 1857 Lamy had
said, "we have no slaves here," the New Mexico legislature had enacted a pro-slavery law in 1859; but this was repealed two years later
and New Mexico was again slave-free. "We have condemned, and put
slavery from among our laws. It is not congenial with our history,"
declared the governor in December 1861.

General Sibley, earlier the United States Army commander in New
Mexico, had defected to the Confederacy and was now in Texas. His
brother-in-law, General Canby, received the Federal command in New
Mexico. As the summer advanced, Canby set about strengthening the
Rio Grande forts with his few regular soldiers and the more numerous
conscripted native and immigrant New Mexicans. Troop movements
faced violent harassment from Indians who raided trails and towns.
News from the south was disquieting—Sibley was about to move his
large invasion force up from Texas. Travellers went about at extreme
peril.

But fortunately, Colorado was quiet, and when Lamy heard late in
the autumn of 1861 that Machebeuf was dangerously ill in Denver,
he sent Ussel, the pastor of Taos, to bring Machebeuf to Santa Fe for
proper care. Ussel went at once, taking a youth as his aide. They went
by horseback across the distance of over three hundred miles, and
found Machebeuf weak but walking about his garden patch with a
cane. He had fallen ill of "mountain fever" in September at California
Gulch and for two months had been unable even to say Mass. Because
of the war, there was no mail service to New Mexico, but some travellers had taken news of his condition to Santa Fe. He kept Ussel for
two weeks, and then feeling strong enough for the journey, returned
with him to New Mexico. "The thought of a visit to Santa Fe seemed
to act like a tonic in building him up," said Ussel. After a long re-

union with the bishop, Machebeuf went on to spend almost all of December with his old parishioners in Albuquerque, "where the care and good old wine of Father Paulet" quickened his recovery.

He thought New Mexico was "in a bad way." The Texan armies had already taken two Rio Grande forts, Apaches and Navajos were on the rampage and new reports came every week of their latest acts of violence. When Machebeuf went for a few days to the bishop's ranch a band of forty Indians passed within a mile of the place, attacked the shepherds at night, and stole all their sheep. A year before, sixty people had been massacred in a parish west of Albuquerque. Smallpox was still ravaging the population. More than a thousand children had lately died of it. Machebeuf went on his way back to peaceful work in Colorado in January 1862.

Lamy reported these and other troubles to Purcell as the invading Confederate Army pressed its way up the central valley of the territory, after "two very important posts [Fillmore and Stanton] were given up with provision, arms and all to a handful of Texans." Since then New Mexico had raised three thousand volunteers, but as there was no money with which to pay them, they were "very much discontented," and nobody knew whether or not they would join the Army regulars to stand against a "large force of Texians who are now 150 miles south from Sta. Fé."

For Sibley's brigade was nearing Fort Craig south of Socorro, and in a few days defeated the United States troops under Canby in day-long battle near the mesa of Valverde. Leaving Canby behind in his now useless fort, Sibley resumed the march to Albuquerque. How soon might he be in Santa Fe? As he went, he sustained his forces by taking the crops and goods of the countryside—sheep and cattle, first—and one citizen filed a claim stating that Texas troops had pillaged "all his chili, corn, wheat, carpets, bed covers, ear rings, ladies' breast pin, hogs, shirts, covered trunks, chinaware, 2 ovens and lard." Albuquerque was a major United States Army depot, and Sibley counted on capturing great quantities of quartermaster's stores when he should arrive there; but taking the town without meeting resistance, he found the Army warehouses in flames, and his expected plunder destroyed.

Santa Fe could do nothing but wait, for the main body of troops which was to have defended it was immobilized at Fort Craig down country, and the local conscripted "volunteers" had little organization and less will to fight. On 4 March Mother Magdalen was dismayed to see two houses next to the convent burning in a high wind which drew the flames and smoke toward her building. It was a store of flour which, to deny it to the enemy, was being destroyed. Just beyond were haystacks in the government corral, and if the fire reached them, the convent would be doubly in danger. The fire did not light upon the convent, though it burned all day. On the same day, the territorial governor, his staff, and a handful of troops, and the national flag, left Santa Fe to be reestablished at Las Vegas, beyond the immediate range of the invasion. The sisters watched them go by on the old street of the Santa Fe Trail, and Mother Magdalen exclaimed, "You can imagine better than I can describe what I felt on seeing all our troops leave [with] that banner under whose shadow I had been reared. . . ."

Six days later on Monday, 10 March, eleven enemy soldiers appeared in Santa Fe. They were all former citizens of the capital who had gone south to join the Confederacy at La Mesilla, and they now returned as advance party for the invaders. They were followed on the next Thursday by seventy more, and then in ten days by two hundred. The invaders placed their artillery in strategic positions, which suggested to the nuns that a battle for Santa Fe was to be expected, and they feared for their convent.

The Confederate bivouacs were all about the convent wall, and along the little Santa Fe Creek which ran by it. One day a Texas soldier climbed to the roof of the convent school and entered by a window overlooking the street. He called out asking if the room were occupied. Opposite, he found another window overlooking the courtyard, and looking down, saw some of the sisters. At that he went out as he had come, and the Mother Superior complained to Lamy, who notified the Texan commander that such incursions must stop, and they did. But because of the Confederate soldiers coming and going all day long, the convent school could not receive the day pupils, and classes were suspended. General Sibley had returned to the city to command the occupation where he had served before as resident.

One of his first acts was to seize all funds in the territorial treasury which, as the *Gazette* drily stated, were "appropriated either to the General's private use or for some other purpose." Another of his moves was to seize the keys of the printing office of the Santa Fe *Gazette,* and still another was to arrest "Mr. Parker," proprietor of the Fonda Hotel, for reasons not made public. Confederate troops were billeted in the old Governor's Palace on the Plaza. Sibley was pleased to be with his old friends at Santa Fe again, and was entertained agreeably, though he failed to gain recruits for his cause. He lingered in Santa Fe, and was seen at the fandangos and dinners, quite as though he were again legitimately stationed in town, when he should have been organizing his men and marching on to Fort Union and beyond. He had the delaying temperament of a heavy drinker and, they said, had been in no condition to lead the battle at Valverde a few weeks earlier, but had turned the command over to Colonel Tom Greene. Meanwhile, better use of the critical moment was being made by the miners of Colorado.

For at the request of Governor Connelly of New Mexico, Governor Gilpin of Colorado had organized a regiment—the 1st Colorado—to hurry south to defend Fort Union, drive back the Confederates, and tear down their "piratical bunting" which flew over the rebel headquarters at Santa Fe.

At last, after about three weeks, Sibley gave the order to move, and on 25 March the Texans under Major Pryor moved out on the Santa Fe Trail toward Glorieta, Apache Canyon, and Fort Union beyond. To their amazement they were faced on 26 March in Glorieta Pass by the 1st Colorado. A six-hour engagement followed which halted the Texan advance, though neither side could claim the day. The Texans were astonished at meeting "instead of Mexicans and regulars . . . *regular demons,* upon whom iron and lead had no effect, in the shape of Pike's Peakers, from the Denver City gold mines." A truce was declared for both sides to help their wounded and gather their dead.

The Confederate battalion commander at Santa Fe ordered the printing, on the *Gazette*'s captured presses, of General Orders No. 4 for distribution to the field troops, congratulating his men on their "victory" at Glorieta. In a dilution of the Napoleonic style, and with a touch of St John, hoping to inspirit his somewhat disillusioned forces, he declared, "Soldiers—I am proud of you. Go on as you have commenced, and it will not be long until not a single soldier of the United States will be left upon the soil of New Mexico. The Territory, relieved of the burdens recently imposed upon it by its late oppressors, will once more, throughout its beautiful valleys, blossom as the rose, beneath the plastic hand of peaceful industry."

Two days later the battle was resumed in Apache Canyon further east, and ended in the total rout of the Texans when their supply depot was destroyed by a flanking movement brilliantly commanded by a Colorado preacher turned battalion commander—Major John M. Chivington. The Colorado regimental historian said that the reverend major's raid was "the irreparable blow that compelled Texans to evacuate the Territory. Its audacity was the principal cause of its success."

For without their supply train, in a land so poor, the invaders were now helpless. They fell back on Santa Fe; and at Loretto, the nuns indoors heard them passing all night long, but until daylight did not know whether they heard Union or rebel troops, but as morning came, saw by their uniforms that they were Texans. "Some came on horseback, others on foot, and other were almost dragged to the city. All were in a most needy and destitute condition in regard to the commonest necessities of life," said the Reverend Mother. For some days the sick and wounded Texans were nursed by various women of Santa Fe, a "praiseworthy" act, said the liberated *Gazette* when it resumed publication on 26 April.

The Texan army left Santa Fe on 8 April, never to return; the Confederate design for riches and empire, through the conquest of New Mexico, Colorado, and California, was destroyed; the Civil War was ended in the wide lands of the diocese; and in due time the Union forces reentered the capital.

A Colorado soldier measured the bishop's church, which had "three or four of the finest sounding bells in the world." He stood "spell-bound by their influence," and went on to reflect upon "the awful power of the Catholic Church in the dark ages, the overwhelming influence of the clergy obtained by keeping the masses in ignorance and practicing on their feelings through the confessional, the unswerving devotion of the priestly orders to her advancement and glory, weighed against which the rights of whole nations were as a feather." He entered the church to observe the service and the people who "if they were not deeply impressed with the mummery enacted before them they still preserved a respectful attention." There were nearly eight hundred, all natives but a few soldiers.

On Monday, 20 April, the citizens of Santa Fe raised the national flag again in the Plaza. A large crowd heard a salute fired by Captain José Sena's Volunteer Company, and "great animation pervaded the spectators," reported the *Gazette*. A patriotic address followed, and an ode was read, "Our Flag," by E. Williams, a copy of which was handed to the paper for publication. An appropriate verse cried,

> *We know no rebel vile, can wrench*
> *Our banner from its stand.*

A few days later, now free of anxiety, the Mother Superior led her sisters and pupils on a walk to the foothills of the mountains for a picnic "close to a spring of crystal water." They all climbed the "highest mountain" [read: foothill] and "from there we could see the whole of Santa Fe." To add to their picnic lunch, the bishop had given them wine and baskets of peaches. The convent trees were "laden with flowers," and Mother Magdalen expected they would soon have plenty of fruit.

ix.

Emergencies—Denver and Return

BUT THOUGH THE TEXANS were thrown back, rumors persisted that they might return. Federal troops under General James H. Carleton marched from California to Tucson, expecting to find the enemy there, but the town was undefended. Carleton's column continued eastward to garrison New Mexico, where they expected once again to meet the enemy, this time at La Mesilla, but there learned the news of the Confederate retreat. Carleton relieved Canby of the territorial command in October, and despite the rumors, New Mexico, like Colorado, was immune to Civil War incursions.

Lamy resumed his pastoral visits, now in the northern reaches of the diocese. He blessed two new churches in new parishes. They were made of the usual "poor fabric of mud," but it was the best they could do with what they had, he said, and he thought the buildings looked well enough. There were seven others under construction elsewhere, and the total of new churches or chapels for the years of his work so far was close to thirty. He said it took great patience to build such places, but he was proud of his missioners who led the labors, and their constructions were models for the local country. They built in other ways—travelling miles between their various stations, and, in Santa Fe, even teaching Latin.

Farther to the north, the war had effects in Utah. To hold the road to California against any conceivable Confederate move along it, Federal troops occupied Salt Lake City in the fall of 1862. The Mormon country was under Machebeuf's direct jurisdiction, which brought it into Lamy's diocese. News from Denver came regularly—there was a weekly mail service, and Machebeuf was "well and stirring as ever," said the bishop, noting that Machebeuf wanted two more priests, the work was heavy, in Central City alone there were a thousand Catholic voters in the last election. But there was no one to send him. At least Machebeuf was able to make his own incessant journeys about the Rocky Mountains in perfect security, as Colorado was untouched by the war, and even the Indians were quiet. New mines were still being found, but business was almost wholly concerned with helping with war supply. Machebeuf felt that England was on the verge of declaring war against the States—"offended in her rights," presumably because of the sea blockade; and he believed Canada had already made immense preparations for defense against an American invasion.

But Indian campaigns against the New Mexico ranches and cross-country trails increased after the Civil War troop activity ceased; and the open country was less safe than ever for all those ways of life foreign to the marauding Indians. Towns were almost cut off from each other. Farms were despoiled of their crops. Overland parties too often ended up as scattered rubble of person and material in awful stillness on the exposed vastness. The diocese was in "unhappy condition."

Still, there was little use in waiting for ideal conditions. The scale of need, the expanse of territory, were too great. It was suddenly good news that the California Jesuits were thinking of migrating to Arizona to live with the Indians there—the Papagos, Pimas, Maricopas. At the suggestion of Bishop Amat of Monterey, Father Luis Bosco of Santa Clara, California, wrote to Lamy in the summer of 1862 to ask whether Santa Fe had plans for establishing a permanent mission at San Xavier del Bac, and if so, whether support for himself and some companion Jesuits, to be assigned by their superior, Father Villiger of the California missions, might be forthcoming. It was evidently a response to Lamy's letter to Father Sopranis written in St Louis and carried to him a year ago by Father De Smet. Arizona, still abandoned, would soon have to claim Lamy's own presence. He must first see what was there, and then imagine a future for it.

Presently came another letter from California. Villiger wrote to state, first, that there was as always a distressing lack of men to send into the field—the Jesuit colleges were increasing rapidly on the coast, and priests were needed there as teachers. But, he thought, he might find people to send, under two provisions—first: that Lamy would provide travelling expenses for their journey to San Xavier del Bac; second: that the Arizona mission would be attached to Santa Fe. Therefore, if three priests and one brother were to be assigned to Arizona, would the local population sustain them with food, clothing, and the like? Or, he added, perhaps something to eat for lunch would be enough in the way of food. He hoped for a reply to be sent to him at Rome, where he would soon be.

Lamy was able to reply to these inquiries satisfactorily; and he was thinking of two long new journeys—one to Arizona and the West, in this year of 1863; the other, to Rome, in 1864 to make his regular *ad limina* visit to the Pope.

Meanwhile, another missionary bishop appeared in Santa Fe—the

Right Reverend Josiah Cruickshank Talbot, of the North West Diocese of the Protestant Episcopal Church, who had come down by stage from Colorado. A dreadful trip. Drunken and profane passengers singing obscene songs, all packed in with no room to move; extended runs with most infrequent stops, though the stage drivers were courteous and efficient. There was at least one comfort on the way—a pause at the Hôtel Française (*sic*) at Fort Union.

But then, Santa Fe! Talbot saw everywhere "loose morals," and "universal concubinage," and "open adultery," of which "priests and people alike" were guilty. From all he heard, though, Bishop Talbot was able to credit Lamy with "cleaning up" the corrupt clergy, though he still thought the Church bled the natives for ritual services, including baptisms, for which, actually, the cathedral bells rang out (for a fee). On 3 July the two bishops met in the office of Captain McFerran at Fort Marcy and had a "pleasant conversation about the territory," but when another person entered the captain's office, Lamy withdrew. Bishop Talbot made a note that Lamy and "indeed many of the people of the town" knew ahead of time that "we were on our way here . . ."

Perhaps the weekly mail from Colorado? But it was not always prompt, and Lamy was sharply concerned when in mid-summer he received a letter from Denver dated some time before, written in an unfamiliar hand, to say that Father Machebeuf had been the victim of a shocking accident in the mountains when his carriage had fallen from the narrow road to precipitous rocks below. The letter gave few details, but Machebeuf's condition was clearly dangerous, and Lamy concluded that he might not live. If he was to see him, Lamy must leave for Denver within the hour. He left so precipitately that he neglected to take a supply of rations. A servant rode with him. By noon the next day they appeared in Mora, where Father Salpointe was pastor. Lamy told him the news, and asked him to go along to Denver. The invitation became an order when Salpointe proposed taking a couple of hours to prepare food for the overland ride: Lamy said they would take the remains of lunch on the table and leave at once. It was enough for one meal.

Salpointe could only agree. He was a full-bodied man with large dark eyes and a thick thatch of dark hair which gave him a boyish look. He had an observant, original habit of mind, a keen practical sense, and a Frenchman's taste for a well-set table. Lamy's austere habits—exaggerated by his present haste—led Salpointe to remark that "the Bishop, who could do with one meal a day even at home, provided he had a cup of black coffee and a piece of bread morning and evening, always objected to making ample provision of victuals for traveling." As a result, hurrying to Denver, the little party had to live for the most part on game which they hunted and cooked (without salt) though when infrequently they came to a habitation they did supply themselves with rations. Water was scarce, and they had the plains traveller's familiar disappointment when a deep and beautiful catch basin turned out to contain brackish water; but a few miles further on, they found fresh water, and the next day they came to the Huerfano River and the ranch of a friend, who was able to tell them that Machebeuf was beginning to recover from his accident, though it seemed that he would be somewhat crippled for life.

The relief in this, tempered though it was, gave Lamy a sense of ease, and he pursued the rest of his way to Denver at a more leisurely pace, setting the next day's goal at the new town of Pueblo, only twenty-five miles farther on. When they reached there expecting from promoters' maps to see "a second New York, with splendid streets and blocks [read: business buildings], parks and public gardens," they saw only "a few miserable huts of frame," on one of which, scrawled in charcoal, was the primal word "Saloon." They decided not to spend the night in Pueblo but moved two miles beyond on the banks of a little river, a place "indeed very beautiful." They were at the foot of Pike's Peak, and now nothing lay between them and Denver but grand plains. They moved on, seeing the first habitations at Cherry Creek near Denver City, and after ten days, at last knocked at Machebeuf's door in Denver. In a few moments the door was opened by Machebeuf himself, on crutches.

His astonishment and joy were rewarding. He had had no word that Lamy was coming. The old friends made much of their reunion, and Lamy learned what had happened in the accident. Machebeuf, returning from Central City in his buggy on a precarious, narrow, rocky road chipped out of the mountainside, had met a train of supply waggons. When he drove close to the outside edge to let them pass, he miscalculated, the buggy slipped, and he was thrown down the slope to the rocks below. His right leg was broken at the hip. People took him to a house nearby on the ridge, a doctor was called, the leg was set, but for many months he would be unable to say Mass. Raverdy was still with him, active in the town parish and the mountain missions.

Lamy, writing to Purcell afterward, said, mistakenly, "No bones were fractured. the doctors say that he will get well." But they were wrong. Machebeuf would be a cripple for life, could never ride again, and would have to go about all his work by carriage. With his characteristic habit of adding interest to events, he was inclined, in his letters thereafter, to say, "Pray always for the poor cripple."

The bishop spent five days with him, touring the area, visiting

Central City again, where there were more parishioners than at Denver, and if they as yet had no church, they had a "fine bell." He blessed the neat brick church of Denver, with "quite a number of Protestants" present, and gave a homily at the end of the pontifical Mass. The choir deserved "great credit." Everything had grown. "What a change from my first visit two years ago," wrote Lamy. All of it required "all the energy of Father Machebeuf (and you know he is not lacking in that) to attend to all the wants . . . in Colorado Territory."

Reassured about his confrère, Lamy left again for Santa Fe, going now by way of Ute Pass, the Fountain Valley, and the Garden of the Gods. Once again at the Huerfano, he saw settlers from the south, all of whom were learning English. Again the overland travel was the same—unremitting alertness on the road, not only for Indians, but for outlaws, who, taking advantage of the state of war, were on the increase; spare rations and hunter's luck, now good, now poor. Salpointe said he thought "this mode of life exceedingly hard, because I was still young in the missions." But looking at Lamy, he saw that all of it "seemed of familiar occurrence to my Bishop." In the end, the younger priest spoke for them both when he said, thinking gratefully of unseasoned rabbit meat cooked on a stick in the open air after a day's ride in distance that seemed hardly to diminish by nightfall, "so good a cook is hunger."

As Lamy returned home in late summer, the authorities in New Mexico were putting into action a strong, often pitiless program of defense against the Navajos and Apaches which included plans to gather them on reservations where their constantly mounting warfare against the Mexican and Anglo-American citizens and the peaceful Pueblo Indians would be impossible; or if that should fail, then—but the words of the territorial governor, himself a long-time New Mexican resident, and of General Carleton, in command of the military department, stated the case flatly. Governor Connelly declared that the aim of the government "should be so directed as to keep these sons of the forest within proper limits and either maintain them as paupers, teach them the arts of civilized life and oblige them to sustain themselves, or, on the other hand, exterminate them." The general said, "It may be set down as a rule that the Navajo Indians have long since passed that point when talking would be of any avail. They must be whipped and fear us before they will cease killing and robbing the people."

Colonel Kit Carson was called from Taos to active service and given troops to wage a war of attrition and spoliation against the Navajo. He burned their wheat and corn fields, chopped down their peach and other bearing trees, systematically working to starve the Indians. Indians inclined to be peaceful had been given until 20 July of that summer to surrender. Through the summer and winter many gave up and trudged in great misery to Fort Canby in eastern Arizona, later to be moved, along with thousands more, to the newly established fort named for General Sumner, in southeastern New Mexico, at a site called the Bosque Redondo (or "circular grove"). Carleton defined his purpose in this move: "to send all captured Navajos and Apaches to" the reservation "and there to feed and take care of them until they have opened farms and become able to support themselves, as the Pueblo Indians of New Mexico are doing." It was to be an experiment in changing a whole culture. For the rest—resistant Apaches—Carleton issued orders that: "All Indian men of the Mescalero tribe are to be killed whenever and wherever you can find them . . . If the Indians send in a flag and desire to treat for peace, say to the bearer that . . . you have no power to make peace; that you are there to kill them wherever you find them . . . The Indians are to be soundly whipped, without parleys or councils, except as I have told you."

Lamy was among those who most deplored the savageries which made the diocese, and its territories, almost ungovernable in both civil and religious affairs. A year earlier one of his young French priests, the Abbé Martin, as he called him, was murdered by Navajos who attacked a caravan in whose vanguard he rode. He had been wearing a cloak over his cassock, and if they had seen him as a priest, said Lamy, they would not have harmed him. As it was, instead of robbing his body in their usual way, they "respected him and left." Lamy had known Indian warfare for twelve years, and yet he felt for the marauders, and he prayed that the death of young Martin might "deserve the conversion of his murderers and of the whole tribe."

In the field it was often an unequal struggle. A young officer wrote from Fort Craig on the Rio Grande to his wife in California on 24 August 1863:

My Dear Wife
 On Saturday last, the 22nd inst, I returned from my Indian Expedition, having been absent since July 23rd, just 31 days. It was a very tedious march, travelling all the time through mountains and valleys, having no other roads than Indian trails to follow—and nearly the whole country which my command passed over had never been seen by white men before. My expedition did not accomplish much, as I saw the Indians but once—they were driving about 8,000 sheep which they had stolen. I chased them for 31 miles, when I overtook them, and fought them for half an hour. I only had with me five soldiers, two Mexicans, and myself—eight in all, whilst they numbered between sixty and eighty. When I overtook them it was almost dark, and I was nearly a hundred miles from the rest of my command; so after fighting them for half an hour, I could do nothing more than let them go without getting

the sheep. The only casualty on my side was a horse shot, while we killed two probably three of the Indians. . . . So you see I have smelt gunpowder, and come out of it safe. The[y] are the Navajo tribe. . . .

Across such country, amidst such hazards, Lamy, a few weeks afterward, was on his way for a journey of half a year which would give him his first sight of Arizona, and beyond.

VIII

THE PAINTED LAND

1863–1867

i.

Across Arizona

HE RESOLVED TO GO AS FAR as San Francisco, where he would respond in person to the Jesuit inquiries about Arizona and New Mexico, and ask for men. With Father Coudert, the pastor of Albuquerque, as his secretary and companion, he set on his longest overland journey since Durango. On 20 February 1863, Arizona had been separated from New Mexico as a territory when Lincoln signed the act of establishment voted by Congress. This creation did not affect Arizona as a part of the diocese of Santa Fe. Now Lamy, who knew the western lands only by hearsay, would see for himself this great new third of his spiritual domain.

Leaving Santa Fe on 27 October with Coudert, he went down the river to Albuquerque, stayed a day or two, and then, from Isleta, turned west across the tawny desert. He came to Inscription Rock, also called El Morro, and found carved in its sandstone face many names of other travellers, including that of Juan de Oñate, the colonizer of New Mexico, who recorded that he had "passed by here *(pasó por aquí)*." If, as once stated, another name was scratched into the rock—"Bishop J. B. Lamy, 1863"—no trace of it remains.

The two riders turned north to Fort El Gallo, where the garrison was commanded by Lieutenant Colonel Don Francisco Chaves. The bishop spent a few days there while three companies of dragoons, Major Willis commanding, made ready to march westward. Lamy and Coudert were to join the troop movement. They went by way of the pueblo of Zuñi, where Lamy spent a week. He was joyfully received, administered the sacraments, including confirmation, and slept on the flagstone floor of the pueblo governor, Juan Séptimo. The stone floor, intended as the ultimate in hospitality, resulted in an attack of rheumatism for the visitors. They saw the Zuñi scalp dance, which went on continuously during their visit, to celebrate the recent killing of Navajo marauders. The Zuñis called the bishop "Tata," and watched him leave with the troops for a long open crossing to the next known watering place, which was thirty-six miles away. But in the flat desert, unseen from even a little distance, with no sign of a watercourse, they came upon a fresh natural well rising from a spring deep down within almost perpendicular walls, and so ample that even the horses could pick their way to the water. They called it Jacob's Well, and stayed by it for two days, to rest men and horses. On the third morning they woke under a quiet fall of four inches of snow, which was melted by the great sun during the day as they moved on.

Lamy was a good rider, erect in the saddle. Patient in travel as in other things, he still pressed forward as well as he could, to make the hard country yield up to him its blind ways. He was now in Arizona, somewhere in the northern third of the territory. It did not look like the New Mexico he knew, with its pale grass plains, its long green thread of the Great River valley, its wooded mountains. Here in Arizona the immense distances showed other colors—blue far away, but nearer to, the mountains often looked like frozen fire, under bare colors of rose and ochre and char, and the desert was more barren, and its earth too recalled dead fire in its hues. It looked like a painted land. The valleys showed walls striped like agate. One mountain range after another seemed to deny future escape. Those colossal earth wrinkles from afar made grand statements of beauty in form and atmosphere; but once entered, presented endlessly tortuous ways, caprices of weather, and repeated barriers to progress, all inducing a sense of captivity on a dishuman scale. How was progress measured in such lands? In the open desert, how slowly the mountains ahead seemed to change and come closer—day after day the rider would seem always to be within sight of the same mountains. Often the way ahead vanished through heat waves into the very sky. The pace of travel was so slow as to compel contemplation in anyone given to thought in any degree, and, in some, could serve as an awesome entry into the religious spirit in a time when the work of God was admittedly divine and, on that account alone, wonderful to behold. How ten-fold desirable then, to conquer, or at least survive, hardships in the midst of wonders in honor of a purpose believed in beyond one's own life.

Lamy's military escort had other duties than those of protecting him, for they had reconnoitering to do, and reports to investigate, which made their pace of travel slower than Lamy's needed to be. Coming to the Little Colorado River, he met a train of goods waggons belonging to one of the Armijos of Albuquerque; and bought from the party a waggon with mules and all its merchandise. The waggon drivers entered his service with their vehicle, and Lamy took leave of the troops in order to travel faster. He now had his two saddle-horses, an ambulance with two mules, the waggon with its eight mules, two men with two mules, and a tent, and he led his party out on its own across a wild land in a state of uncontrolled Indian warfare. He kept everyone on the lookout at all times, for the Apache used the bare country itself for cover as no one else could, and might appear between one minute and the next out of nowhere. The party could go no faster than the fastest mule's walk; but they were not subject to delays of days at a time.

They suffered from cold, for they were in high altitudes and winter was drawing on. One night Lamy and Coudert were nearly killed by noxious air caused by live coals in a pan set inside their tent by a solicitous Mexican to keep them warm. They reached fresh air only just in time. Another night, Lamy had to walk about until daylight to keep his feet from freezing, for an icy storm was raging and no fire burned. One day they joined a party of Mexican raiders bound for Cañon del Diablo, which Coudert thought ill-named as it was so cold and far from hell.

For two hundred miles they had been gazing at San Francisco Peak and at last were on its foothill slopes. There they were met by Major Willis's command, who had arrived earlier by another route; and one night in the black silence they heard an unearthly scream. It was the hunting cry of a mountain lion who was only fifty feet from the camp and its animals.

Moving again, Lamy and his people met a Tonto Apache party who, being outnumbered, kept the peace, saying only, "How do you do, tobacco?"; and the caravan crept on to the great labor of crossing the Cañon de la Vivora. Its near side could be descended only with the utmost labor, for it was precipitous—the waggon wheels had to be lashed immovable and each vehicle held back in the descent by forty soldiers. Going the reverse way, this cañon wall could never be ascended. It was a place of no returning. Lamy amiably said that they had crossed the Rubicon, and sold his ambulance forthwith to Major Willis, who was ordered to establish Whipple Barracks and remain. It was to be a new Army post erected to protect the gold and silver miners at nearby Walker (later Prescott) in the very center of Arizona, amidst formidably enclosing mountains.

Until 20 December Lamy remained there, exploring the neighboring mines, and fishing for trout, and then with his little caravan he set out for Granite Creek near the very crest of Granite Mountain. Coming through a heavy snowfall he arrived there on Christmas Eve. A miner offered him his own cabin, eight feet square, which was put up out of parts of wooden packing boxes. The snow blew in through the cracks. It was where Lamy and his seven men would take shelter. It was also where, on the next morning, Lamy offered the Mass for Christmas Day.

> *Deus firmavit* [he intoned in the Collect],
> *orbem terrae, qui non commovebitur:*
> *parata sedes tua, Deus, ex tunc,*
> *a saeculo tu es,*

and praying to God on a wintry mountain of granite, the words told him of how the Lord founded the solid earth, and how it would abide immovable, and how firm was the throne of God even before the world began, and how God was from all eternity. . . .

For as he wrote to Paris, "On Christmas Day, we were able to celebrate the Holy Sacrifice, attended by twenty or twenty-five people kneeling on earth covered with the nighttime's snow. We were on the slope of a mountain, surrounded by forests of russet oaks, silver firs and cedars." The altar was improvised from old planks and set up within his cabin, and was canopied by freshly cut evergreen boughs. Only a few men could kneel inside the cabin—the rest were outside in the cold. It was so cold that a fire was lit in the cabin, and several times Lamy had to bring the chalice with its wine and water to be thawed by the stove. Snow was falling, and so much came through the packing-box walls to fall on the altar that continually it had to be brushed away. Enacting the center of his belief and surrounded by the natural Gothic of the mountain heights—pointed firs and pinnacles of rock—he was a countryman at home.

It was soon time to move on again. He had distributed mail entrusted to him at Santa Fe to bring to some of the miners. He doubted —and so did Major Willis—that gold in great quantities would be taken at Walker, because of a scarcity of water. The miners put much hope on spring freshets to bring them what they needed to wash out the gold. Lamy left his vestments and Mass vessels and two horses with a local resident, Don Manuel Irrizarri, provisioned his small party for six days, bought fresh horses from miners, and set out for the Mojave Indian country. This lap of his journey would take him across the great Mojave Desert, and before he reached the Indian village he had gone along for thirteen days.

One night an Indian tried to steal the horses of Lamy and Coudert. If he had succeeded, the bishop and his people would surely have died trying to cross the desert on foot. They came safely to Fort Mojave and rested for a few days; then with new mounts and supplies were taken across the Colorado River by ferry to continue the journey to

California. They had expected natural forage on the way, but no grass grew, and meeting by chance a Californian on his way eastward to Fort Mojave were able to buy fifty pounds of corn from him for twenty-five dollars. They passed across great mountain rises, thinking each might be the last; but another always loomed ahead. They saw a curious desert tree—the palm of St Peter—which grew as high as fifty feet; and they found on one of the plateaus so many hares and rabbits that they could catch them with their hands. But at last they reached the last plateau, and looking down the abrupt slope to the west, saw at its base a fair-sized California city. It was San Bernardino, a town built by the Mormons, which they reached by way of a well-made road down the mountain.

There Lamy found an old parishioner of his from Ohio who had gone to settle in California, an Irishman called Quinn. In his happiness at the reunion, Quinn gave every hospitality to Lamy and Coudert, and when they had to leave by stage coach for Los Angeles, he assumed the care of Lamy's men until he should return. The trip to Los Angeles was luxurious after weeks in the saddle.

In Los Angeles, Bishop Amat was glad to see Lamy, but when asked about the business of obtaining priests for Arizona, for which Lamy had made his extended journey, replied that two Jesuits had already gone to Tucson—one of them Father Bosco, who had written to Lamy, the other Father Messea. It was gratifying news, and there was now no reason for Lamy to go up the coast to San Francisco on the same mission. The travellers remained eight days with Amat, who showed them the whole vicinity, took them to see the Pacific at San Pedro, and to visit the mission of San Gabriel, with its great groves of orange and lemon trees, which showed together scented flowers, unripe fruit and ripened. It was a place of ease, the air then pure, the light clear, the land beguiling.

But now Tucson awaited. Returning to San Bernardino, Lamy and Coudert found Mr Quinn again, and with his help stocked all equipment for a hard entry into another wilderness, now to the southeast. Once again it was the familiar succession of desert and mountain, repeated through weeks. They noted that one lone passage was across a desert below the level of the seacoast they had left—Death Valley. They proceeded by way of minuscule settlements no longer on the map—La Paz, White Water, Aguas Calientes, Indian Wells, Weaver. Their route lay in a great diagonal across lower Arizona from the Colorado River toward Tucson. They met almost no one, saw few settlements, once came to a cluster of only two families to whom Lamy brought the Mass.

In the Weaver Mountains southwest of Walker he halted while

Coudert, with a companion, went fifty miles to the north to retrieve the vestments, vessels, and horses left at Walker with Don Manuel Irrizarri. On his route north Coudert and his companion went with particular caution, for there was news of Indians about. On reaching Granite Creek safely, they were asked immediately by Don Manuel,

"Where do you come from?"

"From Weaver."

"What news have you of the massacre on the road?"

"We heard of no massacre."

But word had come to the Creek the night before of how three Americans and five Mexicans, who had left Walker to go to Weaver, had been killed, scalped, and mutilated by a band of Tonto Apaches.

At a certain point, the road between Weaver and Walker divided, one part passing to the east, the other to the west, of a great hill. Which route had Coudert taken? The eastern side, said Coudert, which explained the survival of himself and his companion; for the massacre had occurred on the western side, where they would have met the Tontos. At Weaver, Lamy heard of the massacre and mourned Coudert and his rider as surely lost. But after a week they were safe again in Weaver, having passed on the way—this time they chose the western road of the hill—the graves of the victims, buried there by a large party of men from Walker who were out on the land now to avenge their dead friends. Coudert brought the sacred objects with him—but not the horses, for these, and all the livestock belonging to Don Manuel, had been stolen by Indians on a raid.

Tucson was still two hundred and fifty miles away. The monotony of danger—danger from the desert nature, with its sky heat doubled by its reflection from the hard barren crust of the earth; the scarcity of water; and, as attested by abandoned ranches seen now and then, and the remains of mine machinery and overland waggons left to rust and rot, danger from the always travelling Apaches—was unremitting. Campers often travelled during much of the night when the temperature dropped; and with the return of the sun, which heated the air so that it scorched the mouth and throat, the travellers would pause to rest during the hottest part of the day. As a mountain drew clouds together out of its vast exhalations of transpiration, so the desert called forth violent hot winds which rose and carried choking dust over whole provinces.

But if progress was unimaginably slow, there was something stronger than what tried to impede it. A lone dweller in the Arizona wilderness wrote of Lamy: "He stopped a day with us as he was returning from California, a frank agreeable fascinating gentleman with the bonhomie of the Frenchman and the earnestness of the typical Christian." He saw Lamy clearly. "A man of works rather than words, whose field of work is an empire, his diocese stretching from Denver to Mexico, from the Rio Grande to the Colorado."

At last, on 19 March 1864, Lamy and his party drew into El Charco del Yuma, thirteen miles from Tucson, and were met by Father Messea, one of the two who had come from Santa Clara. A mounted squad fired rifle salutes, and they all proceeded to Tucson to be met two miles from the village by Father Bosco, "with as much pomp as the city could afford." They proceeded to the unfinished church, whose sanctuary Bosco had roofed with canvas, while the rest was open to the sky. The bishop's blessing came upon the little crowd assembled to receive him.

Though he thought that one day there would be a large population there, the town was then meagre in numbers and comforts. A survey and mining expeditioner in the same year saw it as "a city of mud boxes, dingy and dilapidated, cracked and baked into a composite of dust and filth; littered about with broken corrals, sheds, bake-ovens, carcasses of dead animals, and broken pottery; barren of verdure, parched, naked, and grimly desolate in the glare of a southern sun. Adobe walls without whitewash inside or out, hard earth floors, baked and dried Mexicans, sore-backed burros, coyote dogs, and terra cotta children; soldiers, teamsters, and honest miners lounging about the mescal-shops, soaked with the fiery poison; a noisy band of Sonoran buffoons dressed in theatrical costume, cutting their antics in the public places to the most diabolical din of fiddles and guitars ever heard." The best accommodations one could possibly expect, he said, were the "dried mud walls of some unoccupied outhouse, with a mud floor for his bed; his own food to eat and his own cook to prepare it; and lucky is he to possess such luxuries as these. . . . The Apaches range within three miles of this place," but the presence of troops, and the counter-raids by the usually peaceful Papago Indians of the region, kept a semblance of security over the village. But its general state, and the ruined remnants of happier times a century ago when it had been "a good-sized town" under Mexican rule, spoke plainly of how it had been reduced by the Sonora/Arizona Indians of the recent past. The days were so hot that a soldier reported how "from 11 o'clock in the morning until 3 or 4 in the afternoon everybody closes their windows and door and sleep, because it is too hot to move about. It is the sleepiest place I ever saw. . . ."

Lamy remained there almost a month, administering baptisms and confirmations to hundreds both at Tucson and at San Xavier del Bac, south of town, where Messea was pastor to its Indians, to the number of four thousand, as Lamy estimated. He thought the church with its adjacent convent "scarcely damaged," and he found the church interior embellished with frescoes and well-executed sculpture. Machebeuf had begun its repair two years earlier. The wonder was that it survived so well as it did after its abandonment in the eighteenth century. In the 1740s a visiting Franciscan saw how that had to be, for reasons both practical and mysterious. "There are many and powerful medicine men here and they slay one another. The missionaries who have resided here have become bewitched and it was necessary to withdraw them before they should die."

The mining engineer was "surprised to see such a splendid monument of civilization in the wilds of Arizona," and he described the rich Churrigueresque façade, the two high bell towers, one of which was domed, and the high dome over the crossing. He saw the two Jesuits from California, who entertained him well, and gave him an "enthusiastic account" of all they planned to achieve in a lifetime of work there. He heard the Indian women "sing in the church with a degree of sweetness and harmony that quite surprised" him.

To the south lay the old Mexican garrison of Tubac, and a few miles farther on the same road, the abandoned mission of Tumacácori. In his turn, Lamy visited both places, passing near Tubac the rusting witness to an Indian raid on a mining supply train: an old boiler by the roadside which never reached Tubac, where gardens and groves of acacias, peach trees, and willows, and flowing water once sustained a northern Mexican mine, and where now all was "ruin and desolation wherever the eye rests." Tumacácori also gave evidence of a once beautifully designed and maintained outpost on the Santa Cruz River. But now its farm buildings, corrals, fences, bake-houses, and the large mission church with its little clay burial chapel within the cloister, were empty to the wind and sun and drifting desert, as Machebeuf had seen, and Lamy now saw.

He was now, by his own observation, master of the realities of all his spiritual empire; and in the second week of April, he and Father Coudert, with their little party, joined with a detachment of several companies of dragoons who were setting out for the Rio Grande forts. The eastward passage was as slow as all the others, but was without unusual incident; and at La Mesilla ("a town a little larger than Los Angeles, and built in the same style—adobes—and peopled by the same nation—Mexicans," according to an officer of Carleton's earlier march) Lamy took his leave of the Army escort and moved a few miles upriver to spend a few days at Las Cruces, where he "was warmly received by the people." There he gave confirmation, and then moved on to Doñana (the village) and Fort Selden, for the same sacrament.

One final hard lap of the six-month journey and its three thousand miles still lay ahead. It was the Dead Man's March—that ninety-mile stretch of waterless desert separated from the Rio Grande by a mountain range. Lamy, Coudert, and the train started from Selden in the evening and rode until midnight, when they stopped at Perrillo a little while, and then moved on to the Dead Man's Spring for the next day. From there they paid a call at Fort McRae three miles from the river —for the long desert march was over; and paused next at San Marcial on the river itself. Fort Craig lay a little way farther north, and there Lamy and Coudert left their companions and rode on alone toward the village of San Antonio.

It was late in the day—the fourth day since leaving Mesilla. Coudert, glancing at the bishop, became alarmed. Lamy was suddenly so weak that he could not stay in the saddle. Coudert helped him to dismount. He seemed hardly to breathe. He lapsed into a semi-coma. Coudert did what he could for him, but there was every sign that Lamy was about to die, lying on the earth as night fell. It was as if the past six months had exhausted him forever. It seemed certain that he could not travel any farther.

But mysteriously, the complete prostration receded as quickly as it had come. Lamy became conscious; he could breathe and move again. Presently—it must have been by a supreme act of will—he remounted his horse, and soon, with Coudert, was fording the Rio Grande to the west bank and moving toward Socorro, where they came to the parish rectory at three o'clock in the morning. The rector, Father Bernard, was absent, but they entered to sleep, and Bernard returned during the morning and cared for his guests. By mid-afternoon, Lamy felt ready to ride again; went upriver to Jojita for the night, forded the river again next day to the east bank, paused at Tomé, and reached Albuquerque to spend the night. On the day following, they halted at Bernalillo, and late in the next day, rode into Santa Fe. It was the twenty-eighth day of April 1864. The bishop with his aide had been absent for six months and two days. Now in his very bones, he had the new lands of the West; and he had seen the parish of Tucson have its beginning. He was within a few months of turning fifty years old. His spare, weathered body had been almost spent in the journey.

Welcoming him home, the *New Mexican* newspaper said, "The Bishop is an energetic, working and faithful steward. Favored are the spiritual flocks, who have so thoroughly upright, just and wise a shepherd. . . . We learn he procured from California, two Italian priests, of qualifications and usefulness, who have come to Tucson. . . . Much good, we trust, will result from his labors. . . . Though somewhat weather-beaten, he appears in fine health and spirits. His friends, and the members of his church, rejoice to see him again."

All the harder, then, when he learned in August that Father Bosco, at Tucson, in failing health, had returned to California and, since the one could not safely cross the desert alone, nor the other alone tend the whole mission, had taken Father Messea with him. Arizona, after all, was once again abandoned.

ii.

Hospital and Schools

LAMY RETURNED from the arduous freedom he loved to administrative affairs of the sort which had long plagued him. He was obliged once again (as years ago) to write Barnabo that six or seven "miserable priests" whom he had had to suspend might send "a certain petition" against him to the Vatican, which was accordingly warned. "The good is done through a great deal of pain and opposition of all sorts; Providence permits it to try us and to keep us in humility." The Propaganda duly noted and circularized his alert within the Vatican bureaux.

In another familiar matter—"Allow me to remind you of the claim I made once or twice [*sic*] concerning certain places between the diocese of Durango and that of Santa Fe. Five years ago I obtained a decree from Rome on this subject but Mgr. of Durango wished to interpret it in another way"—and the old wrangle went on again: Lamy repeated his arguments that all territory, including the three river villages southeast of El Paso which belonged to New Mexico for civil administration, must belong to the bishop of Santa Fe for ecclesiastical affairs. A Roman secretary duly digested the letter for his superiors: "He asks that—" and silence followed.

The bishop reported to the Society at Paris about the progress in erecting new churches and chapels, described once again the process of making sun-dried bricks of clay, and noted that some of the new buildings could hold as many as a thousand people. The earthen cathedral of St Francis had undergone only repairs to its interior. "As soon as it is possible," he wrote, referring for the first time to one of his greatest desires, "we hope to be able to begin a new church that would look more like a cathedral than the present one . . ." That, of course, lay some years in the future. Another matter could not wait for long. There was "still a greater need of a hospital."

It was, then, necessary to find the people for a hospital staff. There was already a building—his own second residence. It stood in the enclosed park behind the cathedral and ran along eastward from the Governor's Palace. This he would give over to those whom he would ask to establish the hospital, if only they would come.

He wrote to Mother Josephine, the Superior of the Sisters of Charity at Cedar Grove, near Cincinnati, opening his correspondence with an offer of terms and conditions if she could spare some of her sisters for Santa Fe. Under routine administration, she would raise the matter with her archbishop—Lamy's old friend Purcell, who would pose no objections. Preparations followed through the year. He wrote to Spalding at Baltimore, to say that in the previous autumn—before his departure for Arizona—he had expected a group of Sisters of St Joseph to arrive at Santa Fe to open an orphan asylum, but none came, though the motherhouse had offered their services. Could Spalding help him to find nuns for the purpose?—a discreet way of suggesting that a word from him to the Josephines might suffice. . . . Meanwhile, Father Ussel had gone to France seeking Christian Brothers and priests: would the Society in Paris see to his expenses?

In the north, Machebeuf, lame but busy, was establishing chapels and congregations in the new Colorado towns which were "springing up on all sides." He hoped that when Colorado should become a diocese, as it must, its new bishop would find all prepared for him. In his duty, Machebeuf planned to make a trip to raise money. Lamy gave him papers of authorization, but in the end, Machebeuf sent Raverdy, and himself remained at home, as he did not feel equal to strenuous travel.

In 1 August, having taken stock, Lamy asked Rome to excuse him from the required visit *ad limina* to the Pope—his absence would seriously impede progress just then in New Mexico, and more than that—he had no money to pay for such an expensive journey. In the same letter, he felt a new opportunity should be exploited: Zubiría, whether dead or retired, was no longer bishop of Durango. Now, "there is a chance to clear up" the long-standing territorial problem, "as there will be a new bishop in Durango. . . . *Please reread* my former letters in which I explained all my reasons. . . . please see that we get a new decree. . . ." Greater patience seemed called for at his desk than in the slow passages over the barren distances with all their sudden mortal strikes—a year ago a young priest had been murdered by Indians, another only two months ago.

After three months at home, he was again in the field, going now to visit the Navajo and Apache Indians gathered on the reservation of the Bosque Redondo at Fort Sumner on the Pecos River in south-eastern New Mexico. He travelled in company with General Carleton and staff. The general, as author of the reservation plan to pacify and reeducate the bellicose Indians, was to make an inspection of the more than eight thousand Navajos and Mescalero Apaches at the Bosque, and the four hundred soldiers who kept them under control while try-ing to teach them new habits of dwelling, farming, and living together. Education in the white man's terms was to be given the captives.

During Lamy's long absence in the West, Eguillon, his vicar general, had been asked by "the officers" to "establish schools to civilize" the Indians "by means of Christianism. The government work is done, but not ours." On his return, Lamy had sent a priest and two assistants in minor orders to Fort Sumner, and told the Society "we have great hopes to do good amongst them. The Government seems determined to make them live in these reservations and nowhere else. They (the Indians) see the missionaries with a good eye, and no doubt we shall succeed with them, especially the youth . . ."

But a sad spectacle met him at the Bosque Redondo. The Indians were subdued enough, except among themselves—the Navajos (by far the larger Indian contingent) and the Apaches were hostile to each other. Both tribes were survivors of furious vengeance brought against them by the Army and the citizenry, whose spirit had been expressed in the Santa Fe press—"Go it citizens! Give the enemy no rest. Chase him, fight him, subdue him, kill him when necessary in defense of life, family, property and security"—the same purposes long held by the Indians in their own terms, whether against Spaniard, Mexican, or eastern American. Once he had the Indians, Carleton gentled his policy, fought for their protection, sustenance, and future, against civilian factions both in New Mexico and in Washington. Seeing them with a vain and proprietary eye, he said they were now "the happiest people I have ever seen."

But "My dear wife," wrote a soldier from Fort Sumner, "this is a terrible place . . . The Rio Pecos is a little stream winding through an immense plain, and the water is terrible, and it is all that can be had within 50 miles, it is full of *alkili,* and operates on a person like castor oil—the water, heat it a little, and the more you wash yourself with common soap the dirtier you will get. . . ." It seemed an insuper-able task to haul supplies for twelve thousand people—soldiers and Indians—over the plains during wartime. Carleton sent strong appeals to Washington: "These Indians are upon my hands. They must be clothed and fed until they can clothe and feed themselves"—for he still hoped they would take up the agrarian life of the ancient Pueblo people. He called for cattle drives to bring beef to the reservation over the empty plains—the actual beginning of the cattle trails of New Mexico. Though a major of volunteers selected the site on the Pecos, with its groves of cottonwoods, and saw the construction of fine officers' quarters and barracks, and thought it "the most beautiful Indian fort in the United States," the wretchedness of the interned people was plain to see.

Lamy was moved. What he might hope to do was help to give a future through education to the three thousand Indian children of the Bosque. He saw his school, with its priest, begun. But when—as throughout his active lifetime—he appealed for federal funds to pay teachers, they were not granted; and in any case the experiment of the reservation on the Pecos was abandoned when after five years the reservation was relinquished by order of Secretary of War U. S. Grant. The Navajo people went back to their mountain and desert homes. Lamy saw them as human beings, "interesting, intelligent, and laborious." They saw themselves in the spirit of their place, for going home in 1868 at the end of what they always called "the long walk," they said, "When we saw the top of the mountain [Mt Taylor] from Albuquerque we wondered if it was our mountain, and we felt like talking to the ground, we loved it so, and some of the old men and women cried with joy when they reached their homes."

When he returned to Santa Fe, Lamy heard from Rome that he was excused by Pius IX from making his obligatory *ad limina* visit for another three years. Astonishingly, the same letter assured him that the Doñana dispute had long since been settled in his favor. Could this be so? Would word from Durango be required also? But if there was anything which could not be expedited, it was that issue. In one more responsive to his touch, Lamy saw his own schools proliferate, even if, as he said, "we have to proceed a little at a time"—so he declared at the end of 1865.

Though there were no public schools in the territory, Lamy and his teachers were reaching out to more and more young people by the month. The Santa Fe schools had five hundred pupils, and the Loretto Academy of Our Lady of Light had to enlarge its rooms and grounds every few years. The demands were ahead of certain supplies—Lamy had to ask Archbishop Spalding to investigate why his order for school books had not been filled by Messrs John Murphy, though he had sent them three payments. The newspaper said editorially that the nuns had "the complete confidence of the community at large." The Mother Superior gave the character and terms of her establishment in a decorous advertisement in the paper:

CONVENT OF OUR LADY OF LIGHT.

This Institution is under the direction of the Most Rev. Bishop John B. Lamy.

The establishment for the education of Misses, is located in the most beautiful part of the city. The building is commodious and is surrounded by a large garden which affords ample room for the scholars to take exercise in.

The culture of the intellectual faculties of youth and the training of them in the paths of virtue, being the important duties confided to the Sisters, they will take every care to instruct their pupils in those branches which constitute a useful and refined education, and above all, in the principles of the Catholic Religion and the duties which it imposes.

The discipline is mild and parental, and at the same time strict and positive. The Sisters will take particular care of the health and welfare of scholars.

The branches taught in this Institution are: Orthography, Reading, Writing, Grammar, Arithmetic, Geography, History; and for the more advanced; Astronomy, with the use of the globes, Natural Philosophy, Botany, &c. &c.; also Needle Work, Bordering, Drawing, Painting, Music on the Piano and Guitar, Vocal Music and French.

Pupils are taught and speak in the English and Spanish languages, equally.

TERMS.

Boarding and tuition one year $300; one half payable in advance.

Lessons on the Piano, per month,	$7.50
" " Guitar "	4.00
" In drawing and water painting, per month	2.00
" In Italian Painting "	2.50
" In Artificial flowers "	2.00
" In French "	3.00

The scholastic year begins on the first of November and ends on the last Thursday of August.

The correspondence of pupils is subject to inspection.

No deduction in charges is made except in cases of absence for three months.

Parents or Guardians of scholars will furnish them with clothing, bed and bed clothes, napkins, knife, fork, spoon, tumbler, plate, cup, towels, wash basin, combs, brushes, &c. &c.

For all information in regard to this Institution, call upon, or address by letter, the Mother Superior, M. MAGDALENA.

Santa Fe, September 17, 1865

What was more, the Santa Fe Lorettines, now with several members to spare, colonized Mora, Taos, and Denver with new convent schools across the diocese, where such refinements as instruction in astronomy ("with the use of the globes"), bordering, Italian painting, and artificial flowers, along with more basic subjects, had never been known. Lamy's nuns were as indefatigable as he in crossing the open country on miserable roads, and when they set up their little schools far away, children, and the future, responded. At Mora, where Father J. B. Salpointe was pastor, it was thought "very creditable to [the sisters] that they are making so many efforts to instruct and elevate the characters of the young girls who are advancing to womanhood," and it was hoped that "the teachers will receive the support and kindness of the people."

The schools for boys were also advancing with the arrival of additional Christian Brothers; and Lamy was particularly encouraged when Ussel, the pastor of Taos, arrived in Santa Fe, bringing twelve seminarians from Lyon. They had come by way of Denver, after a rousing journey. In the Atlantic, they had met a fearful storm lasting four days and nights; crossing the plains—in winter, a poor time to try it—they had been attacked twice by Indians, and had skirted peril in a snowstorm. But all were in good health, *"grâce à Dieu,"* and what was more, four Christian Brothers came with the party. Lamy could not adequately tell his gratitude to the Paris Society for their helping in paying for the passage of such invaluable additions to his human resources.

It would seem that Paris understood his problems better than Rome; for in March 1865 he was obliged to write to Barnabo at the Propaganda: "In your letter of November 9, 1864, you gave me hope that the affair"—was it possible that this was still being agitated?—"of Doñana county would soon be decided. Last December I visited our possessions in this county, but as half is under the jurisdiction of Durango, I saw that there were difficulties arising from policy differences, especially for marriages. Here are the names of the places that Mgr. de Durango does not want to cede: La Mesilla, Picacho, Los Amoles, La Mesita, La Ysleta, San Elizario. There are about 4000 people in all. The American military commandant in New Mexico told me recently that I should take possession of these places for since the new regime in Mexico [i.e., the administration of Benito Juárez's anti-clerical party] the difficulties will be greater between the priests under the jurisdiction of Durango, but residing in New Mexico, and the American civil authorities. To avoid this trouble it is urgent that the county of Doñana be put under the jurisdiction of Santa Fe in the necessary places. . . ."

There was another disappointment in territorial affairs—the restoration of the mission of Arizona. Mindful of the dangers he had both seen and heard of, Lamy hesitated to make an assignment there a matter of ordering anyone to go. Without prejudice, he left it to volunteers; and in the spring of 1865 three proposed themselves. One could not be spared—he was building two schools at Mora. But two others, Fathers Lassaigne and Bernal, proposed themselves, and were sent off down the Rio Grande to Las Cruces, there to find an expedition west-going, which they could join, since to go alone would be the utmost folly. In Las Cruces, they found no organized trains willing to face the Apaches. All travel had been stopped, and after three weeks of trying to find a way westward, they returned to Santa Fe and their old duties. Arizona must wait again.

But life was quotidian—small matters as well as large made up its fabric. A busy man noted his reminders anywhere. On the back of a letter which Machebeuf had sent on to him from the Messrs Daugherty, Carriage Makers, of St Louis, regretting that Denver had cancelled its order for an overland ambulance, Lamy jotted down in pencil his reminders for Holy Week 1865:

> *Cathedr. vespers*
>
> *
>
> *Meeting ladies society*
>
> *
>
> *Festival Easter tuesday*
>
> *
>
> *ladies for Reath [wreath]*
> *for decorations Monday & Tuesday*
>
> *
>
> *Mass every day in h. at 8 (Confessions)*
>
> *
>
> *Attend high Mass on thursday—at 8*
>
> *
>
> *prayers, lecture & Benediction at 7—*
> *(Candles) Good Friday at 9—acl. at 8 o.c.*
> *14 Stations—H. Saturday*
> *H. water—from E.S.*
> *1 Mass at 8—h.m. at 10*

But if affairs naturally centered in one's own life, the larger world must enter also. "We have a weekly mail which crosses the plains in fifteen days, from Leavenworth to Sta. Fe." Local society kept its own flavor, however, and the Santa Fe paper regretted that "at a fandango, a few evenings since, two of the females became insulted and enraged at each other," and further deplored "that American men and women present endeavored to inflame the ill will and violence of the two women, the one against the other, and that a ring was formed and knives placed in the hands of each, for a desperate fight." The event was known in frontier parlance as a "lady-fight."

iii.

Christmas Eve: Attempted Murder

A LITTLE OVER A YEAR after negotiations had begun between Santa Fe
and Cedar Grove, four Sisters of Charity arrived in Santa Fe on 14
September 1865 to begin the realization of yet another of Lamy's long
views. They were Sister Superior Vincent, and Sisters Pauline, Theo-
dosia, and Catherine. The bishop was away when they appeared, but
all preparations had been made for them, and they moved into his
own large house which had been readied for them. He retained two
rooms for his own use until he should find other quarters. They had
come by rail and boat from Cincinnati to Omaha; and from there to
Denver by stage coach. Sister Catherine had sharp memories of the
stage trip. The coach was built for four people, eight were crowded
into it, the heat was great, they all suffered from thirst, the jolting
was worse than that of a runaway freight train, she was sure, and with
all that, there was the unceasing and exhausting alert against Indian
attacks. For "the luxury," she recalled, they had to pay twenty-five
cents a mile. In Denver the four nuns stepped down at Planter's Hotel,
but when Machebeuf heard of their arrival, he sent his carriage to
take them to the comforts of his Loretto Convent. From Denver they
had a coach all to themselves with only the Indians to worry about.

What they found in Santa Fe was described by one of their community who came later but heard much. This was Sister Blandina,
who by her own animated account was for a long time at the center of
leading events in the diocese. "Imagine," she told, "the surprise of
persons coming from places where houses are built with every convenience and sanitary device, suddenly to find themselves introduced
into several oblong walls of adobe, looking like piled brick ready to
burn, to enter which, instead of stepping up, you step down onto a
mud floor; rafters supporting roof made of trunks of trees, the roof
itself of earth which they were told had to be carefully attended, else
the rain would pour in; door openings covered with blankets; the
whole giving you a prison feeling; a few chairs, handmade and painted
red; a large quantity of wool which they were assured were clean and
for their use; no stoves, square openings in corners where fires could

be built—all those things were to constitute their future home. Where
the bare necessities of life were to come from was an enigma to them.
Strangers to the country, the customs, and the language, do you wonder that a lonesome feeling as of lingering death came over them?"
Blandina always valued vivid overstatement to obtain her effects, for
she went on to say: "Can you doubt that it would have required the
presence of an angel to convince them that the preparations made for
them were princely? Yes," she cried, "so they were, for the time and
country. This had been the Bishop's Palace, which he had given up,
so that the Sisters might have easy access to the Cathedral!"

Lamy returned home a little over two weeks later and found the
new sisters "well and cheerful." He supposed they had written to Cincinnati about their new situation, and if everything appeared "strange
to them," he was sure they would "soon be reconciled." They were
already learning "the Castellano" and would soon be talking freely
with everyone. Their energy was exemplary, they had barely arrived
when they had placed an advertisement in the paper announcing that
the Sisters of Charity had set about opening a hospital for the needy
and infirm of the city. Two of the nuns had been nurses back East in
the Civil War.

Their situation, as Lamy gave it, was encouraging—they had at least
twenty rooms, "such as the country can afford," and a garden and three
large yards, all enclosed. The hospital joined the cathedral at the rear,
so they would not have to go outside to enter the church. A little
spring-fed stream ran through their property. The whole place was a
monument to the memory of Father Avel, who, dying of the poisoned
chalice, had left a legacy of three thousand dollars to found a hospital;
and Lamy had used the fund to buy a piece of property which he later
sold for a sum applied to the present establishment. In return for his
house, the nuns were to pay him the first two thousand dollars they
might have available. Purcell had advanced a thousand dollars for
their westward journey. The four Sisters of Charity were living in
"apostolic poverty."

It was good to feel the response of Santa Fe to the hospital settlement. The American population was generous in support of it, the
territorial legislature voted a subsidy of one hundred dollars a month
to St Vincent's, and General Carleton offered the hospital two thousand
dollars provided it would be available to sick soldiers. Talented citizens were getting up a benefit concert, with proceeds to go to St
Vincent's. Lamy believed they would be ready to open the hospital
in the coming January 1866.

It was a season of deep snows. Santa Fe's mountains, all the slopes,
were richly white against the gold and blue of the winter skies. Over

the whole town drifted the pungent scent of piñon smoke from the baked fireplaces of every house. The newspapers carried stories of great suffering on the plains. Six soldiers were killed or scalped four miles above Fort Dodge in Kansas. On the Arkansas River ice was twelve to eighteen inches thick. Two trainmen—the railroads were slowly advancing westward—froze to death on Bear Creek in Kansas. Twenty waggon trains were halted at one time by icy streams and high blizzards, a stage was delayed twenty hours at Pawnee Fork on the Arkansas, another was delayed for a day at Little Cow Creek near Fort Larned, and the oldest plainsmen believed this was "the hardest winter they [had] ever experienced."

Christmas Eve at Santa Fe was bitter cold. Midnight Mass in the cathedral was over by two o'clock in the morning. Lamy was asleep in his room at one end of the hospital. Like the usual ground-floor rooms in adobe houses, it opened directly onto the covered *portal*. His *mayordomo* slept in the next room. In the cold and quiet of the un-lighted night, a man, hungry and freezing, perhaps even drunk after Christmas celebrations, opened the door of Lamy's room, entered, and said, showing a revolver,

"Give me fifty dollars or I will kill you."

Lamy knew his voice, and so did the *mayordomo*, who was awakened by the sound, for the intruder was one of the bishop's employees. The *mayordomo* leaped out of bed and hurried into the bishop's room. Lamy said to him,

"Take him out and give him fifty dollars."

The *mayordomo* took the man outside and sent him off, refusing him the fifty dollars. In a few minutes, the man broke into a room nearby where two priests lived. One was ill—"very much reduced and weak." Both were asleep in the freezing cold. The wandering intruder went to their fireplace and began to fumble about to build a fire. It awoke the sick priest, who thought it was his companion who was striking matches.

"What are you building a fire for?" he asked.

This awoke the other priest, who replied,

"I am not making a fire"—and then realizing that there was a stranger in the room, he ran for the door. The stranger cried after him,

"If you don't give me something to eat, I will kill you!" and not waiting for an answer, fired his revolver at him, hitting him in the neck. Then, going to the bed where the sick man lay, he shot him twice, once in the head, once in the leg. The shots aroused others, they came, the man was arrested, and taken off to jail. Reporting the event —ATTEMPTED MURDER read the headline a week later—the *Gazette* said, "Both the wounded men are doing well and are in a fair way to recover."

Lamy mentioned the affair to Purcell, though he supposed the sisters "will have written you what a narrow escape I had on Christmas Eve. . . . Gracias a Dios que nos ha libertado. Even our Deacon who had received two shots and who according to all appearances could not survive is getting quite well. . . . It is in great measure owing to the good care of the Sisters that he has got over." With the letter he sent Purcell a cheque for a thousand dollars in repayment of the travel loan given to the Sisters of Charity, and added, "in this territory we are going slow as in the old fashion. whilst in the States you go at Full Speed on your railroads or steamboats, we can hardly raise here an ox team. But what can we do, we must try to put up with such order of things as Divine Providence is pleased to dispose. Our good Sisters of Charity are sometimes a little down hearted because everything with us goes so very slow . . ."

The end of the year did not pass without an impassive reminder to Rome: "I am taking this opportunity to observe to Your Eminence that I have not yet received the decision of the question of Mesilla and the places nearby which I have already mentioned to you."

As the new year opened, a new start seemed possible for Arizona. Earlier, the parish priest of Mora, John Baptist Salpointe, had volunteered to go when he could be spared in New Mexico; and now Lamy, who had received him from Clermont in 1859, accepted his offer, and added three other volunteers: Fathers Francis Boucart and Patrick Birmingham, and a young Mr Vincent as schoolteacher. The dangers of the journey to Tucson had not abated—they were in everyone's thoughts. Hardly a week went by without reports of atrocities on travellers' paths everywhere in the diocese. Lamy asked General Carleton if he could provide military escort for the new mission party, and the general agreed to protect them as far as Camp Bowie—the limit of his military jurisdiction. From that point, Salpointe, the head of the mission with the title of vicar forane, or rural dean, must manage for whatever protection he could find.

Like his prelate, and others before him, Salpointe and his men set out downriver on their assignment. With a four-horse waggon driven by a Mexican, the three priests, mounted on horses, left Santa Fe on the afternoon of 6 January 1866. Along the Rio Grande, they often stayed overnight with ranchers or in the little river towns, for until they reached Fort Selden, where the westward turn would come, they did not feel in need of troop protection, though solicitous, if tactless, friends had assured them that in their general venture, "they were going to certain death."

Again, the vast land had its surprises. Encamped for the night above Coronado's old region of Bernalillo, they met a strange electrical storm, during which "long aigrettes of electricity . . . shone without interruption on the ears of the horses." Salpointe remarked that this, with the roar of the Rio Grande in flood nearby, and the dense darkness of the night, made all seem "weird and ominous." The very landscape as they advanced was dotted with the old unpromising place names—Dead Man's March (where they barely avoided a skirmish with Indians), Dead Man's Spring, Soldier's Farewell. But the country was magnificent, and Salpointe took pleasure as an amateur botanist in seeing new flora and identifying them later with their Latin terminology.

From Selden to Bowie they were safely escorted by Carleton's troops. At Bowie, the commanding officer assumed their safety and brought them to Tucson on 7 February 1866, after they had been a month on the river and desert trails. Their reception was quiet—their arrival while expected had not been scheduled. Not much could have been done about it in any case. Tucson was as poor as ever, with its six hundred inhabitants, its unfinished church still unroofed, its lawless life, and the extremes of poverty and high prices in miserable contrast. Salpointe was happily received, however, and set to work forthwith in conditions far less promising even than those of Santa Fe in 1851 and Denver City in 1860. All his early efforts met discouraging results. An attempt to roof the church with timbers from mountains forty-six miles away failed because of heavy snows which blocked the transport of logs. A school promptly founded at San Xavier del Bac for the Papago Indians and Mexicans there was forced to close in two months for lack of money, and Vincent the teacher and the pastor Father Boucart returned to live at Tucson. The school was reestablished there. An effort to provide a mission at Yuma on the Colorado River under Birmingham and Boucart failed when the two priests, attacked by fever, had to abandon the place, and Salpointe for a time was the only priest left in Arizona.

Yet he held on, aided by new colleagues, and with a barely tenable gain here, another there, Lamy's pattern of colonization slowly took root: missions first, schools next, amenities of charity next, and in due time, as a result of the combination of these, a slow emergence of civilized life, to match both the needs and contributions of an always increasing population of prospectors, traders, and finally, town-makers.

In Colorado, where he went on a pastoral visit in May, Lamy could see how a colony made its way, even through troubles. Denver had been swept by fire two years before, but in destroying the wooden shacks of the city's first life the disaster resulted in new, more sightly and permanent buildings of brick and stone. Mountain flood had done its work, too, for soon after the fire, Cherry Creek, usually dry, had risen with a sudden crest of twenty feet which had swept away houses, tents, bridges, in the lower parts of the city. Rebuilding was rapid, and Lamy found Machebeuf busier than ever, though lame, and carrying out his long day's work by buggy, and rarely able to dispose of his paperwork at night before eleven.

He took Lamy everywhere, principally to Central City, to lay a cornerstone of the new church, to administer confirmations (he found the children "well prepared"), and there, also, to dismiss an Irish priest who was making trouble. The old friends gave a pontifical High Mass together, with Machebeuf as deacon and Raverdy as subdeacon, on Trinity Sunday, the bishop preached, and Lamy admired Machebeuf's new bell—it weighed two thousand pounds, "very fine," which had been cast for him in St Louis. Lamy could inform Machebeuf that he had an answer to his restrained inquiry of last December about Durango: the Vatican said it had "repeatedly" asked explanations of Durango for its delay in obeying orders issued earlier to transfer the disputed lands to Santa Fe. But—this after fifteen years—the Secretary of the Propaganda added, "I'll wait for a while for his reply, and after having received it, I shall present immediately the explanations of both sides to the final judgement of the Sacred Congregation."

Matters proceeded more swiftly in the New World. Colorado was growing fast in population and capital. The mines "inspired such confidence in the capitalists of New York and Boston that two railroad companies were rivalling each other in activity and energy to reach the foot of the Rocky Mountains." Machebeuf reported that he was certain it would take only a year or eighteen months until it would be possible to ride to New York by rail in five or six days in the new palace sleeping cars. *Days:* how many ox and mule trains had they known which took as many weeks simply to cross the plains between the diocese and the Missouri River?

It was plain to see how Colorado was swiftly taking on a character in contrast to that of its parent see. New Mexico remained largely Mexican; Colorado was flooded with an Anglo-American population of wholly different style, energy, and values. Already Denver was richer than its cathedral city of Santa Fe. A change must soon come. Lamy foresaw Colorado as independently a vicariate apostolic; and there would hardly be any doubt that Machebeuf must be its first bishop. The friends discussed the matter frankly; though nothing could be considered settled until after a number of official acts had been promulgated. Nevertheless, in his impetuous way, Machebeuf could not resist writing home to mention the prospect.

On his way home overland to New Mexico after a stimulating Denver visit, Lamy paused halfway to Santa Fe on the River of Las Animas—the Souls, or as French trappers called it, the Purgatoire, and the Americans, corrupting this, the Picketwire. There he inspected a large new church going up, of adobes, and now saw this humble material as durable and suitable, as well as inexpensive. After a brief pause at Santa Fe, he went down the eastern plains of his lands. They were sparsely settled. But there were still Navajos and troops at Fort Sumner, in the Bosque Redondo, and he went there to visit them. He had to travel two hundred and fifty miles without seeing a house, "camping *à la belle étoile* and exposed to be scalped at every step." At a water hole, he and his small party came upon "some clothes, camping articles etc with fresh human blood on them," and were told that four men had been killed there on the night before by Navajos. "This happened," he said, "within 12 miles of Fort Sumner where there are 5 companies of soldiers."

Presently he moved on southwestward travelling on a military road which connected Fort Sumner with Fort Stanton in the Capitan Mountains. It was a stretch of a hundred and twenty miles farther. From far away he could see the Capitan range lying east and west, and at its west end, through a great notch in the mountain profile, called Capitan Gap, where the road ran, the distant crown of the Sierra Blanca showed pale blue against the light. He gave his duties to the garrison at Fort Stanton and then made his way to the old royal road along the Rio Grande. In all, on this great circle trip he travelled over nine hundred miles, gave confirmations in twenty-four settlements, most of them new places, and found seven new churches, on one of which, it having just been completed, he bestowed the episcopal blessing. The open mystery of a handful of human lives working to survive and grow into community in a land so bare, hazardous, and beautiful, held him fast; and he gave back to it the mystery of faith.

IX

ROME AND BATTLE

1867

i.

Rome—An Accounting

FIVE MONTHS AFTERWARD the bishop was in Rome to make his postponed visit *ad limina* to Pius IX, and to carry out a commission given to him by the hierarchy of the United States assembled in their second plenary council at Baltimore. Travelling toward the council, which convened on 7 October 1866, and bringing Coudert with him again as his secretary, Lamy paused at Mt St Vincent in Ohio to ask for additional Sisters of Charity. His little hospital staff were "doing well" but the need would grow; and, further, he wanted to found an "industrial home" in which native girls could learn proper trades by which to support themselves.

At the sessions in Baltimore, the bishops surveyed the state of the Church in the United States. Among the matters discussed were new dioceses in the rapidly developing lands of the West. Proposals for creating apostolic vicariates for Colorado and Arizona came up. Lamy spoke several times on these and other subjects. His hard-gained experience, his weathered dignity, came strongly through his simple discourses; and his fellow bishops, much impressed by him, voted to name him as the courier who would carry to the Pope the record of their meetings. Though it was not specified, the expenses of his journey must have been paid by the council, even though he was already planning on going to Rome in his own duty. Such aid was welcome to an administrator who had to count every dollar.

While the conciliar documents were being given proper form to submit to the Pope, Lamy was in New York; and at last, when they were ready, he sailed, with Coudert, in a French steamer on 17 November, and was given his passage without charge. Crossing to Brest in nine days, he found the voyage pleasant, and proceeded at once to Paris, where he stayed three days in preliminary talks with the Society concerning his needs for the return journey homeward. His next stop was in Auvergne, where he spent a few days in old familiar places. When he told of his experiences, he seemed in a somber mood because of the weight of his debts.

Meantime, at Rome, his arrival was anxiously awaited by Cardinal Barnabo, who, said the American Father McCloskey, who was Rector of the North American College in the Via dell'Umiltà, "doubtless has nightly visions of the Venerable Bishop of Santa Fe wending his way too slowly to Rome with Baltimore's 'big book' and its interpretation under his arm. Woe be to him if he has lost the precious documents for if he has, he need never again show his face in Baltimore." But before this letter went off to Purcell in America, a postscript was crowded in—Lamy had arrived on 16 December.

Rome, as ever, was a city of grand contradictions of circumstance. In the intricate struggles of the Italian kingdoms to be united under Victor Emmanuel, Rome and the papal dominions were still under the threat of the King's armies and Garibaldi's genius. Until a few weeks before, the troops of Napoleon III had been in Rome to protect the papal position; but they had been withdrawn in early December, and Pius was left with only his own mercenaries—largely Frenchmen. But uncertainty reigned, an invasion was possibly imminent, and if it came, the Pope was calmly resolved to escape; though some hoped he would resort to defiance and artillery, even as the people rejoiced that the French emperor's army had gone, and that their liberty was restored, as they believed. A great majority were in favor of the revolutionary movement of the King and his supporters; but meanwhile, as Lamy saw, everyone proceeded with preparations for the great Christmas festivals quite as though "all Italy was humbly submissive at the Feet of the Holy Father."

Lamy was given rooms at the North American College. Early in the day after his arrival, he heard of a ceremony which was about to take place at St Peter's—the beatification of a certain Benedictine, and hurried to find a place in the crowd, as Pius IX officiated. The Pope gave a short allocution in Italian which Lamy "understood well," and which "left us all electrified and cheerful." Later, Lamy, dressed not in prelatic violet but in "a plain black cassock," managed after "some difficulties, to be admitted to the Kissing of the feet," when all who passed by the Pope received the pontifical benediction. As Pius was in the act of blessing Lamy, he said to him, smiling warmly,

"But you are a bishop!"

Lamy told him his name and diocese.

"Oh!" Pius went on. "You were at the great council of Baltimore—forty-five bishops and archbishops. I received your telegraphic dispatch, and I hope you bring us the decrees of that Council."

The Pope's suite—cardinals and lesser prelates—were, said Lamy, "surprised and at the same time pleased at the familiarity of the H. Father toward a missionary Bishop just arrived, sans ceremony, from the wild territories of the W.S. [S.W.] of America. . . ."

Three days later he had his private audience with the Pope, accompanied by Coudert. Pius was "extremely cheerful," and on receiving the richly bound copy of the Baltimore decrees from Lamy, exclaimed, "What beautiful things they make in America!" turning the volume over, looking at it, opening it. Lamy thought him full of confidence in the face of the political dangers which threatened the Papacy. On a later day Lamy "had the honor of serving the Holy Father's Mass and of assisting him at the altar. . . ."

In himself, Lamy was a living link between the "wild territories" of the Great American Desert and the sumptuous masterpieces of liturgical art, architecture, protocol, and ritual which gave papal Rome its character. He was now at the center and source of his belief, which had given him his share of responsibility, and his image of the expression of human community at the summit of its style. For centuries great imaginations had served, through all the arts, as in all civilizations, man's explanation, through his received idea of God, of the central design of life. The magnificence of papal Rome was essentially no more than homage to the invisible glory of the eternal. The arts of man reached toward God and in return a spirit akin to the divine entered into their masters. Christian Rome was faith made manifest and superb—while faith itself remained as simple and life-sustaining as water in the desert. Amidst domes and colonnades, and vistas of worked travertine, corridors of saints and vaults of miracles painted by genius, pageants of splendor to delight the eye and edify the conscience, great chambers whose volumes and proportions exalted not man but God, Lamy, belonging to all this as a bishop, made his initial report to the Vatican of his first fifteen years of effort in a land where dimension was measured by deserts and mountains, and man's works were largely the result of mixing water, earth, straw, and the heat of the sun, shaped by the palm of the hand, whether to become shelter, chapel, or cathedral.

The substance of the report was much the same as that which he had submitted also to the Society for the Propagation of the Faith at Paris. He let facts speak for themselves, but the bloom of growth was over all he described. Civilization was emerging under his touch. It might have done so under another leader, representing another system of values; but the fact was that there was no other, and it was left to him to lead the way. The spirit of growth in religion created the model of growth in all other beneficial expressions of society. For the bishop was not content to preach charity—he must enact it, and lead others to enact it, using all the daily materials of life, however poor. By a simple extension of his own character, Lamy, in expressing his own faith and carrying out his charge, also created for the old Spanish kingdom a sense of enlightenment through which for the first time in all her three centuries her people could advance their condition and so become masters instead of victims of their environment. What he had to tell Rome on 16 January 1867, as he had already told Paris, was a simple chronicle with here and there an unconscious note of eloquence.

He said his diocese was very much spread out, being about three hundred leagues from north to south, and almost as much from east to west. He had been able to repair most of the old churches, and build eighty-five new ones, all of adobes. The cathedral at Santa Fe was nothing more than an old mud church, slightly repaired. It was very poor, as was the episcopal residence. None of them had any "architectural character," but "thanks to God" were well frequented. The total number of churches and chapels was one hundred thirty-five.

He had three schools directed by the Christian Brothers in full prosperity. Those of Santa Fe never had fewer than two or three hundred pupils, who were taught English, Spanish, reading, writing, geography, Latin, history, music, and arithmetic. All the missions had schools, at least during the winters. The Loretto Sisters maintained five schools. Their first novitiate for postulants was numerous, many novices belonging to the first families. Another school was run by the Sisters of Charity. In addition to elementary subjects taught in English and Spanish, the sisters gave lessons in painting, music, and embroidery. There was the beginning of a seminary at Santa Fe under the direction of a priest. The number of students had never surpassed six and so far only four had been ordained as priests.

The diocese already had six convents of nuns. They supported themselves from the income of their schools. The nuns lived under religious rule and were bound by vows of poverty, chastity, and obedience. They were not cloistered. A year ago a hospital and orphanage had been opened by four sisters of St Vincent de Paul.

The chief difficulties in his mission lay in maintaining connections with the outside world, and of these, the greatest was the passage of the immense plains which isolated the diocese from the rest of the United States. After crossing the ocean, and then travelling six hundred leagues by rail, the most trying and costly part of the journey had yet to be passed. Up to that point, he and his people had been able to make use of the comforts of civilized countries; but from there on, they had to travel nine hundred miles without seeing a hut or even a bridge, all the while being exposed to Indian arrows. The savages rarely failed to attack caravans, even very large ones. He remembered how in the autumn of 1855 six of his Brothers of the Christian Doctrine, coming to found schools, crossed the plains. As a precaution they joined a train of five hundred open waggons, loaded with provisions and merchandise for New Mexico. The prairie voyage took two and a half months, and the travellers were attacked several times by Indians, despite the defense offered by the twelve hundred men of the caravan, and a number of people were killed or wounded. The expenses of such travel were enormous—one had to buy everything, animals, waggons, provisions, camping equipment. In New Mexico, they had only the most rigorously necessary things to sustain life, and he meant, literally, bread and meat. There were no factories. Most of the inhabitants raised sheep and cattle—at little profit, probably because of the Indians who stole the flocks and herds, and killed the shepherds and cowmen, or took them prisoner. Yet the prairies were vast and beautiful, and Providence had placed countless droves of buffalo upon them, which provided food and hides for half a million people—the Plains Indians.

Three territories comprised the diocese of Santa Fe at present. The Catholics numbered between 130,000 and 140,000, divided between New Mexico (110,000 Mexicans, all Catholic, and 15,000 Catholic Indians), Colorado (8000 Mexicans and Americans), and Arizona (7000 Indians and Mexicans among whom, as on all sides, there were some good and some bad). He had fifty-one active priests where he had come to find nine. Eleven were either retired or deprived of their priestly functions. Fourteen were Mexican, thirty-one French, and six others from different European countries. He expected to take eight or ten back to Santa Fe with him now. With his present number of priests who administered to a Catholic population so spread out, they could hardly make visits to the villages at any great distance from the missionary residence. He could use more than a hundred priests if he could maintain them once they had arrived in the diocese. In New Mexico, besides the enumerated Catholics, there were four to five thousand Americans, more atheist than Protestant, three or four hundred Jews, and thirty thousand unsettled Indians, barbarous and "almost cannibalistic." There were thirty-one missions or jurisdictions. In seven churches and five chapels the priest was in residence and kept the Blessed Sacrament in the tabernacle.

He had made three pastoral visits to Colorado, only one into Arizona. On that one he travelled over three thousand miles on horseback. In many places, he and his companions had to sleep under the stars, and often had to go sixty or seventy-five miles without water, when he would walk to rest his horse. Despite all such endurances there was reward in meeting faithful souls in the wilderness who had not seen a priest for many years.

He told of the Christmas Mass on the snow-covered side of that mountain in Arizona, and brought the account of the journey full circle until he came to Tucson and San Xavier del Bac, whose history and condition he described. He noted Aztec ruins, and those left also by Spaniards who had been forced to abandon Arizona in the eighteenth century because of the ferocity of Apache warfare. One of his strongest impressions of Arizona found its way into the report as he described the great saguaro cactus, and recalled that travellers had told how the word "Arizona" was the Indian word for "land of the cactus," and he thought "the etymology sounds truthful enough." Anyhow, the gigantic cacti, by their beauty, form, and great height, were the most interesting of their species, often taking the form of a many-branched candelabrum, with the circumference of the trunk measuring a metre. The plant yielded an exquisite fruit, which the Indians gathered by means of a long pole to which a sickle was lashed. At a distance, immense forests of these cacti "appeared like a troop of giants armed for a battle."

Colorado was much colder than Arizona. Out of its cold heights its great rivers came pounding out into wide valleys to cool the meadows. Thousands of farmers were already in possession of its most beautiful valleys, and the cereals they grew were among the territory's main resources, along with gold and pasture lands. Silver fir and cedars covered the towering mountains up to the timberline.

New Mexico had an older non-Indian population than either of his other two territories. Generations of families had been born there to raise their children, their flocks, and keep their lands. These—the Mexicans of Spanish descent—were well disposed toward religion, wanted the sacraments, revered their clergy, and willingly went about the tasks of building the church whose plan had been drawn and given them by their pastor. If the church building was of "a poor style, nevertheless it is the best monument of the place." Indians in the pueblos, he said, were very fond of their priests. In one pueblo, when the pastor was to be moved elsewhere, they pleaded with the bishop that he stay in such a way that he could not refuse them. The young priest, alas, was not destined to remain with them much longer—he died of a brain fever soon afterward. In respect of the roving tribes, the government had a plan to maintain them on reservations. He had already sent priest-teachers to one such with some success.

As to general observations—social abuses mainly in the moral sphere would be the hardest to cure. Their main causes arose from the bad examples which the worshippers of his diocese had witnessed, scandals emerging particularly from the old clergy. A larger number of priests, good priests, would be the best cure for this, as well as for ignorance. He regretted to report that he had neither chapter house nor cathedral canons. Item: no neighboring bishop had interfered in the exercise of his jurisdiction. Item: he had held three diocesan synods in the past twelve years. Item: regular visitations in the diocese could not be made to accord with Canon Law because of the great distances, the conditions of the roads, and the dangers of Indian attacks which often destroyed caravans and killed travellers. Still, as circumstances allowed, episcopal visits were made each year to one or another part of the diocese. Item: some income reached the chancery from the raising of animals which certain parishioners gave instead of actual money in tithes—four thousand dollars, approximately.

Communication was still difficult between New Mexico and the rest of the United States, and transportation was exorbitantly expensive. But looking to the future, the bishop (older now, fifty-two years of age, gray-haired, more gaunt and weathered than ever) felt the excitement of all who built in harmony with the forces of their times. Railroads were advancing from the west in California and from the east in Missouri and Texas; and when they should meet, the condition of things would be entirely changed. Mines could be worked, stock raised and shipped, cultivation of produce increased; laborers would be better paid, they could construct houses and churches as in the East. Factories might well be established—woolen mills to use the product so plentiful in that country. In time his mission would without doubt find extension and a way of sustaining the great, heavy loads which were always found in new undertakings. "Providence will never abandon us"—his conviction was clear.

Through all his report there seemed to show a love of the desert and mountain Southwest which had gradually cast its spell over him. Knowing his immense land in the same terms as any other frontiersman, he loved it the more for seeking out, and surviving, its hazard and its challenge. The report was taken under advisement less for this value than for its hard facts.

While in Rome, in his endless pursuit of new helpers, Lamy asked Barnabo for his influence in recruiting Jesuits for Santa Fe, saying he had without avail been asking the Society of Jesus for men for thirteen years. The cardinal, an administrator, told him to put the request in writing. Undoubtedly it was then forwarded to the current general of the Jesuits, Father Beckx, who, when Lamy called on him a few days later, at once assigned him three priests and two brothers, out of the province of Naples. They were Fathers L. Vigilante, as superior, Rafael Bianchi, and Donato M. Gasparri; and brothers Prisco Caso and Rafael Vezza. They were to sail for America with the bishop in May.

ii.

Madame Bontesheim and Bureaucracy

LAMY HAD A FEW MORE DETAILS of business to complete with Barnabo, and one of historical piety—which cardinal or prelate, he asked, could tell him where to find the keys to the chapel which contained the chains of St Peter?

Oh, surely Cardinal Clarilli would know, replied Barnabo.

But Clarilli did not know, nor did others whom Lamy asked, for he was given several different directions. Nobody seemed to know how to reach the great relics.

If only he had consulted an example of that living institution in Rome, who reappeared with every generation—the pious and tireless matron who was often in her self-created system more effective at getting things done in the grand confusions of the Vatican bureaucracy than the members of the Curia. At the time, there was a Madame Bontesheim whom Father McCloskey described as "a General of division, who summons us Captains and marches us hither and thither. She is indeed a famous woman" to whom the chains of St Peter would have been a trifle to manage. But gossip had it that she was busy with what she called "a respectable scrape" concerning "one of those wandering nuns" who was trying to enlist members for a new convent which consisted only of herself as Mother Superior and one other nun, in Liberty, Texas. A young American girl was greatly drawn to the venture; Madame Bontesheim tried to prevent her going, but "failed most signally in effecting a separation between the Mother Superior and the girl."

In any case, Lamy saw her in another affair when she marched him to recite his "experiences" to a hall full of novices of an order of nuns. How ever had she discovered him in a city full of bishops? But her skill was famous. He was ready enough to describe his distant life for Madame Bontesheim, and also for his fellows at the North American College, whose rector said, after he departed Rome, "we miss very much his interesting and graphic descriptions of his missionary life among the Indians. He is full of Americanisms, and his imperfect knowledge of English and his quaint way of describing things afforded us many a hearty laugh. With all his dove-like simplicity he has quite enough of the Serpent's cunning, and it would have amused one to see the skill with which he evaded the approaches of an Italian who wished to go to Santa Fe, believing it, no doubt, to be an appendage of New York or Philadelphia, the only places a large number of these gentry ever heard of."

In the third of the audiences which he granted Lamy, Pius IX gave him permission to leave Rome and it was remarked that "the Holy Father has been very kind to him." Toward the end of January 1867, Lamy sailed for France from Civitavécchia. He would spend three months preparing for his homeward expedition in Paris and Lyon— and also in replying to certain critical comments on his report which came from Barnabo three months later. The cardinal granted that pastoral visits in the Santa Fe diocese might be difficult, but "wishing to encourage your solicitude," he suggested to Lamy that his visitations be made more often and more thoroughly. He thought the same about holding diocesan synods. As for education—teaching skills and the fine arts were well enough, but the cardinal "was surprised in not finding any mention in the proposed study schedule about the instruction in Religion." There were other, lesser criticisms.

If Lamy briefly despaired of making anyone halfway around the world see his lands and their problems, he preserved his "dove-like simplicity" and promptly replied from Paris. Concerning pastoral visitations, he said that now with his new increment of Jesuits he hoped to be freer to travel about his territories more regularly, and also to hold synods every two years. In the matter of religious education—he had simply neglected to make specific mention of what perhaps "it was not necessary to explain": that in all nine of his establishments of schools or orphanages, religion was being taught regularly with "great success"; the teachers were "clerics themselves." Disposing of the few remaining inquiries, he was respectful—and swift: for it had been noted in Rome that he thought matters there moved too slowly. "The Roman *piano, piano,* does not suit the Bishop of the Navahoes. . . ."

Working between Paris and Lyon to complete his homeward party, Lamy with evident satisfaction was finally able to catalogue its members: in addition to the five Italian Jesuits, he had enlisted a priest and a deacon at Rome, six seminarians from Clermont, and two more Brothers of the Christian Doctrine—twenty-one in all, not counting himself and Coudert, his secretary. In America he would add several

more nuns from Loretto, Kentucky, to his charges. It was a grand increment, and in Rome, by the tone of his letter describing his efforts,
they thought he was "making hay while the sun shines."

Once again he had to appeal to the French Society for increased
financial help in paying for the transport of his people. All expenses
had increased, and while grateful for the unfailing aid he had always
received from Paris and Lyon, he thought it necessary, in asking for
more, to repeat his familiar description of the conditions of westward
travel in the United States—its distances, costs, dangers, and hardships.
At last he was ready; and with his twenty-one *"sujets"* ("individuals"),
as he always called them, he sailed from Le Havre on 9 May 1867, on
the "magnificent sail and steam vessel" *Europa*. The crossing was mild
until on 19 May the *Europa* encountered a violent storm off New-
foundland in a "gulf" which the sailors referred to as "The Devil's
Place." For a while the ship was in extreme peril, and all on board
suffered; but she made port safely on 23 May, coming up the Narrows
to New York early in the morning. There before Lamy's new collection of strangers, lay unknown America and their separate fates.

· · ·
iii.

Homeward

TWO DAYS LATER they were at Baltimore, where Lamy left the seminarians, including his nephew Anthony Lamy, who was Marie's
brother, for further study with the Sulpicians, and boarded the railroad train to St Louis for three days of "remarkable" luxuries and
comforts. By 2 June they were in St Louis, where three Loretto nuns
and two Christian Brothers joined the party. After four days of shop-
ping and outfitting, the bishop was ready to lead the way West. He
had twenty mules, two small waggons, and five "light ambulances,"
and two saddle-horses. "This outfit," he said, "cost us near $5000" (in
today's money at least twenty thousand). June seventh found the party
in Leavenworth, as guests of Bishop Miège, who now had a large house
where all the men were put up, and where he gave them every comfort. The nuns—two Sisters of Charity and the three Lorettines—
stayed at St Vincent's Academy. Two Jesuits joined the group there—
including one of the Italians from Naples—and also going along were

a student, Paul Beaubien, from St Louis University, the bishop's young business agent, Jules Masset, and two Mexican servants, Antonio and Antonito: twenty-six in all.

Lamy considered which trail to follow over the plains. He had hoped to take the northern fork of the Santa Fe Trail, by way of the Smoky Hill River, Bent's Fort, and the Las Animas River in order to meet with Machebeuf in Colorado. But all reports indicated that the warring Indians were more active there than elsewhere. Through that summer, the whole prairie seemed continuously afire with Indian furies; for after the Civil War, emigrants were again pouring to the West, threatening the Indian supremacy in his own domain; and the Indian was striking back with ferocity and skill. So continuous was the struggle, so active was the Army in newly established forts along the westward trails, that the eastern papers carried every day a regular news report with the running headline of "The Indian War."

Lamy decided it would be prudent to abandon the northern route and to set out directly to the southwest toward the familiar ford of the Arkansas River to the west of Fort Dodge, Kansas, at a place known as Cimarron—one of two crossings a few miles apart, the other being near the later settlement of Ingalls. This was the path most often used by the waggon trains for Santa Fe and Chihuahua; and in the summer of 1867 Lamy heard that there were many such caravans on the plains. In the company of one or another of these westbound his people would be safer than alone.

The party left from Leavenworth on 14 June. Four days later they reached a Jesuit mission at St Mary's of the Pottawatomies, where in good company they rested for six more days. Leaving there on the Feast of SS Peter and Paul—29 June—they moved on across the southern reach of the Smoky Hill River, and there they entered upon the prairies proper, bidding "adieu to civilization." That river, said one of the missioners—it was Father J. Brun, who wrote letters based on his diary—"marked the boundary of the Indian territory, a river sadly famous for the piracies and massacres committed by the savages."

Soon after that crossing, while the bishop's party were encamped, four mounted Indians suddenly appeared. They were painted, wore loops of necklaces and feathered headpieces; and at their belts each had a little mirror which he always carried. Asking for tobacco and coffee, they sharply scrutinized the waggons and the people of the caravan, and departed in silence as suddenly as they had come. "They were spies," said Brun.

He had a stranger's eye and word for the disturbing newness of all that the party encountered. After the eastern travel and its comforts, he now saw "the reverse of the medal." The miseries of the sea were replaced now by those of the land, and they were worse than the ocean storms. He had his list: to sleep on the bare earth under open sky; to use your boots for a pillow; to live in the mud (they met with two weeks of almost unceasing torrential rains); to hump along on a horse all day under a burning sun; to be on the alert at every instant for savages; then, to sleep without supper; to rise and depart without breakfast; to suffer torture by mosquito; to go ten or twelve miles looking for a ford at a river before making camp, fighting the currents which might carry away waggon and cargo. And the exhaustion! What would be the worst misery in ordinary life counted for nothing in the most usual events of the journey. "We asked ourselves," he noted, "whether to laugh or cry." But *pleurer?*—No! he declared stoutly.

They had trouble with straying animals, and herders who got lost looking for them and had to be searched for as well. Once, far off, they thought they saw in a great dark mass far ahead of them an army of Indians massed for the attack. Lamy climbed up on a waggon wheel and gazed through his telescope—it was a relief to see that it was a large caravan bound east from Santa Fe whose members had been as frightened and for the same reason as Lamy's party.

Eventually they overtook a large caravan of eighty waggons, including those of Jewish merchants of Santa Fe, with men well armed, going their way; and the two parties joined together. The better to protect Lamy's people and provisions, Captain Francisco Baca, who commanded the traders' train, divided it into two columns, assigning one to each side of the bishop's party.

According to Captain Baca's scouting parties, there were evidences of a great body of Indians—perhaps a thousand strong—coming together for attack. A hollowing sense of increased danger pervaded the caravan.

On Sunday, 14 July, Lamy said Mass and preached on two seriously related topics—one was "the necessity of bearing with fortitude the evils of this world," and the other was the absolute requirement that all must give "strict obedience to orders." For now they began to see little detached parties of Indians reconnoitering and retreating, over and over again, "not unlike those wolves which are said to gather far and near to attack strayed sheep in the desert."

But now another trial—one familiar to prairie voyagers—came to afflict the train: cholera was epidemic on the plains—almost all trains were infected, including a few of Lamy's waggoners, and presently the disease was spreading up and down the straggling and slow-going line, chiefly among the Mexican carters. A priest who travelled part-way with Lamy saw how he "was always the same, affable, in good spirits, stout-hearted, passing his courage along to his missioners." Such steadiness was needed in the atmosphere of uncertainty and in the face of obstacles which the party encountered. Lamy had been assured of military escort from Fort Harker. He sent a detachment to notify the commander that the train was approaching; but the rivers were in flood after the weeks of heavy rainfall and Lamy's men never reached Harker. He went on toward Fort Larned. A detail of troops came to meet him, but because of the cholera, their officer imposed a quarantine and sent the train on a detour away from the fort. Once again, without soldiers, the long train resumed the plodding march to the southwest, drawing away into the low undulations of the distance, where the heat of the sky and the reflected heat of the earth met in a glassy waver which absorbed the line of the horizon and which either enlarged any object entering the mirage, or erased it from sight, as if it had never existed.

iv.

Prairie News

READERS of the New York *Herald,* on Friday, 19 July 1867, turning to page four where the running headline of THE INDIAN WAR appeared as usual, were shocked to read a "Special Telegram to the Herald" announcing

> Capture of a Train near Fort Larned, with a Bishop, Ten Priests and Six Sisters of Charity—The Men killed and Mutilated, and the Women Carried Away.

The dispatch went on to particulars:

> Leavenworth, Kansas, July 18, 1867
> (6 o'clock P.M.)
> A train was captured last Sunday, near Fort Larned, by the Indians. Bishop Lamy, ten priests and six sisters of charity accompanied the train as passengers, en route to Santa Fe. The men were killed, scalped and shockingly mutilated. The females were carried away captives. This information comes through reliable sources.

The news went rapidly across the prairies, and from Topeka Father
Defouri wrote to the Society at Lyon what he had heard of the "horri-
ble death of Mgr. Lamy." Reporting the failure of troops to serve as
escort, Defouri stated that he had no details beyond the information
that the party had been massacred without mercy, but added, "we
know that the body of Mgr. Lamy was horribly mutilated, ten priests
were staked out and scalped. The rest were taken prisoner. The poor
sisters, what horror! to be slaves at the mercy of these savages; dragged
from village to village to be subjected to every kind of outrage and
probably to die lashed to the post of torture. Let us draw the veil
over it all, and pray."

At Trinidad, Colorado, the pastor, Father Vermare, heard the same
story at his outpost near the New Mexican border, sorrowed for those
who had been slain, and for their families and colleagues in France,
and held a requiem Mass in his mission chapel for the dead bishop
and his companions.

v.

The Battle of the Arkansas Crossing

THE PLAINS WERE ALMOST LEVEL. There was little or no evidence of
rock. As they would start out on the trail in the morning, they could
see perhaps fifteen miles ahead the actual end of the day's march. The
dimension of this limited vision governed their sense of time and
space, and commanded their patience in new terms. The south wind
prevailed and often threw obliterating dust across the vast spaces and
anything that moved across them. Imprisoned in distance itself, the
travellers could find escape only through the inner self—faith in their
purpose, whether that of layman or priest or nun, even as they were
open to every danger of land, sky, and human attack.

As nearly as the trail allowed they had followed the Arkansas River
with its great bends. It was, after the first half of the plains crossing
westward, the main source of water, until it must be left behind at
the final crossing west of Fort Dodge. The troops at that post were also
ordered to quarantine the caravan because of the quick contagion of
cholera.

As darkness was falling on 17 July, the bishop's train halted for the

night. Men began to unharness the draft animals. Others were preparing the camp. It was never clear whether darkness was a blessing
or a further danger. Before the picket lines and the temporary corral
had been formed, fifty Indians suddenly as if created in that instant
appeared from the west and attacked the halted company with
showers of bullets and menacing yelps of battle. The surprise was
complete, but the Mexican drivers returned the Indian fire, leaped
on their mounts and gave chase to the Indians, who in their usual
tactics had ridden by to ready themselves for a return attack. The
Indians vanished, and the traders returned to their camp. The attack
had been a scouting raid. The camp kept extra watch all night and
moved out again with daylight.

Farther west, they met trains—one large, one small—coming from
Santa Fe with soldier escorts which had been sent out from Dodge.
They had been attacked an evening earlier by elements of the same
Indian party. There had been casualties—two men killed, three
wounded, some of them troopers, and after two hours the Indians had
retired. It was now clear that all the approaches, east and west, to the
Arkansas River crossings in the Cimarron stretch were under the constantly moving control of the Indian bands. They were like cloud
shadows, now seen, now invisible, according to the contours of the
open land as they swept across it.

The trail to the river showed many roughly parallel waggon tracks,
as everywhere else on the prairie route. A caravan could be expected,
by anyone watching, to follow a known course. Lamy knew the path
from having used it before. He knew it when they were coming close
to the Cimarron crossing. He rode up and down the column giving
strict instructions to all his people. By general consent he was acknowledged as a commander of the whole train, and his orders were taken
by the merchant traders and the Mexican waggoners alike. He created
a common nerve of understanding, and the purpose of it, as everyone
understood, was defense. They moved warily along on the morning
of 22 July. It was a dry day—hot, dusty. The combination of space,
and unvaried slow movement over seemingly empty land, was often
hallucinatory, especially as travellers strained to see, on all sides, that
which remained expertly hidden.

At mid-morning—they said it was about ten o'clock—word came to
Lamy, and the sisters in their waggon, that young Jules Masset was
suddenly writhing with abdominal cramps. He was sweating. His fever
rose. It was cholera. One or two of the Santa Fe merchants went to his
waggon to do what they could for him. Massaging his belly to ease his
cramps, they could only watch him sicken rapidly as the morning went
by and the train made no halt for the nooning. Toward two o'clock

they came to the low rises beyond which lay the Arkansas River. They soon saw the river and its opposite bank.

The water ran, heavy with silt, in a channel which was part of a much wider dry bed. The approach from the left bank, where the waggons came, was wide and sloping gradually to the ford. The whole crossing was perhaps fifty yards wide. The opposite bank was more abrupt and the trail led from the river and past a grove of cottonwood trees. Tall fox-colored brush grew on both sides, and short, tawny grass, and prickly bushes with black stems and branches and parched leafage. The water was pale, reflecting the hot white sky, and the white salts of alkali showed along the brink. In the far distance ahead were low, pale blue ridges. If the hot south wind blew, it lifted heavy dust—almost sand—from the banks and threw it over everything, so that the general effect was a monotone of pale earth color.

At two o'clock the train broke the line and formed a semicircular camp, with its long side based as closely as possible on the northern bank of the river. The passenger waggons and animals were in the center, surrounded by a stockade of cargo carts close together. Sentries were posted at once to watch in all directions. One Mexican waggon forded the river without incident—though there were sinkholes and quicksand, and the current was more vagrant than it looked. The waggon, which included in its cargo kegs of brandy, rose to the crest of the opposite bank near the trees where low grass grew. The drivers left it there and returned to camp without seeing what the sentinels saw—two Indians lying "on their breasts in the weeds, like snakes," watching the waggon as it crossed. When enough more had crossed, leaving a divided defense, they evidently meant to make a signal for attack and take the rest of the train before it could move.

A detail of fifteen men was sent out to scout the land behind the low rises above the camp. In almost no time the scouts came tearing back to camp pursued by hundreds of Indians. Two of the scouts were almost taken, but escaped by riding in a wide circle back to the river. The camp was still settling into its routine for the usual brief nightly halt. Lamy's preliminary orders now took hold. There were about ninety armed men in the train; they were at once ready at their stations, with loaded rifles, and on order, they fired at the Indian pursuit.

The battle was formed.

The Indians withdrew to range themselves seven or eight hundred yards away on the low crests. From that main body two small bands rode off, one to the river above the camp, the other below. They crossed the river and met at the stranded waggon. Breaking into it they found the brandy, smashed a keg, and drank.

From the rear, the main body of the Indians charged down upon the camp and were met with a great salvo from the American rifles, which were effective at long range. The attack drew back. A few fallen Indians were surrounded and carried away in the retreat, as Indians always retrieved their dead or wounded. Once again in order, the Indian phalanx flowed down the low slope but again was forced back. Their arms had less range than those in the caravan—they carried bows and arrows, rifles, and, said the bishop, *"pistoles à six coups"*— six-shooters. They were splendidly mounted and rode wonderfully, concealing themselves all but for feet and hands behind their horses' bodies as they galloped past the riflemen in the waggons. When they fired, their bullets fell "like hail" but without taking serious effect.

As the battle flowed back and forth in fury, confusion, outcry, sweat, and dust, Jules Masset, knowing that he was dying, began to call out for his mother. Lamy was told of his state. The word went also to one of the Sisters of Charity—it was Sister Mary Augustine—who said she would go to the suffering young man. Told which was his waggon, she began to thread her way along the ground between other waggons. She said the arrows flying all about her sounded like "a disturbed beehive." She reached him and gave him what comfort she could, and before he died, one of the priests came to attend him, while the battle went on outside. (In all, ten persons died of cholera on the journey, and were buried on the plains.)

Now the attackers resorted to a variety of ruses to bring the defenders out of their waggon-fortress. John Geatley, an armed waggoner, said, "The situation was appalling—it appeared we were to contend with all the savages south of the Platte River." The Indians drove up from behind the northward ridge a large herd of cattle they had stolen from the train which had been attacked the day before. They hoped the traders would venture out to capture the cattle. But no one went. Again, a file of Indians rode past the camp, with "incredible agility," to invite a foray into combat. Lamy harshly ordered no one to budge from his post within the stockade. They fired from their places, and he fired with them. The Indians retreated again, only to return in force time and again.

The din was appalling. Those huddling within the waggons, seeing nothing of what went on, but hearing the impact of bullets and arrows on the waggon wheels, the fusillades, and the war cries from one side and the shouted orders from the other, saw in their minds a struggle even worse than the actual one. One of the nuns—the youngest, Sister Mary Alphonse, a Lorettine eighteen years old—was in an extremity of terror. They heard the drumming hooves advance and retreat, hoping that every retreat would be the last; but the sustained onslaught continued for almost three hours. How much longer could it be resisted?

Finally, the main body of the warriors drew away, leaving behind a few small bands who rode back and forth in challenge. But the defenders knew that the surest trick of the Indians was to simulate a retreat, wait for lowered caution, or even emergence of a beleaguered force, and then to resume the attack in new ferocity, often victoriously. But presently there was no Indian in sight.

In the lull about thirty men ventured out of the waggons on to the open space between the camp and the ridge to inspect the battlefield with its scattered trophies—wounded or dead horses and their saddles, bridles, moccasins stitched with dyed quills, necklaces of shells and wampum, arrows, rawhide quivers. In a flash, a line of Indians rode down upon them from nowhere, and the traders barely made it safely back to the waggons.

During one of the charges, a warrior among the Indians was—so a man in the waggons thought—a young white man whom he identified as Charley Bent, the son of the one-time Governor Bent of New Mexico. It was a curious discovery, for young Bent had been educated in Catholic school and college of the Middle West and the East, but had chosen to join the raiding Indians in their plains life.

Toward evening, the Indian groups crossed the river to assemble near the stranded Mexican waggon, which they plundered, cracking open more brandy, and set about getting drunk. One Indian dashed back and forth across the river crying toward the camp, *"Amigos! Amigos!"* but no one responded; and far into the darkness, the traders continued to fire at the Indian bivouac on the far bank. After dark, the caravan animals had to be fed, and were cautiously taken to graze along the river's edge outside the camp. Indians observed this, and some swam over under darkness and in as much quiet as possible tried to stampede the herd. But Lamy's sentinels, whom he kept strictly at their posts, heard them coming, drove them back with rifle fire, and the animals were brought back into the corral. It seemed almost a signal that the battle was over when the Indians set the lone waggon on fire.

Presently all was quiet.

It had been a "terrible day," said Father Brun, "these seven hours of combat." The pious Mexicans of the train considered that they had been saved by the presence of a bishop and his priests, as ministers of grace. Beyond that, it was Lamy's skill and example which had most acted to save the expedition, in support of Baca's command.

Early the next morning, in all caution, the crossing of the river by the entire train began, and took most of the day. They marched until late. There was no sign of the enemy. As they came to their slow halt and the making of camp, the young Sister Alphonse lost all her strength. The bishop was called by the other nuns who attended her. She was dying. Lamy "assisted her for death." She lived during the night, and at the assembling of the train for the next day's march, she begged that her body not be left by the train but be taken on to Santa Fe for burial, for she was mortally afraid that the Indians would desecrate her grave if they found it. She died at ten o'clock on the morning of 24 July. Lamy wrote of her that "she was a girl beautifully educated, and a true model of piety and of all the virtues . . . she died of terror" endured in the battle. Her last wish could not be observed— there was always the chance of contamination by the cholera; and toward evening, with Lamy assisting one of the priests, she was buried by the trail, in a rude coffin fashioned out of some planks taken from a waggon. A wooden cross was put at the head of her grave. In a few years this disappeared; but someone found her grave anyhow, near the still-visible ruts of the trail, and not far from the tracks being newly laid for the westward advance of the railroad; for where she was buried, the prairie grass grew higher than that all around.

The train moved on, presently crossed the Cimarron River, and days later came to Trinidad, where they read in the Denver *Gazette* how the bishop and the other men had all been massacred, and the religious led away as captives; and where Father Vermare told them he had sung a requiem Mass for them all. "It is thus," wrote Father Gasparri, one of the Jesuits in the party, "that history is written." Actually, the massacre report had been denied within a few days by the New York *Tribune,* and Defouri and Vermare had written hastily to Europe to relieve those who grieved for Lamy and his people. The Secretary of War, General U. S. Grant, issued a statement confirming the falsity of the report, and a Washington dispatch stated that it had been the work of "wretches who manufacture lying dispatches and send them broadcast over the country with cold-blooded malice"—the purpose being to inflame public feeling against the Indians the better to have the war of extermination against them intensified and, pre- sumably, the western lands opened more readily to settlers. "The ob- ject in view has been too well accomplished. The indignation of the public mind against the poor Indians has been fired."

Lamy and his people came into Santa Fe during the evening of Assumption Day, 15 August. Despite a heavy rainstorm, people began to assemble to ride out "on the States road" to meet him, and as he entered the city he was greeted by all the bells of Santa Fe, and a Te Deum in the cathedral sung by Vicar General Eguillon. The bishop had been absent for almost a year, and his plains voyage, with all its storms, had taken sixty-two days. "His whole caravan was saved through his foresight, nerve, and kindness," Defouri told Paris. Lamy himself wrote the Society that in a few days he would send the details of the "long, laborious, and dangerous voyage across the prairies," but now he would merely report his arrival, as, at the moment, he felt "a little tired."

X

INCREASE

1868–1874

i.

A Quiet Conscience

LIKE HIMSELF, SO LONG AGO, coming in his youth to the alien land of Ohio, his newcomers were soon assigned to duties, whether in church, mission, school, convent, hospital. Time, in his absence, finally brought peace to Taos, for three weeks before his return, so Lamy was told, Padre Martínez had died in Taos on 27 July. The *New Mexican* declared him "universally loved by all who knew him. Taos county has lost one of her most worthy citizens and will sadly lament his loss." He had been buried, according to his wish, in his own oratory, with Father Lucero "acting as pastor of the schismatics."

In his will, listing his property and its disposition, Martínez revealed himself as one of the richest natives of New Mexico, for his holdings of farming and grazing land, and sheep, cattle, and goats. In a codicil made a month before his death, he reaffirmed his view of himself. ". . . I have complied with my ecclesiastical ministry with fidelity and good faith, in whatever I could, to the best of my knowledge; many years I dedicated myself to interested study of the science of religion, to learn to serve my God, Creator, and Saviour, that my body may descend in tranquillity to the silence of the grave, and my soul may appear and rise up to the divine tribunal, with clear satisfaction that I have done all that I could to teach the minds of my fellow citizens, bringing them temporal good, and, above all, their spiritual benefit; all because that is the way it has been dictated by my Christian religion that I profess, convinced of its truth and sanctity. My conscience is quiet and happy. God knows this to be true. If any of my fellow citizens and neighbors complain that I have injured them this may have been through mental error; but not with the intention of my heart. A human creature is weak but I have never had any intention of injuring anybody. In my nature I have been inclined to do good. I will present the testimony of my works in documents, So Help Me God."

ii.

Two New Bishops

BY THE NATURE of where he worked, the bishop's life showed a constant alternation between the physical life of the outreaching land and a binding duty to the desk in his whitewashed office in the adobe house on the cathedral grounds where, almost entirely in his own hand, he kept up a flow of letters to Paris, Lyon, Cincinnati, St Louis, Rome. Soon after his return he was reporting to Paris that he was immediately opening in very important places two new schools for boys, with the four new Christian Brothers who had come home with him. Counting the one already at work in Santa Fe, this made three such schools. In Santa Fe and elsewhere the sisters already had four schools and were about to open a fifth. The hospital was progressing, if with "mediocre materials." In mid-autumn thirty priests assembled from all quarters of the diocese for a pastoral retreat—some came through dangerous territory from as far away as a hundred fifty and two hundred miles to attend, and two of the new Jesuits had given a mission in the cathedral city with the church full, day and evening. With all such successes to recount, Lamy felt justified in citing the extraordinary expenses of his latest journey westward, which had been ruinous: he was obliged to ask for an advance of twelve thousand francs out of the Society's allotment to him for the next year. He had a good record of repayment; and his work spoke for itself.

Of Barnabo, at year's end, he felt it was time to ask whether the proposed separate establishments of Colorado and Arizona each with its own bishop, as proposed by Baltimore and discussed at Rome, had been approved. The reasons had already been given, it was clear that no single bishop could properly attend to the growth of the three territories together. There was a limit to any man's strength. Lamy would continue to spend his as long as it was there; still sinewy, strong, and effective, he was prematurely worn; and the robust good looks which gleamed forth during his early times as bishop were now tempered by permanent signs of hard endurance. His eyes were still brilliant but were set deeper in his head, his cheekbones showed more sharply, his jaws more squarely.

The answer from Rome soon came.

Machebeuf was notified by Barnabo informally of his designation as vicar apostolic of Colorado and Utah, with the title of Bishop of Epiphany *in partibus infidelium*. Before the Roman bulls reached him with his official appointment, he was full of reasons for declining it. Physically he was feeling miserable—his old injury was acting up, he had to use a cane, saying Mass was a great problem. Moreover, the Irish in his parish were actively hostile to him, for one reason because of "my quick and passionate temper," as he said, and for another, because he had asked Lamy to dismiss the Irish priest at Central City a few years earlier. For still another, he had on the orders of the archbishop of St Louis opposed the Fenian Brotherhood, an Irish-American secret society devoted to political agitation for the independence of Ireland from England. This was a costly position for Machebeuf to take, for it meant that the Fenians—and the Irish immigration to the mines had been large—refused to contribute to the upkeep of the church. Worst of all, Machebeuf's finances were in dreadful trouble, and would continue to be throughout his active work. In a word, he was uneasy about becoming a bishop under all such disadvantages until a Jesuit friend persuaded him that his duty was to accept, and his self-respect required him to work to balance his financial affairs rather than leave this to a successor.

Soon, then, he was off to Montreal looking for a priest to elevate to the post of his vicar general; and in mid-summer, he was consecrated in Cincinnati by Purcell with two other Auvergnats as co-consecrators—Bishops Rappe and De Goesbriand, who had come to America with him and Lamy decades before. Lamy was not present in St Peter's in Cincinnati—he would have been, but the journey was "so far and so costly" that he could afford neither time nor money for it. By that time Machebeuf was reconciled to his "heavy burden," and, in the regular practice of the western bishopric, he was soon homeward bound with a new increment of five Loretto sisters to add to the seven already at work in Denver.

For Lamy it was a lightening of his own load when he could send a paper on 21 September 1868 to Machebeuf to say officially that he was "happy to turn over to [Machebeuf's] jurisdiction the Catholics of Colorado Territory who were before in our diocese." Soon after arriving in Denver, Machebeuf made a tour of his own vicariate, and extended it with a visit of a few days to see Lamy at Santa Fe. Both now bishops—who were those untried youngsters who had run away one day before dawn in Clermont in their early twenties?

But Arizona and the nuisance of the boundary quarrel were not so promptly settled as the status of Colorado. Bishops for both territories had been proposed in Baltimore, and supported by arguments in Rome, and Lamy urgently had put forward Salpointe to be elevated to the mitre and given a vicariate apostolic in Arizona. The Propaganda seemed ready to act on Lamy's advice—but Salpointe had somehow heard of what was being readied for him, and immediately wrote to Barnabo begging that the erection of an episcopate for Arizona be deferred. While Lamy argued for it, giving strong territorial reasons for its establishment, and endorsing Salpointe in all personal matters, Salpointe presented such disclaimers of his own unworthiness and such a different picture of the actual conditions in Arizona that the Vatican abided by his advice and the matter lay dormant.

Lamy refused to leave it at that. He officially renewed his proposal for Arizona. His first choice was still Salpointe ("very successful in studies at Mont-Ferrand, received no degrees, had not been a professor, efficient as a missioner, spoke French, English, Spanish, Latin, Greek; exhibited the highest degree of prudence as vicar general of Santa Fe; in good health, honest, patient, able in financial affairs; persistent; excellent reputation, never any kind of moral trouble; mild and loved by all"). Father Lawrence Bax of St Louis came second ("native of Holland, spoke Dutch, French, English, Latin and Greek, prudent, thrifty, stable in character, never involved 'contra mores,' zealous builder of churches, excellent administrator"). Third was Father John Baptist Rallière ("highest honors at the Clermont seminary though holding no academic degrees, eleven years a most successful missionary in New Mexico, spoke French, Spanish, English, Latin, Greek, efficient pastor of souls, excellent health, honest, discreet, prudent, never anything in his actions against moral principles, built several churches and schools").

But Lamy was determined upon Salpointe. He wrote the Baltimore archbishop, now Martin John Spalding, to urge the cause upon Rome. Salpointe's "humility" must not be allowed to stand in the way. Moreover, Arizona actually had more Catholics now than Colorado; and, surely, the Roman creation of Arizona as a vicariate apostolic with its own bishop would necessarily define the actual boundaries of his territory, and there, at one final stroke, the assignment of the *Condado* [Mesilla] Doñana could be specified, and the old tiresome boundary indecision be resolved. "It would be a very fair way to cut short that question which has caused and still causes many troubles and misunderstandings," wrote Lamy. It was a pity that Salpointe in his protest had "represented the state of affairs in a different light." But the fact remained that what would belong to Salpointe consisted of two counties, "one of Texas, the other of New Mexico." Finally, Lamy stated that "I am too far distant to visit those places."

He was, in the end, persuasive. Rome declared Arizona separate from New Mexico as a vicariate and named Salpointe after all, on 25 September 1868, and the effective instruments reached Lamy two months later. He forwarded them at once to Salpointe in Tucson, but an additional document still was not included, and Lamy wrote to request it: it should be a bull authorizing Salpointe to take jurisdiction of "the two counties," El Paso in Texas (i.e., the American town of that name and its downriver villages) and the famous *Condado* of Doñana which reached all the way across both New Mexico and Arizona.

But the old issue was not yet to be settled. Rome had written a few months ago asking the new bishop of Durango—it was now José Vicente Salinas succeeding Zubiría and inheriting the struggle—asking (once again!) for "a report" about those territories, but had received no reply. Even before his elevation, Salpointe himself had twice journeyed to Durango (in the pattern of Lamy and Machebeuf before him) to see Salinas and persuade him to yield on the strength of papal documents long since sent to Lamy. But both journeys—dangerous as always, each requiring fifty days' round trip from Tucson—had resulted in nothing, as Bishop Salinas had been absent both times. The problem, now by its protraction attaining the dignity of a scandal, must continue. Nevertheless, Lamy had fostered "two religious colonies" for "Mgr Machebeuf and Mgr Salpointe," making "great sacrifices" to establish them; for both territories would prosper materially more rapidly than New Mexico as the years advanced. Salpointe, receiving word of his elevation, began to make plans to go to France for his consecration. In a final orderly transfer, Machebeuf would be relieved, in 1871, of his responsibility for Utah, when Archbishop Alemany of San Francisco agreed to add that territory to his own.

To put an end to isolation—it was the goal of the whole desert West, and Lamy, with everyone else, saw the need of this, and welcomed every advance in communication, saw its portents, and rejoiced with measured calm when the telegraph reached Santa Fe in the second week of July 1868. News would come more quickly. There was also now a daily mail which connected with the advancing railhead now three days away to the East (at Sheridan, Kansas), and three times a week the four-horse Concord coaches of the Denver and Santa Fe Stage Line connected the two cities by a three-and-a-half-day run. "But with all this," he told Purcell, "Santa Fe is dull, we might say almost dead, that there is nothing doing except two small newspapers which seem to predict great things for the future of New Mexico."

If he sounded skeptical, not so the *New Mexican,* which, becoming a daily paper with the advent of the telegraph, printed a euphoric editorial contrasting the state of the desert West of twenty years ago with the present. "The idea that all this vast central half of the American continent was then or was ever to be valuable to man, had not gained much if any ground, and all west of the 'Big Muddy,' to most people, was a *terra incognita*. But these twenty years past have wrought wonderful revolutions in the mysteries of the 'Great American Desert.' New Mexico was certainly known as *existing* twenty years ago—that is all. . . . But, moving with the line of civilization through the wilderness . . . are the wonderful developments of the grand handiworks of man and the energies of capital, invigorated by enterprise. Santa Fe, that twenty years ago was seventy or eighty days travel from the Missouri river, is now within three days of the western terminus of the iron track and the railroad car. . . . Twenty years ago it is probable that there were not two thousand Americans in New Mexico. Today, there are not less than from twelve to fifteen thousand. The condition of the people native in New Mexico is greatly improved since that day. Life to them is, for the most part, of a more cultivated and more elevated character. Education struggles to break the bonds of ignorance, and religion moves onward with its wondrous softening and christianizing influences. 'Westward the star of empire' has taken 'her course,' and New Mexico is within the range of its glorious influences. . . ."

But if the bishop was paid indirect respects in the editorial, he must still report, not in a spirit of pessimism, for this was never his way, but in his sober realism, that "the thousand of emigrants that were to come to our territory don't seem to have moved yet we have then to resign ourselves to go on slowly as in old times." Meanwhile, a newspaper item reflected a new turn in the popular culture, with a listing of a "collection of select novels" to be had at two dollars a volume, including such titles as *Dear Experience* by Ruffini, *Out of His Head*, by Aldrich, *The Alchemist,* by Balzac, *Who Breaks Pays* (paper cover), *LuLu,* by M. C. Walworth, *Don Quixote de la Mancha, Wa-Wa-Wanda* (anon.), *From Hay-Time to Hopping* (anon.), *Sprees and Splashes,* by Morford, and *Tactics; or, Cupid in Shoulder Straps, A West Point Love Story.* A month later, the paper reported: "Bishop Lamy is making some much needed improvements around the ancient church of the Parroquía in this city"—referring to the old clay cathedral of St Francis.

The improvements were actually preparations in clearing the area of the old church for the beginning of construction on a new cathedral, to be built of native stone, of which Lamy had first spoken in 1864. For he had never changed his response to the mud constructions of New Mexico—though he understood as he deplored the necessity of making them from their humble materials. But to him a chapel, a church, a cathedral above all, should rise to the glory of God as more than a "stable of Bethlehem"; and with his own memory of the high architectural art whose tradition he had inherited, he must, whenever he could manage it, build his cathedral out of another vision than the local one. Byzantium and ancient Rome would still speak through him. There was suitable native stone to be had near Santa Fe. Ochreous limestone for the exterior could be quarried in the Arroyo Saís, and the light volcanic stone for the vaults in the Cerro Mogino within a few miles of the city; and for the interior walls, a heavy granite could be taken from the low hills in the country where the bishop's land lay seventeen miles away on the Santa Fe Trail [the site of the present railroad junction of Lamy, New Mexico]. Preliminary donations were solicited, and the response, though modest, was enough to encourage Lamy to proceed with his plans. The *New Mexican* announced that the cornerstone would be laid on Sunday, 10 October 1869.

In a general way, it was known what Lamy wanted—the Romanesque style was decided upon from the start. There were few detailed architectural plans, or engineering drawings; all that was technically certain was that the new cathedral would be constructed around and over the old earthen church, and foundation footings were accordingly placed outside the walls of old St Francis's. As the new stone walls would rise, they would gradually hide the adobe elevations; there would for years be a complete church within one on the outside, unfinished. With that much to go on, a cornerstone could be set down as a promise.

The cornerstone contained gold, silver, and copper coins; newspapers of the day; official historical documents naming the public officers of the nation, state, and cathedral—President Grant, Governor Pile, and Bishop Lamy. Enclosed also was a list of the first donors to the building fund which gave the names of all those giving twenty-five dollars or more. Lamy led off with a donation of $3000. The sister of the late Rural Dean Ortiz gave $2500, and also presented to the cathedral many altar vessels and ornaments of great value, which brought to mind those missing ever since Vicar Ortiz had departed from his Santa Fe duties in 1852 taking with him certain religious articles of the parish church of St Francis, claiming them as his own. The list of first donors included the Mother Superior Mary Magdalen of the Lorettines ($500), the Spiegelberg brothers ($500) and many other non-Catholics, and members of the once-rebellious Armijo family of Albuquerque.

There was talk of a façade with two towers a hundred feet high, and a dome eighty-five feet high at the crossing of the transepts, and a nave two hundred feet long. The cornerstone was blessed after vespers on its Sunday, and on the following Saturday, the city awoke to learn that it had been stolen, and its contents rifled, never to be recovered. The act might have served as a forecast of the halting history of the cathedral church; but the fact was, Lamy had begun the construction, and all its later vicissitudes could seem only a repetition of the pattern of his whole life in the diocese where there was always trouble enough in the moment briefly to obscure the increase of his achievement over all the years. In dealing with stones as well as men, distance as well as hazard, his patience was still equal to his strength as the new decade of 1870 approached its turn.

He knew his joys, also. His brother Etienne's son, Anthony, who had come with him last time from France, to study in the Baltimore seminary, was now in Santa Fe, and the reunion of this nephew with his older sister, Marie, Sister Francesca of the Loretto convent, brought a sense of family to them all. Anthony, the seminarian, was twenty-four when he came to Santa Fe. He and Marie had kept their family ties only through correspondence since they had been parted—she to go to America when he was still a very small boy. Now when he arrived in Santa Fe and went to the Loretto convent, and she was sent to meet him in the parlor, he cried, "Marie! I am Anthony!" and they made a strong alliance in family love. The nuns noticed that whenever Anthony came to call, Sister Francesca always had a new piano piece ready to play for him.

iii.

Vatican Council

SALPOINTE AND MACHEBEUF had expected to travel together to Europe in 1869. There were two great events calling them there. One was Salpointe's coming consecration by his old bishop, the now aged Féron, in Clermont; the other was to present themselves to Pius IX as new bishops. On his way, Salpointe went east from Tucson, planning to turn north to Santa Fe and there take leave of Lamy. But he found Lamy at Las Cruces, and the two rode by stage together to Santa Fe, while Lamy gave certain errands to his younger suffragan to carry out for him in France. Salpointe coached on to Denver to meet Machebeuf, who had to disappoint him—fire had destroyed St Mary's Academy in Denver and Machebeuf could not leave just yet. But he promised to hurry away soon afterward in order to attend Salpointe's consecration in Clermont. This, too, failed to happen, as Machebeuf missed his sailing on a French steamer and had to wait a fortnight in New York for the next one. He arrived in Clermont a day after the consecration. But there were moments of jubilation still to enjoy, and Machebeuf was positively harassed by dinner invitations which he could not refuse.

One of Lamy's most important charges upon Salpointe, now the vicar apostolic of Arizona with the title of Bishop of Dorylla *in partibus infidelium,* was to find and engage for Santa Fe an architect and some skilled stonemasons who would undertake to proceed with the building of the new cathedral, for the earlier contractor-architect—an American—had proved inefficient in the laying of the foundations, which were already shifting. Salpointe found his men. They were Antoine Mouly and his son Projectus, who in turn found stonecutters. All would go to Santa Fe to work on the new shell of the stone cathedral. For the rest, the two vicars apostolic returned to old scenes in Clermont and Riom. With emotion, Machebeuf "officiated and confirmed" in the college where he "had been educated nearly forty years ago." Six seminarians of Mont-Ferrand actually did not wait for solicitations, but approached Salpointe asking to go with him to Arizona. He promptly accepted their offer, which was approved by Bishop Féron as, said Salpointe humorously, a favor not to be denied a guest.

Three days after Machebeuf's arrival the two new bishops set out together for Rome, arriving in 23 July. They remained for twelve days, saw Pius IX three times and discussed their vicariates with him in detail. The Pope examined maps of Colorado and Arizona and heard reports of how much was to be done in the desert and the mountains —so much, in fact, that he dispensed them both from remaining in Rome to take their places as bishops in the forthcoming Vatican Council of 1870, the preparations for which were resounding throughout St Peter's and all Rome.

"You cannot wait for the Council," said Pius, "you have too much to do to organize your vast dioceses." He paused with a gleam in his eye, and added, amiably, "In any case, being only young bishops, you have not yet much experience and could not give us much assistance!"

Machebeuf later noted, "How true was this remark—of course." They returned to France passing through Pisa, Florence, Milan, over the Simplon Pass, and into Geneva. Salpointe continued his journey directly to America, but Machebeuf paused in Ireland, calling at the colleges of All Hallows', Carlow, Kilkenny, and Maynooth, where students for holy orders in each place were eager to go to Colorado with him; but he lacked funds to pay their way and he had to leave without them. Salpointe, on the other hand, sailing from Brest on the *City of Paris* on 18 September had secured for his colony five seminarians, three deacons, and twelve subdeacons.

Lamy, in his turn, set out for Rome and the Council. Barnabo had passed from the scene, and his successor, Giovanni Cardinal Simeoni, must become familiar with the world pastorates under his Sacred Congregation of the Propaganda Fide. Presented with a questionnaire from him, Lamy gave in abbreviated form much the same information as he had laid before Barnabo in 1867.

When the first Vatican Council was convened by Pius IX on 8 December 1869 in the wide and lofty north transept of St Peter's, Lamy was in his place among the six hundred bishops in white mitres and copes who were seated on ranks of tribunes at right angles to the papal throne which stood at the far end of the chapel. Red cloth covered the seats for cardinals, green those for the bishops. Flemish tapestries were hung on the walls. A great pedimented partition painted to simulate marble, and reaching across the whole mouth of the transept and halfway up to the gold coffered vault, separated the scene of the Council from the public spaces of the basilica. But though it was only a screen, it had great double doors, and these, by the Pope's order, were left open so the wandering public could hear the liturgical events of the opening session, and in the crowd those used to doing so sang the responses with the assembled prelates. Eighty thousand people thronged St Peter's and joined in with the *Veni Creator* as it was intoned at the temporary altar facing the Holy Father. The vaults themselves so far above, and the distant walls with their gray marble pilasters, and the very floors of gray lilac, seemed to be the actual source of sound of the antiphonal choirs and the murmuring public. In the midst of this, the single voice of the celebrant was a small thread of supplication wavering into the gray and golden spaces. Silver dust in the upper vastness made farther what already seemed distant in the arches and vaults, the domes and cupolas, the glimpses of side aisles. All the attendant magnificence was a material analogy for the power of spiritual intention. As such, it was expensive, and gave rise to the famous witticism of Pius IX, who, touching on the dominant issue of the Council, hinted, at the same time, that the affair was costly, when he said, "I don't know whether the Pope will come out of this Council fallible or infallible; but it is certain that he will be bankrupt."

As for the proceedings, in which beyond simple attendance Lamy seemed to take no active part, they were, despite the grand good humor, charm, and vitality of Pius, tumultuous and disorganized. Factionalism was everywhere. Procedure was obstructive rather than helpful. Archbishop Peter Richard Kenrick of St Louis wrote after three months of it, "Most of us are very tired of Rome and would willingly leave it. . . . Nothing has been done. The Body is too big for work, unless divided into Sections, and those who had the management of matters were, and are, unwilling to attend to the suggestions made to them by those who had experience in similar assemblies"— possibly citing the order and dispatch of the American bishops in their Baltimore synods.

"The Council appears to have been convoked for the special purpose of defining the Papal Infallibility and enacting the proposition of the Syllabus as general laws of the Church. Both objects are deemed by a minority, of which I am one, inexpedient and dangerous, and are sure to meet with serious resistance. The men of both parties are considerably excited; and there is every reason to fear that the Council, instead of uniting with the Church those already separated from it, will cause division among ourselves most detrimental to Catholic Interests. . . ."

Tempers ran so high that when the bishop of Bosnia, in his turn on the rostrum, spoke against the infallibility motion as inimical to Christian unity, he was assailed with cries of "Let him come down . . . He is Lucifer, anathema, anathema . . . He is another Luther, let him be cast out," and "Come down, come down"; and, vigorously protesting, he came down. "No wonder," said a later commentator, "no wonder Cardinal Newman dismissed [such aspects of] the council's proceedings as 'a grave scandal.' " The American bishops in general were against the doctrine of infallibility, which was finally promulgated in July 1870; but by then Lamy was gone, his view on the issue unknown. On a tablet which was placed on a wall of the basilica, his name was included with those of the bishops attending.

For his chief concern in Rome was once more, even in the unpropitious atmosphere of the Council which must have disrupted ordinary administration, the scandal of his territorial claim, still in abeyance after two decades. He wrote a new memorandum for Simeoni, who was not so familiar with the case as Barnabo had been.

He reviewed the entire history of the matter, bringing it up to two years ago, when on the creation of the vicariate apostolic of Arizona, the whole disputed area had been assigned by the Vatican to Salpointe.

"This, however, did not yet eliminate the inveterate evil, since the Bishop of Durango [Salinas] has not yet relinquished his jurisdiction, despite all the official Apostolic papers . . ." and so on and on. "Therefore I ask, and insistently ask, the Sacred Congregation that before I leave for America the eminent Cardinal Prefect of this congregation issue an official document in which the jurisdiction be given to the Apostolic Vicar of Arizona over the counties of El Paso, Doñana (or Mesilla Valley)," and he asked for this in duplicate copies, one to go to Salpointe, the other to Salinas in Durango, whose delivery he, Lamy, personally would assure through "a trusted hand." He specified further that henceforth all the priests in the area should receive their priestly faculties from Salpointe only. "The time is certainly come that there must be an end to all this for the good of our Faith," and a powerful endorsement was added by Archbishop Kenrick, who wrote on it, urgently asking that *as soon as possible* the request therein be granted and "the whole matter be settled once and for all." Lamy, with two other American bishops, was granted leave to return to his diocese "on account of the urgent wants" there.

He left for Auvergne, and there, on the first Sunday after Easter 1870, he reconsecrated the parish church of Lempdes, the home of his childhood faith and his mature vocation, where considerable renovation had been done. He was also to bring back a loan of twelve thousand francs which Machebeuf had asked his brother Marius to raise for him. Machebeuf was anxiously in debt for a brick church, and for the travel expenses of two or three Irish priests who were coming over after all, and for two freight consignments which were impounded by customs until he could pay the duty on them.

Homeward bound, Lamy sent one more bolt of argument to Simeoni in the territorial matter; for he had received certain information at Lyon which seemed to suggest strongly that Salpointe had come to the end of his endurance, and, unless the matter were settled immediately, would resign as apostolic vicar of Arizona—may, in fact, already have sent in his resignation, which would not "surprise" Lamy, for he knew him well. Salpointe might not suffer in futility the dismissal of all the efforts he had made on his own part to resolve the affair with Durango. Could Arizona be expected to slip away once again, until a third start on her spiritual colonization would have to be undertaken? As in all affairs between the field and headquarters, time alone could tell; and Lamy returned to America, and a peaceable crossing of the prairies, much of the way, now, by the railroad, and arrived at Santa Fe to receive the usual welcome on 23 June 1870.

iv.

Follies and Dangers

SALPOINTE DID NOT RESIGN—but neither was the Durango dispute resolved out of hand. A year later, Bishop Salinas wrote a long letter to the Vatican declaring that he would agree to ceding the locality of "Mesilla"—but not Doñana or "El Paso," which embraced the three downriver villages so long ago delegated to Lamy by Odin. His argument was that the "El Paso district" was not in United States territory but in Mexican; and if he gave over spiritual jurisdiction of them to an American bishop, "sooner or later it would come to this: the forcible entry of those people [i.e., the North Americans] into the Republic [of Mexico] whose ancient tendencies, as we all know, are already manifest as to their eventual absorption of the entire frontier of Mexico." His fears were not groundless—there had been some agitation in Congress at the time of the 1846 war for the annexation of all of northern Mexico.

But Bishop Salinas was confused by nomenclature, as his predecessor had been, for Mesilla and Doñana were practically interchangeable terms, and "El Paso," designating the Mexican town south of the Rio Grande, had also been used since 1858 as the name of the settlement plotted in that year on United States land north of the Rio Grande. Moreover, he seemed not to recognize that the three villages once belonging to Mexico had become part of the North American possession when the course of the river had shifted and had passed to the south of them, thus leaving them north of the boundary line in the river's midstream. Salinas avowed that he would obey the Pope, whatever the decision, but until he had direct orders, he would hold his present position—and territory. Lamy told Rome that unless Salinas acceded, Salpointe would lose "half of his already poor diocese." Moreover, Salpointe was concerned with that which, "by right," belonged to him, "as he is in American, and not Mexican Territory."

Rome once again issued an Apostolic Letter naming "El Paso" and "Doñana better known as Mesilla Valley" as part of the vicariate of Arizona, and had sent a copy to Tucson. Was it over at last?

Salpointe once again journeyed to Durango to see the bishop and show him the papal order, after twice notifying him by mail without effect. Surely the actual papal document in hand would be "sufficient," wrote Salpointe to Simeoni, "to show the will of the Holy Father and let his intentions take full effect. But"—he went on—"things turned out differently, and I am hesitant to relate this." For the fact was that, after having actually read the Roman bull, Salinas "lost his composure and used words which had no reverence and refused to give the requested jurisdiction unless he received direct word from the Roman Curia . . ." Salpointe returned home hoping that Rome would support him by sending the papal order direct to Salinas. Further, he served notice that so far as he was concerned, he would carry out his duties in the disputed lands in full obedience to the decree of Rome, using the Mexican priests who remained in "Doñana," though trouble could be expected of them.

Legally, the affair seemed done with; but in 1874 local residents of Las Cruces in the *Condado* petitioned Rome for "a foreign bishop" and "foreign priests" to establish a diocese at the city of Chihuahua who would minister to the old sore spot. But as this presumed territorial ties to Mexico instead of the United States, nothing came of it, and the Mexican mails must at last have carried to Durango the decree of cession to which Salinas bowed.

The twenty-three-year-old dispute was finally over.

Meanwhile, Salpointe asked Rome for a coadjutor bishop to help him in his far-flung duties; but this was not granted him.

In 1871 Lamy had the happy opportunity to ordain his nephew Anthony, who was assigned first to Taos, later to Abiquiu, and finally to Manzano. The bishop was now concerned largely with consolidations of works long begun. He went east as far as Baltimore to raise funds for the cathedral, and was grateful to "the two good ladies who gave me the gold buttons and the box of jewelry." On his way home he paused in his old parishes in Ohio, and between the two visits was given "near $400." In St Louis the donation was $275, and he gave thanks for all such generosity, "considering the sad circumstances of the Chicago fire which occurred at the very time" he was making his appeal. Bringing three more Loretto sisters and a deacon from Santa Fe whom he had sent East for study, he came to Denver, found Machebeuf "as lively as ever," and was snowbound there for eight days before he could turn homeward to Santa Fe.

There the cathedral walls were slow in obscuring the old earth church within. Local masons had been trained by the Moulys, and scaffolding stood clear at the top of San Francisco street, and rows of cut stone, marked for placing, lay on the cathedral grounds. But it was slow, slow—and the cost seemed at times impossible to meet.

But the schools, convents, hospital, and orphanage were making their gains, and the bishop took his meals with the orphans, whose flour and fuel he personally supplied. Lamy and Machebeuf grieved over the news from France—the empire at war, the defeat, the disorders of the commune—*"Nos pauvres compatriotes."*

Excitement seized Santa Fe and the whole West—and even a portion of the financial marts of New York and San Francisco—when a tremendous discovery was announced in 1872: precious stones, mostly diamonds and rubies, were suddenly found lying on the very surface of the Arizona desert. The "diamond fields" made news everywhere. Santa Fe papers were at first skeptical, then intrigued, at last in full cry of enthusiasm as they reported developments. Jewel experts in New York, London, and San Francisco had authenticated certain gems submitted for inspection by the discoverers and promoters of the great find. Parties of experts were led circuitously in blindfold to the fields and once there were allowed to see and to pick up gems from the earth. Stock speculation fed on its own excitement, there were fortunes to be made. But in a matter of months it was all over, for Clarence King, United States geologist, left his survey along the fortieth parallel, went to visit the rich sites with an associate, and promptly proved that the fields had been "salted" with a few real rubies and diamonds, while what were native were only garnets of small size, all too common to certain parts of Arizona. The affair was a swindle, and never more clearly so than when, among the "salted" jewels, prospectors found diamonds already cut and faceted. If the event had the air of an episode out of the cultural loam which produced Mark Twain and some of his moods, the sardonic style of public wit was present in an editorial item in the *New Mexican* for 16 December 1873:

A BUTTON

Presented to Governor Arny by Thos. V. Keams, which was found on a trail in the diamond country of Arizona, was sent by the Governor to the Smithsonian Institution and he has received the following letters in regard to it:

SMITHSONIAN INSTITUTION
Washington, D.C.   Nov. 14, 1872.

My Dear Governor: I send you what they have written me about the button from New York, and with this the article itself, as you probably may wish to add it to your museum of historical curiosities.

> Very truly yours,
> SPENCER F. BAIRD.

Gov. W. F. M. Arny, Santa Fe, N.M.

New York, Nov. 12, 1872.

My dear Professor Baird: I enclose the button. An old button maker from England says that they were made in Birmingham, England, before 1820. Mr. Steele of the Schofield Button Manufactory Co., Conn., says that there is a pattern of a button at their factory made for a South American Republic forty-five years ago. The legend is "República de Columbia, Marina." The Columbia consul says that about 1817 Columbia had a navy and a uniform button. I think it reasonable to say that this button was a Columbia navy button 1817 to 1820.

Yours truly,
AMORY EDWARDS.

Who will solve the question how that button got to the unexplored region of Arizona? Did the marines of the Republic of Columbia visit there in search of minerals, garnets, etc.?

Follies and dangers were not far separated. The cattle trade was steadily increasing, and inviting Indian attacks. In mid-summer 1872 thirty thousand head of cattle crossed New Mexico northward out of Texas. Two of the droves were attacked, and Apaches were suddenly more active in town and out. In Santa Fe, a reporter "noticed a band of Apaches curiously threading the streets and peering into private and public doors and windows. Those who imagine that the Indian is stoical and utterly oblivious to all that passes about him when beneath the eye of the 'paleface,' should have seen these wide-eyed, gaping mouth bummers, turning over children and colliding with posts and obstacles along the sidewalks as their faces were turned in a fixed stare and no noticeable emotion towards a fancy show window, a gay dress or some other equally common sight. Unlike the pueblos they were a filthy, cutthroat looking lot."

In the open ranchlands—in one instance only three miles from a United States fort—Apache raiders murdered and mutilated their victims: "his face was cut off (nose, mustache and beard)," and settlers called for harsh military reprisals. Elements of the grotesque continued in contrast to the life of grace and amenity which Lamy, and others, worked hard to bring to the local life. The Santa Fe Plaza in the autumn of 1872 was "never so dirty as now." Hay waggons and bull trains came there not only to sell their goods but also to camp, whose "debris" annoyed "the most frequented promenades and the most central business parts of the city." Citizens finally made a volunteer force to clean "the disgraceful appearance and . . . eye-sore." All the roads leading out of Santa Fe were barely passable by daylight, and not at all by night, and nothing was being done to improve them. Now and then a high wind drove stinging dust across the city, but as often as not was followed by a day so clear and air so mountain-pure and quiet that the citizens breathed deeply of the natural well-being which was as true of Santa Fe as its other qualities.

And when there was a feast of particular reverence to be observed, when splendor was appropriate, the bishop could officiate at the altar of an adobe church, vested in chasuble, maniple, and stole of white moiré, studded with precious stones, embroidered in red crosses, and laced and braided with gold bullion. The vestments had come from a Jesuit church in Paris as a donation to the mission of New Mexico.

Growth in what Lamy had begun continued now almost as if by natural law—all but the cathedral, where work went haltingly. The bishop often took the midday meal with the workers, serving them himself. Still, he could report in 1872 that including churches under construction he now had one hundred and eighty, and that he had forty private schools under instruction by priests, and five Loretto convents, whose schools were prospering, and that the Christian Brothers had up to two hundred and fifty scholars; and in the following year, that the first Santa Fe convent of the Lorettines had ordered the start of construction on their own new chapel, to cost thirty thousand dollars. It was to be Gothic in style, after the original inspiration of the Sainte Chapelle in Paris, however far short of the original the local style must necessarily fall. Projectus Mouly, who was the son of the architect of the cathedral, undertook the chapel. It was a serious responsibility for a youth of eighteen, especially since his architect father could not even work with him—Antoine Mouly was going blind, and eventually had to be returned home to France. In 1873 there was again discouraging doubt that construction of the cathedral could continue—the *"petite cathédrale en pierre"*—for lack of money. Times were hard in New Mexico, worse there than in the nation, where at large a severe financial depression brought panic to investors and failures to banks. On Lamy's cathedral, at one time, only ten men could be asked to work for pay.

V.

For the Pueblos

IN THE MID-1870s, A COMPLEX CONDITION involving the federal government, the Pueblo Indian culture, the state of education, and the Catholic and Protestant Churches in New Mexico and Arizona, gave high concern to both Lamy and Salpointe. The federal government regularly appointed agents for Indian affairs in the various western regions. The agent was to supervise education, among other factors of Indian life. In New Mexico, the agent welcomed the natural interest of the Protestant Churches in missionizing Indians, and in certain pueblos appointed resident teachers who were non-Catholics. But the Indian religious conversion dating from the days of the conquistadors was Catholic; and everywhere vestiges of the Franciscan teachings were present in the pueblos. Inroads upon these alarmed Lamy, particularly since he found evidence of neglect of even the simplest educational duties—quite apart from religious instruction itself—by the lay teachers.

In Arizona, Salpointe had no resources with which to counter the vigorously active free public schools which with continuing emigration were springing up in his area. Both bishops wrote to their sustaining Society in France describing the threat to Catholic teaching, and also stating the need to provide Indians with education in common knowledge indispensable to the modern world whose styles and standards followed the United States culture wherever it went. "At great sacrifice" Lamy stationed extra priests in the pueblo missions, but his view of a solution was a more ample one than that of simply increasing his teaching assignments.

It was his hope that he, rather than a layman appointed by Washington, might be made actual agent for the Pueblos. If this could be managed, he could then revive not only the Catholic culture of the Indian towns, but he could also create a comprehensive system of schooling now sadly lacking among the Indians. He moved to lay his plan before the proper authority in Washington. This turned out to be Brigadier General Charles Ewing, who came of a family which had belonged to Lamy's parish in his early Ohio mission days; and now the general, who was a child of six years when Lamy had last seen him, was stationed at the War Department, Washington, in the bureau which superintended Indian affairs.

In 1873 Lamy had already sent Ewing a preliminary report about the Pueblos. To acquaint him more fully with the Pueblo nature and tradition, the bishop now gave much time to composing what he called a "Short History of the Pueblo Indians of New Mexico," which he addressed to Ewing in February 1874. It was an essay of about ten thousand words. In his opening lines, he declared, "Now I am prepared to give you information satisfactory, I think, for any candid mind, based upon history, old records, manuscripts, traditions, with citations of the author they are taken from. There are no facts of history better proved," he went on, "than that the civilization of our

Pueblo Indians is contemporaneous with the discovery of New Mexico by the Spaniards who brought with them the Catholic faith and within a few years converted most of the Indians."

The "Short History" then went on to give an account of Pueblo life in colonial New Mexico throughout the two and a half centuries before his own arrival at Santa Fe in 1851. He touched upon the Pueblo Rebellion of 1680, saying that "the expulsion of the Spaniards from the country was, no doubt," caused partly by "the oppression and many abuses of the conquerors upon the Indians." With the Spanish restoration of 1692, the Pueblo missions were resumed until the withdrawal of the Franciscans early in the nineteenth century. In his own time he had done what he could to revive them; but the management of Pueblo life by United States civil authority had not been helpful and in some cases had been disastrous.

For one thing, in a pueblo where a Protestant faction had grown up among the Indians, hostility between its members and those of the Catholic majority had come about, so that a miniature religious war divided the community once so unified in its Christian beliefs, even while the ancestral pagan religious practices continued—those ways which lay at the heart of the Pueblo design of life. Further, Lamy was convinced that Indians could only be taught, at first, through the Spanish language in which they were proficient, and that their knowledge of English would have to come later. But the government lay teachers spoke only English, and the Indian children comprehended little enough of what they heard in school. Finally, in one pueblo which he cited, and used as an example (it was Laguna), the lay teacher held class only a few times in eight months, and gave himself leaves of absence for weeks and months at a time, for which he drew a hundred dollars a month, and "had a fine time of it." No wonder Lamy had been asked for Catholic teachers by some Pueblo authorities.

Now what he proposed to Ewing was that the government grant him a modest subsidy to set up a system of education in the Pueblos— he gave a brief description of all those in the Rio Grande region—at a cost of five hundred dollars for each of the twelve principal towns, or a total of six thousand dollars. This would be enough to "pay a teacher in each village, and also to procure some benches, tables, stationery, books, etc. The conventos or priest's residences could serve for school-rooms." For another six thousand dollars, he would be able to bring thirty or forty boys and girls a year to the sisters' and brothers' schools at Santa Fe and elsewhere, and pay for their room, board, clothing, and supplies. If the plan were approved, it would be well to include two thousand dollars more for an agency house in Santa Fe, where the Indian parents could stay when they came to town, "for if the Government gives us the agency for the Pueblos, we are sure to have some Indians every week, if not every day." One more detail: if the far-distant Moquis (seven pueblos) and the Navajos on their reservation were to be included, "it would take at least $4000 more." He hoped that by the means suggested, "the schools would be well attended and good results could be obtained with good management, prudence, and"—a phrase which bespoke his character and practice— "entire patience."

Lamy's proposal for his Indian agency came to nothing. Salpointe's alarm over free public (non-sectarian) education had no relief. Neither man had any deep experience of the American tradition of the separation of Church and State in all its implications. Lamy seemingly did not recognize that public tax monies could not be administered within the walls, actual or doctrinal, of the Church. But though he failed in his Indian plan, he once again revealed his sense of compassion, and his view of the needs of the community in his care.

vi.

Hard Times

IN THOSE LATER YEARS, Lamy said many times that the great poverty of his people would never be relieved until the arrival of the railroad, making transport and export, communication and cheaper goods, possible. He looked eagerly to the day when Santa Fe would be connected to the world by the speediest form of travel. Six regional or local railroad lines were optimistically incorporated for New Mexico in 1870—the South Park, the Eastern Colorado, the Merino Valley, the San Juan, the Galisteo, and the Santa Rita railways—but there was little enough product within the state to make them succeed as feeder lines unless they could connect with a main transcontinental line.

In 1874 tracks from the East were nearing Trinidad, Colorado, on the very boundary of New Mexico. But how slowly they came! It appeared that local businessmen, who stood most to gain by the coming of the transcontinental railroad, held back when asked to contribute through local bond issues to the expenses of building the line. Eastern capital, accordingly, was not in a hurry to invest alone. It was odd—every place which had prospered already had the rails.

Denver had known prodigious growth with all its industrial components—gas lines, street cars, water power, fire department, even city beautification, though it was true that many of the thousands of miners who had roared into Colorado failed to "strike it rich," and took their way out of the new state. But by then Denver relied on more than a single industry, and Machebeuf was as busy, ingenious, and lively as ever—though now and then his "passionate temper," as he himself called it, marred the happy animation of his rule. He had a spat with a nun, who viewed him as "very impulsive." One day she all but accused him of being a liar, or, as she put it, of "telling her a falsehood." There was fake nicety in the language, and her own impulsiveness, to which she admitted, earned her a suspension by the bishop. He was on record as being against women's suffrage—a form of independence, after all—and had printed a sermon against it and its agitators, who were "short haired women and long-haired men." In the end, Sister Fidelis agreed that she had gone too far.

Machebeuf's relative prosperity was in great contrast to the condition of New Mexico. In 1874 because of drought the harvest had failed so extremely that Lamy reported how one third of the population was suffering from famine. Resources were so scarce that not only was work on the cathedral threatened, but construction of a new hospital which Lamy had planned to build in four fine lots behind the cathedral had to be postponed.

In such hard times, it was, then, something of a surprise when added burdens were suddenly proposed for Santa Fe by Archbishop Peter Richard Kenrick of St Louis. Writing to both Machebeuf and Lamy on the same day, he proposed the separation of the see of Santa Fe from the province of St Louis, and the erection of a new province under an archbishop at Santa Fe, with Colorado and Arizona, and possibly Montana, as its suffragan dioceses. Machebeuf immediately forwarded his letter from Kenrick to Lamy; and Lamy noted in its margins, as to Montana, "no," and as to the whole proposal, "I would wait," and returned it to Denver. He elaborated these views in a direct reply to Kenrick.

First describing the character of the populations, and the numbers of Catholics in the Southwest, Lamy went on to state his opinion: ". . . it is safer to wait a few years." At the moment, apart from Denver, the Church's population was overwhelmingly Mexican. He thought that increasing immigration would bring more Anglo-American and German constituents to create a broader base of growth in the new society slowly emerging in the western territories. He believed that new natural boundaries would create themselves—the southern portion of Colorado combining with the northern part of New Mexico, and the northwestern portion of Texas with the southern portion of Arizona; and then each of these would require a new vicariate apostolic with its own bishop, in addition to those prelates already established in Santa Fe, Denver, and Tucson. Concerning Montana, he was decidedly of the view that it was much too far away from Denver, even, not to mention New Mexico, to be appropriately joined to Santa Fe. But he said, otherwise, "when these changes are made, then Sta F. will be the proper loc. for an archbc"—sending to Machebeuf his abbreviated notes for the full reply to Kenrick.

He had given, quite impersonally, his advice. Whether it would be followed no one could yet say. Episcopal synods and Vatican consistories would make their own decisions. Meanwhile, to celebrate Lamy's twenty-fifth anniversary—his silver jubilee—as bishop, Santa Fe was witness to ceremonies, both sacred and social, held with "pomp and rejoicing."

He had other quieter pleasures. On a fine hillside in the Tesuque Cañon about three or four miles from town, he had acquired in 1853 the small country property where he could retire for rest, meditation, concentrated work. There he had built a small lodge, consisting of two rooms—one a tiny chapel with its altar for his daily Mass, the other his combined sitting room and bedroom. He called it the Villa Pintoresca. It had a vast view of the Jemez Mountains, and nearer, the golden-pink barrancas of the eroded sandstone screens above Española. The play of light over all these at any time was marvellous, but especially so in early morning and in evening. The little *estancia* was his delight. He liked to receive people there. The road to it between the foothills and in the cañon of the little Tesuque River gradually grew more passable. "Good work has been done on the Bishop's ranch road," said the newspaper. "It forms one of the best rides out of the city. This is the work, we presume, of Bishop Lamy." Though other people rode, Lamy often walked the whole way to the lodge.

XI

ARCHBISHOP

1875–1880

i.

The Archbishop

KENRICK AND HIS ASSEMBLED BISHOPS, meeting in St Louis, went counter to Lamy's advice, and sent their recommendations to the Vatican: Santa Fe should become a metropolitan see, with Lamy as its first archbishop, and the apostolic vicars Machebeuf of Colorado and Salpointe of Arizona as his suffragans. On 12 February 1875, Pius IX, in consistory, decreed the establishment as proposed, named Lamy for the pallium, and bestowed a red hat upon an American for the first time. This was Archbishop John McCloskey of New York.

Lamy was absent on a ten-day pastoral visit when a letter came from Purcell to congratulate him on the promotion; but Lamy had not yet received any official notification. By April the news was general, and Machebeuf pointed out to his sister that the new province of Santa Fe had three bishops, all of them Auvergnats.

Affairs took Salpointe to New York during the spring, and there he was given a papal mission to carry out; for Monsignor Caesar Roncetti, who had arrived in New York to present the cardinal's biretta to McCloskey, brought also the pallium for Lamy, but after his voyage from Rome did not feel equal to the further journey to Santa Fe to bestow upon Lamy the badge of his new office. Instead, discovering that a bishop suffragan to Santa Fe was in town, Roncetti asked Rome to approve his giving the pallium to Salpointe for delivery to Lamy. The permission was granted, and Salpointe returned to New Mexico carrying the visible symbol of the rank of archbishop, with which Lamy would be solemnly vested.

The pallium signified that its wearer participated "in a particular way" in the very institution of the Pope's supreme pastoral office. It was worn only by patriarchs, primates, and archbishops. Unchanged since the sixth century, its form consisted of a collar made of a white woolen band "three fingers wide" which could be placed over the head upon the shoulders of the wearer. Lappets of the same width as the band hung from it front and back. It was woven and made according to ancient ritual and symbol. The wool was taken from two white lambs representing Christ, the Lamb of God, and the Good Shepherd. The lambs were blessed on the feast of St Agnes, 21 January, in the saint's basilica on the Via Nomentana at Rome, and the bands were woven from their wool by the Benedictine nuns of St Cecilia in Trastevere, who completed the fabric by embroidering six black crosses of silk on collar and lappets. The finished pallium was blessed by the Pope in St Peter's on 28 June, the eve of the feast of SS Peter and Paul, and was then placed in a silver urn, and the urn deposited in a cabinet under the Altar of the Confession over the tomb of St Peter, there to remain until taken away for presentation. An investiture of the pallium always followed celebration of the Mass and taking of an oath of allegiance to the Pope by the new recipient. The Latin word meant both cloak and pall. The pallium was buried with its holder. All arrangements went forward for Lamy's reception of it on 16 June 1875.

ii.

Jubilation

AT DAYBREAK nine puffs of cannon smoke followed by the thump of shots broke over Santa Fe from Fort Marcy on its height. The salute was followed by strains of music sounding from the bishop's garden, where the band of St Michael's College serenaded him in front of his house. Newly placed evergreen trees traced the lines of the streets. Since early morning, the living elements of a procession were seen gathering in the side streets where sodality banners stirred and shone in the fine air—it was a beautiful spring day. At nine o'clock there was movement around the cathedral. Clergy in vestments were gathering there, twenty priests who had been able to come from their distant missions, and the two bishops from Denver and Tucson, and the new archbishop himself. The old cathedral, within the yet incomplete shell of the new, was too small to receive the great crowd which was expected; and the investiture would take place in the open courtyard at the rear of St Michael's College next to the ancient chapel of San Miguel in College street.

Gradually the procession took form in Cathedral Place, and in its slow march went swaying down San Francisco street, glistening in color, sparkling with the gold of fringes and passementerie and bright ribbons and flowers carried in baskets, on the earthen street between the low adobe houses with their always flaking and always renewed walls. Over the low roofs rang the music of the Eighth Cavalry Band at the head of the march. The long line reached all the way back to the bishop's garden. Its head turned left to cross the little river of Santa Fe and proceed up College street. In the college patio the colonnades of the porticoes were twined with garlands of pine bough. An altar, backed by draped American flags, was waiting. Tribunes for the prelates and tents for the clergy and civil and military dignitaries were ranked near the altar. Holy societies with their banners, and girls in white, and boys wearing red ribbons, and nuns and brothers in their habits, and men and women of the laity, all escorted the archbishop, who walked beneath a "magnificent" purple canopy lately received from France. The college patio was large, and five thousand people filled it when the prelates were in their places of honor.

Hobbling his way to the altar, Machebeuf, who had come from Denver part-way by train, part-way by "a wretched coach," began to sing the pontifical High Mass, and the long chant of the liturgy drifted upon the open air. In all decorum and in such degree of splendor as the old poor city could provide, the solemn celebration brought pride to all present. After the Gospel the vicar general, Monsignor Eguillon, preached in Spanish, drawing a parallel between the ascent of David to the throne of Israel and the elevation of Lamy to the rank of metropolitan of the new province of Santa Fe. Salpointe gave a sermon in English. At the end of Mass, Machebeuf reminisced in English, speaking of his lifelong friendship with Lamy and his work side by side with him, and thirty-seven years found voice in his words.

Then the slender, fine figure on the central throne came forward to be robed in pontifical vestments. He knelt before Salpointe, who stood at the altar on which the pallium lay under a veil of red silk. Salpointe intoned the papal documents he had brought from New York, and finishing with those, took the pallium and faced the kneeling archbishop, on whose shoulders he placed it, saying,

"For the honor of Almighty God and the Blessed Mary, ever virgin, of the holy apostles, Saints Peter and Paul, of our Lord Pope Pius IX of the Holy Roman Church, and of the Church of Santa Fe confided to your care, we deliver to you the pallium taken from the tomb of Saint Peter, which signifies the plenitude of episcopal power, with the title and name of Archbishop, which you shall use within your church on certain days, as is determined in the privileges granted by the Apostolic See."

After bowing to Salpointe, Lamy turned to the people, and, thanking them all for the esteem and respect their presence showed for him, he spoke of what had come that day from Rome.

"If such honors," he said, with diffidence which was noticed, "had been the lot of such cities as New York, Boston, Philadelphia, which count their Catholics in hundreds of thousands, even by the half million, in the forefront of progress, which breathe wealth and life through every pore of the social body, what would be astonishing about that? But that the universal Father of the faithful has deigned to cast his eye upon our poor town of Santa Fe, lost in deserts and unknown to the whole world, is a favor which should arouse our feeling of the most lively gratitude toward the Sovereign Pontiff." He then paid a "neat tribute to the free republican institutions of the country," and the ceremony ended with the singing of the Te Deum, after which the excited throng conducted Lamy to his residence.

The day of celebration was one third finished. In the garden, a pavilion with tables had been set up for one hundred particular guests invited by the attending clergy. A fountain played between the tables, while the Eighth Cavalry musicians, in full-dress dark blues with light blue trousers and white gloves, provided continuous music. Many toasts sounded over the grand boards, and reached their climax when Acting Governor William G. Ritch (it was seen as meaningful that he, a Protestant, was warm in his praise of Catholic affairs) rose to speak a grave, courteous address containing learned allusions. The acting governor also later wrote a dispatch on thirty pages of foolscap for the New York *Herald,* doing the event, and his own efforts, full justice.

He rapidly sketched New Mexican history, beginning firmly if inaccurately with the Aztecs, and proceeding through the conquistador period to the present, included a sketch of Catholic culture in America deriving from the colony of Lord Baltimore. It was an easy step to a reference to America's freedom of religion. History obliged him to touch upon the condition of New Mexico at the time of Lamy's arrival, which so many there present could well remember—"the entire absence of any institutions of learning worthy of the name, and, to state it mildly, the not very flattering state of society among priests and people alike"; since when, he was quite certain, it would not be regarded as undue commendation when he said the "reforms, the general elevation of the moral tone, and the general progress . . . are very largely, and in some cases, entirely due to the wholesome precepts and examples which have shone forth upon this people from the living presence of the later Bishop, now the Archbishop of Santa Fe . . . the conservator of the public good . . . to know whom was only to admire and respect." By his presence and actions, Lamy, said the speaker, had brought recognition of the "worthiness of this people" from the Supreme Head of "the oldest and most numerous of Christian denominations," a denomination which had been chronicled by a Protestant historian, as "a Church which was great and respected before the Saxon had set foot upon Britain, before the Frank had passed the Rhine, when Grecian eloquence still flowed from Antioch, when idols were still worshipped at Mecca. Gentlemen, I thank you for your kind attention." The author telegraphed the *Herald* that "the address of Governor Ritch was delivered with distinct enunciation, and in a clear full voice; and was listened to with close attention and at the close cheered most spiritedly."

Lamy replied with a few words of thanks, and extended his encouragement to his priestly colleagues there present, and the celebration was adjourned until four o'clock, when Lamy and people came together again for the consecration of the archdiocese to the Sacred Heart, a sermon, and benediction of the Blessed Sacrament.

The evening belonged to the people. The plaza, most of Santa Fe, was illuminated by *farolitos* and *luminarios,* the cathedral was fronted with four illuminated transparencies showing portraits of Pius, Lamy, Machebeuf, and Salpointe, the cavalry band filled the plaza with a fine blare, there was a balloon ascension, the sky was full of fireworks, and Major José Sena, who was largely responsible for the organization of the day, spoke in Spanish, and the Hon. William Breedon in English. Everyone was present, everyone had contributed: "Jews and Protestants rivaled each other in the breadth of their generosity." The affair passed beyond a religious event, and was taken to heart as a *"fête nationale."* It ended with a torchlight procession which escorted Lamy from the plaza back to his garden house.

Dutifully expressing his thanks to the Pontiff and reporting the events of the day to Rome, Lamy contented himself with remarking that all of them were "equally brilliant," and that the investiture had been accomplished "with all the solemnity which our poor capital allowed us." He was soon concerned with simpler matters, for daily life had its claims also, and it was observed in a day or two that he was "painting and kalsomining his residence in a very tasteful manner . . . which gave a most pleasing relief to the primitive adobe."

Anthony Lamy, the pastor at Manzano, Valencia County, had been unable to go to Santa Fe to see his uncle receive the pallium—in fact, had not even heard of the event until the archbishop mentioned it to him in a letter afterward. "We live here in Manzano," wrote Anthony to his sister at the Santa Fe convent, "in a desert & separated from the rest of mankind at least in communication. . . . You must not forget to send me a good description of the great ceremony which took place in Santa Fe for I dont expect it from anybody else." Sister Francesca kept him happy by writing often, for they had much feeling for each other, and she never forgot how she would play him a musical treat in his earlier visits to the convent. Late in 1875, he wrote her that he had been to the "Rio Bonito"—in the Capitan country southeast of Manzano—visiting the villages and Fort Stanton. At the fort he went to the cell of "a poor fellow condemned to death & stayed with him for more than an hour giving him all the spiritual consolation in my power." He had done this against advice, for there was fever about and he himself was not feeling well. But he continued to visit the condemned man and at the end, rode in the same cart with his body to consign it for burial. Already ill, Anthony was open to contagion; caught the fever; and died on 7 February 1876, at the age of twenty-nine.

The archbishop was notified. The bells of Santa Fe tolled for Anthony Lamy. The Loretto sisters knew who was dead, but none could face telling Sister Francesca. It was her uncle who came to her and said,

"Marie, the bells are tolling. They are tolling for your brother."

The nuns said that she never again touched her piano.

...

iii.

A Mile a Day

THE DESERT NATURE at its best was held in a precarious balance of rainfall, the growth of grass and other vegetation, and the survival of people and animals. In good years, there was barely supply for modest enterprises. In bad, everything was sadly affected; and protracted drought such as held the land in a long sort of breathless pause in the seventies and eighties was a calamity touching upon the lives of all. Lamy repeatedly described such a condition to his lifeline in Paris. In a single season forty thousand lambs starved to death when the grasses failed. Other crops for human use died of the heat and the dry, with the result that a number of outlying missions had to be abandoned, for there was nothing to sustain the missioner when the people had all they could do to keep themselves alive. In the hot sand-storms which came with the drought, a diarist noted that the "bottom of the Rio Grande appeared as if smoking," for the river itself was dry in many places. Pastoral visits were risky when water was scarce in the great overland stretches, and not only the settlements but the Apaches and other raiders felt the privations, and once again opened their persistent campaigns of depredation, for they were not people who grew food for themselves, but ranged to prey upon the produce of the town Indians and the villages and ranches of the old settlers. The Army mounted expeditions, notably against the leader of the southern New Mexico Apaches, the notorious and skillful Victorio, and Fort Stanton was in a state of constant alert, as troopers rode out to do battle in the White Mountains and the Capitan Range, and the deserts which lay athwart the Rio Grande.

And, too, in the desert and mountain nature, lay the opposite excess —that of sudden cloudburst when the drought gave way to violent floods which did faster and even greater damage in a few days than a decade of drought. The rude bridges of the Rio Grande were often destroyed in spring floods and some had to be renewed annually; and if a promising little crop was rising in the valley fields, it was wiped out by the tearing waters, and the riverside villages of earth were some-times engulfed and melted away into the fast, tumbling muddy flow of the river into which all mountain tributaries were tipped so violently. In one town five hundred families were flooded out in 1884.

Again, then, travel to certain of his districts was impossible at such times for Lamy; and for all the causes of his troubles of a material nature, he was certain that the principal cure would be the completion of the railroads, transcontinental and local. The lines would imme-diately unite communities now separated by hazardous journeys made alone and in the open. Indians would be far less effective against iron locomotives and thickly ribbed wooden coaches and heavy speed. Goods and produce could be brought quickly to needy populations. A web of easy communication would appear. In the nation, railroads had followed the pioneer waggon trains; and settlement and prosperity and stability had followed railroads. The same must come—he knew it would come—to New Mexico, as it had come already to Colorado, and even, from the west, to Arizona. But how slow was the progress, and how great the obstacles, while he continued to make his exhaust-ing trips by horseback, with his black leather sling bag, or in a buggy, which held his travelling trunk of slats of pale wood covered with horsehide to which the hair still clung, and which was lined with printed wallpaper, which he had bought in Lyon from Mm Condamin Fils, in the Quai St Antoine, the *Fabrique de malle et articles de voyage en tous genres.*

It was no wonder, then, that he was one of the strongest workers in the promotion of the railroads for New Mexico. As he summed it up for Paris, trying as always to make them *see:* "Our territory, although in U.S. is separated from other provinces owing to its remote situation and being surrounded by Indian tribes with no railways, no navigation, scarcely a few bad roads. The nearest seaport is about 450 leagues away, and the railway 100 leagues."

But in 1875, coming in what seemed like agonizing slowness to the New Mexicans, but like titanic speed to the railroad workers, the line which was to be the Atchison, Topeka and Santa Fe was advancing at a rate of a mile a day after passing Las Animas, Colorado—the river settlement which Lamy had come to so often on his horse. In Boston, President Nickerson of the railroad wired orders in 1878 to the railhead at Topeka, "Go on as rapidly as possible to Raton Pass. When that is sure we shall organize this end and go through. We mean . . . business. . . . There will be no looking back." A day later he had a shrewd, impersonal thought: "See if we can not save something by employing Mexican labor." The *New Mexican* kept a sharp eye on rail progress, and saw with approval "the speedy extension of the rails southward as far as Santa Fe" which would open up "the wealthy regions of Southern Colorado, New Mexico and the San Juan mines."

It was all the more a stunning disappointment when instead of coming to Santa Fe, the railroad, reaching a natural turning point for the capital, merely established there a way station which they called Lamy after the bishop's former property there, and moved directly on to Albuquerque. It appeared that certain citizens of Santa Fe, knowing the usual "good thing" in business, had bought property along the old Santa Fe Trail by which the rails would most naturally have approached Santa Fe, and had demanded a price for it which the line refused to pay. The engineering difficulties for the line to the capital were also more expensive than anticipated. Santa Fe was dismayed. Of all times when a commercial lift was needed it was the worst in which to discourage the benefits which the rails would bring. There was depression in the country as a whole, and it was especially acute for New Mexicans. No native workers were used in the line construction after all. Herds and flocks were starving to death. Near-famine conditions prevailed in parts of the diocese. Somehow the railway must be brought to town.

A committee was formed, with Lamy as a member, and a bond issue was proposed to the people to finance a spur line from Lamy junction to the capital—a distance of seventeen miles. The archbishop was the first to sign the petition circulated to the voters. The *New Mexican* strongly urged its approval. It would be expensive—the Topeka treasurer of the line estimated that it cost $12,000 to lay a mile of track. Santa Fe voted its bond issue of $150,000 by a vote of three to one. The future was coming after all.

Its immediate terms, necessarily, were all which Lamy and the others saw. When the rails were ready, he said, "the working of the mines, the raising of the flocks, the cultivation of vineyards, will change entirely the condition of things. We will be able to employ laborers at more reasonable wages, construct houses and churches as in the east. We may probably see factories established in this country, where wool is to be obtained in great abundance. In this general increase of resources, this mission will without doubt find extension and a way of sustaining the great, heavy loads, which are always found in new undertakings."

Who was not excited by the news that "the monster engine to be used on the switchback over the Raton Pass, on the Atchison, Topeka and Santa Fe railroad, has arrived at Atchison on its way west"? Built at the Baldwin locomotive works in Philadelphia, it weighed 188,200 pounds, and would pull a train of seven loaded cars over the mountains. In Santa Fe, the people were topically and "justly proud of the elegant [new] establishment which is known to the admiring public as the Broad Gauge, and patronized by all who prefer the genuine article to a miserable compound." The finest wines, liquors, and cigars were to be had there. "Hospitality is said to be part of a gentleman's religion," mused the *New Mexican*. "If this be correct, Stimson, of the Broad Gauge, must be a very religious gentleman," and evidently the public continued to make the Broad Gauge their headquarters, to enjoy "all the luxuries served in such a superb manner by Joe and Harry."

On 9 February 1880, ex-Governor George T. Anthony of New Mexico telegraphed to President Nickerson at Boston: "Atchison, Topeka, and Santa Fe are united by an unbroken band of iron, and a continuous path of commerce." The *New Mexican* trumpeted "NEW MEXICO'S TRIUMPH," and added, "the Old Santa Fe Trail passes into oblivion." The last spike was driven by General Edward Hatch, representing the Army establishment in the territory, by Chief Justice L. Bradford Prince, and by the territorial governor, General Lew Wallace, who was occupying the old palace in the plaza and working on the final chapters of *Ben Hur*. A parade with bands, flags, school children, citizens, and carriages celebrated the event, and all were told, in florid oratory, of the day's significance. A month later Governor

Wallace was able to write to the Secretary of the Interior, "It gives me pleasure to report New Mexico in a state of quiet. A large immigration is pouring in under inducement of rich mineral discoveries and increased railroad facilities."

Lamy felt almost immediately an easing of material concerns. The railroad system granted all clergy free passage and half rates for the shipment of goods and supplies for church and school. In the continuing drought, famine was averted by the freighting of food. Prices of everything dropped. The towns to the south were connected to the main east-west line by New Mexico's internal railroad companies. Trains for the east left Santa Fe every morning at eight, with "sleeping car berths secured at station." Trains for Albuquerque and the south departed daily at three in the afternoon.

Maintenance of the lines called for a large labor force, but as yet, few of the native New Mexicans were employed by the main railroad. Lamy wrote to the company asking that they be recruited for the well-paying work, saying "let them bring their wages to their families and let them secure the necessities of life and honest comforts to which a family have a right." There could be blessings in material things. In 1880, on 17 March, the first train of the Southern Pacific went west to reach Tucson. As it connected with the long spur of the Santa Fe reaching from Belen to El Paso, travel to Arizona was now possible in great comfort. A year later Lamy and Machebeuf and a Father Phillips of the Denver diocese were carried in Pullman Palace coaches to Tucson, for the first time with dispatch and safety, there to pay a visit to their old confrère Salpointe.

iv.

Styles

LIKE ANYONE moving from his own culture to an alien one, Lamy brought his with him, and when conditions allowed, he bestowed what he believed to be its best character upon an environment new to him. He had not been alone in viewing the adobe style of New Mexican construction as primitive, often barbaric, by its very nature subject to rapid deterioration. Even so, he could recognize the native appropriateness, in surroundings of poverty and social simplicity, of the New

Mexican style which was so directly derived from the hive-like enclosures seen in the terraced towns of the Pueblo Indians; and it was only natural that the Franciscan friars, the Spanish colonizers of the sixteenth century, coming into the strange land, with few engineering resources or imported building materials, should build their own churches and houses after the manner of the Indians. New Mexico's isolation for centuries embedded the style of these as a tradition, which served the Spanish and later Mexican settlements well. Harsh necessity caused even European Spaniards to do with what was to be had, even if they remembered the great shrines and palaces, the castles and *estancias,* of Spain, and would have had them again if they could.

But Lamy came with a time of growing communication and transport, with a fixed vision of what was seemly. The Romanesque, the Gothic, the mansard styles of France were what had always enclosed the religious activities of his early life; and at Santa Fe, when it was time to build, it was the manner of these that he brought to his low-storied earthen city—the reminders of France which affected the whole material character of a place as his French clergy were affecting its spiritual life. That a remote imitation was all that could be managed he would have been willing to agree. But even so, in his view, what he wrought seemed more suitable, more beautiful, than what he had found.

Twentieth-century immigrants from the Anglo-American East and elsewhere found the old New Mexican atmosphere appealing for its very difference from the commonplace sophistication of their brick and wooden cities, with all their mechanical uses; and some held Lamy to blame for the changes in character he had put upon the cities of New Mexico in his time. But what such new settlers saw were not the Santa Fe, the Albuquerque, the Taos, of his time, in all the dusty, desiccated poverty they then showed, where every street was like a section of barnyard, and walls and roofs cracked and shed their substance under long drought and infrequent but violent downpour. Any photograph of Santa Fe in the previous century bore the likeness of a run-down collection of sheds and byres, corrals and poor open fields, irregular paths and alleys and stretches of wall, all in the same color of dried earth mixed with straw; and with only the church building rising higher than the hand of a man reaching to touch the ceiling.

It was this view of the place which had moved the soldiers, traders, and immigrants of the time to their descriptions of the city as a prairie-dog town, a random collection of flatboats grounded on a dusty plain, an enlarged scatter of dusty bricks lying about. If he had been an artist Lamy might have seen what later comers saw in the harmony between the landscape and the human dwellings made from its clay and the undemanding life of the native people. He might have felt the passionate devoutness of the Mexicans as they expressed this in their natively carved and painted devotional pieces, with all the blood and suffering and fear of God which honestly primitive crafts could simulate. These were appropriate for the Spaniard and Indian to venerate, for to them, holy tortures found some luxurious echo in their temperaments. Later collectors loved them less for religious than for aesthetic reasons.

But Lamy knew also the European religious art of his time, which was already turning bland in the spirit of *bondieuserie* reproduced in commercial plaster and print. Machine processes banished aesthetic awe which was the inheritance of sixteen centuries of Christian conviction. So it was that in his labors to reach both economy, utility, and dignity in his monuments to piety and decorum, Lamy drew upon his own native tradition with its inheritance of masterpieces of style in daily use since the thirteenth century—and also on the growing industry which produced plaster saints and lithographed Stations of the Cross. In doing so he wrought results which were admired in their time, when progress meant change, especially in matters of style and taste. It was left to a later age to find beauty inherent in the Spanish colonial and Pueblo traditions of building, and to mingle with these the convenient niceties of plumbing and other technical construction so that prosperous modern settlers were able to have their native culture both ways.

It was the poverty of the environment which prevented high aesthetic achievement of the Old World sort in the bishop's buildings. Falling between two traditions—the grand European and the uncultivated but fervent native—Lamy's style reached only a gesture and a function of devout memory.

Now, as the cathedral began to take shape, the Moorish arches of Spain, as repeated in the French Romanesque in many places such as Vézelay and—closer to the old home—Notre-Dame de Port, and even Lempdes, began to show. "The front," wrote the archbishop too confidently at the start, "is of a variety of stones, yellow and red, representing a mosaic. . . . The front has columns ornamented with capitals on which large figures *en relief* are nicely worked." He was speaking of the ideal, not the real, but what was real enough was that the cathedral had no roof as yet—would not have for years—but he said it would be a "stone arch roof." He estimated that the church would measure two hundred by sixty-six, "all cut stone in the Roman Byzantine style." One of the southwest entrances, observed the *New Mexican*, was beginning "to indicate the fine and massive style of the architecture [and] makes us impatient to see the whole imposing plan completed."

Work was advancing in the nave in 1873, with a wide central aisle separated from two narrower side aisles by the first indications of plain stone columns, which were to be surmounted by Corinthian capitals and connected by semicircular arches which recalled the interior of Notre-Dame de Bonne Nouvelle at Lempdes. The adobe north transept and sanctuary of the old cathedral would have to remain part of the new—it was impossible to know where funds would come from to replace these in addition to the old nave. But the trouble was even more general, for despite all efforts to continue, work on the cathedral was halted from 1873 until 1878. Lamy had already spent fifty thousand dollars and in 1875 he said it would take as much more to complete the new stone section, and a year later he had to report that in fact he would need twenty-five thousand francs a year for seven or eight years to reach the end of the project.

Even at that, he saw that the original plans would have to be simplified—no carved figures could now be expected to take their places in the façade, and the only "mosaic" effect would survive in alternate large red and yellow blocks of sandstone in the arches of door and shallow niches on the ground level at front and sides. The modifications which had to be accepted were planned during the five-year hiatus in the construction. A new architect was found to replace the departed Antoine Mouly, but proved unsatisfactory. The cathedral rectors in turn assumed responsibility for what could be done, and in fact when work was resumed in 1878, directed much of it. But again the progress was slow, falling behind schedule, and again for lack of means to pay for workmen and supplies. In 1881 "the good and saintly archbishop was never in greater need than now."

But during all the intermittent labor on the exterior of the new cathedral, services continued within the old. Going there was like passing through an outer shell to enter an inner tabernacle. The great ornament of the adobe interior was the carved and polychromed stone reredos above the main altar. When Lamy sold the *Castrense* in 1859, he had had the reredos removed from there to the cathedral, and had put the newly arrived Father Salpointe in charge of it to replace an old tinselled altar piece which newcomers had seen with such amazement after the mid-century war. It was fitted into the sanctuary, which as in other native churches narrowed like the head of a coffin, and the adobe plaster embraced it in dusty plainness. The carved stone panels and their faded colors showed the more beautifully for the starkness of the enclosing walls, in one of which a humble wooden door frame opened into the sacristy. The eighteenth-century carving was thought to be "stucco and fresco work" when an American captain saw it in 1881. He gave one of the last descriptions of the interior of the old St Francis Cathedral after he attended Mass there and, later, vespers, on Holy Thursday in 1881.

"I arrived," he wrote, "as the bells were tolling and was fully rewarded for my trouble. The old church is in itself a study (the parroquía) of great interest; it is cruciform in shape, with walls of adobe, bent slightly out of perpendicular. Along these walls, at regular intervals, are arranged rows of candles in tin sconces with tin reflectors. The roof is contained by bare beams. The plaster work of the interior evinces a barbaric taste, but there is much worthy of admiration. The ceilings are blocked out in square panels tinted in green; two of the walls are laid off in pink and two in light brown. The pictures are, with scarcely an exception, tawdry in execution, loud colors predominating, no doubt with good effect upon the minds of the Indians. . . . In one place, a picture of the Madonna and Child represents them both with gaudy crowns of gold and red velvet."

He was fascinated by the styles of the service, both the august and the plebeian. "The vestments of Archbishop Lamy and the attendant priests were gorgeous fabrics of golden damask." The archbishop's throne was a walnut armchair carved in motifs of Victorian Gothic which rose along sides and top to a tall pinnacle flanked by finials resembling miniature pyramids connected by their bases. The arms, seat, and back were upholstered in dark cherry velvet bound by gold tape. The whole—surely the grandest piece of furniture in Santa Fe— stood on casters, and expressed a character of both ceremonial and period style.

"The congregation," continued the captain with growing amazement, "was largely composed of women and children almost all of whom were of Mexican or Indian blood, swarthy countenances, coal black manes and flashing eyes being the rule, although there was by no means a total absence of beautiful faces. Fashion had made some innovations upon the ancient style of dress; cheap straw bonnets and the last Chatham street outrage in the shape of cheap hats were ranged alongside the traditional tapalo and rebosa [sic]." There was an excellent sermon, but the captain could scarcely hear it, for "such an epidemic of coughing, hawking, spitting, and snuffling seized upon the congregation that it was impossible for me, a foreigner, to make out one third of what was being said," which was "utterly ruined in its effect by the continuous barking of the women and children. The sermon over, Archbishop Lamy washed the feet of the twelve altar boys, a custom which I have never before seen in this country."

At various times, Lamy raffled off his horses, his carriage, to gain a little money for the building, and most of the meagre funds regularly due to the archdiocese went for the cathedral expenses. The local citizens were as generous as the times allowed—Major José Sena in the end managed to raise contributions totalling $135,000, the Contreras family gave $10,000, José Leandro Perea $5000, and the Protestants, Jewish, and military residents were responsive with gifts; but there never seemed enough, either of money or time. The Jews of Santa Fe were happy to see the Hebrew symbol for Yahweh carved and set within a stone triangle over the main door, and some said this was done by Lamy out of gratitude for Jewish support—though theologians pointed out that the triangle and the Hebraic letters symbolized the Holy Trinity enclosing the Godhead, a device long known in traditional use by the Church.

In 1884 the new nave would be closed over by the vaultings of the roof, finished in volcanic tufa from the Cerro Mogino twelve miles from Santa Fe. The originally planned dimensions would then be seen in their reduced measure: from the front to the transepts, one hundred twenty feet; width, sixty feet; height of nave, fifty-five feet. The towers first designed to reach upward in three diminishing drums would never have their spires topping off at one hundred thirty-five feet, but would stop short by eighty-five feet—a modification proper for both aesthetic and engineering considerations, since the planned height was out of proportion to the scale of the rest, and the added weight might have caused the spires to fall. The fundamental land of the site, porous with generations of old graves, seemed in a constant state of settling—so much so that the architect finally in charge (it was Machebeuf's nephew Michael) added subordinate arches to uphold the main side arches of the nave to arrest cracking which had already begun. The walls of the nave were not strictly parallel—a possible reflection of the original conformation of the old adobe walls which they were to replace, and which, in their imprecision, had given such touching evidence of the craftsman's hand upon the very surface.

The year 1884 would mark a great stage, however inconclusive, in the work of making the cathedral, when an extraordinary enterprise took place. The stone enclosure was complete as far as the adobe sanctuary and side chapel. Old St Francis's stood complete within the new; and now the citizens of Santa Fe, on a volunteer basis, came to take down, brick by brick and timber by timber, the original church; and for weeks carried these elements out the new stone door to waiting waggons until nothing was left of the original nave, and the new columns and arches and vaulting were revealed in their stark, plain, but fine symmetry. The new walls were joined to the earthen walls of the old transepts. The cathedral had its complete interior, made of both new and old; and in an eloquent way its contrasting styles and materials spoke for the history—heritage and experience—embraced by Lamy's life. In the dirt floor of the sanctuary (compacted dust carpeted over) Lamy would finally direct that two graves be dug and walled with concrete where the archbishops of Santa Fe would lie, the graves to be in line with the epistle side of the high altar.

The French inheritance was most fully realized when the Chapel of Our Lady of Light at the Loretto convent was completed in 1878. Of a much smaller scale than the cathedral, the chapel represented less of a continuing burden financially. Young Projectus Mouly had given it his time as architect during the five-year lapse of construction on St Francis's. It was believed that the chapel was built after memories of the Sainte Chapelle in Paris; and in greatly more humble terms—heavy where the original was light, stolid where the other was elegant—it did make certain allusions to its great model. It rose, slender and narrow, in the Gothic style, with rows of finials along the tops of the walls against the steep-sloping red roof. The chapel was twenty-five feet wide and seventy-five deep, including the sanctuary. Shallow stone and mortar buttresses stood against the walls at symmetrical intervals. An extended crown-like needle rested on top of the roof—though at the sanctuary end rather than above the center of the nave as in Paris. There was a rose window in the façade, and the main door was arched and decorated with trefoils and free-standing articulated pilasters. Arches and lesser windows were set in the front under the sharply angled roof line. The ochreous gray stone like that of the cathedral, and the volcanic material for the roof, came from Lamy's nearby quarries. Windows of stained glass had been ordered from France and were installed in time for the consecration performed on 25 April 1878, by Monsignor Eguillon, vicar general, and chaplain of the convent.

The Loretto sisters saw the work proceed without interruption, though there were certain difficulties. Projectus Mouly was an energetic worker—he once rode to Denver on a burro to obtain a rotary stone crusher—and he was also an artist with a strong vision. When certain "persons in authority criticized his work" as architect and engineer of the chapel, asking for changes in the design, he took offense, refused to agree to alterations, resigned, and, declared a watchful and sympathetic nun, fell into bad company. He wrote to his father in France telling what had happened, even giving reassurances that his new companion, with his fault (probably drinking), of which the father knew, would not endanger him. But it was not long until Projectus died of pneumonia in St Vincent's Hospital.

Yet work on the chapel continued without interruption; and the sisters by their prudent financial management of their income-producing school evidently faced no such crises as Lamy with his cathedral. They imported from France a harmonium for the choir loft—an instrument by Debain, who described himself as *"Inventeur de l'harmonium,"* and one who held a patent "By appointment to the Emperor." With an oak veneer case, a single manual, and two carpeted treadles, the harmonium had, in addition to the usual stops, several which made "effects" possible—a saxophone (after the horn invented in Belgium in 1840), a musette or bagpipe, accordion, a celesta, and, for ardent moments, the *tremblant.* The entire chapel "so creditable to the Territory," said the *New Mexican,* was "entirely due to the efforts and consideration of Archbishop Lamy, who has given the work from the commencement his personal attention and supervision." He was so often at the construction site that, as with the cathedral builders, he would take his lunch with the masons and carpenters of the chapel. Completed before any of the other foreign buildings of the city, the chapel by itself gave a strong first statement of the forces of change.

More were to come. A few weeks before the Loretto chapel was dedicated, the Christian Brothers began to demolish their old college farther up the lane known as College street. In the middle of the month the cornerstone was laid for a two-storey building with a third storey incorporated in a mansard roof. A tall central cupola rose at the center. The walls were made of adobes—the college quickly became celebrated as the tallest adobe building erected in the Southwest. It stood just south of the old chapel of San Miguel, which was in a dilapidated condition since its adobe towers had collapsed during a strong storm, to lie in heaps of rubble against the front. The new college rose upon the contributions raised by Brother Botolph, the president. Various parishes and towns gave money, many individuals gave sheep, others oxen, heifers, a goat, lumber, until the building cost of $19,362 was met. With that structure, once again central France came into view. In its long, three-tiered façade, its Mansard roof, its ranks of symmetrical windows, it was akin, even if remotely, to the seminary of Mont-Ferrand, where the archbishop and so many of his clergy had taken their studies; and in its long dim narrow corridors, ribbed in dark wood, with classrooms and faculty quarters on the first two floors, and dormitories on the third behind the gable windows, it brought the very image of a propriety never before seen in such purpose at Santa Fe.

It stood also as strong evidence of the achievements in education of the Brothers, under the rule of their order across the world; and the other New Mexico cities where they maintained schools could see St Michael's as the monument to an ideal of education which, even as later secular schools and colleges came rapidly to life, first helped the territory to join the world. Again the visible character of Santa Fe knew change from the old manner of three centuries of flat earthen roofs where grass took seed.

The last of the religious buildings to come with Lamy's program of building in the alien style was the academy of the Loretto sisters. It stood just to the south of the unfinished cathedral, and was completed in 1881. Again, it was a building of adobe, rising sixty feet to three storeys, with a pointed cupola supporting a cross. Its manner reflected mid-nineteenth-century continental architecture, with a mansard roof faced in slate from St Louis which Mother Magdalen in one of her last official acts went personally to buy and bring home. Again the sisters, with Lamy's firm support, proceeded on their own to create a building of dignity, decorously in harmony with the sophisticated idiom of its time, in contrast to the simple fabrications of Santa Fe, which in outline so often resembled the drawings of children unencumbered with any but local, and locally sufficient, manners. Conviction and energy saw the venture to a successful finish. "We started our own brickyard and opened our own quarry," said Mother Magdalen, "had our own lime burnt to order and our own lumber sawn by our own natives. . . ."

The adobe walls were plastered in stucco. Carved wooden cornices and window frames and porch details gave the building a strict charm; and now the chain of Lamy's buildings reached from Cathedral Place up College street and across Santa Fe Creek to the new St Michael's College. All of these loomed over the town. All served the imperatives of the now expanding society; and all finally made the next invasion of style—that of the eastern Americans with their red brick houses, their middle western Victorian commercial and domestic buildings— seem like a proper expression of the times: the territorial epoch which finally made Lamy's edifices less exotic, until the twentieth century's rediscovery and adaptive restoration of the original character of Santa Fe's first three centuries.

With the greater facilities of the new St Michael's College, Lamy began an experiment in the education of a small group of Indian youths from the Pueblos. The federal government, at public expense, was already sending young Indians to two Protestant Indian schools— one at Albuquerque, the other at Carlisle, Pennsylvania. Lamy was concerned for the loss of their religious belief and habit by these students; and in 1878 he was able to persuade the government to guarantee one hundred dollars each to pay the expenses of twenty-two students who would be enrolled in a special department of the college. It was a small beginning, but it was expected to increase as the learning of the Indian youths proved itself. One priest who examined the class was "astonished at their remarkable proficiency in reading and writing English and Spanish." He was equally impressed by their progress in arithmetic, and he cited their otherwise commonplace gains because it was thought and said by many "that the Indian is sluggish and slow in learning, whereas the reverse is the case," which could be proved by every mission school in the pueblos—but the priest-teacher could visit the pueblo classes only once a month.

Yet when the time came for the government to send its promised payment for the Indian scholars at Santa Fe, nothing was sent, and all efforts, including a memorial to Congress, failed to obtain the funds. The Commissioner for Indian Affairs at Washington—one Price—wrote that "he could not entertain the idea." Lamy bitterly concluded that the whole government was as anti-Catholic as the President—U. S. Grant. Since neither the college nor the archdiocese could afford the needed twenty-two hundred dollars for the young Indians' annual expenses, much less look forward to an expansion of the program, the special Indian class was dropped after a year. The government schools, "under the special direction of Presbyterians and Methodists," prospered and grew with public funds.

Lamy's other schools—those of the Lorettines, the Sisters of Charity, the Christian Brothers, the Jesuits, variously in Santa Fe, Taos, Los Alamos, Albuquerque, Socorro, and elsewhere—made their way steadily, responding to immigration from the East, and to good management.

At the Santa Fe Loretto convent there was a change of administration: Mother Magdalen Hayden, who had accepted the post of superior on the bank of the Missouri River in 1852, was obliged by rheumatic ill health to resign her post. She was succeeded by Marie Lamy, who became Mother Francesca. Now approaching full middle age, she had grown into a capable maturity, and her appointment was popular with her sisters. She and her uncle remained as close as ever in affection and temperament; and their sense of family was sustained by the nearness of Marie's surviving brother Jean and his wife, who lived in Santa Fe for some years. Mother Francesca, continuing the policies of her predecessor, was able to offer new courses of instruction added since those announced in earlier years, and now the making of young ladies (of whom "propriety of deportment, politeness, and personal neatness" were required), would include the arts of "Wax flowers, materials furnished, $20 per course"; "Artificial or Hair flowers, $10"; "Harp, $30"; "Guitar, instrument furnished by pupil,

$40." Non-Catholic pupils "were not required to assist at the religious instruction given to the Catholics."

The Sisters of Charity, led by the energetic Sister Blandina Segale, pressed forward with the building of an "industrial school" at Santa Fe, which was the last project erected under the supervision of young Projectus Mouly. It was opened in 1880 with a festival concert, with Mr Wedles at the piano, and a vocal solo by Mrs Dr Symington; but its career was inauspicious, and after a few years it was obliged to close down.

At the same time, a non-sectarian academy was flourishing. Founded in 1877, it was in its fourth year in 1881, with distinguished overseers including Bishop George K. Dunlop of the Protestant Episcopal Church, Acting Governor Ritch, Chief Justice Prince, and members of the leading families of Spiegelberg and Catron. Strong new elements of the society were in their turn reaching for amenity as Lamy had done since the beginning of his work in the vast and disorderly diocese. With the coming of the railroads and new settlers, the Southwest was drawn more closely into the national character; and a diversity of styles in ways of expression was inevitable, and, under the idea of the federal republic, desirable. But the Great American Desert was slow to lose all of its Spanish colonial and western frontier nature.

v.

Atmospheres

VERY MUCH A CITIZEN of his capital, Lamy—many spoke of him as the "first citizen"—was open to visitors, and was also frequently seen walking in the plaza or taking his way to errands. The town he saw was as lively as ever, but there was a sense of good government for New Mexico ever since the arrival of Lew Wallace to preside in the Governor's Palace in 1878. "It appears that the Territory has been afflicted, as most new Territories are, with a ring of rascals, who congregate about the seat of government and pluck the tax-payers in every possible way. Wallace has smashed this ring right and left, and has his pay in the gratitude of the people."

The governor was seen as "above reproach, a man of strong principles, and a student of humanity." He set about halting the Lincoln

County War in southeastern New Mexico, where rival factions were terrorizing the country, with William Bonney, a youthful murderer calling himself Billy the Kid, as the leading criminal. Wallace posted an award of five hundred dollars for his capture, and Bonney responded—so said Mrs Wallace—by declaring, "I mean to ride into the plaza at Santa Fe, hitch my horse in front of the palace, and put a bullet through Lew Wallace." One of her friends warned her to "close the shutters at evening, so the bright light of the student's lamp might not make such a shining mark of the governor writing till late on *Ben Hur*. . . ." But instead, Bonney was brought to Santa Fe and jailed. Later he was returned to Lincoln for trial, escaped from the old courthouse after killing two guards, and was shot to death himself by Sheriff Pat Garrett in a dark room at Fort Sumner.

The peace was broken also in Arizona, where Salpointe was working to build a hospital. Not only Apaches, now, but "cow boys" were on the rampage in cow-stealing raids. Apaches also in southern New Mexico and Utes in Colorado were sowing terror again. Wallace asked Washington for authority to raise troops, but the War Department replied—in the face of his report of outrages—that it had "no information as to the nature of the outbreak or number of hostiles," and permission was denied. Satisfactions must remain merely personal, then. *Ben Hur* had been published, the first edition of five thousand copies was instantly exhausted, and "the author smiles." Lamy received an autographed copy from General Wallace, with whom he was on excellent terms.

Business was quickening, the city was expanding. Lamy "heartily" endorsed the growing manufacturing interests of Santa Fe. The Church owned considerable property by now, and that part which contained the cathedral, the hospital, and the orphanage, offered a logical site for the extension of the street running east from the plaza. A committee was planning to call upon him to grant the right of way for Palace avenue, and he was known to be willing. The street would run all the way to the eastern limits of the city, into the very foothills of the mountains. By the opening up of the new thoroughfare, the hospital would stand on the very edge of the street. Railroad promotion was also in the air, and one diarist ironically thought new spur lines would depopulate Las Vegas and Santa Fe, and he noted also "a large hotel scheme" for the ruins of Pecos. "Schemes," he said, "and scheming, and nothing else." In a later generation, a churchman, viewing the mission field of New Mexico, thought it good, but added that "the theology of the dollar was more in vogue there than that of Saint Thomas. . . ."

The energies of self-awareness were strong enough by 1883 for

Santa Fe to mount a Territorial Exposition commemorating the history of three and a third centuries of New Mexico, arbitrarily dating 1550 as the founding year—though at that time no white men were in the region. A wooden exhibition hall was erected, the rafters and walls were draped with patriotic bunting and an abundance of American flags, and boughs of pine were interlaced with rafters and joists. Exhibits traced the history of the area since the time of Cabeza de Vaca, and open booths set forth the products of the territory. Great pyramids of fruits, vegetables, preserves, and handiwork were laid on tables. Glass cases held examples of Indian crafts and historical objects, Indian blankets hung on the walls, and an occasional Indian in ceremonial dress stood among the black broadcloth figures of his conquerors. Minerals of all kinds were displayed, and merchandise, including knitted hammocks, sewing machines, office supplies, and, through placards inviting orders, Chickering pianos. Japanese lanterns hung from the beams and a fountain in a cement octagonal bowl played at the center of the hall. The whole was "a novel and interesting sight," and it spoke of the progress for which the territory was reaching in civil and economic affairs.

Susan Wallace, of Indiana, thought Santa Fe, "though dirty and unkempt, swarming with hungry dogs," yet had "the charm of foreign flavor, and, like San Antonio, retains some portion of the grace which long lingers about, if indeed it ever forsakes, the spot where Spain has held rule for centuries." Citizens of a newer strain could have a "pleasant evening" at singing parties held in the evenings at the First National Bank, while deploring "ugly music" which issued forth from saloons. The Union Restaurant in lower San Francisco street advertised meals at all hours for thirty-five cents, and those who wanted to drink beer in the shade or roll ten pins could go to Miller's Summer Garden in South Santa Fe street, or meet their friends for spirited conversation of an evening at the brewery. "In the evening took oysters," recorded the diarist, and all knew that Miller's received fresh oysters daily—Mallory's famous "Diamond" brand of Baltimore oysters. By day, one "saw Pueblo Indians on the streets, fine fellows, clad in white with hair tressed behind and hanging down on each side. Driving a herd of burros." Burros were everywhere, most of them bringing bundles of piñon wood from the hills, many of them used for riding, and a troop of "Burro Cavalry" was maintained by the United States garrison.

In 1880 citizens watched as the "new gasometer and conduit" were being erected to bring gas for lighting to the central streets and the plaza, and a year later, the telephone reached Santa Fe. President Rutherford B. Hayes paid a visit to town, and Lamy was in the forefront of the reception mounted for him. Despite an outbreak of small-pox in epidemic proportions in 1883, when Lamy issued a pastoral letter directing priests to prevent public funerary display of those who died of the highly contagious disease, the vicar general of the arch-diocese predicted that New Mexico would in time, when better known, become "the great sanitarium of the United States," citing its "eleva-tion, its dry atmosphere, its mineral and hot springs," as cures for pulmonary diseases. If people died of such in New Mexico, it was, he said, because they had come there too late.

Marvels were known—a priest galloping near Pecos saw a curious quadruped; followed; captured it; found it to be a "wild girl"—a child—who had disappeared years before from her home. Her parents came and recognized their daughter Carmela. And matters for pity: in 1881, Lamy's old adversary, the ex-priest Gallegos, was brought to St Vincent's Hospital after suffering a stroke. He made signs asking for something. Many guesses were made as to what he wanted, to all of which he indicated "No!" until at last someone said "priest," and he brightened, and Monsignor Eguillon, at the cathedral, was sent for, but arrived too late to see Gallegos alive and to bring him anything but prayers for the dead and—most likely—conditional absolution. Lamy, on another occasion, was "cast down with sadness" when his nephew and namesake, returning from a trip out of town, shot to death the French architect François Mallet, who had tried to offer unwelcome attentions to young Lamy's wife. The murderer was acquitted.

In another claim on Lamy's loyal sympathy, the archbishop's old friend and mentor, Purcell of Cincinnati, needed tactful help in deep trouble. During the financial panic of 1873, deposits of personal savings had been given into Purcell's care, and he in turn had given his brother custody of the monies, who in turn had trusted others. The finances of the archdiocese were in disorder; and finally Rome concluded that Purcell must be relieved of all financial management. To accomplish this as considerately as possible, the Propaganda Fide wrote to Lamy saying that the Pope had ordered the appointment of a coadjutor for Purcell to be made at once, with the right of succes-sion; and Lamy was now given a delicate mission: "I ask that you, following your old custom, visit the Archbishop and relate this deci-sion to him, and suggest that during the next provincial Synod a suitable person, especially well versed in temporal matters, be pro-posed [as coadjutor to Purcell]; and in this way the honor of the Church would be preserved, and by using discretion and the most considerate of means, the needed arrangement be achieved. . . ." The matter was resolved accordingly; but Purcell, in an extremity of embarrassment, went into retirement at the convent of the Brown County Ursulines. To what active and well-loved older colleague could Lamy write thereafter of his problems, hopes, modest successes?

Machebeuf, to the north, offered a complication in 1879 which resulted from the very growth of Colorado; for with the new Leadville mines far to the west in the Rockies, his duties were more arduous than ever—and he, lame and suddenly aging, was unable to be as active as he needed to be; and he asked Lamy to petition Rome to appoint a coadjutor bishop for the vicariate apostolic of Colorado to share his work.

Denver had settled into a steady rate of growth. Machebeuf had recently built a two-storey brick house for a new Loretto school which contained also meeting rooms for the parish sodalities; and two other new schools were opened in Pueblo and Conejos, again under the sisters from Kentucky. The Sisters of Charity hospital at Denver was going along nicely, and it was a "miracle" that these same sisters had already opened another in Leadville, where Machebeuf found it so difficult to go in his buggy.

Leadville was early Denver all over again—and if anything, even more active. The mines of California Gulch were marvellously rich, miners came swarming to the number of fifteen thousand in the winter of 1879, and by summer, Machebeuf thought there would be as many as thirty thousand. At ten thousand feet of altitude, the snows lasted late, and he saw people kneeling in the snowy street outside the single small church when there was no room for them inside during Mass. He began the construction of a brick church in 1879, named after the Annunciation, and people would boast that—using their mountain altitude—its steeple was the highest in the world. The whole town faced to the west a great range of mountains with year-round snow on its rocky peaks. Leadville stood on its height in a shallow cup and to the east, there were mild hills, and a bracing sense of Alpine meadows about the town, as quiet and peaceful as the streets were crowded and noisy. Coaches, waggons with linen hoods, carts, drays, men on foot in crowds, filled the streets. Leadville had its bank, its bookstore, and its Tabor Opera House, where Emma Abbott sang in *Fra Diavolo,* and disappointed the miners with her restrained presentation of the "bed scene," and Oscar Wilde lectured on aesthetics to their respectful mystification.

And all about the willful business of the town were the shacks of the mines, with their sluices, heaps of tailings, little trackways for ore carts, and the obscure narrow, low tunnels which burrowed into the hillsides to bring forth wealth in such amount that after one single strike a certain miner and his partners were justifiably incorporated for twenty million dollars. It was clearly a region which must be serviced; and Lamy, followed by Salpointe, strongly recommended to Rome that Machebeuf be given his coadjutor—and indeed, Lamy proposed again the matter of raising Denver from a vicariate apostolic to an episcopal see. Candidates were nominated for bishop coadjutor and the Curia took the matter under unhurried advisement. Machebeuf made what journeys he could—preferably, now, by railroad, but even this had its vexations; for going by rail to his southern Colorado town of Alamosa to administer confirmation, he confidently left his luggage containing his cassock, mitre, crozier, the holy oils, and his episcopal seal, in the railroad station. The station burned to the ground overnight, and all that was left to Machebeuf was "his little seal," with its engraved motto, *Auspice Maria*.

XII

GARDENER AND APOSTLE

1880–1885

i.

Relief

MACHEBEUF WAS NOT THE FIRST BISHOP of the Santa Fe province to ask
for a coadjutor—Lamy had already done so in 1876, making an appeal
which his two suffragan bishops had signed with him as they met in
council. Supporting his request, he stated, "Reasons for asking this
favor are the following: advanced age, because he is already 62 years
of age; besides the petitioner's health is not firm, which makes the
visitation of his diocese barely possible. The visitation of the diocese
in these days has to be made more frequently and thoroughly. The
boundaries are so far flung and the faithful so widespread that to
travel requires a long time, and is so difficult, that he alone cannot do
all these things, together with regular administration to the needs of
the faithful, which increase day by day. To this add the many ordinary
duties—creation of new parishes and care of them. This requires quite
a bit of study and preparation; to find and train new pastors and provide for their support. . . . I would like to add that the Most Reverend
Vicar Apostolic of Arizona can hardly make the long arduous journey
across deserts [between Arizona and Santa Fe] without endangering
his life. In view of all this we hope that the Holy Father will accept
our petition favorably which we most sincerely ask Your Eminence to
convey to him. . . ."

He closed by nominating as coadjutor the pastor of the cathedral,
Father Johannes Augustus Truchard of the famous bass voice. Lamy's
petition vanished into the labyrinths of the Vatican and for years there
was no response.

There was none, either, to a proposal which he and his bishops made
at the same time: this was for the establishment of a third vicariate
apostolic under Santa Fe. It was to consist of the southern counties of
Doñana, Grant, Lincoln, and El Paso. The first three belonged to New
Mexico, the fourth to Texas. But all were under the authority of

Salpointe at Tucson, with a population of 90,000 persons. Las Cruces, roughly at the center of the district, could be the seat of the new bishop, who would minister to these lands far more readily than was possible either for Lamy or Salpointe. If any final resolution were now needed, the creation of the vicariate, which in the end would surely become a diocese, would also dispose of any lingering claim to the *"Condado"* of southern New Mexico and Arizona by the Mexican bishops.

Rome promptly replied with a routine request for the usual lists of candidates. Lamy sent none. The matter rested until he paid his last visit to Rome in 1878, and what then was more urgent for him was to be granted the appointment of a coadjutor to come to his aid. He asked "repeatedly" for this; for he felt himself gradually losing the strength which had served him so well for the years of encompassing his domain. Evidently he did not yet look like an old and incapable man—but he knew what effort of will it now took to meet even simple duties. He saw himself become forgetful in little matters. He must insure the succession at Santa Fe, and the continuation of what he had begun. Rome asked him for the usual nominations, then; he said he would comply; but meanwhile, he withdrew his earlier request for the new vicariate of the *"Condado,"* and returned to Santa Fe.

In mid-winter 1880, the city was alarmed to hear that the archbishop was suddenly taken ill—seriously ill. For five weeks he was close to death, and ready for it. The last sacraments were given him. Mother Francesca stayed with him as often as possible—during one period of five days and nights when he was most ill, she scarcely left him. He was touched, and when feeling easier, he always called her "Marie." But one day noticing that after attending to him she bathed her hands in an antiseptic solution, he turned indignant and cross, and told her formally, "Mother Francesca Lamy, go over there and get Hermana Xaviera (Sister Xavier) to come and wait on me!"—for a sister from Loretto remained at all times in the room next to his. The hospital Sisters of Charity came as experienced nurses to help him, but he sent them away. He preferred the Lorettines. Of these it was Sister Petra whom he kept by him above all others, though Sister Blandina declared that once when he refused his medicine, it was she herself who forced him to take it—"cowed his defiance," as she put it, and declared "that he soon recovered." In March the newspaper reported that he was resting "much easier last evening," and finally in April, though "scarcely able to write, having been very ill for 5 weeks," he told the Society at Lyon "thanks to God, I am still here." In the same letter he reported the state of "terrible drought" which held the land, with great losses of animals, and severe suffering by people and priests.

But if his strength slowly returned, it was now evident that he would never again be as confident and effective as before. Again, in the following year, he "suffered for months," and it had become "an absolute necessity" for him to have a time of rest and repose. "May God spare for a long time this prelate, so necessary to his flocks"—thus the vicar general Defouri.

As soon as he could write, Lamy again pressed Rome for the appointment of his coadjutor. His renewed arguments were both touching and powerful. Since his serious illness of 1880 he had been hardly able to apply himself to matters requiring serious attention. When he tried to go out on pastoral visits, he became ill. He cited again the immensity of his diocese and the hundred thousand people in his charge. He recalled the experiences of desert and plains and Indian hazards. He listed the progress made in all fields, and he gave again a set of names of those whom he recommended to come to his cathedral as aide and successor. They were the Jesuit J. M. Marra of Santa Fe, the French secular priest Peter Bourgade of New Mexico, and Father W. J. Howlett of Colorado (later the biographer of Machebeuf). All had their particular virtues, and if it was wondered why he had not proposed Salpointe, the reason was that he had informally asked Salpointe if he would serve, and Salpointe had asked to be excused.

One loving concern lay heavily upon Lamy in the choice of his successor. "Our Mexican population has quite a sad future. Very few of them will be able to follow modern progress. They cannot be compared to the Americans in the way of intellectual liveliness, ordinary skills, and industry; they will thus be scorned and considered an inferior race. If the bishop who will follow me has not lived among the Mexicans for a long time and if he should not show a strong interest in them, they will become disheartened. Seeing themselves on the one hand under American discipline and, on the other, imagining that the Americans prefer foreigners to them, their faith, which is still lively enough, would grow gradually weaker; and the consequences would be dreadful. The morals, manners, and customs of our unfortunate people are quite different from those of the Americans. With the best possible intentions, those who would not try to understand our [native] worshippers or would not become interested in their well-being, would have trouble in adapting to their spirit, which is almost too primitive." All such reasons induced him, then, to ask for a Jesuit father, in particular one who had already had long experience in that land. Lamy really "loved the native people," said one of them who became a priest in his service.

For himself, the archbishop hoped to resign and retire, and for his remaining years—he believed them to be few—he would keep only the revenue of two houses which he owned and which upon his death would return to the archdiocese. "I have always been poor," he wrote to Lyon, "and I hope to die poor." He asked—once again—that the Pope would grant his petition. In support of it, he enlisted letters to Rome from Cardinal McCloskey of New York and Archbishop Wood of Philadelphia.

In April 1882, Lamy felt that he must meet an engagement to administer confirmations in the Red River Valley to the northeast of Santa Fe. Going out, as so often, on horseback, he arrived at San Miguel so ill with fever that he was unable to say Mass and only with much determination was he able to administer confirmation to a large class of children before he had to return to the house of Don Jorge Chaves and take to his bed. For two days he stayed there, in what were reported to be "agonies of pain"; but on the third day he left his bed and called on the editor of the *Red River Chronicle,* at his office. The editor took him home, and later declared in print, "Archbishop Lamy is a very entertaining visitor." But he had also to add that "the venerable prelate is getting old; he cannot stand long travels over rough roads any more as in days gone by." From Red River, Lamy had planned to extend his pastoral journey down to western Texas but he was forced to give it up and go back to Santa Fe. He did not know how much longer he could meet the land on its own terms.

How slow, how deliberate, the Roman bureaux! He told Simeoni of how he had had to abandon his visit to "a new part of this diocese," and how when halfway there, he had become ill, and had had to "come back home." And "if," he begged, "if my petition won't be granted soon, let me at least be allowed to ask the Holy See to give me authority to name one of my own priests, under faculties by the Sovereign Pontiff, to administer confirmation in those distant parts of the Diocese." He also warned the Society at Lyon that for two years his strength had been waning, and that he found himself unable to apply himself to any serious affairs—even though in appearance he still seemed "robust" and able to carry out his usual journeys by horseback.

And now at last papers flowed back and forth between the Roman Congregation and the American prelates concerning the nominations Lamy had offered. Rome asked Lamy whether he would accept Salpointe as his coadjutor, whom he had not proposed to the Vatican. It was a sudden new direction, and Lamy at once telegraphed that he would "with great pleasure" accept Msgr Salpointe. (It turned out that it was Archbishop Gibbons of Baltimore who had nominated him directly to Rome.) Salpointe was, said Lamy, "the one most fit for this position," and he now hoped for a swift confirmation of the appointment.

But the year went past, and most of the next, and Salpointe remained at Tucson—except for a brief visit to Rome to represent Lamy at a council of American archbishops called by Leo XIII, who had exempted Lamy from attendance for age and infirmity.

Meanwhile, the succession to Salpointe in Arizona had to be determined before he could leave there to live at Santa Fe. His own new appointment was accordingly delayed. The complicated and drawn-out nominating process for a new bishop at Tucson once again was set in motion, with the usual three candidates, and the time-consuming circularization of bishops for their votes. In December 1883, Lamy pleaded with Salpointe: "You know yourself, Monseigneur, that not only my memory, but also my other mental faculties have much declined; the smallest serious effort, worries, cares, difficulties, exhaust me and make me ill. Knowing my reasons, please help me as much as you can. I will always be grateful to you . . ." and he went on to beg Salpointe to convince Rome of his condition, about which, Rome finally agreed that "no doubt can exist."

On 7 April 1884, the Vatican notified Salpointe, and on the ninth, Lamy, that the appointment had been made by Leo XIII, and congratulations showered upon them. Salpointe was the coadjutor designate with right of succession. "As for myself," replied Salpointe, "I do not know whether to congratulate myself for it, since I find myself already too highly placed for my weak talents." His sentiments were not those of the usual expected humility—he had a pragmatic and sometimes acerb temperament, and meant just what he now said. In due course he was invested with the title of Archbishop of Anazarbe, and whenever his successor at Tucson should be appointed, Salpointe would in obedience move to Santa Fe; but meantime, he and Lamy agreed that it would be wise for him to remain in Arizona and himself preside over the orderly transfer of affairs there.

The very knowledge that his burden was already officially lightened, and would soon practically be so, seemed to revive Lamy's energies. In May, quite in his old habit, he set out on a two-week pastoral visit, beginning with the dedication of the new Jesuit church of the Immaculate Conception at Albuquerque. How he loved the open country; was most at home in the saddle; most content when he was able to assist at the process of growth, in whatever degree.

ii.

The Gardener

TIME WAS ON HIM NOW, TO SEE. More spare than before; taller than
average, he was still muscular. Callers—according to the season he saw
many in his garden—saw his dark eyes somewhat sunken, though still
quick to sparkle when he was amused or interested. His jaws and
cheekbones and chin now jutted out like the granite outcroppings of
his old country of Auvergne. His mouth was folded inward—he had
lost teeth. If he had always moved deliberately, now perhaps he went
more slowly than before. He had few personal indulgences; and the
one he loved best, gave most to, received most from, was the garden
behind the cathedral. There his adobe house, with its small chapel,
stood at one edge of the five-acre tract; and there through the years he
had made a haven away from the parched distances of his far-flung
work. It was a silent and living model of what could be done with the
desert; and lying all about it, the city of Santa Fe also bore out his
belief in planting and cultivating what would take root and grow.
Mid-century daguerreotypes of the city showed almost no trees; but in
photographs of the 1880s, the plaza and other streets had bountiful
shade. From many a plains voyage Lamy had brought cuttings of fruit
and shade trees and grape vines all the way in buckets of water, scarce
as it was, to be planted on his arrival home.

The garden was walled with adobes by his first French architects,
who had crafted its main entrance out of native granite. There was a
sparkling fountain, and a sundial stood on a pedestal of polished
Santa Fe marble. Aisles of trees, plants, and arbors led to it from all
quarters of the enclosure. Formal walks reached from one end of the
garden to the other, with little bypaths turning aside among the flower
beds and leading to benches cunningly placed in the shade from which
Lamy and his visitors could see, on the high ground to the north and
east, the old earthen battlements of Fort Marcy, and "the only brick
and modern residence in the city, and a windmill, probably the only
one in the territory." To the west through the branches of his trees he
could make out the long blue sweep of the Jemez Mountains. At the
south end of the garden on its highest ground was a spring which fed

a pond covering half an acre. From the pond flowed little graded waterways to all parts of the garden. In the pond were two small islands on one of which stood a miniature chalet with a thatched roof. Little bridges led to the islands. Flowers edged the shores, and water lilies floated on the still surface, and trout lived in the pond and came to take crumbs which the archbishop threw to them. Now and then he would send a mess of trout over to St Michael's College to be cooked for the scholars.

There was always color in the garden through the warm season, for he chose varieties of plants which would in turn keep new blooms coming. He loved to bring wildflowers in from the country—someone said he "tamed" them in his cultivated beds. There was a plot for vegetables. Many of the trees bore fruit, and he worked season by season to improve their size and flavor. From cuttings of California vines he grew Malaga grapes whose bunches finally measured fifteen inches long. His cabbages and beets were huge, and he once showed three turnips which together weighed twenty-five pounds. His strawberries were so spectacular that he was able to sell them for a dollar a box, giving the proceeds to charity. When he came to live in New Mexico there were almost no fruit trees, for the fruit culture of the Spanish and Mexican colonists had vanished. Bringing in new orchard stocks, he encouraged others to do the same. For each tree he spent ten or fifteen dollars; and for freight—when the trees came by stage—ten dollars a pound. One of his pear trees yielded one hundred and fifteen pears in a season, and his prize cherry tree, which he called the Belle of Santa Fe, bore two crops a year of black oxheart cherries. For a visitor he could pick a peach of five and a half ounces, a pear of eleven, or an apple of sixteen. When he gave a caller one of his prize peaches, it was always with the earnest request that the pit be kept— and planted.

Among his shade trees he cultivated elm, maple, cottonwood, locust, and both weeping and osier willows. There were red and white currants, plums as large as hen's eggs, and flawless Catawba grapes. Every vine leaf, every shrub, was sound, and so were the trees—apple, peach, pear (he espaliered the pears with the help of Louis, his gardener, who was remembered as a "wonderful gardener, a little man"). They said that much of Lamy's original garden stock came from Auvergne. When the yield was bountiful, he would thin out his growths for transplanting.

Within his garden walls, he delighted to receive visitors. The garden was a famous sight in Santa Fe—the other, which he could see at the eastern end of his retreat, was the unfinished cathedral, one of whose towers was rising toward its belfry. He would walk the raked

aisles with his callers, or sitting by the pond throw crumbs to the
trout. A correspondent who signed himself D.T.W. in an eastern paper
had a fine day with the archbishop, who opened for him "a bottle of
the best wine I have yet tasted in Santa Fe . . . it would have passed
for a very fine Burgundy."

They sit by the trout pond, in which Lamy most "delights his soul."
In one corner of the lake, partitioned off from the rest, "is the nursery,
where the baby trout are—little fellows, but as spry as can be." Lamy
has his favorite seat by the main pond. As they talk, the archbishop
commences "throwing bread into the water." The lake, which is as
smooth as glass, now looks as though a thunder shower has suddenly
dropped upon it. Its whole surface is agitated at once. For every crumb
of bread that fell, "I should judge that forty fish rose at once."

So they sat by the lakeside, "the archbishop talking all the time and
abstractedly throwing in his bread, while the beautiful creatures
swarmed from all quarters, even up to our very feet. . . . He kindly
offered a day's fishing, but it would have been murder—as bad as
shooting quails on the ground . . ." The visitor spends two hours with
this "excellent man, and a more pleasant, cultivated gentleman I have
rarely met."

Everyone saw that Lamy loved the work of gardens; but it was plain
that he did not follow it for his pleasure alone. Sweeping the long
shady vista and its bright colors of fruit and flower with a gesture, he
would say that the purpose of it all was to demonstrate what could be
done to bring the graces and comforts of the earth to a land largely
barren, rocky, and dry. To help his fellow citizens follow his example,
he made them many gifts. On one of his westward journeys over the
plains he brought horse-chestnut seeds in a pail of water all the way
from Ohio, and a hundred sapling elms besides. He gave these to be
planted in Santa Fe, and one day his old friend Mrs Flora Spiegelberg
glanced out of her front window in Palace avenue and saw the archbishop planting with his own hands a pair of willow saplings at her
front gate. When he was done with his spading, he blessed the young
trees. In another year he saw English walnut trees planted in the city
from his seeds. In another, a thousand fruit trees were set out in
Santa Fe where there were so few.

If the garden was his principal joy, he did not see it as his exclusively. The pleasure it gave to visitors rewarded him, and what it had
to offer in other ways was at the disposal of those who needed it. One
day Sister Blandina, from the hospital nearby, looked over the wall.
She saw beds of cabbages, turnips, carrots. In the hospital there were
seventy-two patients, thirty-five orphans, and sixteen nuns who had
not "a handful of vegetables" in their kitchen. The garden was quiet

—nobody there. Blandina "made one athletic spring," with heavy skirts and rosary flying, vaulted over the wall and landed near the cabbage patch. There in haste she threw over the wall at least two dozen cabbages, and many more of the smaller vegetables. A little later, she went to Lamy's house in the garden and knocked.

"Come in."

She went in and said,

"I have come to make a confession out of the confessional."

He gazed at her with "that benevolent expression which once seen" could never be forgotten. He saw that she was covered with dust.

"My little sister," he said, "what have you been doing?"

"Stealing, Your Grace. With never a thought of restitution, I dug up enough vegetables from your garden to last us three days."

"And then?"

"Whatever you say," she replied.

"Tell Louis to give you all there are."

She could only say, "Thank you very much." All she ever heard further about the raid was that in a little while he sent sacks of coffee and sugar to the hospital.

Among an occasional visitor was the Swiss-born anthropologist Adolph Bandelier, who brought Lamy news, now and then, of his discoveries. Antiquity was evident everywhere in New Mexico, either exposed and waiting to be recognized, or waiting to be dug up and opened to knowledge. It was not, as in European cultures, continuously assimilated, adopted, modified, and brought along into daily use. Now the newly arrived industrial age seemed swiftly to bypass whole epochs. Bandelier appealed to Lamy's sense of tradition. It was believed that Bandelier became a Catholic. People saw him wearing a clerical collar. When there was a progressive movement launched to raze the old Governor's Palace and replace it with an up-to-date new capitol, Lamy powerfully opposed the idea. Bandelier spent nine months living in a pueblo, slowly becoming a friend and accepted there. His purpose was to discover whether it was true that the Indians had a cult for worshipping snakes. He came away having seen the cult in action, and had his drawings to show in proof. If the snake was a deity, he was also a natural inhabitant, and a priest one day at his altar in San Juan was not prepared for what he saw there near his feet—a huge diamondback rattlesnake coiled in wariness.

So much to talk about with a congenial caller (though sometimes Lamy did not admit all comers, but courteously and briefly stayed them at his door). Somehow an absurd rumor went about in 1881 that he was the owner of a newly discovered and immensely rich gold mine; and he was at some pains to assure Paris and Lyon that there was no truth to it; for such a story could seriously disturb the modest flow of revenue which provided the chief support of his labors. He was prompt and careful in accounting for financial matters —unlike Machebeuf, whose methods were diffuse and impetuous. Month by month, year by year, Lamy made his reports, and gave his hearty thanks for the help which sustained him. When in residence, he worked steadily at his desk. After he drafted his pastoral letters, Mother Francesca copied them for the printer.

One of the Loretto sisters served as the chapel sacristan. It was her duty to summon the archbishop for early Mass. When she rang the rising bell, she would see his light instantly come on, but he was often late appearing in the sacristy, where she waited to serve his Mass. At the altar, he was never hurried, every motion was exact, careful, devout.

The nuns saw how he kept as much time as possible for prayer and spiritual reading. His library gave evidence of much use. Many of the volumes were water-stained from the shipwreck—how long ago? thirty years—was it possible? They were theological works in French, Latin, Spanish, many of them published in the seventeenth and eighteenth centuries, retaining their original bindings of leather and gold, or vellum with quill lettering. The collection included a seven-volume edition of the *Mystica Ciudad de Diós* (Madrid, 1758), that "Divine History of the Virgin Mother of Christ" by the extraordinary nun María de Agreda. She was famous among the faithful for her gift of bilocation by which, in the 1620s, she was able to appear to countless Indians of the Southwest to whom she introduced the cross, though at the same time she visibly remained in Spain at her post as Mother Superior María de Jesús of the Discalced Sisters of St Francis at Agreda, on the border of Aragon and Castile, where she also had time to write. Among his other books, Lamy had his own Thomas Aquinas in several editions of the *Summa*—Latin volumes published variously in 1570, 1790, and 1798. There was a copy in vellum of *Commentaria in Duodecim Prophetas* (Venice, 1704); a *Virgini Deiparae* (Rome, 1633); a *Theologia Moralis (La Croix)* (Venice, 1753); a *Commentarius in Esdram, Nehemiam* (Antwerp, 1645), the wooden cover of which had been cracked in drying after immersion; and a *Commentaria in Proverbia* (Brussels, 1739). All these bore marks of the sea, some permanently warped by the waters of Matagorda Bay. To think—so they marvelled in the convents—of all the bishop's voyages and travels since then! One journey overland added up to three thousand five hundred miles, and if all his days of camping out "under the stars" were reckoned together, they came to more than a thousand.

Near or far, others had claims upon him which he met as he could.

A Taos Indian lay incurably ill in St Vincent's, and knowing he was to die, begged to be sent home to his pueblo. The doctors believed this ill-advised. Lamy heard of the case, directed that the Taoseño be given his wish, put on a cot, the cot into a waggon driven up the riverside road to Taos. The man died soon, but at home. On a heavy snowy day Major Sena's mother lay in bed with a fever. Lamy went to see her wearing the shawl which he put around himself in cold weather. From his garden harvest he carried four fine apples in the breast of his cassock. They were rich in pectin and quinine, good for fever. He put them on the hearth to roast them, chatted with the invalid, and when the apples were ready, peeled them with his pen-knife and, slice by slice, fed them to the old lady. The family said it was "a simple thing," but they always remembered it. Another woman who as a small child received a visit from him when she was sick in bed told how he came to see her. He seemed so tall, all in black, that he terrified her and she burrowed down under the blanket, pulling it over her head. Then she felt him gently pulling it off her face. Sitting by the bed, he said she was not to be afraid, and told her a story. Listening in wonder, she began to feel better.

In the Rosario Chapel stood the Shrine of La Conquistadora— Our Lady of the Conquest. It contained a tiny statue of the Madonna, in painted gesso and wood. She was the patroness of Santa Fe, for she had been brought to New Mexico by Oñate in 1598, taken south to safety during the Pueblo Rebellion of 1680, and brought back by De Vargas during the reconquest of 1692. She was the most venerable sacred object in Santa Fe, and her wardrobe of ceremonial costumes, changed for important feast days, was voluminous, her votive gifts innumerable. She was carried every year in the May procession, when the faithful marched through the streets, pausing at each improvised shrine—there were many of them—set up before house or shop by people who wanted the procession to halt for prayers, when the benign influence of La Conquistadora could be visited upon them.

In the Corpus Christi procession one year the marchers paused in Palace avenue before the house of Willi Spiegelberg to rest for a moment in the heat of the day. They set the decorated and canopied litter of La Conquistadora on the street while they mopped their brows and chatted briefly. The smallest Spiegelberg child—a little girl of four or five—saw the tiny Madonna and, unobserved, ran out to take it up in her arms as she would a doll, and happily returned to the house. The bearers went on their way, and not until they reached the cathedral did they notice that their Madonna had left them. Their astonishment was mixed with fear. They had no explanation for the terrible event. The procession must proceed, another holy figure was found, and the mystery grew with the day. It was not solved until in the evening Flora Spiegelberg went to kiss her daughter good night and found the Madonna tucked neatly in her daughter's bed. "Horrified," Mrs Spiegelberg flew to the archbishop's house to restore the figure with explanations and apologies. Lamy received all with "roars of laughter," and he and his appalled guest had a glass of wine together. (They were old friends—when the Jews of Santa Fe held their holy-day observances, Lamy was usually present.) Comforted, she was able to go home in peace, though her child felt robbed of her new doll. Nothing more was heard of the affair until many months later "a beautifully dressed wax doll" came from Paris, with a note from the archbishop to the little girl to explain that it was "to replace the little Madonna."

Generally companionable, Lamy was easy with his colleagues; though there was a shade of formality in his dealings with Salpointe, such as never obtruded itself in his friendship with Machebeuf. But after all, the younger man had come as a recruit to Santa Fe, while Machebeuf had been to school with him, had arrived with the bishop at the beginning, and with him had faced and overcome the first obstacles of the desert diocese. When these two friends were together, the talk seemed to go racing along. The essence of friendship was never to have enough time to exchange all the ideas and references and memories that wanted sharing. Lamy's quiet bearing was well countered by Machebeuf's vivacity. Where the one had humor under his calm, the other had an extravagance of word and gesture which his priests used to mimic when he was absent. But in essential affairs he was as serious as his superior, and he never asked anyone to undertake a duty which he himself had not already served. Like Lamy, Machebeuf loved the native Mexican people, who repaid them both with dependent respect. In repose Lamy was like a medieval sculpture of a bishop whose eyes saw beyond time; Machebeuf, even in repose, with his small hilarious old face, looked like a carved imp unexpectedly glimpsed as a detail in a pulpit or a capital.

After the railroads came, the two old friends were able to meet more frequently than in harder days.

In the spring of 1884, the Jesuit pastor of San Felipe de Neri in Old Albuquerque sought out one of his nuns—it was Sister Blandina in her genius for being "present at the creation" in any situation.

"I am in trouble," said the pastor. "Can you help me out?"

"What is the trouble, Father?"

It seemed that Lamy and Machebeuf were to arrive on the four o'clock train, were coming to the parish, and there was no cook to prepare their dinner—an archbishop and a bishop! Blandina—so suitably named—assumed the problem. All the local clergy were to entertain the visiting bishops while the music room of the parish house was being turned into a banquet hall—quite possibly it was the great *sala* of the old house of Father Gallegos behind the church— and while the nuns put together a menu to be served at six o'clock. A mood of reminiscence was prescribed by Blandina. It carried through until after dinner when at half past seven the supper room again became a music room, and the eight nuns of the community entered to join the clergy in a *conversazione*.

The archbishop, the bishop, in the principal armchairs, faced a semicircle of Sisters of Charity leaning decorously forward in their little straight chairs. Machebeuf pointed to Blandina and told Lamy how he had first seen her in Trinidad, Colorado, carrying two hods full of plaster to be applied to the new schoolhouse she was having built. The plasterers had gone for the day. The local priest was walking with Machebeuf. She put him to work while Machebeuf watched.

"Do you remember, Sister," asked Machebeuf now, "how annoyed Father Pinto was?"

Amidst the marvelling murmur at this, Blandina, like an experienced hostess, said to Machebeuf,

"Now, Bishop, that you have brought on the conversation about me—give us the pleasure of knowing how you became lame."

To this somewhat odd question, he replied,

"My horse got frightened and threw me with my foot in the stirrup and in this posture the animal dragged me. When the horse stopped, my leg was broken."

If anyone remembered that it was a buggy accident, no one offered a correction. Lamy, taking pleasure in his friend's gifts as a story-teller, said,

"What about the time you dined at one of Harvey's restaurants"— the eating houses maintained at railroad meal stops on the Santa Fe— "and the waiter told you you occupied two seats, and for that reason you would have to pay for two persons?"

The nuns rustled and said,

"Yes, tell us, Bishop."

"Well," said Machebeuf, "it happened at a period when . . . you could take advantage of thirty minutes for dinner. All who wanted to [leave the train and] dine filed into Harvey's dining hall. Some good man took compassion on my lameness and carried my valise. He looked to see where there were vacant places, spying a table where two chairs were not occupied, he placed my valise on one and helped me to seat myself on the other. . . . When the waiter came to collect, he said to me: 'You occupied two seats—your charge is double.' The gentlemen at the table looked quizzically at me and I good-humoredly said: 'Justice is one of the prime factors of our Constitution, hence I will follow its dictates.' "

With that, Machebeuf, opening his valise, said to the waiter,

"Bring dinner for one more—this guest does not want anything damp. Bring equivalents in dry edibles."

And then, Machebeuf said, the men at his table let go a yell "as though a mountain cat were making ready for a spring—the others in the hall joined in the fun. . . ."

Blandina noted that Machebeuf's "lower lip has the expression of a good grandmother who fears she never does enough for all who belong to her. His whole make-up says, 'You may take advantage of me, but I remain poor, lame Bishop Machebeuf, one of the first modern missionaries of the Southwest.' "

Breaking the respectful stillness which followed the anecdote, one of the Jesuit priests said to Lamy,

"Now, Most Reverend Archbishop, it is your turn to tell us something of your earlier days in New Mexico."

How meagre the social life of the listeners; how hungry for converse in such an august visitation. Lamy did his share. He knew the absorbing delight of his listeners in the small events and details of daily life which if they met them well would bring the great things to take care of themselves in harmony. He said,

"Well, you all know that the Vicar Forane Ortiz would not acknowledge me as the rightful person for the see of Santa Fe unless I could show my credentials from the bishop of Durango. So to Durango I went on horseback. The experience of later years made me understand I was safer in going unobtrusively through New Mexico down to Durango, Old Mexico, than if I had a large retinue for protection. At that time the Navajos and Apaches were constantly on paths of destruction warring among themselves and against our native population. Our Mexican people greatly feared the Navajos, and though quite a number of our best families have raised [Indian] children found on the battlefield after Indian attacks, they still are on their guard against whom they raised. You would greatly insult a native by calling him a *Chato Navajo*—flat-nosed Navajo—as they do in anger."

Another Jesuit asked him if he gave confirmation on that trip to Durango.

"Oh, no. That took place some years afterward, when I formulated plans to build a stone cathedral. The bishop of Durango kindly invited me to give confirmation in a number of isolated villages, some of which had not been visited for seven years."

The purpose, of course, was to raise funds to build the cathedral.

In the poor villages, the parents of the sponsors of those confirmed gave him *dos reales*—twenty-five cents. The journey took several months. The sponsors had to be instructed, which took many days, and so did the children. A few of the richer people gave *cariños,* or love tokens—"among them one solid gold brick." He was kindly received everywhere, but the native food was not good for him, especially tortillas. Chili con carne gave one strength. Jerked meat was common. He always carried some bread, crackers, a few hard-boiled eggs. The travel was exhausting, but not any more, since the railroads had come. "But look back from the eighties to the fifties, and it meant purgatorial work. . . ."

Lamy's time in the West spanned all the great changes in the forms of life which followed the American invasion, and he took full advantage of them all. But, too, he represented the still unchanging great world, through Rome. Everyone remarked his affability, "the kindest man you ever saw," said a priest he had sent to the seminary and who lived to be a hundred and remembered him well, and saying it, the little old man had a strike of energy through his whole bird-like body which was like a convulsion of truth. He remembered Lamy's "strong voice," and he thought he remembered that Lamy's speech in both English and Spanish retained a tinge of French accent.

In his lifetime's succession of the opening out of his world, through the perceptions of faith, and the conquest of the physical environment, he showed everyone his gift for reality, which did not preclude appropriate gaiety, and an almost abstract, selfless piety, a "given" which was to remain constant. If his thoughts came to him slowly, they came firmly. Nobody said he was brilliant, but all seemed to reach beyond that to his disposition, which an Army colonel called "lovable," with the added observation that the archbishop, when he believed himself to be right, "could be as firm as a rock." In all his life, his energy was like a force of nature, except for those sometimes inexplicable and sudden spells of exhaustion to the point of serious illness; but there was no hint of accidie in his days—his prodigious, handwritten correspondence, his purgatorial travels, disposed of that tendency of the celibate life.

A sense of his own energy came through his descriptions of the new energies of others, as he saw civilization unfolding under his hand. He —and Machebeuf—were spared the bleak luxuries of skepticism, and he seemed to open the windows of his desert adobe towns upon the world. To live and work without doubts and yet without arrogance— this was to possess a serene balance, like the result of some hidden but all-availing law, with its power to commit, to spend, and to renew its forces. If nobody found him clever or volatile, most people felt that he was strong essentially, and that his main strength was given to his love of God, expressed through the long labors he calmly and justly pursued; and many must have asked themselves why this spiritual dedication was so moving in a *physical* sort of man? Few knew it, but it may have been that the devotion to Notre-Dame de Bonne Nouvelle which he had from childhood was a sort of abiding innocence which animated him all his life. An orator once said on an occasion of compliments that Lamy was "the greatest pacifier he had ever known."

He liked to share what he had—perhaps most of all the freeing outlook and closeness to nature of his little ranch in the Tesuque Cañon. Now and then he would go to St Michael's College in the piercing early morning air of Santa Fe and collect a straggle of boys and walk them out to the Villa Pintoresca, where they could hear his Mass, and a couple could serve it for him. He had made a fish pond there too, and they could fish for German carp which he had had shipped to him; and when he brought the nuns and other friends to the country for a picnic, they were told to pick at will among the peach trees— but to exhaust one place before they raided another. He once called one of the nuns to come to look at a certain flower with him. She thought he might be about to pick it; but instead, he knelt, inhaled its fragrance, and brought her to her knees to do the same. The scattered families who lived in the cañon saw Lamy as he went on foot from the villa to the chancery in the mornings. When he was alone in his lodge, he spent much time reading, and he used his old caravan telescope to sweep the sky, and the unchanging fantasies of the earth forms, near and far, and the constantly changing marvels of light and color at sunrise, in daytime storm and cloud passage and in the fiery fall of evening before the starry dark.

In November 1881, General Charles Ewing—the same who had been unable to further Lamy's plan for the Pueblo agency schools—had put up at the Exchange Hotel in Santa Fe and had gone at once to call at the archbishop's *"palacio."* It was a reunion which bound the early days in Ohio to the decades which followed in the West, for Ewing and his parents had belonged to Lamy's parish in Lancaster, and Purcell had married Charles Ewing and his wife, all of which Lamy recalled. They toured the garden where snow had fallen, and the general picked a flower out of a snowbank to send his wife.

Lamy invited him to see the Villa Pintoresca, and took him there in a buggy. "The Archbishop drove me himself, and he drove like a Jehu [*and the driving is like the driving of Jehu the son of Nimshi; for he driveth furiously—2 Kings 9:20*]. We had lunch at the ranch—a wild beautiful place from which you can see Mountain Peakes covered with snow that are 120 miles away." Lamy took him to the chapel and showed him a chalice set with jewels, "very old probably over 300 years that he found there thirty years ago when he came here first as Bishop of Santa Fe. The old gentleman was very kind and fatherly— talked of my old home when he was a young Priest where he was often kindly cared for, when I was a child only six years old . . . and his visits there as bright places in his missionary life that never grew dim, but to which he turns with pleasure and loves to talk . . ." In his life's fabric there seemed to be no broken thread.

...
iii.
The Apostle

WITH SALPOINTE, HIS COADJUTOR, to share his duties, and to be ready to succeed him if sudden need arose, Lamy was lighter in spirit and more energetic than he had been for some time. His main local concern now was to see the cathedral completed. It stood covered, services were regularly held there, but the towers rose slowly, the sanctuary was still the old tapering, coffin-headed, adobe enclosure which he had found in 1851; and funds were slow to come.

He worked every possibility to bring in more; but it was still an astonishment, given his recent serious illnesses, when he left Santa Fe in 21 July 1884, for another trip of many months in Mexico, to raise money by donation, loan, and the little fees which would come to him in giving confirmations. The prospect of a long journey and hard work in the great land of which his diocese was a physical extension seemed to bring him zest and a return of strength.

Going south by the Santa Fe Railroad, he met with a washout above Socorro—sudden heads of storm water tore away the old silt left ages before by the Rio Grande—and going single file with the other passengers along a sloping path on the bank of an arroyo, he had to walk from the broken track to the other side of the washout where the track resumed and another train was waiting. He was glad that his two valises were not heavy, for he was carrying them, and even at that, had to stop twice to rest in the heat.

A few days later he reached Chihuahua city, travelling by President Diaz's Mexican Central Railway, where thirty-three years ago he had advanced a few miles a day by horse. He was acclaimed on his arrival now, and was taken on a whirl through the city in a carriage, and visited the "beautiful chapel of Guadalupe" where he had said Mass in 1851. He spoke to his host—a rich man—about a loan of a few thousand dollars, but seemed unlikely to receive it. The governor and his staff, and splendid Mexican music from the bands of the infantry and cavalry regiments, paid him respects, and he felt "very well," though the heat was frightful, and there had been no rain for months. A day later he was to go on to Zacatecas, and then to Mexico City. At every stop he was received with "ovations." Word of his arrival was always telegraphed ahead. The archbishop of Mexico, whom he had met at the Vatican Council of 1869, received him warmly, and invited him to give confirmations anywhere in the huge diocese of the primacy.

He went, then, to Puebla, and at every train station, there were delegations of clergy and faithful, and he was taken to the "grand palaces" of the leading citizens. At Puebla, he was dazzled by the magnificence of the churches—the great cathedral with its huge dome, its towering choir and dazzling gold everywhere, and its bells (more beautiful in tone than any he had ever heard in Europe). With the image of his half-stone, half-adobe unfinished cathedral surely in mind, he remarked the decorations, marbles, gilded sculptures, of the Blessed Sacrament Chapel in the cathedral, which alone, he was told, had cost "one million and a half dollars." The golden altar screens of Mexican churches were like nothing anywhere else, and the profusion of churches in city after city was astonishing.

He wrote to Mother Francesca frequently during the tour, sometimes in English, often in Spanish.

In the midst of the alien splendors and the ardent people he encountered, he was mindful of more homely affairs—there were running accounts to meet at Santa Fe, Mother Francesca was to see that a draft on Paris was duly presented to Mr Spiegelberg at the Second National Bank. If Juan, the caretaker at the Villa Pintoresca, needed food for repair work there, it was to be taken to him, and he should bring a horse to Louis the gardener, take him to the villa, and show him how he keeps the place. It was time to lay in firewood for the next winter— let them bring three hundred loads at least—the little bundles which a burro could carry. If there was any money left after paying for the wood, Mother Francesca could keep and use it.

Wherever he went to hold services, Lamy preached. Asked what sort of preacher he was, a priest who knew him well said, "Very good preacher." He wrote his sermons and his retreat reflections in pencil. They were brief, and wherever he gave them, they brought in simplicity of word an often freshly stated idea of the equation possible between

God and man. He was a man of his time and place, and he met its
hard conditions without much comment; but he would not have been
so effective if he had not also been a man of a timeless faith which was
his source of strength and the medium of his humanity as he extended
it to each being in whom he always saw the universal—Indian, Protestant, Jew, or Catholic. He would say:

The divine word is a mirror that discloses to the ambitious all the infidelity
of the world which he serves. It lets him see his ingratitude toward God,
whom he has rejected, abandoned. This divine word is a mirror without taint
that shows the impenitent sinner the danger to which he exposes himself in
falling into the hands of the terrible justice of God.

On 13 August, he came by train in the state of Puebla to a station
where he was met by priests who conducted him on horseback to a
town eighteen miles away at the base of the mountains, "rather cool
and damp." After confirming many hundreds there, he left to go
thirty-six miles deep into the mountains to a town where sixteen or
twenty strong men took away the four horses of his waggon and pulled
it themselves to the church, where "a splendid choir with a grand
organ sang the Te Deum." There he was informed that deeper in the
mountains were two more curacies they hoped he would visit.

In the words of the Epistle we are sons of the Light, for the same reason that
we are Christians. Let us go out of the fog of sin. . . .

Among the throngs who responded to him in Mexico—the greatest
crowds of his apostolate—he seemed to demonstrate that a great priest
was one not less like, but more like, all humanity.

In Zacatlán toward the end of August at least six thousand people
came out to meet him on the road, where on every side he saw green
fields reaching as far as the highest hills. He passed between gardens
and orchards—every kind of fruit but grapes; he supposed the excessive rainfall rotted the vines. There were two grand churches, one of
which "would make a good cathedral. . . ." He confirmed four or five
thousand people there, and invitations kept arriving from other places
asking him to come. He would be at least two more months in the
diocese of Puebla. The local general and the mayor came to dinner at
the pastor's house. In most places, he found, the civil and military
authorities did not enforce "those tyrannical laws of this government
against the Church." If Mother Francesca should write to him—he
was troubled at not having heard from her—let her "put sixteen cents'
worth of stamps."

In another day, he had come to Chiuawapa, where he saw in the local curate a man after his own heart. This was an Indian of fine education and a most neat appearance, who for his eight thousand souls had established schools, educated young men, helped to build and improve the town which was now almost new, including a new church being built to replace an older one—itself very fine, but its roof leaked. The *padre* led his people to "open good roads, plant trees," and he had embellished the place with "a large and beautiful park and a fountain where the water is brought from over ten miles." Lamy had had too many ovations, he said, which made him feel miserable, the fatigue made his work all the harder afterward. "I will be glad when I get through and be able to be in a quiet place."

A humble fervent prayer is necessary to obtain the grace of God that permits us to meet our duties, to practice our virtue, and to avoid sin: keep vigil and pray, find refuge in all humility, put your confidence in God, assure your salvation by your good deeds . . . that is the grace I ask of God for everyone.

Though the work of confirmations left him little time—in one cluster of five parishes he gave over twelve thousand—he took a few minutes every day to write letters. In Ixtacamastitlán they told him, in September, that they had never seen a bishop. Lamy was not astonished to hear this—the remoteness of so many Mexican towns was daunting. For fifteen days, with Mexican companions, he had ridden on horseback, for there was not a single waggon road—nothing but "narrow, rocky paths, and high precipices." It was high, rough mountain country. But he lovingly described the cultivated mountain slopes, where beautiful green fields were seen at altitudes of six thousand feet or more. He saw, even in such a remote place, various kinds of mills for the manufacture of cloth, pottery, paper. The people were admirably simple and full of faith. They were very clean, their style of dress exceedingly plain. They came to receive him with fine flourishes of music, "dozens of violin bows decorated with a great variety of flowers—Mexico is the land of flowers." They overwhelmed him with attentions and invitations. These he had mostly to decline, for after so much work he was beginning to feel tired. On some evenings he could scarcely stir because of extreme fatigue, though, he wrote his niece, "I feel no pain." He retired early, slept soundly, and the next day found himself strong again.

What happened with a missionary who had converted a certain Indian? The Indian, after being well prepared, received the holy Sacraments. The priest left. After a year he returned to the same place and the converted Indian again asked him for communion. The priest told him he would gladly give him communion after he had been to confession. The Indian was horrified, and said to the priest, "Can one sin after being baptized and having had first communion? Thanks to God, I have committed no sin!" Nevertheless, to comply with the precept of the church, he confessed himself. —Oh! that it might happen so with every Christian!

He hoped to be able to hold out—it was now nearly the middle of September—so that he could go to five more parishes which he promised to visit on his way back to Puebla and Mexico City. Luckily these were places along the railroad and his journey would be less tiring. The bishop of Durango had asked him to give confirmations at Chihuahua on his way north— he hoped to be there by 15 October, and by the twenty-fifth in El Paso, and in early November back in Santa Fe, where without much respite he would have to prepare to attend the Plenary Council to be held in Baltimore later in November. Meanwhile, events in Mexico continued in much the same style. He was accorded so many attentions that he felt almost ashamed. Home thoughts: he hoped Mother Francesca had received the money Father Farini was to receive, and also that if she needed them, she would get some eggs from the *ranchito*. She was to pay Juan his wages (and the little boy helper—twenty-five dollars for both) and give them money for grain; and if there was a balance she was to keep it for herself.

As God said to a just man, "I give myself as your reward, because I cannot give anything greater than myself." So also God said to the soul of the reproved, "I myself will be your torment, by separating myself from you, because in the treasures of my wrath I have nothing any more terrible than parting and separating myself from you."

In early October he returned exhausted one evening from a ride of over thirty miles across the "highest ridge of this cordillera." (He was in Zacopoaxtla.) For fear his horse would stumble and fall on the steep, stony, high path, he dismounted, and leading his horse walked down the mountain for at least three miles. Still, from the summit there was a wonderful view of immense peaks near Veracruz—Orizaba and Perote—and he rode through the semi-tropical lands of sugar cane and coffee plants. For more than a month he had seen no waggon road, and there would be one more week of such travel. Even so, the cordillera was thickly settled, there were fine churches everywhere and even "the highest class" of people had truly admirable faith. Every priest whom he met had enough work "as would commonly occupy two or three."

There is no neutrality between the son of God and the world, between the happiness of being one of His disciples and the misfortune to be against Him, in the kind of his enemy.

At last, on 10 October 1884, he would take the train for Chihuahua and the north. He had already written to Salpointe to meet him in New Mexico at some southern railroad station. When he reached home in late October, the *New Mexican* reported his "most cordial welcome," and noted that "during his absence he travelled about 10,000 miles and confirmed 35,000 people—a remarkable feat for the reverend father who is in his 72nd year."

XIII

DAY'S END
AT SANTA FE

1884–1889

i.

Changeover

IN NOVEMBER 1884, Lamy went to Baltimore—by rail, now, all the way—to sit with his fellow American bishops in the Plenary Council presided over by Archbishop Gibbons. Each delegate was to bring two theologians with him. Lamy had none to call upon, or perhaps to spare, from Santa Fe. He asked that two be assigned him by the cardinal. His voice was heard in the debates. It was not so strong as many remembered it. He was more than gaunt—almost emaciated now. His robes hung loosely upon him, and the great size of his skull was accentuated by the outlines of bones and the hollows of his cheeks sculptured by age. His bulky biretta sat high upon his head. His eyes were entirely recessed in shadow, and his face was wholly pale. The long Mexican ordeal, coming after his illnesses and beyond these the lifetime of extraordinary exertion demanded of his so often vulnerable health, had hurried the reckoning which he was ready to meet.

On his return to Santa Fe, he wrote to Leo XIII in December submitting his resignation, with explanations which were sufficient. Now that the succession was insured and vested in Salpointe, Lamy asked again in January 1885 that Simeoni press for the Pope's acceptance of his petition. The request was not yet known to Santa Fe.

Salpointe, after nineteen years in Arizona, returned to Santa Fe in February, now as an archbishop. Lamy at once began to divide his tasks with him. One of his gravest wishes was still to obtain governmental help to establish Pueblo schools; and after discussing the matter with him, Salpointe went to visit the ten nearest pueblos, to examine the state of affairs, and to determine whether such schools would be welcomed by the Indians. Their decision, he found, was unanimously in favor of them. He would now be able to present their case if it fell to him to do so.

Father Peter Bourgade of Silver City had been appointed to succeed

Salpointe at Tucson, and in April he was summoned to Santa Fe to be consecrated by Lamy. Inviting Machebeuf to the ceremony, Salpointe wrote, "Do not forget to bring your mitre, crozier, and pontifical vestments. You know we aren't rich here, and have here only what is needed in our rituals." He told Machebeuf also that Lamy was well enough, but now that he had a coadjutor, he wanted to do nothing. "I can't blame him—he worked long for the right to rest. . . ." The old archbishop assisted by Salpointe and Machebeuf endured the four-hour ritual of raising Bourgade to the episcopate on 1 May, in the half-new, half-old cathedral; and daylong celebrations followed, with a great dinner, fireworks, and artillery salutes, for it was the first ceremony of its kind ever to have been performed in Santa Fe.

Six months after he had offered it, Lamy's resignation was laid before Leo XIII during the papal audience of 28 June 1885. "His Holiness diligently examined the reasons presented by Archbishop Lamy." On 18 July, the Vatican wrote to Lamy that "the Holy Father, with saddened heart, saw the Archdiocese of Santa Fe being widowed by the departure of its good and most worthy Pastor. However, after a close examination of the reasons revealed by Your Excellency, His Holiness has accepted your resignation. Certainly, it seems right and just that Y.E., after all those years of such great and excellent labors in the vineyard of our Lord, should deserve to spend the rest of your life in peace and tranquility. . . . Under your guidance and administration the cause of our faith has made great strides in remarkable growth. . . ."

On the same day, Cardinal Simeoni sent instructions to Salpointe to succeed Lamy immediately, advised him that between them they should arrive at suitable financial arrangements for a pension which would provide a "decent living" for Lamy, and assured Salpointe that at the next papal consistory the pallium would be requested for him.

All formalities accomplished, Lamy was now in a position to take a tablet of faintly blue-lined paper and in the enlarged, deliberate, but still firm handwriting of his seventy-second year, set down the "Resignation of Abp. Lamy and his farewell to the clergy and faithful of the Diocese of Santa Fe," reading:

For some years past we had asked of the Holy See a coadjutor in order to be relieved of the great responsibility that rested on our shoulders since the year 1850, when the supreme authority of the Church saw fit to establish a new diocese in New Mexico, and in spite of our limited capacity we were appointed its first Bishop. Now our petition has been heard and our resignation accepted. We are glad, then, to have as a successor the illustrious Mons. Salpointe, who is well known in this bishopric, and worthy of administering it, for the good of the souls and the greatest glory of God.

What has prompted this determination is our advanced age, that often deprives us of the necessary strength in the fulfillment of our sacred ministry, though our health may apparently look robust. We shall profit by the days left to us to prepare ourselves the better to appear before the tribunal of God, in tranquility and solitude.

We commend ourselves to the prayers of all, and particularly those of our priests who, together with us, have borne and still bear the burden of the day, which is the great responsibility of directing the souls in the road of salvation. Let the latter remember that, in order that their holy ministry be of any benefit, their example must accompany their instructions. It is with pleasure that we congratulate the most of the clergy of this diocese for their zeal and labors; and we desire those who might have failed in their sacred duties may give, henceforth, better proofs of being the worthy ministers of God.

We also commend ourselves to the prayers of the faithful, whose lively faith has edified us on many an occasion. We exhort them to persevere in this same faith, in their obedience to the Church, in their faithfulness to their daily obligations, in the religious frequence of the Sacraments, and in the devotion to the Blessed Virgin Mary, which is one of the most efficacious means of sanctification.

Finally, we hope that the few religious communities we have had the happiness to establish in this new diocese will offer some memento in their prayers for our spiritual benefit.

We ask of all to forgive us the faults we may have committed in the exercise of our sacred ministry, and, on our part, we will not forget to offer to God our humble prayers for all the souls that the Lord has entrusted to us for so many years.

J. B. Lamy, Archbishop

Given at Santa Fe, N.M., on the 26th day of August, 1885.

The letter was read, in Spanish, in all the churches on Sunday, 6 September. In due course, Lamy, no longer entitled Archbishop of Santa Fe, was granted by the Vatican the courtesy title of Archbishop of Cyzicus.

The end of his term of duty was, like each year of diocesan administration, the occasion for a statistical report to the Society for the Propagation of the Faith in France, which bore so great a share of the expenses of the mission districts the world over. For the end of 1885, the annual report from Santa Fe recorded 238 churches and chapels where Lamy, in 1851, had found 66; 54 priests instead of 12 (which was reduced to 9); 2 colleges, 8 schools, many parish schools, Indian schools, a hospital, and an orphanage, where there had been none of these, thirty-four years ago. This was merely the skeleton of his work. The body of his accomplishment stood forth in the whole character of those people to whom he had given himself, and in the gradual effect of their lives upon the society as it changed—the move toward amenity, through respect for three cultures, and ultimately their civilized union.

So long as he was able, the archbishop had pursued his share of this task with a sort of grave passion, extending the graces of education, charity, and civil progress for all citizens, and the blessings of religion for those of his faith, across his domain of responsibility, which at its greatest had measured about one tenth of the total area of the United States. As he gave over his task, he wrote to the Society at Lyon: "In the future, kindly address your letters to Mgr Salpointe, who is taking my place, the Holy See having accepted my resignation. . . . For some years I have felt myself incapable of managing my diocese any longer," and in the same letter, he said fervently, "I take this opportunity to thank you for all you have done for my diocese during the 35 years I have managed it, without which help my mission would not be as it is now. . . . I hope to end my days in the midst of the faithful I have tried to direct into the way of virtue."

ii.

The Old Men

IN YIELDING UP THE THRONE, Lamy told Simeoni that Salpointe would occupy the greater part of the bishop's house, "which is sufficiently comfortable; and he shall also have the few resources of my Diocese. For my support, the rents of a few small houses which have been built near the Cathedral will suffice."

At first, this seemed to Salpointe like a suitable arrangement, and he said as much to Rome, since Lamy "is not asking for any money but will support himself by the rent of some houses he owns in Santa Fe which he wills to the Church." Lamy, he was glad to report, had "no illness," and was "strong enough to walk and travel by horse, but unable to give sustained attention to anything serious. . . ."

But when the next annual allocation of funds came from Paris, there was a requirement of a pension of 7,500 francs for Lamy, along with Salpointe's own salary of the same amount. With all the other fixed expenses, and a debt of 80,000 francs at five per cent interest, the pension was a decided burden.

Yet Lamy did not want it—he persisted in his own plan for his maintenance, which gave Salpointe much to complain of in a letter to Simeoni in November. "His Grace does not wish an annual pension; he is asking to retain, during his lifetime, the interest of the houses and gardens known under the name of property of the Archbishopric, another house in the city, and a property of little revenue in the country. In keeping all this for himself, Mgr Lamy leaves me absolutely nothing, not even a place to stay. During the seven months that I have been here, I have had to accept the poor hospitality that the priest of the cathedral has had the charity to offer me and which, however sufficient for me, is far from being suitable for the position which I hold. On the other hand, I must say that if I am obliged to pay a pension in cash to the former Bishop, should the Holy See oblige me to, I don't know where I would obtain the necessary funds, for money is scarce here. The accounts for the year 1884 show that the revenues of the diocese did not reach $3000.00 which is quite insufficient to insure a livelihood for the present Archbishop and also to permit him to meet the costs of the administration."

Salpointe was quite willing to live in a modest portion of any one of the houses held under Lamy's ownership. But "here again a difficulty is presented. For Mgr Lamy tells me that the diocese is in debt for a total of $15,000.00 which I must take charge of." But how would one raise money for current needs if one had no property to mortgage? "What is more, I could die before Mgr Lamy, but could I by document oblige my successor to accept the position which I will have to accept and which will not be very agreeable?"

Salpointe reminded the cardinal of what he had said in Rome: "I agreed to come to Santa Fe by pure obedience. I resolved not to appear condescending to the wishes of Mgr Lamy and I believe that I have not deviated from that resolve, but it has been very difficult. If it were only a question of my own personal suffering, I would readily submit to it. What bothers me, however, is to see that there are many needs for which the diocese has but few resources. . . . Mgr Lamy wishes to give me the property titles which I mentioned, while keeping the interest for himself for the rest of his life. I will await for a reply from Your Eminence before accepting the documents. The property could give under $1500 per year. . . ."

It was a squabble between two old men grown testy, Lamy at seventy-one, Salpointe at sixty. From Rome, Simeoni reminded Lamy that a friendly settlement was to have been worked out between the retired and the active archbishops of Santa Fe, and he was shocked to discover "recently that nothing has been done in this matter. Moreover, I understand that the Most Reverend Salpointe has as yet received only a single room from the priest of your cathedral church.

Therefore, in order not to force him to live outside the Archiepiscopal Palace, I ask you to assign a suitable part in your Archiepiscopal mansion to the Most Reverend Salpointe." Simeoni then wrote Salpointe: "I think that this letter of mine will be welcomed and accepted by him. . . ."

By the time Simeoni's letters—with their air of restrained exasperation—reached Lamy and Salpointe, the problem had vanished. Salpointe replied at once to say that he was very glad to report that "there is no more difficulty between me and the Most Reverend Lamy." The fact was, Lamy "changed his decision," and gave to Salpointe "all the documents and deeds of all the church property without restriction." Salpointe had found adequate living quarters; and Lamy went into permanent residence at the Villa Pintoresca in mid-summer 1885. There, as he often said, he would be able, far from the hurry of the world, to prepare himself more readily for his mortal end, whenever. So, said Salpointe, it was there that he lived "in the silence of retreat," and he noted that for several years it had been evident that Lamy's powers were slowly fading, though he never complained of any illness.

Lamy returned on 21 November 1885 to invest his successor with the ultimate insigne of archbishop. On that morning Salpointe received the pallium from him in a most quiet ceremony. The new archbishop had planned to hold a solemn pontifical ceremony, bringing his two suffragan bishops to Santa Fe for the event, to be performed for the public to see, and all to bear witness. But there were no means to cover the costs of such grandeur, and no time to wait, for without the pallium he would not technically be able to fulfill his functions as archbishop. In explaining all this to Machebeuf, he reported that Lamy was well.

By now Lamy must have recognized, very probably had accepted, the condition that much of life inevitably was unfinished business. In any case, he would have no choice now but to accept a certain decision taken by his successor soon after the changeover in authority. "So far," declared Salpointe, "as the Cathedral is concerned, it would be imprudent to desire its completion, in view of the poverty of this land and the impossibility of finding funds in the diocese to help in this task." He found the building half completed and the rest almost ready for the permanent joining of the old north transept—in use by the people—to the new portion. What needed to be done at once was to effect the connection to keep out the weather, and to add to the façade enough to give the whole appearance of a church; and all he could ask France for was enough for these modest conclusions. Work on the cathedral was brought to a halt.

In the following year, the towering carved-stone reredos, originally taken from the *Castrense* and installed in the cathedral sanctuary under Salpointe's supervision in 1859, was now curtained away by a false wall of canvas. Lamy's last bestowal of his powers upon the cathedral he had worked to build, as he had his archdiocese, with troubled care, was to come on 7 March 1886, when he blessed the bells from the old adobe north tower which had been newly hung in the corresponding new stone tower. By then, the architect Michael Machebeuf and his wife, with no more to do, had returned home to France.

A strange summer followed—drought was succeeded by cloudbursts, the dry rivers and dusty arroyos suddenly ran with turbulent brown water, and the pueblo church and *convento* of Santo Domingo—one of the largest pueblo missions, with its Franciscan archives dating back to the founding of the colony in 1598—were crumbled away by the Rio Grande, and nothing remained of church, cloister, and archives.

It was satisfying for Lamy to learn in 1886 that one of his disappointments now turned into a success for Salpointe. The new archbishop, convinced by what he had seen in the pueblos, went to Washington to ask the Commissioner of Indian Affairs, one Oberly, for funds to establish pueblo schools. Commissioner Oberly was persuaded by Salpointe's case, gave him contracts in support of four day schools, with a promise of three more to come, together with a contract for a vocational training school for Indians at Bernalillo. The Pueblo villages which received their schools were Acoma, Laguna, Paguate, Santo Domingo, Jemez, San Juan, and Taos.

Affairs to the north were increasingly complicated during the next year or two. Though Machebeuf had asked for a coadjutor on grounds of his infirmity many years earlier, this was not granted to him at the time; but now Rome reconsidered—but for a different reason. Machebeuf's diocesan finances were in disorder, and a younger, abler administrator was needed to salvage the temporal affairs of the diocese which in his optimistic zeal Machebeuf had allowed to run far into debt. The appointment of Father Nicholas Matz as coadjutor in Denver was made without prejudice to Machebeuf; and, in fact, upon a reminder from Lamy in 1887, the Vatican raised Denver from the status of vicariate apostolic to that of episcopal see, and Machebeuf remained as its first bishop; for his lifetime achievements were properly recognized and praised, and on the occasion of his golden jubilee as a priest, in 1886, one of the tributes addressed to him declared that "his history is almost the history of the Catholic church in these mountains," and that "from the Gulf of California to the Mississippi valley the name of Machebeuf is known."

Lamy was at peace at the Villa Pintoresca. He had his books, and his telescope, and his far view of the Rio Grande Valley and the blue

Jemez beyond the pale orange hills of Tesuque. Salpointe kept an eye on the old man's health and reported often to Machebeuf—Lamy had brought him "some magnificent peaches" from the *ranchito,* Lamy was "habitually well."

He had visitors, who saw in him still what an Army captain saw when he had called at the residence in town: "a venerable gentleman, whose finely shaped head, clean-cut features, clear, bright eyes, discover him to be a man of acute intellect and whose gentle smile and modest, courteous manners conceal the great scholar and man of wonderful executive ability he is known to be." Another caller found him "earnestly studying a folio edition of the Holy Gospels, making himself sensitive to the tones of that language which was so soon to be his proper idiom. . . ." Collegians from St Michael's liked to go to see him at the Villa Pintoresca; and when they came, they were, he said firmly, to walk all the way out from Santa Fe, just as he used to do for so many years. (He now had to ride to town and back.) Yes, Archbishop, they would say, yes, Archbishop—but as often as not they rode, until they came to the hill immediately to the south of the ranch; and there they would dismount, tether their horses out of sight, and climb over the hill to the lodge, puffing with contrived virtue.

Sometimes he would go into town, to take his pleasure of the day by greeting people in the plaza, where there were benches under the trees within the white picket fence along the four sides of the little park. If he stayed overnight, he said Mass at six o'clock the next morning, either in the convent chapel, or at St Michael's, or in the chapel at St Vincent's Hospital.

On 4 October 1887, he appeared in Santa Fe to keep the feast of St Francis of Assisi. There was a procession that evening. The traditional stacks of piñon wood burned along the streets, throwing firelight like banners across adobe buildings. The marchers carried lighted candles through the sharp autumn air. In the procession walked the retired archbishop, and it was a wonder to see him again— so thin and white, so frail and faithful—passing through his streets to the cathedral for vespers at the end of the feast.

He was back again on 12 December to dedicate the chapel of Our Lady of Light at the Loretto convent, now at last completed. The unfinished cathedral was in continuous use, and the choir of St Michael's College sang the midnight Mass there at Christmas.

A few weeks later on 7 February 1888, a message came from the Villa Pintoresca. The old archbishop had been taken sick in the country, and asked to be brought into town, where his cold—he said he had a cold—could be treated properly. A carriage was sent at once.

iii.

Day's End

HE WAS BROUGHT to his old, high, square room in Archbishop's House where the white walls were finished at the ceiling with plaster cherubim. Doctors were called—Santa Fe's leading medical men, Symington and Lindell. They diagnosed pneumonia. Lamy's condition gave reason for encouragement. There was some improvement—no call for serious fears. But a few days passed, the pneumonia grew worse, and his strength did not seem to return.

After the first days, then, Lamy, knowing better than anyone what drew near, sent for Salpointe and asked him to administer the last sacraments; and asked him further to give him the indulgence *in articulo mortis.* Lamy said to Salpointe, later,

"Thank you. I was able to follow every word of the prayers you came to say for me. Keep praying for me, for I feel that I am going."

Twice in the following week, Salpointe brought him the viaticum. Two nuns kept watch day and night—one of them was his niece Marie, Mother Francesca. When her hours of vigil were over each time, and she returned to the convent for a little sleep, the students, looking out the windows at Loretto, saw her coming from the bishop's house with her veil dropped over her face.

Early on the night of 12 February Lamy seemed to fall into a restorative sleep, and Salpointe, who had urgent matters to attend to in Las Vegas, felt it safe to go there by the train which left Santa Fe at two in the morning.

But Lamy coughed "considerably" during the night, and toward morning he was restless. At half past five, Mother Francesca called the gardener, Louis Mora, who slept in the adjoining room in case of need. He came and together they turned the archbishop in his bed, for he could not do this for himself, nor even make his wants known. They did what they could to make him comfortable.

At seven o'clock, Louis suddenly said to Mother Francesca that he thought it would be well to send for a priest. Archbishop Salpointe was away, all the other priests nearby were saying their Masses. But a quarter of an hour later, one of them came, and saw what must be done at once, and began to recite the prayers for the dying. Within the half hour, the archbishop came to himself, saw them all, and his niece said he smiled as though he saw a heavenly sight, and died without pain or distress. It was February thirteenth, 1888. In a little while all the bells of Santa Fe began to toll, and soon everyone in the old mountain capital knew for whom.

Humble proprieties followed. Lamy's nephew and namesake, and Father Jouvenceau of the cathedral, and other priests, washed the corpse. The undertaker came to take it away for embalming. At six in the evening the archbishop was brought to the Loretto chapel to lie on a bier in the sanctuary while the members of the community kept vigil all night. He was robed in red dalmatic and chasuble and on his hands were purple gloves. The pallium lay upon his shoulders and breast. A white mitre emblazoned with the Holy Ghost in gold was on his head. His hands held a crucifix. His large amethyst ring gleamed on his right hand. His feet were encased in purple slippers. The altar was fronted in black and silver. Thirty candlesticks were wrapped in black cloth and their candles flickered in the sanctuary. His face was diminished to the size of the skull, but its integument, so close to the bone, held an expression of peace in mortal sleep.

In the morning Lamy was carried on his bier by six priests, led by Salpointe, through the city and its throngs of witnesses. The procession moved from the chapel in College street to Cathedral Place, then across to Palace avenue, around the plaza, and back up San Francisco street to enter the cathedral which Lamy was never to leave again. He lay in state there for twenty-four hours, and they said six thousand people came by to see him, and many kissed his purple slipper. Machebeuf had hurried by train from Denver, Salpointe from Las Vegas. Each of them, and Monsignor Eguillon, the vicar general, said a Mass during the morning. It was Ash Wednesday. All day delegations of priests and religious and laity arrived from the outlying diocese.

On Thursday, 16 February, at nine o'clock, the obsequies began in a solemn pontifical Mass, with Salpointe, Machebeuf, and Eguillon at the high altar before which lay the dead archbishop. The Collect was intoned:

Grant us, Lord, that the soul of thy servant Bishop Juan whom Thou hast withdrawn from earthly toil and strife, may be admitted into the company of thy saints . . .

And at the Secret:

Grant, we entreat thee, Lord, that the soul of thy Bishop Juan, may profit by this sacrifice, the offering of which, under thy ordinance, earns pardon for the sins of all mankind . . .

It was the last occasion to draw together the two friends who together had made their escape into their lives half a century ago. At a certain moment, Machebeuf limped forward to speak—"if speaking it could be called," said the rector of the Denver cathedral, who was present; for Machebeuf was all but inarticulate through tears and sobs. His face was runnelled like that of an ancient of days. He remembered what they had passed through together, the two seminarians, the two curates, the two missioners, "these two vicars"; and what together they had transformed in the immense land which they had loved for its very hardness, where they had spent themselves for the lives, mortal and immortal, of others. Of the two friends, the younger was now gone. Over his corpse the older said that his time would come next, and soon.

Presently the tremendous liturgy of the dead was resumed which by its impersonality brought a sense of triumph over death. After communion, Eguillon, the celebrant, sang:

Almighty God, we pray that the soul of thy servant Bishop Juan may be cleansed by this sacrifice, and that in all time to come he may deserve the remission of sins and respite for his soul . . .

When Mass was over, Salpointe spoke a eulogy in English, Eguillon one in Spanish. At noon the congregation was dismissed. The ring and the crucifix were taken from Lamy's hands, the one to be kept by his niece and eventually to go down through his family, the other to be given to a friend. On the evening of the funeral, the corpse was enclosed in a plain wooden coffin, four days later it was removed to a metallic casket, and then lowered into the narrow crypt before the high altar of the church which the generations have made into the monument over his grave. Dead in his seventy-fifth year, he had been a priest for fifty years, a bishop for thirty-eight.

The next day, when in his memory, his niece, as was her duty, began to lead her people in the *De Profundis* at the end of a meal in the refectory, she began to cry and could not proceed. At St Michael's, his collegians in a resolution described him as "a second Saint Paul" and decreed the wearing of mourning bands for thirty days. Writing to Europe, Salpointe told how Lamy had lived so long, and was so identified with the desert and the mountain West, that all its people, regardless of their religious beliefs, were attached to him, and prided themselves on belonging to him.

Affirmation was the theme of his life. Who knew how much spiritual energy was thoughtlessly inherited, absorbed, and reactivated in later inheritors? Lamy's unquestioning manner of spiritual commitment could seem as natural to him as all the other simply accepted aspects of his daily life and time. What John Henry Newman wrote of St John Chrysostom could be as true of Lamy—"his intimate sympathy and compassionateness for the whole world, not only in its strength, but in its weakness; in the lively regard with which he views everything that comes before him, taken in the concrete, whether as made after its own kind or as gifted with a nature higher than its own. I speak," Cardinal Newman said, "of the discriminating affectionateness with which he accepts every one for what is personal in him and unlike others. I speak of his versatile recognition of men, one by one, for the sake of that portion of good, be it more or less, of a lower order or a higher, which has severally been lodged in them. . . . I speak of the kindly spirit and the genial temper with which he looks around at all things which this wonderful world contains. . . ."

Not a philosopher, not a sophisticate, Lamy was an unquestioning perpetuator of the values of almost two thousand years of faith, set forth in every august expression of liturgy, as well as in the daily simplicities of the peasant village life into which he was born like any other local child—except that upon him were visited a form of energy and a need to express it which other children of Lempdes did not receive. The mystery abides. At Clermont it was recorded, *"Sa mort a été la fin d'un beau jour"*—his death was the end of a fine day.

iv.

Two Summertimes

In the next summertime the archbishop's garden yielded fifteen hundred quarts of strawberries, forty gallons of cherries, one thousand of currants, and two hundred of raspberries; while five thousand shrubs, vines, and young trees which were ready for transplanting from the garden were auctioned for charity in the plaza of Santa Fe.

A year later Joseph Priest Machebeuf died in Denver.

FIDES ET OPERA

SOURCES CONSULTED

A   UNPUBLISHED MANUSCRIPT AND ARCHIVAL MATERIALS

B   MISCELLANEOUS DIRECT MATERIALS
    1   Interviews
    2   Author's Field Drawings and Notebooks
    3   Pictorial Sources
    4   Sound Recording

C   PUBLISHED PRIMARY SOURCES

D   OTHER SOURCES
    Books, Pamphlets, Unpublished Dissertations, etc.

E   SERIALS

A UNPUBLISHED MANUSCRIPT AND ARCHIVAL MATERIALS

(ANNALES) *de l'Oeuvre de la Propagation de la Foi, Paris.* (Citations also from numbers in BALT and TCA.)

(ATSF FILES) *Atchison, Topeka and Santa Fe Railroad. Letterbook files. Topeka, Kansas.*

(BALT) *Baltimore Archdiocesan Archives.*

(BEINECKE) *Beinecke Rare Book and Manuscript Library, Yale University.*

Charlemagne, Brother Walter. *Letters to M. le Chanoine Pierre Lacour, written from Santa Fe. Ecole Massillon, Clermont-Ferrand.*

(CIN) *Cincinnati Archdiocesan Archives.*

(CIN/ND) *Cincinnati Archdiocesan Archives in University of Notre Dame Archives. (Letters of J. B. Lamy; Letters of José Antonio Martinez to Bishop Lamy, 1853–1861; and tracts, circulars, newspaper articles against Lamy 1857–1860 [Spanish]. Letters of J. B. Purcell.)*

(DEN) *Denver Archdiocesan Archives. ("Memoirs"; miscellaneous papers.)*

(DEN/RA) Joseph Priest Machebeuf. *Letters, in hand copies made from originals in Monastère de la Visitation de la Sainte Marie, at Riom, France.*

Robert Dougherty. *Business correspondence, St Louis, 1862–1864.* DEN.

Evangelista, Sister. *Notes on early Santa Fe, n.d.,* DEN.

Ewing, Brigadier General Charles. *Letter, June 1881, to wife. Copy.* BEINECKE.

(GALV) *Galveston Diocesan Archives.*

(GUL) *Georgetown University Library. John Gilmary Shea Collection.*

Hayden, Mother Magdalen. *Excerpts from letters. Extracted by Sister M. Matilda Barrett, archivist, Loretto Motherhouse, Nerinckx, Ky. Typescript. (Note by Sr. Matilda: "Spanish originals in Loretto archives.")* LO.

(HL) *Histoire de Lempdes. Lempdes Parish archives.*

Lamy, Hippolyte. *Mémoire. Lempdes Parish archives.*

Lamy, Juan Bautista, archbishop. *Short history of the Pueblo Indians of New-Mexico, sent to Genl. C. Ewing by the Bishop of Santa Fe. Santa Fe, N.M. February 25, 1874. Ms. copy in the Shea Collection,* GUL. *Another ms. copy, with a few pages missing, is in the Martin Griffin Collection, St Charles Borromeo Seminary, Overbrook, Pa.*

(LO) *Loretto Motherhouse Archives, Nerinckx, Ky.*

Loza, Pedro, Bishop of Sonora. [*Instrument of cession of certain Gadsden Purchase lands to diocese of Santa Fe. Alamos, Sonora, 16 January 1859.*] TA.

(L/SPF) *Lyon Archives of the Société Pour la Propagation de la Foi.*

(L/SPF/ND) *Lyon Archives of the Société Pour la Propagation de la Foi in* ND, q.v.

(L/SPF/TCA) *Lyon Archives of the Société Pour la Propagation de la Foi,* in Texas Catholic Archives, q.v.

. . . *Missions catholiques, les.* L/SPF/TCA, q.v.

(MNM) *Museum of New Mexico, Santa Fe.*

(ND) *University of Notre Dame Archives.*

(NMSRA) *New Mexico State Records and Archives, Santa Fe.*

(NO/ND) *New Orleans Archdiocesan Archives in University of Notre Dame Archives.*

Pettis, George. *Letters written from Arizona and New Mexico, 1862–1864. Ms., Coe Collection,* BEINECKE.

(P/SPF) *Paris Archives of the Société Pour la Propagation de la Foi.*

(P/SPF/ND) *Paris Archives of the Société Pour la Propagation de la Foi in University of Notre Dame Archives.*

(P/SPF/TCA) *Paris Archives of the Société pour la Propagation de la Foi in Texas Catholic Archives.*

(RA) *Riom Archives of the Monastère de la Visitation de la Sainte Marie. Letters of Joseph Priest Machebeuf, 1839–1886, to his sister* [and other materials]. *Typescripts from the originals by Reverende Mère Thérèse Lucie Roy.*

Ritch, William G. *Dispatch to the New York Herald, 21 June 1875, reporting ceremonies elevating J. B. Lamy as Archbishop of Santa Fe on 16 June 1875. Ms. Huntington Library, San Marino, Calif.*

Ronquillo, E. W. *Ms. notes, 1851–1877. Newberry Library.*

Saler, Francis. *Business correspondence (bell casting). St Louis, 1865,* DEN.

Sapp, Francis. *A brief history of the Sapp family in the early Danville community, 1805–1905. Annotated and mimeographed by Homer Blubaugh. Cincinnati, n.d., St Mary's Seminary.*

(SF) *Santa Fe Archdiocesan Archives.*

(SF/ND) *Santa Fe Archdiocesan Archives in University of Notre Dame Archives.*

(SLU) *St Louis University, Saint Pius X Library.*

(SPF/ND) *Archives of the Société Pour la Propagation de la Foi in University of Notre Dame Archives.*

(TA) *Tucson Diocesan Archives.*

Talbot, Rt Rev Josiah Cruickshank. *Diary. Typescript after ms. New Mexico State Records and Archives.*

(TCA) *Texas Catholic Archives.*

(TCA/L/SPF) *Texas Catholic Archives copies of Lyon Archives of Société Pour la Propagation de la Foi.*

Truchard, Jean-Auguste. *Une lettre de M. Jean-Auguste Truchard curé de Santa Fe datée 23 Juin 1875 et reproduite dans La Semaine Religieuse de Clermont du 7 Août 1875 . . .*

(VPF) *Vatican Archives of the Sacred Congregation of the Propaganda Fide. Rome. Documents referred to are coded as follows: Scritt[ure] orig. rif. nelle Congr. Gen., bundles 972 through 974; and scritture rif. nei congressi America Septentrionale, volumes 14 through 22.* The documents are filed chronologically within the classifications. To identify those quoted or abstracted, the date of writing is given in the notes.

(VPF/SPF/TCA) *Vatican Archives of the Sacred Congregation of the Propaganda Fide, papers of the Société pour la Propagation de la Foi, copies in Texas Catholic Archives.*

B   MISCELLANEOUS DIRECT SOURCES

1   INTERVIEWS

Brun-Voyat, Madame (great-great-niece of J. B. Lamy). Lempdes.

Chauvet, M le Chanoine. Nohanet, Puy-de-Dôme.

Fanguet, M l'Abbé, Curé de Lempdes. Lempdes.

Fournier, M le Chanoine. Riom.

García, Rev José S. Trinidad, Colorado.

Raynor, Mrs E. Frank. New York.

Whalen, Mrs Charles. Santa Fe.

2   AUTHOR'S FIELD DRAWINGS AND NOTEBOOKS

(Beinecke Rare Book and Manuscript Library, Yale).

3   PICTORIAL SOURCES

BALT.

Cincinnati Historical Society.

Cincinnati Public Library.

Echols, Isabel, and Johnson, E. Dana, Photograph collection, Santa Fe.

El Paso Public Library, Sarony lithograph.

Hine, Robert V. Bartlett's West, drawing the American boundary. New Haven, 1968.

LO.

Meem, John Gaw. Photograph collection, Santa Fe.

MNM.

New Orleans Historical Museum.

New Orleans Public Library.

Reps, John W. Western city views. Fort Worth, 1972.

Rinhart, Floyd and Marion. American Daguerreian art. New York, 1967.

San Antonio Public Library.

4 SOUND RECORDING

Canteloube, Joseph (arr.). *Chants d'Auvergne. Sung by Madeleine Grey. Odeon, n.d.*

C PUBLISHED PRIMARY SOURCES

Abert, James W. *Western America in 1846–1857, the original travel diary . . . with illustrations in color from his sketchbook. San Francisco, 1965.*

Almada, Bartolomé E. *Almada of Alamos, the diary of Don Bartolomé. Trans. by Carlotta Miles. Tucson, 1966.*

Balthasar, Juan Antonio. *Balthasar, padre visitador to the Sonora frontier, 1744–1745. Ed. and trans. by Peter Masten Dunne. Tucson, 1957.*

Bandelier, Adolph F. *Southwestern journals, 1880–1882 (v. 1). Ed. and annotated by Charles H. Lange and Carroll L. Riley. Albuquerque, 1966.*

Bartlett, John Russell. *Personal narrative of explorations and incidents in Texas, New Mexico, California, Sonora, and Chihuahua, connected with the United States and Mexican Boundary Commission during the years 1850–1853. 2 v. New York, 1854.*

Benavides, Fray Alonso de. *Revised memorial of 1634. Ed. by Frederick Webb Hodge, George P. Hammond, and Agapito Rey. Albuquerque, 1945.*

Browne, J. Ross. *A tour through Arizona, 1864, or, adventures in the Apache country. Tucson, 1950.*

Caesar, Caius Julius. *The Gallic wars . . . with an English translation by H. J. Edwards. The Loeb Classical Library. London, 1939.*

Chateaubriand, Vicomte François-René. *Oeuvres romanesque et voyages. Texte établi, présenté et annoté par Maurice Regard. Paris, 1969.*

Clark, Charles M. *A trip to Pike's Peak, and notes by the way, etc. With editorial and biographical notes by Robert Greenwood. San Jose, 1958.*

. . . Concilia provincilia Baltimori, habita ab anno 1829. ad anno 1849. Baltimore, 1851.

Cremony, John C. *Life among the Apaches. Tucson, 1854.*

Davis, W. W. H. *El Gringo, or New Mexico and her people. Introduction by Harvey Fergusson. Santa Fe, 1938.*

Dickens, Charles. *American Notes. London, 1957.*

———. *The Pilgrim edition of the letters of Charles Dickens (v. 3). 1842–1843. Oxford, 1974.*

Drown, William. *Escorting a bishop.* In: *From everglade to cañon with the Second Dragoons . . . 1836–1875, by Theo F. Rodebaugh. New York, 1875.*

Ellis, Rt Rev Msgr John Tracy, ed. *Documents of American Catholic history. Milwaukee, 1956.*

Emory, William H. *Lieutenant Emory reports . . . a reprint of Lieutenant W. H. Emory's Notes of a military reconnaissance. Ed. by Ross Calvin. Albuquerque, 1951.*

————. *Report of William H. Emory, Major, First Cavalry and U.S. Commissioner, United States and Mexican Boundary Survey, 34th Congress, 1st session, ex. doc. no. 135. Washington, 1857.*

. . . *Fifty Years in a Brown County convent. By a member of the community. Cincinnati, 1895.*

Fulton, Maurice Garland, ed. *New Mexico's own chronicle. Three races in the writings of four hundred years. Adapted and ed. by Maurice Garland Fulton and Paul Horgan. Dallas, 1937.*

Gibson, George Rutledge. *Journey of a soldier under Kearny and Doniphan. Ed. by Ralph P. Bieber. Glendale, 1935.*

Gregg, Josiah. *Commerce of the prairies. Ed. by Max L. Moorhead. Norman, 1954.*

Hollister, Ovando J. *Colorado volunteers in New Mexico 1862. Ed. by Richard Harwell. The Lakeside Classics. Chicago, 1962.*

James, Henry. *William Wetmore Story and his friends, from letters, diaries, and recollections. 2 v. Boston, 1904.*

McCall, Colonel George Archibald. *New Mexico in 1850: a military view. Ed. by Robert W. Frazer. Norman, 1968.*

Marryat, Frederick. *A diary in America. Ed. by Sydney Jackman. New York, 1962.*

Martínez, Antonio José. *Letters (1856–58) (previous publication uncertain); broadsides (in Gaceta de Santa Fe); tracts (Taos, 1859–61). All in reproduction of ms. or typed copies. Santa Fe Archdiocese archives in University of Notre Dame archives.*

Meriwether, David. *My life in the mountains and on the plains . . . Ed. by Robert A. Griffen. Norman, 1965.*

Montoya, Juan de. *New Mexico in 1602. Trans., ed., and annotated by George P. Hammond and Agapito Rey. Albuquerque, 1938.*

Pino, Pedro Bautista, *et al. Three New Mexico chronicles . . . Trans. with introduction and notes by H. Bailey Carroll and J. Villasana Haggard. Albuquerque, 1942.*

Segale, Sister Blandina. *At the end of the Santa Fe Trail. Milwaukee, 1948.*

Smith, George Winston and Judah, Charles. *Chronicles of the Gringos. Albuquerque, 1968.*

Smith, Truman. *Speech of Mr Truman Smith of Connecticut. Delivered in the House of Representatives U. States, March 2, 1848. Washington. 1848.*

Thackeray, William Makepeace. *The letters and private papers . . .* *3 v.* Ed. by Gordon N. Ray. Cambridge, *1946.*

Trollope, Anthony. *North America.* Ed. *Donald Smalley and Bradford Allen Booth. New York, 1951.*

Trollope, Thomas Adolphus. *What I remember.* Ed. *Herbert van Thal. London, 1973.*

Turner, Henry Smith. *The original journals of Henry Smith Turner. With Stephen Watts Kearny to New Mexico and California. 1846–1847.* Ed. by Dwight L. Clarke. Norman, *1966.*

Wallace, William Swilling, ed. *A journey through New Mexico's first judicial district in 1864. Letters to the editor of the Santa Fe Weekly New Mexican. Los Angeles, 1956.*

Woodhouse, Samuel. In: *L. Sitgreaves, Report of an expedition down the Zuni and Colorado rivers. 33d Congress, 1st session. Senate. Washington, 1854.*

Young, John D. *John D. Young and the Colorado Gold Rush. A trip to the gold regions of the Rocky Mountains in the summer of 1860.* Ed. by Dwight L. Smith. *The Lakeside Classics. Chicago, 1969.*

D   OTHER SOURCES

BOOKS, PAMPHLETS, UNPUBLISHED DISSERTATIONS, ETC.

Adams, Henry. *Mont-Saint-Michel and Chartres. Boston, 1933.*

Almada, Francisco R. *Resumen de historia del Estado de Chihuahua. Mexico, D.F., 1955.*

——. *Diccionario de historia, geografía y biografía Sonorenses. Chihuahua, n.d.*

Aubert, Marcel. *Le vitrail français. Paris, 1958.*

Barbour, Sister Richard Marie, S.L. *Light in Yucca Land. Centennial commemorative volume, 1852–1952. Santa Fe, 1952.*

Berenson, Bernard. *The passionate sightseer. From the diaries, 1947 to 1956. London, 1960.*

. . . *The cathedral of St Peter in Chains. Brochure of the cathedral. Cincinnati, n.d.*

Cekosh, Barbara Jo and Ferro, David E. *Once an educational oasis: Loretto Academy in Santa Fe.* In *New Mexico Architect, July-Aug., 1971.*

Chavez, Fray Angelico. *Archives of the Archdiocese of Santa Fe. Washington, 1957.*

——. *The Cathedral of the Royal City of the Holy Faith of Saint Francis. Santa Fe, 1947.*

—— *My Penitente land. Reflections on Spanish New Mexico. Albuquerque, 1974.*

. . . *Colorado state guide. New revised edition. Harry Hanson, ed. American Guide Series. New York, 1970.*

Conard, Howard Lewis. *Uncle Dick Wooten, the pioneer frontiersman of the Rocky Mountain region.* Ed. by Milo Milton Quaife. *The Lakeside Classics.* Chicago, *1957.*

Cuyler, Rev. Cornelius M. *The Baltimore co-cathedral. Minor basilica of the Assumption of the Blessed Virgin Mary. Its history and description.* Baltimore, *1951.*

Darton, Alice. *Bishops and holy men galore. Compiled by Alice Darton, ed. by Father Frederick McAninch. Typescript. Unpublished.* TA.

Defouri, V. Rev. James H. *Historical sketch of the Catholic church in New Mexico.* San Francisco, *1887.*

. . . *Diocese of Columbus, the history of fifty years, 1868–1918.* Columbus, *1918.*

Drago, Harry Sinclair. *The steamboaters, from the early sidewheelers to the big packets.* New York, *1967.*

Dunbar, Seymour. *A history of travel in America.* New York, *1937.*

Emmett, Chris. *Fort Union and the winning of the west.* Norman, *1965.*

Espinosa, Gilberto, *et al. El Rio Abajo.* n.d.

Forrest, Earle R. *Missions and pueblos of the old southwest. 2 v.* Glendale, *1929.*

Gabriel, Angelus. *The Christian Brothers in the United States, 1848–1948.* n.d.

Garraghan, Gilbert J., S.J. *The Jesuits of the United States. 3 v.* New York, *1938.*

Guérard, Albert. *France, a modern history.* Ann Arbor, *1959.*

Hales, E. E. Y. *Pio Nono, a study in European politics and religion in the nineteenth century.* Garden City, *1962.*

Hawgood, John A. *America's western frontiers.* New York, *1967.*

Horgan, Paul. *Great River, the Rio Grande in North American history. Third edition, revised. 2 v.* New York, *1968.*

Horn, Calvin. *New Mexico's troubled years, the story of the early territorial governors. With a foreword by John F. Kennedy.* Albuquerque, *1963.*

Howlett, Rev. W. J. *Life of the Right Reverend Joseph P. Machebeuf, D.D., pioneer priest of Ohio, of Colorado, and Utah, and first bishop of Denver.* Pueblo, *1908.*

Keleher, William A. *Turmoil in New Mexico, 1846–1868.* Santa Fe, *1952.*

LaFarge, Oliver. *Santa Fe, the autobiography of a southwestern town . . . with the assistance of Arthur N. Morgan. Foreword by Paul Horgan.* Norman, *1959.*

Lees-Milne, James. *Saint Peter's, the story of Saint Peter's basilica in Rome.* Boston, *1967.*

Long, Haniel. *A Pittsburgher en route, New Mexico.* In: *The American Caravan, ed. by Van Wyck Brooks, Lewis Mumford, Alfred Kreymborg, Paul Rosenfeld.* New York, *1927.*

Long, Oscar F. *Changes in the uniform of the Army. Washington, n.d.*

Loomis, Noel M. *Pedro Vial and the roads to Santa Fe. Norman, 1967.*

McCann, Sister Mary Agnes. *Archbishop Purcell and the Archdiocese of Cincinnati. Doctoral dissertation. Unpublished. Catholic University of America, 1918.*

McMahon, Joseph Henry. *The order followed in the consecration of a bishop, according to the Roman Pontifical . . . Trans. and ed. by the Rev. Joseph Henry McMahon. New York, 1932.*

Mathew, Archbishop David. *Lord Acton and his times. London, 1968.*

May, J. Lewis. *Cardinal Newman. New York, 1931.*

Maxwell, William. *Ancestors. New York, 1971.*

. . . *The Missal in Latin and English. Being the text of the Missale Romanum with English rubrics and a new translation. Ed. by J. O'Connell and H. P. R. Finberg [with prayers translated by the joint editors and scriptural passages throughout trans. by R. A. Knox]. New York, 1949.*

Mulhane, Rev. L. W. *History of St Vincent de Paul's parish, Mt Vernon, Knox County, Ohio, and also a brief sketch of St Luke's Parish, Danville, Knox County, Ohio. Mt Vernon, 1895.*

Newman, John Henry. *Historical sketches. 3 v. In: v. 2, The Last Days of St John Chrysostom. London, 1873.*

O'Malley, Francis Joseph. *A literary addendum: Willa Cather's Archbishop Latour in reality . . . A dissertation. Unpublished. University of Notre Dame, 1933.*

. . . *Paroissien romain, contenant les offices de tous les dimanches et des principales fêtes de l'année en latin et français. Tours, 1858.*

Pevsner, Nikolaus. *An outline of European architecture. Harmondsworth, 1968.*

Prucha, Francis Paul. *A guide to the military posts of the United States, 1789–1895. Madison, 1964.*

Read, Benjamin N. *Illustrated history of New Mexico. Santa Fe, 1912.*

Rorimer, James J. *The cloisters . . . Third edition. New York, 1963.*

Ruxton, George Frederick. *Adventures in Mexico . . . from Vera Cruz to Chihuahua in the days of the Mexican war. Oyster Bay, 1915.*

Ryan, Rev. Paul E. *History of the diocese of Covington, Kentucky. Covington, 1954.*

. . . *Seventy-five years of service, 1859–1934, an historical sketch of Saint Michael's College. Santa Fe, 1934.*

Salpointe, Most Rev. J. B. *Soldiers of the Cross. Notes on the ecclesiastical history of New Mexico, Arizona, and Colorado. Albuquerque, 1967.*

Schuchard, Ernst. *100th anniversary Pioneer Flour Mills, San Antonio, Texas, 1851–1951. San Antonio, 1951.*

Steadman, Ruth W. *History of Saints Peter and Paul church, Sandusky, Ohio, 1871–1971.*

Stoddard, Whitney S. *Monastery and cathedral in France. Medieval architecture, sculpture, stained glass, manuscripts, the art of church treasuries. Middletown, 1966.*

Trevor, Meriol. *Newman, light in winter. Garden City, 1963.*

Twitchell, Ralph Emerson. *The leading facts of New Mexican history. Cedar Rapids, 1911.*

Underhill, Ruth M. *The Navajos. Norman, 1956.*

United States Department of the Interior. *The national survey of historic sites and buildings. Washington, 1963.*

Wallace, Susan E. *Land of the Pueblos. New York, 1888.*

Warner, Louis H. *Archbishop Lamy, an epoch maker. Santa Fe, 1936.*

E SERIALS

(Dates of issues cited appear in the Notes.)

Catholic Telegraph (Cincinnati).

Chicago Times.

Colorado Catholic (Denver).

Commercial (Cincinnati).

Commercial Bulletin (New Orleans).

Congressional Globe.

Daily Picayune (New Orleans).

Denver Catholic Universe.

Denver Republican.

Gaceta de Santa Fe (Spanish-language supplement in Santa Fe *New Mexican*).

Galveston News.

Hartford Evening Post.

Les Missions Catholiques.

New Mexican (Santa Fe. Variously at different periods titled *Daily New Mexican, Santa Fe New Mexican, Weekly New Mexican Review, New Mexican Review*).

New Mexico Architect.

New Statesman (London).

New York Herald.

Red River Chronicle (San Miguel del Vado, New Mexico).

Santa Fe Gazette.

Santa Fe Register.

Santa Fe Republican.

Santa Fe Weekly.

La Semaine Religieuse (Clermont-Ferrand).

NOTES

Numbers in the left-hand column indicate pages in text. References to sources are located by catch phrases or by general subject (cited in parenthesis).

The original language of a reference in French, Spanish, Italian, or Latin is so identified in the notes. All those without such identification may be assumed to be in English.

In the case of original documents, reference is made, unless otherwise specified, to copies in microfilm, Xerox, or other forms of reproduction.

Abbreviations for collections of sources, or serial works, cited in the notes refer to their full forms as given here:

ANNALES   *Annales de l'oeuvre de la Propagation de la Foi, Paris.* (The series initially bore the title *Lettres édifiantes.*) (Volumes also from BALT and TCA.)

ATSF FILES   *Atchison, Topeka and Santa Fe Railroad. Letterbook files. Topeka, Kansas.*

BALT   *Baltimore Archdiocesan Archives.*

BEINECKE   *Beinecke Rare Book and Manuscript Library, Yale University.*

CIN   *Cincinnati Archdiocesan Archives.*

CIN/ND   *Cincinnati Archdiocesan Archives in University of Notre Dame Archives.*

CD   *Columbus Diocesan Archives.*

DEN   *Denver Archdiocesan Archives.*

DEN/MEMOIRS   *Denver Archdiocesan Archives, Miscellaneous Papers.*

DEN/RA   *Denver Archdiocesan Archives copies of Riom Archives Letters of J. P. Machebeuf.*

GALV   *Galveston Diocesan Archives.*

GUL   *Georgetown University Library.*

HL   *Histoire de Lempdes, Lempdes Parish Archives.*

LO   *Loretto Motherhouse Archives, Nerinckx, Ky.*

L/SPF   *Lyon Archives of the Société pour la Propagation de la Foi.*

L/SPF/ND   *Lyon Archives of the Société pour la Propagation de la Foi in University of Notre Dame Archives.*

MNM   *Museum of New Mexico, Santa Fe.*

ND   *University of Notre Dame Archives.*

NMSRA   *New Mexico State Records and Archives, Santa Fe.*

NO/ND   *New Orleans Archdiocesan Archives in University of Notre Dame Archives.*

P/SPF   *Paris Archives of the Société pour la Propagation de la Foi.*

P/SPF/ND   *Paris Archives of the Société pour la Propagation de la Foi in University of Notre Dame Archives.*

P/SPF/TCA   *Paris Archives of the Société pour la Propagation de la Foi in Texas Catholic Archives.*

RA   *Riom Archives of the Monastère de la Visitation, Riom.* (Letters of J. P. Machebeuf.)

SF   *Santa Fe Archdiocesan Archives.*

SF/ND   *Santa Fe Archdiocesan Archives in University of Notre Dame Archives.*

SLU   *St Louis University, St Pius X Library.*

SPF/ND   *Archives of Société pour la Propagation de la Foi in University of Notre Dame Archives.*

TA   *Tucson Diocesan Archives.*

TCA   *Texas Catholic Archives.*

TCA/L/SPF   *Texas Catholic Archives copies of Lyon Archives of Société pour la Propagation de la Foi.*

VPF   *Vatican Archives of the Sacred Congregation for the Propagation of the Faith.*

VPF/SPF/TCA   *Vatican Archives of the Sacred Congregation for the Propagation of the Faith, papers of the Société pour la Propagation de la Foi, copies in Texas Catholic Archives.*

CHAPTER I

PAGE

3   before sunrise on 21 May 1839   Howlett, 43–44
       Joseph Priest Machebeuf   Howlett, 22–3
       Lamy not well   Howlett, 45
       dressed as laymen   Ibid., 43, 44
       Lamy, younger   Salpointe, 194
       Machebeuf, twenty-seven   Ibid.
       seen and recognized   Howlett, 43
4   in this case it was Machebeuf   Darton, 7
       one more peril   Howlett, 43
       he himself had come away   Ibid.
       drive of over two hundred miles   Machebeuf to father, Paris, 24 May
            1839, in Howlett, 47
5   to reach each other   Caesar, 383–85
       early Gallic settlements   Guérard, 30–31
       most "religious" of men   Caesar, 28
       rivers, woods, springs   Guérard, 29
       Vercingetorix   Ibid., 33–34
6   defenders put the torch   Caesar, 401
       sent for his chiefs   Ibid., 509
7   shrine of St James   Stoddard, 10–11
       (Roman architecture)   Pevsner, 70
8   Rome gave its arches   Rorimer, 1–2
       strong local flavor   Stoddard, 7
       dark volcanic stone   Pevsner, 7

PAGE

9   "the light of Christ"   Aubert (*"La clarté est le Christ"*), ref. to Luke 2:32
color was always an element   Adams, H., 41
mortality is present   Ibid., 30
Save my soul   *Chanson de Roland,* in the original quoted in Adams, H.:

> *Guaris de mei l'anme*
> *de tuz perils*
> *Pur les pecchiez que*
> *en ma vie fis!*

Upon his arm   Ibid.:

> *Desur son braz teneit*
> *le chief enclin*
> *Juintes ses mains est*
> *alez a sa fin.*

10   founding bishop   Darton, 1
by 1262   Stoddard, fig. 350
11   experience in their music   Cantaloube
12   *paysans aisés*   Chauvet, conversations
of their eleven children   Darton, 7
13   Lamy became her familiar   Fanguet, conversations
14   early Auvergne fresco   E.g., Le Puy cathedral
15   Jesuit *collège* at Billom   HL
16   "the Lamb"   Defouri, 30
called him "Whitey"   Howlett, 105; Machebeuf to sister, Sandusky City, Ohio, 26 May 1841, French
pleins de chasmes   DEN, Notes On Early Days
confining regimen   Howlett, 29–30
(revival of religion)   Guérard, 290
17   Tocqueville   Ibid., 294
distinguished himself   HL (*où il se distingua encore par ses talents et surtout par sa vie exemplaire*)
Lettres édifiantes (ANNALES were previously called *Lettres Édifiantes.*) Defouri, 31
(thoughts of . . . missioners abroad)   Salpointe, 197–98
Odin   Howlett, 35
Flaget   Ibid., 36
bishop of Bardstown   Darton, 36
cathedral . . . open log cabin   Darton, 14a
seamed old face   Flaget statue, Bardstown cathedral
18   wish of Pope Gregory XVI   Darton, 6
Machebeuf ordained   Salpointe, 197
Lamy two years later   Ibid.
Lamy at Chapdes   HL
Machebeuf at Le Cendre   Howlett, 32
letter reached Sulpician rector   Ibid., 40
(Purcell recruiting)   CIN, Purcell, letters, n.d.
rector lost no time   Howlett, 40

PAGE

32   Great National Road   Maxwell, 38
(precarious travel)   CIN, Purcell, letters; Mulhane, 80
(Fenwick)   Mulhane, 55

33   "vulgar prejudice"   CIN, Purcell, letters
"preached twice"   Mulhane, 80–81
(Mass in private houses . . . borrowed chapel)   Ibid., 8
"early candle-light"   CIN, Purcell, letters
walking from Danville   Mulhane, 39

34   (letter to Purcell)   CIN/ND, Lamy to Purcell, Danville, Ohio, 16 Sept 1840
(Danville church yet to be completed)   CIN/ND, Lamy to Purcell, Newark, Ohio, 29 June 1842
(details of Danville church and dedication)   Ibid.; CIN, Purcell, letters
(The original St Luke's was destroyed by fire in 1839.)   Mulhane, 83

35   (Purcell to Mt Vernon)   Ibid., 10, 13
rectory opposite church   *Diocese of Columbus*, I, 391–94
impulsive notion   Salpointe in LA SEMAINE RELIGIEUSE, Clermont, 29 Aug 1868, French

36   Lamy assignments   Mulhane, 39
(Lamy, horse)   CIN/ND, Lamy to Purcell, Danville, Ohio, 16 Sept 1840
(Machebeuf, horse)   DEN/RA, Machebeuf to father, Tiffin, Ohio, 24 Jan 1840, French
(mission life details)   Ibid.; Machebeuf, in Howlett, 65, 66, 104, 140–41

37   Danville and Tiffin 80 miles apart   DEN/RA, Machebeuf to father, Tiffin, Ohio, 1 Jan 1840, French
(Lamy, Machebeuf ill)   RA, Machebeuf to sister, Tiffin, Ohio, 7 Oct 1840, French
(Machebeuf rumored dead of cholera)   Howlett, 77
Machebeuf: "I declare to you"   Darton, 18
Lamy: "my Beloved Ohio"   CIN/ND, Lamy, Lempdes, France, 2 Aug 1848
(plans to visit Auvergne)   DEN/RA, Machebeuf to father, Lower Sandusky, Ohio, 26 Mar 1841, French

38   "sacerdotal zeal"   CIN/ND, Lamy to Purcell, Danville, Ohio, 13 Dec 1841
"fervent pastor"   CIN, Purcell, letters
financial depression   Machebeuf to brother, in Howlett, 105–06
(financial depression)   Machebeuf to father, in Howlett, 107; DEN, Machebeuf to sister, Lower Sandusky, Ohio, 2 Mar 1842, French
(Danville rectory)   CIN/ND, Lamy to Purcell, Danville, Ohio, 14 April 1841
(Mt Vernon church)   Mulhane, 14, 40; CIN/ND, Lamy to Purcell, Danville, Ohio, 29 Aug 1841; CIN/ND, Lamy to Purcell, Danville, Ohio, 13 Dec 1841

39   (Mt Vernon church burns)   CIN, Purcell, letters
(Newark church)   CIN/ND, Lamy to Purcell, Danville, Ohio, 29 Aug, 13 Dec 1841; Newark, Ohio, 26 Feb, 26 April, 1842; Danville, Ohio, 6 April 1843

40   (Machebeuf, first Sandusky church)   DEN, Memoir of the Church of the Holy Angels, 15 Oct 1888
(Sandusky steeple)   Steadman; Machebeuf to father, Sandusky, Ohio, 28 Feb 1842, in Howlett, 141
their fellow Auvergnats   DEN/RA, Machebeuf to father, Monroeville, Ohio, 30 Jan 1842, French
(Lamy, Machebeuf exchange visits; Lamy "dear colleague," "neighbor") DEN/RA, Machebeuf to sister, Lower Sandusky, Ohio, 10 Mar 1841, French; CIN/ND, Lamy to Purcell, Danville, Ohio, 29 Aug 1841

41   (Machebeuf self-examination)   DEN/RA, Machebeuf to father, St Alphonso, Ohio, 4 Oct 1842, French
"I am happy"   DEN/RA, Machebeuf to brother, Sandusky City, Ohio, 30 June 1842, French
"when will we finish them?"   Ibid.
(Lamy self-searchings)   ND, Lamy to Purcell, Danville, Ohio, 11 April 1841
to French Canada   DEN/RA, Machebeuf to father, Montreal, 12 Jan 1843, French
(Machebeuf raises money, Quebec)   Howlett, 113
(Machebeuf shipwrecked)   Newspaper clipping, 1843 (attribution untraceable)
Lamy went to see him   CIN/ND, Lamy to Purcell, Danville, Ohio, 6 April 1843

42   (Lamy had four churches)   CIN/ND, Lamy to Purcell, Danville, Ohio, 7 Jan 1844, English, French
(will go begging)   Ibid.; CIN/ND, Lamy to Purcell, St Louis, Mo., 14 Mar 1844
(imbroglio with "Mrs Biddle")   CIN/ND, Lamy to Purcell, Danville, Ohio, 14 April 1846
"there are times"   CIN/ND, Lamy to Purcell, Newark, Ohio, 24 June 1842

43   "way of mildness"   CIN/ND, Lamy to Purcell, Danville, Ohio, 14 April 1841
sick calls   Ibid.
"Latsin pas!"   DEN/RA, Machebeuf to sister, Sandusky City, Ohio, 26 July 1843, French
"gaie, grand, gros, et gras"   Ibid. (I am indebted to F. D. Reeve for the alliterative translation.)
(language shortcomings)   CIN/ND, Lamy to Purcell, Danville, Ohio, 16 Sept 1840, English, French, Latin

44   boarding at Sapp's   Ibid.
(requests for objects)   CIN/ND, Lamy to Purcell, Newark, Ohio, 26 Feb 1842; Danville, Ohio, 7 Jan 1844
thousand persons present   CIN/ND, Lamy to Purcell, Danville, Ohio, 11 April 1841
"did not get scared"   Ibid.
Temperance Society   CIN/ND, Lamy to Purcell, Danville, Ohio, 13 Dec 1841
"yet another thing"   CIN/ND, Lamy to Purcell, Newark, Ohio, 24 June 1842

PAGE

45   (Newark growing)   CIN/ND, Lamy to Purcell, Danville, Ohio, 7
      Jan 1844, English, French
      "hearty and strong"   Ibid.
      Mansfield   CIN/ND, Lamy to Purcell, Mt Vernon, Ohio, 20 Jan
      1844
      (Mt Vernon church under roof)   CIN/ND, Lamy to Purcell, Mt
      Vernon, Ohio, 19 Aug 1845
      (would pledge inheritance)   CIN/ND, Lamy to Purcell, Newark,
      Ohio, 13 Dec 1845

46   300 families   CIN/ND, Lamy to Purcell, Annual Report, n.d.
      (once almost drowning)   CIN, Purcell, letters, n.d.
      (Christmas Mass, Danville)   CIN/ND, Lamy to Purcell, Danville,
      Ohio, 7 Jan 1844
      ("Know-Nothing," "Maria Monk")   DEN, Memoir of the Church
      of the Holy Angels, 15 Oct 1888

47   (Methodists, furious)   CIN/ND, Lamy to Purcell, Danville, Ohio,
      7 Jan 1844
      (Mass, Toledo, private house)   DEN/RA, Machebeuf to sister, Nor-
      walk, Ohio, 26 May 1841, French
      atrocious calumnies   RA, Machebeuf to sister, Sandusky City, Ohio,
      10 Nov 1843, French
      (Machebeuf's father ill)   DEN/RA, Machebeuf to sister, Sandusky
      City, Ohio, 23 Oct 1843, French
      (Machebeuf unable to leave)   DEN/RA, Machebeuf to sister, San-
      dusky City, Ohio, 10 Nov 1843, French
      "two hundred piastres"   Ibid.

48   Farewell, dear papa   DEN/RA, Machebeuf to father, Sandusky City,
      Ohio, 23 Oct 1843, French
      Lamy journeyed to Sandusky   Howlett, 122
      (arrived Le Havre 6 July)   DEN/RA, Machebeuf to sister, Le Havre,
      13 July 1844, French

49–52 (Machebeuf in France and recruiting Ursulines *passim*)   *Fifty Years,*
      32–52

49   to Avignon   DEN/RA, Machebeuf to sister, Avignon, 27 Oct 1844,
      French
      (Machebeuf at Rome)   RA, Machebeuf to sister, Rome, 17 Nov 1844,
      French

50   (audience, Gregory XVI)   Howlett, 128–29
      (Machebeuf at Venice)   RA, Machebeuf to sister, Venice, 30 Nov
      1844, French

51   (Machebeuf and French royal family)   ND, Machebeuf to Purcell,
      Paris, 10 April 1845, French; Machebeuf to sister, Paris, 20 April
      1845, French; Howlett, 134–35

52–53 (Machebeuf and party voyage to the United States)   RA, Machebeuf
      to sister, Paris, 20 April 1845, French; RA, Machebeuf to sister, Le
      Havre, 2 May 1845, French; RA, Machebeuf to sister on board *Zurich,*
      31 May 1845, French; Darton, 24–25; RA, Machebeuf to sister, New
      York, 4 June 1845, French

52   Father Pendeprat   DEN/RA, Machebeuf to sister, Avignon, 27 Oct
      1844, French; Howlett, 140

PAGE

(Rappe advises not to move Lamy)   CIN/ND, Rappe to Purcell, Toledo, Ohio, 1 July 1848
(Lamy home at Lempdes, family settlement, can partially repay Purcell) CIN/ND, Lamy to Purcell, Lempdes, France, 2 Aug 1848

63   (France in "uncertain state")   Ibid.
"some dreadful explosions"   CIN/ND, Lamy to Purcell, Clermont, France, 27 Aug 1848
(Mont-Ferrand seminarians; other recruits)   Ibid.
(Lamy to bring sister and niece to America)   CIN/ND, Lamy to Purcell, Lempdes, France, 2 Aug 1848
(all remember Purcell)   CIN/ND, Lamy to Purcell, Clermont, France, 27 Aug 1848
(Machebeuf's requirements)   RA, Machebeuf to brother, Sandusky City, Ohio, 3 Oct 1848, French

64   (Lamy recruits nuns; to England)   CIN/ND, Lamy to Purcell, Clermont, France, 27 Aug 1848
(bishop of Clermont approves Lamy's sister to go to U.S.)   CIN/ND, bishop of Clermont to Purcell, Clermont, France, ? Sept 1848, French
(niece Marie frightened at sea)   DEN, Sr. Evangelista, "Notes on Early Santa Fe"
(immigration, Irish famine)   RA, Machebeuf to sister, Sandusky City, Ohio, 16 Oct 1848, French; Howlett, 148–49
(Lamy visit to Machebeuf; vine cuttings; objects)   RA, Machebeuf to brother, Sandusky City, Ohio, 10 May 1849, French
railroad had reached Cincinnati   Ibid.

65   (First Baltimore Council)   RA, Machebeuf to sister, Sandusky City, Ohio, 10 May 1849, French
(Treaty of Guadalupe Hidalgo)   VPF, copy, Treaty of Guadalupe Hidalgo, n.d.

66   (Speech of Congressman Smith)   Smith, T.
(Church jurisdiction after Treaty; Zubiría in New Mexico, affairs bad there)   TCA, Blanc to Odin, New Orleans, 23 Jan 1849, French

67   (Rome lets Mexican bishops retain jurisdiction in ceded lands)   Ibid.
(cholera, New Orleans)   Ibid.
(details, Baltimore cathedral)   Cuyler

68   (bishop of Durango—only three visits)   L/SPF, Lamy to L/SPF, Santa Fe, 28 Aug 1851, French (summary)
("the good old man" escaped death)   Ruxton, 164

68–69   (state of church, New Mexico)   Gibson; Abert; Turner

69   (state of church, Texas)   TCA/L/SPF, Odin to L/SPF, Galveston, 1851, French
(Rome rules on extent of Galveston diocese)   TCA, Odin to Barnabo, VPF, Rome, 18 Sept 1851, French
(Baltimore Council report to L/SPF)   L/SPF, U.S. bishops in Council, Baltimore, 14 May 1849, French (copy)

70   *"Beatissime pater"*   VPF, Baltimore Council to Pius IX, Baltimore, 13 May 1849, Latin

70–72   ever since 1630 (*et seq.*)   Benavides, 11, 192

72   (N.M. bishopric proposed 1810)   Pino

PAGE

73 (Lamy on several lists)   VPF, Baltimore Council to Pius IX, 1849, Latin
(Lamy first on list for Santa Fe)   CIN/ND, Eccleston to Purcell, Baltimore, 30 March 1850
cholera not so bad   CIN/ND, Lamy to Purcell, Covington, Ky., 25 July 1850
(establishment, vicariate)   Salpointe, *Soldiers,* 194
(Lamy named vicar apostolic)   Salpointe, LA SEMAINE RELIGIEUSE, French; Councilia Prov. Balt., 273, Latin

74 (the great news—these two vicars)   RA, Machebeuf to sister, on board *Peytona* en route New Orleans, 17 Jan 1851, French
(Machebeuf's dilemma)   Ibid.

75 never to be separated   Ibid.
(Lamy retreat, Ursulines)   *Fifty Years*
(Blanc on Lamy's plans)   CIN/ND, Blanc to Purcell, New Orleans, 16 Nov 1850, French; GALV, Blanc to Odin, New Orleans, 21 Sept 1850, French

76 (Cincinnati 1850s)   Contemporary engravings
(St Peter's, Cincinnati)   Brochure, Cincinnati cathedral; Trollope, T.A., 59, 60

77 "bishop factory"   McCann
(the consecrators)   HL

77-80 (Lamy consecration)   McMahon, *passim*

80 (Lamy's episcopal ring)   Brun-Voyat, conversation with author
Purcell preached   McCann

81 (Rappe tries to persuade)   RA, Machebeuf to sister, on board *Peytona,* 17 Jan 1850, French

CHAPTER III

85 25 November 1850   VPF, Lamy to Barnabo, Santa Fe, 8 May 1864, French

86 mixed passenger list   Darton, 35; RA, Machebeuf to sister, on board *Peytona,* 17–20 Jan 1851, French

86-87 (details, river travel)   Ibid.

87 (Lamy guest of Blanc)   VPF, Lamy to Barnabo, Santa Fe, 8 May 1864, French
"friend and brother"   CIN/ND, Blanc to Purcell, New Orleans, 16 Nov 1850, English, French
(why via New Orleans?)   Ibid.
(Lamy to Mobile)   GALV, Blanc to Odin, New Orleans, 21 Dec 1850, French
(New Orleans, description)   Defouri, 32; photos and prints, New Orleans Public Library

88 (Gulf shipping details)   COMMERCIAL BULLETIN, New Orleans, 4 Jan 1851; DAILY PICAYUNE, New Orleans, 4 Jan 1851; TCA, Odin to Blanc, Galveston, 30 Dec 1850, French

89 (Odin advice for Lamy)   Ibid.

PAGE

90   (Lamy to sail on Army transport; missed it)   RA, Machebeuf to sister, New Orleans, 23 Jan 1851, French
(Lamy takes next ship)   Ibid.
(*Palmetto* cargo)   COMMERCIAL BULLETIN, New Orleans, 6 Jan 1851
(*Palmetto* condemned; Lamy knew it)   MNM, RED RIVER CHRONICLE, 29 April 1882
having left a letter   RA, Machebeuf to sister, New Orleans, 23 Jan 1851, French

91   (Pilot-town, description)   Contemporary print, New Orleans Public Library
(Lamy arrives at Galveston)   TCA, Odin to Blanc, Galveston, 8 Jan 1851, French

91–93   (Odin advises Lamy, Galveston; Lamy sails on)   TCA, Odin to Blanc, Galveston, 10 Jan 1851, French

94   (weather turned result of "norther")   Defouri, 33

95–96   (*Palmetto* wreck, details)   DAILY PICAYUNE, New Orleans, Tuesday, 21 Jan 1851

95   "white with frost"   MNM, RED RIVER CHRONICLE, 29 April 1882
(drunkenness ashore)   Ibid.

96   (Lamy, Negro helper, salvages some books)   Defouri, 33
Capt. James Cummings   DAILY PICAYUNE, New Orleans, 21 Jan 1851
"A Card—to the Public"   Ibid.

97   (Smith—testimonials and reply)   NEWS, Galveston, 14 Feb 1851
(Indianola, a railroad terminal)   Hine, 17

98   (San Antonio, description)   Reps; Schuchard

99   (Lamy losses, asks loan)   L/SPF/ND, Lamy to L/SPF, Santa Fe, 28 Aug 1851
"disastrous beginnings"   ND, Rev James F. Wood to Purcell, Cincinnati, 14 March 1851
"bought bronco mules"   MNM, RED RIVER CHRONICLE, 29 April 1882
gave further thought   TCA, Odin to Blanc, Galveston, 7 Feb 1851
(Machebeuf at New Orleans; death of Margaret Lamy)   RA, Machebeuf to sister, New Orleans, 23 Jan 1851, French

100   (Lamy accident)   Salpointe, in LA SEMAINE RELIGIEUSE
to overtake the soldiers   Howlett, 157
"Lamy will start for Santa Fe"   TCA, Odin to Blanc, 17 Feb 1851, French
during the delay   VPF, Zubiría to VPF, Durango, 1 Nov 1851, Spanish

101   (Lamy, Machebeuf at San Antonio)   *Fifty Years;* Lamy to Purcell, San Antonio, 10 March 1851
Odin had built   L/SPF/ND, Odin to L/SPF, Galveston, 1851, French
(population after 1849)   Ibid.
(Machebeuf visits forts)   RA, Machebeuf to sister, Santa Fe, 29 Sept 1851, French
(Harney and Lamy)   REPUBLICAN REVIEW, Albuquerque, 29 Oct 1870; Darton, 37
(Machebeuf's baggage)   RA, Machebeuf to sister, Santa Fe, 29 Sept 1851, French

PAGE

102   "Lamy . . . won't hesitate"   TCA, Odin to Blanc, Galveston, 13 May 1851, French

102–04   (overland to El Paso, details variously)   Long, O., 174; RA, Machebeuf to sister, Santa Fe, 29 Sept 1851, French; Howlett, 158–59; Lamy to Blanc, El Paso, 29 June 1851. French, tr. in Ellis

103   (El Paso road)   Map, "Reconnoissances of Routes from San Antonio de Bexar, *El Paso del Norte*, etc.," by Bvt Lt Col J. E. Johnston, T. Eng, et al., Philadelphia, P. S. Duval's Lith. Steam Press.

104   (El Paso and adjacent villages, details variously)   Lamy to Blanc, El Paso, 29 June 1851, French, tr. in Ellis; *Fifty Years,* Lamy to Purcell, El Paso del Norte, 29 June 1851; Hine, 30; L/SPF/ND, Lamy to L/SPF, Santa Fe, 28 Aug 1857, French

105–06   (El Paso, description)   Print, Sarony & Co., New York, El Paso Public Library

105   (Lamy wrote pastor at Socorro)   Darton, 38a
    Lamy wrote his official news   Warner, 263

106–08   (northward, El Paso–Santa Fe, details variously)   RA, Machebeuf to sister, Santa Fe, 29 Sept 1851, French; L/SPF/ND, Lamy to L/SPF, Santa Fe, 28 Aug 1857, French

108   (Zubiría at Tomé)   Parish church register, Tomé, N.M.

108–10   (Lamy, reception at Santa Fe, details variously)   L/SPF, Lamy to L/SPF, Santa Fe, 28 Aug 1851, French; RA, Machebeuf to sister, Santa Fe, 29 Sept 1851, French

108   (Juan Felipe Ortiz, description)   Turner, 73

109   (church of St Francis, description)   Abert, 40

110   (drought broken)   Defouri, 34

CHAPTER IV

113   "continue to exercise"   TCA, Blanc to Odin, New Orleans, 23 Jan 1849, French
    (Ortiz denies Lamy authority)   Salpointe, 196; Segale, 164–65

114   news of Lamy's presence   CIN/ND, Martínez to Zubiría, Taos, 28 Aug 1851, Spanish

114–16   (*Castrense* affair)   CIN/ND, Lamy to Purcell, Santa Fe, 2 Sept 1851; Abert, 41; RA, Machebeuf to sister, Peña Blanca, N.M., 31 May 1852, French
    (The *Castrense* has long since been razed and the stone reredos is installed in John Gaw Meem's beautiful church of Cristo Rey in Santa Fe.)

116   (diocese limits)   Howlett, 169

117   (census 1851)   Horn, 25–26
    "stable of Bethlehem"   L/SPF/ND, Lamy to SPF, Santa Fe, 30 Nov 1854, French
    "casa Americana"   Defouri, 42
    (Palace of the Governors)   Davis, 41ff

118   "the most abject"   Pvt. A. T. McClure (?), in Smith, G. W., 121

PAGE

118–19 (New Mexico costumes, customs)   Elliott, in Ibid., 122; Davis, 61–64; Salpointe, 221

119 four Protestant ministers   L/SPF/ND, Lamy to L/SPF, Santa Fe, 28 Aug 1851, French (summary copy)
Juan José "told me"   Bandelier, I, 256–57
"real masters of the country"   Baker, in Smith and Judah, 123–24
$114,050   Frazer, in McCall, 178
to form itself politically   Ibid., 21

120 citizens' memorial   31st Congress, 1st session, Executive Document No. 76 (Senate)

121 hostile to the power   Defouri, 35
"steamboats and steam cars"   Abert, 56
skeptical observer   Turner, 89
New Mexican houses   Abert, 39; Davis, 50–52

121–22 fandangos   Abert, 34–35, 55

122 "troops drunken and reeling"   New Orleans PICAYUNE, 19 Jan 1857, reprint of letter to ST LOUIS REPUBLICAN
funerals   Abert, 34
"all the luxuries"   Ibid., 75
(Santa Fe plaza, stores)   Ibid., 35, 40
hotel   Davis, 42
the local newspaper   SANTA FE REPUBLICAN, 16 Oct 1847

123 Lamy could see   Davis, 42
Fort Marcy   Frazer, in McCall, 120; Abert, 39, 40; Davis, 42
Sumner . . . in open conflict   Horn, 39–41; Frazer, in McCall, 26; Emmet, 116–19
"Navajoes are a terror"   Abert, 43
"the hillsides and the plains"   McCall, 89
sale of Mexican children   Horn, 55

124 "archaic city-republics"   Long, H.
"intelligent, moral, sober"   McCall, 85
parish church   Abert, 40

125 a later churchman   Salpointe, 199–200

126 "not one was supposed"   Turner, 75
"diminution of filth"   McCall, 85
"kindness of the people"   Abert, 71
"mistake to think the country"   VPF/TCA, Lamy to P/SPF, summary, 28 Aug 1851, Santa Fe, French (tr.)
"everything needed to be created"   Salpointe, 201

127 "state of immorality"   P/SPF, Lamy to P/SPF, Santa Fe, 31 Aug 1851, first Annual Report, French
"Mexican national vice"   Ibid.
his own census   Ibid.
eight or nine thousand   L/SPF/ND, Lamy to L/SPF, Santa Fe, 28 Aug 1851, French (summary)
another six thousand Indians   L/SPF/ND, Lamy to L/SPF, Santa Fe, 31 Aug 1851, French (summary)

128 first Franciscans   L/SPF/ND, Lamy to L/SPF, Santa Fe, 31 Mar 1853, French

PAGE

recalled with gratitude   Bartlett, I, 147
expressly ordered by Rome   TCA, Blanc to Odin, New Orleans, 23
 Jan 1849, French
conversed in Latin   Darton, 44

140–41   (Zubiría had written to Lamy, *et seq.*)   VPF, Zubiría to VPF,
 Durango, 1 Nov 1851, Spanish

141   had written in protest   VPF, Baltimore Council to VPF, Baltimore,
 1852, Italian, (summary)
"I knew nothing about it"   Salpointe, 198–99
what had caused the confusion   VPF, administrative memo, 1853?,
 Italian (printed document)

141–43   (discussion of territory)   VPF, Machebeuf to VPF, Santa Fe, 28 Dec
 1859, French

144–45   (Zubiría's letter to Vatican on territory)   VPF, Zubiría to VPF,
 Durango, 1 Nov 1851, Spanish

145   (Durango, aspects)   Ruxton, 162–64; Gregg, 282

146   Lamy impressed Emory   Emory, Report I

147   Rio Grande dry   Ronquillo
expected him home   RA, Machebeuf to sister, Santa Fe, 29 Sept
 1851, French
(Lamy reached Santa Fe 10 Jan.)   CIN/ND, Lamy to Purcell,
 Santa Fe, 1 Feb 1852
speaking wretched Spanish   RA, Machebeuf to sister, Santa Fe, 29
 Sept 1851, French

148   some of the people   Salpointe, 196, 197
"incapable or unworthy"   L/SPF/ND, Lamy to L/SPF, Santa Fe,
 28 Aug 1851, French (summary)
the "greatest number"   CIN/ND, Lamy to Purcell, Santa Fe, 1 Feb
 1852
"good face"   Ibid.
submit by force   Ibid.
the pastor of Pecos   Ibid.
restoring the *Castrense*   RA, Machebeuf to sister, Santa Fe, 29 Sept
 1851, French

149   natives were promised   Darton, 44
(Third Order of Penitence)   Horgan, GR, 376–77; LaFarge, 149–50
Zubiría had been horrified   Zubiría, in Chavez, *My Penitente Land*

150   (Machebeuf retreat)   CIN/ND, Lamy to Purcell, Santa Fe, 1 Feb
 1852
Navajos at peace   Ibid.
doing "pretty well"   Ibid.
"ten little boys"   Ibid.
on this visit   Ibid.
on 5 February 1852   Ibid.

151   seeds, animals, commodities   CIN/ND, Martínez to Zubiría, Taos,
 28 Aug 1851, Spanish
none of such tribute   P/SPF/TCA, Lamy to P/SPF, Santa Fe, 1851,
 French (tr.)

152   (personal misbehavior)   VPF, Machebeuf to VPF, Rome, 1856,
 French

PAGE

gentle admonitions   Howlett, 191
"like spring"   CIN/ND, Lamy to Purcell, Santa Fe, 1 Feb 1852
Father Roothaan   Garraghan (summary)

153   council in Baltimore   CIN/ND, Lamy to Purcell, Santa Fe, 1 Feb 1852
(rich Frenchman's house)   RA, Machebeuf to sister, Peña Blanca, N.M., 31 May 1852, French
took to the road   Ibid.

154   *Vicario Andando*   Howlett, 239
(hopes to see Murphy 1 May)   SLU, Lamy to Murphy, Santa Fe, 1 Feb 1852 (copy)
"pleasure trip on the plains"   Meriwether, 147
stage service   Darton, 47

155   "instead of becoming settled"   Horn, 30
(stages of plains travel)   Davis, 6
P. J. De Smet   SLU, De Smet to Lamy, St Louis, 11 Nov 1851, French
no continuous rail travel   Dunbar, 1088ff

156   council convened   Darton, 49
"decided humbly to ask"   VPF, F. P. Kenrick to Pius IX, Baltimore, 19 May 1852, Latin
the geographical matter   VPF, Baltimore Council to VPF, Baltimore, 1852, Latin
"three small parishes"   VPF, Odin to Barnabo, Galveston, 1 Sept 1852, French

157   the twenty-ninth   VPF, Baltimore Council to VPF, Baltimore, 1852, Latin
(wrote to the Lyon office)   L/SPF/ND, Lamy to L/SPF, New York, 29 May 1852, French

158   his niece   Defouri, 36
set out on 26 June 1852   Barbour, 29
Trollope observed   Trollope, A., 386
Marryat   Marryat, 216ff
Thackeray   Thackeray, III, 594ff

159   his first concern   L/SPF/ND, Lamy to L/SPF, St Louis, 1 July 1852
with courage   P/SPF/ND, Lamy to P/SPF, St Louis, 1 July 1852, French (tr.)
put his trust   Ibid.
good stroke of business   SLU, Lamy legal instrument, St Louis, 10 July 1852

159–60   (orders and purchases)   SLU, De Smet record of account, St Louis, 1852

160   Father Pendeprat   *Fifty Years*, 102
steamer *Kansas*   Defouri, 37
to teach Spanish   Barbour, 31
travelled only by daylight   Drago, 125
anchoring for the night   Ibid., 153

161   cholera was aboard   P/SPF/ND, Lamy to P/SPF, Independence, Mo., 28 July 1852, French

temperament being as it was   VPF, Baca to Lamy, Peña Blanca, 9 Mar 1853, Spanish

felt obliged to report   VPF, Baca to Lamy, Santa Fe, 2 Feb 1853, Spanish

180   another powerful antagonist   VPF, Machebeuf to Martínez, Santa Fe, 3 Feb 1853, Spanish

"I remain satisfied"   VPF, Martínez to Lamy, Taos, 21 Feb 1853 Spanish

notarized depositions   VPF, citizens' depositions, Taos, 9 March 1853, Spanish

181   half the population   Davis, 64–65

"policy of Spain"   Ibid.

"slight change for the better"   Ibid.

"school of the sisters"   CIN/ND, Lamy to Purcell, Santa Fe, 10 April, 1 June 1853

(convent school opened)   Barbour, 36

pupils were instructed   Davis, 41–42

"signs of ecclesiastical vocation"   P/SPF/TCA, Lamy to P/SPF, Annual Report, 1853, French

prospects for missions   Ibid.

182   (appeal for Jesuits)   SLU, De Smet to Lamy, St Louis, 6 Feb 1853

dun the bishop   Ibid.

last year's subsidy   CIN/ND, Lamy to Purcell, Santa Fe, 10 April 1853, English, French

"borrow" two priests   CIN/ND, Lamy to Purcell, Santa Fe, 1 June 1853

in Easter week   CIN/ND, Lamy to Zubiría, Santa Fe, 15 April 1853, Spanish

wrote also in detail   CIN/ND, Lamy to Purcell, Santa Fe, 10 April 1853 (summary)

Purcell would, he hoped   Ibid.

planned to go to Europe   CIN/ND, Lamy to Purcell, Santa Fe, Aug 1853

wrote in similar vein   VPF, Lamy to Barnabo, Santa Fe, 31 July 1853, French

183   he wrote also to another   Darton, 58; Lamy to F. P. Kenrick, Santa Fe, 31 Oct 1853

full status of a diocese   VPF, memorandum, Rome, 18 July 1853; Salpointe, 206

Ortiz, at Durango, had sent   VPF, Rubio to Marini, Durango, 21 July 1853, Spanish

"coldly received"   Darton; Lamy to F. P. Kenrick, Santa Fe, 31 Oct 1853

183–84   (issue of tithes)   VPF, Lamy to Baca, Santa Fe, 17 May 1853, Spanish; VPF, Baca to Lamy, Peña Blanca, May 1853

184   the vast majority   CIN/ND, Lamy to Purcell, Santa Fe, 10 April 1853

"give the last blow"   BALT, Lamy to F. P. Kenrick, Santa Fe, 31 Oct 1853

185   "imposing ceremony"   Meriwether, 155

"most deservedly popular"   Ibid., 161

PAGE

      great deal of hostility   Ibid., 165
      battle against Apaches   Salpointe, 192–93
      Meriwether officially recommended   Meriwether, 165 (note by
        Griffin)
      a recent event   P/SPF/TCA, Lamy to P/SPF, Santa Fe, 30 June
        1853, French
      "the Great Captain"   H. Lamy
186   (details of Santa Fe life)   Davis, 47, 48, 49, 88, 89
      scandalized an Anglican bishop   Talbot
      territorial assembly asked   CONGRESSIONAL GLOBE, 32nd Congress,
        2nd session (Senate), 10 Feb 1853, 551
187   there is great talk   CIN/ND, Lamy to Purcell, Santa Fe, 1 June 1853
      Sunday within the octave   Ibid.
188   plans to go to Europe   BALT, Lamy to F. P. Kenrick, Santa Fe,
        31 Oct 1853
      place enraptured Machebeuf   DEN/RA, Machebeuf to sister, Santa
        Fe, 28 Jan 1854, French
      (word of the elevation)   NEW MEXICAN, Santa Fe, 3 Dec 1853, Spanish
      pastoral letter announced new status   CIN/ND, Martínez, tract,
        Taos, 10 Aug 1860, Spanish (tr.)
189   "dullness of Santa Fe somewhat broken"   Davis, 126–28
      two promising Mexican youths   RA, Machebeuf to sister, Santa Fe,
        22 Jan 1854, French
190   (second pastoral letter)   Newberry Library, pastoral circular, Santa
        Fe, 14 Jan 1854, Spanish
      "exaggerated"   VPF, Machebeuf to VPF, Rome, 1856, French
      (Gallegos affair)   Ibid.
191   Martínez wrote Lamy   VPF, Martínez to Lamy, Taos, 7–8 March
        1853, Spanish
      (Armijo, 950 citizens)   VPF, Armijo and parishioners to Lamy, Al-
        buquerque, 15 March 1853, Spanish
      "rehabilitation"   VPF, Lamy to Armijo, Santa Fe, 17 March 1853,
        Spanish
      Armijo protesting   VPF, Armijo to Lamy, Albuquerque, 30 April
        1853, Spanish
192   "don't want to threaten"   VPF, Lamy to Armijo, Santa Fe, 24 May
        1853, Spanish
192–94   (Machebeuf vs. Gallegos)   RA, Machebeuf to sister, Santa Fe or
        Albuquerque, 1854, French
192   (Gallegos—appearance)   Twitchell (illust.)
194   observing the customs   RA, Machebeuf to sister, Santa Fe, 22 Jan
        1854, French
      so complete was the union   Ibid.
      "did not lack ability"   Ibid.
195   (Gallegos candidate)   Meriwether, 158
      (Gallegos—campaign)   Ibid., 166–72
      election was close   Horn, 48
      (Gallegos's credentials)   CONGRESSIONAL GLOBE, 32nd Congress, 2nd
        session (House), 19 Dec 1853, 62–63
      (victory to Gallegos)   Ibid., 33rd Congress, 1st session (House), 24
        Feb 1854

PAGE

to bring an interpreter   Ibid., 27 Feb 1854, 492

it was another aspect   BALT, Lamy to F. P. Kenrick, Santa Fe, 31 Oct 1853

Zubiría his prelate   CIN/ND, Gallegos to Zubiría, Washington, 2 June 1854, Spanish

197   (description of *sala*)   Abert, water-color sketch facing 41

refused to abandon it   VPF, Machebeuf to Zubiría, Albuquerque, 11 May, 30 June 1854, Spanish; RA, Machebeuf to sister, Santa Fe, 30 Nov 1854, French

198   present a pipe organ   Howlett, 205–06

"Apostolic Prelate . . . class of heroes"   CIN/ND, P. R. Kenrick to Purcell, St Louis, 7 March 1854

(promise of some sisters)   Darton, 59–60

sailed on 29 March   CIN/ND, Lamy to Purcell, Paris, 16 April 1854, English, French

in Birmingham   Ibid.

Newman in Birmingham   Trevor, 51

199   the Ursulines   CIN/ND, Lamy to Purcell, Paris, 16 April 1854, English, French

with the Sulpicians   Ibid.

young New Mexican seminarians   Ibid.

the new Emperor   Ibid.

Eternal City was a meld   Berenson, 18–36, *passim*

200–03   (Gadsden Purchase; "*Condado*" controversy)   Meriwether, 225, 233–238; Horn, 46, 47, 54, 55; VPF, Lamy to VPF, Santa Fe, 1854, Latin; VPF, Baltimore Council, Vatican Memo., 1853, Italian; VPF, Zubiría to Barnabo, Durango, 22 April 1853, Latin, with duplicate of: VPF, Zubiría to VPF, Durango, 1 Nov 1851, Spanish; VPF, VPF to Zubiría, Rome, 17 June 1854, Latin; VPF, Rome, 1854, Vatican printed circular, Italian

202   serious doubts   VPF, VPF to Zubiría, Rome, 17 June 1854, Latin

203   in good health   LO, Hayden to LO, Santa Fe, 21 Aug 1854

acquired some paintings   VPF, secretarial minute, Rome, 27 June 1854, Italian

"open-mouthed only for visions"   James, 109

"capital fellow"   Hales, 18

a dove had repeatedly   Ibid., 20

204   the flagellant brotherhood   SF/ND, Martínez to Lamy, Taos, 27 Nov 1856, Spanish

(description of chalice and case)   LO

wrote from Civitavécchia   VPF, Lamy to Barnabo, Civitavécchia, 30 June 1854, French

205   (names of new recruits)   ANNALES, v 27, 1855

agreed to lend   L/SPF/ND, Paris, secretarial minute, 29 July 1854, French

moved on to Lyon   P/SPF/TCA, Lamy to P/SPF, 1854, French (tr.)

to see his land   P/SPF/ND, Lamy to P/SPF, Paris, 29 July 1854, French (file copy)

206   planned to visit   DEN/RA, Lamy to Soeur Philomène, Paris, 28 July 1854, French

PAGE

       from Le Havre on August first   Ibid.

       Machebeuf had sent   CIN/ND, Lamy to Purcell, camp near West-
          port, 25 Sept 1854

       rainy weather   Ibid.

       "while putting his gun"   Defouri, 48

       "bearded stranger"   Darton, 63–66

207   spell of illness   LO, Hayden to LO, Santa Fe, 4 Nov 1854

       (on 5 October, travel westward)   ANNALES, v 27, 319–21, Lamy to
          P/SPF, Santa Fe, 1 Jan 1855, French

       it was so notable   SLU, De Smet to Lamy, St Louis, 17 Feb 1855

208–09   (dragoons' welcome to Lamy)   Drown

209   call of respect   LO, Hayden to LO, Santa Fe, 22 Nov 1854

       (death of young deacon)   RA, Machebeuf to sister, Santa Fe, 30 Nov
          1854, French; P/SPF/TCA, Lamy to P/SPF, Santa Fe, 30 Nov 1854,
          French (tr.)

       (parish assignments)   RA, Machebeuf to sister, Santa Fe, 30 Nov
          1854, French

       "mon cher Albuquerque"   Ibid.

       (great cost of caravan travel)   L/SPF, Lamy to L/SPF, Santa Fe,
          30 Nov 1854, French

210   number of boxes   SLU, De Smet to Lamy, St Louis, 17 Feb 1854

       left for the East   CIN/ND, Lamy to Purcell, Santa Fe, 1 March 1855

       occasion to visit   *Fifty Years,* 109

       aboard the *Genoa*   Barbour, 32

210–11   (westward journey, 1855)   DEN, Sr. Ann Joseph to Howlett, Floris-
          sant, Mo., 28 Oct 1902; Howlett, 200, 201

211   prayers "in time of war"   SF, pastoral letter, Santa Fe, 18 Feb 1855,
          Spanish (printed circular)

       canonically installed   Darton, 67

211–12   (return of ex-Vicar Ortiz)   VPF, Lamy to VPF, Santa Fe, 1 Feb 1856,
          French; VPF, J. F. Ortiz to Zubiría, Santa Fe, 24 July 1855, Spanish

212   as far south as Tomé   Tomé, N.M., parish records, 7 March 1855

       (report on return of Ortiz *et seq.*)   VPF, Lamy to Barnabo, Santa
          Fe, 1 Feb 1856, French

       "the bell was taken down"   VPF, Machebeuf to VPF, Rome, 1856,
          French

213   withdraw the license; "not all roses"   CIN/ND, Lamy to Purcell,
          Santa Fe, 30 Dec 1855

       new pastoral circular   SF, Santa Fe, Nov 1855, pastoral circular,
          Spanish (printed)

       discipline he had announced   Ibid.

214   a gratifying response   CIN/ND, Martínez to Lamy, Taos, 29 Nov
          1855, Spanish

       twelve older boys   Darton, 68

       begin their Latin studies   CIN/ND, Lamy to P/SPF, Santa Fe, 30
          June 1855, French

       Casa Americana   Barbour, 33

215   friend who never failed him   CIN/ND, Lamy to Purcell, Santa Fe,
          30 Dec 1855

       "most likely Rev. Mr Machebeuf"   Ibid.

CHAPTER VI

PAGE

229   devastating sketches . . . Ortiz, Salazar, Lujan, Gallegos, Martínez
Ibid.
Clementi in Mexico City   VPF, secretarial minute, Rome, 25 June
1856, Italian

230   had never been acknowledged   VPF, VPF to Lamy, Rome, 24 July
1856, Latin
new county named Doñana   VPF/L/SPF, Machebeuf to L/SPF,
Lyon, 7 June 1856, French

231   soldier recorded his view   McCall, 135
Zubiría had given Martínez   SF/ND, Martínez to Lamy, Taos, 1
Oct 1856, Spanish

232   "does not behave well toward me"   Ibid.
"only human thing"   SF/ND, Taladrid to Lamy, Taos, Oct 1856,
Spanish
abused Martínez's reputation   SF/ND, Martínez to Lamy, Taos, 1
Oct 1856, Spanish
"I know how to hit hard"   Ibid.
had Lamy's letter to prove it   Ibid.
published an open letter   Ibid.
a difficult road   McCall, 129, 135
"as a heretic"   SF/ND, Martínez to Lamy, Taos, 1 Oct 1856, Spanish

233   a private oratory   Ibid.
"worse than these two together"   CIN/ND, Lamy to Purcell, Santa
Fe, 3 March 1857, English, French
one Cárdenas   SANTA FE GAZETTE, 3 Sept 1853
"we ask the people"   Ibid., 22 Aug 1853

233–34   (Gallegos' speech to House)   CONGRESSIONAL GLOBE, 34th Congress,
1st session (House), 23 July 1856, 1730ff

234–36   (Otero's speech)   Ibid.

235   "head and front of his offending"   *Othello* I, iii, 81 (paraphrase)

236   (Gallegos unseated, Otero seated)   CONGRESSIONAL GLOBE, 34th Congress, 1st session (House), 23 July 1856, 1730ff
Doñana problem   VPF/TCA, Lamy to Barnabo, Santa Fe, 1 Oct
1856, French (copy); VPF/TCA, secretarial minute, Rome, 1 Oct
1856, Italian (copy)
"excessive" language   SF/ND, Martínez to Lamy, Taos, 17 Nov
1856, Spanish
writ of suspension   CIN/ND, Lamy to Purcell, Santa Fe, 3 March
1857
Martínez defied even this   SF/ND, Martínez to Lamy, Taos, 12 Nov
1856, Spanish

236–37   (Machebeuf and party, France to U.S.)   RA, Machebeuf to sister,
on board *Alma*, 20 Aug 1856, French

237   (Chateaubriand at Niagara Falls)   Chateaubriand, *Atala*, 95–96;
Voyage en Amérique, 696–97

238–39   (Machebeuf and party plains crossing)   Ussel, in Howlett, 212–18

239   on 3 November   RA, Machebeuf to brother, camp near New
Mexico, 3 Nov 1856, French
written permission to sell   VPF/TCA, Lamy to Barnabo, Santa Fe,
1 Oct 1856

PAGE

wrote to congratulate   GUL, Lamy to Barnabo, Santa Fe, 1 Dec 1856, French (copy)

to thank him for his confidence   Ibid.; VPF, Lamy to Barnabo, Santa Fe, 1 Dec 1856; French

"I hope also"   Ibid

240 on 12 November   SF/ND, Martínez to Lamy, Taos, 12 Nov 1856, Spanish

his manner of expression   SF/ND, Martínez to Lamy, Taos, 17 Nov 1856, Spanish

241 probe old injuries anew   SF/ND, Martínez to Lamy, Taos, 27 Nov 1856, Spanish

pour out his troubles   CIN/ND, Lamy to Purcell, Santa Fe, 3 March 1857, French

242 "war to the death"   P/SPF/TCA, Lamy to P/SPF, Santa Fe, 5 March 1857, French (tr.)

(Machebeuf back at Albuquerque)   RA, Machebeuf to sister, Albuquerque, 28 Feb 1857, French

another enormous missive   SF/ND, Martínez to Lamy, Taos, 13 April 1857, Spanish

Martínez wrote to Machebeuf   SF/ND, Martínez to Machebeuf, Taos, 2 May 1857, Spanish

it was no wonder   Taladrid (Un Observante), GACETA DE SANTA FE, issue 42–43

tensions in Taos   SF/ND, Martínez to Machebeuf, Taos, 2 May 1857, Spanish

he set in motion   Darton, 73–74; Howlett, 230–33

243 mounted a guard   SF/ND, Martínez to E. Ortiz, Taos, 22 June 1857, Spanish

243–44 (excommunications of Martínez and Lucero)   Howlett, 230–33

244 a curious tale to tell   SF/ND, J. E. Ortiz to Lamy, Taos, 23 July 1857, Spanish

245 proposing creation of a chapter   VPF, VPF to Pius IX, Rome, 27 Sept 1857, Latin; VPF, secretarial minute, Rome, Jan 1858, Italian

246 Lamy wrote to Barnabo   VPF, Lamy to Barnabo, Santa Fe, Jan 1857, French

"please note"   Ibid.

Barnabo replied   VPF, Barnabo to Lamy, Rome, 11 Feb 1857, Latin

again, in May   VPF, Lamy to Barnabo, Santa Fe, 1 May 1857, Spanish

in his opinion   VPF, Lamy to Barnabo, Santa Fe, 11 Aug 1857, French

he returned to Santa Fe   LO, Hayden, Santa Fe, 20 July 1857

(procession of Corpus Christi)   Ibid.

on the following day   LO, Hayden, Santa Fe, 17 July 1857

246–47 (Machebeuf eastward 1857)   Machebeuf to sister, in Howlett, 221–22

247 he thought Indians   RA, Machebeuf to sister, Kansas City, 8 Sept 1857

met with a disappointment   CIN/ND, Machebeuf to Purcell, Louisville, 26 Aug 1857

Lamy's niece Marie   Ibid.

(description of Marie Lamy)   LO, daguerreotype

gardener from Versailles   RA, Machebeuf to sister, Kansas City, 8 Sept 1857, French

247–48   (Machebeuf trip westward 1857)   Ibid.

248   whose commanding officer   CIN/ND, Machebeuf to Purcell, Louisville, 26 Aug 1857

strange news from Mexico   CIN/ND, Lamy to Purcell, Santa Fe, 1 Sept 1857

might travel to Mexico   CIN/ND, Lamy to Purcell, Santa Fe, 3 March 1857, English, French

(kept bread, crackers *"el bendito frijole"*)   Warner, 280

ten thousand men   CIN/ND, Lamy to Purcell, Santa Fe, 3 March 1857, English, French

conversions   P/SPF/ND, Lamy to P/SPF, Santa Fe, 15 March 1857, French

"no slaves here"   Ibid.

paid what he could   CIN/ND, Lamy to Purcell, Santa Fe, 1 Sept 1857

in his old church of Covington   Ibid.

a thousand francs per year   P/SPF/TCA, Lamy to P/SPF, Santa Fe, 1 June 1857, French (tr.)

Peter Hart   CIN/ND, Lamy to Purcell, Santa Fc, 17 July 1857

249   snows closed direct trail   RA, Machebeuf to sister, Albuquerque, 28 Feb 1857, French

"schools are going on"   CIN/ND, Lamy to Purcell, Santa Fe, 3 March 1857, English, French

given the Lorettines   LO, Hayden, Santa Fe, 10 July 1857

"good Mexican pony"   CIN/ND, Lamy to Purcell, Santa Fe, 10 July 1857

too much to hope   SF/ND, Martínez to Lamy, Taos, 27 Oct 1857, Spanish

wrote also to Ortiz   SF/ND, J. E. Ortiz to Martínez, Taos, 12 Nov 1857, Spanish

Ortiz replied indignantly   Ibid.

250   "money, money, money"   SF/ND, Martínez, in GACETA DE SANTA FE, n.d., Spanish

"profaned the sacred temples"   Ibid.

"one hundred thousand dollars"   SF/ND, Martínez, tract, Taos, 24 Sept 1859, Spanish

a "fanatic"   SF/ND, Martínez, tract, 12 April 1860, Spanish

"this century of light"   SF/ND, Martínez, tract, Taos, 18 June 1860, Spanish

repudiated the bishop   Ibid.

simony; "acting against the laws"   SF/ND, Martínez, tract, Taos, 10 Aug 1860, Spanish

"ravening wolves"   SF/ND, Martínez, tract, Taos, 22 Sept 1860, Spanish

St Thomas Aquinas   SF/ND, Martínez, tract, Taos, 1861, Spanish

CHAPTER VII

255   *La cour de Rome*   RA, Machebeuf to sister (en route westward?), 26 Sept 1858, French

       affair was under study   VPF, secretarial report, Rome, March 1858, Italian

256   Martínez wrote from Taos   SF/ND, Martínez to Lamy, Taos, 29 March 1858, Spanish

       "all the mischief he can"   CIN/ND, Lamy to Purcell, Santa Fe, 1 June 1858

       "Utahs, a powerful tribe"   Ibid.

       "very hard Spring"   Ibid.

       spent four months travelling   P/SPF/TCA, Lamy to P/SPF, Santa Fe, 1 Feb 1858

       Ortiz . . . died suddenly   CIN/ND, Lamy to Purcell, Santa Fe, Jan 1858

       (a necrology)   Newberry Library, "Some Friends," Santa Fe, Jan 1858

257   sent for Machebeuf   RA, Machebeuf to brother, Santa Fe, 16 July 1858, French

       series of loving protests   Ibid.

258   to mark Lamy's departure   LO, Hayden, Santa Fe, 22 July 1858

       "used to such travelling"   CIN/ND, Lamy to Purcell, Santa Fe, 1 June 1858

       first Colorado parish   Conejos, Colo., historical marker

259   Bishop Spalding . . . told Purcell   ND, Spalding to Purcell, Louisville, 24 July 1858

       celebrated the Mass   VPF, minutes, 2nd Provincial Council, St Louis, 1858, Latin

       voted to petition   VPF, VPF to Zubiría, Rome, 9 Feb 1859, Latin; CIN/ND, Lamy to Purcell, St Louis, 13 Sept 1858

       the Vatican, on 10 June   VPF, VPF to Zubiría, Rome, 10 June 1858, Latin

       papal decree   VPF, decree of VPF, Rome, 7 June 1858, Latin

       sent with the letter   VPF, VPF to Lamy, Rome, 10 June 1858, Latin

       a nice technicality   CIN/ND, Zubiría to Lamy, Durango, 28 June 1859, Spanish, Latin

260   "last August third"   VPF, Lamy to Barnabo, Santa Fe, 19 Oct 1858, French

       (Father Avel poisoned)   Howlett, 239–43; P/SPF/TCA, Machebeuf to P/SPF, Santa Fe, 1858, French (tr.)

261   Vatican decree granting him   VPF, secretarial minute, Rome, Dec 1858, Italian

       another in the same month   P/SPF/ND, Lamy to P/SPF, Santa Fe, Feb 1859, French

       relieved Machebeuf   Defouri, 56

       appointed Father Eguillon   Ibid.

       wrote to the vicar general   VPF, Lamy to Barnabo, Santa Fe, 19 Oct 1858, French

PAGE

262   "I have received a decree"   CIN/ND, Lamy to R. Ortiz, Santa Fe,
        1 Sept 1858, Spanish
        (Machebeuf's journey to El Paso and Sonora)   RA, Machebeuf to
        sister, Santa Fe, 28 April 1859, French

263   "do you remember"   Howlett, 290
        Vicario Andando . . . Camino Real   Ibid., 239
        usually took along   Ibid., 238

264   only surviving mission   Defouri 57–58
        "half the buildings"   Hine, 67–68
        when a bishop of Sonora   Howlett, 249
        (Arizona miners)   Browne, 20–22
        "headquarters of vice"   Ibid.
        set out on 20 December   Defouri, 66
        somewhere nearer Arizona   L/SPF/ND, Machebeuf to L/SPF, Santa
        Fe, 1 May 1859, French (ms. copy)

265   "a fitter location"   Browne, 166
        a party of travellers   Defouri, 66–74
        land of the Yaqui   Browne, 243–44

266   "miserable Mexican sea-port"   Ibid, 244, 245
        his interim cathedral   Almada, *Diccionario*

267   he signed the paper   TA, Loza (document), Alamos, Sonora, 16 Jan
        1859, Spanish (ms. copy)

268   a "half-fugitive"   Almada, B., 39
        given a little house   Salpointe, 224
        to build a larger church   L/SPF/ND, Machebeuf to L/SPF, Santa
        Fe, 1 May 1859, French (ms. copy)
        one of the tribal elders   Salpointe, 227

269   (against the crime of murder)   Defouri, 59–60
        he was guarded   Salpointe, 227
        suffering from malaria   Darton, 87
        "Tu capitán?"   Defouri, 73–74

270   24 March   L/SPF/ND, Machebeuf to L/SPF, Santa Fe, 1 May 1859,
        French (ms. copy)
        "congratulated him heartily"   Defouri, 74
        eighteen parishes   Darton, 98
        sending Father Peter Eguillon   P/SPF/ND, Lamy to P/SPF, Santa
        Fe, Feb 1859

271   sending Eguillon   CIN/ND, Lamy to Purcell, Santa Fe, 16 Jan 1859
        (Christian Brothers for school)   Ibid.
        (Eguillon at Clermont)   Salpointe, 210–12
        (Eguillon and party West)   Ibid., 212–18

272   (Lamy receives Eguillon party)   Ibid., 219
        young men had been spared   L/SPF/ND, Lamy to L/SPF, Santa Fe,
        13 Nov 1859, French
        (Machebeuf to Arizona again)   Howlett, 251
        Lamy kept him   Ibid., 257–58

273   began the repairs   Darton, 85–86
        discoveries of gold   Howlett, 286–87

274   what Zubiría demanded   VPF, Zubiría to VPF, Durango, 16 May
        1859, Latin

as a saint   LO, Sister Evangelista
"our little schools"   CIN/ND, Lamy to Purcell, Santa Fe, 16 Jan
   1859
curriculum   Barbour, 43
(Hilaria and the devil)   LO, Hayden, Santa Fe, 23 Nov 1858

283   "smart and fine young lady"   CIN/ND, Lamy to Purcell (fragment),
   Santa Fe, 1859
(schools prospering)   CIN/ND, Lamy to Purcell, Santa Fe, 21 Jan
   1861
three hundred pupils ... effect on parents   P/SPF/TCA, Lamy to
   P/SPF, St Louis, 30 June 1861, French (tr.)
convent property   Barbour, 35; LO, Hayden, Santa Fe, 10 Sept 1861
year before the arrival   VPF, Lamy to Barnabo, Santa Fe, 19 Oct
   1858, French
"adobe hut with four walls"   *75 Years,* 53
presented them with a contract   Defouri, 51–53

284   "pretty good school"   CIN/ND, Lamy to Purcell, Santa Fe, 30 Jan
   1860
"cleanly, joyous, little fellows"   NEW MEXICAN, Santa Fe, 13 Feb
   1864
need for a seminary   L/SPF/ND, Lamy to L/SPF, Santa Fe, 1 Feb
   1858, French (copy)
"war in the west"   CIN/ND, Lamy to Purcell, Santa Fe, 30 Jan 1860
mail service   Machebeuf, in Howlett, 243
communications cut off   CIN/ND, Lamy to Perché, Santa Fe, 7 Jan
   1861, French
twenty men   Ibid.
"reign of terror"   L/SPF/ND, Lamy to L/SPF, Santa Fe, 25 Feb
   1861, French
Navajos descended from Welsh   Hollister, 146
effects of a drought   P/SPF/TCA, Lamy to P/SPF, St Louis, 30 June
   1861
need for a hospital   Ibid.
fainted at the altar   LO, Hayden, Santa Fe, 19 Oct 1859

285   stove in the chapel   LO, Santa Fe Annals, 1858
picnic at his *ranchito*   LO, Hayden, Santa Fe, 21 Sept 1860
still opposition   L/SPF/ND, Lamy to P/SPF, Santa Fe, 1 Feb 1858,
   French (copy)
would rather help   CIN/ND, Lamy to Purcell, Santa Fe, 30 Jan
   1860
Peter's Pence   VPF, VPF to Vatican treasurer, Rome, 27 Aug 1860,
   Latin
repayment by installment   L/SPF/ND, Lamy to P/SPF, Santa Fe,
   25 Feb 1861, French
the tithing regulations   VPF, Lamy to Barnabo, St Louis, 12 May
   1861, French

286   on St Francis's Eve   CIN/ND, Lamy to Purcell, Santa Fe, 20 June
   1859
"some amelioration"   CIN/ND, Lamy to Perché, Santa Fe, 7 Jan
   1861, French

PAGE

tin cup   Darton, 98
reception was festive   Salpointe, 239
287   (Lamy to St Louis via Denver)   CIN/ND, Lamy to Purcell, St Louis, 10 May 1861
288   realigned the boundaries   Darton, 104
"when I arrived here"   CIN/ND, Lamy to Purcell, St Louis, 10 May 1861, French
torn by massacres   CIN/ND, Lamy to Perché, St Louis, 12 May 1861
tension was running high   VPF, Lamy to Barnabo, St Louis, 12 May 1861, French
Anthony Trollope   Trollope, A., 387–88
"troubles" in New Mexico   CIN/ND, Lamy to Purcell, St Louis, 10 May 1861
289   to Father Sopranis   SLU, Lamy to Sopranis, St Louis, 12 May 1861, French (copy)
a forced march   P/SPF/TCA, Lamy to P/SPF, Santa Fe, 30 July 1861, French (tr.)
"troubles" on two fronts   L/SPF/ND, Lamy to L/SPF, Santa Fe, 1861, French
Gazette asked editorially   SANTA FE GAZETTE, 11 May 1861
290   New Mexico spoke out   Horn, 85
conscription   SANTA FE GAZETTE, 14 Sept 1861
"put slavery"   Horn, 100
he sent Ussel   Ussel, in Howlett, 298–99
291   quickened his recovery   RA, Machebeuf to brother, San Miguel (del Vado), N.M., 14 Jan 1862, French
these and other troubles   CIN/ND, Lamy to Purcell, Santa Fe, 27 Jan 1862
filed a claim   Espinosa *et al.*, 119
Mother Magdalen was dismayed   LO, Hayden, Santa Fe, 7 May 1862
291–94   (Civil War, New Mexico)   Horgan, GR, 819–30
292   on the same day   Horn, 102
six days later   SANTA FE GAZETTE, 26 April 1862
feared for their convent   LO, Hayden, Santa Fe, 7 May 1862
one day a Texas soldier   Ibid.
seize all funds   SANTA FE GAZETTE, 26 April 1862
keys of the printing office   Ibid.
"Mr Parker"   Ibid.
troops were billeted   Museum of New Mexico, exhibit caption, Palace of the Governors
Sibley was pleased   Conard, 374–77
293   "piratical bunting"   Hollister, 136
on 25 March   SANTA FE GAZETTE, 26 April 1862
"regular demons"   Hollister, ch. x.
"soldiers, I am proud"   Rittenhouse
its audacity   Hollister, 117
passing all night long   LO, Hayden, Santa Fe, 7 May 1862
294   the sick and wounded Texans   SANTA FE GAZETTE, 26 April 1862
Texan army left   Barbour, 36
measured the bishop's church   Hollister, 213–16

PAGE

raised the national flag   SANTA FE GAZETTE, 26 April 1862
led her sisters and pupils   LO, Hayden, Santa Fe, 7 May 1862
295   rumors persisted   Pettis, 1 Dec 1862; 24 Dec 1862; CIN/ND, Lamy to Purcell, Santa Fe, 29 Dec 1862
resumed pastoral visits   P/SPF/TCA, Lamy to P/SPF, Santa Fe, 2 March 1863, French (tr.)
effects in Utah   Howlett, 320
weekly mail service   CIN/ND, Lamy to Purcell, Santa Fe, 29 Dec 1862
Machebeuf was "well"   Ibid.
thousand Catholic voters   RA, Machebeuf to brother, San Miguel, 14 Jan 1862
296   England was on the verge   Ibid.
"unhappy condition"   VPF, secretarial minute, Rome, 12 July 1863, Italian
suddenly good news   TA, Bosco to Lamy, Santa Clara, Calif., 18 Aug 1862, Spanish
another letter from California   SLU, Villiger to Lamy, Santa Clara, Calif., 28 Jan 1863, Latin
296-97   another missionary bishop   Talbot
297   a letter from Denver   Defouri, 75ff passim
297-98   leave for Denver   Salpointe, 236-37; Howlett, 309-10
298   writing to Purcell   CIN/ND, Lamy to Purcell, Santa Fe, 20 Sept 1863
"pray always"   DEN/RA, Machebeuf to sister, Denver, 13 Feb 1867, French
299   Connolly declared   Horn, 104
the general said   Ibid., 105
300   Carleton defined   Ibid., 106
Martin . . . was murdered   P/SPF/TCA, Lamy to P/SPF, Santa Fe, 2 March 1863, French (tr.)
"My dear Wife"   Pettis to wife, Fort Craig, N.M., 24 Aug 1863

CHAPTER VIII

305-13   (Lamy to California, Arizona, and back)   Defouri, 80ff; Salpointe, 240
306   good rider   Salpointe, 206
308   as he wrote to Paris   ANNALES, Lamy to P/SPF, Santa Fe, 1866, French
he doubted   NEW MEXICAN, Santa Fe, 23 Jan 1864
310   "stopped a day with us"   HARTFORD EVENING POST, correspondent, 20 June 1864
311   "city of mud boxes"   Browne, 129-30
"Apaches range"   Ibid., 135
a soldier reported   Pettis to wife, Tucson, 26 May 1862
baptisms and confirmations   TA, cathedral records, 27 March 1864, Spanish

PAGE

312   "scarcely damaged"   ANNALES, Lamy to P/SPF, Santa Fe, 8 May
        1864, French
        "powerful medicine men"   Balthasar, 79
        "a splendid monument"   Browne, 140
        an old boiler   Ibid.
        "ruin and desolation"   Ibid., 149
        now its farm buildings   Ibid.
        and at La Mesilla   Pettis to wife, La Mesilla, 1 Sept 1862
313   28th day of April   LO, Hayden, Santa Fe, 12 Sept 1864
        welcoming him home   NEW MEXICAN, Santa Fe, 7 May 1864
314   learned in August   Defouri, 61–62
        "miserable priests"   VPF, Lamy to Barnabo, Santa Fe, 8 May 1864,
        French
        duly noted   VPF, secretarial minute, Rome, as of 8 May 1864, Italian
        in another familiar matter   VPF, Lamy to Barnabo, Santa Fe, 8
        May 1864, French
        "he asks that"   VPF, secretarial minute, Rome, as of 8 May 1864,
        Italian
        new churches and chapels   VPF/SPF/TCA, Lamy to P/SPF, Santa
        Fe, 1864–65?, French (tr.)
        "more like a cathedral"   Ibid.
        "still greater need"   Ibid.
315   wrote to Mother Josephine   Defouri, 102ff
        expected a group   BALT, Lamy to Spalding, Santa Fe, 1 March
        1865
        Father Ussel   CIN/ND, Lamy to P/SPF, Santa Fe, 18 June 1864
        Machebeuf, lame but busy   Howlett, 314
        gave him papers   DEN, Lamy to whom it may concern, Santa Fe,
        25 July 1864
        asked Rome to excuse him   VPF, Lamy to Barnabo, Santa Fe, 1
        Aug 1864, French
        in the same letter   Ibid.
        sudden mortal strikes   BALT, Lamy to Spalding, Santa Fe, 12 Sept
        1864
316   travelled in company   Cremony, 209
        eight thousand Navajos   Keleher, 504
        four hundred soldiers   Cremony, 209
        "schools to civilize"   P/SPF/TCA, Eguillon to P/SPF, Santa Fe, 13
        March 1864, French (tr.)
        sent a priest   P/SPF/TCA, Lamy to P/SPF, Santa Fe, 14 Aug 1864,
        French (tr.)
        "Go it citizens!"   NEW MEXICAN, Santa Fe, 31 Jan 1864
        "the happiest people"   Keleher, 407
        "this is a terrible place"   Pettis to wife, Fort Sumner, N.M., 26 Feb
        1864
        "must be clothed and fed"   Keleher, 371
317   (beginning of the cattle trains)   Horgan, GR, 832
        "beautiful Indian fort"   Cremony, 199
        three thousand Indian children   Horgan, GR, 832
        reservation was relinquished   Keleher, 459

PAGE

"interesting, intelligent" BALT, Lamy to Spalding, Santa Fe, 12 Sept 1864

"the top of the mountain" 49th Congress, 1st session, Executive Document (House), 14; Keleher, 502

excused by Pius IX VPF, VPF to Lamy, Rome, 21 Oct 1864, Latin

assured him Ibid.

"a little at a time" CIN/ND, Lamy to P/SPF, Santa Fe, 29 Dec 1865, French (copy)

no public schools LaFarge, 20

five hundred pupils L/SPF, Lamy to L/SPF, Santa Fe, 8 May 1864, French

had to enlarge LO, Hayden, Santa Fe, 12 May 1863

his order for school books BALT, Lamy to Spalding, Santa Fe, 24 July 1865

"confidence of the community" NEW MEXICAN, Santa Fe, 13 Jan 1864

317–18   decorous advertisement NEW MEXICAN, Santa Fe, 18 Nov 1865

318   colonized Mora, Taos, Denver Barbour, 36; LO, Hayden, Santa Fe, 20 Dec 1863; LO, Hayden, Santa Fe, 12 Sept 1864; LO, Hayden, Santa Fe, 14 March 1865

319   "very creditable" Wallace, W. S., 49

schools for boys SPF, Lamy to L/SPF, Santa Fe, 29 Oct 1865, French

encouraged when Ussel L/SPF, Lamy to L/SPF, Santa Fe, 7 March 1865, French

could not adequately tell Ibid.

he was obliged to write VPF, Lamy to Barnabo, Santa Fe, 12 March 1865, French

Lamy hesitated Defouri, 62

one could not be spared Salpointe, 241

320   on the back of a letter DEN, Dougherty & Bro to Machebeuf, St Louis, 7 March 1864

"weekly mail" BALT, Lamy to Spalding, Santa Fe, 30 April 1865

Santa Fe paper regretted NEW MEXICAN, Santa Fe, 23 Jan 1864

321   arrived in Santa Fe CIN/ND, Lamy to Purcell, Santa Fe, 9 Oct 1865

away when they appeared Ibid.

had come by rail Segale, 84–85

"imagine," she told Ibid.

322   "well and cheerful" CIN/ND, Lamy to Purcell, Santa Fe, 9 Oct 1865

advertisement in the paper LaFarge 35

two of the nuns DEN, SANTA FE REGISTER, n.d.

their situation CIN/ND, Lamy to Purcell, Santa Fe, 9 Oct 1865

(memory of Father Avel) Segale, 86

Purcell had advanced CIN/ND, Lamy to Purcell, Santa Fe, 9 Oct 1865

population was generous Ibid.

voted a subsidy CIN/ND, Lamy to Purcell, Santa Fe, 5 Feb 1866

General Carleton offered Darton, 130

a benefit concert L/SPF/ND, Lamy to L/SPF, Santa Fe, 29 Oct 1865, French to open the hospital　　CIN/ND, Lamy to Purcell, Santa Fe, 9 Oct 1865

323　stories of great suffering　　SANTA FE GAZETTE, 10 Feb 1866

"attempted murder" (In the *Gazette* accounts the dialogue passages appeared in indirect discourse. They are given here in direct discourse without changing word or sense.)　　SANTA FE GAZETTE, 30 Dec 1865

324　"will have written you"　　CIN/ND, Lamy to Purcell, Santa Fe, 5 Feb 1866, English, Spanish

impassive reminder　　VPF, Lamy to Barnabo, Santa Fe, 4 Dec 1865, French

a new start　　Salpointe, 342ff

asked General Carleton　　SANTA FE GAZETTE, 17 Aug 1867

title of vicar forane　　Defouri, 62–63

325　had to abandon the place　　Defouri, 64

(fire and flood in Denver)　　Howlett, 315–16

326　Machebeuf busier than ever　　CIN/ND, Santa Fe, 18 June 1866

day's work by buggy　　RA, Machebeuf to brother, Denver, 2 Oct 1866, French

took Lamy everywhere　　Ibid.

dismiss an Irish priest　　Ibid.

new bell　　CIN/ND, Lamy to Purcell, Santa Fe, 18 June 1866

cast for him in St Louis　　DEN, F. Saler to Machebeuf, St Louis, 25 April 1865

restrained inquiry　　VPF, VPF to Lamy, Rome, 5 Feb 1866, Latin

the mines "inspired"　　RA, Machebeuf to brother, Denver, 2 Oct 1866, French

discussed the matter　　Howlett, 334–35

327　River of Las Animas　　CIN/ND, Santa Fe, Lamy to Purcell, 18 July 1866

(troops at Fort Sumner)　　CIN/ND, Lamy to Purcell, Santa Fe, 18 July 1866, English, French

travelled over 900 miles　　Ibid.

331　paused at Mt St Vincent　　Segale, 89

"doing well"　　BALT, Lamy to Spalding, Santa Fe, 11 June 1866

spoke several times　　Defouri, 106–07

CHAPTER IX

sailed . . . 17 November　　Lamy, in Darton, 145

Brest in nine days　　CIN/ND, Lamy to Purcell, Rome, 22 Dec 1866

332　a somber mood　　Fournier　　Conversation with author

anxiously awaited　　CIN/ND, McCloskey to Purcell, Rome, 18 Dec 1866

uncertainty reigned　　Ibid.

proceeded with preparations　　CIN/ND, Lamy to Purcell, Rome, 22 Dec 1866

at the North American College　　Ibid.

PAGE

        beatification   Ibid.

        in the act of blessing   Ibid.

333   his private audience   Ibid.

        "what beautiful things"   Lamy, in Darton, 146

333–37   substance of the report   VPF, Lamy to Barnabo, Rome, 16 Jan 1867, French; P/SPF/ND, Lamy to P/SPF, Santa Fe, 25 Aug 1866, French

337   Jesuits for Santa Fe   VPF, Lamy to Barnabo, Rome, 1 Jan 1867, French

        at once assigned him   Defouri, 107

338   chains of St Peter   VPF, Lamy to Barnabo, Rome, 16 Jan 1867, French

        a Madame Bontesheim   CIN/ND, McCloskey to Purcell, Rome, 26 Jan 1867

        "a respectable scrape"   CIN/ND, McCloskey to Purcell, Rome, 9 Feb 1867

        recite his "experiences"   CIN/ND, McCloskey to Purcell, Rome, 19 Jan 1867

        "we miss very much"   CIN/ND, McCloskey to brother, Rome, 26 Jan 1867

339   "very kind to him"   CIN/ND, McCloskey to Purcell, Rome, 19 Jan 1867

        certain critical comments   VPF, Barnabo to Lamy, Rome, 24 April 1867, Latin

        promptly replied from Paris   VPF, Lamy to Barnabo, Paris, 6 May 1867

        "the Roman *piano, piano*"   CIN/ND, McCloskey to Purcell, Rome, 19 Jan 1867

340   "making hay"   CIN/ND, McCloskey to Purcell, Rome, 9 Feb 1867

        he had to appeal   L/SPF/ND, Lamy to L/SPF, Lyon, Feb 1867, French; L/SPF/ND, Lamy to L/SPF, Lyon, 5 April 1867, French

        "magnificent sail and steam vessel"   TCA, MISSIONS CATHOLIQUES, Fr. M. J. Brun report, Lyon, 1868, French

        (voyage of the *Europa*)   Defouri, 107–08

        left the seminarians   DEN, Lamy to Raverdy, Leavenworth City, 10 June 1867

        "remarkable" luxuries   TCA, MISSIONS CATHOLIQUES, Fr. M. J. Brun report, Lyon, 1868, French

        to lead the way West   DEN, Lamy to Raverdy, Leavenworth City, 10 June 1867

        also going along   Defouri, 108ff

341   which trail to follow   DEN, Lamy to Raverdy, Leavenworth City, 10 June 1867

        "adieu to civilization"   Defouri, 108ff

        "river sadly famous"   TCA, MISSIONS CATHOLIQUES, Fr. M. J. Brun report, Lyon, 1868, French

        soon after that crossing   Ibid.

342   "not unlike those wolves"   Defouri, 108ff

        almost all trains   SPF/ND, Lamy to P/SPF, Santa Fe, 18 Aug 1867, French

        travelled part-way with Lamy   Defouri, 108ff

PAGE

343   escort from Fort Harker   L/SPF/ND, Defouri to L/SPF, Topeka,
      22 July 1867, French
      imposed a quarantine   Barbour, 37
      were shocked to read   NEW YORK HERALD, Friday, 19 July 1867, Vol.
      XXXII, No. 200, p. 4

344   from Topeka Father Defouri   L/SPF/ND, Defouri to L/SPF, To-
      peka, 22 July 1867, French
      at Trinidad, Colorado   L/SPF/ND, Vermare to L/SPF, Trinidad,
      Colo., 10 Aug 1867, French
      troops at that post   Barbour, 37

345   fifty Indians   TCA, MISSIONS CATHOLIQUES, Fr. M. J. Brun report,
      Lyon, 1868, French

345–49   (description of Cimarron crossing battle, passim)   Ibid.; Defouri,
      108–18; Barbour, 37ff; P/SPF/ND, Lamy to P/SPF, Santa Fe, 18 Aug
      1867, French; L/SPF/ND, Lamy to L/SPF, Santa Fe, 8 Sept 1867,
      French

347   in all, ten persons   P/SPF/ND, Lamy, in Defouri, letter to P/SPF,
      Topeka, 19 Sept 1867, French

349   read in the Denver Gazette   Brun, in Defouri, 114
      wrote Father Gasparri   Gasparri, in Ibid.
      report had been denied   NEW YORK TRIBUNE, 23 July 1867
      came into Santa Fe   P/DPF/ND, Lamy to P/SPF, Santa Fe, 18 Aug
      1867, French
      absent almost a year   SANTA FE GAZETTE, 17 Aug 1867
      despite a heavy rainstorm   P/SPF/ND, Lamy, in Defouri, letter to
      SPF, Topeka, 19 Sept 1867, French

350   sixty-two days   Ibid.
      "foresight, nerve, and kindness"   VPF, Defouri to VPF, Santa Fe,
      16 Feb 1884
      "a little tired"   P/SPF/ND, Lamy to P/SPF, Santa Fe, 18 Aug 1867,
      French

                         CHAPTER X

353   Martínez had died   NEW MEXICAN, Santa Fe, 3 Aug 1867
      he had been buried   Defouri, 125
      (Martínez's will)   Warner, 84ff

354   two new schools   CIN/ND, Lamy to P/SPF, Santa Fe, 10 Sept 1867,
      French
      in mid-autumn   L/SPF/ND, Lamy to L/SPF, Santa Fe, 23 Dec 1867,
      French
      extraordinary expenses   Ibid.
      of Barnabo   VPF, Lamy to Barnabo, Santa Fe, 12 Dec 1867, French

355   Machebeuf was notified   DEN/RA, Machebeuf to sister, Denver, 14
      April 1868, French
      reasons for declining   CIN/ND, Machebeuf to Purcell, Denver, 26
      March 1868
      a Jesuit friend   Ibid.

PAGE

off to Montreal   RA, Machebeuf to brother, New York, 6 July 1868, French

consecrated in Cincinnati   *Fifty Years,* 161–63

Lamy was not present   CIN/ND, Lamy to Purcell, Santa Fe, 18 July 1868, English, French

"happy to turn over"   DEN, Lamy to whom it may concern, Santa Fe, 21 Sept 1868

to see Lamy at Santa Fe   Howlett, 347ff

356   Salpointe had somehow   BALT, Lamy to Spalding, Santa Fe, 23 March 1868

the matter lay dormant   VPF, VPF to Salpointe, Rome, 13 Dec 1867

Salpointe   VPF, Lamy to VPF, Santa Fe, 1868, Latin

Lawrence Bax   Ibid.

John Baptist Rallière   Ibid.

more Catholics than Colorado   BALT, Lamy to Spalding, Santa Fe, 26 April 1868

"a very fair way"   Ibid.

"too far distant"   BALT, Lamy to Spalding, Santa Fe, 23 March 1868

357   Arizona separate from New Mexico   Salpointe, 259

an additional document   VPF, VPF to Lamy, Rome, 20 Jan 1869, Latin

asking (once again!)   Ibid.

but both journeys   Salpointe, 261–62

"two religious colonies"   P/SPF/TCA, Lamy to P/SPF, Santa Fe, 1870s?, French (tr.)

a final orderly transfer   RA, Machebeuf to sister, Denver, 6 June 1871, French

telegraph reached Santa Fe   NEW MEXICAN, Santa Fe, 7 July 1868

daily mail   CIN/ND, Lamy to Purcell, Santa Fe, 18 July 1868

four-horse Concord coaches   NEW MEXICAN, Santa Fe, 11 Nov 1868

not so the *New Mexican*   NEW MEXICAN, Santa Fe, 7 July 1868

358   "the thousands of emigrants"   CIN/ND, Lamy to Purcell, Santa Fe, 18 July 1868, English, French

"collection of select novels"   NEW MEXICAN, Santa Fe, 6 Feb 1868

some much needed improvements   NEW MEXICAN, Santa Fe, 17 March 1868

358–59   (stone for the cathedral)   Chavez, SFC

359   laid 10 October   NEW MEXICAN, Santa Fe, 8 Oct 1869

few detailed architectural plans   Chavez, SFC

cornerstone contained   Ibid.

first donors   DAILY NEW MEXICAN, Santa Fe, 8 Oct 1869

360   cornerstone was blessed . . . stolen   DAILY NEW MEXICAN, Santa Fe, 18 Oct 1869

"I am Anthony"   Darton, 183–84

he found Lamy   Ibid., 157–58

361   missed his sailing   RA, Machebeuf to brother, New York, 8 June 1869, French

engage for Santa Fe   Salpointe, 261

"officiated and confirmed"   Howlett, 357–58, Machebeuf to Raverdy, Clermont, 20 Aug 1869, French

PAGE

saw Pius three times   Darton, 159

he dispensed them both   CIN/ND, Machebeuf to Purcell, Paris, 21 Sept 1869

passing through Pisa, Florence   DEN, Machebeuf to Raverdy, Clermont, 20 Aug 1869, French

calling at the colleges   Howlett, 359

362   Salpointe, on the other hand   Darton, 167

gave in abbreviated form   VPF, Lamy to Simeoni, Rome, 1869–70, Latin

362–63   (Vatican Council)   Mathew, 178; Hales, 310–12; Lees-Milne, 317–18

363   Kenrick of St Louis wrote   SLU, P. R. Kenrick to ?, Rome, 6 March 1870

when the Bishop of Bosnia   Johnson, Paul, in NEW STATESMAN, London, 12 Oct 1962

a new memorandum   VPF, Lamy to Simeoni, Rome, 18 Feb 1870, Latin

364   a powerful endorsement   Ibid.

leave to return   SLU, P. R. Kenrick to ?, Rome, 6 March 1870

reconsecrated the parish church   HL

loan of twelve thousand francs   RA, Machebeuf to brother, Denver, 20 April 1870, French

certain information at Lyon   VPF, Lamy to VPF, Lyon, 23 March 1870, Spanish

a peaceable crossing   RA, Lamy to LA SEMAINE RELIGIEUSE, Clermont, 23 May 1870, French

the usual welcome   NEW MEXICAN, Santa Fe, 21 June 1870

365   Salinas wrote a long letter   VPF, Salinas to VPF, Durango, 11 June 1871, Spanish

Salpointe would lose   VPF, Lamy to Simeoni, Santa Fe, 20 Feb 1872, French

Rome once again issued   VPF, VPF to Lamy, Rome, 26 March 1872, Latin

Salpointe once again journeyed   VPF, Salpointe to Simeoni, Las Cruces, N.M., 2 Dec 1872, Latin

366   local residents of Las Cruces   VPF, lay residents to Pius IX, Las Cruces, N.M., 26 July 1874, Spanish

meanwhile, Salpointe asked   VPF, Salpointe to Simeoni, Las Cruces, N.M., 10 Dec 1872, Latin

opportunity to ordain   Darton, 183–84

to raise funds   BALT, Lamy to Spalding, Santa Fe, 6 Dec 1871

367   took his meals   CIN/ND, Sister M. Vincent O'Keefe to Purcell, Santa Fe, 10 Feb 1871

"*Nos pauvres compatriotes*"   L/SPF/ND, Lamy to L/SPF, Santa Fe, 28 April 1871, French

367–68   (diamond and ruby swindle)   NEW MEXICAN, Santa Fe, 1 April, 21 Aug, 22 Aug, 7 Oct, 26 Nov, 30 Nov, 4 Dec, 16 Dec 1872

368   thirty thousand head   NEW MEXICAN, Santa Fe, 21 Aug 1872

Apaches curiously threading   NEW MEXICAN, Santa Fe, 7 Oct 1872

Apache raiders murdered   NEW MEXICAN, Santa Fe, 26 Nov 1872

"never so dirty"   NEW MEXICAN, Santa Fe, 18 Oct 1872

PAGE

a volunteer force   NEW MEXICAN, Santa Fe, 16 Dec 1872
all the roads   NEW MEXICAN, Santa Fe, 24 June 1873
369   chasuble, maniple, and stole   LO, archives
serving them himself   Darton, 197
now had 180   L/SPF/ND, Lamy to L/SPF, Santa Fe, 1 Jan 1872,
French
(private schools, convents)   Ibid.
their own new chapel   Barbour, 38
discouraging doubt   P/SPF/ND, Lamy to P/SPF, Santa Fe, 20 Aug
1873, French
only ten men   CIN/ND, Lamy to Purcell, Santa Fe, 29 Dec 1871
370   inroads upon these   L/SPF/ND, Lamy to L/SPF, Santa Fe, 20 Oct
1873, French
active free public schools   L/SPF/ND, Salpointe to L/SPF, San
Xavier del Bac, 31 May 1873, French
370–72   (Lamy's plan for Pueblos)   Lamy, SH
372   never be relieved   L/SPF/ND, Lamy to L/SPF, Santa Fe, 20 Oct
1873, French
six regional or local   NMSRA
tracks from the East   NEW MEXICAN, Santa Fe, 26 Jan 1874
local businessmen   Ibid.
373   Denver had known   RA, Machebeuf to brother, Denver, 22 June
1872, French
spat with a nun   CIN/ND, Sister Fidelis to Purcell, Trinidad, Colo.,
23 March 1873
against women's suffrage   Howlett, 413–14
suffering from famine   P/SPF/ND, Lamy to P/SPF, Santa Fe, 23
April 1874, French
added burdens   DEN, P. R. Kenrick to Machebeuf, St Louis, 26 Feb
1874 (annotated by Lamy)
elaborated these views   DEN, Lamy to P. R. Kenrick, Santa Fe,
1874
374   his silver jubilee   Defouri, 138
"the Bishop's ranch road"   NEW MEXICAN, Santa Fe, 17 Nov 1874

CHAPTER XI

377   counter to Lamy's advice   VPF, minutes of Synod, Rome, 1875,
Italian
Pius IX, in consistory   Salpointe, 265–66
ten-day pastoral visit   CIN/ND, Lamy to Purcell, Santa Fe, 10 March
1875
Machebeuf pointed out   RA, Machebeuf to sister, Denver, 14 May
1875, French
Monsignor Caesar Roncetti   Salpointe, 265–66
377–78   (on the pallium)   *New Catholic Encyclopedia*
378   16 June 1875   Defouri, in Howlett, 381

PAGE

378–81   (events of 16 June 1875, variously)   Truchard, in LA SEMAINE RE-
          LIGIEUSE, 4 Aug 1875; Ritch; Defouri, in Howlett, 382

381   "equally brilliant"   VPF, Lamy to VPF, Santa Fe, 30 July 1875,
          French
          "our poor capital"   VPF, Lamy to Franchi, Santa Fe, 7 July 1875,
          French
          "painting and kalsomining"   NEW MEXICAN, Santa Fe, 22 June 1875

381–82   Father Anthony Lamy   LO, Anthony Lamy to sister, Manzano, 23
          June, 3 Nov 1875

382   Father Anthony Lamy   Darton, 183–84
          Lamy repeatedly reported   P/SPF/ND, Lamy to P/SPF, Santa Fe,
          1884
          40,000 lambs   P/SPF/TCA, Lamy to P/SPF, Santa Fe, Nov 1883,
          French (tr.)
          missions had to be abandoned   P/SPF/TCA, Lamy to P/SPF, Santa
          Fe, 25 April 1880, French (tr.)

383   "bottom of the Rio Grande"   Bandelier, 142
          (Apaches)   NEW MEXICAN, Santa Fe, 16 Dec, 5 April 1880
          (Rio Grande floods)   L/SPF/ND, Lamy to L/SPF, Santa Fe, 18 July
          1884, French
          (Lamy's trunk)   In museum, Loretto Chapel, Santa Fe

384   as he summed it up   P/SPF/TCA, Lamy to P/SPF, Santa Fe, 1878?,
          French (tr.)
          a mile a day   SANTA FE WEEKLY, 16 Nov 1875
          "as rapidly as possible"   ATSF Files, Topeka, Kans., "Letters," v. 9,
          #878, J. Nickerson to W. B. Strong, Boston, 7 March 1878
          "employing Mexican labor"   Ibid., "Letters," v. 9, 8 March 1878
          "speedy extension"   NEW MEXICAN, Santa Fe, 7 March 1876
          a stunning disappointment   LaFarge, 96
          demanded a price for it   Ibid.
          bond issue was proposed   Warner, 276

385   the first to sign   NEW MEXICAN, Santa Fe, 20 Sept 1879
          cost $12,000 to lay a mile   ATSF Files, Topeka, Kans., "Letters,"
          v. 10, #731, "Geo. L. Goodwin, Tr.," 28 June 1879
          "the working of the mines"   Lamy, in Warner, 179
          "the monster engine"   NEW MEXICAN, Santa Fe, 18 Jan 1879
          "the Broad Gauge"   NEW MEXICAN, Santa Fe, 19 July, 2 Aug 1879
          telegraphed to President Nickerson   NEW MEXICAN, Santa Fe, 14 Feb
          1880
          final chapters of *Ben Hur*   Horn, 216

386   Wallace was able to write   Ibid., 217
          granted all clergy free passage   L/SPF/ND, Lamy to L/SPF, Santa
          Fe, 5 July 1880, French (copy)
          (railroad timetable)   NEW MEXICAN, Santa Fe, 25 Dec 1880
          Lamy wrote to the company   NEW MEXICAN, Santa Fe, 6 Jan 1881;
          Lamy, in Warner, 276
          blessings in material things   Salpointe, 269

388   "the front is of a variety"   BALT, Lamy to Spalding, Santa Fe, 16 Oct
          1875
          one of the southwest   NEW MEXICAN, Santa Fe, 26 Nov 1872

PAGE

389   had already spent $50,000   BALT, Lamy to Spalding, Santa Fe, 16 Oct 1875

twenty-five thousand francs   P/SPF/TCA, Lamy to P/SPF, Santa Fe, 1876, French (tr.)

the original plans   P/SPF/ND, Lamy to P/SPF, Santa Fe, 4 Aug 1873, French

"never in greater need"   CIN/ND, Defouri to ?, Santa Fe, 20 Oct 1881, French (ms. copy)

services continued   Chavez, SFC

reredos removed   Ibid.

389–90   (description of interior)   LO, Bourke, in SANTA FE REGISTER

391   Lamy raffled   LO, Crocchiola, in SANTA FE REGISTER

meagre funds   CIN/ND, Lamy to SPF, received 8 Oct 1883, French (copy)

citizens were as generous   Chavez, SAL

symbol for Yaweh   Chavez, SFC

nave would be closed   Ibid.

their reduced measure   Ibid.

cracking already begun   Ibid.

not strictly parallel   Ibid.

came to take down   Defouri, 144–45

392   two graves be dug   Chavez, SFC

consecration performed   Barbour, 38

rode to Denver   Segale, 113

"criticized his work"   Ibid., 83–84

died of pneumonia   Ibid., 153

393   "his personal attention"   NEW MEXICAN, Santa Fe, 13 July 1875

(building new St Michael's)   *75 Years,* 72ff

394   (building of Loretto academy)   Cekosh, in NEW MEXICO ARCHITECT, July-Aug 1971, 11–15

"our own brickyard"   Segale, 157

Lamy began an experiment   CIN/ND, Lamy to P/SPF, Santa Fe, 31 March 1878, French (copy); L/SPF/ND, Lamy to L/SPF, Santa Fe, 2 Aug 1879, French; Defouri, 53

395   change of administration   Salpointe, 204

would include the arts   NEW MEXICAN, Santa Fe, 13 Jan 1881

396   "industrial school"   Segale, 153

non-sectarian academy   Ibid.

"Territory has been afflicted"   NEW MEXICAN, Santa Fe, 5 April 1880, quoting New Castle, Ind., MERCURY

"above reproach"   Segale

397   posted an award   LaFarge, 100

so said Mrs Wallace   Horn, 208

not only Apaches   NEW MEXICAN, Santa Fe, 30 Oct 1881

Wallace asked Washington   NEW MEXICAN, Santa Fe, 20 Sept 1879

the first edition   LaFarge, 101

an autographed copy   Warner, 295

Lamy "heartily" endorsed   NEW MEXICAN, Santa Fe, 6 Oct 1882

grant the right of way   NEW MEXICAN, Santa Fe, 19 March 1881

new spur lines   Bandelier, 348

"theology of the dollar"   Charlemagne

PAGE

398 (Tertio-Millennial)   LaFarge 120–21; MNM, contemporary photographs
"though dirty and unkempt"   Wallace, S., 14
"pleasant evening"   Bandelier, 143
"ugly music"   Ibid., 181
Union Restaurant   NEW MEXICAN, Santa Fe, 30 Oct 1881
Miller's Summer Garden   NEW MEXICAN, Santa Fe, 18 Jan 1879
"took oysters"   Bandelier, 375
fresh oysters daily   NEW MEXICAN, Santa Fe, 16 Dec 1880
"saw Pueblo Indians"   Bandelier, 73
"Burro Cavalry"   MNM, contemporary photograph
"new gasometer"   Bandelier, 89
Hayes paid a visit   Warner, 276

399 outbreak of smallpox   Ibid., 268
"the great sanitarium"   VPF, Defouri to VPF, Santa Fe, 16 Feb 1884, English
marvels were known   Segale, 146
the ex-priest Gallegos   Ibid., 181
"cast down with sadness"   Darton, 221
needed tactful help   VPF, VPF to Lamy, Rome, 18 March 1879, Latin

400 Machebeuf, to the north   VPF, Lamy to Simeoni, Albuquerque, 5 Sept 1880, Spanish
(growth of Denver and Leadville)   RA, Machebeuf to sister, Denver, 19, 20 Feb 1879, French
(Leadville, appearance)   Contemporary print
Emma Abbott, Oscar Wilde   Colorado State Guide

401 his episcopal seal (the sense of this in English would be "Holy Mary, protect us")   DEN, Rev Brucker, S. J., ms., n.d.

CHAPTER XII

405 Lamy had already done so   VPF, Lamy et al. to VPF, Santa Fe, 1876, Latin; VPF, Lamy to Franchi, Santa Fe, 8 May 1876, Latin
a third vicariate apostolic   Ibid.

406 his last visit to Rome   VPF, secretarial minute, Rome, n.d., Italian
five weeks close to death   L/SPF/ND, Lamy to L/SPF, Santa Fe, 25 April 1880, French
Mother Francesca stayed   DEN, Sr. Margarita Pacheco, "Notes on Early Santa Fe" (typescript)
Blandina declared   Warner, 134
resting "much easier"   NEW MEXICAN, Santa Fe, 28 March 1880
finally, in April   L/SPF/ND, Lamy to L/SPF, Santa Fe, 25 April 1880, French
"drought"   Ibid.

407 "an absolute necessity"   CIN/ND, Defouri to ?, Santa Fe, 20 Oct 1881, French (copy)

PAGE

Lamy again pressed Rome   VPF, Lamy to VPF, Santa Fe, 18 Dec 1881, French

if it was wondered   VPF, Lamy to Simeoni, Santa Fe, 3 April 1882, Spanish

one loving concern lay heavily   VPF, Lamy to VPF, Santa Fe, 18 Dec 1881, French

hoped to resign and retire   Ibid.

408   "I have always been poor"   L/SPF/ND, Lamy to L/SPF, Santa Fe, 3 Nov 1888, French

he enlisted letters   VPF, McCloskey to Simeoni, New York, 22 Dec 1881, Italian; VPF, Wood to Simeoni, Philadelphia, 21 Dec 1881, Italian

so ill with fever   RED RIVER CHRONICLE, 29 April 1882

he told Simeoni   VPF, Lamy to Simeoni, Santa Fe, 16 May 1882, Spanish

warned the Society   L/SPF/ND, Lamy to L/SPF, Santa Fe, 16 Nov 1882, French (copy)

Lamy at once telegraphed   VPF, Lamy to VPF, Santa Fe, 3 April 1882, Spanish

409   had exempted Lamy   VPF, VPF to Alemany and Lamy, Rome, 22 May 1883, Latin

a new bishop at Tucson   VPF, Lamy to Salpointe, Santa Fe, 7 Dec 1883, French; VPF, Salpointe to Simeoni, Rome, 26 Dec 1883, French

pleaded with Salpointe   VPF, Lamy to Salpointe, Santa Fe, 7 Dec 1883, French

"no doubt can exist"   VPF, secretarial minute for Cardinal Luigi Oreglia de San Stefano, Rome, Feb 1884

notified Salpointe   VPF, VPF to Salpointe, Rome, 7 April 1884, Latin

on the ninth, Lamy   VPF, VPF to Lamy, Rome, 9 April 1884, Latin

"as for myself"   VPF, Salpointe to VPF, Tucson, 5 May 1884, French

Archbishop of Anazarbe   VPF, Salpointe to Simeoni, Tucson, Dec 1884, French

he and Lamy agreed   Ibid.

in his old habit   NEW MEXICAN REVIEW, Santa Fe, 19 May 1884

410–12   (garden)   Fulton, 186–87; VPF, Defouri to VPF, Santa Fe, 16 Feb 1884; Warner, 151–55; Mrs E. Frank Raynor, conversations with author; CIN/ND, Cincinnati CATHOLIC TELEGRAPH, 1875?; COMMERCIAL, Cincinnati, 1876; Salpointe, 277; NEW MEXICAN, Santa Fe, 14 Sept 1875; Segale, 115–17; LO, Sr. Margarita Pacheco

412–13   she saw beds of cabbages   Segale, 144–45

413   (history of the missions)   Hodge, in Bandelier, 51

launched to raze   Warner, 279

the cult in action   Segale, 266–70

an absurd rumor   L/SPF/ND, Lamy to SPF, Santa Fe, 9 March 1881, French

for what he saw there   Bandelier, 182

stayed them at his door   DEN, Sr. Margarita Pacheco, "Notes on Early Santa Fe" (typescript)

414   Mother Francesca copied   DEN, Sr. Gertrude, "Notes on Early Santa Fe" (typed transcript)

PAGE

the chapel sacristan   LO, Sr. Margarita Pacheco
at the altar   LO, José Sena, in SANTA FE REGISTER, 8 Sept 1950
spiritual reading   LO, Sr. Margarita Pacheco
his library   MNM, Santa Fe, In-Loan Agreement List of 70 Ecclesiastical Books of the Archbishop Lamy Collection and the Archdiocese
of Santa Fe Collection, 10 Jan 1969
one journey overland   CIN/ND, CATHOLIC TELEGRAPH (Cincinnati)
(1875?)

415   a Taos Indian   Warner, 134
on a heavy snowy day   LO, José Sena, in SANTA FE REGISTER, 8 Sept
1950
wearing the shawl   Warner, 293
who as a small child   Mrs Charles Whelan, conversation with author

415–16   statue of the Madonna   Mrs. E. Frank Raynor, letter to author,
New York, 31 Oct 1956, and conversations with author

416   Lamy was usually present   Ibid.
in the spring of 1884   Segale, 210–13

416–19   (memories of Lamy in person)   Father José S. García, conversations
with author

419   an army colonel   Warner, 267

420   "greatest pacifier"   Ibid., 252
(picnics at the ranch)   DEN, Sr. Gertrude, "Notes on Early Santa
Fe" (typed transcript)
fish for German carp   NEW MEXICAN REVIEW, Santa Fe, 4 Jan 1884
as he went on foot   LO, José Sena, in SANTA FE REGISTER, 8 Sept 1950
telescope   Warner, 295

420–21   (visit of Ewing)   Ewing to wife, Santa Fe, 26 Nov 1881

421–26   (journey to Mexico)   LO, Lamy to sister, letters from Mexico, 22
July, 9 Aug, 14 Aug, 25 Aug, 26 Aug, 10 Sept, 7 Oct, 10 Oct, 1884

423–25   (extracts from sermons)   LO, Lamy, n.d., Spanish

426   "during his absence"   DAILY NEW MEXICO REVIEW, Santa Fe, 28 Oct
1884

CHAPTER XIII

429   wrote to Leo XIII   VPF, Lamy to Leo XIII, Santa Fe, Dec 1884,
Latin
for the Pope's acceptance   VPF, Lamy to Simeoni, Santa Fe, 26 Jan
1885, French
returned to Santa Fe   Salpointe, 272
Salpointe went to visit   P/SPF/ND, Salpointe to P/SPF, Annual
Report, 1885
Bourgade of Silver City (He became the fourth Archbishop of Santa
Fe.) Salpointe, 271

430   "bring your mitre"   DEN, Salpointe to Machebeuf, Santa Fe, 5 April
1885, French
Lamy was well enough   Ibid.

PAGE

       Bourgade to the episcopate   Defouri, 151
       "His Holiness diligently examined"   VPF, VPF to Lamy, Rome, 18 July 1885, Latin
       Simeoni sent instructions   VPF, Simeoni to Salpointe, Rome, 18 July 1885, Latin

430–31   (Lamy's resignation)   CIN/ND, Lamy letter of resignation, Santa Fe, 26 Aug 1885

431   on Sunday, 6 September   Defouri, 151
       Archbishop of Cyzicus   VPF, Lamy to Simeoni, Santa Fe, 16 Oct 1886, French
       annual report   P/SPF/ND, Salpointe to P/SPF, Annual Report, 1885, French

432   "in the future kindly address"   P/SPF/TCA, Lamy to P/SPF, Santa Fe, 26 Sept 1885
       he said fervently   L/SPF/ND, Lamy to SPF, Santa Fe, 26 Sept 1885, French
       "sufficiently comfortable"   VPF, Lamy to Simeoni, Santa Fe, 3 June 1885, Spanish
       a suitable arrangement   VPF, Salpointe to Simeoni, Santa Fe, 19 Aug 1885, French

432–33   (provision of a pension)   P/SPF/TCA, Salpointe to P/SPF, Santa Fe, 6 Nov 1885, French

433   much to complain of   VPF, Salpointe to Simeoni, Santa Fe, 16 Nov 1885, French
       from Rome, Simeoni reminded   VPF, Simeoni to Lamy, Rome, 18 Nov 1885, Latin

434   "I think this letter of mine"   VPF, Simeoni to Salpointe, Rome, 20 Nov 1885, Latin
       by the time Simeoni's letters   VPF, Salpointe to Simeoni, Santa Fe, 26 Dec 1885, Latin
       at the Villa Pintoresca   Salpointe, 275
       Salpointe received the pallium   DEN, Salpointe to Machebeuf, Santa Fe, 21 Nov 1885, French
       "the Cathedral is concerned"   P/SPF/ND, Salpointe to P/SPF, Annual Report, Santa Fe, 6 Nov 1885, French
       the towering stone reredos (The cathedral was not completed until 1897, then by Archbishop Chapelle.)   Chavez, SFC

435   he blessed the bells (The stained-glass windows now in the cathedral were made in Clermont-Ferrand.)   Ibid.
       Michael Machebeuf and his wife   L/SPF/ND, Lamy to L/SPF, Santa Fe, 24 Feb 1885, French
       (destruction of Santo Domingo)   Chavez, *Archives*
       went to Washington   Salpointe, 272
       (Machebeuf's affairs)   VPF, VPF to Salpointe, Rome, 11 March 1885, Latin; VPF, VPF to Cardinal Gibbons, Rome, 7 Sept 1885, Latin; VPF, Salpointe to Simeoni, Santa Fe, 19 Aug 1885
       Matz as coadjutor   Howlett, 401
       reminder from Lamy   VPF, Lamy to VPF, Santa Fe, n.d., French
       Vatican raised Denver   Howlett, 401
       (Machebeuf golden jubilee)   CIN/ND, CHICAGO TIMES, 16 Dec 1886

PAGE

436   reported often to Machebeuf   DEN, Salpointe to Machebeuf, Santa
         Fe, 15 June, 25 Aug 1886, French
       "a venerable gentleman"   LO, Bourke, quoted in SANTA FE REGISTER
       "earnestly studying"   NEW MEXICAN, Santa Fe, 15 Feb 1888
       in the plaza   Warner, 260
       he said Mass   Ibid., 268
       feast of St Francis   Ibid., 137
       dedicate the chapel   Ibid., 297
       carriage was sent   LO, Santa Fe Annals of Mother Francesca Lamy
437–39 (illness and death, and funeral of Lamy)   LA SEMAINE RELIGIEUSE,
         Salpointe to bishop of Clermont-Ferrand, Santa Fe, 21 Feb 1888, issue
         of 17 March 1888; DEN, Sr. Mary, "Notes on Early Santa Fe";
         Warner 296–97; WEEKLY NEW MEXICAN REVIEW, 16 Feb 1888; LA
         SEMAINE RELIGIEUSE, Mother Francesca Lamy to sister, Santa Fe, 15
         Feb 1888; LO, Crocchiola, in SANTA FE REGISTER, n.d.; Howlett, 404;
         Missal, prayers for a dead bishop
438–39 (the ring)   Fournier, conversations with author; Brun-Voyat, con-
         versations with author
438–39 (the crucifix)   LO, J. Francolon to Mother Francesca Lamy, Santa
         Cruz, N.M., 25 March 1888, French
439   (burial)   Chavez, SFC
       she began to cry   DEN, Sr. Evangelista, "Notes on Early Santa Fe"
         (typescript)
       his collegians   Warner, 274; NEW MEXICAN, Santa Fe, 21 Feb 1888
       writing to Europe   LA SEMAINE RELIGIEUSE, Salpointe, Clermont-
         Ferrand, 24 March 1888
440   (Newman on St John Chrysostom)   Newman, *Historical Sketches II,*
         "The Last Days of St John Chrysostom"
       "Sa mort"   LA SEMAINE RELIGIEUSE, Clermont-Ferrand, 1888
       in the next summertime   Warner, 256
       a year later   DENVER REPUBLICAN, 11 July 1889
       FIDES ET OPERA (Faith and Works)   Motto of Lamy's episcopal coat
         of arms

ACKNOWLEDGEMENTS

Acknowledgements

It is a welcome duty to acknowledge my indebtedness to many persons who over the years have generously helped me in the preparatory tasks for this book.

The late Most Reverend Edwin Vincent Byrne, D.D., eighth archbishop of Santa Fe, hoped that a biography of his first predecessor would be written. When I came to him with my plans, he gave me his friendship and confidence, along with vital help in the form of credentials which assured my access to many invaluable archives in the United States and above all those at the Vatican.

In Rome, his accreditation led me to the Very Reverend Fr Frederick Heinzmann, M.M., Procurator General of Maryknoll, and rector of Maryknoll House. In the face of what seemed my impossible request for all existing papers in Lamy's Vatican correspondence, Father Heinzmann brought my appeal before Peter Gregory Cardinal Agagianian, the late Pro-Prefect of the Sacred Congregation of the Propaganda Fide. With extraordinary dispatch, as astonishing to his staff as to me, His Eminence, receiving me one Monday morning in 1959 immediately upon his return from an audience with Pope John XXIII, granted me full access to any archives of the Propaganda Fide which bore upon Lamy. Cardinal Agagianian put me into the hands of Fr Peter Kowalski, S.J., head of the archives, who in turn gave me into the care of Mr Anton Debevec, a most able archival scholar. Mr Debevec supplied me with hundreds of Lamy papers never before consulted for public use. My debt to all these Roman personages is incalculable.

So, too, is my debt to the Most Reverend Lawrence J. FitzSimon, D.D., third bishop of Amarillo, a scholarly historian who for years had been gathering materials for a life of Jean Marie Odin (first bishop of Galveston and later archbishop of New Orleans), which unhappily he did not live to complete. But Bishop FitzSimon's own researches contained a multitude of valuable references to Lamy, and these he gave to me without hesitancy or reservation. In the course of successive years of visits to Bishop FitzSimon in Amarillo, I felt that I had found not only a generous colleague but a wise and witty friend. I am indebted to Fr Ernest Burrus, S.J., of Rome, for sending me to Bishop FitzSimon in the first place.

Archbishop Byrne directed me to the diocesan archives gathered from all across the United States at the University of Notre Dame, where a rich store of material bearing on Lamy and associated persons is kept. There for a month or so I was made welcome as a resident guest of the university by its great president, the Very Reverend Theodore M. Hesburgh, C.S.C., who, like his faculty and particularly his archivist, the late Fr Thomas McAvoy, C.S.C., showed me every kindness. No trouble was too great for Fr McAvoy to undertake on behalf of my studies, always with high good spirits and that associative imagination which is the mark of a true scholar. The experience of living at Notre Dame, even for only a few winter weeks, was one of the happiest by-products of my long search for the archbishop.

I am grateful to the Abbé Garnaud, of the Ecole Massillon at Clermont-Ferrand, for innumerable courtesies and acts of guidance, including an introduction to the Reverend Mother Superior Thérèse Lucie Roy, of the Monastère de la Visitation de la Sainte Marie, at Riom. Mother Thérèse provided me with exquisite copies of the convent's collection of 113 autograph letters written by Bishop Machebeuf to his sister, Soeur Philomène, between 1839 and 1886. (A selection of these letters was translated by Fr W. J. Howlett and used as the basis of his life of Bishop Machebeuf, privately issued in 1908 at Pueblo, Colorado. It was his work which was the biographical source of Willa Cather's novel, *Death Comes for the Archbishop*, as Miss Cather stated in her book *On Writing*, 1949.)

I owe special thanks, too, for aid of various kinds to many others. Fr José S. García, at the age of ninety-nine, my last living link with Lamy (who sent him to Niagara Falls to be educated for the priesthood), spoke with clear and delightful personal recollection of the archbishop. (Fr García, who lived to be a hundred, told me further that his godfather, Kit Carson, gave his parents a twenty-dollar gold piece as a gift for the newly baptized child, which was prudently hidden behind a brick in the García fireplace at Taos.) Senator Clinton P. Anderson of New Mexico, an expert bibliophile and collector in the field of the literature of the West, aided me with particular research facilities through the Library of Congress. I thank Associate Dean Martin Griffin of Yale College for giving my text a most useful critical reading, and for leading me to the archive formed by his great-grandfather, Martin Griffin, at St Charles Borromeo Seminary, where, after years of search elsewhere, I found Lamy's "Short History of the Pueblo Indians," in a manuscript copy of the lost original.

I am grateful for aid of various kinds to Msgr John Tracy Ellis, of the University of San Francisco; Msgr Charles McManus, formerly of St Patrick's Cathedral, New York; Sister Mary Luke, the superior, and the late Sister Matilda Barrett, archivist, of the Loretto Motherhouse, Nerinckx, Kentucky; Msgr Joseph Gallagher, and Msgr P. Francis Murphy, archivist, of the Archdiocese of Baltimore; Fr Frederick D. McAninch, former archivist of the diocese of Tucson; Fr Donald F. Spitzka, C.M., and Fr Thomas Feely, C.M., of St Thomas Seminary, Denver; the Rev Homer Blubaugh, of St Mary's Seminary, Cincinnati; and, in Santa Fe, John Gaw Meem for his long-sustained encouragement; Fray Angelico Chavez; the Loretto Sisters of the Academy of Our Lady of

Light; and, for particularly constant and helpful support, Manuel J. Rodríguez.

For generous professional sponsorship I thank Roger W. Straus, Jr, of Farrar, Straus and Giroux, and Miss Virginia Rice, my highly effective agent for forty-two years (she closed her office in 1973). For admirable editorial response and assistance, I am grateful to Robert Giroux. I thank, too, Donald Berke for his excellent critical and other help on the final draft of the text; the Aspen Institute for Humanistic Studies, under whose auspices and hospitality much of the book was written during my several periods as a Scholar in Residence; and Wesleyan University, where my post as continuing author in residence has provided me with a permanent base for my library, and every opportunity to work on my books. Once again the sustaining faith of Dr Henry Allen Moe, and the Guggenheim Foundation under his presidency, brought me a research grant which furthered my travels abroad in search of material.

I gratefully acknowledge the help of many more people and various institutions, and I list them here alphabetically with all respect: Arizona Pioneers Historical Society; P. Ball, Special Collections, University of Arizona Library; George Barringer, Georgetown University Library; Beinecke Rare Book and Manuscript Library, Yale University (Herman Liebert, former director, Louis Martz, director); Jan Beyer, Georgetown University Library; Edward W. Bisett; Fr Thomas E. Blantz, C.S.C., Archivist, University of Notre Dame Library; Ruth Lapham Butler, Newberry Library; Msgr le Vicaire Général Chaumont, Clermont-Ferrand; M le Chanoine Chauvet, Nohanet, Puy-de-Dôme; Cincinnati Historical Society; Colorado State Historical Society; Fr Cuesta, Cristo Rey Parish, Santa Fe, N.M.; Fr Valdemar Cukuras, Pomfret, Conn.; Most Reverend James Peter Davis, retired Archbishop of Santa Fe; Elaine Delgado Romer; Isabel Echols; Gaylord Donnelley; Stephany Eger, Librarian, History Division, Museum of New Mexico, Santa Fe; Laura A. Ekstrom, Assistant Librarian, Colorado State Museum, Denver; Bruce Ellis; El Paso Public Library; Eleanor S. Ewing; John K. M. Ewing; M. l'Abbé Fanguet, Lempdes, Puy-de-Dôme; Joan Farrell; Catherine Farrelly; M. le Chanoine Fournier, Riom; Msgr Joseph Gallagher, Archivist, Archdiocese of Baltimore; Donald Gallup, Curator of American Literature, Beinecke Rare Book and Manuscript Library, Yale University; José Ignacio Gallegos C., Durango, Mexico; Most Reverend Rudolf Gerken, seventh Archbishop of Santa Fe; S. E. Pierre Cardinal Gerlier, Archbishop of Lyon; Samuel M. Green, Wesleyan University; M l'Abbé Guillot, Secrétaire-Général de l'Evêché, Clermont-Ferrand; Fr Edmund Halsey, former Archivist, St Charles Borromeo Seminary, Overbrook, Pa.; Fr Charles Haluska, Mt Vernon, Ohio; Archibald Hanna, Curator of the Coe Collection, Beinecke Rare Book and Manuscript Library, Yale University; Edna Haran; the late Msgr Edward Hickey, Chancellor of the Archdiocese of Detroit; Virginia P. Hoke, Southwest Reference Librarian, El Paso Public Library; Mr and Mrs Peter Hurd, San Patricio, N.M.; Fr Stanley Iverson, New Orleans; Dr Myra Jenkins, Director, New Mexico State Archives and Records Library; the late E. Dana Johnson, Santa Fe; Mrs Jordan, Cincinnati Historical Society; Kansas State Historical Society (Frank Miller, Nyle Miller, Joseph Snell, Don Wilson); George H. Kennedy; James Kraft; M le Chanoine Pierre Lacour, Ecole Massillon,

Clermont-Ferrand; Richard Lake, Secretary-Treasurer, A.T.S.F. Railway, Topeka, Kan.; Most Reverend Raymond Lessard, D.D., Bishop of Savannah; Mrs
Ralph Levy; Mr and Mrs Goddard Lieberson; David McAllester, Wesleyan Uni-
versity; Fr Kieran McCarthy, O.F.M., Tucson, Ariz.; David McIntosh; Msgr G.
Marchand, Lyon, France; Arthur Martin; William Maxwell; Fr Modell, St
Mary's Seminary, Cincinnati, Ohio; New Mexico Historical Society; Museum
of New Mexico Historical Archives; Museum of New Mexico Library, His-
torical Division; New Mexico State Archives and Records Library; New
Orleans Public Library; Robert Park, Rosenberg Library, Galveston, Tex.;
Francis Pawlowski; Mrs E. Frank Raynor; Fr Joseph A. Reade, Chaplain,
Mt San Rafael Hospital, Trinidad, Colo.; Joseph W. Reed, Jr, Wesleyan
University; Catherine Reese, Ryan Memorial Library, St Charles Borromeo
Seminary, Overbrook, Pa.; Msgr Walter F. Rosenzweig, Tucson, Ariz.; Saint
Louis University, Saint Pius X Library; Richard Salazar, New Mexico Records
Center and Archives, Santa Fe; Thomas V. Schmidt, Reference Division,
Mullen Library, Catholic University of America; Douglas W. Schwartz; Tania
Senff-Norton; John Spike; Fr Stricker, St Mary's Seminary, Cincinnati; the
late Stanley Stubbs; Larry Taylor, Archivist, St Charles Borromeo Seminary,
Overbrook, Pa.; Joaquín del Valle, Mexico City; Fr Norman Whalen, Tuc-
son, Ariz.; Mrs. Charles Whelan, Santa Fe, N.M.; and Bernard Wirth.

INDEX

Index

Hotel de Dunk, 279
Hôtel Française, Talbot at, 297
Howlett, Father W. J., 407
Huerfano River, 278, 287–8, 298–9

Iberia, 7, 11
Imuris, 265
Independence, Machebeuf party on, 53
"Indian War, The," 341, 343
Indianola, 88–90, 94, 96–8
Indians, burial mounds of, 32; fear of,
and raids of, 119–20, 123–4, 133, 138,
154–5, 185, 188, 207, 248, 271, 299, 310,
334–5, 337; Catholic, 127, 205, 226, 311,
335, 370–1; and churches, 136, 151; and
New Mexico, 155, 284, 289, 291, 296,
299–300, 335–6; and Lamy, 163, 185,
210–11, 300, 315–17, 341–9, 370–2; and
missions, 181–2, 205; votes of, 195; of
Taos, 231; and Chateaubriand, 238; and
Machebeuf, 238–9, 247; and Eguillon
party, 272; and emigrants to West, 279;
and Civil War, 290; in Colorado, 295;
and Sisters of Charity, 321; and art, 388;
see also names of tribes
Infallibility, issue of, 363
Innocent VI, Pope, 10
Ireland (Irish), 64, 355, 362, 364
Irrizarri, Don Manuel, 308, 310
Isleta del Sur, on Rio Grande, 93, 104, 108,
156, 244, 305
Ixtacamastitlán, Lamy in, 424

Jackson, Andrew, 53–4, 88
Jacob's Well, Lamy at, 306
James, Henry, and Pius IX, 203
James, St, of Compostela, 7
Jemez, Pueblo school at, 435
Jesuits, 15, 161–2, 182; Gallegos and, 196;
and Sonora, 264–5; Lamy and, 289, 312,
337–40; and Arizona and New Mexico,
296, 305, 309; mission of, 354; schools
of, 395
Jews, 122, 335, 381, 391, 416
John, Gospel of, 9
Joinville, Princess de, 51
Jojita, Lamy at, 313
José, Juan, 119
Josephine, Mother, Lamy and, 315
Jouvenceau, Father, and Lamy's death
438
Juárez, *see* El Paso
Juárez, Benito, 261, 319
Juilliard, N., 205, 209

Julia, Mother, 52
Juvenceau, François, joins Eguillon, 271

Kansas, Lamy party on, 160–1
Kansas, and Kansas City, description of,
155, 238, 270–1, 288–9
Kaws, 155
Keams, Thomas V., and button, 367
Kearny, Stephen Watts, 54, 122, 149
Kenrick, Archbishop Francis Patrick, 156,
183, 195
Kenrick, Archbishop Peter Richard, 158;
Lamy and, 198, 245, 377; council under,
257, 287–8; and Pike's Peak, 276; and
Vatican Council, 363; and jurisdictional
dispute, 364; and Santa Fe, 373–4
Kentucky, 153, 157–8, 198, 257, 259
King, Clarence, and diamond swindle, 367
Kiowas, 155

La Bajada, 108, 132
La Conquistadora, 415–16
La Fonda, 122, 186, 292
La Mesilla, *see* Mesilla
La Mesita, 319
La Ysleta, 319
Laguna, Pueblo school in, 371, 435
Lamy (railroad station), 384
Lamy, Anthony (nephew), 12, 340, 360,
366, 381–2
Lamy, Etienne (brother), 12, 62, 205, 260
Lamy, Hippolyte (nephew), 185
Lamy, Jean (father), 4, 12, 56, 62
Lamy, Jean (nephew), 395, 399, 438
Lamy, Jean Baptiste, to Paris, 3–4, 19, 21;
and parents, 4, 19; illnesses of, 3, 16, 19,
21, 23, 37, 99–101, 103, 147, 206–7, 284–
5, 313, 406–8, 436–8; birth of, 12; childhood and education of, 13, 15, 17; and
Our Lady of Good Tidings, 13, 420;
description of, 16, 109–10, 310–11, 354,
410, 412, 429, 436; and missionary life,
17–18, 34, 36–7, 44–5; ordination of, 18;
to America, 18–24; and language problems, 23, 29, 34, 36, 43–4, 86, 101, 104,
160, 272; in New York, 24, 62, 157, 331;
in Wheeling, 25; and Cincinnati, 25–6,
29–30; at Danville, Newark, Mt Vernon,
and Mansfield (Ohio), 30–1, 33, 36–56;
churches of, 34–9, 42, 44–6, 57–9, 61,
157, 203, 258–9, 268, 286, 295, 314, 327,
334, 369, *see also names of;* financial
problems of, 34, 38–40, 42–4, 96–7, 99,
127, 157, 159, 169–70, 182, 205–6, 213–
15, 221–2, 285, 289, 332, 354, 389, *see*